T0360973

VARIORUM COLLECTED STUDIES SERIES

Mediterranean Encounters, Economic, Religious, Political, 1100–1550

Dr David Abulafia
(Photo: Eaden Lilley
Photography, Cambridge)

David Abulafia

Mediterranean Encounters, Economic, Religious, Political, 1100–1550

Routledge
Taylor & Francis Group

LONDON AND NEW YORK

First published 2000 by Ashgate Publishing

Published 2016 by Routledge
2 Park Square, Milton Park, Abingdon, Oxon OX14 4RN
52 Vanderbilt Avenue, New York, NY 10017

Routledge is an imprint of the Taylor & Francis Group, an informa business

ISBN 13: 978-0-86078-841-6 (hbk)

British Library Cataloguing-in-Publication Data
Abulafia, David, 1949–
    Mediterranean Encounters, Economic, Religious, Political, 1100–1550.
    (Variorum Collected Studies Series: CS694).
    1. Social Interaction – Mediterranean Region – History – to 1500. 2. Mediterranean Region – Social Conditions. 3. Mediterranean Region – Commerce – History – to 1500. 4. Mediterranean Region – Commerce – Religious Aspects. 5. Mediterranean Region – Politics and Government. 6. Mediterranean Region – Religion.
    7. Mediterranean Region – History – 476–1517.
    I. Title.
    909'.09822'02

US Library of Congress Cataloging-in-Publication Data
Abulafia, David,
    Mediterranean Encounters, Economic, Religious, Political, 1100–1550 / David Abulafia.
        p.   cm. (Variorum Collected Studies Series: CS694)
    Includes bibliographical references.
    1. Mediterranean Region – Commerce – History. 2. Mediterranean Region – History. 3. Mediterranean Region – Civilization. 4. Mediterranean Region – Religion. 5. Middle East – Commerce – History. 6. Middle East – Religion. 7. Christianity – Mediterranean Region. 8. Islam – Mediterranean Region – History. 9. Judaism – Mediterranean Region – History. 10. Middle Ages. I. Title. II. Collected Studies: CS694.
    HF3750.7.A543   2000
    382'.09182'2–dc21   00–061793

VARIORUM COLLECTED STUDIES SERIES CS694

CONTENTS

JEWS AND MUSLIMS UNDER ANJOU AND ARAGON

This volume contains xviii + 352 pages

PREFACE

I

Historians at the start of the twenty-first century have again been questioning whether the Mediterranean can be treated as a unity. The publication of *The Corrupting Sea* by Peregrine Horden and Nicholas Purcell has served as a timely reminder of the complexity and diversity of the Mediterranean land and seascape, and of the implications that this has for the development of regional trade, exchanges of population and even the development of religious cults.[1] For those two authors, the Mediterranean must be seen as an interacting collection of 'micro-ecologies', and it is precisely the inability of most areas, notably the smaller islands, to satisfy their basic needs that gives unity to the edges of the Great Sea, leading to the production for exchange of grain, wine, oil, metals, timber and other necessities of life, and also to the migration of people, and peoples, across its open spaces. This volume on *Mediterranean Encounters*, drawing together papers written or at any rate published in the 1990's, is also concerned with interactions across the Mediterranean, and even further afield, as far as the North Sea; but the emphasis here is on human encounters, between men, and occasionally women, from different economic settings, different political backgrounds and different faiths. It has seemed to me vitally important to set side by side studies of the treatment of religious minorities and studies of trade and high politics. It is not just that they took place within the same chronological span, and within much the same geographical area. It is also the case that politics, religion and the economy in the medieval Mediterranean formed a continuum. Historians have to keep reminding themselves of what is obvious, but too often ignored: that their own compartmentalisation of the past was not matched in the minds of those they are examining.

My longstanding interest has been in the ways in which political developments and economic ones influence one another, as can be seen from my books *The Two Italies*[2] and *A Mediterranean Emporium*,[3] concerned respectively with Sicily and Majorca, and from several of the studies in my two previous books in the Variorum Collected Studies, *Italy, Sicily and the Mediterranean*[4] and *Commerce and Conquest in the Mediterranean*.[5] This is especially apparent from two articles with a title beginning 'The Crown and the Economy...'[6] (to which one could now add essay X in this book, on 'Lo Stato e la vita economica'). Here I have also sought to insert in that framework the economic activities of the Jews and Muslims, and the fate they met at the hands of different masters, from the hostile Charles II of Naples at the end of the thirteenth century to the surprisingly *simpatico* Ferrante I of Naples in the fifteenth century. In other words, *pace* Braudel, Horden and Purcell, one must not neglect the significance of human choices and *histoire événementielle* in determining the longer term changes that took place within the Mediterranean world.

Yet there is still so much to be done before we can understand the impact of the different cultures and religions of the Mediterranean shores on the merchants who traversed the sea; or before we can see what role faith played in the expansion of Italian trade across the Mediterranean, in the period of the early crusades. The way forward lies in a combination of closely focussed research pieces, several of which are included here, with broader essays which seek to bring together from a novel perspective (if and when possible) the conclusions of research conducted by scholars up to my own time. It is not a case of either one, or the other. My biography of Frederick II means it is no secret that I regret the way that German historiography has leaned so heavily towards the establishment of precise details, without sufficient attention to broader analysis. But equally, like many historians, I take pleasure in the hunt through the archives and printed sources, and in the realisation that the detail gives sharpness and tone to the broader view, as well as providing the evidential basis for historical arguments. Therefore this book alternates as far as possible between those two types of scholarly article.

II

In the first section, devoted to trade across the Muslim-Christian frontier, I have sought to reinject religious faith into the activities of Italian merchants as they force open the markets of the Levant in the twelfth century (essay II), while also postulating a relationship in which exchange of goods takes absolute priority, and exchange of ideas, in the market place at any rate, is very limited (essay I). Yet this exchange had an enormous impact on the western economy, as can be seen from the study written for the Datini Institute in Prato of the trade in industrial materials such as cotton or indigo, and as emerges from the Catalan tariff lists of the late Middle Ages (essay V).[7] In the same section I home in on some case studies: the building of Genoese ties to Muslim Majorca (essay III), an issue I dealt with in the Spanish but not in the English version of *A Mediterranean Emporium*;[8] the links between Ancona and the Levant, a subject I have already addressed

twice before, but which I examine here in the round, taking on board the
work of the late Eliyahu Ashtor and Peter Earle (essay IV).[9] But I particularly
wanted to include this article, which was published simultaneously in Italian
and English following a conference at the University of Padua, because of
its appendix denouncing the so-called travel diary of Jacob of Ancona, a
work published in 1998 to the accompaniment of grand claims.[10] My
comments on Jacob considerably extend an article I wrote in *The Times* of
London, where space was lacking for a full demonstration of my views.[11]

In the second section I move away from contact between Christian Europe
and the Islamic world to consider the impact of the Italian and Iberian
merchants on the European economy. The panorama extends as far as London
and Southampton (essay VII, a paper originally delivered in Venice), for it
is essential to understand how the Mediterranean interacted with the Atlantic,
just as we have seen it interacting with the Red Sea and Indian Ocean in the
previous essays; Braudel's Mediterranean, after all, extended at appropriate
moments as far as the Atlantic islands and even Cracow.[12] The essential
back-up to these commercial activities was provided by the early Italian
bankers, who are the subject of essay VI, where, in the wake of an excellent
book by Edwin Hunt, I present them not just as bankers but also as merchants
dealing with vital commodities such as grain and wool.[13] Hunt himself made
some use of a study I published in 1981 of Florentine links with Naples,
and it is a pleasure to be able to reciprocate by acknowledging the stimulus
provided by his own work, and that on the Medici business enterprise by
Richard Goldthwaite and by the late Raymond de Roover.[14] It is to the Medici
that I have dedicated essay XI, a study of the role of the Florentine firm in
the local Adriatic grain trade at the end of the fifteenth century, based on a
remarkable portolan's register from Apulia. The aim of this article, first
published in Malta, was not merely to make a marginal contribution to the
understanding of Medici affairs in the age of Lorenzo *il Magnifico*, but
more importantly to stress the significance of short distance trade in basic
commodities, in this case mainly between the Apulian ports and those of
the facing coast of Dalmatia. This picture of intense short distance contacts
needs to be extended to other parts of the Mediterranean: Malta itself is a
good example.

This article fits in with my concern to re-evaluate the role of the Adriatic
in Italian trade (see also essay IV), but it is intended to pick up in a local
setting a much bigger theme which dominates the argument of essay VIII, a
relazione given to the XVIth Congress of the History of the Crown of Aragon
in Naples in 1997. There I aimed to re-assess the pioneering work of Mario
del Treppo on Catalan trade in the fifteenth century, in the light of the
increasing emphasis among economic historians on the importance of local
trade networks, and in the light of arguments about economic decline in the

century after the Black Death; it will be seen that I remain sceptical about the usefulness of the concept of 'decline' in that era, especially when describing the lands of the Crown of Aragon.[15] I have sought to build on the existing and often very inaccessible studies of local trade, and to provide an overall view of trade networks in the western Mediterranean.[16] In sum, I see the reassertion of local systems of exchange as an important sign that the post-plague economy was not in 'crisis' or 'decline', pejorative and loaded terms, but undergoing a fundamental *ristrutturazione*, restructuring, consequent on the demographic and other changes of the years after 1347. To compare the pre- and post-plague economies is to compare chalk and cheese.

In the third section I begin to home in on the Kingdoms of Sicily and Naples, the focus of much of my research. Essays X, XI and XII were designed to pick up and develop ideas outlined in my general account of the life and reign of Frederick II, first published in 1988; in particular, these articles provide fuller annotation than was possible in that book.[17] The article entitled 'Lo stato e la vita economica' was originally delivered as a paper at a colloquium organised in 1989 by Pierre Toubert and Agostino Paravicini Bagliani at Erice, and was conceived in some sense as a follow-up to my 'Crown and the Economy under Roger II'; it could well have carried the title 'The Crown and the Economy under Frederick II'. The paper on the political crusades, which I believe modifies some of the arguments of Norman Housley in his important and stimulating book on crusades against Christian lay powers, was first delivered at Joshua Prawer's seminar at the Institute of Advanced Study of the Hebrew University of Jerusalem.[18]

Essay XII, a paper given at the National Gallery of Art in Washington, DC, leads directly towards the studies of the Jews and Muslims under the later kings of Sicily and southern Italy, which make up the fourth section of this book. In essay XIII, as in essay XII, I seek to link together the treatment of Jews and Muslims.[19] It is a matter for regret that, partly because of intense modern political conflicts, historians have often tended to treat one or the other but not both; one only has to consider the unappetising abuse heaped on one great pioneer in this field, Bernard Lewis, to see how difficult it has been to navigate through such waters.[20] It is my hope that these articles will reveal the advantages in taking both communities together, and seeing how the experiences and fate of one group affected that of the other group. Fortunately, the work of scholars such as Elena Lourie in Israel, David Nirenberg in the United States and Mark Meyerson in Canada is restoring three dimensions to the study of relations between Jews, Christians and Muslims in the Middle Ages.[21] However, there has also been a notable expansion in interest in the history of the Jews in Italy, and essays XIV, XV

and XVI reflect the attention being paid to the Jews of southern Italy and
Sicily, by far the largest communities in medieval Italy. Essay XV, which
has its origins in a lecture given at Trier in Germany, picks up the history of
the south Italian communities to take it beyond the disasters of the late
thirteenth century into a period of economic transformation under the
Aragonese kings of Naples, among whom Ferrante I (Ferdinand I) was a
particular friend of the Jews, in contrast to his cousin and namesake in
Aragon-Catalonia. It is also possible to observe how the atmosphere changed
in Naples following the French invasion in 1494–95, and the seizure of
control by Ferdinand the Catholic in 1502–03. It was also, as essay XVI
tries to explain, a period of intellectual vitality, partly because exiled Jews
saw Naples as a haven; and the Hebrew printing presses of Naples provide
fascinating evidence in this regard.

The final three essays take one into the political convulsions that
accompanied and followed the War of the Sicilian Vespers. The rivalry
between Aragon and Anjou was part of what I have described in a book
published in 1997 as a 'Two Hundred Years' War', with ramifications in the
cultural, economic and above all political life of large parts of the
Mediterranean.[22] Essays XVII, XVIII and XIX look at three theatres in which
these rivalries produced, if only on paper, unexpected political entities: the
plans to create a kingdom for Frederick III of Sicily in Albania and western
Greece, provided he would surrender Sicily to the Angevins (essay XVII);
the incorporation of Genoa within the Angevin dominions, a subject well
reported by the Genoese annalists (essay XVIII); the political complications
that resulted from the existence of a curiously constructed Majorcan kingdom
which was eyed by predatory neighbours in both Aragon-Catalonia and in
France, and which consisted entirely of lands held from the Aragonese and
French rulers (essay XIX). This article, delivered as a lecture at the annual
conference on Majorcan history in Palma in 1998, approaches the history
of the Majorcan kingdom from a different angle to the chapters on political
history in my *Mediterranean Emporium*; my other numerous articles on the
Catalan kingdom of Majorca are, however, all subsumed within that book,
as well as listed in its bibliography, and there was no reason to reproduce
them independently here.

III

I have left out of this volume several studies of the politics of the kingdom
of Naples in the era of King Ferrante I, a subject on which my views are
contining to develop.[23] One or two articles did not really belong to
Mediterranean history and were set aside.[24] I have also omitted essays which
formed part of several big projects, easily accessible, and in some cases
covering similar ground to pieces contained here, though at a more rapid

speed: the volumes on *Gli Ebrei in Italia* in the *Einaudi Storia d'Italia*, to which I contributed three articles on the Jews of Sicily, southern Italy and Sardinia; volumes 5 and 6 of the *New Cambridge Medieval History*, where several survey articles run parallel to chapters in my *Western Mediterranean Kingdoms*, and some methodological pieces which try to integrate the history of Islamic Europe into that of Christian Europe.[25]

It gives me great pleasure once again to thank John Smedley for his help, encouragement and energy in this project. I also thank all the publishers who have willingly agreed to the reproduction of these articles in this book, including Ithaca Press, Reading (essay I), Peter Lang, New York (essay II), the Società Dalmata di Storia Patria (essay IV), Cambridge University Press (essays VI and XIII), Malta University Press (essay IX), the Centro di Studi sull'Alto Medioevo, Spoleto (essay XI), the National Gallery of Art, Washington, DC (essay XII), the Ministero per i Beni culturali e ambientali, Rome (essay XIV), Hahnsche Buchhandlung, Hamburg (essay XV), Frank Cass, London (essay XVII), the Institut d'Estudis Baleàrics, Palma de Mallorca (essay XIX), and all the other editors and publishers who have handled my work in Italy. I am very grateful to Amanda Power, Carolina Lo Nero and Merav Mack for compiling the index in the time left to them by their own research projects, which at the moment they are conducting under my direction. I remain deeply grateful to my colleagues the Master and Fellows of Gonville and Caius College for the splendid facilties that the college still provides after 652 years of its own history. Since some of these papers were delivered at conferences far from Cambridge, it is the least I can do to thank Anna, Bianca and Rosa Abulafia for their patience and understanding while I have been away on my travels, and for their good company when we have crossed the paths of medieval monarchs and merchants on our joint travels.

DAVID ABULAFIA

Gonville and Caius College,
Cambridge, March 2000

Endnotes

[1] P. Horden and N. Purcell, *The Corrupting Sea. A Study of Mediterranean History*, Oxford, 2000, reviewed by me in the *Times Literary Supplement*, no. 5063, 14 April 2000, pp. 9–10.

[2] *The Two Italies. Economic Relations between the Norman Kingdom of Sicily and the Northern Communes*, Cambridge, 1977; Italian ed., Naples, 1991.

[3] *A Mediterranean Emporium. The Catalan Kingdom of Majorca*, Cambridge, 1994; Castilian ed., 1996.

[4] *Italy, Sicily and the Mediterranean 1100–1400*, London, 1987

[5] *Commerce and Conquest in the Mediterranean 1100–1500*, Aldershot, 1993.

[6] 'The Crown and the Economy under Roger II and his Successors', *Dumbarton Oaks Papers*, 37, 1983, 1–14, repr. in *Italy, Sicily and the Mediterranean*; 'The Crown and the Economy under Ferrante of Naples (1458–1494)', in T. Dean, C. Wickham, eds., *City and Countryside in Late Medieval and Early Renaissance Italy. Studies Presented to Philip Jones*, London: Hambledon Press, 125–46, repr. in *Commerce and Conquest*.

[7] Another version of this article appeared in slightly different form as: 'The Impact of the Orient: Economic Interactions between East and West in the Medieval Mediterranean', *Across the Mediterranean Frontiers. Trade, Politics and Religion, 650–1450*, ed. D.A. Agius and I.R. Netton, Turnhout: Brepols, 1997, 1–40. The version published here was accompanied by a discussion, also published, which I have not reproduced, and which may be found in the full *Atti* of the XXIX Settimana 'F. Datini'; but I am grateful to Richard Goldthwaite, Michel Balard and David Jacoby *inter alia* for their helpful comments.

[8] *Un Emporio Mediterráneo. El reino catalán de Mallorca*, Barcelona, 1996, pp. 131–8.

[9] 'Ancona, Byzantium and the Adriatic, 1155–1173', *Papers of the British School at Rome*, 52, 1984, 195–216, repr. in *Italy, Sicily and the Mediterranean*; 'The Anconitan Privileges in the Kingdom of Jerusalem and the Levant Trade of Ancona', *I comuni italiani nel regno di Gerusalemme*, ed. G. Airaldi and B. Z. Kedar, *Collana di fonti e studi*, Genoa: Istituto di Medievistica, 1987, 525–70, repr. in *Commerce and Conquest in the Mediterranean*.

[10] The Italian version appeared as:'Oriente e Occidente: considerazioni sul commercio di Ancona nel Medioevo', *Atti e Memorie della Società Dalmata di Storia Patria*, 26: *Città e sistema adriatico alla fine del Medioevo. Bilancio degli studi e prospettive di ricerca*, 27–46. The English version given here is in fact a translation of my Italian original by Michele Pietro Ghezzo, although the appendix about Jacob of Ancona, pp. 61–6, is in my own English.

[11] 'An Amazing Journey – or Just a Hoax? David Abulafia on the Tall Tale of an Ancient Traveller', *The Times*, no. 66, 061, 1 December 1997, p. 22.

[12] And see Felipe Fernández-Armesto's enormously stimulating *Before Columbus. Exploration and Colonisation from the Mediterranean to the Atlantic, 1229–1492*, London, 1987.

[13] E.S. Hunt, *The Medieval Super-Companies. A study of the Peruzzi Company of Florence*, Cambridge, 1994.

[14] See my 'Southern Italy and the Florentine Economy, 1265–1370', *Economic History Review*, ser. 2, 33, 1981, 377–88, repr. in *Italy, Sicily and the Mediterranean*; R. de Roover, *The Rise and Decline of the Medici Bank, 1397–1494*, Cambridge, MA, 1963.

[15] Cf. here the work of S.R. Epstein, *An Island for Itself. Economic Development and Social Change in Late Medieval Sicily*, Cambridge, 1992.

[16] This version was published in Salerno in advance of the *Atti* of the congress, and its existence owes much to the good offices of Alfonso Leone, Massimo Oldoni and

Gerardo Sangermano. Cf. M. del Treppo, *I mercanti catalani e l'espansione della Corona d'Aragona nel secolo XV*, 2nd ed., Naples, 1972; Catalan ed., Barcelona, 1976.

[17] *Frederick II. A medieval Emperor*, London and New York, 1988; revised eds., 1992, 2001; Italian eds., Turin, 1990, 1993. Unfortunately the German editions of Berlin, 1991 and Munich, 1994 were abridged without advance warning, and they leave out some important parts of the argument, though it was possible to compensate in part in the later edition by adding a chapter on the historiography of Frederick II.

[18] N. Housley, *The Italian Crusades. The Papal-Angevin Alliance and the Crusades against Christian Lay Powers, 1254–1343*, Oxford, 1982.

[19] An Italian version of part of this article appeared as 'La caduta di Lucera nel 1300', *Per la storia del Mezzogiorno medievale e moderno. Studi in memoria di Iole Mazzoleni*, Pubblicazioni degli Archivi di Stato, Saggi, 48, Rome: Ministero per i Beni culturali e ambientali, 2 vols., 1998, vol.1, 171–86.

[20] B. Lewis, 'The Question of Orientalism' in his *Islam and the West,*, Oxford and New York, 1993, pp. 99–118.

[21] E. Lourie, *Crusade and Colonisation. Muslims, Christians and Jews in Medieval Aragon*, Variorum Collected Studies, Aldershot, 1991; D. Nirenberg, *Communities of Violence. Persecution of Minorities in the Middle Ages*, Princeton, NJ, 1996; M. Meyerson, *The Muslims of Valencia in the Age of Fernando and Isabel. Between Coexistence and Crusade*, Berkeley and Los Angeles, 1991.

[22] *The Western Mediterranean Kingdoms, 1200–1500. The struggle for Dominion*, London, Harlow and New York, 1997; Italian ed., Bari and Rome, 1999. I have omitted from this book my article 'Bad Rulership in Angevin Italy: the Sicilian Vespers and their Ramifications', *Haskins Society Journal*, 8, 1999, 115–35, which follows closely what appears in *The Western Mediterranean Kingdoms*; for a different perspective, see my 'Charles of Anjou Reassessed', *Journal of Medieval History*, 26, 2000, 93–114.

[23] Notably 'The Inception of the Reign of Ferrante I of Naples', in *The French Descent into Italy, 1494–5. Antecedents and Effects*, ed. David Abulafia, Aldershot, 1995, 71–89; 'Ferrante I of Naples, Pope Pius II and the Congress of Mantua (1459)', in *Montjoie. Studies in Crusade History in Honour of Hans Eberhard Mayer*, ed. B.Z. Kedar, R. Hiestand and J. Riley-Smith, Aldershot, 1997, 235–49.

[24] 'Un'economia in crisi? L'Europa alla vigilia della Peste Nera', *Archivio Storico del Sannio*, iii, 1998, 5–24; 'Ernst Kantorowicz, Frederick II and England', *Ernst Kantorowicz. Erträge der Doppeltagung Institute for Advanced Study, Princeton/Johann Wolfgang Goethe-Universität, Frankfurt*, ed. Johannes Fried, R. Benson, *Frankfurter Historische Abhandlungen*, Band 39, Frankfurt: Franz Steiner, 1998, 124–43

[25] 'Islam in the History of Early Europe', *Itinerario. European Journal of Overseas History*, 20, 1996, 9–23; and in *Islam and Europe in Past and Present. An Academic Session held at the Dopskerk in Wassenaar on Friday 20 September 1996 to Commemorate the Twenty-fifth Anniversary of NIAS*, ed. W. Hugenholtz and K. van der Vliet-Leigh, Wassenaar: Netherlands Institute for Advanced Study, 1997, 9–23, 67–9; also in *The European Review*, 5, 1997, 241–56; 'Minorities in Islam: Reflections on a New Book by Xavier de Planhol', *The European Review*, 7, 1999.

PUBLISHER'S NOTE

The articles in this volume, as in all others in the Collected Studies Series, have not been given a new, continuous pagination. In order to avoid confusion, and to facilitate their use where these same studies have been referred to elsewhere, the original pagination has been maintained wherever possible.

Each article has been given a Roman numeral in order of appearance, as listed in the Contents. This number is repeated on each page and quoted in the index entries.

I

The Role of Trade in Muslim–Christian Contact during the Middle Ages

I

The subject matter of this paper may seem to demand little justification. In 1962 Aziz Atiyah entitled a slim volume *Crusade, Commerce and Culture*, and had no serious doubts about the link between the three.[1] The evidence is surely clear enough: the arrival of Arabic numerals in Europe, used first by the very notaries who drew up contracts for trade in the Muslim world around 1200; the use in several European languages of commercial terms of Arabic or Persian derivation, such as bazaar, cheque, tariff, traffic, arsenal, *douane* or *dogana*,[2] and, once we enter the nautical world, the Islamic derivation of instruments, astronomical tables and cartographic methods is a common assumption, if not quite a certainty. This is to leave aside additional evidence provided by the vocabulary used to describe various expensive textiles, such as the damasks of Damascus and the *baldechini* of Baghdad, or cloths made from raw materials originally unfamiliar in the west, such as the fustians, partly of cotton, of Fusṭāṭ (Old Cairo).

A further area that Professor Atiyah might have investigated more deeply is the transfer of Arab agricultural technology to western Europe, generally in those areas, such as Valencia and Sicily, that had once been under Arab rule.[3] Seville oranges, bananas, rice, henna and sugar are a few of the products that continued to be produced by Christian conquerors, who also sought to acquire the technical skills required for the glass industry, for glazed pottery production, for the paper industry and possibly for the silk industry from the Muslim world. Such commodities acquired great importance in Mediterranean trade by 1400, and were carried much further afield, via the Atlantic all the way to England; even when produced in lands ruled by Christians, they were often cultivated or fabricated by Muslims or Jews, and their origin in the Islamic world is incontrovertible.

It is an impressive picture which has been qualified most notably by Joseph Needham's assertion that a good deal of what the west supposedly acquired from the Arab world was in reality ultimately of Chinese origin, not least paper and the compass.[4] Much the same could be said to apply to some of the fruits and specialised crops of Chinese or Indian ancestry that have just been mentioned.[5] Even if this were largely true, it would not contradict the assumption that it was from the Muslim world that all or most of this know-how arrived in western Europe; nor would it be easy to prove that in around 1300 or even 1400 western Europeans had much knowledge or understanding of Chinese and Indian culture, Marco Polo notwithstanding. But the idea of western borrowing from Islam by way of the international trade routes needs more careful definition from a western perspective as well as from a Chinese one. It is clear already that a distinction needs to be made between the borrowing of Arabic terms as a result of Christian conquest of Muslim lands, and borrowings actually effected through trade. The use of place-names in the Islamic world to describe particular types of cloth does seem to provide a faint echo of early trade relations, even though terms such as fustian rapidly came to be applied to western copies of what were originally cloths of a single place in Egypt.[6] There is, however, one western institution that provides eloquent testimony to the nature and effect of western trade with the Muslim world in the Middle Ages: it is the *fonduq* or *fondacho*, another word which (though ultimately of Greek origin, in the form *pandocheion*) arrived in Italian and Catalan from Arabic, and which was used to described the inns, warehouses and business headquarters that the western merchants operated in North Africa and other Muslim lands.[7]

The central question I want to pose is what it meant to a western merchant, a Latin Christian reared in an age of constant crusade propaganda, to penetrate the Christian–Muslim frontier not as a soldier but as a merchant. We must therefore start with an act of imagination. To live in the late thirteenth century as a Latin Christian

The Role of Trade in Muslim–Christian Contact

in Majorca was to live among the vestiges of an Islamic civilisation that had been torn apart by the Aragonese–Catalan conquest of 1229. The Muslims were a minority, many of them unfree. To travel from there to Valencia was to stay under the rule of an Aragonese king, but to enter a second world in which Muslims were the majority and in which the royal government treated the inhabitants with well-calculated consideration.[8] But to move from there to Tunis or Alexandria was to enter a third world in which Christian merchants were able to practise their religion only on sufferance, and in which simple daily activities, like the quaffing of wine, were subject to government control. It was a world in which the nature of government interference in economic affairs was entirely different from what was found in Genoa, Pisa or even the strongly interventionist Venice. But above all, it was a predominantly Muslim world in which Christian merchants had daily contact with people of another religion.

In a recent, and in many ways inconclusive, book Philip D. Curtin has talked of the stimulating economic role of 'cross-cultural trade', expressed primarily through the presence of cohesive minorities settled in outstations in the midst of an alien civilisation; among the groups that he cites are the Armenian diaspora, and the Greeks who reached as far south as the Zambezi River as Africa was opened up. Often such groups are strikingly resistant to assimilation, retaining a distinctive religion and/or language.[9] Did similar contact between the Christian merchants and the Muslims in the Middle Ages leave any cultural legacy? In a material sense, certainly, it did: the arrival and imitation in the west of oriental luxury goods is proof of that, though there is obviously a difference between items treasured as curios, and items imitated and even excelled by western copyists. The example of Islamic glazed pottery shows how something at first regarded as exotic became the inspiration for a prosperous local industry in central Italy during the early Renaissance.[10]

The intellectual impact of mercantile contact with the Muslim world is far harder to judge. It will be necessary to take on board the statements of missionaries as well as merchants, notably Ramón Llull of Majorca, eccentrics who used the trade routes to try to convert the Muslims to Christianity. It is possible that Llull's generally good-tempered approach to Islam and Judaism reflects a mercantile culture in which it was difficult to demonise the non-Christian:

contact on the frontier was too persistent, and real friendships could be formed across the religious divide between Christian, Muslim and Jew.[11]

In the first part of what follows I shall outline the process by which western merchants began to penetrate the markets of the Islamic world, taking my discussion up to about 1400. This will mean looking as much at the exports from the west to the Muslim countries as at imports into Europe: the aim will be to show the increasing interdependence of the western and the Islamic economies. I shall then look at the way that communities of Latin merchants operated within the Muslim cities such as Tunis and Alexandria where they had been granted *fonduqs*. Finally, I shall assess the implications of this contact for Christian understanding of the Muslim world.

II

Around 1000 the trade links between western Europe and the Islamic world were few, and were dominated by a small group of cities. One or two of these cities, notably Naples and Marseilles, were very ancient trade centres which had continued to send ships or at least goods to the Maghrib and even the Levant throughout the early Middle Ages;[12] more noticeable, however, are the newer centres, above all Venice and Amalfi, which traced their origins to groups of Roman refugees fleeing the barbarian invasions. In each case, we are looking at trade in small quantities of prestige products. The papyrus of Egypt disappeared from use in western Europe in the eleventh century, but perfumes, spices, cloth and gold were among articles being imported by way of Gaeta in southern Italy around 1012.[13] The southern Italian towns supplied courtly demand in Benevento, Capua, Naples and not least the great ecclesiastical centres at Rome and Montecassino; at this period only small quantities of eastern cloth were filtering north of the Alps. We must not forget, either, that the Byzantine Empire was an alternative source of supply for luxury cloth, and that almost anything under the sun could be bought in Constantinople. It is thus possible that some Islamic products reached the west via Byzantium. Finally, it has to be stressed that the strong stylistic similarities between Byzantine and Islamic silks makes it hard to identify surviving

The Role of Trade in Muslim–Christian Contact

examples found in western Europe as specific imports from Spain, Sicily, Egypt, Syria or Greece. However, some Islamic cloths, silks especially, were certainly arriving in northern France and even northern Germany well before 1100.

The opening up of the Levant trade coincides with the early crusades, and there has been vigorous debate over the importance to the rise of Italian sea-power of the conquest of the Holy Land by the crusaders. Commercial privileges, including promises of tax exemption and quarters in the coastal cities of Palestine, were granted to Genoa, Pisa and Venice, in return for naval help in the capture of Acre, Jaffa, Haifa and eventually Tyre; after the battle of Ascalon, in 1123, Egyptian fleets apparently ceased to pose a great threat to western shipping. In the traditional scenario, new naval powers, Pisa and Genoa, moved in swiftly to take advantage of the commercial privileges that had been granted them, and rose rapidly to a position where they could challenge, if not equal, Venice; better established centres of the Levant trade in southern Italy, such as Amalfi and Bari, failed to participate in the early crusades and thus did not reap the rewards that were offered Genoa and Pisa. The imposition of Norman rule in southern Italy is traditionally assumed to have deprived the region's cities of the political freedom necessary if they were to conduct a vigorous foreign policy aimed at supporting the crusader states.[14]

More recent research has tended to qualify this view in important ways. Pisa and Genoa were not total newcomers to the Levant in the 1090s. They clearly had an active trade in the Maghrib well before 1100. Their merchants occasionally appeared in Alexandria before the First Crusade. These cities saw themselves as front-line statelets with a special duty of clearing the western Mediterranean of Muslim pirates. They had expelled the Muslim warlord Mujāhid from Sardinia at the start of the eleventh century, and alone or together they worked hard against Muslim power in Sicily (attacking Palermo in 1063) and in Tunisia (attacking al-Mahdiyya in 1087). After the First Crusade their enthusiasm for the holy war against Islam in the west did not abate one whit: in 1113–15 the Pisans invaded Majorca and Ibiza with Catalan help; in 1147–8 the Genoese committed themselves to expensive campaigns against Muslim ports in Mediterranean Spain, Almería and Tortosa.

Recent research has also shown that the Holy Land was not the prime trading target of Italian merchants even when they reached the Levant.[15] The Venetians had big interests at Tyre, including landed estates in the environs (later known to have produced sugar cane, a plant that had quenched the thirst of the armies of the First Crusade).[16] But Tyre gives poor access to the interior, since it is cut off from the trade routes leading into Syria by the mountains of southern Lebanon. Acre was better placed, since from there overland routes crossed the rolling hills of Galilee and ascended the Golan Heights before pressing on to Damascus.[17] Acre in particular could function as an outport of Damascus, and Italian merchants gathered there from the mid-twelfth century in order to make contact with Syrian Christians and Muslims bringing goods from as far afield as Mosul. Yet we should not underestimate the bitter struggles that the Italian merchants had to undergo, not with the Muslim rulers of the Middle East but with the Latin kings of Jerusalem, who denied them confirmation of the rights that they claimed in virtue of the treaties drawn up at the time of the original conquest of the coast of the Holy Land.[18] In the 1160s the Genoese demanded, even at the papal court, the restoration of a Golden Inscription supposedly installed in the Church of the Holy Sepulchre in Jerusalem, detailing their special privileges.[19] So bitter was the conflict that in 1163 the Genoese appear to have withdrawn from trade in the Holy Land.[20]

It is now clear that the great age of Acre's trade was the thirteenth century, when changes in the international trade routes as a result of the Mongol conquests in Asia made the overland routes beyond Mesopotamia into Persia, and via Cilician Armenia through Turkey to Persia and beyond, into thriving business concerns.[21] Despite attempts to limit Italian participation on these routes by the rulers of Jerusalem (who saw the penetration of the interior as a threat to their revenues from trade) there were Italian visitors to such centres as Aleppo in the thirteenth century, in search both of luxury goods and of alum, a fixative used by western cloth manufacturers.[22]

But it was the lights of the Pharos of Alexandria that really beckoned. In the twelfth century, Egypt was a major exporter of alum to the west.[23] It was also an important souce of cotton, much of which was not in fact Egyptian but Indian.[24] And here lay the attractiveness of Egypt. It was an access point to a second set of trading networks, to which the Italians did not have access; like

The Role of Trade in Muslim–Christian Contact

Bruges in Flanders, Alexandria was the interchange point between otherwise largely self-contained trading systems, on the one hand the Hanseatic system in the North Sea and Baltic, on the other the elongated trade route via Cairo, the Red Sea and Yemen to India and the Spice Islands. Increasingly fearful of the danger of Christian assaults on Mecca and Medina, the Egyptians closed the Red Sea to non-Muslim shipping. By the end of the twelfth century a new generation of Muslim merchants, the *Karimis*, had gained ascendancy on the India route, taking over gradually from the well-documented Jewish merchants of Fusṭāṭ, the so-called Cairo Genizah merchants.[25]

Pepper and ginger certainly took first place in the Italian spice trade out of late medieval Egypt; it is noteworthy that these products, like much of the exported cotton, were not actually produced in Egypt, but were trans-shipped (and heavily taxed) through Egypt.[26] This is not to deny the gratitude felt by western rulers when they received gifts of Egyptian products from the sultans of Egypt; in 1306 James II of Aragon was sent embroidered and plain cloths in a variety of colours, produced in the state factories in Egypt, and made of silk, linen and cotton; some of the cloths were hand-painted, one possibly with pictures of peaches; the sultan also sent balsam and incense, and some crossbows.[27] The Aragonese–Mamlūk diplomatic exchanges illustrate the efforts made by western princes to keep open the trade routes and to guarantee the safety of Christians in Muslim lands; James II even sought to secure the reopening of Jacobite and Melkite churches in Cairo.[28] But it was normally a delicate enough task to look after the western Christian visitors to Egypt, let alone the native Christian communities.

Christian merchants found themselves in a difficult diplomatic position. On the one hand, there was the fact that they had helped create the Latin Kingdom of Jerusalem, and that they had a considerable stake in its survival. On the other hand, their presence in Acre, Jaffa and Tyre was made more valuable, in commercial terms, by the fact that the ports of the Holy Land were secure bases from which it was possible to make short trips to the Nile Delta. Acre was Alexandria's twin, in the sense that it provided facilities for merchants (and their ships) who intended to make the final hop into Muslim-controlled territory.

Winds and currents helped determine the relationship between

I

Acre and Alexandria.[29] The safest route from Italy to the Levant, from the point of view both of navigation and of immunity from Muslim pirates, was that running round southern Greece, past Crete, and along the island chain towards Rhodes, southern Turkey or Cyprus and the coast of Syria. Some ships did divert from southern Crete directly to the Nile Delta, but few followed the coast of Tripolitania and Cyrenaica, where there were dangerous sandbanks. The result was that a great part of the shipping bound for Alexandria passed the ports of the Latin Kingdom of Jerusalem, once again confirming the special standing of Acre as command centre of the Latin trade network in the Middle East. After the fall of Acre to the Mamlūks of Egypt in 1291, a similar role was assumed by Famagusta in Cyprus, from which trade routes radiated outwards to Laiazzo in Cilician Armenia, to the coast hard by Antioch, to Beirut, and above all to Alexandria and Damietta.[30]

The conquest of eastern markets was also made possible by the readiness with which those markets absorbed western goods. Yet in the older literature the western trading nations tend to be treated as poor relations with little of substance to offer.[31] It is true that until the late twelfth century there was little demand in the Muslim world for western industrial goods; but this changed dramatically as Flemish, north French and even English woollen cloths, made to very high specifications, became the preferred export of the Genoese, Pisans and Venetians to eastern markets.[32] However, the west still depended on Muslim sources for some of the raw materials required in the processing of these goods: alum arrived from Egypt or Syria, and in the late thirteenth century from western Turkey; high quality dyes, notably the bright red grana, came from a variety of sources — in the case of grana, often from Muslim Spain. The growing cotton industry of Lombardy depended, as has been implied already, on supplies of Middle or Far Eastern cotton imported from Egypt and Syria, though there were also supplies nearer at hand in ex-Muslim Sicily and (apparently of a rather better standard) in Malta, which formed part of the Kingdom of Sicily.[33] The conquest of eastern markets by western cloth involved not simply the exploitation of demand for the produce of the mother country among the Franks of the Latin Kingdom of Jerusalem; it also reveals a capacity to create demand at Muslim princely courts. In a sense, the late twelfth century marks the birth of the European

I

The Role of Trade in Muslim–Christian Contact

fashion industry. In 1306 the Mamlūk sultan sent the king of Aragon Venetian linen as well as luxury goods of the Islamic world.[34] The task was facilitated by industrial decline in Egypt and the Islamic heartlands. The theme of industrial decline was the keynote of the work of the prolific Israeli historian of the Islamic economy, Eliyahu Ashtor; but it is hard to explain why this decline took place.[35] Western economic aggression is not a satisfactory explanation, at least on its own, and problems resulting from government intervention in the Egyptian and Maghribi economies must be taken into account too.

Another commodity that western merchants could offer the Muslim world was silver. Here again there have been many misunderstandings.[36] Silver was long seen as a sign of economic weakness: the western world almost entirely abandoned the minting of gold coins after the beginning of the ninth century, while in the Muslim world gold, silver and base metals all circulated. The only Christian kingdoms where a similar position held were those won recently from the Muslims: in some parts of Spain, in Sicily and in the Latin Kingdom of Jerusalem, whose gold coinage was closely modelled on Islamic types. The work of Andrew Watson has indicated, however, that the Muslim countries were short of silver in the early twelfth century.[37] Imports of western silver into the Muslim world, along with the opening of new mines in Khorasan, led to a return to the minting of silver in Syria and North Africa during the twelfth century.[38] The Cairo Genizah documents reveal that a wealthy Jewish merchant, Nahray ben Nissim (fl. 1045–96), carried western silver eastwards in the form of silver ingots.[39] A return to silver meant a return to the freer movement of middle-priced goods, the market for which was restricted by a lack of specie. Of course, another way of describing this process is to say that the balance of trade between east and west always favoured the east in the Middle Ages; such a statement does, however, impose modern economic concepts on the medieval world, and the silver exports must not be seen simply as a drainage of western money eastwards — in a sense, silver too was a commodity, some of which was mined and cast into ingots without being minted as coin.[40] There were also good opportunities for western merchants to buy gold (again, a commodity as well as coin) in the Levant rather more cheaply than they could in the ports of western Europe, and we begin to see an

9

accumulation of Islamic gold coins in royal treasuries as far afield as that of Henry III of England.[41] Muslim gold was thus sometimes used to make very large payments within western Europe, and it was hardly a major revolution when, in 1252, the Genoese and the Florentines resumed the minting of European gold coins, made mainly of gold imported from Muslim lands, after a break of four and a half centuries.[42]

A third group of imports that was much esteemed among the Muslims was armaments. It is hardly surprising that arms appear among the exports to the Latin states in Syria; the scale of exports to Egypt was, however, sufficient to cause scandal throughout the Middle Ages. A type of shield known in Egypt as the *janāwiyya* has been plausibly identified as a shield from Genoa.[43] On occasion whole ships appear to have been sailed to Egypt and sold there, though more common was the trade in timber, vital for the Egyptian army, and in short supply in Egypt itself.[44] Since the great naval defeat at Ascalon at the hands of the Venetians, the Egyptians found it harder to gain access to the timber of southern Anatolia, though raiding parties continued to harass Cyprus, where, again, good timber was to be found. It is clear that the building of a fleet was a far more challenging proposition for the Egyptians than it was for the Italians or even for the relatively sea-shy Byzantines. And no Italian republic was prepared to go to the lengths of offering its fleet to the sultans of Egypt, in the way that the Italians regularly offered fleets in return for commercial privileges to Christian princes — to the Byzantines and to the rulers of Jerusalem.

The result was that the actual privileges the Italian merchants received in Muslim countries were less generous than those which they received in Christian regions. Rather than being granted quarters of towns, they were granted control of a *fonduq*, in which the merchants were confined under curfew at night. The question was one of gaining any access to Egyptian markets, rather than of being given preferential access. Some minor tax reductions were secured, but nothing on the scale of the massive reductions claimed in Constantinople and the Latin east. In 1154–5, the Pisans, perhaps disappointed at their failure to extend their trade rights in the crusader states as far as they had hoped, sent Rainerio Botaccio as ambassador to Fāṭimid Egypt, and were compensated for their pains by promises to grant Pisan merchants safe conduct in Egypt.[45] There

The Role of Trade in Muslim–Christian Contact

are, however, few indications of attempts to penetrate beyond Alexandria and Damietta, though the south Italian merchant Solomon of Salerno, who was a Genoese resident, travelled to Cairo in 1156 to buy lac and brazilwood for a Genoese business partner.[46] In fact, there are several signs that the western merchants approved of crusader plans to establish Latin rule over the Nile Delta: in 1169 the Pisans were lured by King Amaury of Jerusalem into a plan for a joint Byzantine–Frankish attack on Egypt, the prize for Pisa being the promise of commercial privileges in conquered Egypt. But they were back trading in Alexandria in 1174, when an attacking Sicilian fleet surprised a Pisan ship that had arrived from Venice; at the same time, there were apparently Pisans, Genoese and Venetians in the invading fleet.[47] The Egyptians knew that the Italian merchants were involved, and regarded this as a betrayal of the good relations that had been built up over recent years. The original target of the Fourth Crusade, in which the Venetians were so heavily involved, was Alexandria, not Constantinople;[48] and the Fifth Crusade as well as the crusade of St Louis saw the capture of Damietta as the key to the recovery of Jerusalem.[49] Here again the Italians had a commercial stake, though the shameless activities of a group of nineteenth-century forgers, whose bogus charters still have the power to deceive Sotheby's, have perhaps magnified the Italian role out of real proportion.[50] It is certain, too, that the Italians did not always secure the protection they craved. In 1195 and 1200 there were Venetian and Genoese merchants held captive in Egyptian gaols. The Italians were all too easily held hostage for the good behaviour of the mother-city, especially at times of rising tension between the Ayyūbids of Egypt and Syria and the virtually encircled Latin kings of Jerusalem.

The intention here has been to make a very simple point: it was the western merchants who opened up the markets in the Levant. The north Italians were not forced to compete with Muslim merchants operating the same trade routes in reverse direction. Even in the tenth and eleventh centuries, the great age of the Cairo Genizah merchants, Amalfi and other western ports were not apparently visited by swarms of Muslim merchants, though Amalfi itself had a high reputation among Muslims as the western trading station par excellence. In fact, the ample records of twelfth-century Genoa make little reference to Muslim visitors. The major recorded incident in Genoa involving a visit by merchants of probable Muslim origin, themselves agents of a very powerful Muslim prince, actually concerns Sicilian Muslims living a full ninety years after the Norman seizure of Palermo from Islam.[51] It is true that the Jews sometimes acted as intermediaries between the Muslim and the Christian world; but the Jews of Fusṭāṭ, whose trade is so superbly recorded, gave their attention to the India route, to the land and sea trade routes along the coast of North Africa, to trade with Sicily and, in small measure, with southern Italy. What is striking is that the Jewish merchants did not penetrate Genoa or Venice, cities which actually discouraged Jewish settlement.

It was in the western Mediterranean that the role of the Jews as intermediaries took on reality; and it was in this arena that Jews, Christians and in some cases Muslims coexisted in the same cities: Jews and Christians in Marseilles or Barcelona; all three religions in Ciutat de Majorca or Valencia. It is possible, too, that Montpellier in southern France had a small Muslim trading settlement, since fragments of twelfth-century gravestones survive there that are otherwise very hard to explain.[52] It is now necessary to turn to the great arc of lands known to historians of the late Middle Ages as the Crown of Aragon, including Sicily, Sardinia, the Balearics and Montpellier as well as Catalonia, Aragon and parts of southern France. It was from here that a particularly intensive penetration of north-west Africa was launched.

III

Although North Africa was an important source of cloths, it would be wrong to assume that the areas to the west of Egypt had a similar economic profile to Egypt itself. The appeal of African trade lay at least as much in access to supplies of wool, leather and other raw or semi-processed materials as it did in the desire to obtain luxury goods. Morocco even functioned as a granary for western merchants by the fourteenth century, although Tunisia underwent a long economic crisis in which one of the early signs of collapse was the onset of very frequent famines, starting in the late eleventh century. Its towns also gradually succumbed to the industrial malaise which made them increasingly receptive to western finished textiles. The obvious means of payment was gold, as the ability to supply home-

The Role of Trade in Muslim–Christian Contact

produced cloths, and demand for them in an increasingly self-sufficient west, both declined. Western penetration of North African markets perhaps reached its peak when the Catalans and the Italians carved out a monopoly in salt production and transport in the western Mediterranean, so that regular imports of Ibizan salt in exchange for African gold became a satisfying source of profit to the Catalan businessmen of Majorca.[53]

The emergence of the Catalan merchants is one of the great success stories of medieval business. In the twelfth century there was undoubtedly a limited Catalan trade out of Barcelona towards southern France, Muslim Spain and North Africa. The travel diary of the Spanish Jew Benjamin of Tudela, of about 1160, even suggests that Muslim merchants regularly visited Barcelona at this time.[54] However, Catalan fleets played no part in the great naval expeditions against al-Andalus, such as the brief occupation of Majorca from 1113 to 1115. It was a century later, in 1229–35, with the building of a fleet to capture the Balearics decisively in the name of Christendom, that the Catalans became a truly powerful economic and political force in the western Mediterranean. North Africa remained a very high priority for Catalan shipping. Commercial contracts from Barcelona, and a remarkable book of licences for ships leaving the port of Majorca in 1284, confirm the primacy of the Maghrib in Catalan trade at this period.[55] In 1282 the Aragonese conquest of Sicily, valuable both for itself and as a gateway to the Levant, enlarged the area in which Catalan shipping could eventually move freely, even though it by no means marked the inception of Catalan trade with the central and eastern Mediterranean.[56] This position of strength was not significantly weakened in the fourteenth century. The *Llibre de conoxenses de spécies e de drogues e de avissaments de pessoas, canes e massures de diverses terres*, a merchant manual of 1385, probably from Barcelona, refers to seventeen or more ports in the Maghrib and strongly suggests that this was the area of the Mediterranean that the Catalans knew best, other than their home waters.[57] If confirmation were needed, the great number of surviving treaties with the rulers of Tunis, Tlemcen, Bougie and Ceuta indicates the importance of Catalan trade in North Africa to the kings of Aragon and of Majorca, who drew substantial revenues from trade taxes remitted to them by the Muslim amirs.[58] The Catalans possessed more than one *fonduq* in several North

African towns: in Bougie the Catalan king of Majorca gained control of one of the Catalan *fonduqs* in 1302, despite the protests of his kinsman the king of Aragon–Catalonia.[59] There were even cases where the king of Aragon received a share of the trade taxes imposed on all Latin merchants, including Italians and southern French merchants as well as Catalans. This signifies very clearly the political and commercial ascendancy achieved by the Catalans in North Africa during the thirteenth century.

Another source of gold was payment by Muslim charitable organisations for the redemption of captives seized by Christian pirates (Valencia was a great centre of Christian pirates by 1300); however, this was a two-way traffic, and western merchants sometimes found themselves acting as agents for the two Redemptive Orders, the Trinitarians and Mercedarians, who collected funds in western Europe to pay ransoms for Christian prisoners in Muslim Spain and North Africa.[60] The image of the Christian captive in Muslim lands is brilliantly portrayed in such thirteenth-century French romances as *The Count of Ponthieu's daughter*, where the separation of two lovers results from capture and sale into slavery.[61] It was a trade in humans in which the Catalan merchants had a special stake. In addition, Catalan merchants were heavily involved in the trade in Muslim slaves, who were placed on sale in slave markets in Palermo, Ciutat de Majorca and other frontier ports. Many slaves, having been exported from the Muslim world, were then re-exported to North Africa and al-Andalus, so that the Catalans acted as intermediaries between Muslim and Muslim. The sale of the century occurred in 1287, when the Aragonese seized Muslim Menorca and enslaved nearly all those who could not afford to pay for their redemption; the island was almost completely depopulated, though most of its inhabitants did return, if only as slaves, to the Islamic world.[62]

The importance of medieval Catalan trade lies partly in maritime technology: the apparent ease with which Catalan sailors were able to navigate to the Balearics and to Africa in both winter and summer (by 1284) and the advanced cartography of the so-called school of Majorca provide two explanations for the use of Catalan ships even by Genoese and Tuscan merchants seeking to penetrate the markets of North Africa. It has been argued that the Catalans of Majorca were the first Mediterranean sailors to breach the Straits of Gibraltar

The Role of Trade in Muslim–Christian Contact

around 1277 and to establish direct sailings to England and Flanders.[63] What is certain at least is that navigation along the Atlantic coast of Africa developed in the early fourteenth century. Ports such as Anfa (the modern Casablanca) were being visited with regularity around 1330.[64] The Bardi and Peruzzi, the two greatest banks of Florence in the early fourteenth century, turned to Catalan shippers when they sent grain and wine from Sicily to Tunis just before 1300.

The cartographic evidence is, however, very difficult to handle: what survive are the portolan charts of the fourteenth century, in some quantity, and the larger world maps or atlases that were a de luxe extension of the portolan charts, and in some cases formed part of royal libraries.[65] Whether any of these maps were ever used by captains on the high seas is a debated issue. The maps do show similarities to Muslim maps of the thirteenth century, and there is no reason to doubt that such mapmakers as Abraham and Judah (Jafuda) Cresques in fourteenth-century Majorca had access to Arabic geographical sources.[66] They were Jews who could exploit the close cultural and economic links between the Jewish communities of the Balearic Islands and those of North Africa, whence part of the Majorcan community in fact originated. As Felipe Fernández-Armesto has recently stressed in an elegant study of exploration and colonisation before Columbus, the extension of geographical knowledge to include detailed information on the west coast of Africa, as far as the Canaries, and to include also rough data on the gold routes linking black Africa to the Mediterranean, was partly achieved through the physical penetration of these regions by western merchants, Catalan and Italian.[67] Arab geography alone did not solve all the problems of the mapmakers.

Catalan missionaries, seeking to convert the Muslims of the Maghrib to Christianity, did not neglect the opportunities created by the trade relations between the Crown of Aragon and the North African rulers. Dominicans and Franciscans set up schools of Arabic and Hebrew, in which Jewish and Muslim sacred texts were studied in the original, in order to equip the friars for preaching campaigns in Muslim Spain, the Maghrib and, of course, in areas such as Valencia that were now under Christian rule but that retained a large non-Christian population. The most prolific exponent of the mission against Islam was Ramón Llull, born in 1232, who by his death in

I

1316 had set up a school of Arabic in his home island of Majorca, had written a great number of tracts on the relative merits of Judaism, Christianity and Islam, and had gained access to the courts of Majorca, Paris and Rome in attempts to mobilise new Christian missions in North Africa.[68] His own knowledge of Muslim culture was exceptional, though probably not unique; the general mark of his approach was a degree of politeness and respect towards his Muslim interlocutors that perhaps was unique. Once in Tunis, he was able to gain access to the emir's court, and to hold religious discussions with Muslim scholars; but his presence was only tolerated when political relations between Tunis and the Latin west were close and when the ruler of Tunis teased western sensibilities by appearing to hint at his future conversion to Christianity.

IV

It is in Tunis that we can observe the day-to-day interaction of Christian merchants and Muslim rulers. This is in part because of the survival of a remarkable book of minutes by a Genoese scribe, Pietro Battifoglio, dating from 1289.[69] More than three hundred westerners are mentioned in these acts from Tunis, over a period of seven months. Yet the Christian community of Tunis was already very large at the start of the thirteenth century, when the Pisan merchant Leonardo Fibonacci lived there and studied Arabic numerals, on which he wrote a famous treatise in 1202.[70] Tunis is perhaps not typical: the Christian community, consisting of merchants, sailors, mercenaries, loose women, priests and so on, occupied by the mid-fourteenth century a vast area of the city, about equal to the Muslim fortified city.[71] But, precisely because it is an exceptional case, it is worth examining for possible evidence that the merchants of Genoa, Pisa, Barcelona and elsewhere who lived there enjoyed not simply a business relationship with their Muslim hosts.

The evidence of Pietro Battifoglio shows that the problems faced by Christian merchants in gaining recognition of their rights in Tunis were quite severe. On 21 April and on 1 May 1289 the Genoese consul in Tunis, Balianno Embrono, declared to the head of the customs service that the agreements between the city of Genoa and the ruler of Tunis must be respected by that ruler, and that he must

16

The Role of Trade in Muslim–Christian Contact

grant an audience to the consul, as accredited head of the Genoese colony, no less than twice each month.[72] In other words, the consul was having some difficulty in gaining access to the ruler's ear, and yet the latest treaty between Genoa and Tunis dated from as recently as 1287.[73] The guarantees provided by the royal court included a promise of protection for the goods of the Genoese, and of indemnity when they were seized illicitly. A vast sum (20,393 besants) was granted to the Genoese as a refund for damage inflicted by Pisan aggressors on Genoese goods and shipping in the port of Tunis, at La Golette; the ruler of Tunis was liable here since he had failed to give proper protection to his allies.[74] One of the pillaged ships was said to have contained over 2,000 jars of oil. However, wine was an even more sensitive issue, not least since the Genoese were able to operate their own tavern in the *fonduq*. When the amir tried to increase taxes on wine, the consul protested with vigour; afraid of trouble, the consul locked the warehouse where wine was stored, and gave the key to the resident Genoese priest, Tealdo.[75] Such disputes over taxes on oil and wine could erupt in violence: it was apparently easy to mobilise a crowd to hurl not just abuse but sticks and stones at the wine-swilling, pork-eating, uncircumcised polytheists in their midst. The sense of insecurity felt by the Christians in Tunis comes across easily; it was simply not the same existence as they experienced when living in the Italian quarter in Acre or Majorca. Nor did the Italians and Catalans conduct intensive business in the interior of Tunisia. To some extent Tunis functioned as the command post for a local network of trade routes, but the main commercial links were with the Christian world, to Sicily, the Balearics and beyond.[76]

The community of Genoese in Tunis naturally consisted mainly of birds of passage. There were, however, long-term residents: the priest has been mentioned, and it is known that the churches of the different merchant communities were subject to restrictions. Bells were not to be rung and campanili were not to be built, although the Venetians tried hard to build one.[77] They were small chapels, one or more for each merchant community, and another one for the large regiment of Aragonese mercenaries who also lived in Tunis; despite Ramón Llull's wishes, the churches never really functioned as missionary centres, though for about twenty years from 1250 there was a Dominican school of Arabic in Tunis, one of the earliest

I

of those missionary colleges which aimed to teach a knowledge of Arabic and of Islam to future preachers in North Africa and Muslim Spain.[78] It was presumably tolerated because its members sought only to learn from Muslims, and not actually to preach to Muslims. All told, the amirs valued Italian and Catalan trade too much to deny the merchants reasonable facilities; yet the merchants did live in a large, but nevertheless confined, area, and they had to renegotiate their rights regularly. This was an especial problem at the end of the thirteenth century, when the Mediterranean was convulsed by the War of the Sicilian Vespers, and shifting political alliances created great uncertainty about trade prospects.

V

The *fonduq* and merchant quarter thus constituted an island in the Muslim world. It is hard to see how, except in the rare cases of active missionaries seeking to penetrate Islam, these islands were linked by bridges to the surrounding culture. This is not to deny that certain skills in numeracy and cartography did derive from Muslim sources. Trade between Christians and Muslims, conducted by Christian visitors to Muslim lands (and not normally Muslim visitors to continental Europe), had enormous implications for the development of the western economy, as can be seen from the rise of the European textile industries and from the associated changes in the European monetary system after 1252. We can only guess at the extent to which Christian merchants observed and took an interest in the Muslim civilisation they came to know through trade. They travelled to the Muslim lands in search of the products of the east, in search of markets for their own goods and above all in search of profits. Moreover, one of the main attractions of the bazaars of Alexandria was the availability of spices, which had in large measure arrived from beyond the frontiers of Islam, and had been carried all the way across the Muslim world; so too the gold which they sought on the coasts of North Africa had been panned beyond the southern edge of Islam, in black Africa.[79]

While it would be wrong to deny the intrinsic attractions to western buyers of many items produced within the lands of Islam, it is important to remember too that Islam presented a frustratingly large block of lands impeding free access to supplies of non-Muslim

The Role of Trade in Muslim–Christian Contact

regions far to the south and east. As early as 1291, with the Vivaldi expedition to India via West Africa (which never reached its destination) hopes were being expressed of bypassing the Arab countries entirely.[80] The Mongol trade routes also for a few decades facilitated overland links to China that avoided the heartlands of Islam. Thus two hundred years before Christopher Columbus (d. 1506) and Vasco da Gama (d. 1524) merchants saw the Islamic world as much as a physical impediment, as a source of exotic goods and of wealthy clients able to pay in gold.

It was, rather, in those areas of Europe such as Andalusia, Valencia and Sicily where Arab culture survived, at least briefly, the shock of Christian conquest that the economic influence of the Islamic world was most profound. Sicily actually experienced a brief florescence of Arab learning after the Norman conquest; Valencia retained and improved its irrigation systems, still commemorated in the water courts of Valencia City.[81] But even here there is an optical illusion. When in the fifteenth century western merchants visited Valencia and Sicily in search of rice, sugar and up-market fruits, they were buying goods whose production had not necessarily been maintained continuously since Muslim times. Sicilian sugar, henna and indigo were disappearing around 1200, and Frederick II made a determined effort to restore their cultivation, using Jewish labour, in the mid-thirteenth century.[82] The Turkish advances in the eastern Mediterranean were stimulating the planting of so-called Islamic crops in the west, as far west, in fact, as Madeira and the Canary Islands.[83] Valencian irrigation had serviced the needs of grain producers in the thirteenth and fourteenth centuries, and specialised crops apparently grew in importance only in the late fourteenth and fifteenth centuries, even if the know-how had always been there. Even Muslim Granada, a major source of quality fruits, became a virtual economic colony of the Genoese financiers in the fifteenth century, who made Málaga into a major base for Italian and Catalan trade.[84] The lesson of all this is that it was increasingly possible to conduct trade in the produce of the Muslim world without having to set foot in that world. It is true, as has been said, that in formal terms the western merchants never managed to adjust in their favour the balance of trade with the Islamic world. However, following on from the defeat of Muslim navies and from the triumph of western textiles in the Mediterranean, the capture of Arab agricultural technology

I

confirmed the massive ascendancy of western merchants in their trade with Islam by the end of the Middle Ages.

Notes

1 A.S. Atiyah, *Crusade, Commerce and Culture* (Bloomington, Indiana/Oxford, 1962).
2 Atiyah, pp. 240–1.
3 A. Watson, *Agricultural Innovation in the Early Islamic World* (Cambridge, 1983).
4 J. Needham and collaborators, *Science and Civilisation in China* (Cambridge, 1954 onwards), a massive multi-volume work still in progress.
5 Watson, pp. 31–44.
6 Other terms, derived from the absorption and remodelling of Muslim administration under Christian conquerors, do not offer real proof of trade contacts: there are the amirs of Sicily, who developed by the thirteenth century into the office of Admiral; there are also the *rais* or headmen of Latin Syria, and the separate *rais* of the tunny fishing fleets of western Sicily, who are said still to survive. On the former, see L.R. Ménager, *Ammiratis-'Αμηρας. L'émirat et les origines de l'amirauté* (Paris, 1960).
7 Robert Lopez, "The trade of medieval Europe: the South", *Cambridge Economic History of Europe*, revised edn, vol. 2 (Cambridge, 1987), p. 347.
8 See for Valencia the works of R.I. Burns, e.g. *Medieval Colonialism. Postcrusade Exploitation of Islamic Valencia* (Princeton, N.J., 1975).
9 P.D. Curtin, *Cross-cultural Trade in World History* (Cambridge, 1984).
10 David Abulafia, "The Pisan bacini and the medieval Mediterranean economy: a historian's viewpoint", *Papers in Italian Archaeology, IV: the Cambridge Conference*, pt. iv, *Classical and Medieval Archaeology*, (British Archaeological Reports, International Series, 246), ed. C. Malone and S. Stoddart (Oxford, 1985), pp. 287–302.
11 On the general phenomenon of conversion of Muslims in the thirteenth century, see B.Z. Kedar, *Crusade and Mission. European Approaches toward the Muslim* (Princeton, N.J., 1984).
12 R. Pernoud, "Le moyen-âge jusqu'à 1291", *Histoire du commerce de Marseille*, ed. G. Rambert, vol. 1 (1949); P. Arthur, "Naples: notes on the economy of a Dark Age city", *Papers in Italian Archaeology, IV: the Cambridge Conference*, pt. iv, *Classical and Medieval Archaeology*, (British Archaeological Reports, International Series, vol. 246), ed. C. Malone and S. Stoddart (Oxford, 1985), pp. 247–59.
13 M. Merores, *Gaeta im frühen Mittelalter* (Gotha, 1911), pp. 96–8. The debate about the supply of oriental commodities was, of course, given new life by H. Pirenne, *Mohammed and Charlemagne* (London, 1939).
14 See, e.g. A. Schaube, *Handelsgeschichte der Romanischen Völker des Mittelmeergebiets bis zum Ende der Kreuzzüge* (Munich/Berlin, 1906).
15 C. Cahen, *Orient et Occident au temps des Croisades* (Paris, 1983), pp. 123–8.
16 J. Prawer, *Crusader Institutions* (Oxford, 1980), p. 160.
17 The routes thus crossed the present no-man's land between Israel and Syria, passing Banyas in modern Golan, where there was a major castle: *The Travels of Ibn Jubayr*, ed. and transl. R.J.C. Broadhurst (London, 1952), p. 315. Some travellers bound for Tyre stopped in Acre en route (Ibn Jubayr, p. 319).
18 See now Marie-Luise Favreau-Lilie, *Die Italianer im heiligen Land vom ersten Kreuzzug bis zum Tode Heinrichs von Champagne (1098–1197)* (Amsterdam/Las Palmas de Gran

The Role of Trade in Muslim–Christian Contact

Canaria, 1989) for a masterly survey of the relations between the Italians and the kings of Jerusalem in the twelfth century.

19 M.-L. Favreau and H.E. Mayer, "Das Diplom Balduins I. für Genua und Genuas Goldene Inschrift in der Grabeskirche", *Quellen und Forschungen aus italienischen Archiven und Bibliotheken*, 55/6 (1976), 22–95, repr. in H.E. Mayer, *Kreuzzüge und lateinischer Osten* (London, 1983), essay V; B.Z. Kedar, "Genoa's golden inscriptions in the Church of the Holy Sepulchre: a case for the defence", in *I comuni italiani nel regno crociato di Gerusalemme*, ed. G. Airaldi and B.Z. Kedar (Genoa, 1986), pp. 317–35.

20 David Abulafia, *The Two Italies. Economic Relations between the Norman Kingdom of Sicily and the Northern Communes* (Cambridge, 1977), p. 131.

21 On the general problem, see David Abulafia, "Asia, Africa and the trade of medieval Europe", in *Cambridge Economic History of Europe*, revised edn. vol. 2 (Cambridge, 1987), pp. 443–4, and, for Turkey, pp. 455–8.

22 J. Riley-Smith, "Government in Latin Syria and the commercial privileges of the foreign merchants", in *Relations between East and West in the Middle Ages*, ed. D. Baker (Edinburgh, 1973); and, for merchants bound to Aleppo, David Abulafia, "Crocuses and Crusaders: San Gimignano, Pisa and the Kingdom of Jerusalem", in *Outremer: Studies in the History of the Crusading Kingdom of Jerusalem presented to Joshua Prawer*, ed. B.Z. Kedar, H.E. Mayer and R.C. Smail (Jerusalem, 1982), pp. 227–43.

23 Abulafia, "Asia, Africa", pp. 434, 436.

24 For Egyptian cotton, Abulafia, "Asia, Africa", 432; for Indian cotton, see M. Mazzaoui, *The Italian Cotton Industry in the Later Middle Ages, 1100–1600* (Cambridge, 1981), pp. 15, 35 and *passim*.

25 Abulafia, "Asia, Africa", pp. 437–43, and the bibliography, pp. 906–8.

26 See the studies collected together in: E. Ashtor, *Studies on the Levantine Trade in the Middle Ages* (London, 1987); E. Ashtor, *East-West Trade in the Medieval Mediterranean*, ed. B.Z. Kedar (London, 1986).

27 A.S. Atiyah, *Egypt and Aragon. Embassies and diplomatic correspondence between AD 1300 and 1330* (Abhandlungen für die Kunde des Morgenlandes, 23:7) (Leipzig, 1938), pp. 26–34. Further evidence, this time of a physical nature, of interest in fine Egyptian cloths comes from a series of vestments found at the Marienkirche in Danzig (Gdansk): W. Mannowsky, *Der Danziger Paramentenschatz, Kirchliche Gewänder und Strickereien aus der Marienkirche*, vols. 1–4 (Berlin, 1931–8), I, 1:13, II, 1:15; cf. Atiyah, *Egypt and Aragon*, pp. 28–9.

28 Atiyah, *Egypt and Aragon*, pp. 20–5.

29 This is the convincing thesis of J.H. Pryor, *Geography, Technology and War: Studies in the Maritime History of the Mediterranean, 649–1571* (Cambridge, 1988).

30 D. Jacoby, "The rise of a new emporium in the eastern Mediterranean: Famagusta in the late thirteenth century", *Meletai kai hypomnemata, Hidryma Archiepiskopou Makariou III* (Nicosia, 1984), pp. 145–79, repr. in D. Jacoby, *Studies on the Crusader states and on Venetian Expansion* (Northampton, 1989), essay VIII.

31 R.S. Lopez, "Il problema della bilancia dei pagamenti nel commercio di Levante", *Venezia e il Levante fino al secolo XV*, vols. 1–2 (Florence, 1973), I.431–52.

32 David Abulafia, "Maometto e Carlomagno. Le due aree monetarie italiane dell'oro e dell'argento", *Economia naturale, economia monetaria* (Storia d'Italia, Annali, 6) ed. R. Romano and U. Tucci (Torino, 1983), pp. 223–70.

33 For Maltese cotton, see Abulafia, *Two Italies*, 218, 230; A.T. Luttrell, "Approaches to medieval Malta", *Medieval Malta. Studies on Malta before the Knights* (London, 1975), p. 31.

I

34   Atiyah, *Egypt and Aragon*, p. 32.

35   See most conveniently E. Ashtor, *A Social and Economic History of the Near East in the Middle Ages* (London, 1976); E. Ashtor, *Technology, Industry and Trade: the Levant versus Europe, 1250–1500*, ed. B.Z. Kedor (Aldershot, 1992).

36   For a new view, see Abulafia, "Maometto e Carlomagno".

37   A. Watson, "Back to Gold — and Silver", *Economic History Review*, 2, 20 (1967), 1–34.

38   On western sources, see P. Spufford, *Money and its Use in Medieval Europe* (Cambridge, 1988), pp. 109–31.

39   S.D. Goitein, *A Mediterranean Society:* vol. 1 *Economic Foundations*, (Berkeley/Los Angeles, 1967), pp. 153–4; Abulafia, "Maometto e Carlomagno", 253.

40   Abulafia, "Maometto e Carlomagno", 231–6, for the implications; Spufford, 209–24, for the physical realities.

41   P. Grierson, "Oboli de musc", *English Historical Review*, 66 (1951), 75–81; P. Grierson, "Muslim coins in thirteenth-century England", *Near Eastern Numismatics, Iconography, Epigraphy and History. Studies in Honor of George C. Miles* (Beirut, 1974), pp. 387–91; M. Bloch, "Le problème de l'or au moyen âge", *Annales d'Histoire Économique et Sociale*, vol. 5 (1933), pp. 1–34; but cf. Abulafia, "Maometto e Carlomagno", pp. 249–50.

42   R.S. Lopez, "Back to Gold", *Economic History Review*, 2, 9 (1956/7), pp. 219–40; R.S. Lopez, "Settecento anni fa: il ritorno all'oro nell'occidente ducentesco", *Rivista storica italiana*, 45 (1953), pp. 19–55, and 161–98 (and published as a separate volume, Naples, 1955); Spufford, pp. 176–7.

43   Cahen, pp. 133, 176.

44   For an example of a ship being repaired in Genoa and then sailed to Egypt to be sold there, see Abulafia, *Two Italies*, p. 244.

45   K.H. Allmendinger, *Die Beziehungen zwischen der Kommune Pisa und Ägypten im hohen Mittelalter. Eine rechts und wirtschaftshistorische Untersuchung* (Wiesbaden, 1967), pp. 45–54; Cahen, pp. 125–7.

46   Abulafia, *Two Italies*, p. 240.

47   Abulafia, *Two Italies*, pp. 140–1.

48   D. Queller, *The Fourth Crusade* (Leicester, 1978), p. 13.

49   J.M. Powell, *Anatomy of a Crusade, 1213–21* (Philadelphia, 1986), pp. 137–8; the Fifth Crusade did, however, include preparatory expeditions aimed at targets around Mount Tabor in the Holy Land. Joinville's *Life of St Louis* is the major source for the planning of Louis IX's Crusade: *Mémoires de Jean sire de Joinville ou histoire et chronique du très Chrétien roi Saint Louis*, ed. F. Michel (Paris, 1867).

50   David Abulafia, "Invented Italians in the Courtois Charters", *Crusade and Settlement: Papers Read at the First Conference of the Society for the Study of the Crusades and the Latin East and Presented to R.C. Smail*, ed. P.W. Edbury (Cardiff: University College Cardiff Press, 1985), pp. 135–43; some Courtois material was put on sale at Sotheby's in the summer of 1989 on the assumption that it was genuine.

51   Abulafia, *Two Italies*, pp. 247–50.

52   Casts of these stones are on display in the crypt of Nôtre-Dame des Tables, Montpellier.

53   C.E. Dufourcq, *L'Espagne catalane et le Maghrib au XIIIe et XIVe siècles* (Paris, 1966).

54   David Abulafia, "Catalan merchants in the western Mediterranean: studies in the notarial acts of Barcelona and Sicily, 1236–1300", *Viator*, vol. 16 (1985), p. 209, repr. in David Abulafia, *Italy, Sicily and the Mediterranean, 1100–1400* (London, 1987), essay VIII.

55   Arxiu del regne de Majorca, Palma de Majorca, Real Patrimonio, Llicències per a Barques. See A. Riera Melis, "La Llicència per a barques de 1284. Una font important per a l'estudi del comerç mallorquí del darrer quart del segle XIII", *Faventia*, vol. 2 (1980): 91–125, (also printed in *Fontes Rerum Balearium*, vol. 3 (Palma de Majorca, 1978–83);

The Role of Trade in Muslim–Christian Contact

David Abulafia, "Les Llicències per a barques et le commerce de Majorque en 1284", *Les Catalans et la Mer*, ed. H. Bresc (Paris, forthcoming).

56 Fines imposed on Catalan merchants trading with Egypt became a major source of revenue to the Aragonese kings in the early fourteenth century; a supposedly illicit trade was thus transformed into a trade merely subject to additional taxes, and in 1302 these taxes supplied about half the king's known revenue from Catalonia: J. Hillgarth, "The problem of a Catalan Mediterranean Empire, 1229–1327", *English Historical Review*, supplement no. 8 (London, 1975), pp. 7, 41–2.

57 F. Fernández-Armesto, *Before Columbus: Exploration and Colonisation from the Mediterranean to the Atlantic, 1229–1492* (London, 1987), p. 141.

58 For Tlemcen see Dufourcq, pp. 145–56, 311–36.

59 A. Riera Melis, *La Corona de Aragón y el reino de Majorca en el primo cuarto del siglo XIV*, 1: *Las repercussiones arancelarias de la autonomía balear (1298–1311)* (Madrid/Barcelona, 1986), p. 299.

60 The main account of the Mercedarians in the Crown of Aragon is J. Brodman, *Ransoming Captives in Crusader Spain: The Order of Merced on the Christian–Islamic Frontier* (Philadelphia, 1986).

61 *La fille du comte de Pontieu*, ed. C. Brunel (Paris, 1923, 1926).

62 Elena Lourie, "La colonización cristiana de Menorca durante el reinado de Alfonso III el Liberal rey de Aragón", *Analecta sacra Tarraconensia*, 53/4 (1983), pp. 135–86; Ramón Roselló Vaquer, *Aportació a la història medieval de Menorca. El sigle XIII* (Ciutadella, 1980); Micaela Mata, *Conquests and Reconquests of Menorca* (Barcelona, 1984), pp. 9–62. In a paper at the 13th Congress of the History of the Crown of Aragon, Palma de Majorca, September 1987, H. Bresc argued that the events of 1287 were a novelty, marking a new attitude to the Muslims among Christian Mediterranean rulers: H. Bresc, "L'esclavage dans le monde méditerranéen des XIVe et XVe siècles: problèmes politiques, réligieux et morales", *XIII Congrés d'Història de la Corona d'Aragó*, 4 vols. (Palma de Mallorca, 1989–90), 1.89–102; see also David Abulafia, "Monarchs and minorities in the western Mediterranean in the later thirteenth century: Lucera and its analogues", *Christendom and its Discontents*, ed. S. Waugh (Center for Medieval and Renaissance Studies, University of California, Los Angeles, forthcoming).

63 David Abulafia, "Les relacions comercials i politiques entre el Regne de Majorca i Anglaterra segons fonts documentals angleses", *XIII Congrés d'Història de la Corona d'Aragó*, 4.69–79, argues for a continuous series of Mallorcan visits to England and Flanders throughout the early fourteenth century.

64 Dufourcq, Table 3, pp. 596–7.

65 See Fernández-Armesto, p. 151. Indispensable is T. Campbell, "Portolan Charts from the late thirteenth century to 1500", *The History of Cartography: Cartography in Prehistoric, Ancient and Medieval Europe and the Mediterranean*, ed. J.B. Harley and D. Woodward, vol. 1 (Chicago, 1987), pp. 371–463.

66 See the Arab chart illustrated as plate 4 of C. de la Roncière, *La Découverte de l'Afrique au moyen âge: L'intérieur du continent*, vol. 1, published as tome 5 of *Mémoires de la Société royale de Géographie d'Égypte* (Cairo, 1924).

67 Fernández-Armesto, pp. 151–68.

68 The best introductions to Llull are those of J. Hillgarth, *Ramon Lull and Lullism in Fourteenth-century France* (London, 1971), and A. Bonner, "Introduction", *Selected Works of Ramon Llull (1232–1316)*, ed. A. Bonner, vols. 1–2 (Princeton, 1985).

69 Geo Pistarino, ed., *Notai genovesi in Oltremare. Atti rogati a Tunisi da Pietro Battifoglio (1288–1289)*, (Collana storica di Fonti e Studi, 47) (Genoa, 1986). There is also a summary of the acts in G. Jehel, "Catalogue analytique et chronologique des actes du

I

notaire Petrus Batifolius rédigé à Tunis du 20 décembre 1288 au 24 juin 1289", *Cahiers de Tunisie*, 25 (1977), pp. 69–137.

70 C.H. Haskins, *Studies in the History of Mediaeval Science* (Cambridge, Mass., 1924), pp. 249, 259; cf. David Abulafia, *Frederick II. A Medieval Emperor* (London, 1988), p. 254.

71 See the map of late medieval Tunis in R. Brunschvig, *La Berbérie orientale sous les Hafsides*, vols. 1–2 (Paris, 1940–7), I, 339. The first recorded trade representatives of a Christian ruler date from 1117, when Count Roger of Sicily had commercial agents in Tunis, who may, at this period, have been Muslims themselves, though by the late thirteenth century the Christian merchants of Messina controlled a *fonduq* and Sicilian church in Tunis. Bickering between the Sicilian kings and their brothers, the kings of Aragon, over who should control this consulate was one of many irritants creating tension between the various kings of Aragonese origin in the Mediterranean around 1300. By 1231 there was a Venetian consul at Tunis, representing his city's political and economic interests; evidence for representatives of other Italian cities appears soon after this.

72 Pistarino, nos. 68, 87, pp. 99–100, 126; Jehel, nos. 68, 78–9, pp. 99–100, 103–4. There are some very minor discrepancies between the ordering of the documents which result from Jehel's reasonable decision to produce a calendar of acts in chronological order rather than in the order of the documents.

73 L. de Mas Latrie, *Traités de paix et de commerce et documents divers concernant les relations des Chrétiens avec les Arabes de l'Afrique septentrionale au moyen âge*, parts 1–2, vol. 2 (Paris, 1866), pp. 125–7.

74 Pistarino, no. 78, pp. 113–14.

75 Pistarino, no. 1, pp. 3–4.

76 Pistarino, nos. 75, 78, 86, 106, pp. 109–10, 113–14, 125, 153–4, etc.

77 Brunschvig, vol. 1, pp. 452–4.

78 André Berthier, "Les écoles de langues orientales fondées au XIIIe siècle par les Dominicains en Espagne et en Afrique", *Revue Africaine*, 73 (1932), pp. 84–102. Jeremy Cohen, *The Friars and the Jews. The Evolution of Medieval Anti-Judaism* (Ithaca, N.Y., 1982), p. 107, cites the evidence and additional literature; the reality of the existence of the Tunis school perhaps needs further thought.

79 Abulafia, "Asia, Africa", p. 473.

80 Fernández-Armesto, p. 152.

81 T.F. Glick, *Irrigation and Society in Late Medieval Valencia* (Cambridge, Mass., 1970).

82 Abulafia, *Frederick II*, pp. 335–6.

83 Fernández-Armesto, pp. 198–9; C. Verlinden, *The Beginnings of Modern Colonization* (Ithaca, N.Y., 1970) contains several studies of the transfer of agricultural technology from the Mediterranean to the Atlantic; cf. Watson, p. 154, for the Islamic perspective.

84 J. Heers, "Le royaume de Grenade et la politique marchande de Gênes en Occident (XVe siècle)", *Le Moyen Âge*, 63 (1957), pp. 87–121, repr. in J. Heers, *Société et Économie à Gênes (XIVe–XVe siècles)* (London, 1979), essay VII.

II

TRADE AND CRUSADE, 1050-1250

In traditional historiography, the opening of the trade routes linking western Europe to the Levant had enormous repercussions for the western economy. Such authors as Roberto Lopez see the era of the crusades as the period of a commercial revolution, characterized by a greater adventurousness among Latin merchants, a greater sophistication in business techniques, and the effective conquest of the Mediterranean by the shipping of the Italian cities.[1] It would be wrong to confuse cause and effect: the crusades attracted Italian maritime help because the Genoese, Pisans and Venetians had not merely the necessary dedication to the holy war against Islam but also the shipping capacity, the capital and the degree of political organization necessary to turn dreams of the reconquest of Jerusalem into reality. In other words, the crusades were the culmination of a long process of maritime development, and, however great their effect on the trade of the Italians in the eastern Mediterranean, marked only a further stage in the existing process of commercial expansion.

The traditional view of the rise of the Levant trade is based on two foundations. One is the simple chronology: the involvement of the Italians in the great spice trade seems to be visible only in significant degree after 1100. In part this may be an illusion generated by the poverty of the sources for the tenth and eleventh centuries, but it is at any rate clear that many of the wealthy patricians of the twelfth century acquired their political and commercial leadership during that century, helped by the substantial profits they could draw from the spice trade.[2]

---

[1] R.S. Lopez, *The commercial revolution of the Middle Ages, 950-1350*, Englewood Cliffs, NJ, 1971.

[2] For the argument that involvement in the Levant trade only served to strengthen existing élites, see my articles on the Levant trade in my volumes of collected studies *Italy, Sicily and the Mediterranean, 1100-1400* (London, 1987) and in *Commerce and Conquest in the Mediterranean, 1100-1500* (Aldershot, 1993).

2

A second assumption is that the trade of the eastern Mediterranean, and especially of the newly-conquered Holy Land, was fundamental to the trade of the Mediterranean as a whole. The drugs, dyes and spices of the Levant traders are thus seen as the necessary core of the Mediterranean trading system. In the twelfth century, it is assumed, the long-distance trade of the Mediterranean was in essence a luxury trade. A reader of such works as Heyd's *Histoire du commerce du Levant*[3] or of Heynen's study of the origins of Venetian capitalism[4] might be excused for picturing the Levant trader as a purveyor of silks, fine metalwork, pepper and ginger. It is not surprising that historians should look to the areas of trade where the greatest profits were likely to be made; but that does not necessarily mean they were the areas where the volume of trade was greatest - indeed, the simple laws of supply and demand suggest that goods of very high cost are also particularly rare.

The most important challenge to the traditional assumptions about the Levant trade is found in the studies of Claude Cahen.[5] First, he points to the presence of Italian merchants in eastern Mediterranean ports before the First Crusade. Then he emphasizes that Alexandria was generally more important as a centre of trade than Acre or the other ports of the Holy Land. This view in itself is not so revolutionary. The work of the German scholar Adolf Schaube[6] and of the American scholar Eugene Byrne[7] pointed to the use of Acre as a trading entrepôt linking the Frankish settlements in Syria to the more prosperous and desirable market of Egypt. What was postulated was a trading circuit that took western merchants from Italy to Acre, then from Acre to

---

[3]Trans. F. Raynaud, 2 vols, Leipzig, 1885-6.

[4]R. Heynen, *Zur Enstehung des Kapitalismus in Venedig,* Stuttgart, 1905.

[5]C. Cahen, *Orient et occident au temps des croisades,* Paris, 1983; 'Orient latin et commerce du Levant', *Bulletin de la Faculté des lettres de Strasbourg,* 29, 1951, 328-46; 'L'histoire économique et sociale de l'Orient musulman médiéval', *Studia Islamica,* 3, 1955, 95-113; 'Quelques problèmes concernant l'expansion économique musulmane au haut moyen âge', *Studies in the economic history of the Middle East from the rise of Islam to the present day,* ed. M.A. Cook, London, 1970; and so on.

[6]A. Schaube, *Handelsgeschichte der Romanischen Völker des Mittelmeergebiets bis zum Ende der Kreuzzüge,* Munich/Berlin, 1906.

[7]E.H. Byrne, 'Commercial contracts of the Genoese in the Syrian trade of the twelfth century', *Quarterly Journal of Economics,* 31, 1916/17.

Alexandria for the purchase of luxury goods, and then back to Genoa, Pisa or Venice. This is certainly an over-simplification; however, the whole question of the trade between Acre and Alexandria does need to be examined afresh.

First, it is necessary to examine the evidence for pre-existing Italian trade with the Levant. It is generally agreed that before 1100 the principal Latin trading towns active in the Levant trade were Amalfi and Venice. Amalfi has a special role in the literature, because its merchants were described in the Arabic sources as the most active of all Rūmi merchants. In fact, care should be taken with these reports; Amalfi had by the late eleventh century cast off a great diaspora of merchants, present in the south Italian interior, on the coasts of Apulia and Albania, and even in Constantinople, Alexandria and Jerusalem. How many of these merchants actually hailed from Amalfi itself it is hard to say; many were from Ravello, Scala and other neighboring communities, but many may also have been merchants of very varied origins, who sought to benefit from special franchises allowed to the Amalfitans by the Lombard princes of southern Italy, the Byzantine emperors and the Fatimid caliphs. The word 'Amalfitan' thus has some of the connotations of the very loose and inexact use of the words 'Syrian' and 'Jew' to describe merchants in earlier centuries; but in this case it clearly refers to Latin merchants largely of south Italian origin.[8]

These 'Amalfitans' specialized in the import of luxury articles from Byzantium and the Muslim East; they serviced the needs of the great courts of the popes in Rome, of the abbots of Montecassino and of the Lombard princes. Their close links both to the Benedictine order and to the Byzantine world are also visible in the establishment of a so-called 'Amalfitan' monastery of Benedictine monks on Mount Athos. Yet in the tenth and eleventh centuries their trade with the east seems to have consisted in the handling of luxury goods - silks, spices and small quantities of highly priced and highly prized artisan work. It is known that around 1012 the merchants of Gaeta, north of Amalfi, were also

---

[8]David Abulafia, 'Sicily, southern Italy and Sardinia in the medieval Mediterranean economy', in *Commerce and Conquest* cit., I. 7-17.

4

engaged in the trade in luxury articles in the eastern Mediterranean.[9] That the Amalfitans in particular penetrated beyond the major trade routes may appear to be suggested by their presence in Jerusalem at the time of the First Crusade, when according to legend Amalfitan merchants in the besieged city tried to bombard the crusaders with bread. They were sternly ordered to throw stones instead, but by a miracle the stones were transformed into bread and the hungry crusaders were thus fed. More relevant to later developments is the appearance in Jerusalem of an Amalfitan convent, later to become the core of the Hospital of St John.[10] Clearly, however, the Amalfitan presence in Jerusalem is as much or more a reflection of the links between Amalfi and the nearby monastery of Montecassino, which relied heavily on Amalfi for supplies and naval services, as it is evidence for real trade with the Muslims of the Holy Land.[11] It might be suggested that the term 'Amalfitan', when applied to the settlements in Jerusalem as also on Mount Athos has a particularly broad meaning: it means all the Benedictines, many of whom at this period were south Italians, and their suppliers or financial agents, who were generally from Amalfi and neighboring ports.

Amalfi, tied up in the complex politics of Norman Italy, was unable to supply a fleet for the First Crusade, and took long to achieve the status for its citizens that the Genoese, Pisans and Venetians managed to obtain in the kingdom of Jerusalem. In 1161 the bishop of Acre gave land to the Amalfitans for a cemetery, in 1163 the Amalfitans were engaged in a legal struggle over their trading rights at Laodicea [Lattakieh] in the principality of Antioch, and only in 1190 did they receive a commercial privilege in the kingdom of Jerusalem comparable

---

[9]P. Skinner, *Family power in southern Italy. The duchy of Gaeta and its neighbours, 850-1100* (Cambridge, 1994), will be the definitive survey of Gaeta's growth and trade.

[10]For the Knights of St John and Amalfi, see J. Riley-Smith, *The Knights of St John in Jerusalem and Cyprus, 1050-1310*, London, 1967, 36-7; R. Hiestand, 'Die Anfänge der Johanniter', *Die geistlichen Ritterorden Europas*, ed. J. Fleckenstain, Sigmaringen, 1980, 33-47; B. Figliuolo, 'Amalfi e il Levante', *I comuni italiani nel regno crociato di Gerusalemme*, ed. G. Airaldi. B.Z. Kedar, Genoa, 1986, 592.

[11]Cf. H.M. Willard, *Abbot Desiderius of Montecassino and the ties between Montecassino and Amalfi in the eleventh century*, Miscellanea Cassinese, vol. 37, Montecassino, 1973.

to those won by the north Italian cities.[12] By then it seems that the north Italians had established a clear ascendancy in the trade of the Holy Land, and the south Italian merchants, while not insignificant, were unable to exercise the influence over the rulers of the Latin states and their policies that Venice and Genoa obtained.

Yet what this evidence perhaps reveals most strongly is the importance of the religious dimension to the intrusion of the Italians into the Islamic Mediterranean. It is a feature also of the activities of the Pisans, Genoese and Venetians. Venice had earned a reputation as early as the ninth century for its rôle in the struggle against Islam in the Adriatic; probably in 880, and certainly in 992, it won the gratitude of the Greek emperors, who conferred trading privileges on the merchants of Venice. Venice also derived some holy benefits from its Levant trade: the theft of the supposed bones of St Mark from Alexandria was achieved under the cover of trading activities: the bones were smuggled out of Egypt in a pork barrel, which the Egyptian authorities found too offensive to examine carefully. Equally, the Genoese and the Pisans had long-standing experience as warriors against Islam by the end of the eleventh century. This is apparent in the series of Pisan victory songs, commemorating the achievements of the Pisan fleets in expelling the Spanish emir Mujahid from Sardinia at the start of the eleventh century, in besieging Mahdia in 1087, and, after the First Crusade, in launching a new crusade against Almoravid Majorca (1113-5). Other expeditions, for which no Song of Victory survives, were sent against the Saracens in Calabria in 982 and against Muslim Palermo in 1063. With the proceeds of the latter expedition the Pisans started to build their magnificent Romanesque cathedral.[13]

Yet at the same period there was some attempt to trade in the eastern Mediterranean. Samuel Stern, Benjamin Kedar and Gabriella Airaldi have identified Genoese ships that visited Egypt in the tenth and

---

[12]Figliuolo, 'Amalfi e il Levante', 616-21, 656-62.

[13]For a discussion of current views about the emergence of these republics, see my 'Gli italiani fuori d'Italia', *Storia dell'economia italiana*, ed. R. Romano (Turin, 1990), especially pp. 272-5.

eleventh centuries.[14] What is true of Genoa is probably even truer of Pisa: the trade of Pisa may have flowered earlier, and certainly went into decline much sooner, than that of Genoa. The documents of the Cairo Genizah make it plain that there existed an active trade in European silver, often in the form of ingots, on the eve of the First Crusade; one Jewish merchant of Fustat who was involved was Nahray ben Nissim, who flourished between 1045 and 1096.[15]

It is likely, however, that the coast of Tunisia was the main point of contact between Islamic and Latin merchants in the eleventh century: cities such as Mahdia, at the end of the gold caravan routes running from the southern borders of the Sahara to the Mediterranean, were also centres of exchange for the luxury goods of the Islamic world with western bullion and timber. Another important centre of exchange was Sicily, even before the Norman conquest of the 1060s.[16] As well as furnishing luxury goods from the east to merchants of the western Mediterranean, Jewish, Moorish and Christian, Sicily was a major source of grain to north Africa, which was beginning to experience regular famines in the eleventh century. The acquisition of this island by the armies of Robert Guiscard thus had important repercussions for the future of the African cities whose trade and industry were increasingly fed (in the most literal sense) by Sicily.

Hard evidence for trade linking Pisa to Egypt seems to exist in the form of the *bacini,* Islamic pots inserted into the fabric of eleventh-century (and later) Pisan churches. The *bacini* certainly include several spectacular examples of eleventh-century Egyptian ceramic art. A particularly impressive example made in Egypt shows a seated courtier holding a cup; it is inserted in the walls of the church of San Sisto in Pisa, and it is known, in fact, that this church was built or extended after the raid of the Pisans and Genoese on Mahdia on the day

---

[14]S.M. Stern, 'An original document from the Fatimid chancery concerning Italian merchants', *Studi orientalistici in onore di G. Levi della Vida,* Studi e Testi della Biblioteca Apostolica Vaticana, Vatican City, vol. 2, pp. 529-38.

[15]S. D. Goitein, *A Mediterranean society. The Jewish communities of the Arab world as portrayed in the documents of the Cairo Geniza,* vol. 1, *Economic foundations,* Berkeley/Los Angeles, 1967, 153-4.

[16]See my studies in *Italy, Sicily and the Mediterranean* and in *Commerce and Conquest.*

of St Sixtus in 1087, as thanksgivings for the Italian victory. It is quite likely that the ceramics displayed on the façade and tower of the church were booty seized from the quayside at Mahdia by the Pisans. But it is noticeable that many of the pots are not from the region of Mahdia itself, and this does suggest that a great deal of the trade linking northern Italy to Egypt at this period was mediated through Tunisia and Sicily.[17]

The evidence available, skimpy as it is, suggests the following conclusions about the scale of north Italian trade with the Levant in the century before the First Crusade. There was evidently some direct trade between Egypt and Italy in the eleventh century. But there is no evidence that it consisted of regular sailings of large western ships to a variety of Levantine ports. That is a phenomenon of the late twelfth and thirteenth centuries. The earliest activity did not involve the presence alongside the trading expeditions of powerful Italian navies able to secure free access to the trade routes on behalf of merchants from their home cities. The Italians were very much at the mercy of the Muslim rulers, as emerges from the experience of the Amalfitans in 969: during the upheavals that brought the Shi'ite Fatimid caliphs to power, they were accused by the mob of setting fire to the dockyards in Alexandria.

But did the First Crusade actually change all this? Undoubtedly, it opened the door to greater involvement in the Levant trade; generous privileges, such as that received by the Genoese in 1104 or that received by the Venetians in 1123, provided a springboard from which the north Italians established a lively trade through Acre and Tyre. But this trade was not, it will be suggested, created overnight; it grew slowly to a position where it could match the trade of the Latins in Alexandria, and was encouraged in its growth by the remarkable political freedoms enjoyed by the Italians in the kingdom of Jerusalem, which far surpassed anything they could hope to gain in Egypt. It then experienced a real upsurge in the thirteenth century, as a result of the opening up of new trade routes through inner Asia and the creation of tighter bonds between Acre and the lands to the north - Turkey and, beyond that, Persia.

---

[17]David Abulafia, 'The Pisan *bacini* and the medieval Mediterranean economy: a historian's viewpoint', *Papers in Italian Archaeology*, 4, part 4, ed. C. Malone and S. Stoddart, Oxford, 1985, pp.289-91, repr. in *Italy, Sicily and the Mediterranean*.

8

The Italian participants in the First Crusade were moved by strong religious fervor. It is possible, as Cahen has argued, that the Genoese were more fervent in their commitment to the crusade than the Pisans or the Venetians; in fact, the Genoese sources (largely written by the great annalist Caffaro) are simply much more plentiful and vocal, and there are strong hints of religious motives in the Pisan and Venetian sources too. Genoa was an obvious place for crusade preachers to visit. It had close commercial links with the lands of the man who had in a sense been instrumental in organizing the proposed aid to the Byzantine empire out of which the crusade mushroomed: Raymond of Saint-Gilles. Genoa, like Pisa, aspired to establish a commercial protectorate over possible trading rivals in Provence and Languedoc.[18] The Genoese had a long history of trade and settlement in the key south French trading cities, of which Saint-Gilles was one. But in the final analysis, the Genoese were quite simply fired by the preachers. They had already treated the campaign of 1087 to gain control of the trade of Mahdia as a holy war: the Pisan and Genoese participants had visited Rome to receive counsel and blessing from the pope, had subsequently worn pilgrims' purses on the campaign and had been joined by a papal representative, the bishop of Modena. The Pisan *Carmen* composed after the campaign was over compared the Mahdians (*Madianiti)* to the ancient enemies of Israel, the Midianites. So already on the eve of the First Crusade the Italians were depicting themselves as the New Israel, serving God in the conquest of Canaan.[19]

It was the need to organize a crusading fleet that brought the Genoese patricians together into a cooperative system of government, the *compagnia* or commune. At first an ad hoc arrangement, the commune proved its worth and was renewed; Genoa thus owed its rather ramshackle communal constitution to the First Crusade.[20]

---

[18]This point is made forcefully in H.E. Mayer, *Marseilles Levantehandel und ein akkonensisches Fälscheratelier des XIII. Jahrhunderts,* Tübingen, 1972.

[19]Among other editions of the *carmen* see that accompanying the acute insights of H.E.J. Cowdrey, 'The Mahdia campaign of 1087', *English Historical Review,* 92, 1977, pp. 1-29.

[20]I. Peri, *Studi sul comune di Genova,* vol. 1, *Genesi e formaizone del Comune Consolare a Genova,* Palermo, 1951.

And after the crusade had regained Jerusalem, the Pisans were enthusiastic adherents of a new papal project to license the conquest of Majorca as a crusade (1113-5); they received the same privilege for their part in the *reconquista* of the Balearic islands as the pope normally granted to those travelling to the holy places in Jerusalem.[21] Thus the integration of the war against the Moors in Spain into the crusade was partly the work of Italian enthusiasts for the crusading ideal. The same tendencies are visible at the time of the Second Crusade, when, as Giles Constable has shown, the wars in Spain and on the Slav frontier were treated by the papacy, by contemporary chroniclers and by the participants as an integral part of the new crusade to protect the Holy Land.[22] In 1147-9 the Genoese joined the count of Catalonia in a war against the Spanish coastal cities of Tortosa and Almería, both still in Muslim hands. Tortosa was captured, with the result that the southern frontier of Catalonia was at last well protected; Almería, much further to the south, was raided and booty was carried off. The Genoese received a large share of the city of Tortosa, which they had to abandon to the count because the excessive cost of the campaign had virtually bankrupted the city of Genoa. The Italians, alongside the Templars and members of the Spanish Military Orders, thus played a crucial part in the extension of Christian power southwards into Muslim Spain. (This did not prevent them from also making treaties with the Muslim emirs when it suited their trading interests, as in the 1160s with Lupus, ruler of Valencia). But Spain was not at this stage a major trading area of the Genoese, who needed access to its coasts more in order to reach the ports of north Africa, such as Bougie and Ceuta, than in order to acquire the merchandise of al-Andalus.[23] Thus they joined in the *reconquista* partly to open up the routes to Africa, but partly also out of dedication to the holy war that was an integral part of their own history.

---

[21] David Abulafia, *A Mediterranean Emporium. The Catalan Kingdom of Majorca* (Cambridge, 1994), p. 5.

[22] G. Constable, 'The Second Crusade as seen by contemporaries', *Traditio, 9*, 1953; cf. the ever valuable observations of A. Grabois, 'The crusade of King Louis VII: a reconsideration', *Crusade and Settlement: Papers read at the first conference of the Society for the study of the Crusdes and the Latin East*, ed. P. Edbury (Cardiff, 1985), p. 94.

[23] Abulafia, 'Gli italiani fuori d'Italia', p. 278.

Equally, in the conquest of the Holy Land itself we find that material gain was by no means the only attraction to the Italians. Visitors to the museum of the cathedral of San Lorenzo are still shown a massive green glass bowl, the *Sacro Catino,* which the Genoese believed to be the bowl used at the Last Supper; it was seized from the Friday Mosque at Cæsaræa in 1101 by the Genoese invaders. It really is an ancient Roman artefact of around the time of Jesus of Nazareth, but, contrary to the assumptions of the Genoese, was made of glass and not, alas, out of a massive emerald.[24] Might it be suggested that the capture of this spectacular article was as much a cause of wonder and rejoicing in Genoa as the winning of handsome commercial privileges from King Baldwin I of Jerusalem?

The Venetians may seem rather tardy in their response to these new opportunities. At the time of the First Crusade, their fortunes were closely tied to those of the Byzantine emperor Alexios Komnenos, who had of course been instrumental in suggesting to the pope the need for military help against the Turks, a request which culminated in the quite unexpected surge of crusading enthusiasm in 1095. By serving Byzantium, the Venetians were certainly supplying a major part of the aid that Alexios required: he had to ensure that the Turks could not break through to the Aegean and launch pirate ships there (as briefly happened when a Seljuq warlord gained Smyrna); the Venetians were certainly on patrol in the Aegean at the time of the First Crusade. A Venetian chronicle, the *Translation of St Nicholas,* portrays the Venetian fleet blocking the Aegean against intrusions by aggressive Pisan participants in the First Crusade, around 1097; the routes to the Levant from Italy took ships generally into Byzantine waters off Crete and Rhodes, and constantly left the southernmost Greek islands exposed to raids by antagonistic Italian navies.

But even Venice was not forgetful of the higher aims of the crusade. In 1100 up to 200 Venetian ships arrived off the coast of southern Asia Minor on their way to the Holy Land. Before joining the crusade armies, however, they stopped at Myra, in search of the bones of St Nicholas, patron saint of sailors; as they must have known all too

---

[24]H.E. Mayer, *The Crusades,* transl. J. Gillingham, 2nd ed. (Oxford, 1988), pp. 68-9.

well, most of the relics had been seized thirty years earlier by merchants of Bari, who had erected the spectacular Basilica of St Nicholas around their prize. The Venetians were nonetheless insistent that they also discovered some of the saint's bones, and they brought them eventually to the monastery of San Niccolò on the Lido. But not before they had carried the bones south to Haifa, and had participated in a horrendous massacre of the town's Jews and Muslims. Thus here again we seem to see an attachment to the religious dimension of the campaign, expressed in a less direct fashion than by the Pisan and Genoese. As sailors, the Venetians sought the special protection of the patron saint of all sailors, who would guide them to victory in the Holy Land, and ensure thereafter safe passage to their ships: the Venetians too were rewarded with generous commercial privileges, involving the promise of all Tripoli, a third of other towns and complete tax exemption.[25]

But for Venice the really great breakthrough in the winning of mastery over the eastern Mediterranean occurred in 1123-4. In 1118, the Venetians had quarrelled violently with the new Greek emperor, John Komnenos, who refused to confirm the generous grant of tax exemption of 1082. Soon after, momentum began to grow for a new crusade that would secure finally control over the coastal lands of the Latin Kingdom of Jerusalem (Ascalon remained in Muslim hands until as late as 1152). Venice participated both as crusading navy and as vengeful foe of Byzantium, ravaging Byzantine lands en route to the east. Off Ascalon in 1123 the Venetians destroyed the Fatimid fleets sent out from Egypt; soon after they led a victorious assault on Tyre, where in consequence they were rewarded with a third of the city and exemption from all trade taxes. The privileges of the Venetians were then confirmed and extended by the Patriarch of Jerusalem, acting on behalf of the captive King Baldwin II. In 1126 John Komnenos, perhaps fearful of the loss of naval cover previously provided by Venice, renewed and extended the republic's privileges in the Byzantine Empire. Thus by 1126 Venice had won extensive, indeed unparalleled, rights both in Byzantium and in the Holy Land. Despite the occasional courting of Pisa by the Greek emperors (for instance in 1111) neither Pisa nor Genoa obtained in the

---

[25]Abulafia, 'Gli italiani fuori d'Italia', pp. 273-4.

twelfth century so complete a package of tax exemptions both in Syria and in Byzantium.[26]

Some doubt has been cast by H.E. Mayer and M.L. Favreau on the authenticity of the earliest privilege granted by the kings of Jerusalem to the Genoese, of 1101. Genoa insisted that it had received an initial privilege then, granting one third of captured towns and allowing them certain tax exemptions. The Genoese even claimed to have received the right to place a golden inscription in the Church of the Holy Sepulchre, listing their special rights. Whether or not such an inscription, and the attendant rights, existed, it is clear that by about 1160 the Genoese were prepared to argue the case for these rights with enormous energy, setting Pope Alexander III to work in attempts to persuade the reluctant King Amaury of Jerusalem of his obligations to the Genoese.[27] In 1163 the Genoese records mention no trade at all with Latin Syria, and this is surely a reflection of Genoese displeasure at a time when the city was at the peak of its struggle to secure recognition of what it considered its legitimate rights.[28] And this itself suggests that the activation of rights was not as easy as the winning of a privilege. It was not unusual for twelfth-century rulers to dangle impossibly generous offers in front of Italian navies, in order to secure their aid in a project such as the conquest of Sicily or the Holy Land, and then to refuse to confirm these rights after the victory.

Pisa is usually considered to have been in the weakest position of the three Italian cities as far as its privileges to trade in the Latin east were concerned. On the other hand, the Pisan fleet had the dubious advantage of being led by the archbishop of Pisa, Daimbert. But Daimbert's ambitions extended also to rule in the Latin East; he became

---

[26]M. L. Favreau-Lilie, *Die Italiener im Heiligen Land vom ersten Kreuzzug bis zum Tode Heinrichs von Champagne*, pp. 1098-197 (Amsterdam, 1989).

[27]H.E. Mayer, M.L. Favreau, 'Das Diplom Balduins I. für Genua und Genuas Goldene Inschrift in der Grabeskirche', *Quellen und Forschungen aus italiensichen Archiven und Bibliotheken*, 55/6, 1976, pp. 22-96; cf. B. Z. Kedar, 'Genoa's golden inscription in the Holy Sepulchre: a case for the defense', *I comuni italinai nel regno crociato di Gerusalemme*, ed. G. Airaldi, B.Z. Kedar (Genoa, 1986), pp. 317-35.

[28]David Abulafia, *The Two Italies. Economic relations between the Norman Kingdom of Sicily and the northern communes* (Cambridge, 1977), p. 131.

Patriarch of Jerusalem but failed to establish a hierocracy. To some extent, the Pisans were victims of this failure; they depended on him for favors, and gained trading rights at the Patriarch's fief of Jaffa. But Jaffa was simply a less good port than Acre, Tyre or Haifa, and the Pisans only gained full tax privileges at Acre in 1189, in return for providing aid to the Third Crusade. Such a situation did not, however, detract from Pisan success in carving out a highly important place in the markets of the Levant; lack of substantial privileges was amply compensated by the intensity of Pisan penetration of Syrian and Egyptian markets. The unsuspected strength of the Tuscan merchants in the twelfth-century Holy Land has been revealed in a thorough study of the Pisan documentation by Marie-Louise Favreau-Lilie.[29]

Such privileges were a sign (along with the booty of pepper and relics known to have been carried off by the Genoese) of divine grace. It would be quite wrong to assume that the Italians were ever entirely materialistic in their aims, nowhere more so than in the winning of material benefits such as customs exemptions and rights to property in the towns of Syria. These grants were taken as proof of divine blessing, the entry of the New Israel into its inheritance, milk and honey that had turned into gold and spices. They were the just reward of those who had offered their fleets in a higher cause than that of earthly profit. In other words, the Italians came as crusaders first, as merchants second.

None of this is really evidence for extended trade between the Holy Land and Italy in the early twelfth century. We can identify some of the aspirations of the Italian cities, but not whether they were originally fulfilled. The evidence of the Genoese notaries only begins at the end of 1154; Venetian documents do speak of trade in Acre, Tyre and the principality of Antioch, but it is hard to make any quantitative statements on the basis of random survivals of commercial contracts. In any case, it is unclear whether in fact the ports of the Holy Land were more attractive a trading destination than those of the Nile Delta. In 1101 there was plenty of hope among the Genoese that the armies of Baldwin I would sweep into Egypt and establish Latin rule there too; but the sober reality was that Latin resources were far too slim to overwhelm the most densely populated and richest land in the Islamic *oikoumene.* In

---

[29]M.L. Favreau-Lilie, *Die Italiener im Heiligen Land,* cit.

14

1169, King Amaury even tried to secure Pisan cooperation in a highly ambitious assault on Egypt, jointly conducted with Byzantium: this represented an attempt to wean the Pisans away from their known links with the Fatimids in Egypt — more of this shortly.[30]

The position adopted by Adolf Schaube was that by 1150 Italian ships arrived each autumn in the Levant, and put in first at Acre. There they sold their own goods or used western silver to obtain gold, which was in short supply in the west. The fact that the Latin kings of Jerusalem minted gold besants modelled on those of Egypt might be taken as evidence that the western merchants wished to transfer the coins to Egypt, where they would enjoy near parity with the Fatimid dinar.[31] They carried the gold out of the Latin kingdom, primarily to Alexandria, where they bought spices, drugs and other luxury articles. They then returned to the west, perhaps directly without calling in again at Acre. This interpretation was questioned by the Danish historian Erik Bach, who stressed instead the degree to which trade in Acre was directed specifically at Syria.[32] Plenty of Acre-bound merchants did not visit Egypt. This can be demonstrated using the collections of Genoese commercial contracts of the late twelfth century, which offer voluminous information about trade routes and patterns of investment. Further evidence that Acre held its own emerges in more recent research. A stray scribble of 1156, preserved in the archives at Genoa, suggests that Alexandria was only one among several possible targets for the western trader who had come to Acre. Ansaldo Baialardo of Genoa, acting as agent for the great Genoese patrician Ingo della Volta, was instructed to travel east for trade to Syria, then if he wished to Damascus, or perhaps to Sicily, or directly back to Genoa, or to Alexandria and back thence to Genoa via Sicily.[33] Thus it was not automatically assumed that one went from Acre or the other Syrian ports to Alexandria. Indeed, the

---

[30]G. Schlumberger, *Les campagnes d'Amaury de Jérusalem en Egypte*, (Paris, 1906).

[31]A. Ehrenkreutz, 'The standard of fineness of gold coins circulating in Egypt at the time of the crusades', *Journal of the American Oriental Society*, 74, 1954; 'The crisis of the dinar in the Egypt of Saladin', ibid., p. 76, 1956.

[32]E. Bach, *La Cité de Gênes au XIIe siècle* (Copenhagen, 1955); cf. Cahen, 'Orient latin et commerce du Levant'.

[33]Abulafia, *Two Italies*, 224, for the text and comment; also G. Astuti, *Rendiconti mercantili inediti del Cartolare di Giovanni Scriba* (Turin, 1933).

great virtue of Acre was precisely its position on the road to Damascus. Few Italian merchants penetrated into Muslim Syria at this period; the trade privileges at Acre and Tyre may have been intended only for merchants who did not try to cross the frontiers of the Latin states (this was certainly how they were interpreted in the thirteenth century).[34] The native Christian and Muslim merchants came down to the ports of the Latin states from the interior, particularly from Damascus and Aleppo, bearing luxury goods intended for ultimate sale either in western markets or in Egypt. The Latin merchants in the Syrian ports took these goods off them and carried them away on their own ships, not always to northern Italy but also, it is plain, to Byzantium, Alexandria and Sicily, great centres for the consumption of luxury goods. In other words, the Latin merchants even intruded themselves into the trade of Egypt with Muslim Syria. There were, of course, also camel caravans which linked Damascus to Cairo; here, however, the same problem applied; the Latins extended their rule rapidly down to the Gulf of Aqaba, and so even the land trade passed through the territories of the Franks. Occasionally Italian merchants sought to strike southwards from Alexandria. In 1156 Solomon of Salerno, a very wealthy Genoese merchant of south Italian origin, agreed to carry goods from Genoa to Alexandria, sell them there for Egyptian currency, and then go south to Cairo in search of lac and brazilwood.[35] Here we can see the failure of Schaube's thesis clearly spelled out: Solomon went to Egypt, not to Latin Syria, to buy Islamic gold, and there is plenty more evidence of direct trade between Genoa and Alexandria in these years. Between 1155 and 1164, surviving Genoese commercial contracts reveal investments of £10075 in Syrian trade, £9031 in Egyptian, £6689 in Sicilian, £6007 in north African and £2007 in Byzantine.[36] These figures are only the tip of the iceberg, and relate to the prosperous businessmen who had recourse to the notary Giovanni Scriba, from whose hand a register of acts survives at this period. Whether the proportions of trade found in Giovanni Scriba's cartulary is similar to that of Genoese trade as a whole in this period remains unclear. What is certain is that Acre, Alexandria and Palermo dominated the

---

[34]J. Riley-Smith, 'Government in Latin Syria and the commercial privileges of the foreign merchants', *Relations between East and West in the Middle Ages*, ed. D. Baker (Edinburgh, 1973).

[35]Abulafia, *Two Italies*, p. 240.

[36]Bach, *Cité de Gênes*, pp. 50-1.

investments of the Genoese patriciate; and a similar picture probably obtains for Venice, substituting Apulia for Palermo and adding Byzantium to the list.

Alexandria had one major advantage over Acre. This was its position at the head of the routes leading from the Red Sea across to Cairo and up the Nile, along which were carried the spices and cotton of the Indies. Damascus, by contrast, was primarily a supplier of finished goods, such as tempered steel, fine cloths (hence the name damask), some produced locally and some further to the east, in Iraq and Persia. The extraordinary insistence of western consumers on the use of pepper and other eastern spices made Egypt a more important target for Latin merchants. But access to the sources of these goods was entirely closed: the rulers of Egypt became increasingly aware of the danger that Frankish armies and navies might interfere in the Red Sea (where not just trade but the shrines at Mecca and Madina might be threatened); in the late twelfth century the Frankish adventurer Reynaud de Châtillon actually launched a fleet on the Red Sea, while the crusader fort on Pharaoh's island acted as a reminder that the northern tip of the Red Sea was actually in Frankish hands.

For Pisa, however, the failure to win extensive privileges in the Holy Land turned sour the enthusiasm of its merchants for trade in Acre. In 1154-5 a Pisan embassy under Rainerio Botaccio was present in Egypt, and guarantees were obtained of Pisan access to Egyptian markets.[37] There were some tax reductions in force in Alexandria, but it is clear that facilities for the Italians were much less favorable than in the Holy Land. There, they (or at least the Genoese and Venetians) were developing into masters of their own pieces of territory, with their own judges and considerable freedom of movement. In Egypt, conditions were much more difficult. As elsewhere in the Islamic world, the Italians were confined to a fonduk or inn at night, and were kept under close supervision by day. In 1195 Venetians held captive in Egypt were released from captivity; in 1200 Genoese were taken into captivity. It was a parlous existence; but it was commercially the place to be. And in order to strengthen their right to trade in Egypt the

---

[37]K.H. Allmendinger, *Die Beziehungen zwischen der Kommune Pisa und Ägypten im hohen Mittelalter*, Wiesbaden, 1967.

Italians succumbed to the requests of the Fatimids and the Ayyubids for armaments.[38] Cahen observes that a type of shield used in Egypt at the time was called *janawiyah*, that is, the 'Genoese' shield.[39] More important was the supply of timber, which was hard to obtain in Egypt, and the lack of which had a crippling effect on both army equipment and, even more, on the fleet. Egyptian ships had been able, before the capture of the Syrian cities by the crusaders, to sail up the coast to Cilicia and to cut wood there. These supplies were increasingly at risk, and it was apparently not unknown for Genoese shippers to bring not merely wood to Egypt but whole ships, with the intention of putting them on sale, as Solomon of Salerno did in 1159-60.[40] The Pisans were encouraged both in 1154 and later by Saladin to bring timber and arms to Egypt. This trade, though it aroused strong disapproval in the west, did not prevent the Italians from supplying similar goods to the Latin states in the east. By the second half of the twelfth century, the Italians had discovered that they possessed a critical rôle in the supply of strategic materials to the competing powers in the Levant. Thus, despite an agreement with the kings of Jerusalem in 1169, the Pisans were back in Egypt, and were trading in familiar prohibited goods by 1174 at latest. At this point, we seem to see a waning in their original enthusiasm for the holy war, and the gradual triumph of the materialistic motives that most historians attribute to them from the start of their involvement in the crusades. But this was only to follow in a similar direction to many European knights, who showed a decreasing interest in the high ideals of the crusade, between the fiasco of the Second Crusade in 1147-9 and the fall of Jerusalem to Saladin in 1187.

The Third Crusade certainly concentrated the attention of the Italians on Acre in several ways. It spelled the end of the ascendancy of Alexandria. In the first place, the crusaders needed supplies; and they received ample help with ships and provisions from the Genoese. There is ample evidence for heavy Genoese investment in trade with the remnants of the kingdom of Jerusalem in autumn, 1190 and a year later. The Pisans were rewarded with major privileges of tax exemption in

---

[38]For the difficulties of the Italians throughout the period, see Cahen, *Orient et occident*, pp. 124-8.

[39]Cahen, *Orient et occident*, pp. 133, 176.

[40]Abulafia, *Two Italies*, p. 244.

return for their aid during the crusade. Other groups who were offered privileges in return for material help were the Amalfitans, the Marseillais, the Montpelliérains, the Catalans and other merchants of Occitania. The Italians and Provençaux found themselves busy ferrying crusaders, too, including Philip Augustus of France.

After the Third Crusade, attention focused increasingly on a radical new policy towards Alexandria; it was still visited on and off by Italians, but offenses against them seem to have been increasing, and the Venetians helped to lay plans for a great Franco-German crusade against Alexandria. They suspended their trade to build a vast crusading fleet, which in the event sailed to Constantinople and captured the city in 1204. But, as Queller has argued, there is little reason to doubt that around 1202 the Venetians seriously expected to try their hand against Egypt instead.[41] And subsequent crusades against Damietta (captured by the Fifth Crusade in 1218) once again made the point that the conquest of the mouth of the Nile could provide the key to the recovery of the Holy Land.

The argument here has been that the growth of Egyptian trade was in fact a result of the breakthroughs achieved by the north Italians in the eastern Mediterranean in the late eleventh and first half of the twelfth century. There was almost certainly a major expansion in this trade compared to what it had been around 1050, and it was not to lose momentum completely, even with the Third Crusade. This may be explained in the light of several factors. There were goods that Egypt supplied that were difficult to obtain in sufficient quantities elsewhere, such as alum. There was the constant availability of the spices of the Indies. There was the interdependence, at least in times of peace, between Acre and Alexandria in the trade of the Muslim world, described already. There was Islamic demand for western silver, though new silver sources in Iran made this less urgent by the end of the twelfth century. There was the beginning of a gradual decline in the textile industries of the Islamic world, which opened the door to western imitations, such as the fustians of northern Italy (named after Fustat in Egypt!) There was, too, princely demand for the woollen cloth of Flanders. All these factors provided the trade of the Italians in Egypt

---

[41]D.E. Queller, *The Fourth Crusade* (Leicester, 1978).

with enormous momentum. And the Christian dominance of the sea-routes, confirmed with the Venetian capture of Crete (not from the Greeks in fact, but from rival Genoese) meant that by the middle of the thirteenth century the volume of trade with Alexandria was certainly enormous. But equally the volume of trade with Acre had now reached unsurpassed heights. This was partly the result of additional factors. The rise of the Mongol Empire redirected trade northwards across Asia, and made the Black Sea ports and Persia into important staging posts in the trade in eastern luxury items, not least Chinese silks. However, the spice trade remained a largely Egyptian phenomenon. Meanwhile, Acre was able to benefit from easy access to southern Turkey, whence roads ran across to Tabriz and Trebizond. In fact, this also confirmed the special rôle of Acre as an entrepôt between the Muslim cities of the interior, such as Aleppo, and those in the Nile Delta. Interestingly, evidence from San Gimignano shows how Tuscan merchants were active in the thirteenth century in trade between Acre and Egypt, bringing cloth and other goods from bases in the Pisan quarter of Acre.[42] The existence of safe permanent settlements in the Holy Land made it practical for merchants to sail first to Acre, and then radiate outwards, even into Muslim Syria and Turkey. Acre thus became, by 1250, the capital of a whole network of trade routes.[43]

The contention here is that this was a gradual development. The Italian cities could not create their trade with Acre overnight. They simply did not have the manpower and capital to do so. Nor did they have the willpower. They had the religious commitment, but it was not initially directed to material gain. And they had commitments in other corners of the Mediterranean that sometimes (most notably in Egypt) clashed with their commitment to the Latin kingdom of Jerusalem. The Egyptian trade was, in fact, the foundation stone of their Levant trade, and it remained difficult to reconcile the demands of the rulers of Egypt for arms and timber with their duty to the Holy Land. It was there, in

---

[42]David Abulafia, 'Crocuses and crusaders: San Gimignano, Pisa and the Kingdom of Jerusalem', *Outremer. Studies in the history of the Crusading Kingdom of Jerusalem presented to Joshua Prawer*, ed. B. Z. Kedar, H. E. Mayer, R. C. Smail (Jerusalem, 1982), pp. 227-43, repr. in *Italy, Sicily and the Mediterranean*.

[43]Cahen, *Orient et occident*, pp. 192.

20

Egypt, that the interests of materialism triumphed, and they began to worship the god of gold.

III

Gli inizi del commercio genovese a Maiorca e il patto maiorchino-genovese del 1160

La presenza degli italiani nel commercio della Spagna medievale è stata recentemente oggetto di un crescente numero di studi, ed in particolare di un'introduzione magistrale alla problematica per mano di Geo Pistarino[1].

Nei rapporti tra i porti italiani e la Spagna medievale assume particolare rilievo – almeno dopo la conquista catalana del 1229 – la regione balearica: la documentazione è reperibile negli archivi non solo di Genova, ma anche in quelli catalani di Barcellona e di Palma di Maiorca. Tuttavia rimane estremamente rara la documentazione sui primordi della presenza genovese nelle isole Baleari, mentre la presenza pisana già nei primi anni del dodicesimo secolo è molto bene documentata dal *Liber Maiolichinus*, che descrive la breve occupazione di Maiorca e di Iviza da parte dei Pisani e dei Catalani nel 1114[2]. Per gli anni successivi si trovano alcuni riferimenti nelle fonti

---

[1] Il contributo di GEO PISTARINO agli atti del colloquio ispano-italiano è preziosissimo: *Presenze ed influenze italiane nel Sud della Spagna (secc. XII-XV)*, in «Presencia italiana en Andalucia, siglos XIV-XVII. Actas del I Coloquio hispano-italiano», a cura di B. TORRES RAMIREZ e J. HERNANDEZ PALOMO, Publicaciones de la Escuela de Estudios hispano-americanos de Sevilla, vol. CCCXI, Siviglia, 1985, pp. 21-51. Altre collezioni di studi sul tema sono: *Fremde Kaufleute auf der iberischen Halbinsel*, a cura di H. KELLENBENZ, *Kölner Kolloquien zur internationalen Sozial-und Wirtschaftsgeschichte*, vol. I, Colonia, 1970; *Actas del I Congreso internacional de história mediterranea*, in «Anuario de estudios medievales», 10, 1980; in particolare il contributo di M.T. FERRER I MALLOL, *Els italians a terres catalanes (segles XII-XV); València, un mercat medieval*, a cura di A. FURIO, Valenza, 1985; *La presenza italiana in Andalusia nel basso medioevo*, a cura di A. BOSCOLO e B. TORRES, *Studi e ricerche colombiane*, vol. II, Bologna, 1986, e così via.

[2] *Liber Maiolichinus de gestis Pisanorum illustribus*, a cura di C. CALISSE, Fonti per la Storia d'Italia, Roma, 1904.

4

a spedizioni genovesi verso le isole Baleari, come la razzia contro Minorca nel 1146 – spedizione da spiegare nell'ambito della seconda Crociata – e la guerra genovese contro Almeria[3].

Anche se Almeria fu vista come tappa commerciale di qualche importanza, sarebbe azzardato enfatizzare eccessivamente, nella spiegazione di questo fenomeno, le possibilità commerciali offerte dalle isole, che furono viste come base per la penetrazione, oltre che verso le Baleari, verso la Spagna musulmana o verso il Maghrib[4]; per di più, la pirateria maiorchina costituì sempre un ostacolo per la navigazione cristiana nelle acque del Mediterraneo occidentale, come si vede già all'epoca dell'emiro Mugiahid, il celebre signore musulmano di Denia, di Maiorca e (molto brevemente) di qualche parte della Sardegna nei primi anni dell'undicesimo secolo.

Il problema della pirateria musulmana fu ancora grave negli anni venti del Duecento, quando Giacomo d'Aragona stava preparando la sua vittoriosa spedizione contro Maiorca, epoca nella quale, tuttavia, i Genovesi e i Pisani godevano di privilegi commerciali a Maiorca e non volevano, per loro parte, sostenere l'invasione dei Catalani[5]. I molteplici progetti cristiani per la conquista di Maiorca non furono mai determinati dalla ricerca di prodotti isolani, dal momento che l'isola non poteva offrire prodotti di grande rilievo. Essa dipendeva infatti (almeno nell'epoca catalana) dalle importazioni di derrate essenziali, come il grano, per rifornire la capitale, che già sotto il governo musulmano era stata un grande centro di popolazione[6]. Fra le isole minori, Iviza aveva un'importanza globale determinata dal preziosissimo sale, oggetto di esportazioni genovesi nel tardo

---

[3] *Annali Genovesi di Caffaro e de' suoi continuatori*, a cura di L.T. BELGRANO e C. IMPERIALE di SANT'ANGELO, Fonti per la Storia d'Italia, Roma, 1890-1929, vol. 1, pp. 33-35.

[4] Per Almeria, si veda BLANCA GARÍ, *Why Almería? An Islamic port in the compass of Genoa*, in «Journal of Medieval History», numero speciale dedicato a *Aspects of medieval Spain, 711-1492*, vol. XVIII, 1992.

[5] BERNAT DESCLOT, *Llibre del rey en Pere*, in «Les quatre grans cròniques», a cura di F. SOLDEVILA, Barcellona, 1971, cap. 14.

[6] Per la storia delle isole in quest'epoca, si veda G. ROSSELLO BORDOY, *L'Islam a les illes balears*, Palma de Mallorca, 1968; P. GUICHARD, *L'Espagne et la Sicile musulmanes aux XIe et XIIe siècles*, Lione, 1990, pp. 69-70, 181-183.

medioevo, e probabilmente anche nell'undicesimo e dodicesimo secolo, quando il Maghrib divenne centro di scambio fra sale mediterraneo ed oro africano[7].

Divenuta scalo importante per mercanti genovesi, pisani, catalani nel tredicesimo secolo, Maiorca prima del 1200 è quasi sconosciuta agli storici dal punto di vista mercantile[8]. Preziosissimi, per tali ragioni, sono i pochi documenti superstiti nel cartolare di Giovanni Scriba che parlano di Maiorca e Iviza[9]. In contrasto con la maestosa documentazione offerta dal notaio per il commercio in direzione della Sicilia o verso «l'Oltremare», abbiamo solo sei contratti per il commercio balearico: tre per Maiorca e tre per Iviza. L'importanza degli atti di Giovanni Scriba deriva dalla presenza nel commercio maiorchino di alcuni mercanti di primo rango, tra i quali tre dei cosiddetti «Orientali», una volta considerati di origine greca, ebraica o siriana, mercanti in ogni caso che rappresentano il crescente gruppo di commercianti senza radici notevoli nell'antico patriziato[10].

Un contratto del 26 settembre 1156 indica che Bongiovanni Malfigliastro era interessato nel commercio *apud Maioricam*; la composizione della *societas* fu abbastanza complicata, visto che Bongiovanni stava per impegnarvi 16 lire di genovini, come i suoi due colleghi Guglielmo Aradello e Ogerio da Recco, e fu Ogerio da Recco che promise di recarsi a Maiorca portando inoltre la somma di 8 lire di genovini per conto degli altri due e 4 lire e 4 soldi di genovini per conto di Guglielmo Aradello[11]. A quest'epoca Bongiovanni era già coinvolto in una spedizione verso Salerno e la Sicilia,

---

[7] Per il sale di Iviza, si veda J.C. HOCQUET, *Ibiza, carrefour du commerce maritime et témoin d'une conjoncture méditerranéenne (1250-1650 env.)*, in «Studi in memoria di Federigo Melis», vol. I, Napoli, 1978.

[8] Si veda adesso O.R. CONSTABLE, *Trade and traders in Muslim Spain. The commercial relighnment of the Iberian peninsula 900-1500*, Cambridge, 1994.

[9] *Il cartolare di Giovanni Scriba*, a cura di M. CHIAUDANO e M. MORESCO, 2 voll., Roma e Torino, 1935 [in seguito: G.S., con il numero del volume e del documento].

[10] Non vale la pena di riprendere l'argomento contro l'esistenza dei cosiddetti "Orientali", anche se la loro identità esotica fu erroneamente riaffermata in recenti anni da alcuni storici: vedi D. ABULAFIA, *Le due Italie. Relazioni economiche fra il Regno normanno di Sicilia e i Comuni settentrionali*, Napoli, 1991 [ed. orig. inglese, Cambridge, 1977], pp. 314-335.

[11] G. S., I, doc. 141.

6

avendo investito 33 lire di genovini nell'impresa dell'agosto del medesimo anno[12].

Bongiovanni è noto come uno tra i più attivi clienti commerciali del notaio Giovanni Scriba, con investimenti importanti nel commercio siciliano, maghribino, levantino e sardo. In effetti, anche la presenza dei suoi capitali a Maiorca fa parte delle sue ambizioni commerciali più larghe, visto che nel contratto del 26 settembre viene stabilito che Ogerio avrebbe dovuto andare a Maiorca *et inde quo iverit maior pars sociorum suorum cum ligno in quo vadit*.

Maiorca fu soltanto un punto di penetrazione verso l'Africa o la Spagna, e possiamo ipotizzare che le incertezze generate a questo punto dalle attività militari degli Almohadi determinarono un aperto invito ai mercanti a scegliere la loro destinazione quando erano già a Maiorca, che era divenuta il luogo d'asilo di alcuni principi almoravidi, fuggiti dal nuovo ordine almohade nella penisola iberica. Fondamentale fu il desiderio di aspettare, di guardare, di utilizzare Maiorca (come nei secoli posteriori, ad esempio anche all'epoca di Francesco Datini) come punto di osservazione e di informazione sulle possibilità commerciali e sulle attività navali[13].

Il coinvolgimento di Maiorca nel commercio trans-mediterraneo è documentato in un secondo contratto, fra il notaio Giordano e un certo *Maraxi*, per il commercio *apud Deniam, inde Maioricam si velit et a Denia vel Maiorica Siciliam si voluerit et maior pars sociorum suorum iverit illuc*[14]. Il valore del contratto era esiguo, cioè di 15 lire di genovini *in societate* e di un contributo addizionale di 8 lire di genovini da parte di *Maraxi*. La presenza di altri investimenti in questo viaggio risulta dal fatto che il contratto superstite parla degli altri soci di *Maraxi*.

Dobbiamo ammettere una certa perplessità di fronte al nome *Maraxi*, che potrebbe rappresentare uno dei rarissimi nomi musulmani (o ebraici) nel cartolare, e in questo caso si può ipotizzare che egli avesse l'intenzione di viaggiare a bordo di una nave musulmana. Olivia Remie Constable nota che il legame di *Maraxi* con Denia e

---

[12] G. S., I, doc. 106.

[13] D. ABULAFIA, *A Mediterranean Emporium. The Catalan Kingdom of Majorca*, Cambridge, 1994, p. 220.

[14] G. S., I, doc. 487.

Maiorca potrebbe indicare un'origine islamica[15]. Inoltre, va rilevato come la possibilità di penetrare fino alla Sicilia sia un chiaro riflesso dell'accordo firmato nel 1156 fra il comune di Genova e il re Guglielmo I.

Il terzo contratto maiorchino di quest'epoca indica che anche il commercio diretto da Maiorca a Genova era possibile; il celebre Solimano di Salerno, mercante di origine meridionale con cospicui investimenti nel commercio levantino e siciliano, s'interessava a questo punto anche del commercio maiorchino, pur se ad un livello ristretto[16]. Il 20 settembre 1158 egli contrae una *societas* con Ruggero di Chiavica (*Roger de Clavica*) del valore di 45 lire[17]. Come al solito, Solimano investì 30 lire di genovini nell'impresa e Ruggero la metà, prevedendo la divisione uguale dei profitti.

Redatto come tanti altri atti del genere *in domum Solimani*, questo contratto fu in primo luogo rivolto al commercio in Maiorca stessa; ma nel contratto si prevedeva la possibilità che la nave avrebbe potuto dirigersi verso un altro luogo, e anche che la nave avrebbe potuto essere venduta, nel qual caso Ruggero sarebbe stato obbligato a seguire gli altri mercanti coinvolti nella spedizione, gli investimenti dei quali non sono ricordati in questo cartolare.

Ricordiamo come a quest'epoca le acque fra Maiorca e Valencia fossero contese fra il potere almohade e il cosiddetto «Re Lobo», *Rex Lupus*, cioè Ibn Mardanish di Valencia: con lui i Genovesi firmarono un nuovo trattato di pace nel 1161, avendo già nel 1149 assicurato la loro navigazione verso Valencia con un privilegio preliminare. Allo stesso tempo, tentavano di firmare un accordo con gli Almohadi, con lo scopo di permettere il libero commercio a Bugia, centro maghribino che si trovava direttamente a sud di Maiorca (e che fu qualche volta la destinazione di spedizioni dei Banu Ghaniya contro gli Almohadi).

Dobbiamo chiederci se anche Maiorca fu oggetto di tentativi di trovare un accordo, con l'intento di assicurare la navigazione delle navi genovesi verso il Maghrib. La sicurezza delle rotte fu certo già compromessa nel 1159 da una razzia siciliana contro Iviza, interpre-

---

[15] O.R. CONSTABLE cit., p. 109.

[16] Per Solimano, si veda D. ABULAFIA, *Le due Italie* cit., pp. 316-335.

[17] G. S., I, doc. 497.

8

tata talvolta come un tentativo di controllare le vie marittime contro il pericolo dell'espansione almohade [18]. Isolati nel Mediterraneo occidentale, fra la Sicilia, il Maghrib almohade, le forze anti-almohade della Spagna musulmana, i Banu Ghaniya tentarono di neutralizzare almeno alcuni dei loro molteplici nemici esterni. Non sorprende che i signori di Maiorca abbiano cercato in questo momento un accordo con gli italiani, nella speranza di assicurarsi che le flotte di Genova avrebbero scelto altre destinazioni nelle loro guerre antimusulmane. Risulta da una clausola del trattato fra Genova e Federico Barbarossa della primavera del 1162, là dove si parla di Maiorca e Minorca, che era già in vigore un patto con Maiorca, firmato probabilmente nel 1160, visto che la scadenza del patto fu anticipata all'anno 1170 e che tali patti avevano di solito una vita di dieci anni (come per esempio il patto del 1181) [19]. L'esatto contenuto di questo patto rimane puramente ipotetico. La protezione delle isole da razzie genovesi, una clausola importante del patto del 1181, quasi sicuramente vi aveva un rilievo particolare, tenuto conto delle razzie dei Genovesi a Minorca del 1146 e dei Siciliani a Iviza del 1159. È sempre possibile che già nel 1158 le trattative per firmare un accordo fossero in corso, perché la sola informazione su una spedizione genovese verso Maiorca reca la data di questo anno; raramente i commercianti genovesi non colsero l'occasione di approfittare delle spedizioni diplomatiche.

L'importanza del rapporto fra le isole Baleari e Bugia viene espressa in due documenti del 1163, che indicano la presenza di Genovesi nel commercio di Iviza, celeberrimo centro di produzione del sale. Un contratto del 28 agosto 1163 indica che l'importante commerciante Blancardo, probabilmente di origine provenzale (ma non, certamente, un ebreo come altri hanno proposto [20]), aveva l'intenzione di mandare ad Iviza la somma di 40 lire di genovini, per poi commerciare fino a Bugia *aut qua* [sic!] *navis iverit*; il documento indica che i due *socii tractantes*, Fulcone di Pré e Vassallo Raviol, erano già implicati in *societates* con altri mercanti a Genova, presumibilmente per lo stesso viaggio [21].

---

[18] G. Doxey, *Diplomacy, war and trade: Muslim Majorca in international politics, 1159-81*, in «Journal of Medieval History», vol. XX, 1994, pp. 40-41.

[19] G. Doxey cit., p. 48.

[20] D. Abulafia, *Le due Italie* cit., pp. 314-315.

[21] G. S., II, doc. 1084.

Anche Blancardo utilizzò denari forniti dalle sue trattative con colleghi a Genova: A. *Aurie* (cioè Doria) e un certo Pedesemol. Che i due commercianti genovesi abbiano viaggiato verso Iviza a bordo della nave di un certo *Thimonerius* risulta da un atto del 30 agosto dello stesso anno, nel quale Guglielmo Cruseto e Guienzone Bonaminestra contrassero una *societas* di 12 lire e 6 soldi di genovini per il commercio *apud Evençam* [22]. In un altro atto dello stesso giorno i medesimi mercanti stipularono una *accomendacio* del valore di 1 lira di genovini per un viaggio *sana eunte navi qua vado*, che deve indicare un investimento addizionale nella loro piccola impresa di Iviza [23]. I risultati del patto del 1160 sono visibili anche nella lenta ma continua penetrazione da parte dei Genovesi nel commercio di Bugia e di Ceuta, cioè le regioni oltre Maiorca e Iviza, attestata dagli investimenti dei mercanti menzionati negli atti di Giovanni Scriba [24].

L'importanza della regione fu espressa in altri termini in un importante documento del 1162, il trattato fra Federico Barbarossa e il comune di Genova:

> « Et quandocumque domino imperatori divinitus fuerit inspiratum ire contra Sarracenos in toto regno Lupi et regis Maiorice et Minorice, expleto octenio termino, videlicet pacis promisse ipsi regi Maiorice, comune Ianue faciet ei ostem cum sua forcia, et iuvabit eum bona fide, absque fraude et malo ingenio, ad subiugandum ea ad honorem Dei et imperii Romani, ita tamen quod totius terre et pecunie propterea capte vel reddite tertiam partem habeamus totius» [25].

L'ambizione dei Genovesi era in piena espansione, e mirava non soltanto alla conquista del Regno siciliano in lega con l'imperatore, ma anche, come risulta da una clausola del trattato, all'occupazione di Valenza e di Maiorca e Minorca. La possibilità di approfittare del-

---

[22] G. S., II, doc. 1088.

[23] G. S., II, doc. 1087.

[24] D. ABULAFIA, *Le due Italie* cit., pp. 169, 176.

[25] Per il testo del privilegio si veda *Codice diplomatico della Repubblica di Genova*, a cura di C. IMPERIALE DI SANT'ANGELO, 3 voll., Roma, 1936-42, vol. 1, pp. 396-404; D. ABULAFIA, *Le due Italie* cit., pp. 187-189. Una analisi di primaria importanza è offerta da G. DOXEY cit., pp. 46-53.

le difficoltà del regime almoravide in Maiorca, per estendere il dominio genovese oltre la Corsica e la Sardegna fino alle porte della
Spagna, era attraente, ma fu anche un sogno vano[26]. Per spiegare
questi avvenimenti, bisogna anche ricordare i tentativi dei Pisani di
stabilirsi sull'isola in questi anni, e la continua rivalità fra i due comuni per il controllo delle acque attorno alla Sardegna. Ambedue
miravano ad un commercio africano, con una base a Bugia; ambedue vedevano nell'isola di Maiorca la possibilità di ottenere un punto di sorveglianza nel Mediterraneo occidentale.

Nei cartolari genovesi del tardo dodicesimo secolo il riflesso della presenza genovese a Maiorca diviene sempre più chiaro: il cartolare di Oberto Scriba del 1182 contiene dieci contratti relativi al
commercio maiorchino, per un valore complessivo di 851 lire di genovini, subito dopo la conclusione di un trattato fra il governo musulmano di Maiorca ed il comune genovese[27]. Ricordiamo che i testi
superstiti dei privilegi offerti dai signori almoravidi della Maiorca
musulmana ai Genovesi nel 1181 e nel 1188 non sono i primi trattati fra Genova e Maiorca musulmana, mentre il primo patto risale
probabilmente al 1160[28].

Anche i re di Sicilia mirarono per lunghi anni alla conquista
delle isole Baleari, probabilmente nella speranza di sopprimere la
pirateria locale. La documentazione degli anni Ottanta dimostra come, dopo due decadi, la Repubblica di Genova e il piccolo regno almoravide dei Banu Ghaniya avessero trovato un interesse comune
nel respingere altri poteri nella regione: il re Guglielmo II di Sicilia,
che tentò vanamente la conquista di Maiorca nel 1181; l'impero islamico degli Almohadi, contro il quale i Maiorchini rimasero fino ai

---

[26] G. DOXEY cit., pp. 51-52, vede nella clausola un atto di incoraggiamento non
per i Genovesi, che non volevano ritirarsi dai loro obblighi in Maiorca, ma verso i
Catalani, che miravano ancora alla conquista dell'isola. Per parte sua, Percy Ernst
Schramm mise l'accento sull'ambizione commerciale dei Genovesi: P.E. SCHRAMM-
J.F. CABESTANY-E. BAGUÉ, *Els primers comtes-reis*, Barcelona, 1969, p. 34.

[27] D. ABULAFIA, *Le due Italie* cit., p. 222; ID., *A Mediterranean Emporium* cit., pp.
108-110.

[28] L. DE MAS LATRIE, *Traités de paix et de commerce et documents divers concernant les relations des Chrétiens avec les Arabes de l'Afrique septentrionale au Moyen Age*,
Parigi, 1866, pp. 109-113, 113-115.

primi anni del Duecento quasi il solo centro di attiva e continua resistenza nel mondo di al-Andalus [29].

La presenza dei Genovesi nel commercio maiorchino attorno al
1160, e negli anni successivi, fu un chiaro segno della loro abilità di
muoversi fra Almoravidi e Almohadi, fra Siciliani e Tedeschi, fra Pisani e Catalani per assicurarsi il *proficuum quod Deus dederit*.

---

[29] A. Bel, *Les Benou Ghanya, derniers représentants de l'empire almoravide et leur lutte contre l'empire almohade*, Parigi e Algeri, 1903; D. Abulafia, *The Norman kingdom of Africa and the Norman expeditions to Majorca and the Muslim Mediterranean*, in «Anglo-Norman Studies», vol. VII, 1984, pp. 42-45; rist. in D. Abulafia, *Italy, Sicily and the Mediterranean, 1100-1400*, Londra, 1987.

IV

EAST AND WEST:
COMMENTS ON THE COMMERCE
OF THE CITY OF ANCONA IN THE MIDDLE AGES

Some years ago I published two studies on the political and commercial activities of Ancona. One was concerned with the relations between that city and the Byzantine empire at the time of the siege of Frederick Barbarossa in 1173, an event commemorated in the famous tale by Buoncompagno da Segni.[1] The other dealt with the commerce of Ancona with the Levant, in the light of abundant yet at the time little-known[2] records, such as the privilege granted to the merchants of the city at Acre in 1257 and notarial records drawn up in Cyprus around the year 1300 by the Genoese notary Lamberto di Sambuceto, now mostly published thanks to work by Genoese and French authors.[3]

My research on Ancona has convinced me that, even when examining the long-term commercial relations of the city, we must focus on the importance of the relations between the two coasts of the Adriatic in order to

---

[1] D. ABULAFIA, *Ancona, Byzantium and the Adriatic, 1155-1173*, «Papers of the British School at Rome», 52 (1984), pp. 195-216; reprinted in D. ABULAFIA, *Italy, Sicily and the Mediterranean, 1100-1400*, London 1987, ch. IX. For Buoncompagno, see: *BUONCOMPAGNI liber de obsidione Ancone [a. 1173]*, edited by G.C. ZIMOLO, in *Rerum Italicarum Scriptores*, II ed., VI/III, Bologna 1937.

[2] D. ABULAFIA, *The Ancomitan privileges in the kingdom of Jerusalem and the Levant trade of Ancona*, in *I comuni italiani nel regno crociato di Gerusalemme*, edited by G. AIRALDI and B. Z. KEDAR, Genova 1986, pp. 525-70; reprinted in in D. ABULAFIA, *Commerce and Conquest in the Mediterranean, 1100-1500*, Aldershot 1993, ch. XIII.

[3] The editions of notarial records most useful for research on the Anconitans at Cyprus are: V. POLONIO, *Notai genovesi in oltremare. Atti rogati a Cipro da Lamberto di Sambuceto (3 luglio 1300-3 agosto 1301)*, Genova 1982, and R. PAVONI, *Notai genovesi in oltremare. Atti rogati a Cipro da Lamberto di Sambuceto (6 luglio-27 ottobre 1301)*, Genova 1982. Other works were edited by M. BALARD, Genova 1983 and 1984, but deal to a lesser extent with Anconitan matters.

understand the sometimes specialized role that Ancona played in Medieval commerce. Although some authors have seen Ancona as the fifth "maritime Italian republic", there are definite reasons for placing the city on a lower level.[4] Nevertheless, the lack of studies on the so-called "minor" cities in Mediterranean commerce is a serious gap in our understanding of the Mediterranean economy in the late Middle Ages, because the models of Venice or Genoa do not serve to explain the character of trade in the smaller centres, interwoven as they were in a local network of exchange.[5] Recently, also, some authors have shed light on some essential aspects of Anconitan commerce. Examples are the works of Eliyahu Ashtor, known for his capacity to use both Western and Oriental sources, and in particular one of his works on Anconitan commerce in the Levant during the late Middle Ages, based on an analysis of early surviving notarial registers.[6] There are also the works of the German Leonhard, who wrote a highly detailed work on the political and social evolution of Ancona, published by the Institute for German Studies in Rome,[7] and Peter Earle's still valuable works on Ancona in the late 15th and 16th centuries, which expand our understanding of Ancona's external relations with the help of notarial registers in the city's State Archives, during a period of flourishing trade.[8]

These notarial sources are lacking before the late 14th century. We are therefore obliged to use external sources, such as papal registers, which are useful as regards political relations, since Ancona was linked to the Holy See, and documents from Dubrovnik, quoted, for example, in Barisa Krekić's classic study on trade between Dubrovnik and the Levant in the Middle Ages.[9] Also of interest is the so-called travel diary of the Jew Jacob of Ancona who, according to his chronicler, visited the Middle East and even

---

[4] Cfr. *Ancona Repubblica Marinara. Federico Barbarossa e le Marche. Atti del Convegno di studi storici (Ancona, 19-21 aprile 1969)*, Città di Castello 1972.

[5] D. ABULAFIA, *The Levant trade of the minor cities in the thirteenth and fourteenth centuries: strengths and weaknesses*, «Asian and African Studies», 22 (1968), pp. 196-212; reprinted under the title *The Medieval Levant. Studies in memory of Eliyahu Ashtor (1914-1984)*, edited by B.Z. KEDAR and A.L. UDOVITCH, Haifa 1988; reprinted in ABULAFIA, *Commerce and Conquest* cit., ch. XI.

[6] E. ASHTOR, *Il commercio levantino di Ancona nel basso Medioevo*, «Rivista storica italiana», 88 (1976), pp. 213-53; reprinted in E. ASHTOR, *Studies on the Levantine trade in the Middle Ages*, London 1978, ch. VIII.

[7] J.F. LEONHARD, *Die Seestadt Ancona im Spätmittelalter*, Tübingen 1983.

[8] P. EARLE, *The commercial development of Ancona, 1479-1551*, «Economic History Review», s. 2, 22 (1969), pp. 28-44.

[9] B. KREKIĆ, *Dubrovnik (Raguse) et le Levant au Moyen Âge*, Paris/Hague 1961.

EAST AND WEST: COMMENTS ON THE COMMERCE

Zaitun in China, although the diary is certainly a modern counterfeit.[10] It is also clear that the rivalry between Ancona and Venice went back to remote times. In some important ways, it served to stimulate long-distance commerce on the part of the Anconitans, since the problems between the Venetians and the Byzantine empire resulted in friendly overtures being made to Ancona by the Emperor Manuel Komnenos in the second half of the 12th century. Without this political relationship, trade would certainly have developed much more slowly. At that time, according to Greek sources, the Anconitans received from Byzantium money to pay for their resistance to Frederick Barbarossa, who besieged the city twice, believing that Ancona was the means through which the Byzantines were trying to acquire the loyalty of the Italians rebelling against the German empire. Moreover, the Anconitans very probably received trading privileges, the exact reason for which is still unknown, but they increased in importance with the formal submission of Ancona to the Greek empire: ἀκέλευστοι τῷ Βασιλεῖ δεδουλεύκασιν - the Anconitans spontaneously subjected themselves to the Byzantine emperor, as we are informed by the Greek orator Eustathios of Thessalonike, in his praise of the citizens, who had recognized the power of the true Roman Empire, that of Constantinople.[11] According to the Byzantine chronicler Niketas Choniates, the Anconitans were ἰσοπολίταις τῷ γένει Ῥωμαίων, citizens of the Roman empire.[12] The Greek emperor sent considerable quantities of gold to Ancona, in order to buy the support of its citizens and also that of the inhabitants of other cities in the Marches and Lombardy. Pertusi has suggested that, at the end of the 12th century, the Constantinople church of St Stephen was already used as a base for the community of Anconitan merchants, as it certainly was during the last days of Byzantium.[13]

The rivalry between Venice and Ancona is also clearly shown by the records of Venetian statesmen of the times. According to Buoncompagno, at the end of the 12th century Ancona had about ten thousand inhabitants, which is a credible number, as opposed to the population of Venice, which had

---

[10] See appendix.

[11] *EUSTATHII THESSALONICENSIS oratio ad Manuelem imperatorem*, in *Fontes rerum byzantinarum*, I/I, *Rhetorum saeculi XII orationes politicae*, edited by W. REGEL, S. Petersburg 1892, p.111; ABULAFIA, *Ancona, Byzantium and the Adriatic* cit., p. 200.

[12] *NICETAE CHONIATAE historia*, edited by I. A. van DIETEN, in *Corpus fontium historiae Byzantinae, series Berolensis*, XI (1-2), Berlin-New York 1975, p. 202; ABULAFIA, *Ancona, Byzantium and the Adriatic* cit., p. 214.

[13] A. PERTUSI, *The Anconitan Colony in Constantinople and the report of its Consul, Benvenuto, on the fall of the city*, in *Charanis Studies. Essays in honour of Peter Charanis*, edited by A. LAIOU-THOMADAKIS, New Brunswick 1980, pp. 199-200.

perhaps one hundred thousand in the early 12th century.[14] Over the centuries, competition with Ancona was always limited by its relatively small size and by the lack of an economic infrastructure comparable to that of Venice. Already in 1144, the Venetians warned Ancona that, if it should attempt to restrict trade with Pesaro and Fano, the Venetian Republic would help these cities against Ancona (to a certain extent, this protection to Pesaro and Fano was an attempt to restrict the commercial and naval activities of Ancona in the central Adriatic).[15] For these reasons, Ancona's neighbours were subjected to far less onerous requests for naval and military aid than was the case in Istria, a region more securely under Venetian control. In 1151, a brief conflict between Venice and Ancona resulted in the Venetians' confirming the right of Anconitan merchants to travel and trade without restriction in the lands controlled by Venice: in other words, a defeat for Venice. According to Buoncompagno da Segni, the Venetians «semper quodam speciali odio Anchonam oderunt».[16] In addition, Buoncompagno tells us, in 1173, «multi Anchonitani aberant, qui causa negotiandi erant in Alexandria, in urbe Constantinopolitana et Romania».[17] Although this statement cannot be entirely taken at its face value, Ancona's close relations with Byzantium may have resulted in expansion of commerce even in remote places.

There are several indications of trade contacts in the Adriatic in the same period. Already in 1128, a *pagina recordationis* shows that the monks of the Tremiti islands traded as far as Ancona.[18] More important, certainly, were the political and economic links established with Pisa in 1169, which ensured that Tuscan merchants were welcomed in Split and Dubrovnik, and showed the importance for Pisa of a commercial network which, passing through the Marches (primarily through Ancona) penetrated as far as the Balkans in search of silver, slaves and timber. Even more, close links with Pisa (and later with Genoa) offered Ancona hopes of assistance against the Venetian threat.[19] In 1199, the Anconitans signed a trade agreement with Dubrovnik, one of a series of pacts between Dubrovnik and the Italian coastal

---

[14] BUONCOMPAGNI *liber de obsidione Ancone* cit., p. 23.

[15] ABULAFIA, *Ancona, Byzantium and the Adriatic* cit., pp. 204-207.

[16] BUONCOMPAGNI *liber de obsidione Ancone* cit., p. 13; the same attitude on the part of the Venetians may be found in *Historia Ducum Veneticorum*, edited by H. SIMONSFELD, p. 81, in *Monumenta Germaniae Historica, Scriptores* XIV, Hannoverae 1883.

[17] BUONCOMPAGNI *liber de obsidione Ancone* cit., p. 17.

[18] A. PETRUCCI, *Codice diplomatico del monastero benedettino di S. Maria di Tremiti (1005-1237)*, III, Roma 1960, pp. 277-278.

[19] G. GUARNIERI, *Intorno alle relazioni commerciali marittime nel Medioevo fra la Toscana e gli scali adriatici dalmati*, «Archivio storico italiano», 125 (1967), pp. 352-364.

cities of those times.[20] Although the literature on commerce between the Italians in the Byzantine world has always emphasized trade in luxury goods with Constantinople, the presence of Anconitans (and also merchants from Venice and Apulia) in the Byzantine ports of the Adriatic recalls the importance of relatively local links with the western lands of Byzantium, concentrated on more modest but sometimes quite large objectives. In the 12th century, the tendency towards the creation of a system of trans-Adriatic relations was clearly reinforced, as expressed in agreements between Ancona with Trogir in 1236, Zadar in 1258 and 1388, and again with Dubrovnik in 1292.[21]

Clearly, the interests of Ancona were also rooted in the local politics of the Marches, and competition for control of the region's coastline and hills, with Jesi and Osimo inland and Fano and Senigallia on the sea, was complicated by more extended rivalry, between Pope and Emperor, Guelphs and Ghibellines. The Anconitans saw the attempts of Pope Gregory IX to create a papal block in the Marches as an occasion to request his help in their commercial activities. With this aim, as shown by the papal registers of Gregory IX and Innocent IV, the Holy See addressed letters to the Mediterranean powers, stressing that the Anconitans had lived under the protection of St Peter. Of particular interest is a letter sent in 1231 to the Sultan of Egypt, Al-Kamil, in which the pope deplores the fact that Anconitan merchants in Alexandria were victims of severe prosecution, being thrown into prison and their goods confiscated. The letter also indicates that the Anconitans already had some treaty of *fidem et pacem* with the Ayyubid.[22] As shown by a letter written by Frederick II in 1224, there were Anconitan merchants at Acre, and in 1254 Innocent IV, seeking allies in his war against Frederick II, took the merchants of Ancona under his protection, offering very generous privileges to the city and asking the bishop to lend its citizens all necessary help.[23] These hopes were certainly dashed, and only in 1257 was Giovanni d'Ibelino granted the great privilege for Anconitan trade at Acre, as revealed by records now in Maltese archives.

[20] D. ABULAFIA, *Dalmatian Ragusa and the Norman Kingdom of Sicily*, «Slavonic and East European Review», 54 (1976), pp. 414-415, 422; reprinted in ABULAFIA, *Italy, Sicily and the Mediterranean* cit., ch. X.

[21] T. SMIČIKLAS, *Codex diplomaticus regni Croatiae, Slavoniae et Dalmatiae*, III, pp. 12, 209; V, p. 88; VI, p. 620, Zagabriae 1904-5; cfr. ASHTOR, *Commercio levantino* cit., p. 215.

[22] *Annales ecclesiastici ad anno MCXCVIII ubi desinit Cardinalis Baronius, auctore Oderico Raynaldo*, edited by J. D. MANSI, II, Lucca 1747, p. 52, doc. 56.

[23] ARCHIVIO SEGRETO VATICANO (= A. S. VAT.), reg. vat. 21, epp. 43-45, f. 219v; A. THEINER, *Codex diplomaticus domini temporalis s. Sedis*, I, Roma 1861, p. 119.

The pope's attempts to offer Ancona rights to trade in «totam Apuliam et Regnum Sicilie, nec non per omnes terras et aquas ecclesie Romane», conferred in 1245, at a time when the emperor exercised direct control over Apulian ports, came to nothing. Privileges were part of a more extensive plan to offer to political allies of the Pope exemptions and other rights in central Italy and in the Kingdom of the Two Sicilies, in anticipation of the defeat of the papal and Guelph forces.[24] However, the document shows another aspect of Ancona's ambitions in Adriatic trade. This picture also extended to Durazzo, as in 1246 the pope added a privilege for Anconitan commerce in that city, in the hands of the Epirote princes.[25] The pope's explanation for his decision is interesting: Ancona is restricted and isolated by competition on the part of its Ghibelline enemies (for example, Jesi), who threatened port supplies, with the result that external links were essential if the city were to survive. At this point, the impression is that the 1240s were a period of uncertainty and trading difficulties for Ancona. From another viewpoint, more extended contacts are revealed by a papal privilege of 1248, which indicates the presence of a monastery inhabited by Armenian monks in Ancona.[26]

Simple logic obliged the Anconitans to seek political and commercial allies among the enemies of Venice, and it is therefore not surprising that in the conflicts between Genoese and Venetians in the Holy Land during the 12th century - as, for example, the war of San Saba of the 1250s - the Anconitans mainly supported the Genoese.[27] Nevertheless, records indicate that, before 1257, some Anconitans seeking free trade were counted in the warehouses of the kingdom of Jerusalem as Venetians, others as Genoese, and others, more fortunate, as Pisans, who enjoyed the highest exemptions from customs duties. All this was changed by the privilege of 1257.[28] The constitution of the Anconitans as an autonomous corporation, with its own rights and a small piece of land next to the garden of the Genoese, on which to build a church, a palazzo and a lodging-house, reflected attempts by Genoa to improve their standing in the kingdom of Jerusalem. Six witnesses of the privilege of Giovanni d'Ibelino, in 1257, were illustrious Genoese such as Ansaldo Ceba and Gugliemo Spinola, perhaps members of the *haute cour* of

---

[24] A. S. VAT., reg. vat. 21, ep. 46, f. 219v; THEINER, *Codex diplomaticus* cit., p. 119; ABULAFIA, *Anconitan privileges* cit., pp. 530-531.

[25] A. S. VAT., reg. vat. 21, ep. 863, f. 408r; THEINER, *Codex diplomaticus* cit., pp. 124-125.

[26] T. HALUŠČYNSKYJ e M. M. WOLMAR, *Acta Innocentii PP. IV (1243-1254) e Registris Vaticanis aliisque fontibus*, III/IV/1, Roma 1962, pp. 48-49.

[27] G. CARO, *Genova e la sua supremazia nel Mediterraneo*, «Atti della Società ligure di storia patria», 88/I (1974), pp. 34-49, 72-79.

[28] Edition of the text in ABULAFIA, *Anconitan privileges* cit., pp. 560-564.

the kingdom. As in other Jerusalem privileges for Italian trade, the document states that fiscal exemptions enjoyed by the Anconitans were to be limited to trade with Acre itself, and that they would not enjoy privileges if they passed beyond Acre to trade in Saracen lands. Ancona was obliged to offer tax exemptions only to its own inhabitants and to those of the surrounding area, and not (as many other Italians did) to all and any merchants who wished to present themselves to the warehouses as if they were from Ancona. From the viewpoint of the Ibelino government, the importance of the privilege also lay in the requirement to offer, in 1259 (two years later) fifty Anconitan infantry for the defence of Acre, on land and sea. In any case, attempts to protect Acre against rival factions and particularly against the Venetians failed, and in 1259 the Genoese, and doubtless also the Anconitans, departed for Tyre, under the protection of Philip de Monfort.[29]

This was a defeat - if not for Ancona, at least for Anconitan interests. In 1264, in an agreement with Ancona, Venice clearly indicated her intentions with regard to competition, deciding that Ancona was to be limited to commerce in the Adriatic, while commerce with the Levant was virtually suppressed, only the transport of pilgrims to the Orient being permitted to continue. Ancona was no longer permitted to transport *intra culfum* foreign goods, or to send them beyond the Adriatic.[30] In 1274, the Anconitans - unsuccessfully - tried to persuade Pope Gregory X to annul the Venetian treaty. Of importance in the 1264 document is insistence on Venetian control of Anconitan trade in cotton: transport of cotton from Apulia to Venice, along the Adriatic coast north of Rimini and to Dalmatia was forbidden. It is clear that the Anconitans were already heavily involved in the cotton trade, a point fully confirmed by later 13th and 14th century documents.[31]

The records of Lamberto di Sambuceto, a Genoese notary of Famagusta, around 1300, very clearly show to what extent the Anconitans were involved in the cotton trade, and suggest that Syria was the most important source, while Cyprus was the centre of a trading system linking the Italian mercantile communities with Syria, Armenia and Egpyt.[32] A feature of

---

[29] ABULAFIA, *Anconitan privileges* cit., pp. 534-545.
[30] R. CESSI, *Venezia e il problema adriatico* cit., Padova 1943, pp. 75-82.
[31] ABULAFIA, *Anconitan privileges* cit., p. 546.
[32] See editions of records quoted in note 3; also, for the following, ABULAFIA, *Anconitan privileges* cit., pp. 546-558. As regards the problem of Famagusta, see in particular: P. EDBURY, *The Genoese community in Famagusta around the year 1300: a historical vignette*, in *Oriente e Occidente tra Medioevo ed Età Moderna. Studi in onore di Geo Pistarino*, II, Acqui Terme 1997, pp. 235-244 [with an excellent bibliography on pp. 243-244]; P. EDBURY, *Genoese society ca.1300 from the registers of Lamberto di Sambuceto*, in *Die Kreuzfahrerstaaten als multikulturelle Gesellschaft*, Köln 1997, pp. 88-95; M.

these notarial records is their mention of Syrian merchants, that is, Orthodox Christians who had come from Syria to sell Levantine cotton to Anconitan, Genoese, Venetian and other buyers. Cosma and Damiano "de Lezia", perhaps originally from the city of Laodicea (Lattakiah), regularly delivered quantities of cotton to Anconitans like Tomaso de Rogerio. On October 14 1300, Cosma delivered to Tomaso cotton for the high value of 1444 white *bisanti*, for transport to Ancona on a ship belonging to the Anconitan Baron Pellegrini de Galante, and for sale specifically in Ancona. With the profits, Tomaso agreed to purchase supplies «per totam marcham Ancone et totam Ampuliam», with the intention of exporting them to Cyprus.[33] As in those times the Armenians bought wheat from Apulia, with the help of the Bardi family (always present in Famagusta); in this case too grain may have been sought for export to Cyprus. Another possibility is that cloth from the Marches was sent to the Orient, goods woven partly using raw materials from the Orient like cotton, linen and indigo or other dyes imported from the Levant. As Heyd states, the Anconitans exported products of the Marches like oil, wine and fustian, and also Florentine cloth, to the East. Cosma and Damiano de Lezia themselves were also involved in trade with Venice and Dubrovnik although, according to the records of Lamberto di Sambuceto, the cotton trade with Ancona was first on their list: indeed, it would not be an exaggeration to speak of a regular program of investments by Syrian Christian merchants in the Anconitan cotton trade, although some Tuscans like the Pisan Belluco de Belluchis de Accon provided similar services to the merchants of Ancona, in this case sending cotton and sugar to the Marches.[34] Other merchants needed pepper, spices, Oriental cloth and gold, but these were never the main supplies in Ancona's trade with the Levant. In particular, spices did not dominate Levantine trade in Ancona, either then or in later centuries. In October 1301, therefore, we learn that Leonardo Salembene of Ancona declared that he intended to send 45 sacks of cotton to the west, together with 22 cases of sugar, 125 pieces of cloth, and other Oriental products.[35] The trade in slaves from the Orient was not great, but there were

---

BALARD, *L'activité commerciale en Chypre dans les années 1300*, in *Crusade and Settlement*, edited by P. EDBURY, Cardiff 1985, pp. 251-263; D. JACOBY, *The rise of a new emporium in the eastern Mediterranean: Famagusta in the late thirteenth century*, in Μελέται και Υπομνήματα. Ίδρυμα Αρχιεπισκόπου Μακαρίου Γ, I, Nicosia 1984, pp. 143-179.

[33] For the de Lezia, see documents edited by POLONIO, *Notai genovesi in oltremare* cit., docs. 31, 48, 50, 54, 368, 368a etc. (Cosma); docs. 30, 31, 32, 33, 34, 368, 368a, 390 etc. (Damiano).

[34] POLONIO, *Notai genovesi in oltremare* cit., doc. 323.

[35] PAVONI, *Notai genovesi in oltremare* cit., doc. 222.

of course other occasions for the Anconitans to buy slaves, especially from Dalmatia.

Links with Tuscany in the 13th century recall that old commercial relationship between Ancona, Pisa and the Dalmatian cities. It is true that all attempts to enter the spice trade met with considerable hostility from Venice. In July 1349, the Venetians attempted to confiscate Oriental articles transported to Italy by Anconitan and Pisan merchants. According to Ashtor, the Venetians' interest in Anconitan trade focused on the problem of competition in exporting soap. He quotes the resolutions of the Venetian Senate, for example in 1347, according to which soap works in Ancona and the Marches were becoming very numerous, with the result that the price of oil available for the Venetian market had increased by 50% in price, so that the production of Venetian soap fell greatly, due to the lack of oil.[36] One particular problem was soap from the Marches exported on Venetian ships. The Senate, without much success, tried to forbid Venetian ships from transporting Anconitan soap, but again in 1361 it was obliged to take new measures against Ancona. What is striking here is again the importance of exporting local products from the Marches, articles made from supplies obtained from the region around Ancona. Ancona played a very small role in exporting Flemish and French cloth, or other "international" products which passed daily through the markets of Genoa and Venice. There was also fustian cloth from the Marches, woven in part from Oriental raw materials. This tendency towards specialization in local or regional products was widespread in the Levantine commerce of the so-called minor cities. For example, the merchants of San Gimignano were known in the Levant for their saffron, those of Narbonne for honey, those of Messina for wine, and so on.[37] In the case of Ancona, the region providing goods was quite extensive, including several Tusan and Dalmatian cities, but the main role in Anconitan exports was always played by Marches products.

Clearly, the importance of Anconitan imports around 1300 lay in the possibility of supplying the Marches and perhaps also Tuscany with raw products, principally cotton. The testimonies of Lamberto di Sambuceto are amply confirmed in the *Pratica* of Pegolotti, a man who knew the markets of Cyprus very well. Pegolotti adds information on the other markets frequented by the Anconitan merchants, such as Tunis, a centre for oil and canvas. At Constantinople, the Anconitans were known for their soap. Fabriano paper also penetrated international markets, thanks partly to Anconitan merchants. But the most important product in the network of imports from the Orient was cotton. Directed specifically to Ancona, which functioned as a centre for distribution to central Italy, the cotton trade was crucial for the expansion of

---

[36] ASHTOR, *Commercio levantino* cit., pp. 216-217.
[37] ABULAFIA, *Levant trade of the minor cities* cit.

local products like cloth (such as fustian) to the Marches cities, although the Venetians had some sucess in limiting the movements of Anconitan ships to the waters of the central and southern Adriatic.

Pegolotti provides information from a 13th century perspective, although his sources were mostly older. However, the general picture of Anconitan activities in the Orient is confirmed over and over again - for example, in the records of Nicolò de Boateriis, a Venetian notary in Famagusta between 1355 and 1365, and also, for Crete, in the records of the notary at Kandia, Benvenuto de Brixano, who worked at the same time as Lamberto di Sambuceto. In his famous study on Venetian trade in cotton in Syria, Ashtor mentions a cargo ship which, sailing from Alexandria, reached Ancona loaded with 240 sacks of cotton, each weighing 600 Ancona pounds, mentioned in the archives of Francesco di Marco Datini, a merchant from Prato, near Florence. In the same year, a load of 303 sacks of Syrian cotton reached Ancona from Tripoli.[38] Cotton also came from Greece and Turkey and, according to Ashtor (although he never explains why), Syria and Egypt were not, at that time, the most important sources of cotton for the Marches market. But the overall picture indicates considerable quantities.

Commerce with the Levant was indeed strengthened in the late 13th century, after a period of competition between trade via the Black Sea and commerce in the true Levant, i.e., Egypt and Syria, which, after the 1380s, were still the world centre for trade in Oriental products. It appears that the effects of the Black Death on Anconitan commerce were not catastrophic. But the very evident hostile relations between Venice and Ancona greatly influenced the commerce of Ancona itself, and the Venetians hardly doubted that Ancona would win over Genoa in the wars between the two great republics. The danger of being listed among the enemies of Venice was counterbalanced by the possibility of trading in the Levant when the Venetian fleet was away fighting. At that period, the Venetians persisted in believing that the Anconitans had captured and confiscated their ships, and in 1377 the *Serenissima* decided to send an ambassador to Ancona, threatening harsh reprisals.[39]

Shortly afterwards, the war of Chioggia opened up trade with the Levant for the Anconitan merchants, although Ashtor states that war was «only an intermezzo in the centuries-old oppression exerted by Venice on the commerce of Ancona».[40] Venetian pressure remained strong in the early 15th century. In 1422, Venice tried to prevent Ancona trading in Istria and near

---

[38] E. ASHTOR, *The Venetian cotton trade in Syria in the later Middle Ages*, «Studi Medievali», 17 (1976), p. 688, reprinted in ASHTOR, *Studies on the Levantine trade* cit.

[39] ASHTOR, *Commercio levantino* cit., p. 218.

[40] IVI, p. 219.

Rijeka in northern Dalmatia, with the result that the search for timber and other products from the Balkans sold by Ancona to the Orient was restricted. Some references to Anconitan help to Turkish pirates suggests the bitterness of Ancona's hatred of the Venetians. The Turkish conquest of Constantinople did not in fact damage Ancona's long-term trading in the Orient, and after 1459 the presence of Anconitans in Greece, Crete, Syria, Cyprus and Alexandria, with loads of soap, Bergamo cloth, wheat, and even, *horribile dictu*, iron and weapons, is amply documented. Their Levantine commerce in lead, silver, tin and copper also reflects the essential links between Ancona's Levantine trade and its commercial contacts with Dalmatia and its hinterland.

One important consequence of Ancona's entering Levantine commerce was further interest in spices, not only Oriental versions but also Western saffron, although soap from the Marches still remained the most popular produce in the Orient among the goods shipped via Ancona. Other supplies were paper, already an object of trade in 1432, when Jacob Beccarios' ship sailed from Ancona for Alexandria laden with oil, typically one of the products sent to the Byzantine empire and Syria, and, as already mentioned, saffron, produced after the Black Death in large quantities in the Abruzzi, and sent to Zadar and Alexandria on Pietro Matarozi's ship in 1452. As usual, local Marches products played their customary important role.[41]

During the conflict with Venice in 1377, the Anconitans tried to gain the support of the Holy See, under the dominion of which they lived. However, after the Chioggia war, the papacy was more insistent than before in forbidding trade with Muslim enemies in the Orient. Thus, every attempt to settle in the Levant was set about with obstacles, not only in the Orient itself but even in Italy too. In spite of all these problems, Ancona's Oriental trade flourished around 1400. In 1396, Lorenzo Anconetano held a position as consul at Alexandria, although his consulate had perhaps been established ten years previously. In the 15th century many merchants from both sides of the Adriatic, from Zadar and Dubrovnik to Fano and Otranto, chose the protection of the Anconitan consulate which functioned as such for all the non-Venetian Adriatic merchants. Moreover, agreements with Dalmatian cities, as with the industrial cities of Lombardy and with the Catalans, allowed Ancona to create a trade network capable of supplying the Levant with Italian and even Barcelona cloth. The presence of Catalans in Ancona after 1390 indicates how Spanish merchants, first of that city and then of Valencia, sought to use Ancona as a doorway through which to penetrate the Balkans and the Levant.

However, it would be a mistake to exaggerate the number and extent of Ancona's investments in the Orient. Even Ashtor was obliged to conclude that Anconitan commerce in Egypt was normally perhaps one-twentieth of the

---

[41] See tables on pp. 227-229 of ASHTOR, *Commercio levantino* cit.

value of Venetian trade, but this was in a period when Venice clearly predominated in Alexandria and Beirut.[42] Indeed, throughout the 1530s and 1540s, at least one Anconitan ship a year docked at Alexandria. Even more intense was commerce with Greece, whereas the Anconitan colony at Famagusta in Cyprus remained active in the 15th century in supplying their native city with cotton and other Syrian products. The presence of some Anconitan Jews in Famagusta strengthened the economic power of Anconitan merchants in the Orient, although it was to a certain extent limited by the simple fact of Venetian dominion over Oriental commerce: the presence of Anconitans in the Levant, always suspicious of Venetian pressure, was generally only tolerated because the level of investments was low, since the Anconitans mainly specialized in a quite small number of supplies, accepting Venetian supremacy as regards pepper and ginger. However, cotton was always an Oriental product favoured by both Venetian and Anconitan merchants.

These tendencies are confirmed by the late 14th century records analysed by Peter Earle,[43] for whom the years after 1479 were ones of great trade expansion. In his opinion, the early years of the 14th century were those in which «Ancona was still mainly as an important part of a limited excange aconomy within the Adriatic». Earle stresses the rapidity with which this process took place, a result of the flexibility of late Medieval commerce, the capacity to change distant destinations easily without the need to establish massive infrastructures of services or create solid bases for capital investments. With reduced taxes, and freedom of access to the city without regard for the nationality or religion of the merchants involved, Ancona was able to transform itself after 1520 almost into an emporium of the first class. A similarity may be noted with Livorno (Leghorn) in the same period, another example of a port open to all the religions which flourished in the 14th century.

In the late 13th century, Ancona's long-range commerce did not undergo significant changes with respect to that of the late 12th century, as already mentioned. Interest was maintained in Levantine trade, and two or three ships sailed every year for Constantinople and Alexandria. Fabriano paper, oil and soap remained the characteristic goods from Ancona, and the bales of Florentine and Siena cloth also recall the importance of the commercial links between Ancona and the Tuscan cities on the other side of the Appennines. Until about 1520, the Florentines sent their cloth not only to Ancona, but also to other ports in the Marches (such as Pesaro) and to those of the Kingdom of Naples; only after 1520 can we see that this commerce was clearly concentrated on Ancona. In the 14th century, as in the early Middle

---

[42] ASHTOR, *Commercio levantino* cit., pp. 225-227, 253.
[43] EARLE, *Economic development of Ancona* cit., for what follows.

Ages, the Anconitans definitely concentrated on the export of local products such as soap and leather, although volumes reached levels far greater than those of the previous century. Very important, as always, were the close relations with Dubrovnik, and the Dalmatian cities, such as Herceg-Novi, and Valona too remained open doorways for Ancona's Balkan commerce. In that period, Ancona was a true international emporium, where merchants of the Ottoman lands and Western merchants met to exchange their products: «a true frontier between Islam and Christendom», in Earle's words, situated between two worlds and supplying the needs of both, even though Ancona itself was never an important industrial centre.

The extent of Ancona's long-range commerce which I have attempted to depict here was considerable. The fact that relations with Egypt, Syria and eastern Greece were determined by local commerce in the Adriatic between Ancona and other cities of the Marches, and between Ancona and Dubrovnik and other Dalmatian cities, was a constant feature in the economic history of Ancona - a factor which doubtless explains its capacity to resist continual attempts by Venice at restricting such traffic. Moreover, there was a land link with the Tuscan cities - Pisa as early as the 12th century, Florence and Siena in the late 13th century -which facilitated the entry of European cloth on the Balkan and Oriental markets. Oriental merchants obtaining Western industrial products such as Italian paper, soap and cloth, and the West importing raw products such as cotton (partly used to produce Marches cloth) were typical features of Levantine commerce after 1200, and indicate a fundamental change in the relationship between East and West: we may recall that, in the 12th century, the paper used by the notary Giovanni Scriba in Genoa was imported from Alexandria. Ancona too played a role in these essential transformations: even more, it occupies a special place in explaining the relations between distant and local commerce.

Appendix[44]

The publication of the travel diary of Rabbi Jacob of Ancona, who is said to have reached the southern shores of China, mainly by sea, in 1270, several years before Marco Polo, aroused great interest in the British, American and Italian press during 1997.[45] In reality, there were Western visitors to the Far East before Marco Polo who left detailed memoirs of their travels, the friars William of Rubruck and Giovanni di Pian del Carpine.[46] These men, however, set out for the court of the Great Khan in the hope of

---

[44] See p. 51.

[45] J. d'ANCONA - D. SELBOURNE, *The City of Light*, London 1997.

[46] M. KOMROFF, *Contemporaries of Marco Polo*, London 1928; L. OLSCHKI, *Marco Polo's Precursors*, Baltimore 1943.

bringing Christianity to the east, and of building links with the Mongols in order to create a great alliance against Islam. This too was undoubtedly an objective of the Polos when they set out with the Church's blessing and oil from the Church of the Holy Sepulchre in Jerusalem. Jacob of Ancona is, by contrast, presented to us as a merchant whose motives for going east were primarily commercial; as a Jew, he had no interest in promoting world-wide alliances between Chinese rulers and the west; and his destination was Zaitun on the south-east coast of China, a trading station that dwarfed not merely his native Ancona but even Ancona's more powerful rival Venice.

Already Sinologists have found the version of Jacob's diary offered by David Selbourne unnerving, although it is fair to say that Marco Polo too has been accused of errors and invention as well, and even of never actually reaching China at all. Jacob's account seems to have rather little contact with other fragmentary evidence concerning Zaitun. Doubts have thus been raised about the authenticity of a text that is acclaimed on the book jacket as «one of the most important manuscripts ever discovered», and these doubts are all the more serious, since the translator failed to provide a transcription of the original Italian, apart from a few words here and there in acceptably Medieval spelling; there are no photographs of even one page of the original, in a book beautifully illustrated with photographs from mauscripts both Western and Chinese; all we have in the way of a description of the manuscript is the assertion that it is written in an "italic" hand, mixing the Latin, Hebrew and other alphabets, a description of the manuscript that is vague to the point of meaninglessness. Little is said about its provenance, apparently to protect its present owners. None of this inspires confidence.

It has been seen in the main part of this article that Ancona was a town that would have liked to compare itself to Venice, although in fact its Levant trade was probably only worth about one twentieth of that of Venice even in the fifteenth century. The Venetians were constantly busy asserting their own dominance over what they uncompromisingly called the "Venetian Gulf" (to us, the Adriatic), and the time when Jacob is supposed to have travelled to China coincides exactly with a period when Venice imposed on Ancona a severe treaty that was intended to suppress the trade of Ancona with the ports of Syria and Egypt. These were not propitious times for an Ancona merchant to head for the crusader port of Acre, on the coast of the Holy Land, and to try to penetrate beyond into Asia. As already explained, in 1257 the merchants of Ancona had been granted a very handsome privilege for trade in the crusader kingdom by the rulers of that kingdom, a point to which Jacob of Ancona refers. But this was during a bitter war fought out in and around Acre between Ancona's close ally, Genoa and the traditional enemy of both the Genoese and the Anconitans, Venice. The result of this conflict was that the Genoese were forced out of Acre entirely, abandoning their lucrative colony there, which had taken up a sizeable part of the city. Instead they moved to Tyre, further up the coast, and there they still were at the time Jacob is said to have passed through Acre. His own account of the conflict and its effects as recorded by Selbourne is in fact the exact opposite of what is known to have happened: Jacob says that the Venetians were more or less excluded from Acre, while Genoa, Ancona and their friends lorded over the city's trade. This reversal of the facts is certainly an egregious error that immediately casts doubt upon the veracity of the text.

Nor is it the only puzzling statement. Jacob is said to be the grandson of a Florentine rabbi, but around 1200 Florence, then a place of rather limited significance, cannot be shown to have had a Jewish population. At that time, by far the greater part of the Jewish population of Italy lived in the deep south; Florence only became an important centre of Jewish settlement after 1400. The description of the ships used by Jacob - for example, from Ancona to Zadar and Dubrovnik on the opposite coast - bears little relation to the way we know medieval galleys operated and the goods they carried. When he arrives in Dubrovnik, Jacob finds a massive community of Jews, far in excess of what is known to have existed at that time. Travelling through the Middle East, Jacob finds both Jewish and Christian merchants from Italy in such ports as Basra and Siraggi (Siraf), but the latter had lost much of its significance by the late thirteenth century.[47] There is no evidence at all in the many documents we have from the Italian ports at this time that there were colonies of Italian merchants on the shores of the Persian Gulf. We are even told that Jacob's son was a trader based in Aden, and that he came up from there to Basra to marry the daughter of the Italian Jew Isaiah of Ascoli. Yet the glorious days of Jewish Indian traders based in Yemen, acting as intermediaries between Egypt and the Indies, were long past; the Muslims made sure that only Muslim merchants (the so-called karimis) could pass through the Red Sea, partly for fear that infidels might approach too close to Mecca and Medina.[48] In our story, Jacob even returns home by the Red Sea route. This would not have been at all straightforward.

Perhaps the most bizarre aspect of Jacob's business affairs is his choice of partners. We hear of a Venetian Jew who operates a galley and sails in it together with the galley on which Jacob is bound for Acre. Not merely does this raise questions about the intense rivalry between Ancona and Venice, but it contradicts evidence that the galley fleet was the preserve of the Venetian nobility (nor, indeed, were there many Jews in Venice as yet). We also hear from Jacob of galleys setting out on the Indian Ocean, owned by a certain Aaron of Barcelona, the «great Jew of Aragon», titles that improbably mix

---

[47] On Siraf, see R. HODGES, D. WHITEHOUSE, *Mohammed, Charlemagne and the origins of Europe*, London 1983, pp. 145-149.

[48] D. ABULAFIA, *Asia, Africa and the trade of medieval Europe*, in *Cambridge Economic History of Europe*, II, Cambridge, 1987^2, pp. 437-443.

what were then two very distinct political entities (although they shared a single ruler).[49] Much is known about the merchants, Jewish and Christian, of medieval Barcelona, and the idea that any of them traded to China by way of the Indian Ocean in the thirteenth century is completely at odds with all the information we have about the range and interests of Catalan merchants at this period.[50] So too the presence of a Pisan and other western merchants (even a Genoese counting house) at Zaitun at this period is simply unthinkable, whatever Jacob may appear to say, and bears no relation to what we know in detail from other sources; it was only half a century later that a colony of Italians settled for a decade or two in the city.[51]

The only alternative to these objections is to state that this is indeed a revolutionary manuscript, uncovering secrets that the public documents of the great Mediterranean ports kept concealed. But, riewed from other perspectives, it is still a very peculiar text. We know a surprising amount about Jewish travellers from medieval Europe; one twelfth-century Spanish traveller, Benjamin of Tudela, probably reached at least as far as Baghdad, and described China, in vague terms, coloured by myths of gigantic griffins that preyed on sailors in those waters.[52] Several travellers reported on their visits to the lands through which Jacob is said to have passed, and it is very striking how different their outlook was from that of Jacob.[53] One feature they could not help noticing when they travelled through Galilee, Syria and Iraq was the presence of many holy places, sacred to Jews and sometimes to Muslims as well, such as the tombs of the prophets Daniel and Ezekiel in Iraq and Iran. Indeed, to reach Golan and the way to Damascus, it was impossible to avoid some famous Jewish sites. To Jacob, arrival in the Holy Land was the occasion merely for a pious glance in the general direction of Jerusalem. We are told by the translator that he is something of a rationalist, but it is inconceivable that he would have put out of mind the holy tombs in Galilee,

---

[49] On the Jews of Barcelona during this period, see Y.T. ASSIS, *Jewish economy in the medieval Crown of Aragon, 1213-1327: money and power*, Leiden 1997; Idem, *The Golden Age of Aragonese Jewry. Community and society in the Crown of Aragon, 1213-1327*, London 1997.

[50] D. ABULAFIA, *Catalan merchants and the western Mediterranean, 1236-1300: studies in the notarial acts of Barcelona and Sicily*, «Viator: medieval and Renaissance studies», 16 (1985), pp. 209-242.

[51] On Venetians east of Suez, see R. S. LOPEZ, *Venezia e le grandi linee dell'espansione commerciale nel secolo XIII*, in *La Civiltà veneziana del secolo di Marco Polo*, Firenze 1955, pp. 39-82.

[52] *The itinerary of Benjamin of Tudela*, edited by M. N. ADLER, London 1907.

[53] E. ADLER, *Jewish travellers of the Middle Ages*, London 1930, offers a collection of travel reports from Italian, German and Spanish Jews.

especially when he seems so punctilious in his prayers and observance. Thus, he seems quite at odds with the frequent reports of other Jewish travellers.

However, the oddest feature of Jacob of Ancona is the image that he presents of social evils while publicly discussing the state of Zaitun society with the conservative dignitary of the city called Pitaco. We can almost read the account Pitaco gives of the troubles of contemporary society as an invective against twentieth-century habits (indeed, David Selbourne tells us that he was influenced by this text when writing his own book, *The Principle of Duty*). Jacob's own experiences in the Chinese city also reveal the sheer depravity of its inhabitants. Zaitun is given over to uncontrolled sexual freedom. Few women marry as virgins; indeed, we are repeatedly told that young women walk around in immodest, revealing clothes (among them many Lesbians), while sexual intercourse is freely engaged in. This takes all forms, and homosexual acts are presented as entirely normal, equal in all respects to heterosexual love, an attitude that Pitaco deplores. Women, fully empowered, act «like lions», dominating men sexually and in all other ways they choose. Single mothers are a common feature of society; slimming has become a craze among young women. Zaitun even has its own equivalent of modern film stars:

«So depraved are the citizens of Zaitun that the most beautiful of the harlots are considered as goddesses by both men and women, who follow them as they go, while the young seek to copy not only the manner of their clothes or the colours with which they adorn their faces, but the very sound of their voices when they speak or sing».

The city of Zaitun has become dangerous because the streets are full of drug addicts and muggers. Fashions in music have changed for the worse, and all one hears nowadays are raucous sounds from Hell. Euthanasia is freely practised, and no one mourns at funerals (in fact, the ashes of the deceased are carelessly mixed up together). Children are allowed to do as they please, and the view is taken by supporters of the new order that they should be free to pursue their education at whatever speed they wish. No child should be judged to have failed. «Now - says the regretful Pitaco - we live without any guiding idea, trying things here and there, like a blind man».

It is a picture of a society teetering on the brink of the abyss, ignoring the terrible fate that awaits it (the Mongols are only a little way over the horizon), while it immerses itself in hedonism. Yet it might also serve as an account of our own society from the hand of someone who detests modern trends. Thus the highly coloured account of Jacob's exploration of this New Sodom and Gomorrah culminates when he unwillingly finds himself in a sordid night club, «whereupon I saw many obscene things», which he however describes in exhaustive detail. The account of Jacob's exploration of this city of sin is certainly powerfully written. He even looks at one point to the future, offering an unmistakable prophecy of both the Holocaust under a

"New Haman", and the return of the Jews to the land of their ancestors. But the greatest warning Jacob makes seems to be directed not at his own time, nor at our recent history, but at the social condition of the west at the end of the second millennium. Firm evidence of the existence of a manuscript has not been provided. Indeed, there are too many statements attributed to Jacob that do not accord with the exact knowledge historians have of Jacob's time. It seems that David Selbourne has provided the world not with a Jewish Marco Polo, but with a Jewish Gulliver.

V

Industrial Products: the Middle Ages

I. Some problems of definition

When I was asked to present a paper on the industrial products arriving in Europe from the East and from Africa in the late Middle Ages, it seemed a straightforward enough task at least to enumerate them and perhaps even to weigh their significance against one another, allowing for manifold difficuties with the sources. More demanding, certainly, is the question of the economic changes that contact with markets in and beyond the Islamic world engendered in western Europe, though here a long historiographical tradition, culminating in the works of Roberto Lopez and Eliyahu Ashtor, has provided tempting, if not always conclusive, answers for the end of the Middle Ages[1]. But on looking closer at the literature, one finds that the emphasis lies not on the products of the East, but on the way the trade routes were managed by western merchants: going back to the classic work of Heyd, a tradition has been established of studying the institutional and legal framework within which trade could take place, notably the granting of privileges and the acquisition of warehouses and other vital facilities; and some attention has also been given to the volume of trade, as far as it can be recovered from extremely partial figures[2]. The role of particular commodities (industrial and otherwise) has been studied less, and much has been taken for granted, though some important tentative conclusions about the movement of bullion have

---

[1] R.S. LOPEZ, *The Trade of Europe: the South*, in *Cambridge Economic History of Europe*, II, Cambridge 1987[2]; also my own article in the same volume, *Asia, Africa and the Trade of Medieval Europe*; E. ASHTOR, *Levant Trade in the Later Middle Ages*, Princeton (NJ) 1983, and the various collections of Ashtor's articles, notably *Studies on the Levantine Trade in the Middle Ages*, London 1978, and *East-West Trade in the Medieval Mediterranean*, ed. B.Z. KEDAR, London 1986.

[2] W. HEYD, *Histoire du commerce du Levant au Moyen Age*, transl. F. Raynaud, I-II, Leipzig 1885-1886; this is to be preferred to the German original (Stuttgart 1879), in view of the author's further additions.

been offered by Lopez, Day and others [3]. In particular, the insights of art historians and archaeologists have been ignored by economic historians, even when some of the most valuable evidence for the arrival of eastern products in western lands is to be found in such collections as the Museo di San Martino at Pisa [4].

A particular difficulty in approaching this topic is the application of the word 'industrial' to the products arriving from the East and from Africa in medieval Europe. At the risk of repeating points made in other *relazioni*, it has been necessary to adopt the widest possible definition here, embracing processed and semi-processed goods such as drugs and dyestuffs, as well as the products of workshops in the Islamic world: leather goods, ceramics, metalwork, textiles (though silk has been the subject of an earlier Prato *settimana*). Particular emphasis will be placed here on the role of industrial crops, including cotton, flax and indigo; but in order to understand their relative significance in international trade, it will be necessary to refer quite often to the most prominent food flavourings as well, notably pepper and ginger (itself often processed and packed in wooden cassettes). Wax is an important African product which deserves consideration under the heading of semi-processed goods. Imports of alum, used *inter alia* in the textile industry, are also a constant theme that needs to be borne in mind.

To make sense of the subject it is also important to consider briefly the role of frontier societies within what is commonly defined as Europe (notably those of Sicily and of both reconquered Valencia and unconquered Granada) in the trade networks bringing eastern products, or at any rate products characteristic of the eastern markets, to western consumers; the 'agricultural revolution' following the rise of Islam transplanted some distinctive eastern products to Mediterranean lands [5]. Not just eastern plants such as the banana, rice and citrus fruits, but methods for making certain processed goods travelled westwards. Paper is the prime example of such a commodity, with an ancestry that can, as is well known, be traced back to China; imported from Alexandria in the middle of the twelfth century, it was readily available in Mediterranean Spain from local, Valencian, mills by the late thirteenth, and by the fifteenth century the paper of Fabbriano had acquired a significant

---

[3] J. DAY, *The Medieval Market Economy*, Oxford 1987; R.S LOPEZ, *Il problema del bilancio dei pagamenti nel commercio di Levante*, in *Venezia e il Levante fino al secolo XV*, I-II, Venice 1973, pp. 431-452.

[4] D. ABULAFIA, *The Pisan bacini and the Medieval Mediterranean Economy: a Historian's Viewpoint*, in *Papers in Italian Archaeology*, 4, *The Cambridge Conference*, part 4, ed. C. MALONE, S. STODDART, Oxford 1985, pp. 287-302.

[5] A. WATSON, *Agricultural Innovation in the Early Islamic World*, Cambridge 1983.

place in the cargoes of Anconitan merchants bound for the Levant [6]. Glazed pottery, for which the technology did not really exist north of Sicily, or perhaps Rome, in the twelfth century, was being produced in central Italy during the thirteenth century, and had ceased being a curiosity imported from Muslim Spain, Morocco, Tunisia and the Levant [7]. Glass offers an excellent example of an item exported from the East which was followed by the borrowing of the appropriate technology, to the point where western glass easily surpassed eastern in quality; however, the best glass of Murano and its rivals continued to rely on ingredients imported from the Levant.

Whereas several contributions to this *Settimana di studio* look at other regions of the world in addition to Asia and Africa, the geographical concentration of this paper reflects the realities of medieval trade. From the Baltic and eastern Europe there did, of course, arrive in the medieval West a number of highly prized products, notably furs and (though in limited quantities) amber; but the major characteristic of trade with the Baltic and the further reaches of the Atlantic was that finished goods were sent outwards - armaments to the Teutonic Knights in Livonia and Estonia, in exchange for grain, for instance - while imports were dominated by basic foodstuffs, in particular rye and fish, whether herrings from the Baltic Sound or stockfish from Iceland and Greenland [8]. By the late fifteenth century some dyes were being obtained in the Canary islands, where they occupied a significant place in the local economy; and Madeira was to become an important sugar producer [9]. But the rise of Madeira itself reflected the decline in dependence on eastern markets, which were now increasingly under threat from the Turks.

In dealing with these issues, historians have often been content to rely on the rich but problematic information contained in Pegolotti's *Pratica della Mercatura* of the early fourteenth century (though in part reflecting conditions half a century earlier) in assessing what items were available to western merchants in what eastern ports [10]. One problem is that Pegolotti is not by any means unique as a source of such information; many other *pratiche* have been neglected, and their own usefulness is occasionally compromised by the

[6] E. ASHTOR, *Il commercio levantino di Ancona nel basso medioevo*, in "Rivista storica italiana", 88, 1976, pp. 215, 241, repr. in his *Studies on the Levantine Trade*.

[7] D. ABULAFIA, *The Pisan bacini*, cit.

[8] Ph. DOLLINGER, *The German Hanse*, transl. S.H. Steinberg, London 1970.

[9] F. FERNANDEZ-ARMESTO, *The Canary Islands after the Conquest. The Making of a Colonial Society in the Early Sixteenth Century*, Oxford 1982, pp. 69-74; R. CARITA, *Historia da Madeira (1420-1566). Povoamento e produção açucareira*, (Funchal 1989), pp. 187-213.

[10] Francesco Balducci PEGOLOTTI, *La pratica della mercatura*, ed. A. EVANS, Cambridge (Mass.) 1936.

fact that they often seem to have borrowed uncritically from one another: one thinks of Antonio da Uzzano here, whose own *Pratica* dates to 1442 but (in Evans' words) 'offers much the same kinds of information as are to be found in the early parts of Pegolotti's book' [11]. Expressed differently, the *pratiche* cannot be seen simply as 'objective' statements of what was available and accessible in eastern markets, but as an idealised view of what merchants might seek in the East, based as much on out of date reports as upon exact knowledge of contemporary conditions [12]. Similar problems arise with Marco Polo's account of the East, recently once again under attack for its veracity; but for readers in the late medieval West it remained an important account of the place of origin and physical nature of the dyes and spices they received in desiccated or powdered form from a mysterious Orient [13]. Thus the question becomes not simply 'What did western merchants acquire from the East?' but 'What did they think they could acquire from the East?' Similar problems arise concerning north-west Africa, where the magnificent portolan charts and atlases produced in medieval Majorca and Italy convey a sense of awed awareness of the potential of the southern Sahara as a source of gold (in particular); but once again myth and history easily became intertwined, so that information about rulers of the gold lands, such as the fourteenth-century distributor of largesse Mansa Musa, information by now long out of date, was still being replicated in the mid-fifteenth century [14].

Our ability to describe the commodities reaching western markets is limited by the simple fact that contracts for maritime trade do not as a general rule specify the items being carried out from the west, nor those that the travelling merchants are expected to purchase. Partly this reflects the fact that trade was conducted in stages, and the further a merchant went, the more likely it was that he was selling, buying and reselling as he travelled. At best, something can be said about which goods were traded, from the references that do exist in these documents; but any attempt at quantification soon founders, beyond generalities to the effect that pepper was the number one spice and ginger stood at number two; it was food flavourings rather than industrial goods such as eastern cloths that stood at the apex of the distribution system. Documents similar to bills of lading are rare, though some fragmen-

---

[11] *Ibid.*, p. xxxix.

[12] Particular value may, however, attach to several fifteenth-century merchant guides, such as that of Benedetto COTRUGLI, *Della mercatura et del mercante perfetto* (Brescia 1602).

[13] F. WOOD, *Did Marco Polo Go to China?*, London 1995.

[14] E.g. in the great Catalan map in the Este library at Modena, dating from the mid-fifteenth century.

tary documentation of this sort can be found in Marseilles. More revealing perhaps, though not sure evidence in themselves of what actually arrived, are the tariff lists of which several survive from the Catalan ports such as Tortosa and Collioure [15]. These can be compared with tariff lists from the Islamic world, most importantly the twelfth-century *Minhaj* of al- Makhzumi, to which the late Claude Cahen devoted his attention [16]. What is missing is a secure price series for the major imports, although some scholars such as Ashtor have bravely attempted to collate information about prices. This aspect of the imports from the East will have to be left to one side here.

In pursuing this topic a decision has to be made where to draw the line between East and West in describing the late medieval economy. Clearly, the boundaries of Europe as now conceived were not coterminous either with those of Christendom or with those of what might loosely be termed a 'western economy', based until about 1250 on exchanges in silver and dominated by the production of basic foodstuffs, generally, too, lacking the vast metropolises characteristic of the Near and Far East. Fundamental to the discussion that follows is the belief that the Islamic city fulfilled a much wider range of economic functions than most western cities, as a highly diversified centre of trade and industry which evolved in what was often a hostile environment, or at least one which was incapable, or barely capable, of meeting its essential needs. Specialisation and the creation of a vast labour force producing finished goods for a wide variety of markets was thus the key to survival; and this was reflected at every level of economic activity, from the greater diversity of the diet of even lowly city dwellers, to the role of the city as a redistribution centre for exotic goods imported from as far away as the Indies [17]. The Islamic city produced a vast variety of quality goods, and what is perhaps most surprising is the concentration of interest among western merchants on a narrow band of commodities, particularly pepper, though, as will be seen, cotton and indigo acquired an increasingly important position too. Differently expressed, what attracted western merchants to the Islamic world was not simply its own products, but also (at times

---

[15] M. GUAL CAMARENA, *Vocabulario del comercio medieval*, Tarragona 1968/Barcelona 1976.

[16] For this important source, see: C. CAHEN, *Un traité financier inédit d'époque Fatimide-Ayyubide*, in "Journal of the Social and Economic History of the Orient", 5, 1962, pp. 139-159; ID., *Contribution à l'étude des impôts dans l'Égypte médiévale, ibid.*, pp. 244-278; and in particular ID., *Douanes et commerce dans les ports méditerranéens de l'Égypte médiévale d'après le Minhadj d'al-Makhzumi, ibid.*, 7, 1964, pp. 217-314; also, H. RABIE, *The Financial System of Egypt A.H. 564-741/A.D. 1169-1341*, London 1972, pp. 11-12.

[17] On Islamic cities, see I. LAPIDUS, *Muslim Cities in the Later Middle Ages*, Cambridge 1984[2].

primarily) the produce that was trans-shipped through Muslim lands from much further to the East.

The different character and needs of the Islamic city generated a different relationship with the surrounding countryside to that generally found in the West; such centres had developed in western Europe in the early Middle Ages, but primarily in areas under Muslim rule: Córdoba, Seville, Palermo are the three giants that fall into this category; and what is noticeable about them is that Christian conquest steered the economy in a new direction, back to the production and distribution of basic bread grains, and away from the more diverse range of foodstuffs and textile fibres (most significantly, cotton) earlier characteristic of these cities and their surrounding regions [18]. Nonetheless, vestiges of the old order can be identified in Christian centres seized from Islam such as Valencia and its *horta* (*huerta*) or Majorca, still a major source of dried fruits some time after their conquest. Although there appears to have been a serious contraction of cotton production in Sicily after about 1200, cotton remained a significant export in the thirteenth century, carried aboard Catalan ships towards Barcelona, for processing in Catalan workshops. Techniques as well as raw materials moved westwards: it is now considered likely that the art of knitting travelled along such routes from Old Cairo to Muslim and Christian Spain; by the fifteenth century knitters' guilds existed in Barcelona itself.

The imitation by western producers of eastern products lessened dependence on eastern markets for high quality cloths and other goods. Western merchants could even sell their imitations in the East to those who had once produced similar items. Whereas before 1200 western merchants had expressed interest in luxury cloths produced in Egypt and Syria, by 1300 their interest was more heavily concentrated on the dyestuffs available in the East; they were selling to Levantine consumers cloths they themselves had produced using the dyes, and in some cases the raw fibres, they had bought in eastern markets. It is not necessary to accept every aspect of Ashtor's fervently held belief in the industrial decline of the Middle East in the late Middle Ages to acknowledge how profound the process of substitution was: at one end of the spectrum, the silks of Tuscan, Lombard and Ligurian workshops came to supplant those of the Muslim East and China (though the process was a slow one, with the Sforza dukes of Milan massively extending Lombard mulberry plantations in the late fifteenth century); at the other end

---

[18] T. GLICK, *From Muslim Fortress to Christian Castle*, Manchester 1996.

of the spectrum, humdrum fustians took their name from the virtual capital of the Islamic world, Cairo (in its form of Fustat, the name given to Old Cairo); and elsewhere on the spectrum of quality there were the western *baldacchini*, named after Baghdad, and other good quality textiles now produced in Italy, Flanders or Germany. The spread of imitative silks began early, while Islam still dominated the Mediterranean, and resulted in al-Andalus in the bizarre habit of manufacturing local silks carrying standardised Islamic designs (themselves of Persian and Coptic ancestry) and the blatantly erroneous label 'made in Baghdad'. In the case of textiles produced in Christian lands, however, the success of the cloth exports towards the Levant, 'dumped' on eastern markets, Ashtor insisted, was sufficient to alleviate significantly the outflow of silver bullion, since the West had few other products to offer eastern consumers apart from humble items such as wood and base metals (banned under papal edicts which sought to limit the eastward flow of armaments). Indeed, it was these humble items, plus slaves, that had dominated the primitive Levant trade of the Amalfitans around 1000.

II. *The role of cotton*

Trans-Mediterranean traffic in the centuries before the rise of the Italian republics is recorded in the letters of, and may well have been dominated by, the so-called Genizah merchants of Fustat (Old Cairo), analysed by Goitein[19]. Goitein's primary interest lay in the India trade, bringing spices and luxury cloths up the Red Sea for redistribution towards Tunisia, Muslim Sicily and al-Andalus. Incidentally, he revealed a strong interest in flax, cotton and silk, the latter of which constituted a standard form of investment around 1050; flax and cotton were seen by the twelfth-century writer al-Makhzumi as prime exports of Egypt [20]. The major change that occurred after 1100 was a double transformation in the management of the trade routes, so that the Indian Ocean and Red Sea routes came increasingly under the control of the Egyptian Muslim *karimi* merchants, while the Mediterranean sea routes were conquered by the fleets of Genoa, Pisa and Venice; at the same time, rising wool production in the West necessitated more and more intensive searches for the most suitable fixative, alum [21]. This was to be found in the twelfth century,

---

[19] S.D. GOITEIN, *A Mediterranean Society. The Jewish Communities of the Arab World as Portrayed in the Documents of the Cairo Genizah*, I, *Economic Foundations*, Berkeley/Los Angeles 1967.

[20] C. CAHEN, *Douanes et commerce*, cit.

[21] C. CAHEN, *L'alun avant Phocée. Un chapitre d'histoire économique islamo-chrétienne au temps des croisades*, in "Revue d'histoire économique et sociale", 41, 1963, pp. 433-447; H. RABIE, *Financial system*, cit., pp. 82-85.

as the *Minhaj* of al-Makhzumi shows, in Egypt itself, though attention shifted to the mines of Phocaea in Turkey by the late thirteenth century; it was only in the mid-fifteenth century that large, high quality alum mines were identified in the West, at Tolfa. Similarly, potash was in demand among western textile producers, while alkaline ashes for soap production (again linked to the textile industry) were an interest of Anconitan merchants in the Levant during the late Middle Ages; the Anconitans form a group of particular interest, since by 1300 cotton and ancillary items needed for the textile industry were their main import from the Levant, rather than the spices favoured by most other Italian merchants [22].

In addition to dyestuffs, the West became increasingly dependent on eastern sources for certain textile fibres, especially cotton [23]. In the twelfth century, the Genoese were still able to export very significant amounts of cotton from Sicily, and it is possible that at this stage it was cotton rather than grain that drew them so enthusiastically into treaty relations with the Norman kings of Sicily from 1156 onwards, though it is generally agreed that the quality of Sicilian cotton remained relatively low [24]. Equally, the island's capacity to supply cotton contracted as traditional Arab agricultural practices were supplanted by a feudal régime which laid emphasis on the extraction of rent from staple crops; as wheat production expanded, cotton plantations, and the necessary skills, went into decline. There were still Catalan merchants in mid-thirteenth century Sicily who went there to buy cotton, while Genoa, Milan and Pavia were still bringing in Sicilian cotton in the late fourteenth and fifteenth centuries [25]. The small Sicilian dependency of Malta appears to have continued to produce cotton of better quality throughout the Middle Ages (increasing its production significantly in the fifteenth century); but it was Egypt, Syria and ultimately India that became the major sources for raw cotton (in wool form or spun into fibre) used in western industries [26]. Indeed, it was the Arabs who first made cotton the everyday wear of inhabitants of the Middle East. It was they who encouraged the planting of cotton during

---

[22] E. ASHTOR, *Commercio levantino di Ancona*, cit.; D. ABULAFIA, *The Anconitan Privileges in the Latin Kingdom of Jerusalem and the Levant Trade of Ancona*, in *I comuni italiani nel regno crociato di Gerusalemme*, ed. G. AIRALDI, B.Z. KEDAR, Genova 1986, pp. 525-570.

[23] M.F. MAZZAOUI, *The Italian Cotton Industry in the Later Middle Ages, 1100-1600*, Cambridge 1981.

[24] D. ABULAFIA, *The Two Italies. Economic Relations between the Norman Kingdom of Sicily and the Northern Communes*, Cambridge 1977.

[25] M.S. MAZZAOUI, *Italian Cotton Industry*, cit., p. 32; D. ABULAFIA, *Catalan Merchants and the Western Mediterranean, 1236-1300*, in "Viator", 16, 1985, pp. 209-242.

[26] M.S. MAZZAOUI, *Italian Cotton Industry*, cit., pp. 14- 27.

V

Springtime, alternating it with winter wheat or barley, and developing soph-
isticated irrigation networks so that normally dry soils could be used to good
effect. Areas that played a notable role in cotton production in the early
Islamic world included the coastline of Syrian and the outskirts of Damascus
and Acre [27]. Mazzaoui has noted that in some parts of Syria a monoculture
developed by the thirteenth century, based around the production of cotton
for export; certain of these ares lay within the political control of the Latins
themselves, as rulers of the Kingdom of Jerusalem [28]. Egypt, on the other
hand, was famed more for the quality than the quantity of its cotton, and flax
remained the major industrial crop exported from the region, in twenty-two
identifiable varieties. In fact, much of the cotton cloth worn in Egypt seems
to have been made from imported raw materials. Similarly, the coast of North
Africa contained both cotton plantations and workshops transforming the
fibres into finished cloth, notably at Tunis (where a mixed cotton-linen weave
was common) and at Sijilmasa, terminal of the gold caravans arriving from
the southern Sahara. What we are thus observing is the widespread use of
cotton to satisfy the elementary clothing needs of the population of the Islamic
lands.

The fashion for cotton was not, however, confined solely to the *dar
al-Islam*. By the mid-twelfth century signs exist of a north Italian cotton
industry that was processing the imported raw cotton of Sicily, Africa and
the East. A Genoese tariff list indicates that Alexandria, Antioch and Sicily
were sources of cotton around 1140. There are enough references to cotton
in the earliest notarial contracts to survive in Genoa (Giovanni Scriba,
1154-64) to make the significance of this product in the Levant trade
abundantly clear. In fact, Mazzaoui says: 'references to both raw cotton and
Italian cotton cloth in Genoese notarial contracts of the second half of the
twelfth century and the opening decades of the thirteenth occur with a
frequency that suggests a phenomenal growth rate in the early stages of the
industry'. Notarial acts from Cyprus, dating to around 1300, reveal the intense
interest of the merchants of Ancona, acting in conjunction with Christian
Syrian merchants, in the supply of Levantine cotton to cloth producers in
central Italy [29]. In Genoa, as in Marseilles and Barcelona, one aim of the cotton
importers may have been to supply the shipping industry, in need of heavy

[27] A. WATSON, *Agricultural Innovation*, cit.
[28] M.S. MAZZAOUI, *Italian Cotton Industry*, cit., pp. 35- 38.
[29] D. ABULAFIA, *Anconitan Privileges*, cit., pp. 551-558.

canvas-type cotton cloths (apparently producing much later on the English words *jeans*, from 'Gênes', and *denim*, 'de Nîmes'). Nor was the use of cotton confined to clothing and naval equipment. Wax candles were produced with cotton wicks, in the Arab fashion; there is also a possibility, though opinions differ, that cotton (*bombax*) was an important ingredient of early forms of paper (*carta bombacynis*), even though other textile fibres, especially linen, seem to have become more important from an early stage.

A second stage in the development of the European cotton industry began in the late fourteenth century, with the emergence of a south German cloth industry, based especially around Ulm, which became a major importer of raw cotton via Venice, seat of the *fondaco dei Tedeschi* [30]. Where appropriate, mixed linen and cotton fustians incorporating local or foreign flax were also produced; all this was to the detriment of the north Italian cotton industry. What is impressive is that the means now existed to transport considerable quantities of eastern cotton across the Alps; the late fourteenth and fifteenth centuries were not, as far as this industry was concerned, a period of recession, at least in Germany. Some reflection of changing circumstances can be seen in Ashtor's classic study, 'Observations on Venetian trade in the XIVth century', where he was able to show that around 1380 there was a significant increase in the volume of Venetian trade in cotton out of Greece, Crete, Syria and Egypt. A whole new line of cogs had to be established in consequence[31]. Even so, Ashtor considered that this was only the beginning of what was to grow prodigiously in the fifteenth century into a major department of Venetian trade.

In sum, the emergence of the cotton industry in the West was a chapter in a longer process which saw western producers supplant those of the East, drawing from the Levant the raw or semi-processed materials they needed, but creating their own textile industries which transformed the fibres into cloth. Still, this was not possible without dependence on the East for fixatives, notably alum, and colourings, notably indigo. Such products were long to play a major role, alongside the leading condiments, in the 'spice trade' with the Levant.

---

[30] M.S. MAZZAOUI, *Italian Cotton Industry*, cit., pp. 139-146.
[31] E. ASHTOR, *Observations on Venetian Trade in the Levant in the XIVth Century*, in "Journal of European Economic History", 5, 1976, pp. 533-586.

V

III. *Indigo and the Levant trade*

The significance of dyestuffs in the Levant trade can be observed further if we examine the important place of indigo in East-West traffic, with the help of a new study by Jenny Balfour-Paul [32]. Indigo was much in demand both in East and West. Large quantities were produced in India, from which its name derived: it was the Indian product *par excellence*; but such was the pressure of demand that by the twelfth century it was readily available from new sources in Syria, Egypt and Yemen. It is recorded as a local product in the Palestinian city of Jericho in the tenth century. Al-Baghdadi in the years around 1200 was much impressed by the sheer quantity of indigo produced in Egypt, but he was less impressed by the quality, which was inferior to that of India. *Color indicus in Aegypto conficitur*, Frederick Barbarossa of Germany was informed by an emissary to the Ayyubid court [33]. The diffusion of indigo should thus be seen as part of the wider dissemination of eastern crops that followed the Islamic conquest of the southern shores of the Mediterranean. But Spain itself was always dependent on imports of this dyestuff; under Muslim rule, the Jewish merchants of Almería were particularly active in the indigo trade, as they were in the silk trade and associated areas of business. In 1252 the dyers of Valencia, steeped in Islamic tradition, still preferred 'Baghdad indigo', which a Catalan buyer in 1385 said was 'the best of all', though the Catalans also handled Persian and Egyptian varieties. What this seems to mean is that Baghdad retained its special place as the emporium through which top quality indigos from further East were redistributed westwards. At times Baghdad indigo was taxed in Italian ports at twice the rate charged on less perfect strains [34].

Institutional factors also helped the spread of indigo: in the eighth century and after, the Abbasid choice of black as the colour of the régime meant that they had settled on a colour which could only effectively be produced from an indigo base. Good quality black remained something of a luxury in East and West for several centuries. Indigo was also a key component in many of the rich colours being produced in the West, such as purples and vivid greens, which were used to dye the prestige woollen cloths of Flanders and northern Italy, in conjunction with madder and other high grade ingredients. It was preferable to woad (to which it is closely related botanically); and the

---

[32] J. BALFOUR-PAUL, *Indigo in the Arab World*, Richmond 1997.
[33] *Ibid.*, pp. 20, 22-4.
[34] *Ibid.*, pp. 23, 28-9.

disappearance of the puple *murex* shellfish made it the most valuable colouring agent after saffron. There were, it is true, several false indigos derived from mulberries and blueberries, but it was oriental indigo that was always especially prized for its vivid hues. Since it arrived in the form of small cakes, it was difficult for purchasers to understand that they were handling a plant product, and for many centuries it was assumed to be of mineral origin. Nor should its role in the arts be ignored here: indigo had an important place in the paintings of the Italian schools in the fourteenth century, as can be seen clearly in the work of Simone Martini. It was used in art as in life as a signifier of luxury. So too was ultramarine of special importance in art, though not practical for use in cloth dyeing. It derived from semi-precious *lapis lazuli*, mostly of Persian origin; a method for making this colour is described in a thirteenth-century work attributed to Frederick II's astrologer Michael Scot and now preserved in Cambridge in the library of Gonville and Caius College; alchemical treatises are a neglected source for information about eastern products such as alum and gemstones [35].

Colouring agents from the Islamic world and beyond were of capital importance to the western medieval artist [36]. In this sense many a spectacular 'Madonna and Child' reveals a heritage from the Levant trade. In eleventh century al-Andalus, Muslim Spain, was a prime source of fine colours, especially saffron and *kermes* (*qirmiz*), even though indigo, brazilwood and lac were not locally available, and were imported by the Genizah merchants and their colleagues, arriving in Almería in the early twelfth century; the Andalusi merchants appear to have been notorious for their demand for brazilwood around 1060, a period in which the luxurious *taifa* courts were flourishing all over Spain. *Kermes* and *grana*, two very similar insect based dyes, were imported from Spain, as was the best cinnabar, a native red sulphide of mercury. The name *kermes* itself gave rise to the term 'crimson', while the identification of *grana* with tiny insects or worms is the source of the word *vermiculum* or 'vermilion'. Red could also be derived from brazilwood and lac, items which contantly appear in the baggage of the medieval spice merchant. Brazilwood in combination with lye potash or alum produced quite different shades of red, and the use of alum guaranteed a warmer colour. Daniel Thompson, in his fundamental study of *The Materials and Techniques*

---

[35] GONVILLE AND CAIUS COLLEGE, CAMBRIDGE, MS 81/214.

[36] D. THOMPSON, *The Materials and Techniques of Medieval Painting*, New York 1926, contains invaluable information on colouring agents.

of medieval Painting observed that 'the amount of brazil wood colour used in the Middle Ages both for painting and dyeing was colossal', vastly exceeding even the much handled insect dyes. For example, it was employed in the reddish purple ink favoured by some Italian humanists [37].

IV. *The evidence of the tariff lists*

Indigo and cotton, then, help define the nature of the problem. Raw or semi-processed materials for the cloth industry occupied a prime role in the traffic from the Levant towards western Europe after about 1150. Taking a stance around 1300, several sources identified so far allow us to examine the movement of goods at different stages in the journey from East to West. Marco Polo identifies centres of production in the Indies for the most exotic and furthest travelled goods; Pegolotti indicates the transfer of oriental goods from eastern Mediterranean ports to Italy, Catalonia and southern France, and the tariff lists from Catalonia document the arrival of these products in western Europe. It thus makes sense to begin at the westernmost extremity, with these tariff lists, and to move the focus gradually eastwards until reaching the point of production. It is therefore necessary to emphasize that the Catalan documents record, explicitly or implicitly, a particular intense contact with North Africa, rather than with the Levant. Christian merchants of course faced similar problems in North Africa to those they experienced in the Middle East: their confinement in close quarters; the periodic confiscation of goods (often a good source of information about what was in their warehouses); interruptions as the result of embargoes and crusades. However, trade with the Maghrib was less obviously dominated by high value goods such as spices. In some cases, western merchants found themselves able actually to supply Maghribi consumers with spices acquired in the Levant, particularly as the domination of Mediterranean waters by Catalan and Italian navies became more complete.

An early example of a tariff list comes from Valencia in 1243, shortly after the Catalan conquest [38]. It may thus reflect the commercial needs of a large Islamic city as much as it does those of a new settler population, (the Muslims were removed from Valencia proper, but they rapidly established a *morería* outside the walls). It is also very difficult to be sure which way certain

---

[37] As well as *ibid.*, see on dyes obtained in Spain O.R. CONSTABLE, *Trade and Traders in Muslim Spain*, Cambridge 1994 (Spanish ed., Barcelona 1996).

[38] M. GUAL CAMARENA, *Vocabulario*, doc. 3, pp. 69-74.

products were flowing, since the region had an established reputation as a source of specialised crops. However, the reference to a tax on paper must reflect the movement of paper from Xàtiva (Játiva) out of the Kingdom of Valencia, while it is clear that pepper and some of the cloths mentioned (from Lleida, Narbonne and elsewhere) were imports from further to the north. Mastic, gum amd wax could originate from several sources, but wax was certainly imported in very significant quantities from the Maghrib towards Majorca and the south of France in this period. Among dyestuffs, the famous *grana* was, as has been seen, a characteristic product of late medieval Spain, while saffron had a special role, here and in Italy, as the major spice and dyestuff produced in the West for export to the East. A further tariff list from Valencia of about 1271 indicates that alum of Aleppo in Syria, as well as Castilian alum, was taxed at 8d per load *(carga)*; this item of course had special importance in the cloth finishing industry, and demand for alum rose as the textile industry of Barcelona and its neighbours expanded. Cotton was also arriving in the city, though its origin can only be the subject of speculation: as has been seen, some Sicilian cotton was being handled at this period by Catalan merchants trading to Barcelona, but Muslim Spain and the markets of Alexandria (which themselves drew on sources as far East as India) cannot be excluded either.

The series of *lezde* or *leude* from Collioure, the outport of Perpignan, starting around 1249, are perhaps a better guide to the arrival of goods in Europe from the Islamic lands, since at this end of the Catalan world Islamic agricultural techniques had not struck any roots, and it is therefore easier to be sure of the foreign origins of the goods mentioned in the tariff lists [39]. Major items imported appear to have been pepper, wax, alum, ginger, cinnamon, cloves, lac, brazilwood, indigo, vermilion, coral, sugar, saffron, mastic and of course silk: largely a familiar mixture of dyestuffs and food flavourings. But there were also many humbler local products such as eels and hake that attracted the same tax rate of 2s 2d per *carga* in 1249 (the rate for the leading products fell to 2s 0d in 1252 and 1297/8) [40]. This was the top tax rate and may plausibly be taken as an indication which items were seen as the most valuable ones by the Crown (which maintained a substantial castle in the port, still in place). In the 1297/8 *lezda*, alum of both Aleppo and

---

[39] *Ibid.*, doc. 4, pp. 75-80. On Collioure, see D. ABULAFIA, *A Mediterranean Emporium. The Catalan Kingdom of Majorca*, Cambridge 1994 (Spanish ed., Barcelona 1996), pp. 126-127, 142- 143, 153-135, 166-167, 259-261.
[40] GUAL CAMARENA, *Vocabulario*, docs. 9 and 24, pp. 102- 197, 161-169.

Vulcano (in the Aeolian islands) appear, the former taxed at twice the rate of the latter, not surprisingly in view of its superior quality. The picture presented by the *lezda* documents from Collioure, which include several further tariff lists from about 1365 and later, is remarkably consistent, and this in itself serves as a warning: it was easier to insert items into the list than it was to delete them from it, since it was often difficult to know whether an item that had not been seen for some years would eventually reappear.

When looking at finished products passing through Collioure, and also taxed at 2s 2d, it seems that the great majority were textiles originating in southern France or Flanders, but high quality 'Cordovan' leather was also traded through the port, and, as Gual Camarena pointed out, at this period much of it was brought not from Andalucia but from North African ports such as Bougie (Bijaya) [41]. The *lezda* of Collioure in fact establishes a hierarchy of goods, with localised products such as linseed oil, pastel, salted fish (still a speciality of the region), tartar of Urgell in the Catalan interior, butter (*manteca*), cheese, figs of Alacant, Tarragona, Majorca, Málaga (then still under Muslim rule) and elsewhere, lentils, peas and beans, all attracting lower rates of taxation than the prestige goods brought from the Maghrib and the Levant. Of course, it remains uncertain whether the goods described actually arrived in the port in significant quantities. However, the strategic position of Collioure at the point where Catalonia and France converged gave it privileged access to goods crossing the Mediterranean and to those, such as northern cloths, that were being exported across the Mediterranean. It is not surprising that the contemporary *lezda* of neighbouring Perpignan, or that of 1284 from the same city (now administrative capital of the new Majorcan kingdom) lays far more emphasis on the arrival of northern cloths, often finished in the city, and less on the network of maritime exchanges that linked Collioure to the Islamic world [42]. The 1284 *lezda* classifies as *totz auers de Leuant* pepper, ginger (*gingibre gros o menut*), incense (*ensens*), wax, cotton and sugar, though it cannot really be assumed that in all cases these items were brought from the East. In other sections of the same document there figure cloths from Alexandria, which Gual thought might well have been produced in other centres, merely imitating Egyptian models [43]; several types of cloth (*bagadels, boquerans, camelotz*) identified as *d'Outramar*, probably not just the crusader states *Outremer* but the Levant as a whole, but rather

[41] *Ibid.*, pp. 281-282.
[42] *Ibid.*, doc. 16, pp. 142-147.
[43] *Ibid.*, p. 196.

few references to alum, which twice appears in the form of *alum de Bolcan*, that is, the alum of the Lipari islands, rather than that of Egypt or Turkey [44]. By contrast, in the *lezda* of Tortosa, of 1252, there is quite a strong emphasis on the import of spices, as well as *alum de pluma*, alum from North Africa (that of Phocæa does not figure in the Catalan tariff lists): pepper, cumin, aniseed (*batafalua*), cedar wood (*citoal*), wax, ginger, cinnamon, cloves, lac, brazilwood, nutmeg (*nous noscades*), as well as colouring agents such as indigo, vermilion, *grana*, resins such as mastic and gum arabic, prepared flavourings of rose and violet. Once again more local products including cheap alums, and middle range foodstuffs such as cheeses, wines and dried grapes (*azebib*), tended to attract markedly lower tax rates [45]. It should be borne in mind that in the mid-thirteenth century the Catalans were not market leaders in the Levant trade, and the presence of many of these goods in the Catalan ports is not proof that all were brought directly from the Levant; still, there was some contact with the East, and there were significant intermediary trading stations at Palermo and Tunis, where such goods were readily available. It is therefore striking that the tariff lists do not simply survive from the major ports of the Catalan world (Barcelona, Tarragona, Collioure), but also from small trading centres such as Cambrils, from which a *lezda* list survives dating to 1258 [46].

It is hazardous to assume that, simply because an item appears at the top of the list of taxes chargeable, it must have been the most important. Ordinances for trade through Barcelona of 1271 do start their list of taxable imports with pepper and ginger, but several dyes are also very prominently placed:

> *Primerament carga de pebre, e de gingebre, e de lacha, d'encens, de breyl, de nous d'exarch, de cubebes saluatges, de citoual, de succre: prenen los corredors per corredures per cascuna carga VIII diners del comprador e altres VIII diners del uenedor, e per cascuna carga d'aquests auers XVI diners de reua.* [47]

The tariff list then mentions indigo *de Bagadel* and *de Golf*, which indicates the prestigious 'Baghdad indigo' and indigo from the Persian Gulf[48]. As the textile industry of Barcelona took off from about 1300 onwards,

[44] *Ibid.*, pp. 200-202.
[45] *Ibid.*, doc. 8, pp. 94-102.
[46] *Ibid.*, doc. 11, pp. 110-113.
[47] *Ibid.*, doc. 14, p. 127.
[48] *Ibid.*, p. 337.

demand for high quality dyes also began to soar. Tariff lists from Saragossa indicate that indigo also penetrated to the inland capital of the Aragonese kingdom [49].

A further perspective on these commodity movements is provided by an invaluable document from Marseilles, dating to 1296, in which a law suit is initiated against a galley master named Guillem Franc; he insisted on obtaining written texts of the bills of lading for two sea journeys made in 1289 from Marseilles and Aigues-Mortes to Majorca by a group of Provençal and Italian merchants, from Marseilles, Piacenza and Genoa [50]. The Piacenzans had loaded on board pepper, lac and *porcellanas*, while Provençal merchants had contributed wine, lac, incense, cinnamon and *porcellanas*; a Pisan had added cloves and aspic as well. On the second voyage a more varied cargo included ginger, coral and textiles. Altogether this is the sort of cargo one would expect to find on a galley of this period: small quantities of high value goods which could be carried by a ship ill-suited to bulkier products. It is striking that these goods were being taken out of western Europe through Majorca, itself a major springboard for penetration into the markets of North Africa; the document thus illustrates the increasingly important intermediary role acquired by western merchants in trade between the Middle East and the Far West of Islam (Granada, Morocco, Algeria). However, Guillem Franc did not apparently cover that leg of the journey himself, preferring to load goods in Majorca for import into continental Europe: cloves, already taken out to Majorca, were also part of his cargo on his return, indicating the complexity of the routes by which eastern spices reached and were distributed in the western Mediterranean; other products were more characteristic of the western Mediterranean as a whole, such as fine treated leathers, probably from the Maghrib, semi-treated cowhides, cheeses, dates and wax; cumin was available both from Levantine and local markets (such as the Maltese archipelago). Particularly interesting are the *porcellane* or cowrie shells (apparently named after their shape, similar to that of a baby piglet); these were exported towards Majorca and the Maghrib, and they originated in the Indian Ocean, but were in demand in West Africa where they functioned as a means of exchange [51]. For the Latin merchants, the sale for specie of humble cowrie shells in North Africa was literally a golden opportunity. Similar evidence that western merchants acted

---

[49] *Ibid.*, docs. 10 and 19, pp. 107-110, 152-156.

[50] Discussed in D. ABULAFIA, *Mediterranean Emporium*, cit., pp. 116-117, using L. BLANCARD, *Documents inédits sur le commerce de Marseille*, I-II, Marseille 1880-81, II, pp. 451-455.

[51] *Ibid.*, p. 117; cf. J. HOGENDORN, M. JOHNSON, *The Shell Money of the Slave Trade*, Cambridge 1986.

as intermediaries carrying industrial produce of the eastern lands to other Islamic destinations is provided by the references in the notarial cartulary of Amalric, of 1248, preserved in Marseilles, to the export from Marseilles of cotton bound for Ceuta in north-west Africa. But it is clear that the emphasis lay on the carriage of semi-processed or unprocessed goods, rather than on finished items made in Africa and Asia.

V. *Pegolotti's Mediterranean*

The function of the Mediterranean ports such as Aigues-Mortes, Palermo, Barcelona and Ciutat de Mallorca was not simply the redistribution of eastern goods towards the European continent, and of European goods (notably textiles) towards the Islamic world; in addition they functioned as bridges linking the central Islamic lands with the Maghrib and what remained of al-Andalus. The conquest of the Mediterranean by the Italian and Catalan navies catapulted the merchants of Genoa, Barcelona and the Tuscan cities into mastery over the distribution of eastern spices in north-west Africa, Islamic Spain and also those parts of the former Byzantine Empire where they operated trading stations. Equally, loss of mastery over the routes leading to the Levantine ports engendered new decisions about where to turn for the eastern produce on which western consumers had become increasingly dependent. An image of the trans-Mediterranean links at a critical moment in the struggle for mastery over the Levant is supplied by Pegolotti's *Pratica*.

Pegolotti provides not merely a summary of the taxes payable across the Mediterranean, but also a summation of material that already existed in written form. His debt to a Pisan brokers' tariff of 1323, and apparently also to documentation available to him from Flanders, has been noted by his editor, Evans [52]. In addition, the references to Acre as an active port make it abundantly clear that he based part of his account of Syrian trade upon manuals in use before the fall of the Latin Kingdom of Jerusalem in 1291, and the subsequent abandonment of Acre as a transit port for the Levant trade[53]. His image of Acre is one of a centre for the export of pepper (cited, as usual, in first place), ginger, wild brazilwood (*verzino*), indigo and cotton, whether in the form of thread or 'wool' (*cotone filato, cotone mapputo*); mercury (*argento vivo* or quicksilver) also passed through both Acre and Alexandria [54]. The list of spices and dyes is very similar to that found in the

---

[52] PEGOLOTTI, *Pratica*, cit., pp. xxvi-xxxvii.
[53] *Ibid.*, pp. 63-69.
[54] *Ibid.*, pp. 63-64.

V

Catalan tariff lists: lac, zedoary, mastic, mace, nutmeg, cinnamon all appear. Although he refers also to salted meats and both cattle and buffalo leather, it cannot be presumed that these were travelling westwards from Acre, which was also a major centre for the redistribution of western imports to Alexandria and Syria; Sicilian ham and bacon appears to have been in demand among the Christian inhabitants of the Latin East [55]. One spice, saffron, which Pegolotti mentions under the heading of Acre, was clearly imported from San Gimignano and other centres in central Italy, while sugar exports to the West were balanced by honey imports from the West (notably from Ancona, and, to judge from other evidence, Narbonne as well) [56]. He indicates a supply line carrying spices and also pearls to Barletta in southern Italy, later on a major Venetian base [57]. In describing Alexandria, Pegolotti mentions some additional eastern goods, notably cassia bark, 'dragon's blood' (another dyestuff) and tamarind, from India [58]. Hidden among the great catalogue of spices available in Egypt we also find soap, rice, raisins, sal nitric and other products which were counted as *spezie* by medieval merchants. His list reads as a veritable pharmacopoeia of the medieval Mediterranean. It is interesting to observe that western merchants in Alexandria also appear to have handled Maghribi products such as *scorza di Buggiea*, a type of cinnamon substitute from Bougie, acting presumably as intermediaries between north- west Africa and Egypt, rather as they have already been observed acting as intermediaries in the trade in *porcellane* between the Levant and the Maghrib[59]. It is important to recall that Egypt drew commodities from further East for resale to Italian and other western merchants, and also produced its own versions of several of those commodities. The *Minhaj* of al-Makhzumi from the late twelfth century makes plain the active export of locally produced spices such as cumin; Egypt was also a source of emeralds at certain periods. Most ghoulish of all its products was what Pegolotti called *munmia*, desiccated mummy powder, which was used as a medicine throughout the Mediterranean region, and was regarded even by rabbis as a permissible drug,

---

[55] *Ibid.*, p. 64.

[56] *Ibid.*, p. 64; for San Gimignano saffron, see D. ABULAFIA, *Crocuses and Crusaders: San Gimignano, Pisa and the Kingdom of Jerusalem*, in *Outremer. Studies in the History of the Crusading Kingdom of Jerusalem*, ed. B.Z. KEDAR, H.E. MAYER, R.C. SMAIL, Jerusalem 1982, pp. 227-243; for Narbonne honey see D. ABULAFIA, *Narbonne, the Lands of the Crown of Aragon and the Levant Trade 1187-1400*, in *Montpellier, la Couronne d'Aragon et les pays de Langue d'Oc (1204-1349). Actes du XII⁰ Congrès d'Histoire de la Couronne d'Aragon, Montpellier, 1985* = "Mémoires de la Société archéologique de Montpellier", 15, 1987, pp. 189-207.

[57] PEGOLOTTI, *Pratica*, p. 66.

[58] *Ibid*, p. 70.

[59] *Ibid.*, p. 70.

since the human bodies from which it was derived now counted as no more than the dust of the earth [60]. Gum arabic derived, at least in its purest forms, from either East or West Africa, and its presence in the markets of Alexandria is thus testimony to links down the Red Sea to the Zanzibar Coast.

A not dissimilar picture emerges from Pegolotti's treatment of Famagusta, which in the early fourteenth century took over from Acre as the major way station for western merchants attempting to trade with the Levant, and which could be used either as a base for penetration into Cilician Armenia, Syria and Egypt, or, during periods of strictly enforced embargo against the Mamluk ports, as a collection point for goods illicitly crossing the lines; Pegolotti's image of a vibrant centre of exchanges, to which he devotes an especially large amount of space in his book, hardly fits the modest needs of Famagusta itself, or the requirements of the down-at-heel Lusignan rulers of the kingdom [61]. At the very start of the fourteenth century a particularly active group of Syrian Christian merchants regularly carried cotton there for resale in Ancona and other Italian ports, and various types of cotton (in addition, as it happens, to local Cypriot wool) are mentioned by Pegolotti. The author had spent upwards of five years on the island, and it is this part of his survey of the Mediterranean that perhaps inspires most confidence in its accuracy. He even observes what sort of bottles are to be used for Cyprus syrups, and in what sort of cases they are to be packed [62]. The presence of these syrups is evidence that at a mid-point in the long journey from East to West some of the spices were being processed into concoctions, made without any doubt using the sugar of Cyprus to which Pegolotti also devoted much attention. For it seems clear enough that the major Levantine centres trading with the West exploited their position by developing local industries for the production of drugs, sweetmeats and syrups or jams: the *zenzeverata da mangiare* attributed to Alexandria appears to fulfill this role, though some arrived from India already packed in little wooden cassettes (Pegolotti was worried that confusion might result concerning the weight of ginger packed with and without covers) [63].

Further to the west, in the Maghrib, Pegolotti's picture lays far less emphasis on spices; Tunis attracts his attention as a centre of exchange for cotton, linen, wool, canvas and such modest foodstuffs as carobs, nuts, oil

---

[60] *Ibid.*, p. 70.
[61] *Ibid.*, pp. 77-102.
[62] *Ibid.*, pp. 317-318.
[63] *Ibid.*, p. 70.

(often imported from Italy) and chestnuts; he says little about Tunis as a source of wax [64]. From the Tunisian island of Jerba, a Sicilian possession for much of this period, oil alone seems to have been sent across the sea to Palermo and Messina [65]. Some characteristic products of this region, such as leather, wool and pottery, hardly aroused his interest. He is uninformative about trade through Ceuta, Bougie and other major ports of the Maghrib, though he does note the sale of *magaluffa*, wild goat hides (an unfamiliar term to his contemporaries, for he takes the trouble to explain it), in Safi, a port on the Atlantic coast of Morocco, which was also a source of grain; and he indicates that merchants penetrate into the interior as far as Meknes, Fez and Rabat [66]. He also discusses the trade of *Niffa*, that is, Anfa or the modern Casablanca (*dar el-Beida*), which had become a significant port for trade with the West by this period [67]. 'Morocco' leathers completely dominate the picture: cowhides, whether from grown cattle or young calves; camelskins; goat and lambskins; but wax, wool, almonds and grain were also available. At Arzila there was apparently some trade in indigo, alum and ivory, and a local bark appears to have been exported to the western Mediterranean as a cinnamon substitute (*erba d'uscian*) [68]. Ivory, often under the title *denti di Liofante*, appears several times in Pegolotti's work, as far East as Acre, but evidently Africa was a significant source, and surviving artefacts from Sicily and Spain reveal that this traffic had antecedents in the tenth, eleventh and twelfth centuries [69]. It is not surprising to find 'elephants' teeth' among the goods attributed to the markets of Majorca by Pegolotti [70]. Overall, though, North Africa presents a very different picture to that available either for the Levantine ports or for southern Spain (whether reconquered Seville or unconquered Granada and Málaga). Seville appears in Pegolotti as a redistribution centre for spices such as pepper and ginger, hardly surprisingly, given its access to the Mediterranean trade routes via the Straits of Gibraltar, and its entrepreneurial role between the Mediterranean and the Atlantic trade routes; and very striking is the role of that 'Mediterranean Emporium', Majorca, which, true to its function as a centre of exchange for any type of

[64] *Ibid.*, pp. 130-136.
[65] *Ibid.*, p. 137.
[66] *Ibid.*, pp. 273-274.
[67] *Ibid.*, p. 275.
[68] *Ibid.*, p. 276.
[69] *Ibid.*, pp. 63, 69, 78, 123, 141, 294.
[70] *Ibid.*, p. 123.

goods entering the western Mediterranean, from the Levant, the Atlantic or from the European and African land masses, could supply almost anything that originated in the Islamic world and beyond:

> *Pepe tondo, mandorle sanza guscio, cera, cotone mapputo, giengiovo, lacca e gherbellasi, allume, verzino scorzuto, cannella, grana d'ogni ragione, zucchero in pani, e polvere di zucchero d'ogni ragione, cassia fistola, tartero cioè gromma, incenzo d'ogni ragione, galla d'ogni ragione, comino, gomerabica, vernice.*
>
> *A cantara della terra vi si vendono: Argento vivo, e vermiglione cioè cinabro, e mele d'ape, e lino, e sapone in pezze, e stoppe, e carne, e saime insalate, e fichi secchi dell'isola, e gli altri a sporta che dè essere cantaro 1 della terra; indaco d'ogni ragione salvo del golfo, e mondiglia di verzino, e avorio d'ogni ragione, e denti di liofante, e mastico, turbitti, zettoara, zucchero candi, chitirra cioè draganti, orpimento, galbano, zolfo, tamerindi, mirra, sene, timiame è incenso di greci, zafflore, erba da vermini, landano, lisciadro cioè salarmoniaco, polvere d'oriallo, tuzia, biacca, verderame, guado, agnellina di Maiolica, agnellina di San Matteo, lana e agnellina d'Inghilterra, agnellina di Maiorica* [71].

The impression is of a vast mingling of goods, which barely merit any form of classification into categories; but dyestuffs certainly have a prominent place in the list, and their marriage with English, Spanish or Balearic wools brought prestige to the Catalan textile industry. Later Pegolotti points to the arrival also of Barbary leathers, *zibibbo* or raisins (mentioned also in Pisan tariff lists of this period as an import into Majorca), and North African wool (*lana di Garbo*). Drugs and dyes include myrobalan, 'dragon's blood', sandalwood, rhubarb and mummy powder [72].

Cotton, of course, figures prominently in Pegolotti's work; raw cotton, he says, was being sold at Tana in the Crimea, an important Venetian base; Mazzaoui notes that this picture is confirmed by a trade agreement between Ancona and Dubrovnik of 1372, setting a tariff of 6d per *centenario* for cotton imported from *Gazaria* (i.e. the former land of the Khazars) and Tartary. Pegolotti actually provides a rank order of cotton producers in Syria, ranging from Hama in Syria, and its close rival Aleppo, down to Cyprus and Lattakiah (Laodicea). Mazzaoui's view is that western purchasers were unable to penetrate far into the interior to obtain cotton from such sources as Persia and

---

[71] *Ibid.*, p. 123.
[72] *Ibid.*, p. 124.

Turkestan, and that Syrian cotton was thus the Middle Eastern cotton with which they were most familiar. Transport costs for such a bulky commodity meant that merchants who penetrated as far as Tabriz were not likely to buy cotton there. Certainly, the Venetian colony established in Aleppo after 1207/8 seems to have seen pearls, gemstones and cotton as its main targets. However, sea routes that penetrated deep into cotton producing areas could be exploited to bring the commodity from very far afield: the Ragusan and Anconitan interest in Crimean cotton has already been mentioned, and they also made contact with sources in the Caucasus. After 1300 Anatolia became an important source of inferior quality cotton. In addition, it seems logical to argue that much of the cotton purchased in Egypt around 1300 was in fact obtained from India, and carried along the sea routes up the Red Sea. In that case significant quantities of Indian cotton may periodically have been available in the West.

For information about the Indies there was no more popular source of information after 1300 than Marco Polo's description of his return journey to the West, in which he offered descriptions of large numbers of products the origins of which could only previously be the subject of guesswork. Thus he describes the high quality of Ceylon's brazilwood, and refers to the excellent buckram cloths available from the Malabar coast:

> In this kingdom there is great abundance of pepper and also of ginger, besides cinnamon in plenty and other spices, turbit and coconuts. Buckrams are made here of the loveliest and most delicate texture in the world. Many other articles of merchandise are exported. In return, when merchants come here from overseas they load their ships with brass, which they use as ballast, cloth of gold and silk, sendal, gold, silver, cloves, spikenard and other such spices that are not produced here. You must know that ships come here from very many parts, notably from the great province of Manzi, and goods are exported to many parts. Those that go to Aden are carried thence to Alexandria[73].

Gujarat is praised for its indigo, cotton and leather, both goat and buffalo hides, as well as unicorn skins! Embossed leather mats are a local speciality; indeed, 'in this kingdom are produced leather goods of more consummate workmanship than anywhere in the world, and of higher value'. Cambay is another important export centre for buckram cloth, cotton and indigo, and

---

[73] MARCO POLO, *Travels*, ed. and transl. R. LATHAM, Harmondsworth 1958, p. 290.

356

Marco Polo cannot even be bothered to name the other products traded there, the list is so vast.

VI. *Hardware from the East*

Further evidence of commercial, or at any rate diplomatic, contact with the East is provided by the survival in the West of metalwork, ceramics and glass of eastern origins. Some scholars who favour a diffusionist approach have argued that the development of Limoges enamels betrays eastern influence, and that the aquamanile, a common form of cast bronze animal sculpture, is copied from Islamic models; certainly some aquamanili, such as a famous example that long stood high on the roof of Pisa Cathedral, were acquired in the Middle Ages from Muslim courts, whether in Spain, North Africa or Egypt, along with metal basins and bowls that still occasionally survive. [74] Similarly the evidence of the ceramic *bacini* incorporated in the towers and façades of the churches of Pisa and several other Italian cities seems to reveal regular contact with the ports of the Islamic Mediterranean, though some (such as those at the church of San Sisto) were most likely acquired by piracy, notably the Pisan-Genoese raid on al-Mahdiyyah in 1087. Tin glazed wares of such high quality finish were not produced north of Lazio; on the other hand, it is hard to press the claim that these were all especially costly items. Some may have arrived as ballast in the bottom of Pisan trading vessels. By about 1200 *bacini* were arriving from Egypt, Tunisia, Morocco, Spain and Sicily; and western technology only began to catch up in the thirteenth century, when comparable glazing methods were developed in Tuscany. At that point the Pisan churches turned more and more to local products in order to decorate the exterior [75]. Meanwhile some Islamic jars were certainly reaching the West, as archaeological evidence shows, perhaps as containers for higher value goods. By the late Middle Ages, Muslim Spain and Valencia had become significant sources of high grade glazed pottery, so that 'hispano-moresque' tableware was found in Medicean Florence, in Bruges and in England; the techniques of production were, however, imitated first by Spanish Christians and then in central Italy. The history of glass making reveals that, as with ceramics, the West was able to learn its skills from the East, in this case developing them to a new peak: by the late fourteenth century the West was exporting glass to the Mamluk realms, while

---

[74] J.W. ALLAN, *The Influence of the Metalwork of the Arab Mediterranean on that of Medieval Europe*, in *The Arab Influence in Medieval Europe*, ed. by D.A. ANGIUS, R. HITCHCOCK, Reading 1994, pp. 44-62.
[75] D. ABULAFIA, *Pisan bacini*, cit., pp. 287-296.

the alkali used in glass production at Murano were themselves derived from the Levant. Ashtor saw this as another example of the failure of the Levant to sustain the technological lead it clearly possessed in the early Middle Ages. Of course, there were other finished goods produced in the East which were of a quality that could not be mimicked in the West. Celadon wares of great delicacy were filtering through the Islamic world to decorate the tables of the kings of Sicily in the thirteenth century, to judge from archaeological evidence at Lucera in Puglia. A century ago, the National Museum in Dublin acquired an early fourteenth-century Chinese porcelain vase, the 'Fonthill Vase', which was probably brought to Europe by a diplomatic mission around 1338. Since then it has peregrinated through Hungary, Naples (possibly) and France [76]. Its high relief decoration suggests that it was itself a great rarity in China, not to mention the West. In other words, it was a curio, even for the Chinese; it serves as a reminder that the surviving artefacts cannot be assumed to be typical of the products of the East reaching Europe, most of which ended up in the dyer's vat or as food flavourings.

VI. *Conclusion*

By the beginning of the thirteenth century a shift in the economic relationship between East and West was already becoming visible. Demand for eastern cloths was beginning to decline, while demand for raw materials, notably cotton, grew, in order to satisfy the needs of an Italian cotton industry which would, by 1400, become well established north of the Alps as well. In addition, western producers were beginning to find a good market for their own woollen cloths, from as far away as Flanders and England, as well as Italy and Catalonia, in North Africa and the Levant. Some of the Mediterranean wool producers were, indeed, making use of raw wool from the Maghrib. As western cloth production grew, to satisfy demand both in the Christian West and in the Islamic lands, so too demand for high quality dyestuffs to colour the best European cloths grew. This demand could only in part be met locally; apart from saffron, the best colouring agents had to be acquired through trade with the Levant, though most of them, especially indigo, hailed from far to the East. In addition, the fixatives and mordants used in the processing of cloth, especially alum, could be found in the East. Thus the history of the European textile industry reveals a complex inter-

---

[76] J. CHAPMAN, *The Fonthill Vase* in "The Irish-Chinese Cultural Society Newsletter", 3, December 1981; I am grateful to Professor Seymour Phillips of University College, Dublin, for his kindness in providing a copy of this little known study of the vase.

dependence between workshops producing the best woollens, fit for a king (or sultan), and merchants bringing westwards materials that were essential to the industry's success. Less prestigious, but equally dependent on supply lines from the East, was the developing cotton industry in western Europe.

The resale in the East of goods partially manufactured using raw materials from the East marked, in Ashtor's eyes, the great triumph of western technology and commercial expertise over that of the Islamic world. It also alleviated the outflow of silver bullion, even though it seems clear that the balance of payments continued to favour the Levant throughout the Middle Ages. Yet another approach might be to see the relationship between East and West as one of a growing mutual interdependence. Janet Abu-Lughod has argued that in the period 1250 to 1350 a global economy was coming into being, only to be disrupted by the shock of the Black Death [77]. Her arguments partly depends on the traditional emphasis placed on the trans-Asia trade routes created as a result of the Mongol conquests in Asia; another view might be that the great spice trade through the Indian Ocean to Alexandria was never seriously replaced by the new Asiatic routes carrying silk and slaves. But that is not to deny signs of a global economy coming into existence, bringing together in a common enterprise the Christian and Islamic shores of the Mediterranean. That common enterprise was the textile industry, both luxury woollens and humbler cotton cloths. The evidence presented here suggests that in some sectors of the western European economy the presence of items imported from the East was of critical importance to further expansion. The political, cultural and religious barriers across the Mediterranean proved permeable; cotton, indigo and alum were the agents binding together East and West.

---

[77] J. ABU-LUGHOD, *Before European Hegemony. The World System, AD 1250-1350*, New York 1989.

The impact of Italian banking in the late Middle Ages and the Renaissance, 1300–1500

Over twenty years ago, when I was undergoing my initiation in research in Italian economic history, I went to cash a cheque drawn on the London bank of Messrs Coutts and Company, founded as recently as 1692, in the marble halls of a great Italian bank situated on the Piazza dei Banchi at Genoa. My own transaction, involving the acceptance of a paper document drawn on an account over a thousand miles away, was itself the lineal descendant of the business transactions carried out in that Piazza and in the other banking centres of medieval Italy seven centuries earlier. But an even stronger reminder of the medieval heritage was provided by the woman in the queue ahead of me, who was apparently cashing her savings of gold coins for modern Italian lire; each one of her coins was carefully assayed by the bank clerk before being accepted. Such images are, of course, deceptive if they are thought to imply that the great banks of medieval Italy inhabited marble halls or possessed staffs of the gigantic size found in modern banks. The Genoese bankers of the thirteenth century operated from small booths containing *banci* or *tabule*, exchange tables, on which transactions were conducted.[1] The magnificent surviving palaces of the Peruzzi or Medici in Florence may say something about the wealth of the great banking families of late medieval Tuscany, but little space within these palaces was given over to banking operations. Besides, the oldest bank in present-day Italy, the Monte dei Paschi di Siena founded in 1472, descends from the pawnbroking office of late fifteenth-century

Siena, and it is to similar origins that other very old banks in Italy, such as the Banco di Napoli, must primarily be traced.

Indeed, any approach to the problem of banking and capitalism in late medieval Italy must contend with several fundamental problems. In the first place, there is the question of definition of terms. The application to late medieval Italy of language that has long been adapted to the needs of a modern industrial economy is unavoidable; but it affects even the use of so basic a term as 'banking', a term which in fact originated in this very period and place. Of the Medici firm a distinguished economic historian has flatly insisted: 'it was not a bank in the modern sense of the term', concerned in the first place with deposits and extended loans;[2] it will be seen in this discussion that I have preferred where possible to employ such terms as 'company' or 'firm' to describe the Florentine banks. The use of the epithet *bancherius* to describe businessmen who specialized in the exchange or handling of money (including deposits) can be found in Genoa as early as the twelfth century, though these individuals, like any Genoese with cash in hand, also invested in trading expeditions and bought or sold cloth. There were certainly several types of money specialist, ranging from the moneylender or pawnbroker who concentrated his attention on small loans, often aimed at peasants or artisans in need of short-term credit, to the collectors of papal taxes, *mercatores camere*, who were able soon after 1200 to transmit funds from England, Ireland, even Scandinavia, as far as Rome.[3] Pawnbrokers, for their part, were intrinsically involved in the running of shops selling a great variety of goods, mostly but not exclusively unredeemed second-hand objects such as metalwork or textiles. Ecclesiastical disapproval of usury meant that it was unusual for a moneylender to live exclusively off the charging of interest, which would need to be masked as part of wider transaction costs.[4] Indeed, exchange transactions were generally regarded as non-usurious on the grounds that exchange rates fluctuated, and the element of uncertainty meant that the banker was not 'buying time' by charging interest at an agreed rate, but was providing a risky service to his clients, for which he could legitimately claim a reward. It was also a widespread, and just about licit, custom in Genoa and elsewhere to agree upon a fictitious settlement date for a loan, subject to the charging of a penalty for breach of contract.[5] The existence of such mechanisms does not prove that the Church had no influence on the development of banking; rather the opposite was the case: bankers were constrained by the law of the Church, and some of their most prestigious operations, such as the handling of the papal account, were the source of little direct profit, but rather of prestige. The pope was a 'loss leader' for those bankers who serviced his account. At the top end of the scale too there is little evidence that individuals or companies concentrated on the handling of money, to the exclusion of other commercial transactions such as the sale of cloth or foodstuffs. The pure banker, in the sense of an individual or group of individuals who lived almost entirely off the profits of exchange transactions, certainly existed in such cities as thirteenth-century Siena, Piacenza or Asti; but it must be stressed that the major banks of the Italian late Middle Ages were much more than banks: commodity transactions, often on a massive scale, as well as investment in wool workshops, not to mention the operation of tax farms, were all part of the range of profit-making activities that made the Bardi and Peruzzi famous in the early fourteenth century and the Medici in the fifteenth.[6]

It is generally agreed that the profits to be made in banking were derived in the first instance from exchange transactions, although claims have been made for the primary role of moneylending rather than moneychanging. Certainly, the importance of exchange facilities grew as the trade routes through France to Flanders became more active; the Champagne fairs became the major centre for exchange dealings in the thirteenth century, and it is increasingly clear that the function of Champagne as a clearing house was facilitated by the growing sophistication of Italian techniques for the transfer of money. Early forms of bill of exchange can be identified by 1200, and particular credit in the development of the banking activities of the fairs must go to the bankers of Asti, Piacenza and other north-west Italian centres, who acted as intermediaries between Genoese or other Italian merchants and the cloth producers of Flanders and northern France. The exchange transactions could and did mask the charging of interest rates, a factor which makes the compilation of tables of exchange rates between medieval currencies an extremely challenging task.[7] There is no need here to examine the full range of options which enabled a Florentine bank to make a loan in Florence in florins and to recover (by means of a notional triangular network of exchanges) capital and interest again in florins, without incurring the wrath of the Church. For the primary objective of the larger banking enterprises was neither deposit taking nor the provision of local credit, but the accumulation of profits through charges on exchanges and transfers. How lucrative this could be is apparent from, say, the profits of the Milan branch of the Medici in 1459 on exchanges conducted with the Geneva fairs: £3,043 13s 4d, or 10% of the gross profits of the branch; but it is also important to note that sales of silks, brocades, English wool, jewellery and belts produced 42% of profits.[8] In other words, the more purely mercantile side of Medici company business was often especially lucrative. It will be seen that the operation of banking business alongside the sale of luxury goods or foodstuffs is a fundamental feature of the great Florentine banks of the late Middle Ages.

Here it is proposed to concentrate on those big Florentine banks, the Bardi, Peruzzi, Medici and so on, between about 1300 and about 1500, that is, between the emergence into clear light of the Peruzzi and the fall of the Medici bank in 1494. This is partly for lack of intensive study of banking in other Italian centres, though good recent work by Edward English has illuminated the banking history of thirteenth-century Siena, and a major study of banking in Venice is expected shortly from Reinhold Mueller.[9] Lucca too has been a focus of attention in the thirteenth and fourteenth centuries, especially at the hands of Thomas Blomquist, while its banking links to England have been studied from the evidence in London by Richard Kaeuper.[10] Indeed, the links between the Italian bankers and the English crown have long been a well-researched theme. Other kingdoms have fared less well: the Italian presence in Spain is best known from sixteenth-century evidence, and much more attention needs to be paid to Genoese and Florentine links with Castile, even after the magisterial opening studies of Federigo Melis.[11] Florentine bankers in southern Italy first became a focus of interest in the work of Georges Yver, way back in 1903, on the basis of a vast body of Neapolitan documentation, now sadly laid waste; but it will be seen that the role of the Florentines in southern Italy is now being re-emphasized in the latest research.[12] Moving later, the activities in fifteenth-century Naples of the Strozzi bankers of Florence are well documented, thanks to the researches of Alfonso Leone;[13] but there are still vast gaps, for instance the lack of a full-scale study of those great rivals to the Medici, the Pazzi. It should be mentioned, however, that pawnbroking in Italy, especially the Jewish loan banks of the late fourteenth and fifteenth centuries, has been closely and effectively analysed in a number of studies; these include a celebrated survey by Léon Poliakov which reveals how intense was the discussion in ecclesiastical circles about the legitimacy of permitting the Jewish *banchieri* to function, and how persistent were Franciscan attempts to establish loan banks which were free of the taint of 'usury'.[14] It is not, though, intended here to dwell long on this predominantly 'down market' type of banking, but rather – for reasons that will rapidly become obvious – on activities related to the exchange of money on an international scale.

Despite these examples of much-valued research, there is a strong impression that the history of early Italian banking has gone into recession. Long favoured in the entourage of *Annales*, the study of the history of trade and banking has given way to the study of the mental world of the merchant. Economic historians of Italy have been anxious, in recent years, to provide a broader analysis of the factors allowing for growth or promoting recession in the much-debated post-Black Death era; it is here that the work of Richard Goldthwaite and John Day has achieved especial significance, and Goldthwaite has also written a characteristically clear and thoughtful essay on the Medici and fifteenth-century capitalism, offering new perspectives on attitudes to competitiveness in the fifteenth century.[15] All the same, it is a surprise to be reminded that many of Armando Sapori's classic studies of early Italian banking date back over fifty years, though they are still much cited; it is actually sixty years since he published his ground-breaking edition of the banking records of the Peruzzi.[16] The pioneering studies of Raymond de Roover, a businessman turned business historian, have established a firm outline of the development of the Medici bank; his full statement of the bank's history was published in 1963,[17] while a preliminary study appeared as far back as 1948.[18] In 1954 he could write: 'In recent years, more progress has been made in the history of banking, perhaps, than in any other field of economic history. Moreover, most of the publications which are responsible for this advance in our knowledge have been devoted to banking in the Middle Ages.'[19] The reality was, in fact, that much of the most striking progress had been made by de Roover himself, and since his death in 1972, and the publication by Julius Kirshner of a collection of de Roover's key articles in 1974, the study of medieval banking has shifted its emphasis, so that the analysis of theories of usury has remained a significant area of research (notably at the hands of Kirshner), while business histories of medieval companies have been rather rare. A major exception, however, is the publication in the autumn of 1994 of Edwin Hunt's study of the Florentine Peruzzi; like de Roover, Hunt approaches his subject from the vantage point of years spent in business, and his work raises important issues concerning the role of banking activities, as such, in the overall business profile of what we are accustomed to call the Florentine banks.[20]

Hunt insists that it is more appropriate to term the Bardi, Peruzzi and Acciaiuoli of fourteenth-century Florence 'super-companies' than banks, in view of the geographical range of their activities, stretching as far afield as England, Spain or the Aegean, and in view of the enormous range of economic activities that they encompassed. If commodity trading was indeed the major preoccupation of the Peruzzi, then the image of the company as simply the Peruzzi Bank is inadequate. Hunt points out that a study limited to Florentine dealings with the English kings or the popes will conclude that the Peruzzi or Bardi were in the first instance bankers or wool merchants; a study that looks closely at their Mediterranean connections will suggest that they were very large general merchants; a study that homes in on Florence will see them as manufacturers as well as traders. Hunt says: 'to focus only upon specific aspects of the businesses produces results like those of the fabled three blind men trying to understand the nature of an elephant'. Nor should it be forgotten that several Florentine banks took care to invest in real estate, whether as a buffer against hard times or, more likely, as a sign that the company was operated by respectable individuals with roots (ancestral or invented) in the countryside. Thus the range of activities was as wide as circumstances allowed, from the purchase of a narwhal's horn to the management of customs taxes in the ports of the Kingdom of Naples. It would be a cardinal error to single out what by modern standards are regarded as banking operations from the full range of business concerns conducted 'in the name of God and profit' by the Florentine bankers. Emphasis will therefore be placed here on the relationship between investment in long-distance trade or in manufacturing and the money side of these companies' business.

It is essential to understand what these companies were not. They were not permanent establishments with plant. Marble halls, it has been seen, were definitely not part of their equipment, which, at its most basic, consisted of their account books, especially the secret account books which survive for the Peruzzi and, later on, the Medici. Although heavily involved in the grain trade out of southern Italy, the Peruzzi possessed neither ships nor wagons nor mules for the transport of these goods, for all these would need to be hired. Even the prime warehouse which they used in Florence was leased for three or four years at a time; though part owned by a member of the Peruzzi family, he was not a partner or employee of the firm. The Peruzzi and their rivals were not permanent in another respect: the companies consisted of short-term partnerships which were periodically renewed (allowing thereby for redistribution of capital shares), though the actual process of dissolution and renewal did not interfere with continuing business.

Cash flow and the management of trade were, of course, indissolubly linked, and it was precisely the careful accounting and substantial assets that these companies possessed that made it possible to operate on a Europe-wide scale, arranging for the long-distance transport of prodigious amounts of wool, cloth and grain; cloth imported for finishing in Florence tied up capital, and even when the cloth was prepared it still had to be re-exported towards consumers in Naples or North Africa. Cash was therefore, as Hunt demonstrates, often immobilized for long periods, and the difficulties faced by the Florentine banks from the 1330s to the great crisis of 1343 are more easily comprehensible in this light.[21] Equally, the growth of the Peruzzi company has to be attributed to a cumulative process whereby the trading profits of the 1280s and 1290s inspired confidence among possible investors. The reorganized company of 1300 raised capital of £124,000, of which £54,000, nearly 44%, had been injected by outsiders; and interest bearing deposits at 7 or 8% attracted still more capital.[22]

Yet it was arguably the political ties of the Florentine banks, or at least of the Florentine city government (just now in constant flux), that did most to establish the Bardi, Peruzzi and Acciaiuoli as the most powerful and wealthiest banks of the Middle Ages, easily surpassing even the fifteenth-century Medici. The divisions within Italy between Guelf and Ghibelline factions, the former broadly pro-papal, and divisions among the Guelfs between so-called White and Black factions, generally served the interests of those Black Guelf banks that identified most strongly with the papal cause, and which were able to sustain the pope's hard-pressed finances at a time of bitter conflict between the Angevin rulers of Naples and the Aragonese kings of Sicily.[23] It was difficult to steer a safe course between the competing monarchs of Naples and Sicily, or between France and England; what is impressive is that the leading Florentine banks were able to maintain important trading ties with rulers constantly at odds with one another, all of whom were desperate for the credit and other financial services that the Bardi and Peruzzi could offer. The Florentines, for their part, were determined to gain privileged access to the grain supplies of southern Italy and Sicily, or to the wool of England; loans to the rulers of these lands lubricated the trade routes, and were justified through the commercial opportunities they created, certainly not through the payment of interest (which was at best negligible).[24] Such loans also provided direct access to the most demanding consumers, who were themselves arbiters of taste for their wealthier subjects; it is likely that sales of fine cloth and other luxury items at the courts of debtor princes were made highly profitable by the insistence on charging inflated prices for luxury goods, as the unstated cost of granting hefty loans. Yet it is not difficult to see that this was also a precarious state of affairs, as events around 1340 began to reveal: close ties to Edward III of England drew the bankers into a financial morass and contributed significantly to the shattering bankruptcies of 1343.[25]

In July 1335 the Peruzzi possessed five agents in England, four in France, four at Avignon, four in Flanders and six in Sicily, but in the Kingdom of Naples they had eleven: six based in Naples and five at the grain exporting station of Barletta.[26] South Italian grain was indeed a major preoccupation of the Peruzzi, as it was for all Florence: the city is said to have been able to feed itself from local supplies for only five months out of twelve in a normal year, during the early fourteenth century, which was a period when there were many famine years too; and the Florentines were active in supplying wheat from Sicilian or Apulian stocks to other areas as well, as far afield at Cilician Armenia.[27] The Acciaiuoli were not far behind the Peruzzi in their close attention to southern Italy, with nine agents at Naples and Barletta in 1341 and three in Sicily; their coverage of northern Europe, though far from negligible, was slighter than that of the Peruzzi; and it is noticeable that the three great banks were not averse to co-operative ventures from the very start, whether in financing cotton shipments from Cyprus to Ancona and Venice, or grain shipments from Sicily to Tunis: they were not exclusively concerned with trade towards Florence, and had good links to leading Catalan shipowners, to Genoese or Venetian cloth-dealers, or to whichever merchant offered the specialities that they needed to conclude an elaborate business deal.[28] They did not assume that they alone had the capacity to see a transaction through from start to finish. In other words, they possessed a range of specific functions in trade and finance, and did not seek to rationalize the conduct of international trade by bringing ancillary commercial activities (such as ship-chandling) under their control; some of these skills were in any case famously tied to other commercial centres such as Barcelona, Venice and Genoa.

Nowhere is this sense of definite, limited objectives truer than in the case of investment in the woollen industry. The Peruzzi and Bardi were active in the export of English wool, whether to Flanders, to feed that region's looms, or, increasingly, towards Italy, where good imitations of Flemish cloth were being produced, especially the Florentine *panni alla francesca*, by the 1330s.[29] Spain and North Africa also featured prominently as sources of wool. But the Peruzzi did not control the process of woollen cloth production once the raw materials had arrived in Florence; an exceptionally elaborate putting-out system was operated by the *lanaiuoli*, relying on artisans who worked at home on the multiple process of cleansing, carding or spinning, dyeing, weaving and finishing Woollen cloth sold back by *lanaiuoli* could then be distributed along the trade networks dominated by the companies, notably in the Kingdoms of Naples and Sicily.[30] Occasional direct control of wool workshops by the Peruzzi and other banks should not confuse the picture: their investment in the running of a woollen cloth firm was a business opportunity like any other, and if profits failed to meet expectations there was no reason to pursue the project permanently. Of course, there were smaller banks which placed a heavier emphasis on the woollen cloth industry of Florence; the Alberti bank, closely studied by Sapori and de Roover, seems to have grown out of a cloth importing firm, and retained a *bottega della lana* in 1321–3, in which they had invested over £12,000, yet the shop appears to have been liquidated by 1325 before re-emerging a couple of years after that.[31] Thus even those who placed large investments in cloth were not necessarily committed to the unremitting pursuit of that objective, despite its fundamental importance in the Florentine economy. Practical interests, notably profitability, naturally took first place. It would perhaps be true to state that the companies were so well attuned to an economy which throve on putting out, selling, reselling, exchanging that the complex chain of cloth production was not something they would have sought to control from top to bottom. They were simply not monopolists; the idea of in some sense 'rationalizing' the process of industrial production, in an age when factories were to all intents non-existent, had no part in their economic planning. Both in industry and in commerce they were careful to concentrate on the areas of expertise they were known to possess.

The Peruzzi, Bardi and Acciaiuoli gained special strength from the fact that they were in the first instance family operations, but even so they drew on board non-family shareholders (who were even for a time a majority in the Peruzzi company, around 1335).[32] Yet by no means all leading members of the Peruzzi clan were involved with the company. The importance of the extended family in the political and economic life of the Italian urban aristocracy can scarcely be exaggerated. But nearly as important as family ties was the principle of loyalty that bound the staff of the early Florentine companies together, as well as the efficient methods of book-keeping, whether strictly worthy of the title 'double entry' or not, that enabled the central offices to measure the success of the multifarious enterprises in which the company engaged. On this note, it should also be emphasized that the Medici were rather exceptional in maintaining family continuity over a whole century, as a result of a series of genealogical accidents which preserved a single line of inheritance from Giovanni di Bicci at the end of the fourteenth century to Lorenzo il Magnifico at the end of the fifteenth.

As far as it is possible to identify a coherent plan of operations, our evidence is mainly derived from the organizational structure of the great companies: the Bardi, perhaps in view of their size, were particularly ready to allow branch managers extensive discretion, while the smaller Buonaccorsi, number four in the ranking of early fourteenth-century Florentine banks, were rather more tightly managed from the centre.[33] Of the Peruzzi, Hunt says: 'the Florence management centralised *policy* but was prepared to decentralise *execution* within the constraints established by policy.' Decisions had to be made whether a branch would be operated by a partner or a factor, and indeed where it was worthwhile operating a branch of what size. A chairman or *capo* in Florence presided over developments, but it remains unclear how far decisions were made by the *capo* and his close associates on an *ad hoc* basis; this seems most likely, and any idea of a formal company board, meeting regularly in Florence is of course a modern fantasy. Shareholders, rather than lingering in Florence, often travelled as far afield as England to negotiate business and to monitor the performance of branches abroad. In the other direction, Francesco Forzetti, who spent something like forty years as manager in charge of the Palermo branch, was occasionally brought to Florence on business.[34] By the fifteenth century, significant variations can be seen in the overall structure of banks, with the Medici, for instance, operating their branches as notionally independent firms. Indeed Goldthwaite concludes that what was striking by that time was precisely the 'lack of structure' in the banking system: 'their common interests were little served by corporate organisation'. Trust was an essential feature of the operation of any bank, and yet it was based not so much on legally binding documents as upon family relationships and other intimate ties, which could transcend even the bitter political rivalries within the Italian cities or between one city and another. Associated with this was a lack of a genuinely competitive spirit; this was not a mental world Weber or Tawney would perhaps have found it easy to describe.

The principles according to which a banking company should operate were enunciated with supreme clarity in Leon Battista Alberti's *Della Famiglia*, begun in 1432, the work of a highly gifted *uomo universale* who was also a member of a leading banking dynasty:

> Just look at the house of Alberti: as it excels in all professions, so also in this one, pecuniary though it might be, it has flourished in western Europe and in many different parts of the world, always with honesty and integrity; hence we have acquired no little fame among all nations and a pre-eminence not incommensurate with our merits. For in all our business dealings no one was ever found who would permit even the slightest malpractice. We have always observed the greatest simplicity and the plainest truth in every contract; and thus we have come to be recognised as great merchants both in and outside of Italy, in Spain, in the West, in Syria, in Greece, and in all the ports of the world.[35]

Thus the Alberti (in this idealized picture) retained their strong pride in family, and set alongside it an insistence on honesty; together these were the recipe for success, though Leon Battista also had to admit that it was easier to counsel the employment of relatives than to secure their services. As well, the Alberti had taken care to avoid the mushroom growth which had in the end destroyed the Peruzzi and Bardi.[36] It is noticeable that the Medici were not able to draw into the management of their bank significant numbers of their own relatives; nor did the major partners and managers outside the Medici clan succeed much better in drawing in their own relatives. Indeed, it was the quarrelsome, inefficient management of the latter-day Medici bank, and the lack of central control by a *capo* preoccupied with high politics, that fatally eroded the Medici enterprise at the end of the fifteenth century.

There is no need here to reopen the debate on the fall of the Florentine companies in 1343. That they had greatly over-extended themselves is clear, and that a lesson was learned by later banking enterprises emerges from the more modest scale on which their successors, such as the Alberti and eventually the Medici, were content to operate.[37] Glossy royal or papal accounts were seen increasingly as a liability to be avoided where possible, though politics never ceased to intrude: there was no great reason for the Medici to open a glossy new branch in Milan except to foster political ties with Francesco Sforza, duke of Milan, around 1450.[38] This branch was housed in a magnificent palace presented to the Medici by the duke of Milan, adorned with sculptured medallion portraits of the duke and duchess, so that, as Goldthwaite remarks, 'it seemed more suitable for a diplomatic residence than for the working headquarters of a firm'. Indeed, it was arguably neglect of the traditional pursuit of profit which helped bring down the bank in 1494, after decades during which Lorenzo the Magnificent had concentrated his attention on political issues rather than on the family firm.[39]

It would be a mistake to exaggerate the importance of the Medici bank in either Florentine or European affairs. That it was a smaller enterprise than the Peruzzi or Bardi 'super-companies' is well known. Its capital formation in 1451, of 72,000 florins, was not in fact so exceptional: Goldthwaite cites a figure of 53,600 florins for the company of Carlo Strozzi in 1367, and Filippo Strozzi was worth about 70,000 florins when he died in 1491.[40] Indeed, what is more striking than the slight lead obtained by the Medici over other Florentine banks is the large number of banking and trading enterprises overall, so that nearly 140 Florentine firms can be identified operating in late fifteenth-century Lyons. In other words, the Medici were the largest, but not gigantic, fish in a well-stocked and capacious pool. Goldthwaite points out provocatively that 'the history of international banking and commerce in Medicean Florence could be written without so much as mentioning the Medici – and such a study would be a healthy corrective to the current historiographical situation'.[41]

Still, it is the Medici who have attracted the attention of both political and business historians, and their firm will have to be used as an example for want of anything more 'typical'. The Medici display the same diversification into manufacture as so many of the earlier Florentine banks: from 1431, they possessed a wool workshop, opening a second workshop in 1439.[42] This was a period when Florentine woollen manufactures had long passed their peak, and it is not surprising to find them investing also in silk production, acquiring a majority share in what proved a profitable undertaking. In 1441 the two wool shops accounted for one tenth of the assets of the Medici bank, and the silk workshop another tenth. As late as 1491 Lorenzo de'Medici was still prepared to invest in the Florentine wool industry, and it seems that even in the difficult years following his death, French invasion, Medicean exile and revolution under Savonarola profits from the investment accumulated. Demand for silk was particularly healthy in the fifteenth century, and the industry had moved far beyond its early west European base of Lucca; but, whereas Florence had once been master of the woollen industry in Italy, it now had to fight for its place in the silk markets alongside not only Lucca but Genoa and non-Italian centres. The Medici supported not just their own silk workshop but the silk shops of other Florentine entrepreneurs; in 1477 two chests of velvet silk were sent by the Medici to Naples, but none of the silk was actually produced in the Medici workshop.[43] (So too Filippo Strozzi's company was closely involved in the wool trade, and happily bought and sold in transactions with independent workshops, which the firm never sought to monopolize).[44] De Roover concluded that the industrial investments of the Medici 'never yielded more than a small fraction of the total profits derived from business ventures'.[45] Of course, some of the profits of overseas branches were derived from sales of cloth, but the contrast between the profits of the workshops and the profits drawn from banking activities (understood in the widest sense) is striking: between 1397 and 1420 banking and foreign trade produced 143,348 florins, whereas the woolshops produced 8,472 florins, a mere 5.5% of gross profits.[46] Between 1420 and 1435 the revenue from the woolshop accounted for just over 3% of profits; over the next fifteen years, taking the silk shop into account as well, the textile manufacturing arm was producing 10% of profits. Yet these were not negligible sums, and it would be wrong to be misled into ignoring them by over-stressing the massive profits from banking and general trade, which were themselves sizeable at this period.

What was crucial was an ability to adapt to changing economic circumstances, in the aftermath of plague and sudden population loss. Increasingly, there is a tendency to discard the gloomy view of an 'economic depression of the Renaissance' once forcefully presented by Roberto Lopez and Harry Miskimin, and to lay stress on the process of economic reconstruction that characterized the late fourteenth and fifteenth centuries.[47] New economic relationships had to be formed in an age of growing regional specialization; it was also a period in which periodic shortages of specie wreaked havoc in the money markets, especially in regions such as Catalonia where conservative economic policies were generally pursued and innovation came only late. Florence too was caught up in this drastic readjustment, as the shrinking of wool production amply reveals; traditional trading links towards Flanders were compromised by economic difficulties in the Flemish cloth towns, so that they now had little to offer the Florentines in the way of commodities. The bullion famine affected Flanders more, perhaps, than other regions of Europe.[48] Indeed, one effect was the decline of business through Bruges, which would lose its importance as a money market, having already lost its importance as an exchange centre in international trade. Bruges was thus in the long term no more a success story for the Medici than it was for other investors, and the closure of the Bruges office of the Medici bank by Lorenzo de'Medici in 1480 put to an end a history of growing losses.[49]

On the positive side, the lack of heavy dependence on Flanders and England for wool and cloth resulted in a greater diversification of trading enterprises, as Florentines searched for raw materials in areas that had earlier been relatively neglected, such as southern Italy and Spain, both of which were experiencing a massive expansion of wool production. The increasing complexity of international exchanges kept bankers busy, and often in profit, but it also obviated the need for dangerously intimate relations with foreign rulers such as the king of England, who could soak up a perilously high proportion of working capital; a broad portfolio of investments and a broad spread of branches meant that a crisis in the fortunes of one agency did not spell disaster for the entire enterprise, as had occurred in the age of the Bardi and Peruzzi. This process of dispersal meant that no single bank tended to grow disproportionately large, and none was able nor sought to dominate the market in (say) raw wool.

In any case, the Medici found that opportunities for growth were not always as they had anticipated. The successful establishment of the Lyons fairs by Louis XI of France diverted business away from Geneva, and the 1460s saw the Medici reacting carefully to changed circumstances, maintaining offices for a while in both centres, until it became obvious that Lyons was the victor.[50] An early example of failure to make headway is provided by the history of the Naples branch, never itself an important branch, but one which must have seemed, in the light of past Florentine penetration of the region, to hold out promising opportunities; in some years before the liquidation in 1426 the branch made an apparent loss, while political upheaval in the south Italian kingdom made prospects increasingly uncertain. There was a long delay before a Naples office was reopened, in 1471, and here political motives may well have played an important part, with Lorenzo de'Medici hoping to keep an eye on the unpredictable King Ferrante of Naples. If that was the intention, returns were poor indeed, for Ferrante joined the papal conflict with Medicean Florence that followed the Pazzi conspiracy in 1478, and only after a famous visit to the king of Naples did Lorenzo restore peace – and his bank branch. In the meantime Medici assets were confiscated, and the branch continued to be a source of concern even after radical reorganization under the name 'Lorenzo Tornabuoni and Company'.[51] It seems likely that lending to the royal court and the nobility risked going out of control. And here, indeed, is the core of the problem, for after 1479 Lorenzo the Magnificent was determined to maintain cordial relations with Ferrante of Naples. Any losses suffered in Naples were a part payment for the peace of Italy, which was soon to fall apart, with disastrous results not merely for the royal house of Naples but for the Medici and their bank, when the French invaded Italy in 1494–5.[52]

It remains to ask how developments in Italian banking influenced the growth of 'capitalism'. Historians of banking have been understandably reluctant to pursue the term capitalism very far; de Roover used it to indicate primarily the search for profitability. Goldthwaite has rightly stressed the lack of emphasis on competition among firms and the absence of any real preoccupation with the exercise of power, a statement that is strengthened rather than weakened by the gradually declining performance of the Medici bank in the age of Lorenzo il Magnifico. A more elaborate definition, which has been pursued here, would seek to examine the role of the banks in investment in manufacturing, or in other profit-making activities which would result in the mobilization of a significant workforce. Here it is difficult to show that the Florentine banks had a special role. What is striking about them is precisely the way that the Peruzzi and Medici saw investment in cloth workshops as one among many viable business opportunities; but if the viability of the enterprise was called into question, then they were prepared to shift their investments to other types of activity. This largely reflects the fragmented system of cloth production, which in any case was subject to guild intervention. The creation of cloth factories was unthinkable, while the contraction of markets for the fine Florentine cloths of the 1330s necessitated a shift towards investment in silk workshops, in the age of the Medici. But it was not the Medici who were responsible for the expansion of Florentine silk production. Arguably the Bardi and Peruzzi had played a significant role in the provision of English wool, when available, to Florentine looms, but that was only for a brief period, and represented the apogee of an already well-developed woollen cloth industry on which the bankers drew, as merchants seeking to satisfy the needs of foreign consumers, but which they had not

VI

32

really created. This is not to deny their crucial role in servicing the long-distance trade in wool, cloth and grain, and their success in gaining access to the most prestigious, if also the most penurious, purchasers in Europe. The commercial and financial network they created provided an increasingly vital back-up for the trading activities of their fellow-Italians and of native merchants throughout Europe. Thus they did not in fact mould or seek to mould the shape of the European and Mediterranean economy in the late Middle Ages, even though within specific regions, notably England and southern Italy, they helped stimulate production of foodstuffs and raw materials for export. Striking commercial expansion was, indeed, possible without the existence of comparable financial networks, as the example of the German Hansa reveals.[53] But whereas the Baltic and North Sea emerged as a well-integrated set of markets fairly closely co-ordinated by the Hansa, the Mediterranean and western Europe for any number of reasons lacked similar integration and co-ordination. One of the elements that did provide a degree of wider co-ordination was the Italian financial network which, as has been seen, existed not simply to service the specific needs of cities such as Florence, but to provide valuable expertise in the handling of money, the rapid transmission of funds and the bulk purchase of wool, grain and so on. It was the pursuit of these specific skills that was the source of success for the Florentine companies in their heyday.

Notes

1 For the Genoese banks, see Roberto S. Lopez, *La prima crisi della banca in Genova* (Milan, 1956).
2 Richard A. Goldthwaite, 'The Medici Bank and the World of Florentine Capitalism', *Past and Present*, 114 (1987), pp. 3–31.
3 E. Jordan, *De mercatoribus camerae apostolicae saeculo XIII* (Rennes, 1909); W. E. Lunt, *Papal Revenues in the Middle Ages*, 2 vols. (New York, 1934).
4 There is a growing literature on usury; see, e.g., B. Nelson, *The Idea of Usury. From Tribal Brotherhood of Universal Otherhood*, 2nd edn (Chicago, 1969); J. T. Noonan, *The Scholastic Analysis of Usury* (Cambridge, Mass., 1957); J. Le Goff, 'The Usurer and Purgatory', in *The Dawn of Modern Banking*, Center for Medieval and Renaissance Studies, University of California, Los Angeles (New Haven, 1979).
5 See, e.g., David Abulafia, *The Two Italies. Economic Relations between the Norman Kingdom of Sicily and the Northern Communes* (Cambridge, 1977), pp. 272–3.
6 See the incisive comments of Edwin Hunt in his *The Medieval Super-Companies. A Study of the Peruzzi Company of Florence* (Cambridge, 1994).
7 The problem of exchange rates has been raised in a critique by R. Mueller of P. Spufford's exchange tables: 'The Spufford Thesis on Foreign Exchange. The

Evidence of Exchange Rates', *Journal of European Economic History*, 24 (1995), pp. 121–9, as against P. Spufford, W. Wilkinson and S. Tolley, *Handbook of Medieval Exchange*, Royal Historical Society (London, 1986).

8 Raymond de Roover, *The Rise and Decline of the Medici Bank, 1397–1494* (Cambridge, Mass., 1963), p. 266.

9 Edward D. English, *Enterprise and Liability in Sienese Banking, 1230–1350* (Cambridge, Mass., 1988).

10 T. Blomquist, 'The Dawn of Banking in an Italian Commune: Thirteenth-Century Lucca', in *The Dawn of Modern Banking*, R. W. Kaeuper, *Bankers to the Crown. The Riccardi of Lucca and Edward I* (Princeton, N.J., 1973).

11 Melis was ever conscious of the importance of links between Spain and Tuscany. See *inter alia* F. Melis, *Industria e commercio nella Toscana medievale*, ed. M. Tangheroni and B. Dini (Florence, 1989); F. Melis, *I mercanti italiani nell'Europa medievale e rinascimentale*, ed. H. Kellenbenz and L. Frangoni (Florence, 1990); F. Melis, *L'economia fiorentina del Rinascimento*, ed. B. Dini (Florence, 1984); but especially the collected studies in F. Melis, *Mercaderes italianos en España* (Seville, 1976).

12 G. Yver, *Le commerce et les marchands dans l'Italie méridionale au XIIIe et au XIVe siècle* (Paris, 1903).

13 A. Leone, *Il giornale del Banco Strozzi a Napoli (1473)*, Fonti e Documenti per la Storia del Mezzogiorno d'Italia, vol. 7 (Naples, 1981).

14 L. Poliakov, *Jewish Bankers and the Holy See*, transl. M. Kochan (London, 1977).

15 Goldthwaite, 'The Medici Bank'; see also J. Day, *The Medieval Market Economy* (Oxford, 1987), a collection of Day's articles.

16 A. Sapori, *I libri di commercio dei Peruzzi* (Milan, 1934); A. Sapori, *The Italian Merchant in the Middle Ages* (New York, 1970), lacking however, the fine bibliography of the original French edition.

17 De Roover, *Rise and Decline*.

18 Raymond de Roover, *The Medici Bank. Its Organization, Management, Operations and Decline* (New York, 1948).

19 Raymond de Roover, 'New Interpretations of the History of Banking', *Journal of World History*, 2 (1954), p. 38, repr. in Raymond de Roover, *Business, Banking and Economic Thought in Late Medieval and Early Modern Europe*, ed. Julius Kirshner (Chicago, 1974), p. 200; this volume is a collection of de Roover's most important articles.

20 On this, see Hunt, *Medieval Super-Companies*.

21 *Ibid.*, pp. 156–229.

22 *Ibid.*, pp. 128, 259–60.

23 A useful account of these conflicts can be found in E. Léonard, *Les Angevins de Naples* (Paris, 1954), and, for the Catalan-Aragonese in Sicily, see C. Backman, *The Decline and Fall of Medieval Sicily* (Cambridge, 1995); also David Abulafia, 'Southern Italy and the Florentine Economy, 1265–1370', *Economic History Review*, 2nd ser., 33 (1981).

24 For wool, see E. Power, *The Wool Trade in English Medieval History*, ed. M. M. Postan (Oxford, 1941).

25 Hunt revises the classic interpretation of A. Sapori, *La crisi delle compagnie mercantili dei Bardi e dei Peruzzi* (Florence, 1926).

26 Raymond de Roover, 'The Organisation of Trade', in *Cambridge Economic History of Europe*, vol. III (Cambridge, 1963), p. 86, table II.

27 Abulafia, 'Southern Italy', p. 385.

28 For the involvement of the Florentine banks in the grain trade to Tunis, see David Abulafia, 'Catalan Merchants and the Western Mediterranean', *Viator*, 16 (1985),

34

pp. 233–5; David Abulafia, 'A Tyrrhenian Triangle. Tuscany, Sicily, Tunis, 1276–1300', *Studi di storia economica toscana nel Medioevo e nel Rinascimento in memoria di Federigo Melis*, Biblioteca del Bollettino storico pisano, Collana storica, vol. 33 (Pisa, 1987), pp. 53–75.

29 H. Hoshino, 'The Rise of the Florentine Woollen Industry in the Fourteenth Century', in N. B. Harte and K. G. Ponting (eds.), *Cloth and Clothing in Medieval Europe. Essays in Memory of Professor E. M. Carus-Wilson* (London, 1983), pp. 184–204.

30 Hunt, *Medieval Super-Companies*, pp. 51–7, 67, 170–2.

31 Raymond de Roover, 'The Story of the Alberti Company of Florence, 1302–1348, as Revealed in its Account Books', *Business History Review*, 32 (1958), pp. 14–59, repr. in de Roover, *Business, Banking*, pp. 39–84.

32 Hunt, *Medieval Super-Companies*, pp. 184–5.

33 For the Buonaccorsi, see M. Luzzati, *Giovanni Villani e la compagnia dei Buonaccorsi* (Rome, 1971).

34 On Forzetti, see Abulafia, 'Tyrrhenian Triangle', pp. 70–2.

35 E. Cochrane and J. Kirshner, *The Renaissance*, Readings in Western Civilization, vol. 5 (Chicago, 1986), p. 95.

36 For the early history of this firm, see de Roover, 'The Story of the Alberti Company'.

37 For banking in the era after the fall of the Bardi and Peruzzi, see in particular Y. Renouard, *Les relations des papes d'Avignon et les compagnies commerciales et bancaires de 1316 à 1378* (Paris, 1942); Y. Renouard, *Recherches sur les compagnies commerciales et bancaires utilisées par les papes d'Avignon avant le Grand Schisme* (Paris, 1942); the same author's collected *Etudes d'histoire médiévale*, 2 vols. (Paris, 1968), also offer a great deal of germane material.

38 Goldthwaite, 'The Medici Bank', pp. 29–30.

39 De Roover, *Rise and Decline*, pp. 365–9.

40 Goldthwaite, 'The Medici Bank', p. 16.

41 *Ibid.*, p. 17; cf. Goldthwaite's earlier remarks too, pp. 4–6.

42 De Roover, *Rise and Decline*, pp. 174–89.

43 *Ibid.*, pp. 186–93.

44 For the Strozzi in the fifteenth century, and particularly their operations in Naples, see Richard Goldthwaite, *Private Wealth in Renaissance Florence* (Princeton, N.J., 1968), pp. 31–73, especially pp. 53–7.

45 De Roover, *Rise and Decline*, p. 193.

46 *Ibid.*, p. 47.

47 R. S. Lopez and H. Miskimin, 'The Economic Depression of the Renaissance', *Economic History Review*, 2nd ser., 14 (1962), pp. 408–26; the most successful case-study to challenge the depression argument is that of S. R. Epstein, *An Island for Itself. Economic Development and Social Change in Late Medieval Sicily* (Cambridge, 1992).

48 J. Day, 'The Great Bullion Famine of the Fifteenth Century', *Past and Present*, 79 (1978), pp. 3–54, repr. in Day, *Market Economy*.

49 De Roover, *Rise and Decline*, pp. 346–57.

50 *Ibid.*, pp. 279–311.

51 *Ibid.*, pp. 254–61.

52 For the political setting, see David Abulafia (ed.), *The French Descent into Renaissance Italy, 1494–95* (Aldershot, 1995).

53 P. Dollinger, *The German Hansa* (London, 1970).

VII

Cittadino e *denizen*: mercanti mediterranei a Southampton e a Londra*

In apparenza, per lo storico dell'economia medievale vi sono pochi argomenti di studio più promettenti dei rapporti fra l'Inghilterra e il Mediterraneo. Le eccellenti risorse del Public Record Office di Londra possono, in teoria, essere abbinate alle fonti notarili di Genova o di Firenze, e rivelare uno stretto rapporto che risale ad un'epoca ancor più antica dell'apertura, verso il 1277, dello stretto di Gibilterra ai vascelli genovesi. Malgrado ciò, negli ultimi trent'anni, i contatti con il Mediterraneo sono stati oggetto di scarsa attenzione, rispetto al lavoro imponente dedicato all'economia agraria. Secondo Postan, i mercanti italiani ebbero un impatto abbastanza limitato sull'economia inglese[1]. È vero inoltre che le dimensioni modeste delle città, Londra esclusa, rendeva la loro incidenza sulle campagne circostanti più limitata che in Francia o in Germania.

Purtroppo, il diradarsi delle ricerche sul commercio internazionale

* I miei vivi ringraziamenti a Stefan Epstein ed a Rita Astuti per la loro collaborazione nella preparazione della versione italiana del mio testo.

[1] M.M. Postan, *Medieval Trade and Finance*, Cambridge, 1973, pp. 335-41; vedi M. Prestwich, *Italian Merchants in Late Thirteenth and Early Fourteenth Century England*, in *The Dawn of Modern Banking*, Center for Medieval and Renaissance Studies, University of California, Los Angeles, New Haven, 1979, pp. 77-104 [edizione italiana: *L'alba della banca. Le origini del sistema bancario tra medioevo ed età moderna*, Bari, 1982]. Altri contributi importanti sui banchieri italiani in Inghilterra sono: E.B. Fryde, *The Deposits of Hugh Despenser the Younger with Italian Bankers*, in «Economic History Review», ser. 2, III (1950-1), pp. 344-62; A. Beardwood, *Alien Merchants in England, 1350-1377*, Cambridge, Mass., 1931; E. Russell, *The Societies of the Bardi and Peruzzi and their Dealings with Edward III*, in *Finance and Trade under Edward III*, ed. G. Unwin, Manchester, 1918; C. Johnson, *An Italian Financial House in the Fourteenth Century*, in «Transactions of the St Albans and Hertfordshire Architectural and Archaeological Society», n.s., I (1901-2), pp. 230-4; R. Kaeuper, *Bankers to the Crown: The Riccardi of Lucca and Edward I*, Princeton, N.J., 1973, R. Goldthwaite, *Italian bankers in medieval England*, in «Journal of European Economic History», II (1973); R. Kaeuper, *The Frescobaldi of Florence and the English Crown*, in «Studies in Medieval and Renaissance History», X (1973); G. Holmes, *Florentine Merchants and England*, in «Economic History Review», ser. 2, XIII (1960-1); ai quali si deve aggiungere M.D. O'Sullivan, *Italian Merchant Bankers* in cui la prospettiva è altrove: sui mercanti mediterranei residenti in Inghilterra ed attivi nel commercio fra Inghilterra e Mediterraneo, o fra Inghilterra ed i suoi vicini atlantici. Utile per i secoli XIII e XIV è T. H. Lloyd, *Alien Merchants in England in the High Middle Ages*, Hassocks, Sussex, 1982, oltre che con il suo *The English Wool Trade in the Middle Ages*, Cambridge, 1977. Per il secolo XVI, vedi G.D. Ramsay, *The undoing of the Italian Mercantile Colony in Sixteenth-century London*, in *Textile History and Economic History. Essays in Honour of Miss Julia de Lacy Mann*, ed. N.B. Harte and K.G. Ponting, Manchester, 1973, pp. 22-49.

dell'Inghilterra ha provocato un grave sbilanciamento negli studi. Londra, in particolare, è stata trascurata: una trascuratezza ampiamente compensata, d'altronde, dall'esistenza di studi su gruppi di mercanti stranieri, quali i castigliani e i ragusei, in tutta l'Inghilterra[2]. Esistono poi ricerche eccellenti su Southampton, come lo studio di Ruddock sui mercanti italiani[3], e l'indagine archeologica sulla città di Platt, che molto ha contribuito a chiarire i rapporti sociali all'interno dell'élite mercantile[4]. In questa comunicazione, dunque — anche per mancanza di tempo — esporrò soprattutto i risultati relativi a Southampton, per quanto piccola fosse quella città. Mi propongo dapprima di descrivere la crescita di Southampton nel suo complesso; poi di esaminare più da vicino la comunità locale degli italiani, e di osservare la loro integrazione nella più ampia comunità di mercanti; infine di analizzare ancora altri imprenditori del Mediterraneo, che in gran numero scelsero Londra come base di attività, per verificare fino a che punto l'immagine di Southampton possa essere trasferita altrove. Si sosterrà che la fluidità delle condizioni sociali delle città inglesi facilitava l'insediamento e, ove lo si desiderasse, l'integrazione dei mercanti stranieri nella società urbana locale, in modo che uno o due forestieri, divenuti cittadini di un centro urbano inglese, potevano aspirare persino alle cariche più elevate. Cittadini inglesi potevano far sposare le proprie figlie con stranieri, e questi potevano intrecciare legami personali con chiese locali e finanche con signorie di campagna.

Si tratta di una situazione interessante, perché recenti ricerche suggeriscono che alcuni gruppi di mercanti forestieri prosperarono lontano da casa sulla base della loro identità collettiva di stranieri, distinti per cultura e probabilmente per lingua dalla società in cui si insediarono — lo studio ambizioso di Philip Curtin sullo «scambio interculturale» tenta di legare insieme l'intero globo, ed è ozioso suggerire che proprio l'Inghilterra sia rappresentativa di più vaste esperienze[5]. Tuttavia, il processo esaminato in questa sede è, in un certo senso, quello della *perdita* dell'identità di gruppo, dell'assimilazione in una società ospite, e voglio semplicemente aggiungere che esso merita altrettanta attenzione della *conservazione* di un'identità di gruppo da parte di armeni, ebrei e altri.

Southampton

Benché nel XV secolo le fortune di Southampton dipendessero in larga misura dagli italiani, non furono solo loro che la resero importante. Southampton crebbe nella sua scala odierna solo dopo la conquista

---

[2] G. Williams, *Medieval London, from Commune to Capital*, Londra, 1963, parla poco degli italiani.
[3] A. Ruddock, *Italian Merchants and Shipping in Southampton, 1270-1600*, Southampton, 1951.
[4] C. Platt, *Medieval Southampton, the Port and Trading Community*, Londra, 1973.
[5] P. Curtin, *Cross-Cultural Trade in World History*, Cambridge, 1984 [edizione italiana: *Mercanti. Commercio e cultura dall'antichità al XIX secolo*, Roma-Bari, 1988].

normanna dell'Inghilterra nel 1066, ed i suoi stretti legami con la Francia si evincono dall'esistenza di una delle principali vie medievali, la via Francese, *French Street*[6]. Vi erano traffici commerciali e di passeggeri molto intensi con la Normandia, la Guascogna e le Isole Normanne, tutte rette per un certo periodo dalla Corona inglese. Un fattore caratterizzante la comunità mercantile inglese (anche a Londra) è l'esistenza di un patriziato commerciale molto mutevole. Le grandi famiglie di Southampton del XII e dei primi del XIII secolo, come i de Puteo, non sopravvissero fino ai secoli XIV e XV; il tasso medio di sopravvivenza, se così possiamo chiamarlo, era di circa tre generazioni. Apparivano nuovi patrizi, ed i loro predecessori cedevano loro il potere in città e il comando sulle rotte commerciali; così, nel tardo Trecento, dopo una disastrosa incursione francese (1339) e le distruzioni della Peste Nera, emerse un nuovo patriziato, guidato da famiglie quali i Fetplace, i James e i Payn[7]. E ciò perché il vecchio patriziato trasferì, lentamente e di propria iniziativa, i suoi interessi altrove — soprattutto nella terra con l'acquisto (per esempio) di tenute rurali sui confini meridionali dello Hampshire.

I nuovi patrizi erano spesso immigrati. Ve n'erano provenienti dalla Cornovaglia, dall'Inghilterra meridionale e dal Galles. Nel frattempo i borghesi più ricchi aspiravano a posizioni sociali più elevate. Nel 1430 William Soper, un mercante di primo piano che aveva legami commerciali con il Mediterraneo, intrattenne il capitano e i patroni delle galee fiorentine nella sua casa di campagna a 5 km da Southampton. Così, persino, l'uomo d'affari veniva attratto dalla vita del gentiluomo di campagna lontano dalle attività della città.

La mobilità della società di Southampton (ma analoghe risultanze si hanno per Londra) va sottolineata. Fino alla metà del XV secolo, italiani e spagnoli potevano essere accolti in Southampton virtualmente alla pari: potevano acquisire la cittadinanza locale, come potevano ottenere la nazionalità inglese tramite lettere regie di naturalizzazione (*denization*)[8]; ammogliavano la prole con cittadini inglesi, erano ammessi alle alte cariche cittadine. In un certo senso, gran parte del patriziato di Southampton era di origine forestiera: forse non italiana, dal momento che in molti casi proveniva dalle isole Normanne, dalla Cornovaglia o da altre zone che facevano capo a rotte commerciali che partivano a raggera da Southampton. È un'immagine familiare anche in altre città d'Europa: una società relativamente aperta che accoglieva nei ranghi dell'aristocrazia cittadina coloro che erano in possesso di mezzi finanziari, con maggior riguardo alle loro capacità economiche che alle loro origini. Alla metà del Quattrocento, è vero, vi è un abbandono di questo atteggiamento. I tentativi dei mercanti inglesi di egemonizzare i rapporti com-

---

[6] Platt, *Medieval Southampton* cit., pp. 7, 48-50.
[7] *Ivi*, pp. 92-130, 238-9, 246-7, 254-5.
[8] Su questo, vedi la discussione di A. Beardwood, *Mercantile Antecedents of the English Naturalization Laws*, in «Medievalia et humanistica», XVI (1964), pp. 64-76, e di C.T. Allmand, *A Note on Denization in Medieval England, ibid.*, XVII (1966), pp. 127-8.

merciali che legavano Southampton al Mediterraneo vennero accompagnati da vessazioni sui mercanti italiani residenti in Southampton[9]. Forme simili di xenofobia erano tutt'altro che tipiche di quel periodo.

Va sottolineata anche un'altra caratteristica di Southampton — ossia che era una città piccola secondo i parametri mediterranei: meno di 1000 abitanti verso il 1100, forse 2500 nel 1300, soltanto 1600 nel 1377, per crescere molto lentamente fino a quasi 2000 nel 1524[10]. Di conseguenza la richiesta locale di importazioni dal Mediterraneo era piuttosto ridotta. Southampton era importante come emporio per due ragioni. Fungeva, a volte, da porto sussidiario di Londra, per la convenienza che esportatori italiani e spagnoli avevano di abbinare una sosta in un porto inglese con una visita nelle Fiandre. L'accesso a Londra era limitato dai banchi di sabbia della foce del Tamigi, e in ogni caso portava a deviare dalla rotta di Fiandra; alcune navi italiane o spagnole attraccavano a Sandwich, nel Kent, più vicina a Londra di Southampton; ma Sandwich non diventò mai un centro importante del commercio o dell'insediamento italiani. Nel tardo Trecento e nel Quattrocento Southampton acquisì ulteriori motivi di attrazione: dava accesso diretto ai villaggi lanieri del Cotswold a ovest di Oxford; alimentava un commercio vivace di tessuti inglesi e talora anche di lana grezza[11].

Tuttavia per i mercanti inglesi di Southampton il commercio principale era quello locale di generi alimentari, di metalli (in particolare lo stagno della Cornovaglia), di tessuti per il mercato interno; gli italiani e gli spagnoli erano decisamente più coinvolti nel commercio di transito, soprattutto per Londra, ad esempio, nella vendita di spezie orientali, a consumatori ben più distanti dello Hampshire. I mercanti inglesi mantenevano una complessa rete di comunicazioni nell'Inghilterra meridionale, fino alle cittadine dell'interno, come Oxford e Marlborough e ai porti della Cornovaglia e del Devon. I mercanti locali maneggiavano certamente grosse quantità di merci portate per mare dal continente; carichi di vino francese rifornivano i mercati dell'Inghilterra meridionale, e soprattutto questi mercati dipendevano da italiani e catalani per il trasporto di allume dal Levante fino ai centri tessili inglesi. A Southampton i Fetplace, i James e i loro soci prendevano in consegna partite di merci italiane, indirizzandole pressoché ovunque, eccetto che a Londra. Nel 1439-40 Walter Fetplace, un buon amico degli italiani di Southampton, inviò grosse partite di guado, arrivate su navi genovesi, verso alcune cittadine di provincia; ma non spedì quasi mai delle merci a Londra[12]. La divisione di ruoli tra forestieri e autoctoni funzionò piuttosto bene nel XIV secolo e durante gran parte del XV, finché i Payns e altri mercanti di Southampton non tentarono di impadronirsi del controllo degli affari dei forestieri.

[9] Ruddock, *Italian Merchants*, cit., pp. 162-86.
[10] Platt, *Medieval Southampton*, cit., pp. 262-3.
[11] O. Coleman, *Trade and prosperity in the fifteenth century: some aspects of the trade of Southampton*, in «Economic History Review», ser. 2, XVI (1963/4), pp. 9-22.
[12] Platt, *Medieval Southampton*, cit., pp. 156-7, 238-9.

L'epoca migliore per gli affari italiani a Southampton è il tardo XIV e il primo XV secolo. I primi tentativi di commerciare attraverso questo porto da parte di veneziani, maiorchini e fiorentini furono un fallimento: le prime galee veneziane raggiunsero Southampton nel 1319, ma scoppiarono disordini tra i marinai e gli abitanti della città[13]. Così gli inizi del commercio italiano a Southampton non furono di buon auspicio. Neppure la crisi dei Bardi e Peruzzi, di cui Edoardo III era in parte responsabile, funse da stimolo agli affari italiani in Inghilterra; i genovesi (nonché i catalani) fungevano in larga misura da portatori di lana per conto dei mercanti fiorentini; e il crollo delle maggiori ditte commerciali di Firenze in Inghilterra provocò di conseguenza un'ulteriore contrazione del commercio italiano con l'isola[14]. Il commercio tra Italia e Inghilterra, come dice Ruddock, aveva raggiunto il suo punto più basso alla vigilia della Peste Nera[15]. I genovesi si accorsero solo gradatamente delle opportunità create dal ritiro fiorentino; insediandosi al loro posto ottennero un ampio controllo delle esportazioni di lana nel tardo Trecento, e si interessarono lentamente anche della produzione tessile inglese, man mano che questa si espandeva. Passando dall'uso delle galee a quello di *cocche* e *caracche*, furono in grado di abbassare i tassi di nolo per merci voluminose come l'allume e la lana; erano pure costretti a far uso di Southampton o di una stazione costiera simile, perché le loro navi erano troppo grosse per affrontare la lunga foce del Tamigi[16]. Nel 1378 vi furono persino dei progetti di creare un fondaco (*staple*) per l'Europa settentrionale a Southampton, che sarebbe così diventata il luogo di passaggio stabile di tutta la lana di proprietà genovese. L'emissario genovese che si recò da Edoardo III con questo progetto in mente fu assassinato nelle vie di Londra da mercanti inglesi, che temevano una riduzione del giro d'affari nella capitale e nello *staple* già esistente a Calais[17]. Queste difficoltà furono accentuate dai disordini della Guerra dei Cent'Anni, ove l'aiuto genovese ai francesi era fonte di notevole imbarazzo per quei mercanti genovesi che miravano a commerciare con l'Inghilterra. Ma egualmente le difficoltà d'accesso ai Paesi Bassi portarono i veneziani a ristabilire i convogli marittimi per l'Inghilterra nel 1394, con una spiccata preferenza per Southampton rispetto a Londra; a loro si unirono la neonata marina fiorentina, i catalani e a un certo punto persino delle navi napoletane[18].

È ora di esaminare più attentamente le carriere di alcuni degli immigrati italiani di Southampton. È chiaro che vi erano molti mercanti che si fermavano per poco; ci interessano di più i domiciliati a lungo termine, il nucleo della comunità italiana. Verso il 1400 questa consisteva di

---

[13] Ruddock, *Italian Merchants*, cit., pp. 22-8.
[14] A. Sapori, *La crisi delle compagnie mercantili dei Bardi e dei Peruzzi*, Firenze, 1926.
[15] Ruddock, *op. cit.*, pp. 35-6.
[16] *Ivi*, p. 36.
[17] B. Z. Kedar, *Merchants in Crisis: Genoese and Venetian Men of Affairs and the Fourteenth-Century Depression*, New Haven, 1976, pp. 31-7.
[18] Ruddock, *Italian Merchants*, cit., p. 67.

una dozzina circa di mercanti, senza contare le famiglie e la servitù (che spesso era pure italiana), cosicché la popolazione italiana della città contava tra le 50 e le 100 persone, all'incirca il 5 per cento della popolazione totale[19]. La colonia londinese era certamente molto più ampia, mentre a metà del XV secolo il gruppo di Sandwich contava soltanto 3 o 4 mercanti. A Southampton non pare esservi stata una chiesa degli italiani e neppure, per gran parte del tempo, un console che rappresentasse qualcuno dei tre principali interessati — fiorentini, genovesi e veneziani. Né esisteva un quartiere esclusivamente italiano in quella che era, in ogni caso, una cittadina molto piccola. Il mescolarsi di italiani e inglesi era espresso inoltre nei legami di matrimonio e di amicizia tra stranieri e indigeni, nonché nella frequente naturalizzazione dei forestieri e nella loro partecipazione al governo di Southampton. È ben vero che nel XV secolo il governo regio tentò di imporre un controllo più stretto sui mercanti forestieri, con l'insistere perché abitassero presso un ospite indigeno; ma a Southampton era frequente che mercanti locali ben disposti dichiarassero di ospitare un certo numero di forestieri, anche quando è più che probabile che questi continuassero ad abitare nei propri locali affittati[20]. Là dove invece questa ospitalità aveva effettivamente luogo, pare che essa abbia rafforzato il legame tra indigeno e straniero e portato ad una maggiore cooperazione negli affari.

Osserviamo prima i toscani. Vi sono poche indicazioni di una presenza fiorentina nel Trecento, malgrado l'attività intensa a Londra; i Bardi presero in affitto alcune case in città, ma è nel XV secolo che si rende visibile una presenza costante di fiorentini. In questo periodo essi affittavano generalmente uno dei palazzi più imponenti della cittadina, West Hall[21]. Ma già nei primi anni del Quattrocento i fiorentini stavano varcando il confine che divideva lo straniero dall'indigeno. Bartolomeo Marmora aveva moglie inglese e ottenne delle lettere di naturalizzazione da Enrico V nel 1417; in seguito, la sua vedova sposò un mercante del luogo molto preminente, William Overy[22]. Negli anni '20 Paolo Morelli, di Firenze, succedette al Marmora nella posizione di primo mercante fiorentino a Southampton, guadagnando pure lui il rispetto degli uomini d'affari locali. Sposò una donna italiana, ma visse circa 30 anni in Inghilterra, con base a West Hall in Southampton, e funse da principale agente fiorentino in città. Trattava poche merci a proprio nome, ma maneggiava quantità cospicue di prodotti mediterranei: seta grezza siciliana, tessuti rifiniti, come velluti dell'Italia settentrionale, vino dolce e frutta secca dal Mediterraneo orientale, riso e cotone[23]. In questo senso Morelli è Southampton: le sue attività incarnano le funzioni di questo emporio — spedisce i beni di lusso mediterranei lungo le vie per Londra, permette agli italiani di Londra di perseguire senza distrazioni i propri

---

[19] Ruddock, *Italian Merchants*, cit., pp. 118-31.
[20] *Ivi*, cit., pp. 97-8, 156-8, 190-3.
[21] Platt, *Medieval Southampton*, cit., pp. 269-70.
[22] Ruddock, *Italian Merchants*, cit., pp. 121-2.
[23] *Ivi*, pp. 98-105, 122-3.

fiorenti affari nella capitale. Egli agiva per conto dei veneziani oltre che dei fiorentini, in un periodo, gli anni '40, di traffici ridotti tra Venezia e Southampton; nel 1442 vendette del vino di Andrea Corner veneziano al socio fisso dei mercanti italiani, Walter Fetplace, e ai suoi compagni. Infine, quando commerciava per conto proprio, Paolo Morelli tendeva a seguire le vie segnate dai mercanti inglesi, piuttosto che dagli italiani, in Inghilterra: inviava vino guascone e portoghese alle cittadine dell'Inghilterra meridionale per via di terra, e investiva in viaggi di navi inglesi o portoghesi che ancora non si spingevano in quell'epoca fino al Mediterraneo. Ruddock suggerisce che Morelli era probabilmente il prototipo degli agenti fiorentini in Southampton a quell'epoca[24]. Così i legami, matrimoniali e commerciali, di Antonio Guidotti con la ricca famiglia Huttoft suggeriscono che la ricchezza di questa trovava origine non tanto in affari locali quanto in investimenti italiani[25].

La carriera di Christopher Ambrose esemplifica l'integrazione degli stranieri nella società-ospite. Raggiunta Southampton nel 1462, ben presto egli divenne l'unico agente fiorentino in città; trattava vino, tessuti, cuoio, allume, guado, con un forte interesse per le merci di lusso del Mediterraneo, che vendeva a titolo personale a consumatori nobili. Aveva rapporti con mercanti inglesi delle città meridionali, come Salisbury e Winchester. Mostra così un maggiore interesse nel commercio personale che non Paolo Morelli; ma, da un altro punto di vista, è molto più inglese — nel 1472 si naturalizzò e diventò cittadino a pieno titolo di Southampton. Qui la sua ricchezza e affidabilità gli portarono ulteriori vantaggi, perché nel 1483 fu eletto sceriffo, e in seguito, nel 1486 e nel 1487, tenne la carica più elevata: quella di sindaco (*mayor*)[26]. In effetti, il veneziano Gabriele Corbet era diventato sceriffo un trentennio prima di Ambrose, ma nessun altro italiano sembra essere diventato sindaco. Come Gabriele Corbet, egli visse nella grande casa di *la Chayne*, ma era proprietario di immobili anche in altre zone della cittadina, tra le più ricche e alla moda: si servì della posizione di naturalizzato per acquistare terreni che come straniero non poteva tenere in allodio; lasciò un figlio che continuò a fare affari a Southampton[27].

La comunità genovese a Southampton era più ampia: negli anni '30 vi risiedevano diversi agenti degli Spinola; ben presto si aggiunsero dei Cattaneo e dei Grimaldi. L'insediamento genovese raggiunse il suo apice nel 1458, quando la crisi provocata dalla competizione inglese nel commercio del Levante ebbe come conseguenza il ritiro di diversi fattori genovesi da Southampton[28]. Vi era un forte sentimento antistraniero, generato da una fazione politica che tentava di strappare il governo

[24] Ruddock, *Italian Merchants*, cit., p. 102.
[25] Platt, *Medieval Southampton*, cit., pp. 242-3; vedi anche A. Ruddock, *Antonio Guidotti*, in «Papers and Proceedings of the Hampshire Field Club and Archaeological Society». xv (1941-3), pp. 134-42.
[26] Platt, *op. cit.*, pp. 229-30.
[27] Ruddock, *Italian Merchants*, cit., pp. 160-1; Platt, *op. cit.*, pp. 229-30.
[28] Ruddock, *op. cit.*, pp. 175, 185.

VII

cittadino dalle mani dei Fetplace e dei loro alleati. Gli interessi degli Spinola furono da allora in avanti rappresentati dal solo Benedetto Spinola, ma questi sopravvisse alla tempesta e nel 1485 si naturalizzò dientando cittadino di Southampton. Diventò pure un mercante locale, non molto dissimile nelle sue attività personali dai suoi colleghi inglesi; commerciava lungo le coste meridionali inglesi, fino alla Francia del Nord e alle Fiandre[29].

L'emergere, fin dal 1457, della concorrenza inglese sulle rotte del Levante, segnò l'inizio di un lento declino del commercio italiano attraverso Southampton. È dunque sorprendente trovare una famiglia genovese che mette radici a Southampton proprio in questo periodo: i Marini, che in origine operavano a Londra, compaiono come residenti sulla costa meridionale dal 1481, quando Gioffredo de' Marini affitta una piccola casa per £ 1 l'anno[30]. Ben presto divenne tanto ricco da pagare quasi dieci volte tanto per la residenza un tempo maestosa di precedenti mercanti fiorentini, West Hall, che divenne pertanto la dimora della famiglia. Gioffredo era uno specialista in merci mediterranee di lusso, benché si occupasse pure di coloranti, pesce e altri prodotti dei Paesi Bassi. Dall'Inghilterra esportava naturalmente tessuti, oltre che cuoio e stagno o peltro. Al contrario di Morelli, dunque, si concentrò sul commercio in proprio; vi sono scarsi indizi che fosse agente di qualcun altro. Nel 1500 i suoi successori a West Hall, in particolare i cugini Brancino e Niccolò de Egra, indirizzarono i propri favori sui patroni inglesi piuttosto che italiani: e inviavano merci nel Mediterraneo sulle navi locali che dominavano sempre più il commercio marittimo inglese. Vi erano, in poche parole, molte meno navi genovesi in arrivo a Southampton, e inoltre Brancino Marini preferiva le navi inglesi a quelle italiane — tanto più quando si doveva scegliere tra una galea veneziana, con i suoi noli elevati, e una *carrack* inglese. In questo modo Brancino non faceva che imitare i mercanti locali: i beni a bordo della *Charity* e della *Julian*, due navi inglesi in arrivo dal Mediterraneo alla fine del 1504, erano quasi tutti di proprietà di mercanti di Southampton. In effetti lo vediamo sempre più integrato nel mondo commerciale inglese, tanto più in fretta ora che gli Italiani si erano in larga misura ritirati da Southampton. Brancino era l'unico italiano a caricare merci su navi locali in partenza per Bordeaux e altri porti francesi; tra il giorno di S. Michele del 1500 e quello del 1501 si servì di 15 navi inglesi, di 2 iberiche e solo di una nave italiana. Pochi anni dopo, quando il conflitto con la Francia impedì ogni accesso al Mediterraneo, e praticamente interruppe ogni legame con i mercati esteri, Brancino tentò di entrare nel commercio al dettaglio locale; ma non era naturalizzato, e gli stranieri erano rigorosamente esclusi da queste attività. Fu multato per il tentativo di sfidare le leggi cittadine e pare che si sia ritirato, disgustato, a Genova.

Niccolò de Egra, invece, rimase a Southampton, sopravvivendo alla

---

[29] *Ivi*, pp. 125, 183, 216.
[30] Per i Marini, vedi Ruddock, *Italian Merchants*, cit., pp. 232-54.

guerra francese e abitando a West Hall. Intorno al 1516 egli era, per citare Ruddock, «soltanto un piccolo mercante che a malapena sopravviveva»[31] ; ma il lento aumento degli affari e la sua decisione di richiedere la naturalizzazione, nel 1519, lo misero al riparo dal rischio di morire d'inedia. Mantenne stretti legami con le Fiandre e la Francia settentrionale e occidentale, e commerciò con la Bretagna, la Rochelle e Bordeaux. In un caso, una nave tornò dalla Francia carica unicamente del suo guado. Tuttavia mantenne i contatti con italiani a Londra e nel Mediterraneo, come con Antonio Bonvisi di Lucca; commerciava a titolo personale con il Mediterraneo, esportando panni e stagno, acquistando vini dolci — cosicché per i Marini, alla metà degli anni '20, gli affari mediterranei divennero forse di nuovo predominanti. In seguito a complesse riparazioni fatte a sue spese, West Hall diventò rapidamente una delle case più belle della città: era un segno del suo desiderio di far colpo sui cittadini con il suo successo. Morì nel 1544 esprimendo la volontà di essere sepolto nella chiesa di St. John, vicino a West Hall — non nella chiesa degli italiani, perché non ce n'era una nel suo quartiere molto benestante. Anche la moglie, Anna, pare italiana; lasciò al figlio Gerardo una tenuta (*manor*) a Woolston che aveva acquistato nella vecchiaia. Entro il 1600, la famiglia dei Marini era diventata pura *gentry* inglese, radicata a Woolston e ben lontana dagli impegni del commercio mediterraneo[32].

È chiaro che i Marini non sono un caso tipico. Arrivano tardi e commerciano in un periodo in cui vi sono pochi italiani residenti o di passaggio a Southampton. Tuttavia la loro vicenda offre interessanti punti di confronto con quella degli immigrati fiorentini e genovesi di epoche precedenti. È evidente che la naturalizzazione portava con sé dei vantaggi; in un'epoca di difficoltà economiche non sorprende neppure trovare che gli italiani assimilati adottino la medesima strategia commerciale dei mercanti locali — si concentrano su traffici più ristretti, oltre Manica, e fanno largo ricorso a navi inglesi[33]. In effetti, vi sono indizi che gli italiani fossero portati a naturalizzarsi con più entusiasmo proprio nei momenti in cui le loro fortune a Southampton, o altrove, parevano maggiormente minacciate — da concorrenti inglesi, ad esempio.

Abbiamo visto toscani e genovesi; l'esperienza veneziana mostra delle analogie. Gabriel Corbet, uomo di mare, si naturalizzò nel 1431, avendo in precedenza servito Enrico V in mare, forse durante la campagna di Agincourt del 1415. Corbet pare un esempio dell'italiano integra-

[31] Ruddock, *Italian Merchants*, cit., p. 241.
[32] *Ivi*, p. 254.
[33] Cf. l'esperienza dei mercanti di Montpellier, attivi nel commercio da Lynn in Norfolk, al nord di Cambridge, fino alla Norvegia, nel 1304/5: non si può parlare, forse, di una colonia permanente di provenzali-mercatori in Inghilterra, ma la loro presenza, anche temporanea, sulla rotta scandinava indica pienamente come i mercanti mediterranei potevano inserirsi nel commercio atlantico, senza dubbio con l'intento di fornire merci specializzate (per esempio falchi) ad altri imprenditori mediterranei: Lloyd, *Alien Merchants*, cit., p. 94.

to, che mantiene qualche legame commerciale con l'Italia, ma che si occupa altrettanto del commercio della Manica e dell'Atlantico. Non era un mercante di grandi ricchezze, sebbene acquistasse la grande casa detta *la Chayne*, oltre ad altre proprietà urbane[34].I servigi resi alla città culminarono nella sua elezione come sceriffo nel 1453, poco prima di un'esplosione di sentimenti xenofobi, che però si concentrò più a Londra che sulla costa meridionale. In effetti, le sommosse contro gli stranieri del 1456-57 nella capitale, furono di qualche beneficio per Southampton: le galee veneziane cominciarono ad attraccare nel suo porto, e vi fu persino una proposta, d'accordo i capi locali delle comunità italiane in Inghilterra, di trasferire gli affari da Londra a Winchester, ad un tiro di schioppo da Southampton[35]. Negli anni '90, con la nomina di un console distinto per Southampton, i veneziani andarono un passo oltre a quanto avessero mai fatto genovesi o fiorentini. Nel 1495 il console in Southampton, Almoro Gritti, fu catturato da pirati francesi insieme al capitano delle galee veneziane, presso cui si era recato nel porto. Quando venne nominato un nuovo console a Southampton, il senato veneziano scelse Thomas Overy, un inglese; più tardi troviamo un genovese coll'incarico di console veneziano. Il ruolo secondario di Southampton nel commercio atlantico di Venezia e il numero molto ridotto di veneziani residenti furono forse fra i motivi per la nomina di consoli non veneziani[36].

Eccetto che per il consolato veneziano, vi sono scarse prove di una vita organizzata all'interno delle comunità italiane a Southampton. È possibile che i veneziani prediligessero in particolare la chiesa di St. Nicholas, ai margini della città; fu lì che diversi marinai schiavoni furono sepolti verso il 1491 in una tomba piuttosto elaborata, decorata con i simboli degli Evangelisti[37]. Ma la chiesa di S. Nicola non era nulla di più di una piccola e semplice cappella. I fiorentini tentarono di abbellire un'altra chiesa di Southampton, quella di St. John, al centro della zona commerciale, frequentata sia da indigeni che da stranieri: nel 1467 il capitano e i patroni della flotta di galee fiorentine, nonché altri membri della nazione di Firenze in Inghilterra, offersero alla chiesa una serie di arazzi[38].

Come si è visto, gli italiani non abitavano neppure in un quartiere distinto. In genere avevano casa nelle vie sud-occidentali della città, le più vicine al porto, in una zona residenziale dove fra i vicini si contavano le maggiori famiglie del luogo. Dislocati altrove c'erano alcuni artigiani italiani, emigrati da Lucca e da altri luoghi, che venivano ben presto accettati dalla comunità, come membri delle arti. Legati alle famiglie di mercanti italiani, vi erano servitori della medesima origine. Maria Moriana ebbe la sfortuna di avere come padrone una persona

---

[34] Platt, *Medieval Southampton*, cit., p. 268; Ruddock, *Italian Merchants* cit., pp. 160-1.
[35] Ruddock, *Italian Merchants*, cit., pp. 166-9.
[36] *Ivi*, pp. 136-8.
[37] *Ivi*, p. 132.
[38] *Ivi*, pp. 131-2.

inaffidabile come Filippo Cini di Venezia, che prima tentò di venderla e poi cercò di frodarla di £ 20. Esistono le prove pure della presenza di schiavi presso queste famiglie italiane[39].

Quegli italiani che tentavano di diventare cittadini di Southampton trovavano pochi ostacoli; era addirittura più difficile non diventarlo, come dimostrano le vicende di Brancino de' Marini, cui non fu permessa la vendita al dettaglio perché si ostinava a mantenere la condizione di straniero. La cittadinanza e la naturalizzazione erano due cose distinte, ma collegate — l'una locale, l'altra su un piano nazionale. Se un cittadino non era oriundo, generalmente doveva poter dimostrare di essere stato naturalizzato dalla Corona, dopo aver chiesto alla Cancelleria delle lettere di *denization*[40]. Poteva richiedere l'esenzione da tasse e restrizioni imposte agli stranieri, come l'obbligo formale di risiedere presso un ospite indigeno; ma doveva anche pagare le tasse locali — come peraltro tendevano a fare tutti i residenti da lunga data, fossero stranieri o indigeni.

Londra e i mercanti mediterranei

Non si intende inferire che Southampton costituisse un microcosmo di Londra. Le comunità italiane della capitale erano molto più ampie, e rette da consoli; hanno lasciato il segno nella *Lombard Street* della City odierna. Purtroppo non hanno lasciato uguale segno negli studi recenti, e per poter osservare i mercanti di Londra all'opera si dovrà suddividerli per «nazione», e poi concentrarsi su alcuni individui eccezionali. Inoltre, il lavoro recente più sistematico si è occupato di spagnoli e ragusei, non degli italiani; come verrà chiarito, i primi avevano legami molto stretti con i colleghi d'affari italiani[41]. Come in precedenza, il nucleo di questa discussione riguarderà i modi attraverso cui mercanti stranieri di spicco vennero assorbiti dalla comunità ospite di Londra o, talvolta, di Southampton.

Un avvenimento di primaria importanza per il commercio anglo-spagnolo fu, chiaramente, l'apertura dello stretto di Gibilterra verso il 1277[42]. Il risultato non fu soltanto la creazione di un legame marittimo

---

[39] *Ivi*, pp. 127-30.

[40] Beardwood, *Mercantile Antecedents*, cit., pp. 64-76.

[41] Per i castigliani, vedi Wendy Childs, *Anglo-Castilian Trade in the Later Middle Ages*, Manchester, 1978, e T.F. Ruiz, *Castilian Merchants in England, 1248-1350*, in *Order and Innovation in the Middle Ages. Essays in Honor of Joseph R. Strayer*, ed. W.C. Jordan, B. McNab, T.F. Ruiz, Princeton, N.J., 1976, pp. 173-85, ristampato in spagnolo sotto il titolo *Mercaderes castellanos en Inglaterra, 1248-1350*, in T.F. Ruiz, *Sociedad y poder real en Castilla en la Baja Edad Media*, Barcelona, 1981, pp. 201-224. Per i ragusei vedi V. Kostić, *Dubrovnik i Engleska, 1300-1650* (Srpska Akademija Nauka i Umjetnosti, monografie, CDLXXXVIII), Beograd, 1975.

[42] R.S. Lopez, *Majorcans and Genoese on the North Sea Route in the Thirteenth Century*, in «Revue belge de philologie et d'histoire», XXIX (1951), pp. 1163-1179; A. Lewis, *Northern European Sea-Power and the Straits of Gibraltar, 1031-1350*, in *Order and Innovation*, cit., pp. 139-64. Vedi anche la tesi di dottorato di Wendy Burnham su '*The Genoese and the Opening of the Sea-passage to Flanders and England*', Università di Cambridge, 1975.

anglo-italiano e fiammingo-italiano. In diversi modi, anche il commercio della Spagna settentrionale ne beneficiò, perché mercanti baschi della Castiglia settentrionale furono in grado così di inserirsi nel commercio di mediazione a lunga distanza[43]. Si aggiunga il fatto che cominciò a svilupparsi il commercio tra l'Andalusia, nonché la Spagna mediterranea, e l'Inghilterra, che convogliò le frutta di qualità e altre merci di semi-lusso a Southampton e a Londra[44]. Il commercio anglo-iberico differiva da quello anglo-italiano per la mancanza di interessi da parte dei castigliani per la lana inglese. Con l'espansione delle esportazioni castigliane e la contrazione di quelle inglesi, le Fiandre trassero una parte sempre crescente delle loro materie prime dalla Mesta, e non v'è alcun dubbio che fossero le Fiandre, piuttosto che l'Inghilterra, a costituire l'attrazione primaria per il commercio castigliano in direzione della Manica nel tardo XIV e nel XV secolo. La casa-madre settentrionale di castigliani e catalani si trovava a Bruges, e poteva accadere che essi regolassero da lì le loro dispute a Londra, o i negoziati con la Corona inglese[45].

Ciononostante la Corona inglese era ansiosa di concedere favori a singoli mercanti iberici. Andrés Perez de Castrogeriz iniziò a commerciare da Burgos e dalla Guascogna negli anni 1270, si fece conoscere presso la corte regia, e fu inviato in missione diplomatica in Castiglia da re Edoardo II[46]. Perez è un esempio precoce di un mercante iberico residente a Londra, in un arco di quasi 50 anni, protetto e favorito dalla Corona e in grado di ricambiarne i favori: Andrés Perez tentò persino di organizzare dei prestiti a beneficio dello squattrinato sovrano. Alla sua morte, nel 1325, si era trasferita a Londra una seconda famiglia, probabilmente da Vitoria, capace di raggiungere alcuni dei traguardi di Pérez. Fernand Manion diventò cittadino di Londra nel 1324, commerciò con le Fiandre, e in Inghilterra acquisito persino delle terre e prese moglie[47]. Quest'ultimo personaggio è forse eccezionale per il grado di integrazione nella vita inglese, come cittadino di Londra e proprietario fondiario. Childs suggerisce che una delle ragioni per cui le dimensioni dell'impresa iberica restarono modeste è che gli affari erano divisi tra Londra e Southampton, per non parlare di Sandwich e di altri centri minori, per cui nessuna singola grossa comunità si sviluppò in un luogo solo[48]. Tuttavia, gli iberici erano già in grado di ottenere lettere di protezione per alcuni membri della loro «nazione», e persino l'esenzione da alcune tasse a Londra e a Southampton.

---

[43] Per i baschi, J. Heers, *Le commerce des Basques en Méditerranée au XVe siècle (d'après les archives de Gênes)*, in «Bulletin hispanique», LVII (1955), pp. 292-324. R. Collins, *The Basques*, Oxford, 1986, pp. 239-43.

[44] David Abulafia, *Les relations commerciales et politiques entre le royaume de Majorque et l'Angleterre selon la documentation anglaise*, comunicazione al XIII° Congrés de la Historia de la Corona d'Aragò, Palma de Mallorca/Menorca, settembre 1987.

[45] W.B. Watson, *Catalans in the Markets of Northern Europe during the Fifteenth Century*, in *Homenaje a Jaime Vicens Vives*, vol. II, Barcelona, 1967, pp. 787-813.

[46] Childs, *op. cit.*, pp. 229-30; Ruiz, *Castilian Merchants*, cit., pp. 178-9.

[47] Childs, *op. cit.*, pp. 227-8; Ruiz, *op. cit.*, p. 179.

[48] Childs, *op. cit.*, p. 203.

Alla fine del XIII e agli inizi del XIV secolo, i catalani ed i maiorchini spedivano allume e esportavano lana per conto degli italiani, e proprio la loro relativa scomparsa, e la riaffermazione di una presenza castigliana in Inghilterra entro i primi del Quattrocento, rappresentano le due facce di una stessa medaglia[49]. I carichi di allume continuarono ad arrivare, sotto il controllo di castigliani o italiani, ma in Inghilterra la contrazione delle esportazioni di Londra fu bilanciata da un'espansione della produzione tessile che attrasse gli uomini d'affari castigliani, prima più interessati alle merci fiamminghe[50]. Malgrado ciò, essi non utilizzavano necessariamente navi proprie. Verso il 1440, Alfonso Dios de Gabralyon, probabilmente di Siviglia, fece uso assiduo di galee e *carracche* italiane; si concentrò sull'esportazione di tessuti inglesi, in partite uniche di 48 panni per volta. Altri andalusi seguirono percorsi simili, mostrando un profondo coinvolgimento nel commercio del vino, sia guascone che del Mediterraneo.

Le lotte tra le maggiori potenze influenzarono pesantemente il commercio estero in Inghilterra durante il tardo XV e il XVI secolo, e provocarono gravi danni ai traffici anglo-iberici; tuttavia i mercanti di Dubrovnik (Ragusa) si introdussero nel commercio inglese proprio nel momento in cui italiani e iberici avevano difficoltà a mantenere i contatti. Una piccola e autonoma repubblica sotto tutela ottomana, con accesso ai Balcani controllati dai turchi oltre che ai porti italiani, poteva accedere al commercio inglese senza complicazioni politiche. La comparsa di un numero significativo di ragusei nella Londra cinquecentesca ci ricorda i vantaggi ottenuti da Dubrovnik dalla sua imposta neutralità politica. Relativamente ai vent'anni che seguono il 1515, Kostić scrive che «vi è ragione di credere che in questo periodo il ruolo dei mercanti di Ragusa nell'esportazione dei panni inglesi nel Mediterraneo orientale fosse superiore non solo a quello dei veneziani, bensì anche a quello di tutti i mercanti stranieri in Inghilterra messi insieme»[51]. Dubrovnik non mirava tanto a rifornire un proprio mercato desideroso di ottenere tessuti del Nord, quanto di far proseguire le sue importazioni inglesi verso i consumatori dei territori ottomani a Oriente. Fra i beni maggiormente importati da Dubrovnik vi erano i vini dolci e la frutta secca della Grecia; il carattere fondamentale dei carichi differiva ben poco, dunque, da quello delle galee veneziane più antiche, benché le navi ragusee avessero spesso una capacità doppia delle galee[52]. Parrebbe pertanto che il sostantivo inglese *argosy* [grande flotta di navi mercantili] derivasse nel XVI secolo non dagli argonauti di Giasone, bensì dal nome di Ragusa, patria di queste navi massicce e sempre presenti[53].

---

[49] Per i catalani, vedi Abulafia, *Relations commerciales* cit.; anche Lloyd, *Alien Merchants*, cit., pp. 162-4.

[50] Cf. Ruiz, *op. cit.*, pp. 175-6.

[51] Kostić, *Dubrovnik*, cit., pp. 113, 576; vedi anche Ramsay, *op. cit.*, pp. 28-9, 37-8, 48; F.W. Carter, *The commerce of the Dubrovnik republic, 1500-1700*, in «Economic History Review», ser. 2, XXIV (1971), pp. 370-94.

[52] Kostić, *Dubrovnik*, cit., p. 569.

[53] Vedi *The Oxford English Dictionary*, alla voce *argosy*, mentre *The Oxford Dictionary*

VII

Tuttavia, il commercio di Ragusa con Londra gettò le sue basi ai tempi delle galee veneziane. Negli anni 1430 e 1440 Ivan Manević si trasferì dalla Dalmazia a Londra, unendosi alla comunità italiana e importando tessuti veneziani e orientali sulle galee di stato, ed esportando panni e lana inglesi. Si naturalizzò inglese e diventò uno dei più importanti mercanti di origine straniera a Londra. Divenuto suddito della Corona, allargò i propri interessi per comprendervi l'esazione delle tasse sulla produzione tessile nel Somerset, Dorset e Wiltshire, e acquistò case e terreni a Londra, nelle contee vicine e nella regione del Salisbury. Quando morì a Londra nel 1465 fu sepolto nel convento agostiniano[54]. È probabile, ma non del tutto certo, che fosse di Dubrovnik, ma la città come tale non dominava ancora il commercio dei mercanti dalmati nel Nord. I suoi profitti derivavano dal commercio mediterraneo in generale. E il grado con il quale estese i suoi interessi finanziari dal commercio alla terra — spesso nelle zone da dove traeva la sua lana o i suoi panni — ricorda il comportamento degli italiani a Southampton. A partire dal 1530, dei Ragusei, come i fratelli Brailović (Evangelista) o la famiglia Naljesković, iniziarono a lasciare un segno più profondo. Marin de Nale aveva importato panni inglesi a Dubrovnik ai primi del Cinquecento; i suoi tre figli, Nikola, Augustin e Ivan, suddivisero i propri affari tra Londra, Dubrovnik e Venezia — un sistema che rammenta quello dei Rothschild di qualche secolo posteriore. Entro il 1541, Nikola era diventato uno degli stranieri più ricchi, e abitava nell'area di Lombard Street, nella parrocchia di St. Nicholas Acon, una zona molto frequentata dai veneziani. Si naturalizzò, acquistò proprietà immobiliari in Inghilterra e fu coinvolto nel commercio locale di frumento e legname[55]. Di nuovo vediamo all'opera il processo di naturalizzazione: non soltanto un mutamento di condizione giuridica, da straniero a naturalizzato, ma una trasformazione degli interessi economici, con un maggiore coinvolgimento in affari di natura locale, e soprattutto nell'acquisto di terra.

Fu però Nikola Gucetić (de Gozzi) a raggiungere in questo periodo la maggiore preminenza nella colonia ragusea in Inghilterra. Nel 1570, un quarto circa dei panni inglesi inviati a Dubrovnik erano stati forniti da Gucetić; le sue importazioni erano dominate dalle industrie dei panni di lusso dell'Italia settentrionale, e comprendevano velluti di Genova, tessuti di seta e anche gioielli. Visse in Tower Ward in condizioni di indubbia agiatezza; non si sposò mai, e alla sua morte nel 1595, a Londra, lasciò £ 30.000, di cui una parte non insignificante fu inviata come legato alle chiese di Dubrovnik. Una ricchezza tale era probabilmente senza rivali nella comunità di Londra di questo periodo, con la sola eccezione di Sir Orazio Pallavicino, genovese naturalizzato e consigliere della regina Elisabetta; Gucetić fu l'unico straniero cui si chiese di donare £ 300 per la difesa dell'Inghilterra contro l'Armada spagnola;

---

of English Etymology ha confuso Ragusa di Sicilia con Ragusa-Dubrovnik.

[54] Kostić, *op. cit.*, p. 572.
[55] *Ivi*, pp. 238-61, 586-7.

ma fu l'ultimo raguseo a raggiungere vette così vertiginose, perché i suoi eredi gestirono male i suoi affari, oltre al fatto che, in generale, il commercio raguseo con l'Inghilterra iniziò a decadere verso il 1600[56]. Ciò riflette forse un declino commerciale di Dubrovnik stessa, l'abbandono dei traffici da parte del patriziato urbano e lo sviluppo di una mentalità da *rentier*.

La cronologia della presenza ragusea a Londra è chiaramente fuori fase rispetto a quella degli altri principali gruppi di mercanti mediterranei. D'altronde è pure chiaro che l'esperienza ragusea del XVI secolo ha punti di contatto significativi con quella precedente di italiani e spagnoli. I «milionari» di Dubrovnik non erano autosufficienti: godevano di contatti stretti e frequenti con altri mercanti stranieri, e commerciavano non solo con la loro città d'origine, ma con tutto il Mediterraneo. Essi mostrarono pure un certo grado di integrazione nella società ospite, con esempi di naturalizzazione, legami personali con la Corte ed un rapporto di patronato con chiese inglesi.

Italiani a Londra

Infine, gli italiani a Londra: tanto numerosi, e tanto poco studiati, che sarà necessario prendere due soli esempi, agli estremi opposti del nostro periodo, ognuno dei quali ha ottenuto il riconoscimento da parte degli storici di essere uomo di ricchezze e abilità eccezionali; entrambi erano originari di Genova: sir Antonio Pessagno e sir Orazio Pallavicino.

Antonio Pessagno

La famiglia di Antonio Pessagno giunse in Inghilterra verso il 1300, membri di un illustre casato genovese impegnato nell'attività non del tutto eccezionale di importazione di allume ed esportazione di lana[57]. Antonio era un uomo ambizioso, e già dal 1310 si era reso conto che far prestiti al re gli avrebbe fruttato privilegi eccezionali. Venne stigmatizzato nella corrispondenza privata dei Frescobaldi sia per la sua malvagità che per la sua influenza sul re, paragonabile soltanto a quella dell'odiatissimo beniamino regio, Piers Gaveston. Agli inizi del 1313, il re gli aveva ceduto il controllo di diversi transiti doganali in Inghilterra e Guascogna, oltre a diritti sulla produzione di stagno della Cornovaglia. In Inghilterra aveva legami molto stretti con mercanti genovesi e della Francia meridionale, ma non fu in grado di farsi apprezzare dalla giunta cittadina di Londra, la quale — malgrado, o per via di una richiesta della Corona di favorirlo — addirittura respinse la sua domanda di cittadinanza nell'aprile 1312. Così, invece, ottenne l'esenzione dalle tasse sugli stranieri direttamente dalla Corona, poche settima-

---

[56] *Ivi*, pp. 262-99, 587-90.
[57] Natalie Fryde, *Antonio Pessagno, King's Merchant of Edward II*, in *Studi in memoria di Federigo Melis*, Napoli, 1978; non ho visto la tesi di dottorato su Pessagno, opera di Diane Owen Hughes, presso l'Università di Yale.

ne più tardi, e il re dimostrò che poteva scavalcare i mercanti londinesi se egli lo voleva. Tutto ciò accrebbe la tensione tra Pessagno e i londinesi. In ogni caso era la corte reale che Antonio si trovò sempre più a rifornire. Nell'aprile 1312 gli veniva assegnato il titolo di «mercante regio», e intorno a questi anni inviava spezie, gioielli e tessuti mediterranei alla corte di Edoardo, affidandosi ai suoi contatti genovesi; come diversi altri fra i primi mercanti spagnoli, fungeva anche da fornitore di cavalli da guerra, vino e persino frumento. Dopo il fallimento dei Frescobaldi fu in grado, congiuntamente a mercanti della Guascogna, di Cahors e di Toulouse, di inserirsi nello spazio lasciato aperto dai banchieri forestieri, e tra il 1310 e il 1319 pare avesse prestato al re non meno di £ 145.000. Buona parte di questo denaro Pessagno dovette cercarla altrove: questa somma supera di gran lunga le sue possibili risorse. Egli stesso si rivolse ai Bardi e ad altri banchieri fiorentini che gli sarebbero succeduti come stretti associati dei Plantageneti. Con l'aiuto del papa guascone Clemente V, Pessagno organizzò il finanziamento della campagna di Edoardo II in Scozia, che culminò con la sconfitta umiliante a Bannockburn.

Compiti tali furono accompagnati da ricompense adeguate: fu fatto cavaliere, com'era dovuto ad un membro della nobiltà genovese, e gli fu concessa la tenuta (*manor*) di Lambeth, lungo il fiume, sul lato opposto di Londra. E, infine, gli venne offerto l'incarico di siniscalco della Guascogna, insieme alla signoria su Créon e sull'isola di Oléron nella Francia occidentale. Fu la sua incompetenza come siniscalco che determinò il suo richiamo in Inghilterra e la rottura con Edoardo II — il quale, ciononostante, gli restava sempre pesantemente debitore. Di conseguenza Antonio si mise dalla parte dei nemici di Edoardo durante i violenti sommovimenti del 1327.

Antonio Pessagno è un caso estremo: un mercante che fu in grado, da solo, benché non soltanto con le proprie risorse, di far fronte alle necessità finanziarie di un monarca affamato di soldi e nello stesso tempo preoccupato di non rivolgersi per aiuto ai *lords* o ai *commons*. Il re aveva poche remore, parrebbe, a trattare Pessagno alla pari di un nobile inglese, e qui vi era forse un parziale riconoscimento che, nella società d'origine, Antonio Pessagno era egli stesso un aristocratico. La dipendenza da mercanti e banchieri stranieri irritava la nobiltà inglese — ma non era, o non era del tutto, una questione di disprezzo del modo di vita mercantesco, del lucro e delle pratiche usurarie. Ai primi del Trecento il problema era politico: qui vi era un re che evitava di dipendere dai suoi consiglieri di diritto, dai pari del regno, e si rivolgeva invece a stranieri, al guascone Gaveston e a finanzieri italiani.

La carriera di Pessagno va confrontata con quella di un altro genovese, residente in origine a Londra: sir Orazio Pallavicino, membro di una famiglia con una lunga tradizione commerciale in Inghilterra[58].

---

[58] Per quello che segue, vedi Lawrence Stone, *An Elizabethan: Sir Horatio Palavicino*, Oxford, 1956; cf. Ramsay, *op. cit.*, p. 44.

Servì la regina Elisabetta, alla fine del secolo XVI, in veste di finanziere di guerra, diplomatico e agente segreto, e aiutò la monarchia a superare i difficili anni della guerra con la Spagna. Alla base delle fortune di Orazio c'era il commercio dell'allume: suo padre aveva ottenuto la concessione del monopolio delle miniere papali di allume di Tolfa, e Orazio fu posto a capo del ramo di Anversa dell'azienda paterna. Di nuovo l'allume, dunque, gioca un ruolo nel coinvolgimento genovese nell'Europa settentrionale, ma in maniera ben diversa: Orazio Pallavicino operò per creare un monopolio sulle riserve di allume, vendute all'ingrosso agli olandesi, ma garantite da prestiti inglesi; e, in un periodo di forte conflitto tra cattolici e protestanti, si ritrovò dalla parte di inglesi e olandesi nella guerra con la Spagna. Guadagnandosi rapidamente i favori della corte inglese, fu inviato in missioni diplomatiche vitali presso gli alleati protestanti dell'Inghilterra, in Germania. Nel 1585 ricevette le lettere di naturalizzazione; nel 1587 fu fatto cavaliere, e in seguito aiutò a progettare le difese inglesi contro l'Armada spagnola — insistendo persino, da buon genovese qual era, a salire sui vascelli inglesi per guidarli nella lotta agli spagnoli. Era un notevole esperto di strategia navale, ed aveva idee molto chiare su come provocare il blocco della Spagna e delle Indie occidentali, idee che la regina Elisabetta (figura indecisa e sempre sovrastimata) non fu in grado di apprezzare a sufficienza. Tra gli stranieri, per i suoi prestiti alla Corona egli aveva un concorrente soltanto in Nikola Gucetić, di Ragusa: Gucetić era il più ricco straniero a Londra, Pallavicino il più ricco naturalizzato.

Per poter osservare l'integrazione di sir Orazio nella società inglese è più utile esaminare piuttosto la sua posizione a Corte: egli era annoverato fra i più potenti magnati del paese al momento dello scambio di doni per l'anno nuovo con la regina. Nel 1589 la regina gli dette in cambio dei suoi doni un regalo di argenteria dorata; soltanto quindici altri cortigiani ebbero pari favori. Il suo regalo era stato una spilla incastonata con diamanti, opali e perle. Ma sir Orazio manteneva anche contatti stranieri; uno dei suoi amici più stretti era il genovese Prospero Spinola. Continuò a scrivere le sue lettere in italiano, lasciando l'incombenza della traduzione in inglese al suo segretario. Sposandosi, scelse in moglie la figlia di un ricchissimo mercante di Anversa, Anna Hooftman Eychelberg, membro di una famiglia di nuovi ricchi con un passato di scarso rilievo. E, soprattutto, verso la fine della sua vita, si allontanò da Londra e dalla corte per trasferirsi in una proprietà che aveva acquistato a Babraham, appena fuori Cambridge. Negli anni '90 si trasformò in un completo gentiluomo di campagna inglese.

Uno dei problemi che gli si ponevano era quello religioso, in un'Inghilterra guidata da una regina ostile alla chiesa cattolica. È possibile che in gioventù fosse stato un cattolico fervente, ma le circostanze politiche, se non la propria coscienza, modificarono il suo orientamento: la rabbia del Papato per l'abilità da lui mostrata nell'amministrazione del monopolio dell'allume papale, a scapito degli interessi del Papato stesso, lo portarono a rispondere con denunce che indussero il Papa a chiedere a sua volta al governo genovese di assicurare sir Orazio nelle mani dell'Inquisizione — senz'alcun successo. Pallavicino si spostò lentamente verso il protestantesimo, giungendo infine ad un esplicito anticattolicesimo. In un certo senso, faceva quello che gli veniva imposto. La posizione dei mercanti italiani in Inghilterra non era facile quando si trattava di religione. Nel 1576, l'ambasciatore portoghese organizzò dei servizi religiosi cattolici, aperti agli stranieri o anche a inglesi ricusanti. Ma persino in questo caso le autorità inglesi tentarono di intervenire in maniera ufficiosa. Nei primi anni '80 Pallavicino, come altri italiani, evitò semplicemente di recarsi in chiesa. Ma le autorità non erano soddisfatte neppure di questo. La lenta conversione al protestantesimo esprime chiaramente la sua progressiva transizione da ricco finanziere e diplomatico straniero a gentiluomo di campagna naturalizzato.

Orazio Pallavicino

Di Orazio Pallavicino, Stone dice che «era più cittadino d'Europa che di qualsiasi altro paese». Gli italiani, e altri mercanti del Mediterraneo, presenti in Inghilterra tra il 1200 e il 1600, di rado troncavano i propri legami con i loro compatrioti, benché potessero forse farlo i loro discendenti, spesso metà inglesi per nascita. Ma gli italiani non opposero neppure forti resistenze all'assimilazione. Fino alla metà del XVI secolo professavano la stessa fede degli inglesi, cosa che non si verificava invece per molti dei loro soci d'affari nel Mediterraneo, musulmani e greci. Con gli inglesi condividevano, a partire dalla metà del Quattrocento, l'uso delle navi inglesi; e prima d'allora dividevano il commercio in uscita da Southampton per l'Inghilterra meridionale, lasciando quello locale agli inglesi e tenendo per sé il traffico londinese di merci esotiche.

Giacché, in effetti, vi erano ben poche barriere all'assimilazione, non sorprende trovare molti italiani, spagnoli e ragusei che le attraversano in diversi modi. Potevano naturalizzarsi inglesi e diventare borghesi di Londra o di Southampton, cambiando status di fronte alla legge e all'esattore. In altri casi il mercante spostava il fulcro dei propri affari, e seguiva gli inglesi nei mercati d'oltre Manica o li accompagnava nel commercio locale attraverso l'Inghilterra meridionale. Non invasero in gran numero questi mercati, e per questo motivo non infastidirono troppo quando cominciarono a commerciare su basi locali. Il loro capitale e le loro conoscenze commerciali erano a volte, invece, estremamente apprezzate da compagnie inglesi meno solide con cui si associavano. Per di più, i maggiori mercanti forestieri scoprirono di essere mariti apprezzati, e a questi l'élite di Southampton non chiuse neppure le alte cariche di sceriffo e *mayor*.

Diventando cittadini e naturalizzati, o in diversi altri modi, i mercanti del Mediterraneo riuscirono a farsi accettare dalla comunità inglese. Questo non stava a significare l'abbandono della loro identità originaria di genovese, fiorentino, veneziano, castigliano o raguseo. Significava l'assunzione di una seconda identità, alternativa, che coesisteva senza troppe difficoltà con l'esistenza di origini remote. E la composizione in continuo mutamento della comunità d'affari inglese significava che, per gran parte di questo periodo, vi era disponibilità ad accettare sangue nuovo, inglese e straniero, nei ranghi del patriziato urbano. I mercanti del Mediterraneo erano visti, soprattutto a Southampton, come collaboratori più che come competitori; e pure fra gli stranieri questa era spesso la visione prevalente — con il risultato che si creò il fenomeno del mercante in un certo senso anglo-italiano o anglo-spagnolo.

VIII

L'ECONOMIA MERCANTILE NEL MEDITERRANEO OCCIDENTALE
(1390ca.-1460ca.): COMMERCIO LOCALE E A LUNGA DISTANZA
NELL'ETÀ DI ALFONSO IL MAGNANIMO*

I

Ogni tentativo di descrivere i rapporti economici che collegavano le sponde del Mediterraneo occidentale nella prima metà del XV secolo è vincolato a parecchie limitazioni. In primo luogo, a quel tempo il Mediterraneo occidentale non costituiva un sistema chiuso, ed uno degli aspetti principali del commercio della regione che deve essere discusso è l'impatto di correnti commerciali dirette fuori della regione stessa, sia verso il Levante sia verso l'Atlantico, sul carattere degli scambi commerciali che avevano luogo nel Mediterraneo occidentale. In altre parole, è importante capire il ruolo di intermediario del Mediterraneo occidentale come canale che collegava l'Europa atlantica all'Oriente e l'Europa continentale all'Africa. E, dopo tutto, questo intendiamo servendoci del termine mar Mediterraneo, il mare fra le terre, ma anche di fatto un mare tra i mari. Città come Valencia e Ciutat de Mallorca erano importanti non solo come fonti o acquirenti di merci, ma anche come punti di approdo per il traffico tra l'Italia e lo stretto di Gibilterra e oltre.

Accanto a questa vi è una seconda considerazione. Alla stessa epoca, il tardo Medioevo vide un cambiamento di attenzione tra i mercanti che ricercavano merci tradizionalmente associate coi mercati orientali e il Mediterraneo occidentale, così come le acque intorno a Gibilterra divennero fonte più frequentata di prodotti come lo zucchero, che prima si reperiva sui mercati orientali. La disponibilità nella Spagna meridionale di frutta secca di buona qualità rimediò alle difficoltà incontrate nel trovare accesso ai mercati dell'ex-Impero bizantino, ed ebbe effetti significativi sulla prosperità dei regni di Valencia e Granada. È quindi possibile parlare della crescente importanza commerciale del Mediterraneo occidentale alla fine del Medioevo. Più in generale, possiamo riscontrare dopo il 1350 una tendenza alla specializzazione regionale all'interno dell'Europa occidentale, che ebbe significative implicazioni per le reti della distribuzione commerciale; la specializzazione locale nella produzione di coloranti (come lo zafferano) o di commestibili specializzati (come il riso) stimolò anche il commercio regionale di beni primari come il grano, che do-

---

* Questo articolo è una versione notevolmente accresciuta della relazione *L'economia mercantile nel Mediterraneo occidentale nel periodo di Alfonso il Magnanimo*, tenuta al XVI Congresso internazionale di Storia della Corona d'Aragona, Napoli 1997.

vevano essere trasportati in quelle aree le quali tendevano a specializzarsi in prodotti meno fondamentali. In particolare, l'abbandono di terre agricole e la loro conversione in pascoli portarono ad una maggiore reperibilità all'interno del Mediterraneo occidentale di lane di qualità molto diverse, dalla *dogana delle pecore* dell'Apulia o dagli ovili di Aragona, Castiglia e delle Baleari. È pertanto difficile cercare dove si possa trovare qualche traccia di tali cambiamenti nelle rotte del commercio a breve distanza lungo le coste del Mediterraneo occidentale.

In terzo luogo, ogni esame di questo periodo deve prendere in considerazione il classico dibattito, cui hanno dato vita con grande vigore Lopez, Miskimin e Cipolla, sulla "depressione economica del Rinascimento", un dibattito dominato a lungo dai pessimisti, i quali sostenevano che la fine del XIV e l'inizio del XV secolo avevano visto l'economia dell'Europa occidentale trovarsi in serie difficoltà, soprattutto per la contrazione delle industrie maggiori e il crollo del commercio; più recentemente tuttavia gli ottimisti hanno ripreso forza, nella ricerca di segni di continuazione della vitalità anche in aree come la Sicilia e l'Italia meridionale, a lungo prese ad esempio della depressione economica[2]. La visione più ottimistica ha attirato gli storici della Corona d'Aragona, i quali, come ha osservato Iradiel, sono stati fortemente colpiti dalla crescente importanza di Valencia nel commercio internazionale, che abbiano o no accettato anche prove per il grave declino di Barcellona. In parte, la difficoltà è stata quella di tentare di generalizzare circa una vasta rete di economie, insieme interdipendenti a parecchi livelli cruciali e distinte in molte caratteristiche fondamentali; come è stato appena visto, anche all'interno della comunità catalano-aragonese esistevano notevoli differenze nei risultati economici, che includevano crisi monetarie a Barcellona assenti invece a Valencia, con la sua diversa circolazione. Analisi regionali, che sottolineavano il grado di integrazione economica a un livello locale, come gli importanti studi di Stephan Epstein, hanno decisamente rimesso in questione la nostra capacità di descrivere l'Europa occidentale come una singola economia monolitica[3].

Questo problema sembra puntare in una direzione assai differente rispetto al punto di partenza: l'immagine del Mediterraneo come il "mare in mezzo", in grado di collegare tra loro territori europei ed africani, sembra a prima vista convivere difficilmente con quella di una serie di economie regionali, sempre più capaci di provvedere ai propri bisogni.

---

[2] R.S. LOPEZ-H.A. MISKIMIN, *The economic depression of the Renaissance,* in «Economic History Review», 1961-62, con risposta di C. Cipolla, ibid., 1963-64.

[3] S.R. EPSTEIN, *An island for itself. Economic development and social change in late medieval Sicily,* Cambridge 1992 (trad. it. *Potere e mercanti in Sicilia,* Torino 1995).

In un senso profondo, l'economia del Mediterraneo occidentale dei primi anni del XV secolo deve essere compresa alla luce della tensione tra questi due aspetti: fra il ruolo globale del Mediterraneo occidentale come punto di incontro delle rotte commerciali che andavano in tutte le direzioni, e la tendenza delle rotte locali di questo periodo ad affermarsi in modo sempre più decisivo. Tali differenti aspetti, come diventerà chiaro, non sono incompatibili; ma ciò che può apparire come una ritirata in alcune aree del commercio del Mediterraneo occidentale può essere reinterpretato come un cambiamento nel carattere degli scambi della regione, che non rivelano né depressione né collasso, ma uno sfruttamento sempre più efficiente di risorse locali per soddisfare bisogni regionali. Così nelle isole Baleari possiamo scoprire una notevole espansione sia nella produzione di lana grezza (in particolare a Minorca, come osserva il Melis) sia nella produzione di panni finiti a Maiorca[4]. Quel che risulta visibile qui è un processo di razionalizzazione attraverso il quale la fonte della materia prima grezza e il centro di produzione dell'articolo finito tendono a collaborare più strettamente. Esempi simili possono essere citati per la Sicilia, per la Francia meridionale e altrove in questo periodo. Anche nell'Europa settentrionale è ben visibile verso il Quattrocento il cambiamento dall'utilizzazione di materiali grezzi, come i coloranti, prodotti a grande distanza, al basarsi sulla produzione locale. Dalla grande epoca dell'approvvigionamento a lunga distanza di beni che precedette la Morte Nera, arriviamo ad un momento in cui le reti del commercio a breve distanza erano utilizzate con maggiore intensità, ottenendo notevoli riduzioni delle spese generali ed esaltando l'uso di risorse all'interno di regioni relativamente piccole, come la Sicilia, le acque del Tirreno oltre Amalfi o la Catalogna marittima. Importanti contatti commerciali, come quelli tra Maiorca e i due continenti di Europa e Africa, erano mantenuti da innumerevoli piccoli vascelli, che andavano avanti e indietro per tutto l'anno. La storia del commercio del Mediterraneo occidentale in questo periodo non può certamente essere presentata semplicemente in termini di "grandi correnti commerciali" dominate dalle galee o altre grandi navi. Tutto ciò naturalmente ebbe un effetto sulle opportunità di fare affari offerte ai mercanti specializzati nel commercio a lunga distanza, e creò disagi in qualcuno dei centri classici di tale commercio, specialmente Genova e Barcellona. Anche qui inoltre, prima della morte di Alfonso il Magnanimo, vi sono segni di un significativo adattamento alle mutate circostanze economiche e politiche, accelerata dalla politica adottata dallo stesso re d'Aragona.

---

[4] F. MELIS, *Aspetti della vita economica medievale. Studi nell'Archivio Datini di Prato*, Siena/Firenze 1962, pp. 635-729.

Un'ultima considerazione introduttiva riguarda la saggistica esistente. Non si può prendere in esame questo tema senza tener conto dei classici lavori sui mercanti catalani di Mario Del Treppo o su Genova alla metà del XV secolo (1447-66) di Jacques Heers[5]. Entrambi furono pubblicati per la prima volta negli anni Sessanta e riflettono in modo assai diverso l'impostazione degli storici dell'economia della scuola delle *Annales* allora dominante, incluso un forte interesse per l'accurata esposizione di dati statistici. Ma nella brillante opera di Del Treppo, in particolare, possiamo vedere un vigoroso tentativo di caratterizzare le fasi principali dell'espansione e della contrazione del commercio di Barcellona del Quattrocento; mentre l'interesse per gli sviluppi a lungo termine, più marcato che nell'opera di Heers, offre una suggestiva intelaiatura per la descrizione del Mediterraneo occidentale nel XV secolo: l'enfasi parigina sulle strutture, visibile nell'opera di Jacques Heers, Claude Carrère[6], Jacqueline Guiral[7] e in altre, ha talvolta oscurato questi significativi cambiamenti periodici. In altre parole, ogni asserzione a proposito dell'economia mercantile nel Mediterraneo occidentale ai primi del XV secolo è destinata ad avere il carattere di un commento all'eminente libro di Del Treppo, per non parlare di Bresc[8], Leone[9], Iradiel[10] e molti altri che hanno pubblicato le opere maggiori dopo la prima edizione dell'opera *I mercanti catalani e l'espansione della Corona d'Aragona,* e non c'è bisogno di scusarsi per l'impostazione largamente storiografica che sarà qui adottata.

Il fondamentale riesame offerto da Del Treppo dei punti di forza e di debolezza dell'economia catalana all'inizio del XV secolo e la relativa posizione di Carrère, su alcune questioni di fondo non diversa, hanno prodotto una rivoluzione nel giudizio sul regno di Alfonso il Magnanimo e dei suoi successori. In particolare, le eccezioni sollevate da Del Treppo alle posizioni di Jaume Vicens Vives e Pierre Vilar sul "declino economico" della Catalogna alla fine del Medioevo è di notevole rilievo sulla più vasta

---

[5] M. Del Treppo, *I mercanti catalani e l'espansione della Corona d'Aragona nel XV secolo,* Napoli 1967, (nuova ed.1972 cui ci riferiremo in seguito) e ed. catalana: *Els mercaders catalans i l'expansiò de la corona catalano-aragonesa,* Barcellona 1976; J. Heers, *Gênes au XVe siècle. Activité économique et problèmes sociaux,* Parigi 1961; nuova ed. abbreviata: Id., *Gênes au XVe siècle. Civilisation méditerranéenne, grand capitalisme, et capitalisme populaire,* Parigi 1971.

[6] C. Carrere, *Barcelone. Centre économique à l'époque des difficultés, 1380-1462,* 2 voll., Parigi/L'Aia 1967.

[7] J. Guiral-Hadziiossif, *Valence. Port méditerranéen au XVe siècle, 1410-1525,* Parigi 1976.

[8] H. Bresc, *Un monde méditerranéen. Economie et société en Sicile, 1300-1450,* 2 voll., Roma/Palermo 1986.

[9] M. Del Treppo-A. Leone, *Amalfi medioevale,* Napoli 1977.

[10] Cfr. nota 25.

VIII

questione se l'Europa occidentale registrò una recessione seria e globale dopo la Morte Nera[11]. Ad ogni modo, l'immagine che domina il libro di Del Treppo è quella di un commercio di alto valore e lunga distanza dei mercanti catalani e dei loro concorrenti in aree differenti: Oriente, Fiandre e Inghilterra, ma soprattutto in Sicilia e a Napoli, l'ultima delle quali offre la prova irrefutabile dell'abilità dei mercanti catalani nel rispondere alle nuove opportunità di affari create dalle conquiste di Alfonso il Magnanimo.

Dove sarebbe possibile aggiungere qualcosa all'analisi di Del Treppo è nello studio del commercio a breve distanza e dedicherò attenzione agli studi su alcuni casi di collegamenti lungo la costa della Catalogna, tra la Catalogna, Maiorca e l'Africa, e lungo le coste del mar Tirreno, allo scopo di vedere come gli scambi negli scali più piccoli con imbarcazioni modeste alimentassero le vie del grande commercio, e di chiedermi (senza promettere una risposta) quale fosse il significato complessivo degli scambi locali nelle reti commerciali del Mediterraneo occidentale al tempo del re Alfonso. Questi scambi non sempre valevano la pena della spesa extra di un contratto di assicurazione, e per questa ed altre ragioni non è sempre facile rintracciarli. Si vedrà che alcune connessioni commerciali assai significative erano mantenute con mezzi che all'epoca sembrava poco più di un sistema di cabotaggio: i collegamenti tra Spagna continentale, Maiorca e il Nordafrica dovranno essere analizzati sotto questa luce. Inoltre, ciò che viene descritto qui non è certamente di più della piccola punta di un grandissimo *iceberg*. Dopo aver esaminato alcune prove del commercio a breve distanza, sarà possibile muovere gradualmente la lente verso il prestigioso commercio di lusso a lunga distanza, che ha maggiormente attirato l'attenzione degli storici. Chiaramente questo è solo l'inizio della storia, poiché tempo e spazio precludono lo studio del commercio interno; studi sulle fiere dell'Italia meridionale, specialmente ad opera di Alberto Grohmann, chiariscono il significato delle reti di distribuzione regionale sotto la protezione della monarchia o dei più grandi principi[12]. Ogni valutazione dell'industria dei panni di lana deve ovviamente tener conto delle

---

[11] P. VILAR, *Le déclin catalan au bas moyen âge*, in «Estudios de Historia Moderna», 6 (1956-59), pp. 1-68; J. VICENS VIVES, *An economic history of Spain*, Princeton N.J. 1969, con capitoli di rilievo ristampati in *Spain in the fifteenth century 1369-1516*, a c. di R. Highfield, Londra 1972, pp. 31-57, 248-275.

[12] A. GROHMANN, *Le fiere del regno di Napoli in età aragonese*, Napoli 1969; altre opere che si occupano del commercio interno includono gli studi sulla Sicilia di Bresc ed Epstein già citati e (per l'Italia meridionale) E. SAKELLARIOU, *The Kingdom of Naples under Aragonese and Spanish rule. Population growth and economic and social evolution in the late fifteenth and early sixteenth centuries*, tesi in Ph.D., Università di Cambridge 1966.

strade che avviavano la lana grezza giù dalla Castiglia, dagli altipiani d'Aragona e dagli ovili d'Apulia verso i mercati che rifornivano le città sedi delle industrie tessili[13]. Insomma, vi sono ampie aree che ancora necessitano di una mappatura. Questa relazione non fornisce la pianta, ma qualche idea su come potrebbe apparire. E, data l'ampiezza dell'area da disegnare, mi è sembrato opportuno concentrarmi sui territori compresi nell'orbita della Corona di Aragona, inclusa l'Italia meridionale ed anche, per ragioni che diventeranno ovvie, i tradizionali mercati catalani nel Nordafrica. Domande simili possono essere poste circa il commercio marittimo locale in Liguria, Provenza e lungo le coste della Maremma, ma non mi è stato possibile dedicarmi allo stesso modo a queste aree.

II

La prima tappa è l'Italia meridionale. Un interessante studio sul commercio locale nelle acque del mar Tirreno è stato fornito da Del Treppo e Leone nel loro libro *Amalfi medioevale*[14]. L'analisi di Alfonso Leone degli atti notarili riguardanti il commercio marittimo amalfitano nel XV secolo non lascia dubbi sul fatto che la grande stagione della navigazione amalfitana verso gli angoli più lontani del Mediterraneo sta per finire. Fra il 1388 e il 1494 troviamo la registrazione di 97 viaggi a Salerno e nel Cilento, 70 verso la Calabria, 30 per la Sicilia, 13 a Napoli, e viaggi occasionali verso Gaeta e la Puglia; oltre le acque del Regno ci sono pochi segni di attività, e solo Roma (20 viaggi, specialmente tra il 1443 e il 1468) sembra essere stata una destinazione significativa a nord dei confini del Regno, mentre la Catalogna e la Sardegna figurano assai raramente; il viaggio in Catalogna (1398) sembra di fatto un'impresa genovese. Quanto al Levante, Leone ha trovato solo un riferimento ad un viaggio per Alessandria nel 1408, ma di una nave di Gaeta. Leone sottolineava l'importanza dei piccoli porti del Cilento, come Santa Maria di Castellabate e, in particolare, Agropoli, come sbocco per i prodotti agricoli della regione; vino, grano, olio, lino erano tra i più ricercati prodotti della regione, i quali partivano di lì per le fiere di Salerno.

Con questi *standard*, l'intenso commercio con la Calabria sembra quasi appartenere all'ambito degli scambi a lunga distanza; qui c'era un gran-

---

[13] J.A. MARINO, *Pastoral economics in the Kingdom of Naples*, Baltimora 1988 (ed.it. Napoli 1992); J.A. FERNANDEZ OTAL, *La Casa de Ganaderos de Zaragoza en la Edad Media (siglos XIII-XIV). Aportaciòn a la Historia pecuaria del Aragòn medieval*, tesi di dottorato (microscheda), Saragozza 1996.
[14] Cfr. nota 9.

de interesse per la pesca del corallo e delle acciughe, come per i panni di lino e il cotone grezzo; Pizzo, Nicotera e in particolare Tropea erano punti focali della navigazione amalfitana diretta a sud. Comunque, la caratteristica principale di questo commercio era il fatto che prevedeva anche soste regolari in centri costieri molto più piccoli, dove modeste partite erano comprate e vendute, *in emendo vendendo et alia faciendo*; e il livello degli investimenti non era affatto alto, con un'oncia qui, due là, cosicché appare del tutto eccezionale un contratto di commenda del 1460, secondo il quale un mercante di Ravello ricevette 171 ducati da Coluccio Coppola di Scala ed anche panni ed altri beni per commercio in Calabria. È più notevole, forse, il livello di investimento nel commercio siciliano, diretto all'acquisto di formaggio, tonno salato, zucchero, grano e lana. Si ha inoltre l'impressione di una regolare attività nella movimentazione di prodotti di prima necessità, piuttosto che il tentativo di riprendere il ruolo degli antenati di questi mercanti nel commercio di lusso che aveva costituito una parte importante dei loro affari nell'undicesimo secolo.

Pochi mercanti stranieri furono attirati da Amalfi: fra il 1394 e il 1468 ci sono riferimenti a 26 Genovesi e 15 Catalani che vi fanno affari; tra il 1443 e il 1468 troviamo anche 9 Pisani, un Fiorentino e due Francesi. Risulta che il maggiore interesse dei genovesi era per il mercato del cotone grezzo e la disponibilità di cotone lavorato in Amalfi e dintorni, come la *carta bombagina* di Scala e i fustagni prodotti a Maiori e dintorni. Gran parte del cotone veniva da *Ultramare*, identificato da Leone con territori turchi, benché indicasse tanto la Siria quanto l'Egitto; così i Genovesi erano in grado di rifornire Amalfi e la sua regione con le materie prime necessarie alle industrie locali. Ci sono pervenuti 20 contratti del periodo 1443-1468 relativi alla vendita di cotone effettuata da mercanti stranieri in Amalfi; vendite di panni da parte di mercanti forestieri sono più frequenti dopo il 1469, benché fossero certamente presenti anche in contratti anteriori. Acquisti più modesti di mercanti genovesi comprendevano *strutto di porco* o lardo, che sembra sia stato un acquisto assai popolare, e legno di castagno[15].

Anche la presenza di un significativo numero di mercanti delle città delle vicinanze e di quelle più lontane del Regno diede vita alle attività commerciali di Amalfi; fra il 1395 e il 1468, vi sono testimonianze su 58 visitatori da Salerno e dal Cilento, come pure un significativo numero da Napoli e dalla Penisola Sorrentina (benché siano rare quelle di visite di commercianti amalfitani a Napoli). Molti mercanti siciliani venivano a comprare legno di castagno e a vendere il formaggio dell'isola. Ad Amalfi

---

[15] Dati desunti dal contributo di LEONE in *Amalfi medioevale* cit., parte II.

era assai attivo il mercato di tessuti, ma prevalevano quelli di media o bassa qualità. Fra il 1443 e il 1468 furono registrate 544 compravendite di stoffe e al primo posto vi sono quelle di cotone. In confronto alla ricca documentazione sulla fiera di Salerno del 1478, ci sono poche tracce di panni di qualità provenienti da Perpignano, Maiorca ed altri importanti centri di produzione di panni di lana di buona qualità, e certamente i mercanti amalfitani erano relativamente rari tra la folla della fiera di Salerno. *Amalphitanos quondam magnos fuisse negotiatores*, nelle parole di Flavio Biondo; ed anche per Masuccio Salernitano la città aveva perduto le glorie del passato[16].

Dire che Amalfi nel XV secolo era l'ombra di quello che era stata in passato non significa che i cambiamenti economici del periodo successivo alla Morte Nera fossero responsabili dei mutamenti del carattere del commercio della città. Quello che interessa qui è precisamente l'immagine fornita da Amalfi di interessi commerciali fortemente localizzati, e di una concentrazione su beni primari di basso pregio, come panni a buon mercato e generi alimentari. L'immagine di Amalfi nel XV secolo è poi sorprendentemente diversa da quella, mitica o reale, dei secoli precedenti; nelle parole di Mario Del Treppo, «potrebbe trattarsi di un qualunque porto della costa tirrenica, o di quella adriatica, Scalea, Vibo, Manfredonia, ecc., solo che questa città si chiama Amalfi, e il nome evoca immagini di grandezza e di opulenza, traguardi di espansione fascinosi e lontani»[17]. Così Amalfi del XV secolo è interessante perché non è più atipica, ma è diventata tipica della navigazione tirrenica del periodo.

III

Spostandoci all'estremità occidentale della nostra regione, sono accessibili dati analoghi e mostrano come in un grande centro commerciale, Barcellona, affluisse anche un piccolo traffico locale di materie prime grezze. Anche qui è inevitabile la sensazione che il movimento di legno, panni, generi alimentari e materie prime restò vitale nel primo Quattrocento. Possiamo seguire passo passo due studi che sottolineano questa dimensione della vita commerciale della Catalogna tardomedievale. Roser Salicrù i Lluch ha esaminato i conti della *Lleuda de Mediona* a Barcellona dal febbraio 1434[18] e uno studio poco conosciuto di Mario Zucchitello ha

---

16 Citato in ibid., p. 5.
17 Ibid., p. 3.
18 R. SALICRÙ I LLUCH, *El tràfic de mercaderies a Barcelona segons els comptes de la Lleuda de Mediona (febrer de 1434)*, Barcelona 1995 (Anuario de Estudios medievales, annex 30).

preso in esame il commercio di Tossa de Mar, sulla costa a sud di Girona, con Barcellona negli anni fra il 1357 e il 1553[19].

Tossa era un piccolissimo centro commerciale, con una popolazione stimata nel XV secolo di poco più di 300 abitanti ed è esattamente in questo fatto il significato del lavoro di Zucchitello: l'analisi accurata di un piccolo centro la cui primaria funzione commerciale consisteva nel rifornire Barcellona e perfino Valencia di generi alimentari e materie prime. In aggiunta, i suoi capitani e mercanti più fortunati ottennero per sé un modesto ruolo nella rete che riforniva Barcellona, e in un più lungo termine, Valencia, di prodotti di base. I documenti di *guiatge* a Barcellona rivelano movimenti regolari di grano da Barcellona a Tossa nel decennio 1430-40 ed un commercio piuttosto frequente di pietre da macina. Un attivo commercio di cabotaggio collegava la Francia meridionale con Barcellona, attraverso i porti di quella che ora è nota come Costa Brava; Narbona era un frequente punto di partenza, il che forse riflette l'interesse per il grano di Linguadoca, benché il grano attirasse questi mercanti anche verso Tortosa e Tarragona. Di gran lunga più rari erano i viaggi per le isole; nel 1440 Jaume Darder *menor* viaggiò sulla sua *barca* di 40 *bòtes* (botti) verso Ibiza, ritornando via Barcellona, e il suo parente Joan Darder approdò a Maiorca lo stesso anno con un battello un po' più piccolo, toccando di nuovo al ritorno la capitale catalana. Ma non vi è testimonianza di altri viaggi in mare aperto prima del 1514. Questi erano viaggi brevi sia come distanza sia come durata; Jaume Darder *menor* va e viene da Narbona nel 1446, ma nel 1439 ha fatto un viaggio più ambizioso da Valencia a Tossa via Barcellona su una *barca* di 40 *bòtes*. Nel 1453 lo troviamo che viaggia da Collioure a Barcellona e il suo carico include grano. Lo stesso, o un omonimo, trasportò lana e riso da Valencia a Barcellona nel 1454. Era uno dei più attivi mercanti e capitani di mare di Tossa registrati nei documenti di Barcellona. Vicenç Tomàs commerciò regolarmente su e giù per la costa, caricando legname per la Francia sul suo *lleny*, e ancora il centro della maggior parte del commercio della cittadina è una limitata area costiera tra Barcellona e Narbona, servita da piccoli battelli da 20 a 50 *bòtes*.

L'aspetto più caratteristico del commercio *tossenc* era comunque il rifornimento di legna e carbone a Barcellona dalle foreste alle spalle di Tossa. Le fonti analizzate da Zucchitello parlano di 600 *bòtes* di legname trasportato da Jaume Darder *menor* da Tossa e dintorni a Barcellona fra il 1439 e il 1447. Un altro mercante che già conosciamo, Vicenç Tòmas, fornì 900 *bòtes* nello stesso periodo. Costoro erano tra le figure più im-

---

[19] M. ZUCCHITELLO, *El comerç marìtim de Tossa a través del port barcelonì (1357-1553)*, Tossa de Mar 1982 (Quaderns d'estudis tossencs, 2).

portanti, ma vi erano anche forestieri che andavano a Tossa a comprare legname; nel 1442 Tossa era la quarta più importante piazza di legname registrata nei documenti di *ancoratge* di Barcellona analizzati da Carrère e per molti anni sembra aver fornito quasi 1000 *bòtes* di legname alla capitale. Benché questa cifra la collochi in qualche modo dietro la *leader*, Matarò, capace di fornire due volte e mezzo e anche tre volte questa quantità alla capitale, il legname era evidentemente la maggiore risorsa di Tossa: varie specie di *quercus, arbutus* e *pinus* evidentemente impiegate in gran parte nella produzione artigiana. Un'altra espressione dell'importanza del commercio del legname è data dall'osservazione che tra i centri relativamente più lontani da Barcellona, Tossa era la più importante, e chiaramente molto regolare, fonte di legname[20]. Per quanto riguarda i prodotti del mare, documenti più tardi, a partire dal 1467, mettono in luce l'importanza del pesce nell'economia locale, includendo sia il tonno sia specie molto più piccole; tuttavia le acque catalane, come vedremo tra poco, non erano per nulla l'unica fonte di pesce per Barcellona.

Anche il grano affluiva alle coste della Catalogna dalla Francia meridionale, suscitando l'attenzione di grossi mercanti come Johan Fortis, il quale poteva avere significativi interessi anche nelle forniture di grano da Sardegna, Sicilia e dalla valle dell'Ebro e la capacità di organizzare in più la redistribuzione del grano acquistato su mercati lontani come Rodi e Venezia. La Francia meridionale, in ogni modo, sembra essere stata la maggior fonte di grano per Barcellona in questo periodo, offrendo possibilità di guadagno anche a mercanti più modesti con spazio da riempire sui loro vascelli. Così vi erano anche innumerevoli mercanti minori con base a Tortosa, Tarragona, San Feliu de Guixols ed altri porti lungo la costa di Catalogna, Linguadoca e Provenza, che ebbero un ruolo fondamentale, come ha mostrato Del Treppo, nell'approvvigionamento di Barcellona: uomini come Pere e Bernat Viner, i quali ogni anno tra il 1440 e il 1446 stipularono dozzine di contratti di assicurazione per arrivi di grano nella capitale da Agde, Arles ed Avignone[21]. Spesso tanto i proprietari delle navi quanto i mercanti, si può ragionevolmente supporre, erano di gran lunga più numerosi di quel che rivelano esplicitamente i documenti rimasti. Le testimonianze sulla navigazione da Tossa in questo periodo riguardano sempre *llenys, llauts* ed altri vascelli di media o piccola stazza. Ad ogni modo, qualche idea sulla comparsa di vascelli più grandi, adibiti al trasporto di maggiori quantità di merce su queste rotte, si può ricavare da un modello votivo del XV secolo di una *nau,* dedicato da un marinaio di Matarò ed ora conservato nel Museo Marittimo di Amsterdam; è sorta una

---

[20] Ibid., pp. 75-78.
[21] *I mercanti catalani* cit., pp. 383 e 395-397.

questione se rappresenti un tipo di nave più tipicamente mediterraneo o atlantico, ma vedremo che la *nau* svolgeva preziose funzioni praticamente su tutte le rotte del commercio marittimo catalano[22]. Quella che va sottolineata è l'esistenza, accanto alle navi grosse, di una folla di vascelli più piccoli che attraversavano le acque del Mediterraneo occidentale parecchie volte ogni anno.

La documentazione da Barcellona a partire dal 1434, raccolta da Salicrù, per il traffico di merci come il pesce allarga il quadro presentato tanto da includere orizzonti nuovi e inaspettatamente vasti. Il traffico di merci modeste come le sardine salate non era semplicemente un fenomeno localizzato, ristretto ad acque facilmente accessibili fuori della Catalogna, benché ricche di acciughe e sardine. La *lleuda* di Mediona era pagabile a Barcellona da parte di mercanti non barcellonesi; la documentazione superstite viene da Lent, un fatto che può spiegare la predominanza particolarmente rilevante del pesce nel febbraio 1434, ed anche l'assenza di registrazione di importazione di carne. I conti delle tasse di Mediona sono preziosi in quanto offrono un'immagine assai diversa del commercio di Barcellona rispetto alla documentazione del commercio a lunga distanza di beni di lusso[23].

Il pesce, salato e secco, aveva un ruolo molto importante nella dieta dei Catalani del XV secolo. Era durevole, leggero di peso e il suo basso costo creava una domanda costante. Analizzando le cifre delle tasse municipali solo sul pesce fresco, Salicrù è in grado di mostrare che in un anno tipico, verso la fine del regno di Alfonso il Magnanimo, gli abitanti di Barcellona devono aver consumato in parecchi anni pesce fresco per un valore di almeno ₤ 16.000, mentre i quantitativi di pesce salato proveniente dall'Atlantico su navi basche, galiziane e portoghesi erano altrettanto imponenti, e vi sono indizi di un cambiamento verso un maggior consumo di pesce secco e salato e di una riduzione della domanda di quello fresco. Vi era un particolare interesse per le sardine, seguite dai merluzzi (*merluza, lluç*), mentre erano altrettanto ricercati tonno e anguille. La presenza galiziana in questo commercio era rafforzata dalla

---

22 *Het Matarò-Model. Een bijzondere Aanwist*, Maritem Museum Prins Hendrik, Rotterdam 1982; *Evocacions a l'entorn de la Coca de Matarò*, Barcelona s. d.; H. WINTER, *Die katalanische Nao von 1450 nach dem Modell im Maritem Museum Prins Hendrik in Rotterdam* BURG BEZ. Magdeburg 1956, (trad. cat. *La Nau catalana de 1450 segons el modell del Museu Prins Hendrijk de Rotterdam*, Barcelona 1986; J. W. VAN NOUHUYS, *Het Modell van een Spaansch Karveel uit het begin der 15ᵉ eeuw inhet Maritiem-Museum "Prins Hendrik" in Rotterdam*. Bijlage van het Museum-Verslag 1930; P. TAKAKJIAN, *Thoughts on a 15th. c. Caravel*, in «Model Shipwright», n. 72, 1990, pp. 4-14.

23 SALICRÙ discute le sue sensate conclusioni sulla documentazione in *El tràfic* cit., pp. 3-219.

pronta disponibilità di sale della produzione atlantica, dalla Bretagna a nord al Portogallo al sud. Si affermò una vera e propria industria galiziana del pesce salato, capace di rifornire i mercati mediterranei con le sue eccedenze. Vale la pena anche di insistere sul fatto che nel tardo Trecento e nel Quattrocento ci fu un generale incremento della domanda di alimenti ricchi di proteine, i quali erano più facilmente reperibili in regioni spopolate dalla Morte Nera, poiché anche chi disponeva di mezzi modesti era in grado di seguire una dieta più variata. Come Barcellona, anche Maiorca e Valencia divennero in questo periodo importanti centri di richiesta di pesce galiziano. I conti di Mediona sono anche ricchi di registrazioni di importazioni di olio, miele, legname, metalli e oggetti di metallo, cuoio e pelli, coloranti per l'industria tessile; i conti forniscono dunque l'immagine di una città affamata di generi alimentari e materie prime, il cui commercio non è semplicemente dominato dal traffico di panni di media e buona qualità, mentre appaiono anche questi e le spezie. Lontano dalla Quaresima, c'era anche un attivo commercio di carne salata, come i prosciutti siciliani. Tutto ciò mette in un canto anche l'eccezionale importanza del commercio del grano; a questo proposito, come ha insistito Del Treppo, non deve essere sottostimato il ruolo delle fonti di approvvigionamento della Francia meridionale, anche se Sicilia e Sardegna erano possibili fonti alle quali Alfonso il Magnanimo incoraggiava i Barcellonesi a rivolgersi[24].

Questi frammenti documentari dell'Italia meridionale e della Catalogna suggeriscono che la storia del commercio mediterraneo non può essere scritta soltanto nel quadro della movimentazione a lunga distanza di merci di alto valore, la quale tende ad essere di gran lunga più regolarmente registrata, specie in contratti di assicurazione. Innumerevoli transazioni di basso valore, nelle quali il mercante e il padrone della nave erano spesso la stessa persona, rifornivano di cibo le città marittime e assicuravano ai centri più grandi l'accesso alle materie prime di cui abbisognavano per l'industria tessile, delle costruzioni navali e così via.

IV

Mettendo da parte la breve distanza, cioè il commercio locale praticato con piccole navi per le fortune delle città più grandi, non è difficile vedere che un notevole cambiamento si produsse nel bacino del Mediterraneo quando Valencia emerse come prospero e popoloso centro di commercio internazionale, dal 1380 circa in poi. Un meditato studio di

[24] *I mercanti catalani* cit., p. 395.

Paulino Iradiel, pubblicato per la prima volta nel 1991 e riedito recentemente in un volume di saggi sul commercio delle città spagnole del Mediterraneo, è stato di grande aiuto per spiegarci che cosa stava accadendo[25]. Valencia ebbe infatti un ruolo composito, perché non fu semplicemente capace di fiorire come approdo per il traffico dall'Italia verso Granada, il Marocco, il Portogallo e le Fiandre, ma fu polo di attrazione anche come centro di produzione di generi alimentari speciali come frutta secca, vino e riso; la sua emergente industria tessile fu una fonte di profitti con cui poté essere acquistato il grano siciliano. Essa fu capace così di trarre beneficio dal generale cambiamento, già citato, della corrente di affari dalle regioni dominate dai Turchi verso aree più ad occidente, capaci di rifornire di merci simili i mercanti occidentali.

Valencia diventò la base di una comunità internazionale di mercanti, in un modo mai realizzato da Barcellona, in larga misura a causa di misure protezionistiche che risalivano ai tempi di Giacomo I e furono promulgate ancora sotto Alfonso il Magnanimo. Fiamminghi, Tedeschi, Milanesi, Toscani controllarono settori importanti del commercio della città, mentre la comunità originaria dei mercanti musulmani (la più illustre famiglia era quella dei Bellvis) rimaneva ridotta. In effetti, si ha l'impressione complessiva di una città i cui traffici dipendevano pesantemente da capitali stranieri; in questo senso l'ascesa di Valencia non fu esattamente un successo dei suoi abitanti. Per i mercanti stranieri, l'attrazione di Valencia, che divenne ancora più forte nel periodo della guerra civile successiva alla morte di Alfonso V d'Aragona, era data dalla sua buona posizione sulle rotte a lunga distanza dirette fuori del Mediterraneo, certamente migliore di quella di Barcellona. Dal 1436, le galee veneziane dirette ad Aigues-Mortes e nel Nordafrica si servivano regolarmente di Valencia come base. Come risultato, prodotti locali come la bellissima ceramica ispano-moresca trovarono spazio nelle stive dei vascelli in viaggio per l'Italia, l'Inghilterra e le Fiandre, e nel XV secolo venivano fabbricati servizi da tavola su ordinazione di clienti come i Medici di Firenze[26]. Valencia si trovò al posto giusto al momento giusto ed ebbe le risorse appropriate da utilizzare. In aggiunta, fu

[25] P. IRADIEL, *Valencia y la expansiòn mediterrànea de la Corona de Aragòn*, in *En las Costas del Mediterràneo Occidental. Las ciudades de la Penìnsula Ibérica y del reino de Mallorca y el comercio mediterràneo en la Edad Media*, a c. di D. Abulafia e B. Garì, Barcellona 1997, pp. 155-169 (rist. da *La Corona d'Aragò: el regne de València en l'expansiò mediterrànea 1238-1492*, Valencia 1991, pp. 81-88; cfr. anche GUIRAL-HADZIIOSSIF, *Valence* cit.

[26] Per il commercio della ceramica, cfr. l'eccellente catalogo bilingue della Mostra tenuta in Castelnuovo a Napoli, settembre-novembre 1997: *Valenza-Napoli. Rotte mediterranee della ceramica. València-Napols. Les rutes mediterrànies de la ceramica*, Napoli/ Valencia 1997.

creata una rotta commerciale per il Levante, ma Iradiel osserva che a trarne vantaggio furono navi e investitori maiorchini e castigliani. Già sotto Martino I, la città era in grado di offrire considerevoli sovvenzioni per le campagne italiane del re d'Aragona, sovvenzioni che crebbero per pagare le campagne di Alfonso il Magnanimo nel Regno di Napoli. La base dell'espansione commerciale di Valencia fu il bisogno della città di bilanciare il suo precario rifornimento di derrate alimentari con le risorse disponibili in materia di prodotti più specializzati, un aspetto dell'economia cittadina che orientò Valenza verso il commercio mediterraneo; una volta dimostrata la capacità di soddisfare i bisogni alimentari, erano gettate le basi per un periodo di significativa espansione demografica; anche così, la situazione restò precaria, e Earl Hamilton osservò forti oscillazioni del prezzo del grano a Valencia durante il XV secolo[27].

In ogni caso, è essenziale sottolineare anche l'importanza del commercio di cabotaggio nella creazione della prosperità di Valencia: dai porti a nord di Valencia fino a quelli catalani (come la già descritta Tossa) e oltre, fino alle acque occitane, *barcas*, *llauts* e *balleners* esploravano le coste in cerca di generi di necessità come grano, legname ecc. Il cabotaggio rese facilmente accessibile anche Ibiza, l'isola del sale, e un'intensiva penetrazione del Nordafrica fu condotta da navi che seguivano una rotta circolare attraverso la Granata musulmana giù verso i porti di quella che ora è l'Algeria e poi di nuovo su, spesso per la via di Maiorca (per suo conto, come vedremo, intimamente legata al Nordafrica), per tornare a Valencia. La penetrazione in Africa ampliò il ventaglio delle merci disponibili negli stessi mercati di Valencia, cosicché la città fu in grado di introdurre prodotti maghrebini nelle rotte del commercio a lunga distanza che passavano attraverso di essa; l'Africa era anche una significativa fonte di schiavi, sia per l'uso domestico sia per quello agricolo, un fenomeno che rifletteva la generale mancanza di manodopera di quel periodo. Gli Ebrei e i *conversos* di Valencia erano attivamente impegnati nell'esportazione di vino verso il Nordafrica, spesso per la via di Maiorca. Ma sicuramente il più chiaro segno del successo di Valencia in questo circuito commerciale è la forza globale della sua divisa aurea, che rifletteva gli intimi legami con il commercio africano dell'oro anche in un momento in cui le altre città europee potevano aver incontrato difficoltà nell'accesso al rifornimento d'oro. Hamilton è giunto alla conclusione che Valencia fu quasi unica alla fine del Medioevo per la sua monetazione d'oro e d'argento[28]. Ciò che colpisce è l'indipendenza della rete commerciale che ali-

---

[27] E.J. HAMILTON, *Money, prices and wages in Valencia, Aragon and Navarre 1351-1500*, Cambridge, Mass. 1936 (rist. Filadelfia 1975) pp. 55-59.
[28] Ibid., p. 40; ma cfr. anche pp. 17-26.

mentava Valencia da quella di Barcellona, e di conseguenza l'indipendenza dell'economia valenzana dalle tendenze catalane.

Prendendo in considerazione l'importanza del Maghreb per il commercio di Valencia in questo periodo, è quasi una sorpresa riesaminare le
statistiche fornite da Mario Del Treppo per il commercio di Barcellona in
Barberia, basate sulla documentazione dei contratti di assicurazione. Esa-
minando il periodo tra il 1428 e il 1493, egli mostra che ci furono 459
contratti registrati per commercio con la Sicilia (220 dei quali per Palermo), 336 con la Francia meridionale (spesso collegati al traffico di grano),
334 con la Sardegna, 240 col Levante, 212 col Regno, mentre il numero
delle assicurazioni per il Nordafrica, 106, è addirittura lievemente inferio-
re a quello delle visite nelle Fiandre e in Inghilterra[29]. Alessandria, che
conta come parte del Levante (65 visite), supera di gran lunga Orano (19),
Tunisi (17), per non considerare destinazioni classiche come Bugia (6) o
Tripoli (1)[30]. In altri termini, la Barberia contava solo per l'1,8% del commercio assicurato fuori da Barcellona nel 1428-29, un insignificante 0,2%
tra il 1436 e il 1446, e un più rispettabile 9% tra il 1453 e il 1461[31]. Negli
stessi anni, gli investimenti nelle rotte del Levante, di Sicilia e delle Fiandre erano incomparabilmente più notevoli. Il quadro complessivo ricorda così quello disegnato dagli storici dall'antico commercio genovese che
hanno studiato i primi contratti notarili del XII secolo; anche allora i contratti per il Levante e la Sicilia tendevano a prevalere, perché le condizioni permettevano un facile accesso, mentre il commercio locale è certo
significativamente trascurato nelle registrazioni[32]. In altre parole, vi erano
circostanze che costringevano i mercanti a registrare accuratamente questi contratti e, verso il XV secolo, ad assicurarli; ma naturalmente vi era la
tendenza ad assicurare merci inviate lungo le rotte più pericolose sulle
navi ritenute meno sicure, e all'inizio del XV secolo i premi d'assicurazione per le galee in viaggio verso il Nordafrica restavano più bassi di
quelli per le navi rotonde a vela.

È chiaro che le basse cifre del commercio barbaresco non riflettono la
più ampia realtà dei contatti col Nordafrica, le cui difficoltà diplomatiche
non comportarono interruzioni a lungo termine nei contatti, e i consola-
ti catalani continuarono a funzionare nei porti del Maghreb. Né i porti
barbareschi erano considerati particolarmente pericolosi: Del Treppo
osserva che un premio d'assicurazione del 3-5% soltanto suggerisce che

---

[29] *I mercanti catalani* cit., p. 157.
[30] Ibid., p. 159, tabella II.
[31] Ibid., p. 148, tabella I.
[32] Per questo problema, cfr. D. ABULAFIA, *The two Italies*, Cambridge 1977 (trad. it. *Le due Italie*, Napoli 1991).

36

gli accessi al Nordafrica non erano ritenuti danneggiati da seri problemi di pirateria; il premio è spesso più basso di quello caricabile su viaggi per la Francia meridionale e la Sardegna. Nota Del Treppo: «Il confronto tra i premi dell'itinerario francese e quelli dell'itinerario africano (spesso assai più lungo perché includeva Tunisi e Tripoli), parla senza dubbio in favore della maggiore sicurezza di quest'ultimo»[33]. Le navi che si sa hanno visitato il Nordafrica seguivano talvolta complicate rotte circolari, come la *nau* di Ca Torra nel 1452, le cui possibili destinazioni includevano Tortosa, Valencia, Malaga, Almeria, Tripoli, la Sicilia. Altri contratti d'assicurazione rivelano viaggi di ritorno che passavano per la via di Maiorca[34].

Molte delle navi menzionate nei documenti d'assicurazione per il Nordafrica erano delle *naus*, con una *galea* occasionale che ottenne un premio più basso, e questa stessa nave appare spesso su altre rotte sia per le Fiandre, Genova o Venezia; molto meno dicono i contratti circa le più piccole *llenys* e *barcas* le quali erano state a lungo attive nel commercio che collegava Barcellona a Maiorca e al Maghreb. Ci si può chiedere allora quanto questi battelli fossero tipici della navigazione giornaliera che collegava le terre spagnole all'Africa. La documentazione del commercio africano, o la sua relativa mancanza, è certamente in stridente contrasto con la situazione alla fine del XIII e all'inizio del XIV secolo, quando si può sostenere che il Nordafrica ebbe il primo posto nel commercio marittimo catalano. Inoltre ciò contrasta col quadro che abbiamo per il XVI secolo, quando la preoccupazione per la sicurezza sulle rotte africane, tra gli altri fattori, sfociò in una severa contrazione del commercio barcellonese col Maghreb. Sotto Alfonso V, è vero, il commercio con l'Africa era causa di qualche preoccupazione, benché ciò che interessava Alfonso nelle sue trattative con Tunisi fosse l'acquisto obbligato di grandi quantità (15-20.000 salme) di grano siciliano. Tale fatto getta tuttavia poca luce sulla perdurante fortuna di mercanti dal suo territorio spagnolo verso il Nordafrica. Un altro fattore che potrebbe essere invocato per la contrazione del commercio africano con le regioni catalane era la caduta della domanda di lana africana, quando la produzione sotto la Corona di Aragona e in Castiglia era salita a prodigiosi livelli. I Maiorchini dunque non erano più particolarmente interessati alle lane di Barberia, o perché ne producevano in proprio o perché le compravano nella vicina Minorca, punto di attrazione anche per Francesco Datini di Prato. Altri prodotti nordafricani tuttavia, come il cuoio e naturalmente l'oro, conservavano le loro attrattive.

La risposta al problema della mancanza di documentazione sui con-

---

[33] *I mercanti catalani* cit., p. 487.
[34] Ibid., pp. 708-709.

tratti d'assicurazione del commercio col Maghreb può, in effetti, risiedere nel maggiore risalto che tali contratti davano a imprese su larga scala in navi capaci. Tuttavia il carattere del commercio maghrebino con la Catalogna era sotto certi aspetti alquanto diverso da quello con Maiorca. Come si può vedere già tra la fine del XIII e l'inizio del XIV secolo, esisteva una rete annuale fluida e rapida di rotte mercantili che collegavano Barcellona a Maiorca e quest'ultima ai porti del Nordafrica; come si è visto, anche Valencia nel XV secolo creò una propria rete non dissimile, che raggiungeva tanto Maiorca quanto Malaga e Almeria. Passando dai contratti d'assicurazione di Barcellona ai documenti di Maiorca, studiati da Sevillano Colom e da Macaire, emerge un quadro differente[35]. Il Nordafrica continuava a dominare nei *viatges* concessi a Maiorca durante il regno di Alfonso: dal 1416 al 1419, furono rilasciate 42 licenze di commercio col Maghreb; dal 1440 al 1450 sono 101, benché in seguito si registri un calo. Nel 1445, il 58% dei *guiatges* maiorchini riguardano il commercio col Maghreb, benché in genere la cifra fosse più bassa. In effetti, le cifre sono anche più notevoli tra 1400 e 1411, quando furono rilasciate 444 licenze, una media di 37 all'anno, in un'epoca in cui le scorrerie dal Nordafrica contro Maiorca diventarono una difficoltà costante[36]. L'analisi di Macaire degli affari di Astruch Xibili, ebreo maiorchino che era anche un attivissimo assicuratore, mostra come i suoi forti interessi nel commercio di Barcellona, Valencia, Sicilia e Sardegna fiorissero accanto ad un intenso coinvolgimento nei traffici col Nordafrica; come nei secoli precedenti, Ebrei e *conversos* erano fortemente interessati al commercio tra Maiorca e il Nordafrica. I registri del notaio Anthoni Costanti, che coprono gran parte della prima metà del secolo XV, indicano un commercio intenso di panni esportati nel Maghreb (196 documenti) e importazioni di cera, cuoio e oro. Non vi sono meno di 391 visite identificabili di navi salpate da Maiorca per destinazioni nordafricane; 311 di questi viaggi (l'80%) erano effettuati su navi delle Baleari e solo 20 su navi di Barcellona, 18 su navi genovesi e 14 su navi castigliane. Sono anche presenti piccole imbarcazioni di città minori della Catalogna come Blanes e San Feliu de Guixols, a sottolineare il fatto che questo commercio non era molto diverso come caratteristiche rispetto al cabotaggio costiero già analizzato. Il porto africano preferito fu Algeri (102 visite), seguito da Tunisi (56) e, non molto distaccati, da centri come Tenes, Collo,

35 F.S. COLOM-J.P. MOUNTANER, *Historia del puerto de Palma de Mallorca*, Palma de Mallorca 1974; P. MACAIRE, *Majorque et le commerce international (1400-1450 environ)*, Lille 1986; non sono riuscito a consultare P. MACAIRE, *Majorque et le Maghrib au XVe siècle*, 2 voll., tesi di dottorato, Univ. di Paris-Nanterre 1977.
36 COLOM, *op. cit.*, pp. 188-190.

38

Bugia. Tenes fa anche molte apparizioni nei documenti di *guiatges*, come Algeri[37].

Il quadro ricorda per certi aspetti quello già tracciato del commercio locale: una grande quantità di piccoli vascelli che salpano giorno dopo giorno, con a bordo mercanti certamente in cerca di mercati per panni catalani e maiorchini, ma anche di fare incetta di merci africane come la cera da rivendere nell'Europa continentale. In altre parole, la mancanza di un gran numero di contratti d'assicurazione da Barcellona per il commercio nordafricano riflette la natura caratteristica di tale commercio, il quale era condotto a tappe, con Maiorca, o certamente Valencia, come punti di approdo[38]. La penetrazione catalana nel Maghreb, come ha supposto Colom, non diminuì nel XV secolo, a dispetto degli alti e bassi causati dalla politica del re Alfonso (l'invasione di Djerba nel 1435, per esempio), guidata tanto dai suoi interessi in Sicilia, Italia meridionale e Mediterraneo occidentale quanto dall'attenzione per quelli iberici nel Maghreb.

V

Del Treppo apre il suo libro con una citazione del XV secolo: il commercio del Levante era il *foment, cap e principi de tot lo negoci*; in più, *perturbats los afers de Levant, en gran part son desviats tots les altres*[39]. Per Del Treppo, il commercio col Levante funge da barometro, fornendo una guida sulla salute complessiva dell'economia della Catalogna o almeno di Barcellona; «quella del Levante restava dunque ancora la più importante corrente del commercio internazionale di Barcellona, che ad essa era debitrice di tutte le sue fortune e della prosperità della sua classe dirigente»[40]. Il problema difficile è precisamente quello del rapporto fra le attività commerciali di questa "classe dirigente", specialmente i Barcellonesi coinvolti nelle aspre contese delle fazioni della *Biga* e

---

[37] MACAIRE, *op. cit.*, pp. 411, 426-427; cfr. D. ABULAFIA, *A Mediterranean Emporium. The Catalan Kingdom of Majorca*, Cambridge 1994, p. 228.

[38] Sono lieto di apprendere che questo quadro è confermato dalle ricerche molto interessanti di M.D. LOPEZ PEREZ in presentazione a questo Congresso: *Mallorca y el Mediterràneo en la primera mitad del siglo XV: el àrea maghrebì*, il cui sommario è stampato nei riassunti delle comunicazioni, Napoli 1997, pp 94-95; cfr. anche ID., *La Corona de Aragòn y el Magreb en el siglo XV (1331-1410)*, Barcellona 1995.

[39] A. DE CAPMANY, *Memorias historicas sobre la marina, comercio y artes de la antigua ciudad de Barcelona*, a c. di E. Giralt e C. Batlle, Barcellona 1961-62, vol. II, p. 535, doc. 370.

[40] *I mercanti catalani* cit., p. 1.

della *Busca*, e il più vasto mondo del commercio catalano, il quale comprendeva città grandi e piccole lungo le coste catalane e valenzane e nelle isole del Mediterraneo ed aiutava i più ricchi mercanti di assicurare che i centri maggiori come Barcellona e Ciutat de Mallorca fossero regolarmente rifornite dei prodotti indispensabili. Senza dubbio, il livello degli investimenti in Oriente nel corso del XV secolo è imponente, benché su quelle rotte i concorrenti italiani, specialmente i Veneziani, fossero generalmente in una posizione dominante. Comunque, all'interno delle reti commerciali dei Catalani erano un elemento decisivo anche più modesti sistemi attivi nel Mediterraneo occidentale nella distribuzione di beni essenziali e nella rivendita di merci acquistate al di fuori della regione dei compratori, nel Maghreb, nella Francia meridionale, in Spagna e altrove. È chiaro che il benessere economico della comunità catalano-aragonese all'inizio del XV secolo non si può misurare guardando solo Barcellona, quale che sia il punto di vista sul suo supposto declino: non si può ignorare lo spettacolare successo di Valencia e, per un certo periodo, di Ciutat de Mallorca, Perpignano e altri centri.

Anche importante è la rivelazione di Del Treppo che la conquista di Napoli da parte dell'Aragonese aprì nuovi e vivaci mercati per i mercanti catalani; essi colsero l'opportunità per accedere a Napoli e all'Italia meridionale, tanto più in quanto furono capaci di riempire il vuoto lasciato dai Fiorentini. Nei contratti d'assicurazione di Barcellona sono registrate 137 visite a Napoli, superata da Palermo (212) e Alghero (186) nella graduatoria delle città toccate da navi di Barcellona[41]. A Napoli il commercio catalano sembra aver alimentato le locali rotte di cabotaggio, che, come abbiamo visto, si estendevano fino al Tevere a nord e in Calabria a sud, sempre nelle mani di operatori locali su scala relativamente piccola (il vino rosso di Calabria era spesso ottenuto via Tropea). Soltanto dopo la conquista, i Catalani cominciarono a prendere sul serio il commercio dell'Italia meridionale, in opposizione a quello della Sicilia. L'entusiasmo del re certamente ebbe un ruolo significativo nell'espansione dei collegamenti tra Napoli e Barcellona; nel 1445 Alfonso V era ansioso di vedere stabilito un collegamento regolare mediante due galee, una pagata da lui e l'altra dai suoi tre Stati iberici. Inoltre, i mercanti catalani stabilitisi a Napoli non erano uomini nuovi o operatori su piccola scala, ma uomini d'affari già affermati nel commercio del Mediterraneo occidentale, il più noto dei quali è forse Johan de Torralba[42]. Gaspar Muntmany, altro nome di rilievo, stabilì rapporti d'affari tra Napoli e Tunisi negli ultimi anni del regno di Alfonso e nei primi di Ferrante; non fu la successione di Ferrante

[41] Ibid., p. 159, tabella II.
[42] Ibid., pp. 757-827.

ad un Regno di Napoli separato a condurre ad un declino di tali rapporti, ma la crisi interna della Catalogna che culminò nella guerra civile. Meno evidente la presenza dei Valenzani, ma proprio dall'Aragona vennero importanti finanzieri come Felipe de la Cavalleria, membro di un'importante famiglia di *conversos,* a lungo vicina alla Corona. Comunque il più importante arrivo non fu di carattere umano: fu il panno catalano, perché fu trovato un sostanzioso nuovo mercato per i panni di lana prodotti a Barcellona, Maiorca, Perpignano e altrove. Nel periodo 1447-1469, il 75,8% delle esportazioni catalane registrate nel Regno consisteva in panni catalani, mentre solo il 3% era di panni non catalani e qui possiamo vedere Johan de Torralba attivo nel suo trasporto da Ibiza al Regno[43].

Merci più modeste come pesce ed altri generi alimentari appaiono poco frequentemente; Napoli dunque non era integrata nel reticolo di distribuzione che si irradiava dalla Catalogna per il trasporto di questi prodotti, mentre, come abbiamo visto, c'era un attivo commercio locale nelle mani di mercanti di Gaeta, Amalfi e molti altri centri. L'importazione di panni catalani e valenzani nei territori italiani di Alfonso fu incrementata dalla sua decisione di pagare i soldati in panni, una scelta accorta che sottolinea la sua comprensione di importanti questioni economiche, come è anche evidente nelle sue ordinanze tese a dare assoluta priorità alla flotta catalana. Questo concetto è contenuto in una lettera del dicembre 1451 citata da Del Treppo, nella quale Alfonso esprimeva il suo desiderio di portare a termine il *redreçament dela mercaderia en nostres Regnes* con l'aiuto di *una mutua e reciproca contractacio e comerci deles coses al us dela vida principalment necessaries*[44]. Anche i tentativi di far acquistare da parte dei Catalani più grano dalla Sicilia che dalla Francia meridionale possono far parte dell'immagine di un re il quale, avido di danaro, nella sua ricerca di finanziamenti cominciò a comprendere qualcuna delle potenziali relazioni economiche all'interno del suo vasto dominio.

Inoltre, le solide radici di questa rete commerciale sono altrove. Il Mediterraneo orientale era anche la sede dell'umile cabotaggio, il cui volume resta impossibile da misurare, ma il cui ruolo nella distribuzione delle merci *al us de la vita principalment necessaries* era assolutamente essenziale. Ci sono ancora molte questioni irrisolte concernenti la relazione tra il commercio a breve e quello a lunga distanza; in particolare, è molto difficile delineare paragoni con i secoli precedenti, per i quali la documentazione è in genere anche più frammentaria. Ma certamente vale la pena di porre le questioni. Mi sono qui proposto il fine di spostare il bilan-

---

[43] Ibid., pp. 211-213 e 216.
[44] Ibid., p. 603.

cio del nostro tema fuori dalle "grandi correnti" e di recuperare qualcosa di quella *routine* giornaliera di traffici lungo le coste della Spagna mediterranea, nell'Italia meridionale, sulla rotta delle isole, verso il Maghreb, di quella rete che contribuì a fare del Mediterraneo occidentale al tempo di Alfonso il Magnanimo un mare aperto al commercio.

IX

Grain Traffic out of the Apulian Ports on behalf of Lorenzo de'Medici, 1486-7

I

The intention here is to introduce some documentation concerning the grain trade in the central Mediterranean at the end of the fifteenth century which raises more general questions about the way in which local commerce functioned, and the role of international companies such as the Medici in that commerce. The theme is, in part, the relationship between the grain producing lands of the Italian South and the islands and towns on the opposing shore of the Adriatic; an analysis of this material might also, therefore, serve as a model for similar mainland-island relationships in the same period, such as the grain traffic between Sicily and the dependent Maltese islands. In particular, it will be seen how the role of locally born merchants must not be underestimated in looking at the trade in wheat in the late medieval Mediterranean, even when at the same time we are observing the presence of the biggest trading firms of the fifteenth century.

The involvement of the Florentines in the grain trade of Apulia can be traced back to the end of the thirteenth century. As the political alliance between the Guelfs of Florence and the Angevin rulers of Naples grew ever more intimate, so did the commercial ties, ensuring a market for Florentine cloths in Naples, but also, very importantly, providing Florence with a regular source of good quality wheat from the fields of Capitanata and other grain producing areas of the Neapolitan kingdom. By 1300 the three great Florentine companies of the Bardi, Peruzzi and Acciaiuoli were obtaining from the kings of Naples generous export privileges, exempting them (even) from some of the major trade taxes, and enabling them to transfer prodigious quantities of the so-called *grano ciciliano* to their home city.[1] Without this regular food supply it is hard to see how Trecento Florence could have survived, let alone maintained its phenomenal expansion as a centre of trade and industry: according to an early fourteenth-century source it could only feed itself from local resources for on average five months out of twelve, and southern grain had the enormous advantage of being versatile in its use and easy to preserve (hard wheats being by definition dry, and therefore resistant to rot).[2] The dependence on Naples was accentuated by the difficulties Florence faced in its dealings with Aragonese Sicily, another obvious source of grain, though even there Guelf Florence sealed some improbable business deals with the island's Ghibelline-allied rulers. As for Capitanata, this had been targeted as a good source of grain by the rulers of southern Italy since at least the time of Frederick II. The fields around Lucera were regarded as an especially important source of wheat, and Frederick II had even been prepared to supply oxen and other necessities to the deported Sicilian Saracens who inhabited Lucera, in order to maximise production. Much of the grain produced in the

Capitanata for export was then channelled towards Manfredonia, the port established, as its name suggests, by King Manfred of Sicily (d. 1266) close to the ancient harbour of Siponto; Manfredonia, without a change of name (despite recalling the mortal enemy of the house of Anjou) remained afterwards a vital nexus in the Apulian grain trade. Additionally, the expansion and consolidation of the *masserie*, the state farms characteristic of south-eastern Italy in the Angevin period, ensured a continuing emphasis on production for export, with the state as a major beneficiary.[3] As for the direct involvement of the government in the export of premium grade wheat from Apulia, this can be demonstrated in detail from the late thirteenth century onwards, beginning with Charles I of Anjou's interest in the grain trade between Venice and Apulia.[4] A 'grain weapon' came into being, with rulers such as Robert the Wise (d. 1343) showing themselves willing to deny Venice access to Apulian grain if the Serenissima did not co-operate with Angevin political aims in the Italian peninsula and even further afield.[5] Yet despite the importance of the grain traffic to Florence, Venice and other large towns, the Apulian grain trade also supplied much nearer markets. Bariš Krekić has demonstrated how important to Dubrovnik (Ragusa) was regular provision in Apulian grain, given the lack of extensive local supplies;[6] Albania, too, could be the beneficiary of the Apulian grain trade, when the kings of Naples were seeking to extend their influence to its shores. Of course, there were ups and downs in the Apulian grain trade, and it is likely that the years after the Black Death saw a decline in demand for southern wheat in the depopulated cities of northern Italy, though by no means a collapse. After the arrival of the plague, land was freed for other uses than grain production (a trend already, perhaps, visible in pre-plague Tuscany, as dependence on outside grain supplies became increasingly convenient). Apulia became as famous for its sheep as it was for its grain; and under Alfonso V of Aragon (d. 1458) a massive expansion in the sheep population took place in Apulia, with the crown benefiting enormously by way of the *dogana delle pecore*. The more diversified diet of the post-plague population reduced the significance of grain production; but local specialisation also meant that areas were given over increasingly to other products (in the Abruzzi, for instance, saffron; in Malta there appears to have been a significant recovery in cotton production). This acted as a stimulus to short distance grain traffic, of the sort we shall shortly be examining. As Stephan Epstein has argued in the case of post-plague Sicily, we can see complementary relationships developing between neighbouring regions, so that the Val Demone was able to concentrate on the production of wine and cloths for the domestic market, while other parts of the island were still clearly important producers of wheat surpluses, which could be traded internally.[7] Generally, we can think of the late fourteenth and fifteenth centuries as a period in which short distance inter-regional trade comes into its own; we should thus be very cautious of assuming that a decline in long distance trade, or crises in the big banking houses, are symptomatic of a general crisis in commerce.[8] Particularly in the late fifteenth century, conditions were changing in ways that would favour grain producers. Population recovery was at last taking a hold in Sicily, and, as current research reveals, in southern Italy as well.[9] The international market in grain was reviving, but so too was the internal market, as well as demand from neighbouring regions.

II

These are fundamental considerations that need to be borne in mind when examining the *Copia quaterni Bernardi de Anghono magistri actorum penes magistrum portulanum Apulie de tractis extractis in anno quinte indictionis a portibus civitatis Manfridonie, Baroli, Trani, Vigiliarum, Melficte, Iuvinaczi, Bari, Mole, Sancti Viti de Polignano et de portu Polignani tam per extra Regnum quam infra.*[10] This notebook, recording the grain traffic out of Manfredonia and the Apulian ports, consists of fifty-six pages, and carries the date 1486, though the fifth indiction in question ran from 1 September 1486 to 31 August 1487. It has been edited in the series of *Fonti Aragonesi* published by the venerable Accademia Pontaniana of Naples (which was coming into existence at the very time the document was drawn up). Its editor, Catello Salvati, notes that the document falls into several parts: the first eleven folios are concerned with *tratte*, permits for the export beyond the *Regno* of wheat and other grains from Manfredonia, during most of the year that the document covers; a further section of five folios lists the wheat movements aimed at the internal market within southern Italy, including wheat labelled *pro usu Curie*. We then move to the other ports, with extensive material on Barletta and Trani, and some material towards the end of the document on Bisceglie, Molfetta and smaller centres.[11] Although the document is described as a *copia*, it is possible that this means it was compiled from a mass of documents, such as the original texts of the *tratte*; there are interpolations and corrections which suggest that it is not simply a transcription from an existing register.[12] On the other hand, the entries have the character of abridged minutes:

Die eodem concessa fuit licentia Antonio de Granita de Manfridonia extrahendo de dicto portu et ferendum extra regnum cum navigio Luce de Luca de Catera de tumulis viginti quatuor frumenti

carri 0, *tomoli* 24
[Quat., p. 13][13]

The document thus appears to function as an account book, listing the totals exported *in curribus et tumulis*, and enabling the central administration to tot up the figures for exports out of the Apulian ports in the fifth indiction.

The simple fact that the document is in Naples, and that it represents the results of record keeping in several Apulian ports, suggests that it was copied to meet the needs of central government under King Ferrante (Ferdinand) I of Naples (reigned 1458-94).[14] The office of portulan was, by the Aragonese period, a well established one, which can trace its origins back to Norman times. Given the importance of revenues from trade to the royal fisc in the Neapolitan kingdom, it is not surprising that this official was expected to watch out for smugglers, to check that only permitted quantities of grain were passing through the ports, and to ensure that the royal court was adequately supplied with the food it needed.[15] The portulan was expected to denounce to the royal Sommaria in Naples those who offended against the export regulations. Salvati considers that the Maestro Portulano of Apulia resided at Barletta in the fifteenth century, though his documentation partly dates from as early as 1293. In any case, one duty of the portulans was to keep a note of the concessions made by the crown to licensed exporters, and to record their use of these concessions. Salvati points out that the entries in the register here under examination did not generally cite royal privileges, except in those cases, such as that of Lorenzo de'Medici, other foreign trading houses, and special concessions to monastic houses, which were sanctioned by special instructions from the central government.[16] Ordinary merchants of more modest means were covered by blanket instructions that so much grain might be exported at any one time; the task of the portulans then became that of ensuring that the total exported did not exceed the stipulated maximum, but there was no need to check the credentials of each merchant by asking them to produce a royal privilege; instead they appear to have had the power to grant the merchants the licences to export which they sought: *concessa fuit licentia*, followed by the merchant's name. The basic principle appears to have been that of 'first come, first serve'. What the crown wanted was to shift the grain. It called implicitly on the services of all the grain merchants and shipowners of Apulia, and of their partners in Dalmatia and elsewhere, to help in this massive task. The portulans did not normally specify the destination of the grain whose export they recorded; but they did consistently note the name of the beneficiary of the export licence, the name of the port from which export was permitted, the owner of the ship and the quantity of grain being exported, which they then summarised for accounting purposes at the end of the brief entry.

III

In order to understand the role of Lorenzo de'Medici in the grain export traffic out of Apulia, it is now necessary to consider the fortunes of the Medici branch in Naples. Fortunately, Raymond de Roover analysed the documentation in Florence, largely collected for him by Florence Edler de Roover.[17] Neither shows any awareness of the south Italian documentation, however, apart from an article by the noted Apulian historian Carabellese.[18] The early history of the Medici in Naples in fact brings together the great names in Florentine trade and banking: in 1400 Giovanni di Bicci de'Medici and Benedetto di Lipaccio de'Bardi used as their factor in Naples Castellano di Tommaso Frescobaldi, and his assistant was probably a member of the Tornaquinci family. By 1402 the Medici had three factors in Naples and Gaeta, but business in Naples was conducted in fact in the Bardi name.[19] In the early fifteenth century, the Naples branch had to struggle to show itself useful. De Roover remarks: 'on the average, profits barely exceeded 760 florins per annum over a period of approximately twenty-one years extending from 1400 to September 1, 1420'.[20] In addition to poor profits, there was the problem of the internal strife within the kingdom of Naples, now suffering from the poor management of Joanna II and her ministers, as well as from conflict between *condottieri*; in 1426 the Naples branch was actually closed down, and it remained shut until 1471. Even then there were continued difficulties, and an office they maintained in Apulia, at Trani, was given the task of co-ordinating food purchases in Bitonto, Gallipoli, Monopoli, Ostuni and Terlizzi, where Medici factors were posted. Lack of resources threatened a crash just when the Pazzi conspiracy and the outbreak of war between Ferrante of Naples and Florence in any case sundered all business ties between the Medici and the Neapolitan kingdom. Medici property in the Apulian out-stations was confiscated, but most of the records of the bank were saved from Ferrante's men, with the result that the Aragonese government could not recover for itself the debts and goods it had hoped to acquire.[21] Lorenzo de'Medici, however, had the political sense to see that his war with Naples was of benefit to no-one, and he made a famous visit to Naples in 1479, entering the lion's den in the hope of creating a newly intimate relationship with Ferrante of Naples; in this he succeeded, and the results for Italian politics were a significant realignment.[22] Ferrante genuinely mourned Lorenzo's death in 1492, seeing it rightly as a sign that the old order was coming to an end in the Italian peninsula.

The advantages were also commercial. The Medici bank was restored in Naples; however, there was still no sign that the Naples branch would make a profit, especially since there were old debts to be repaid (some arising from the venture in Apulia already mentioned); in 1483 a loss of 30,000 ducats was being predicted. The War of Ferrara also had a disruptive effect between 1481 and 1484. The Second Barons' Rebellion of 1485 also disrupted seriously the internal life of the kingdom, and the document under investigation here dates from the period of reconstruction after the civil conflict.[23] At this point King Ferrante must have been keen to encourage the export trade, and the resulting revenues; and he evidently saw in the financial operations of the Medici a way of stimulating the kingdom's grain exports: this emerges from the references to royal privileges in favour of Lorenzo de'Medici, which will be discussed shortly. In any case, in 1486 the Medici operations in Naples were restarted yet again under the management of a trusted agent of the Medici, Francesco Naso, who had struggled manfully to keep the bank afloat before and after the Pazzi crisis.[24] The new company operated in the name of Naso, and the Medici did not agree to give their name to the Naples branch; in any case Naso died in 1489. Thereafter the Naples branch became ever more closely tied to the Rome branch, operating from 1490 under the name of Giovanni Tornabuoni, and was absorbed by the Tornabuoni when the Medici bank failed in 1494. De Roover notes that the Naples office seems to have been making loans to the royal court around this time, and that this was a departure from the practice long ago advised by Cosimo de'Medici; probably it reflects a need to cultivate good relations with King Ferrante. Politics was intruding more and more into the operation of the Medici bank, which in any case no longer benefited from the serious interest of Lorenzo de'Medici.[25] Though the Naples branch was never especially important compared to branches much further afield, its fortunes and misfortunes provide an interesting index of the evolution and decay of the Medici Bank as a whole.

IV

The first general feature of the portulan accounts of 1486-7 is the high profile of local merchants and, no less strikingly, shipowners; the general assumption has been that south Italian merchants had long given way on the significant international trade routes to the 'big fish' of Venice, Genoa and Barcelona. Francesco Coppola, the count of Sarno and confidant of Ferrante I, was undoubtedly an exception; his prominence in mercantile affairs emerges clearly from the fact that he is the one really active native merchant at the well documented Salerno fair of 1478.[26] He was soon to meet his end as a result of his perhaps surprising participation in the great baronial rebellion of 1485. Otherwise, it is assumed, there is not much to say about native merchants. Bari and its neighbours had had their heyday in the pre-Norman period, but were now simply the targets of foreign businessmen, notably the Venetians, with their major installations at Barletta and Trani. Venice indeed aspired to such influence that it sought on several occasions to establish mastery over the key Apulian ports, and its acquisition of Molfetta and other centres during the French invasion of 1494-5 was the realisation of long harboured dreams.[27] However, more localised trade evidently did remain in the hands of both merchants and shipowners from Apulia itself, as well as a significant number of Dalmatian wheat carriers.

It makes sense to begin by analysing some data from the first part of the register of 1486-7, that dealing with the export trade out of Manfredonia. The aim here is not to provide a statistical treatment, which would raise the question whether 1486-7 is typical of other years of King Ferrante's reign (which is unlikely, in view of the recent rebellion); but rather the aim is to convey some sense of the rhythm of trade through observing its personnel. Thus in October 1486 Troiano and Francesco *de Buctunis* of Trani were given the right to export a sizeable cargo of *carri* 40 of wheat on the ship of Giliberti *de Buctunis*, which was to be operated by Giovanni de Rico of Molfetta [Quat., p.3]. The same ship was also being used by other combinations of investors, such as Palumbo de Gello and Giliberto *de Buctunis*, who wanted to shift *carri* 6, *tomoli* 18 of wheat [Quat., p. 3]. These were clearly reasonably big operators, since they also made use of a Venetian ship to move over 500 *carri* of wheat on 3 November 1486 [Quat., p. 4]. Pietro di Barletta exported grain using his own ship in December 1486 [Quat., p. 4]. In addition to south Italian merchants, there is also a prominent group of Dalmatian merchants and shippers. Nicola Radi Nicolai of Dubrovnik exported from Manfredonia a small quantity of wheat at the end of October, 1486; he used a ship of his own, while Allegretto Michele of Dubrovnik used a vessel operated by another Ragusan merchant [Quat., p. 4]. Not surprisingly, the exports from Manfredonia were often managed by Manfredonian merchants. The castellan Pietro Baccharo used as his procurator Dionisio de Florio of Manfredonia, who himself made use of Luigi Capuano; here we find the crown intervening to allow the castellan to export from the estates close to his base at *castri Rogi* [Quat., p. 5]. Baccharo also made use of Ragusan merchants and shipowners, exporting *carri* 55, a sizeable amount, on the ship of Marco of Dubrovnik. This ship was also favoured by the castellan of Manfredonia itself, Geronimo Michele [Quat., p. 6] (Geronimo also sent wheat within the kingdom [Quat., p. 21]). Among other Dalmatian vessels we find shipping from Korczula (*Corzula*) and Šibenik (*Scivinico*), as well as Kotor (*Cathera*) and Krk (*Vergla*) [Quat., pp. 7-8, 15, 17]. But it was Lesina nearby on the Gargano peninsula which had a particularly prominent role in the shipping of grain out of Manfredonia [see e.g. Quat., pp. 7-9]. A royal letter permitted Francesco Palmieri of Naples, with Tommaso de Franco of Manfredonia as his agent, to export *carri* 27, *tomoli* 28 of wheat from the *Regno* on the ship of Matteo of Lesina; the royal privilege was dated September 1486, but the export took place in April 1487 [Quat., p. 12]. There was a large merchant fleet from Lesina, including vessels that carried both large and small cargoes: *carri* 90, and also a mere *tomoli* 9 [Quat., p. 16]. We can thus see the shipowners gradually making up their cargoes until they were satisfied that the vessel was adequately loaded. Barley also figured among the exports carried on boats of Lesina, but in much smaller quantities [Quat., p. 16].

There was also an active internal trade in grain within the *Regno*, in which not surprisingly native merchants had a very high profile. Giacobello *de Chianola* of Viesti took *carro* 1 of grain from Manfredonia to Viesti aboard a ship of his home town [Quat., pp. 17-18]. We also find businessmen from Lipari engaged in the internal grain trade [Quat., p. 17]. Barley as well as wheat made its way from Manfredonia down to Monopoli [Quat., p. 18]. The Pistoiese merchant Giacomo Rosso and his agents were given royal permission to take *carri* 68 of wheat all the way to Naples, under the terms of a royal privilege of 6 September 1486, which was acted upon the very next day [Quat., p. 18]; another cargo of 124 *carri* was recorded under the names of Giacomo Rosso of Pistoia and Niccolò Lippo of Florence two days later, 'ferendum infra regnum cum sayectia Philippi Policastri de Liparo' [Quat., p. 19]. Giacomo Rosso was in fact one of the most persistent exporters of Capitanata grain towards Naples; the quantities cited in each licence are large – 41 *carri* here, 74 *carri* there, 53 *carri* elsewhere [Quat., p. 19]. But his ships came from diverse places, including Barletta, such as the ship of Elia di Maffeo, which we learn from a neighbouring document was under the command of Marco Primo of Dubrovnik [Quat., p. 20]. Rosso de'Rossi of Pistoia used the ship of the Ragusan Luca Poli for internal trade in wheat; Rosso's business partner was a Manfredonian, Gabriele di Franco [Quat., p. 21]. The royal portulan Tommaso Barono also exported grain under licence, in the direction of Naples, on the same ship [Quat., p. 20]. An interesting exporter is the *Consolato mercatantl de Manfredonia*, the local board of trade, which in late November took *carro* 1 of wheat out of Manfredonia *infra regnum*.

Similar images of co-operation between Tuscans, Dalmatians and *regnicoli* could be gleaned from the documentation in the same register concerning other ports than Manfredonia. Barletta (*Baruli*) reveals to view merchants of Molfetta, Trani, Manfredonia and Barletta itself; several merchants known from the Manfredonia entries reappear in the Barletta ones [Quat., pp. 25-50]. Trani is well represented among places of origin of non-Barlettan merchants [see e.g. Quat., pp. 32-3]. We meet again Giliberto *de Buctunis*, engaged in a complex manoeuvre which involves the loading of *carri* 40 of grain in Barletta, its transfer to Manfredonia, and its re-export from the kingdom on another vessel [Quat., p. 29]; this type of operation seems to have been relatively frequent, since other merchants adopted the same method [Quat., p. 30-1]. It was probably linked to the export trade towards the Dalmatian towns, as some of the participants in this trade were from Dubrovnik: Simone Caliste *de Ragusio* and Giovanni Allegretti *de Ragusio*, the latter of whom has already been encountered in Manfredonia [Quat., p. 31]. Equally, some traffic passed from Barletta to Trani for re-loading on other ships, a point to which it will be necessary to return [Quat., p. 32]. Giliberto *de Buctunis* is also seen making use of a shipper from Split (*Spalatro*) [Quat., p. 29]. Pietro *de Iudeis* of Barletta may well be one of the *neofiti*, descendants of forced converts of *circa* 1290; the *neofiti* formed an important and still well defined business community in Apulia, and his cargo of 289 *carri* was certainly a sizeable one [Quat., p. 30]. An unconverted Jew appears among those loading wheat on the ship of Geronimo da Bari in May 1487, under the terms of a royal privilege of the previous October; the aim is to export the grain to Venice [Quat., p. 73].

So too the picture holds firm for Trani. The duke of Calabria, the future King Alfonso II, used a merchant and shipper from Trani to shift *carri* 5 of wheat in July 1486 [Quat., p. 43; a marginal note indicates that this entry was erroneously listed under Barletta]. It is the constant litany of references to Ragusan merchants that strikes anyone looking at the document. Occasionally bigger business intrudes, with a few Venetian ships [Quat., p. 51]; it is interesting to compare here some evidence from Bari, in the same register, which reveals that the Venetian merchant Alvise (*Alloysio*) Giovanni Marin was allowed to take a small quantity of wheat *apud Dalmatiam* on the ship of Marco *de Trau*, that is, a ship owned by a man from Trogir (and neighbouring documents also indicate shipments by Trani merchants explicitly to Dalmatia [Quat., pp. 73-4]). Manfredonia was still being used for reloading [Quat., pp. 51-2]. As well as wheat, some beans were exported through both Trani and Barletta [Quat., pp. 60-2, 31, 42], as well as significant amounts of barley through Barletta [Quat., p. 35]. One market for the beans appears to have been Dubrovnik, since in July 1487 an export of beans from Barletta took place which was financed and shipped by men of Ragusa [Quat., p. 42]; more significantly, a section of the register given over to small exports from Trani lists large numbers of Dalmatian ships which were carrying Apulian beans, chickpeas and biscuit out of the port, including boats from Dubrovnik, Kotor, Split and Zadar [Quat., pp. 60-5]. The quantities are not in themselves large, and many of the boats may have been quite small (some were described as a *barcha* or *grippo* [Quat., p. 64]), or they must have given space to other commodities, notably grain, as can be seen in those cases where the shipper is known from entries relating to wheat exports. However, it is the very regularity of this trade in the less glamorous foodstuffs that is striking. Cumulatively, it was certainly thought worth recording. Some of these products were also traded within the kingdom; we encounter 24 *tomoli* of chickpeas bound for Manfredonia on a *barcha*, that is, a smallish vessel [Quat., p. 64]; even in these cases, the shipper might be an outsider, such as Cola *de Catara*, evidently from Kotor in modern Montenegro, or Perrico *de Spalatro* from Split [Quat., p. 64].

V

Most of the evidence cited so far does not concern the Medici. Yet a considerable number of the register entries do mention Lorenzo and his firm. Indeed, the very last two entries, the only ones for Porto Polignano, deal with Medici business. In the former, Angelo Sereno of Monopoli takes out of the port, on the ship of Stefano *de Sepa* of Trani, *carri* 7 of wheat, 'for which he paid in cash for four and for three *carri* they are to go into the account of lord Lorenzo de'Medici' [Quat., pp. 78-9]. The entry is a bizarre mix of Italian and Latin, the language of all the other entries except the very final one. This reports in the vernacular that 'per lettera del loco tenente del maestro portulano so extracte da lo porto de Polignano per cunto de Medici' for twelve ducats of gold 13 *carri*, at the hands of Angelo Sereno and his associate Ranaldo de Barisano (most likely a south Italian name) [Quat., p. 79]. It is hard to believe that this is not the tip of a much larger iceberg. How large the iceberg is emerges from the constant reference to Lorenzo de'Medici and his firm throughout the register. On 11 January 1487 licence was given at Manfredonia to Lorenzo de'Medici and to Francesco Naso, who, as has been seen, ran his operations in the south, and to Naso's procurator Benedetto Benincasa and via him to Troiano *de Mectulo* of Manfredonia, to export 20 *carri* 12 *tomoli* of wheat from the *Regno* on the ship of Gregorio Stefani of Split; 'et sunt in parte pagamenti ducatorum decem milium de oro vigore licterarum regiarum factarum in civitate Neapolis die XVII octobris 1486' [Quat., p. 5]. Are we to conclude that this export was in part paid for by the restitution of Medici property and rights that had followed the making of peace in 1479? In any case, it is clear that the king was only too happy to offer the Medici business opportunities. On 29 January 1487 the Medici with Rosso de'Rossi of Pistoia exported 40 *carri* of wheat on a ship operated by a Neapolitan [Quat., pp. 6-7]. They acted for the castellan of Manfredonia in respect of the export of an identical amount, the very same day [Quat., p. 7]. The Medici sent wheat out of Trani, aboard a Ragusan ship, in September 1486, drawing on the thousand *carri* the king had permitted them to export at this point [Quat., p.50]. Again and again the entries that refer to the Medici mention one, or even more, royal privileges that entitle them to export large quantities of grain [Quat., pp. 51, 52-3; 'iuxta tenorem duorum regiorum privilegiorum'].

The overall quantities of grain they could export were impressive; but the quantities of grain in each shipment were generally on the large side as well, when compared to the business conducted by local merchants: over 71 *carri* for the Catalan ship. Naso seems to have set up a regular rhythm of purchases of about forty or fifty *carri*, as one can see in March 1479 [Quat., p. 10]; the interest in Dalmatia suggests that the Medici, like everyone else, were seriously interested in the carrying trade across the Adriatic, to Kotor, Šibenik and elsewhere, and their aim was not simply to supply Florence, Naples, Venice or Barcelona [see e.g. Quat., pp. 12-15]. When they sent 45 carri on board the ship of Francesco Nicolai of Kotor in May 1487, this was in partial settlement, again, of the 10,000 ducats mentioned earlier [Quat., p. 15]. The same royal letters were cited when they exported 26 *carri* from Barletta aboard a Ragusan ship, in November 1486 [Quat., p. 27], and 55 *carri* 6 *tomoli* from Barletta aboard a Venetian ship a few days later [Quat., p. 28]. This commerce included barley as well as wheat, in large quantities: 80 carri in December 1486, out of Barletta on a Ragusan boat [Quat., p. 28]; 106 *carri* were added only a few days later, in January 1487, aboard another ship of Dubrovnik, and their interest in this commodity remained stronger than that of other merchants [Quat., p. 32]. Like other merchants, they used Manfredonia as a transhipment point for wheat exported from Barletta [Quat., p. 31, a document which refers to the notary Bernardo de Anghono, author of the surviving register].

In February they made a bundle of deals, involving a ship from Korčula, another one from Barcelona (*cum navi Galzarani Andree de Barzillona*), and a third vessel, the *barcha Ioannis Alloysii*, probably Venetian [Quat., p. 9; cf. for this boat p. 32]. These deals appear both under the heading of Manfredonia and under that of Barletta in the register; later too this Catalan ship appears in the entries for Trani [Quat., p.53]. Especially striking is a list of quantities of barley that the Medici were to offload in Manfredonia after it had been transported there in a flotilla of small barques; sailors of Ragusa and of the Apulian ports were to take the goods to the ship of Giovanni Alvise *Buscayno*, probably the same Venetian, for outward passage beyond the waters of the *Regno* [Quat., pp. 32-3]. This may be the same figure who appears in July 1487 as *Iohannis Augustini de Venetiis*, a possible mistranscription of the common Venetian name Alvise or *Aloysii*, itself a form of 'Louis'. Similarly arrangements were made to load up the ship of Galzerano of Barcelona with 38 *carri* of wheat [Quat., p. 33]. Links to Korčula are expressed in a series of documents revealing the use of the ship of Gevellino *de Corzula* in the trade in wheat and barley from Barletta in March 1487 [Quat., p. 34], as well as references to a ship from Korčula in the entries for Trani, carrying a sizeable cargo of 90 *carri* on behalf of the Medici and their associates [Quat., p. 57]. Bisceglie was occasionally used by the Medici exporters; there:

> Die XIII februarii concessa fuit licentia Benedicto Beneincasa procuratori domini Francisci Naczi pro parte magnifici Laurentii de Medicis et pro eo notario Marino Tachia extrahendi et ferendi extra regnum cum navigio Francisci Iacobi de Corczula de curribus frumenti triginta quinque et sunt in excomptu ducatorum 2000 ex debitorum iuxta tenorem licterarum Regie Camere Summarie et duorum regiorum privilegiorum.
>
> [Quat., p. 65, with minor textual amendments]

Another island which furnished ships used by the Medici was Rab (*Arbo*) [e.g. Quat., p. 58]. Rosso de'Rossi, another Tuscan, appears as a close business partner of the Medici; he had the right to export 370 *carri* of barley under the terms of a privilege of King Ferrante

IX

34

of 13 December 1486, and on 19 March 1487 arrangements were made to extract 25 *carri* on the account of the Medici, under the terms of an existing agreement with Rosso [Quat., p.35]. Similar deals brought Rosso and Naso together in the wheat trade [Quat., pp. 36-7]. The Medici renewed their privileges to export from the kingdom in April 1487; an entry in the register from later that month indicates that Lorenzo and Francesco Naso had been granted the right to export 1,400 *carri* on 6 April 1487; from this they were taking 65 *carri* out of Barletta on Gevellino's ship, another 40 *carri* on the ship of Marino Luca and 200 *carri* on the ship of Sansonetto di Iacobuccio of Trani [Quat., p. 39], as well as further quantities later on [Quat., p. 40]. Others too benefited from royal privileges, and that of the Medici was large but not outstandingly so. Ramon *de Paretes*, evidently a Catalan (represented by the Catalan Lorenç Pedralbes) had been granted the right to extract wheat worth 5,500 ducats by letters issued in Naples on 16 October 1486 [Quat., p. 40; cf. pp. 72-3 for his exports to Venice]. Ramon had close ties to the Medici as well, jointly exporting over 133 *carri* in August 1487, and drawing on a privilege of King Ferrante of 2 April 1487; this was the third part of an agreed export of grain worth 14,000 ducats [Quat., p. 43]. It is easy to see that the king of Naples was keen to do business with those who had the resources to finance large scale exports from the kingdom. Catalans were no less welcome than Florentines, as can be seen from a series of export permits issued in Barletta for trade within the kingdom [Quat., pp. 48-9]. Ferrante took an acute interest in such matters, partly as a result of the encouragement of his faithful counsellor Diomede Carafa, who argued that a king could not be poor who had wealthy subjects.[28]

VI

The intention here has been to show how the Medici branch in southern Italy, at least as far as its Apulian trade was concerned, was well integrated into the trade networks that existed in the region at the end of the fifteenth century. Just as the native merchants were heavily involved in the traffic to and from Dalmatia, so too were the Medici. Just as native merchants exerted much energy supplying local markets within the *Regno*, so too did the Medici. The scale of their activities does indeed seem far larger than that of the local merchants with whom they did business. They constituted, of course, a firm with formidable buying power even in its declining years; they also benefited directly from the political links that had made Ferrante of Naples, once so antagonistic to Florence, now its enthusiastic ally. This alliance was only strengthened in these years, as Milan allowed its traditional alliance with Naples, founded in the last years of Alfonso the Magnanimous and Francesco Sforza, to fall into desuetude. Ludovico il Moro, the future duke of Milan, in 1486 already possessed a ducal title which he derived from the Sforza lands in Apulia: he was duke of Bari.[29] But if anyone was maximising the profits to be gained from the Terra di Bari and the grain lands of Apulia, it was his rival Lorenzo de'Medici; and even then it was clearly difficult to make the Naples branch as profitable as had been hoped. Politics rather than economics kept the Medici at work in the grain trade of Apulia, which seems to have supplied Adriatic and south Italian markets rather than Florence itself, as had been the case instead under the Angevin kings of Naples. Certainly, we are looking at small-scale operations by comparison with those of the Bardi and Peruzzi nearly two centuries before. Whereas their south Italian business had been the basis on which the earlier Florentine companies had achieved greatness, the Medici, more modest in size, appear to have regarded Naples and Apulia as good business only insofar as their trade there kept King Ferrante in good humour.

NOTES

1   David Abulafia, 'Southern Italy and the Florentine economy, 1265-1370', *Economic History Review*, ser. 2, 33, (1981), 377-88; repr. in David Abulafia, *Italy, Sicily and the Mediterranean 1100-1400* (London 1987).

2   Domenico Lenzi, *Il Libro del Biadaiolo*, ed. G. Pinto (Florence 1978), 317, and Pinto, introduction, p. 73.

3   M. del Treppo, 'Prospettive mediterranee della politica economica di Federico II', in *Friedrich II. Tagung des Deutschen Historischen Instituts in Rom im Gedenkjahr 1994*, ed. A. Esch and N. Kamp (Rome-Tübingen 1996), 329-30.

4   N. Nicolini, *Codice diplomatico sui rapporti veneto-napletani durante il regno di Carlo I d'Angiò*, Regesta Chartarum Italiae (Rome 1965).

5   David Abulafia, 'Venice and the Kingdom of Naples in the last years of Robert the Wise', *Papers of the British School at Rome*, 48, 1980, pp. 186-204; repr. in Abulafia, *Italy, Sicily and the Mediterranean*.

6   B. Krekić, 'Four Florentine commercial companies in Dubrovnik (Ragusa) in the first half of the fourteenth century', in *The Medieval City*, ed. H. Miskimin, D. Herlihy, A. Udovitch (New Haven 1977), 25-41; see also for relations between Dubrovnik and Apulia M. Spremić, *Dubrovnik e gli Aragonesi 1458-95* (Palermo 1986) [original edition: *Dubrovnik I Aragonci, 1458-95* (Belgrade 1971), especially pp. 143 and 160 of the Italian edition, where Dr Spremić stresses the importrance of the Ragusan fleet for the transport of Apulian foodstuffs.

7   S.R. Epstein, *An island for itself. Economic development and social change in late medieval Sicily* (Cambridge 1992)

8   David Abulafia, 'L'Economia mercantile nel Mediterraneo Occidentale: commercio locale e commercio internazionale nell'età di Alfonso il Magnanimo', *XVI Congresso Internazionale di Storia della Corona d'Aragona, Napoli-Caserta-Capri, 18-24 Settembre 1997: La Corona d'Aragona ai tempi di Alfonso il Magnanimo*, Tema 3: Centri propulsori dell'economia e della finanza, A: Introduzione [in press]; also published in *Schola Salernitana*, 2, 1997.

9   E. Sakellariou, *The Kingdom of Naples under Aragonese and Spanish rule. Population growth and economic and social evolution in the late fifteenth and early sixteenth centuries*, thesis for the degree of Ph.D., University of Cambridge, 1997.

10 *Fonti Aragonesi*, a cura degli Archivisti Napoletani, vol. 6 (Testi e documenti di storia napoletana pubblicati dall'Accademia Pontaniana, ser. 2) (Naples 1968), 3-79.

11 *Fonti Aragonesi*, vol. 6, 'Introduzione', pp. viii-ix.

12 *Fonti Aragonesi*, vol. 6, 'Introduzione', p. xiii.

13 References to entries in the text of this register are henceforth given in the body of this article, in square brackets and prefaced by the word: Quat.]. For the weights and measures, and Ferrante's attempts to unify them according to the standard of the *tomolo* of Brindisi, see Sakellariou, *Kingdom of Naples*, pp. 143-8.

14 There is no biography of Ferrante; see however the material in *The French Descent into Renaissance Italy 1494-95*, ed. David Abulafia (Aldershot 1995); also E. Pontieri, *Per la storia di Ferrante I d'Aragona, re di Napoli*, 2nd ed. (Naples 1969); J.H. Bentley, *Politics and culture in Renaissance Italy* (Princeton, NJ 1987)

15 *Fonti Aragonesi*, vol. 6, 'Introduzione', p. xv.

16 *Fonti Aragonesi*, vol. 6, 'Introduzione', p. xvii.

17 R. de Roover, *The rise and decline of the Medici Bank 1397-1494* (Cambridge MA 1963).

18 F. Carabellese, 'Bilancio di un'accomandita di casa Medici in Puglia del 1477 e relazioni commerciali fra la Puglia e Firenze', *Archivio storico pugliese*, vol. 2 (1896), 77-104.

19 De Roover, *Rise and decline*, p. 254.

20 De Roover, *Rise and decline*, p. 255, and table 50, p. 256.

21 De Roover, *Rise and decline*, p. 258.

22 There are many accounts of Lorenzo's visit to Naples in the modern literature, some of which seem tacitly to accept that he was risking

everything out of love for the republic, which was certainly what he said in a letter of 7 December 1479: 'All I desire is that my life, my death, my prosperity, my misfortunes, may contribute to the welfare of my native land'. But it is hard not to believe that he knew exactly how cordial his reception was going to be. For a qualified interpretation of the traditional view, see for instance the ancient study by E.L.S. Horsburgh, *Lorenxzo the Magnificent and Florence in her Golden Age* (New York and London 1908), 244-52; for the traditional view in its full-blooded form, see the popular work by H.R. Williamson, *Lorenzo the Magnificent* (London 1974), 188-94.

23 The classic account of the rebellion and of Coppola's end is in C. Porzio, *La congiura dei baroni*, various editions since 1586: Naples, 1964, Milan, 1965, Venosa, 1989, etc. For important Florentine dimensions, see H. Butters, 'Lorenzo and Naples', in *Lorenzo il Magnifico e il suo mondo. Convegno internazionale di studi (Firenze, 9-13 giugno 1992)*, ed. G.C. Garfagnani, Florence, 1994, pp. 143-51; H. Butters, 'Florence, Milan and the Barons' War (1485-1486)', in *Lorenzo de'Medici. Studi*, ed. G.C. Garfagnani (Florence 1992), 281-308; H. Butters, 'Politics and diplomacy in late Quattrocento Italy: the case of the Barons' War (1485-1486)', in *Florence and Italy. Renaissance Studies in honour of Nicolai Rubinstein* (London 1988), 13-31. These excellent studies do not, however, touch on the activities of the Medici bank in the kingdom of Naples.

24 De Roover, *Rise and decline*, pp. 257-9.

25 De Roover, *Rise and decline*, p. 260.

26 A. Silvestri, *Il commercio a Salerno nella seconda metà del Quattrocento* (Salerno 1952); A. Sapori, 'La fiera di Salerno del 1478', *Bollettino dell'Archivio storico del Banco di Napoli*, 8 (1954), 51-84, repr. as 'Una fiera in Italia alla fine del Quattrocento: la fiera di Salerno del 1478', in A. Sapori, *Studi di storia economica (secoli XIII-XIV-XV)*, 3rd ed. (Florence 1967); A. Grohmann, *Le fiere del Regno di Napoli in età aragonese* (Naples 1969), 225-34, 464-90; David Abulafia, 'The Crown and the economy under Ferrante I of Naples (1458-94)', in *City and Countryside in late medieval and early Renaissance Italy. Studies presented to Philip Jones*, ed. T. Dean and C. Wickham (London 1990) , 125-46, and especially pp. 140-5, repr. in David Abulafia, *Commerce and Conquest in the Mediterranean 1100-1500* (Aldershot 1993).

27 C. Kidwell, 'Venice, the French invasion and the Apulian ports', in *The French Descent*, ed. Abulafia, pp. 295-308.

28 Abulafia, 'Crown and the economy', pp. 129-33; Diomede Carafa, *Memoriali*, ed. F. Petrucci Nardelli (Rome 1988).

29 N. Ferorelli, 'Il Ducato di Bari sotto Sforza Maria Sforza e Ludovico il Moro', *Archivio Storico Lombardo*, 41 (1914), 389-468; F. Tateo, *Storia di Bari dalla conquista normanna al ducato sforzesco*, (Rome-Bari 1990), 157-8.

X

Lo Stato e la vita economica

Il primo problema nel discutere le politiche economiche di Federico II è decidere se il termine stesso « politiche economiche » sia accettabile. Esso ha indubbiamente l'autorità che deriva dall'uso regolare: James Powell ha intitolato una monografia *Medieval Monarchy and Trade: the economic policy of Frederick II in the Kingdom of Sicily*; un titolo siffatto implica un legame particolare tra l'interesse regio nel commercio ed il carattere complessivo del coinvolgimento di Federico nelle vicende economiche.[1]

In un articolo che era in parte una replica all'opera di Powell, Erik Maschke parlò di *Die Wirtschaftpolitik Friedrichs II. im Königreich Sizilien*; l'orientamento della trattazione di Maschke è che l'interesse di Federico nelle vicende economiche fosse guidato dalle necessità fiscali almeno tanto quanto lo fosse dall'interesse per il benessere degli abitanti del Regno.[2] È anche possibile che la reputazione gonfiata di Federico come principe protorinascimentale abbia indotto gli storici a presumere che quelli tra i suoi atti politici che ebbero un percepibile effetto sull'economia della Sicilia fossero parte di una visione coerente e previdente del ruolo dello Stato nella vita economica.[3] Eppure è noto come soltanto all'epoca del moralista poli-

---

[1] J. M. Powell, *Medieval Monarchy and Trade: the economic policy of Frederick II in the Kingdom of Sicily*, in « Studi medievali », ser. 3, 3 (1966), pp. 420-524.

[2] E. Maschke, *Die Wirtschaftpolitik Friedrics II. im Königreich Sizilien*, in *Vierteljahrschrft fur Social- und Wirtschaftgechichtc*, 55 (1966), pp. 289-524; ristampato in *Stupor Mundi. Zur Geschichte Friedrics II. von Hohenstaufen*, a cura di G. Wolf, seconda edizione (Darmstadt 1982), pp. 349-394 (l'articolo non appare nella prima edizione, del 1966). Cfr. anche F. M. De Robertis, *La politica economica di Federico II di Svevia*, in « Atti delle seconde giornate federiciane », Oria, 16-17 ottobre 1971 (Società di storia patria per la Puglia, Convegni, 4, Bari 1974), pp. 27-40.

[3] Per una critica della tradizionale adulazione di Federico II, cfr. David Abulafia, *Federico II. Un imperatore medievale* (Torino 1990). In questo saggio ho tentato di concentrare l'attenzione il più possibile sugli aspetti delle sue politiche che non potevano essere trattati nel libro, per mancanza di spazio o per altri motivi;

tico Diomede Carafa, alla fine del secolo XV, accadesse che un sovrano dell'Italia del sud, in questo caso Ferrante di Napoli, applicasse princìpi astratti alla gestione regia dell'economia.[4] Le stesse dichiarazioni di Federico sul fondamento logico di particolari politiche sono abbastanza chiare: « compiti chiari e incalzanti rendono il denaro molto necessario per la nostra Corte ».[5] Leggermente più sensibile all'interesse dei suoi sudditi è, forse, la sua affermazione del 1238, che così inizia:

Volentes igitur, (ut) privatorum labor fisci nostri proficiat comodis et fiscalium rerum compendia vice mutua labori respondeant subiectorum...

ma anche qui l'enfasi è sui vantaggi di cui il fisco potrà godere.[6]

Un secondo problema, evidenziato in maniera particolare nell'analisi di Maschke, è l'incapacità di collocare in un contesto più ampio le politiche economiche attribuite a Federico II. Non soltanto manca un qualsiasi parallelo con sovrani contemporanei come Giacomo I di Aragona-Catalogna, che, secondo quello che ci si potrebbe aspettare, poteva condividere un interesse nei profitti del commercio, ma neanche è posta alcuna attenzione agli antecedenti normanni delle politiche di Federico, né alla sopravvivenza di queste politiche sotto gli Angioini e gli Aragonesi.

Powell insiste maggiormente sul contesto normanno, in particolar modo sulla legislazione normanna, ma la ricerca in questo campo è progredita in modo significativo dopo che egli stesso ne scrisse. Ad ogni modo, sono convinto che i frammenti che sopravvivono delle leggi siciliane forniscano piuttosto un'immagine idealizzata che un'utile guida allo studio effettivo. È necessario invece mettere a confronto quanto stava avvenendo sul suolo di Sicilia verso il 1200 con i decreti di Federico sull'agricoltura e il commercio giunti fino a noi.

In questo saggio mi prefiggo di trattare le seguenti questioni. Dirò qualcosa sugli antecedenti normanni delle politiche di Federico nel *Regno*, con la deliberata intenzione di dimostrare una continuità più ampia di quanto Maschke presumesse. Quindi cercherò di far luce sulla natura dell'interesse di Federico in settori specifici dell'economia

dove l'argomento coincide, ho tentato di equilibrare fornendo riferimenti assai più completi di quanto fosse possibile nel libro.

[4] David Abulafia, *The Crown and the Economy under Ferrante of Naples* (1458-1494), in *City and Country in late medieval and Renaissance Italy*, a cura di C. Wickham e T. Dean (Londra 1990), pp. 125-46; cfr. J. Bentley, *Politics and Culture in Renaissance Naples*, Princeton, N. J., 1987.

[5] *Registrum Friderici* (cfr. la nota 7), 267.

[6] *Acta imperii* (cfr. la nota 7), 1.820.

siciliana, in particolare il commercio del grano e la produzione agricola differenziata. Ulitizzerò come testi chiave un gruppo di documenti tratti dai Registri di Federico II, pubblicati per la prima volta da Carcani nella sua edizione del Registro del 1239-40, e da Winkelmann nella sua raccolta di estratti di Registri smarriti di Federico II conservati negli archivi Angioini a Marsiglia.[7]

Infine, intendo considerare la sua cooperazione nel commercio del grano con i mercanti del nord Italia, la cui attività nel *Regno* in questo periodo ha dato luogo soltanto a studi limitati: quello di Heymann Chone del 1902, e quello meno importante di Cesare Imperiale di Sant'Angelo del 1923.[8] Comunque, non mi propongo di ripetere le mie precedenti considerazioni sulla politica monetaria di Federico II, che è in ogni caso argomento di un nuovo studio di Lucia Travaini.[9]

L'obiettivo di Federico, costantemente perseguito negli anni '20 e '30, era di restituire alla Corona i diritti che essa aveva posseduto al tempo del Re Guglielmo il Buono. I genovesi devono poter apprezzare *quod tempore felicis memorie regis Guillelmi secundi, consobrini nostri, extitit consuetum.*[10] Così anche lui ritorna alla pratica normanna nella gestione globale della vita economica dei suoi sudditi. La sua legislazione sull'usura delle *Costituzioni di Melfi* ripete un testo di Guglielmo II, esso stesso derivato dalle deliberazioni del Terzo Concilio Lateranense del 1179.[11]

Sebbene sia sempre difficile essere certi delle condizioni in cui le tasse commerciali normanne fossero imposte, abbiamo la testimonianza di Andrea di Isernia, che scrive nel periodo angioino, secondo il quale il sistema di tassazione del *Regno* potrebbe essere diviso nei *nova*

---

[7] C. Carcani, *Constitutiones regum regni utriusque Siciliae mandante Friderico II imperatore per Petrum de Vinea Capuanum Praetorio Praefectum et Cancellarium... et Fragmentum quod superest Regesto eiusdem Imperatoris Ann. 1239 e 1240* (Napoli 1786) (citato come *Registrum Friderici*, seguito dal numero di pagina, è da preferirsi alle successive trascrizioni di Huillard-Bréholles); E. Winkelmann, *Acta imperii inedita*, 2 volumi (Innsbruck 1880-5), vol. 1, 599-720 (citato come *Acta imperii*, seguito dal numero di volume e di documento).

[8] H. Chone, *Die Handelsbeziehungen Kaiser Friedrichs II. zu den Seestädten Venedig, Pisa, Genua*, Berlino 1902; C. Imperiale di Sant'Angelo, *Genova e le sue relazioni con Federico II* (Venezia 1923) – che tratta in larga misura l'aspetto politico (allo stesso modo la politica del secolo XIII e quella del XX).

[9] David Abulafia, *Maometto e Carlomagno: le due aree monetarie italiane dell'oro e dell'argento*, in «Storia d'Italia», Einaudi, Annali, 6: Economia naturale, economia monetaria (Torino 1983), pp. 223-70; ristampato in David Abulafia, *Italy, Sicily and the Mediterranean, 1100-1400*, Londra 1977, capitolo 4; Abulafia, *Federico II*, pp. 184-8.

[10] *Acta imperii*, 1, n. 758.

[11] *Lib. Aug.* I, tit. 8, vi.

jura dei Normanni e Hohenstaufen, ed i *vetera jura* le cui origini si perdono in tempi remotissimi.[12] Un buon esempio di *vetera jura* è la tassa commerciale nota come *commercium*, *plateaticum* o (al tempo di Federico) *jus dohane*. Il nome normanno ricorda il bizantino « kommerkion », tassa che spesso giungeva al 10%.[13] Il tasso effettivo fu lievemente modificato in eccesso e in difetto dai sovrani post-normanni, ma il principio di una tassa *ad valorem* sui beni che entravano ed uscivano dal *Regno* rimase attivo; inoltre, la monarchia controllava gelosamente il diritto dei mercanti esteri di riesportare beni importati ma non venduti, accordandolo quale speciale privilegio sia sotto i due Guglielmi che sotto Federico II. Certe altre tasse hanno vicine corrispondenze nel Mediterraneo contemporaneo: l'*anchoraticum*, imposta sulle navi al momento in cui esse entravano in porto, condivide il suo nome con la Catalana *ancoratge*, e ha antecedenti molto antichi.[14]

Quel che è significativo riguardo alle tasse normanne è che il governo poteva effettivamente imporle in misura considerevole; esse proprio non esistevano sulla carta.[15] La creazione sotto Ruggero II di un'amministrazione centralizzata che estese gradualmente il suo controllo sull'intero *Regno* trasformò i diritti di *ripaticum*, *scalaticum*, *plateaticum* da risorse signorili in manifestazioni tangibili della realtà della monarchia siciliana.

In altre parole, si diede vita gradualmente ad un monopolio regio sulle più importanti tasse commerciali, ma la sua base risiedeva nelle pratiche tradizionali della amministrazione locale longobarda, bizantina e musulmana. I *vetera jura* erano, è abbastanza evidente, non i diritti di un governo unitario del quale i Normanni erano i successori, ma una confusione di diritti di origini varie; sotto i Normanni e gli Hohenstaufen vediamo un tentativo lento e intermittente di razionalizzare questi diritti, ma perfino un potente governo centralizzato si trovava di fronte ad ostacoli in questo campo. Nel 1187 Guglielmo II dovette ammettere che i tentativi di imporre lo *jus passagii* nell'Italia meridionale erano ostacolati da esponenti della piccola aristocrazia, i quali riscuotevano manifestamente il denaro per se stessi;

---

[12] *Constitutiones regni utriusque Siciliae, Glossis ordinaris, Commentariis excellentiss. I.U.D. Domini Andraeae de Isernia, ac Bartholomaei Capuani* (Lione 1568), 14.

[13] David Abulafia, *Le Due Italie. Relazioni economiche fra il Regno Normanno di Sicilia e i Comuni Settentrionali* (Napoli 1991), pp. 88, 112, 130, 146, 174, 369.

[14] Vi sono parecchi registri di *ancoratge* nell'Arxiu del Regno di Maiorca, Palma, ma niente di questo tipo prima del secolo XIV lì o in Sicilia.

[15] David Abulafia, *The Crown and the Economy under Roger II and his successors*, in « Dumbarton Oaks Papers », 37 (1983), pp. 1-14, ristampato in Abulafia, *Italy, Sicily and the Mediterranean*, cit., capitolo I.

così l'intera tassa fu abolita.[16] Questa fu una pronta soluzione al problema dell'interferenza baronale nei diritti regi; la monarchia era più preoccupata dell'offesa all'autorità regia costituita dall'esistenza di baroni arroganti di quanto fosse ansiosa di assicurarsi il ricevimento di una rendita potenzialmente considerevole dalle strade e dai ponti dell'Italia meridionale.[17]

Era anche una questione di senso politico non meno che fiscale per i Normanni, l'incoraggiare il riassetto del suolo nella Sicilia propriamente detta. Si è generalmente d'accordo sul fatto che il periodo dell'invasione normanna della Sicilia, che seguiva la micidiale guerra tra gli emiri musulmani sull'isola, vide uno spopolamento ed un abbandono di buona terra agricola.[18] Ruggero I tentò di assicurare alla chiesa di Catania quei contadini saraceni che erano fuggiti da quelle terre che adesso le appartenevano durante il caos del periodo di invasione. Era ovviamente facile per i contadini trovare terre vuote più ad ovest.

Inoltre, stimolati forse dal particolare privilegio di Urbano II per Ruggero I nel 1098, i sovrani normanni tentarono di trasformare la Sicilia da isola prevalentemente musulmana in isola prevalentemente cristiana, e di creare nell'isola un nucleo latino: non semplicemente una direzione latina nel governo e nella chiesa, ma una popolazione latina nella regione rurale.[19] Nel 1091 la chiesa di Lipari-Patti stava già cercando coloni latini. Quello che doveva essere un nucleo fedele si rivelò però fonte di conflitto sociale quando i capi lombardi, in particolare Ruggero Sclavo, attaccarono i musulmani negli anni '60 e li cacciarono o li trucidarono nella Val di Noto. Ma il principio che la terra siciliana dovesse essere messa a disposizione degli agricoltori latini, che l'avrebbero coltivata in condizioni di notevole libertà, rimase attivo dal periodo normanno a quello angioino. Secondo Henri Bresc, questa libera popolazione latina fornì il nucleo di una nuova *nation sicilienne* la quale avrebbe espresso la propria identità politica in maniera estremamente vigorosa nel 1282.[20] La mia impressione personale è che i latini che si stabilirono in colonia gravitarono, almeno all'inizio, verso le piccole città della Sicilia orientale, come Randazzo, e sempre più verso le grandi città di

---

[16] Abulafia, *Crown and Economy... Roger II*, cit., p. 9.
[17] Abulafia, *Crown and Economy... Roger II*, cit., p. 10.
[18] M. Aymard e H. Bresc, *Problemi di storia dell'insediamento nella Sicilia medievale e moderna, 1100-1800*, in «Quaderni storici», 24 (1993), pp. 945-76.
[19] Abulafia, *Crown and Economy... Roger II*, cit., pp. 11-13.
[20] Per la più completa esposizione di tale concezione, cfr. l'opera magistrale ma anche controversa di H. Bresc, *Un monde méditerranéen. Economie et Société en Sicile, 1300-1450*, 2 volumi (Roma-Palermo 1986), in special modo il secondo volume.

Messina e Palermo; la colonizzazione della regione rurale fu per la monarchia più difficile da compiere. Quel che è abbondantemente chiaro è che nei duecento anni fino ai Vespri siciliani la Sicilia, ed alcune parti dell'Italia meridionale, sperimentarono una rivoluzione demografica. Particolarmente importante fu la colonizzazione da parte dei liguri che provenivano dall'entroterra di Savona (i quali lasciarono la propria impronta su parecchi dialetti siciliani) e da parte dei lombardi del sud Italia, che provenivano dal territorio di Amalfi. Anche se i singoli stadi non possono essere osservati da vicino, l'emigrazione, il ripopolamento, ed i fattori ad essi connessi, trasformarono la Sicilia musulmano-greca nell'isola cattolico-romana, di lingua in gran misura italiana, che poi continuò ad essere.[21] Tutto questo fu conseguito con l'incoraggiamento regio.

L'importanza della nuova colonizzazione fu, naturalmente, tanto fiscale quanto strategica e religiosa. I sovrani normanni mantennero gran parte dell'isola di Sicilia sotto il loro dominio; dei profitti ricavati dal commercio del suo grano si discuteva con ammirazione dall'Egitto alla Germania; e nel secolo XII c'erano anche in Sicilia come a Malta piantagioni estensive di cotone che attiravano mercanti da Genova, Fustat ed altrove. L'imponente ricerca basata sui riscontri forniti dalle terre di Monreale ha indicato che verso il 1200 i tipi più differenziati di agricoltura stavano lasciando il posto ad una forte concentrazione nella produzione di grano, per rifornire le grandi città della Sicilia ed i mercati d'esportazione.[22]

Chiaramente vi sono pericoli nel generalizzare, perfino per quel che riguarda terre estese come quelle di Monreale, ed è plausibile che la Val Demone non perse mai la sua caratteristica di fonte di tessuti di media qualità, vino ed altri beni relativamente differenziati.[23] Per la corona, comunque, la principale causa di ansietà nei primi decenni del secolo XII era non tanto ciò che si stava producendo sulle terre del re, ma il fatto che le terre del re fossero o meno nelle mani del re. Dovette passare mezzo secolo prima che sforzi decisi venissero fatti per arrestare l'avanzato declino normanno in questo tipo di agricoltura. Avremo modo di affrontare tali argomenti più in dettaglio.

Il primo importante tentativo da parte di Federico II di tornare

[21] David Abulafia, *The end of Muslim Sicily*, in *Muslim under Latin rule. A comparative perspective*, a cura di J. M. Powell (Princeton, N. J., 1990), pp. 103-33.
[22] H. Bercher, A. Courteaux, J. Mouton, *Une abbaye latine dans la société musulmane: economies, sociétés, civilisations*, 34 (1979), pp. 525-47.
[23] Un'energica difesa di questa concezione in S. R. Epstein, *An Island for Itself*, « Past and Present », Cambridge 1992, sull'economia siciliana nel tardo Medioevo.

alle politiche fiscali di Guglielmo II avviene nel 1220; ma è difficile giudicare le conseguenze economiche delle leggi Capuane. L'abolizione, dalla morte del re Guglielmo, dei vecchi tributi doganali, potrebbe aver giovato ai mercanti indigeni. Si è sostenuto che Federico desse qualche aiuto alle città dell'Italia meridionale – fin dal 1215 egli conferì diritti di tassa ai cittadini di Trani.[24] Ma la sua propensione ad abolire tributi doganali ingiusti riflette la sua convinzione del bisogno di affermare l'autorità regia, piuttosto che un desiderio di stimolare il commercio del *Regno* E, mentre riduceva i costi del commercio, egli continuava a mantenere uno stretto controllo dei governi delle città in Campania e Puglia. Il diritto di Napoli ed altre città di mantenere un proprio comune consolare fu revocato.[25]

La maggior parte degli storici ritiene l'estensione dei controlli sul movimento delle merci da parte di Federico più ampia di quanto fosse stata praticata dai Normanni. Giusto, ma bisogna ancora porre in rilievo le continuità. Un controllo sui movimenti del sale si ritrova sotto Ruggero II, sebbene nel suo regno esistessero manifestamente saline sia private che regie. Nel 1134 egli accordò ai monaci di San Salvatore a Messina il diritto di prendere un'imponente quantità di sale l'anno – 100 *salmae* – dalle saline di Faro. E negli anni '20 i monasteri stavano ancora acquisendo diritti su saline nell'area di Siponto.

Ma il decreto del 1231 sembra certamente onnicomprensivo al riguardo.[26] Scrivendo a « universibus habentibus sal » a Siponto, Salpi, Cannae, Barletta, Bari, Brindisi, Taranto ed altre regioni vicine, Federico parla di *totum sal, quod apud quoscunque vestrum poterit inveniri*

---

[24] Powell, *Medieval Monarchy*, cit., pp. 451-2.
[25] Questa immagine sarebbe più infausta se potesse veramente essere dimostrato che Napoli, Amalfi, Bari e gli altri porti avevano compiuto progressi sostanziali nel commercio marittimo durante la minorità di Federico, ma la presenza della rivalità genovese nell'ovest e di quella veneziana all'est lasciò Amalfi almeno immobile; essa può non essere andata in declino (se seguiamo Coniglio ed altri: C. Coniglio, *Amalfi e il commercio amalfitano nel medioevo*, in « Nuova rivista storica », 38-9 [1944-5], pp. 100-14), ma si ritrovò sempre più confinata al commercio nel Mediterraneo occidentale. Tale relegazione è simbolizzata, forse, dal pagamento trimestrale di 1.000 tarì fatto da Pietro Capuano di Amalfi a Federico II per il consolato siciliano a Tunisi, verso il 1241 (*Acta imperii*, 1. n. 878). Una ulteriore riprova dell'atteggiamento di Federico nei riguardi del commercio del sud-Italia nel 1231, quando egli acconsentì a concedere ai cittadini di Amalfi di portare generi alimentari fuori dalla Sicilia, unicamente in questo caso per il loro sostentamento. Così essi non dovevano riesportare ciò che avevano acquistato (*Acta imperii*, 1, n. 774). In effetti, gli amalfitani furono un elemento importante nell'amministrazione regia; forse quel che vediamo qui è un cambiamento interno ad Amalfi, città i cui dirigenti abbandonarono il commercio in favore del servizio pubblico. Una tale trasformazione fu causata solo indirettamente da Federico. Vedi anche Abulafia, *Le Due Italie*, cit., pp. 12-20.
[26] Abulafia, *Crown and Economy... Roger II*, cit., p. 5.

in ipsis partibus, ac etiam totum, quod amodo in futurum fieri conti-gerit in maritimis et in partibus memoratis.
Successive lettere rendono chiaro che non fu solo la Puglia a ricevere tali ordini; la corona aspirava ad un monopolio totale su tutto il *Regno*. In particolare, Federico mirava a fissare il prezzo del sale. Diede istruzione ai suoi ufficiali di comprare sale ad un prezzo stabilito (un quarto di oncia per *centenarium*, usando l'unità di misura di Siponto).[27] Quello che il privilegio non dice è che tutte le saline sono state « nazionalizzate »; il sale deve essere venduto alla corona, che poi lo rivenderà ad un suo prezzo particolare. Naturalmente, molte saline, forse la maggior parte, furono poste sotto il controllo regio, ed in questo senso è possibile dedurre che la produzione, così come la vendita della merce, fosse controllata sempre più strettamente; ma ancora non ci si trova veramente in presenza di quel vasto cambiamento rispetto alle tradizionali pratiche normanne che alcuni studiosi hanno supposto. Lo stesso si può dire degli *jura* imposti su ferro, pece, tonno ed altri prodotti del suolo e dei mari di Sicilia; Federico ristabilì vecchi diritti, in maniera più uniforme ed efficace di quanto forse i Normanni fossero stati capaci di fare.[28] Il principio di fondo rimase lo stesso. Il re aveva potere di amministrazione sui prodotti del sottosuolo, parte della ricchezza che Dio aveva donato al regno; e lo stesso valeva per i prodotti della pesca.[29] Sistemi paralleli di controllo esistevano in altri stati del Mediterraneo quali l'Egitto.[30] La realtà era, nondimeno, che tali diritti avevano dovuto spesso essere recuperati pezzo per pezzo, e le grandiose dichiarazioni sul controllo degli approvvigionamenti di sale non si concludevano che in una condiscendenza solo momentanea. Una lista di diritti del giugno 1231, ritrovata nella Terra di Lavoro, specifica che la curia ha diritto ai *magni pisces* come lo storione e le lamprede, a una parte del contenuto del carniere del cacciatore nella *Terra Cancie*, e che essa riceve una parte del pesce portato a Castellammare; ma l'impressione è di una vasta lista di particolari diritti lungo tutto il sud dell'Italia, piuttosto che di un completo controllo (per esempio) di tutto il pescato e sulle tenute di caccia.[31] Una tale descrizione assomiglia molto a quello che abbiamo dei « monopoli » normanni.

Quanto erano efficaci questi provvedimenti? Una lettera dell'estate 1238 al giustiziere degli Abruzzi suscita dei dubbi. I nobili ed

---

[27] *Acta imperii*, 1. n. 773.
[28] Abulafia, *Crown and Economy... Roger II*, cit., p. 6.
[29] Abulafia, *Federico II*, cit., pp. 34-5; cfr. 42.
[30] H. Rabie, *The financial System of Egypt*, A. H. 564-741 / A. D. 1169-1341 (Londra 1972), pp. 82-8.
[31] *Acta imperii*, 1. n. 783.

i prelati locali importavano sale dalla Puglia e *de imperio*, cioè dall'Italia imperiale, e diminuivano l'acquisto dai depositi regi di sale.[32] Naturalmente, la monarchia era interessata in primo luogo all'effetto che ciò stava avendo sulle entrate regie. I profitti della vendita del sale erano certamente tutt'altro che trascurabili. Il 12 giugno 1231 si ordinò che il sale dovesse essere venduto all'ingrosso ad un prezzo pari a quattro volte quello a cui era stato comprato, e ad un prezzo pari a sei volte il prezzo originale se venduto in piccole quantità.

Federico era giunto alla risoluzione di far sì che il sale divenisse una più importante risorsa fiscale del *Regno*. Nel caso del ferro, la proporzione di acquisto e vendita doveva essere di 2/3.[33] Il sale era di importanza sufficiente ad assicurare che i lavoratori delle raffinerie di Siponto fossero dispensati dal servizio nelle galere regie.[34] A volte, inoltre, il prezzo stabilito era troppo alto, e non più tardi del 1239-40 Federico era preparato a diminuire il prezzo delle sue scorte quando i suoi funzionari lo avvertivano che i beni non si smaltivano. « Fate del vostro meglio per noi », era la sua risposta: il prezzo poteva essere abbassato se ciò significava che la tesoreria reale avrebbe veramente ricevuto il denaro di cui aveva così tanto bisogno. La grande disperazione per il denaro in quel periodo si ripercuote nella maggiore veemenza delle guerre di Federico con il papato ed i ribelli lombardi.[35]

Il sistema di controlli su alcuni altri prodotti era meno ambizioso. Il grano, gli ortaggi, il lino e la canapa, sia che fossero coltivati nelle terre demaniali sia altrove, erano soggetti ad una tassa di un dodicesimo, generalmente (così sembra) in natura; inoltre, coloro che ne avevano il diritto potevano disporre dei prodotti come credevano.[36] Un effetto collaterale di questo decreto fu che dovettero essere costruiti depositi ad hoc per accogliere i beni.[37] Questa istituzione può essere paragonata ai magazzini installati nei porti del *Regno*, dove i mercanti dovevano depositare i propri beni dietro pagamento di una tassa. In Sicilia i porti ed i depositi deputati ammontavano a sette nel 1231, compresi Palermo, Messina, Trapani e Sciacca.[38] Non sembra esserci prova che anche i Normanni adottassero tale pratica, sebbene essa fosse già diffusa in altre parti del mondo mediterraneo prima del

---

[32] *Acta imperii*, 1. n. 819.
[33] *Acta imperii*, 1. n. 786.
[34] *Acta imperii*, 1. n. 789.
[35] Abulafia, *Federico II*, cit., p. 277.
[36] *Acta imperii*, 1. n. 787 (i).
[37] *Acta imperii*, 1. n. 787 (ii)
[38] *Acta imperii*, 1. n. 790.

1200, e continuata in Sicilia sotto gli Angioini e gli Aragonesi.

Comunque, Federico incontrò opposizione alla linea politica di autorizzazione del commercio d'oltremare solo attraverso porti designati. I mercanti che avevano comprato cibarie sulla costa di Sicilia o nell'interno desideravano spostare i propri beni direttamente dalla più vicina costa al riparo, ed erano perfino preparati a pagare di più per il privilegio, ma il governo centrale rifiutò di autorizzare questo cambiamento.[39] È lecito supporre che la corte reale ritenesse di non poter sovrintendere al commercio fuori dai porti minori.

Rivolgendo la nostra attenzione alla gestione dei porti, possiamo contare su una notevole quantità di elenchi di tariffe relativi al regno di Federico. Un confronto tra gli elenchi per Siponto e per Napoli – per un piccolo porto specializzato in sale, ed uno grande che commerciava tutti i beni – suggerisce che la perequazione delle tariffe era stata largamente raggiunta nel 1231. È probabile che tale uniformità fosse meno accentuata sotto i Normanni. Anche se è così, la tariffa di Napoli termina con il commento che se la consuetudine in questi luoghi è di riscuotere più tasse su certi beni, sia fatto ad ogni costo. Lo *jus dohane*, anteriormente *kommerkion*, si era adesso stabilizzato al 10% per i saraceni, ma solo al 3% per i cristiani (gli ebrei non vengono citati). In altre parole, la tariffa preferenziale di cui godevano i genovesi dopo il trattato del 1156, e di cui godettero gli abitanti di Messina dopo la loro rivolta alcuni anni più tardi, fu adesso estesa a tutti i cristiani, *tam cives quam exteri*. Questo era l'importo dovuto in entrata, ma le tariffe per coloro i quali lasciavano i porti si applicavano in egual misura ai cristiani ed ai saraceni. In sostanza, c'era un carico leggero sugli alimenti esportati, cosicché il formaggio e vari tipi di noce erano tassati dell'1%, ma c'era una tassa moderata su spezie come pepe, lentischio, zenzero e indaco, per le quali era dovuto il 3%. Il lino fu tassato al 2% ma una sostanza lanosa chiamata *lana ierosolimitana* o *ultramarina* pagava il 4%, ed il cotone filato non meno del 10%.[40] Nel settembre del 1231 la corte reale diede ulteriori istruzioni perché a Napoli « a mercatoribus Romanis non est aliquid requirendum »; non c'è spiegazione, ma il particolare privilegio accordato ai Romani può essere una ricompensa per il sostegno da loro fornito durante la « guerra delle chiavi » contro Gregorio IX; oppure può riflettere i tentativi dell'imperatore di comportarsi generosamente nei riguardi del Papa ora che la guerra era finita.[41]

---

[39] *Acta imperii*, 1. n. 925, del 1247-8 (?).
[40] *Acta imperii*, 1. n. 790. Ulteriori istruzioni ai *dohanerii* in *Acta imperii*, 1. nn. 792 (Barletta e Trani), 793 (Napoli), 795 (Trani).
[41] *Acta imperii*, 1. n. 793.

Federico mantenne l'interesse dei suoi predecessori per i laboratori della seta e per la produzione specialistica tessile. Quasi non sorprende che il sovrano che commissionava parecchi dei superbi abiti ora nella « Weltliche Schatzkammers » a Vienna, dovesse aver agito così.[42] Un decreto del giugno 1231 collocò il commercio della seta su un piano analogo a quello del sale; ma il fatto che Winkelmann avesse ragione o meno di intitolare il documento in questione « Der Handel mit Seide wird monopolisirt » è un punto controverso. Quel che il testo dice è che la seta nella Val di Crati, in Puglia ed in Calabria deve essere venduta ad un certo *Churulie et socus Ebrei de Trano*, la cui impresa è stata avviata per rivendere la seta *ad opus curie*. Naturalmente la corte di Federico è particolarmente preoccupata che i beni siano venduti ad un prezzo favorevole. Una simile società di ebrei fu avviata a Capua, composta da due operai esperti il cui compito era di sovrintendere alle tintorie di Capua e Napoli; essi dovevano assicurare che le giuste tasse fossero imposte su seta, filato di lino, fustagno ed altri tessuti.[43] Il fisco regio aspirava a portare tutti i laboratori di coloranti sotto la propria direzione, e per quanto possibile, a concentrare le tintorie della Terra di Lavoro nei due centri di Capua e Napoli. Di nuovo potremmo domandarci se questo sia stato veramente un tentativo di rilevare integralmente tali laboratori in tutto il *Regno*, come Winkelmann ipotizza, ma il decreto interferì con i diritti dei vescovi dell'Italia meridionale, ai quali in diversi casi era stato accordato dai Normanni il controllo sugli Ebrei e sulle loro tintorie. Sarebbe anche azzardato presumere che gli ordini di Federico fossero parte di un tentativo di rinvigorire l'industria delle esportazioni. Federico era interessato alle sete ed ai tessuti finemente colorati perché ve ne era bisogno a corte, perché le forniture erano intermittenti e di qualità variabile, e perché erano costosi da acquistare o produrre. I suoi decreti devono essere visti come un tentativo di istituire nuovamente laboratori regi sul modello normanno, anche se essi non facevano più parte del palazzo reale. Una riserva analoga dovrebbe forse essere fatta riguardo alle fabbriche di lana avviate dagli Angioini di Napoli; le forniture a basso prezzo per la corte reale ebbero la precedenza sulla rinascita economica.[44]

Possiamo renderci conto molto da vicino dei veri interessi di Federico se esaminiamo una lettera del 1247 circa, mandata in risposta

---

[42] J. Deér, *Der Kaiserornat Friedrichs II*. (Berna 1952), specialmente pp. 75-9.
[43] *Acta imperii*, 1. n. 796.
[44] S. R. Epstein, *The textile industry of late medieval Sicily: a colonial economy?*, in « Journal of Medieval History », 15 (1989).

ad una relazione di un certo Giliberto Abbate sulle condizioni di Malta e Gozo.[45] La lettera dà un'idea di ciò che la corona si aspettava di ottenere dalle proprie terre in un'area che non era di rilevante importanza commerciale.[46] È comunque ammesso nella relazione *quod homines insularum ipsarum vivunt aliis moribus et constitucionibus, quam alii homines regni nostri Sicilie*, e sebbene questa affermazione sia stata citata per riferirsi alle idiosincrasie di linguaggio ed organizzazione sociale tra i maltesi, queste parole possono anche indicare che la maniera in cui la corona traeva i propri redditi da Malta era in qualche modo atipica. La corte di Federico era disposta a tollerare queste differenze a condizione che non causassero noie, in altre parole perdita di reddito.

Gli *jura dohane Malte terre et maris*, che sono imposti sui beni venduti ed acquistati, sono di 1.900 tarì l'anno, e di 500 tarì a Gozo. Ammettendo che questa sia una tassa in media del 3% (anche se oscillante, come altrove, tra l'1 ed il 10 in casi specifici), ciò ci induce a supporre che il valore totale del commercio attraverso le due isole fosse di circa 6.900 once l'anno. Ma il valore di tutte le tasse ricavate dall'isola era stimato in 14.681 tarì (poco meno di 500 once) ogni anno, cifra che includeva le tasse sulle tintorie (1.060 tarì), sul prodotto dei giardini e dei frutteti (2.921 tarì per Malta propriamente detta), ed altre attività economiche, alcune delle quali sono difficili da individuare.[47] I *villani curie*, che sembra siano stati un gruppo di condizione sociale bassa, principalmente o interamente musulmano, pagava un quarto del proprio prodotto alla curia, la quale lo usava per mantenere 150 soldati e marinai che sorvegliavano le tre roccaforti sulle isole, che erano probabilmente Mdina, la cittadella su Gozo (la moderna Vittoria), e Birgu (la moderna Vittoriosa, e specificamente Castel Sant'Angelo). La *baiulacio* consisteva probabilmente in piccole multe ed imposte, la *sorta* può essere stata una tassa sui giochi d'azzardo, la *barbaria* era forse una tassa sui barbieri, la *madia* una tassa sul traghetto che collegava Malta a Gozo; la *cusia* era una tassa sui sarti; la *conciaria* una tassa sui conciatori; la *cabella tubarum* presumibilmente una tassa sui menestrelli (seb-

---

[45] *Acta imperii*, 1. n. 938.
[46] A. Luttrell, *Approaches to medieval Malta*, in *Medieval Malta. Studies on Malta before the Knights*, a cura di A. Luttrell (Londra 1975). Nonostante un competente esame del documento da parte di Luttrell, che analizza le cifre riguardanti la popolazione in esso riportate, sono stati trascurati importanti aspetti della relazione.
[47] *Acta imperii*, 1. n. 938. Le altre tasse su Malta sono: tubarum, 88t; barbarie, 340t; cabelle baiulacionis et sorte, 1390t; cusie (sic), 540t; villanorum curie, 2516t; apothecarum, 100t; cabelle corbinorum, 150t. Le altre tasse su Gozo sono: barbarie, 80t; cabelle tubarum, 170t; cabelle madie, 300t; tabelle (sic) baiulacionis et uxorte (sic), 600t; cusie, 145t; villanorum curie, 584t; centimulorum curie nostre, 89t. Cfr. anche A. Vella, *Storja ta' Malta* (Valletta 1974), p. 79.

bene in quel caso fosse sorprendentemente produttiva); non si riesce a dare una spiegazione alla *cabella corbinorum*.[48]

L'impressione è quindi di una vasta gamma di tasse su una varietà molto ampia di attività economiche, alcune specifiche delle isole, come il servizio dei traghetti, ed altre caratteristiche dello stile di Federico quanto alla gestione dell'intero *Regno*, come la tassa sulle tintorie.

Da quando Malta e Gozo annoveravano 33 famiglie ebree, e da quando il rapporto tra gli ebrei di Malta e quelli di Gozo (25 famiglie contro 8) eguaglia la proporzione tra il reddito proveniente dalle tintorie su Malta e Gozo (800 contro 260), è probabile che qui come altrove la colorazione dei tessuti fosse la principale attività degli ebrei.[49]

Comunque, la popolazione delle isole era molto eterogenea riguardo alla religione. Accettando la variante proposta da Luttrell per la trascrizione del testo angioino corrotto di Winkelmann, abbiamo 1.047 famiglie cristiane a Malta e 233 a Gozo, e 681 famiglie musulmane a Malta contro le 55 di Gozo. Non è chiaro se l'ammontare per quel che riguarda i musulmani includa pure 144 *servi Gerbini*, contadini provenienti da Gerba o dal Maghreb, i quali badavano alle greggi ed alle bestie da soma della curia. Sembra certo che la parte musulmana della popolazione di Malta sia diminuita in modo significativo a partire dal secolo XII, periodo in cui secondo tutte le testimonianze storiche l'elemento cristiano era ancora irrilevante. Questi mutamenti rispecchiano la già menzionata e più generale trasformazione della popolazione siciliana, tranne per il fatto che a Malta (ed anche a Pantelleria) essi sopravvennero più lentamente. Federico incoraggiò l'insediamento cristiano a Malta; egli vi mandò nel 1224 gli abitanti ribelli di Celano, nei lontani Abruzzi, secondo quanto dice Riccardo di San Germano; mentre la popolazione musulmana era in parte ridotta dalla vendita in schiavitù, se la vendita di una giovane ragazza maltese a Genova nel 1248 può essere assunta come significativa in tal senso.[50]

Le implicazioni economiche dell'espulsione dei musulmani dalla Sicilia propriamente detta erano note alle corte di Federico, che aspirava a salvaguardare i mezzi di sussistenza dei coloni saraceni a Lucera. Nel 1230 Federico offrì ai saraceni di Lucera l'esenzione completa da *plateaticum, jus dohane, passagium* ed evidentemente da qual-

---

[48] H. Bresc, *The Secrezia and the royal patrimony in Malta*, in Luttrell, *Medieval Malta*, cit., p. 134.
[49] Per gli Ebrei di Malta, cfr. G. Wettinger, *The Jews of Malta in the late Middle Ages* (Valletta 1985), che fa un breve riferimento a questo documento a p. 6.
[50] R. S. Lopez, *La vendita d'una schiava di Malta a Genova nel 1248*, in « Archivio storico di Malta », 7 (1935-6), p. 391.

siasi altra tassa regia, nell'intera Italia meridionale[51] (non è sorprendente che della Sicilia propriamente detta non si faccia cenno; la corte reale nutriva qualche perplessità di fronte alla possibilità che i musulmani di Lucera potessero tornare in patria, e causare ulteriori fastidi).[52] Sarebbe abbastanza facile produrre questo fatto come prova che Federico dimostrava un particolare favore verso i musulmani mantenendo fede alla propria immeritata fama di « sultano battezzato ». Già a fianco delle testimonianze storiche tratte dal Registro imperiale del 1239-40, in cui Federico offre squadre di aratri alla comunità di Lucera, sembra un altro tentativo di garantire a questa comunità dei sicuri mezzi di sussistenza, tutt'al più perché essa era formata in parte da ex ribelli alla sua autorità che egli adesso si proponeva di trasformare in sudditi docili. Secondo il Registro imperiale, la comunità saracena di Lucera doveva ricevere un migliaio di armenti, sia addomesticati che selvatici, e doveva essere fatta una lista dei musulmani che ricevevano una donazione. L'idea era di vincolare la colonia saracena al suolo, « così come stavano le cose al tempo del Re Guglielmo ». La questione, quindi, non era semplicemente quella di incrementare le entrate dalla regione di Lucera: si andavano delineando anche importanti motivazioni politiche.[53] D'altro canto, uno dei problemi generati dall'estinzione dell'Islam siciliano fu la creazione di grandi aree vuote le quali smisero di produrre reddito dal momento in cui cessarono di produrre grano ed altri beni. Perciò nell'autunno del 1231 Federico emise un appello perché i coloni venissero in Sicilia, ed offrì la completa esenzione dalle tasse per dieci anni. Lo scopo era di portare tranquillità al Regno *cuius specialior nos cura sollicitat*.[54]

Sebbene i saraceni fossero stati largamente spinti fuori dalla Sicilia dopo la creazione della colonia di Lucera, arrivavano ancora immigranti dal Nord-Africa: non musulmani ma ebrei. La preoccupazione di Federico era di non perdere l'abilità agricola del mondo islamico, ed aveva poco da temere dagli ebrei, i quali non avevano una propria organizzazione politica e non dovevano fedeltà ad un sovrano rivale. Il Registro imperiale del 1239-40 indica chiaramente queste relazioni. Gli ebrei provenienti dal Nord-Africa, probabilmente dell'isola di Gerba, dovevano impiantare e condurre piantagioni, così come introdurre la coltivazione di indaco, alcanna e « vari altri semi che crescono nel Nord-Africa e che ancora adesso non si vedono

---

[51] *Acta imperii*, 1. n. 763.
[52] *Registrum Friderici*, 295.
[53] *Registrum Friderici*, 307; Abulafia, *Federico II*, cit., pp. 277-8.
[54] *Acta imperii*, 1. n. 799.

crescere in Sicilia ». Questa osservazione sembra confermare quanto già si è sottolineato per Monreale, dove le tecniche agricole portate in Sicilia dagli arabi erano scomparse sin dal 1200. Metà del prodotto degli ebrei doveva essere pagato alla Corona; essi erano trattati come « servi della Camera »; erano soggetti (come i saraceni di Lucera) al testatico di origine musulmana, ed a tasse sul vino e sui « coltelli », cioè sul cibo macellato concesso dalla religione ebraica. Il *Secretus* di Palermo, Oberto Fallamonaco, si preoccupava che la Sicilia potesse attrarre troppi di questi immigranti, e per questa ragione il loro futuro non fosse reso affatto troppo sicuro: il vivaio di palme doveva essere dato loro in affitto per non più di cinque o dieci anni. La corte voleva evidentemente tenere d'occhio da vicino la situazione, che era tra quelle che giovavano maggiormente agli interessi del sovrano, e doveva essere tenuta informata dei redditi ricevuti dalle nuove colonie ebree.[55] Inoltre furono richiesti altri coloni, all'apparenza non ebrei: a Riccardo Filangieri, il rappresentante imperiale in Terrasanta, fu richiesto di mandare in Sicilia due uomini esperti nella produzione di zucchero, per far rinascere un'altra industria che aveva probabilmente patito un grave declino dopo l'espulsione dei musulmani.[56] Anche i vigneti di Messina non producevano tanto quanto la corte esigeva, e qui furono predisposte indagini; quest'area, da lungo tempo cristiana, e che si stava specializzando in un prodotto poco preferito dai musulmani, non era neanche esente da difficoltà economiche. Ma bisogna porre l'accento sul fatto che l'interesse di Federico era fiscale più che economico. Fu dimostrato un certo interesse a che il peso delle imposte non cadesse sui più poveri; ma lo scopo era di trovare i mezzi più ingegnosi per incrementare il reddito e ridurre i costi.

Fino a che punto le politiche di Federico dovrebbero essere viste come un tentativo di costruire nel *Regno* un'economia strettamente integrata e autosufficiente? Probabilmente tale ipotesi non merita affatto credito. Federico riconosceva l'importanza del commercio internazionale come fonte di reddito per la corona. Quando incoraggiava le industrie specializzate, lo faceva almeno qualche volta con un occhio ai risparmi finanziari che queste misure avrebbero comportato per la corte: il suo interesse nell'industria della seta e nelle tinture come

---

[55] *Registrum Friderici*, 290-1.
[56] *Registrum Friderici*, 291; cfr. 347 sul consumo di zucchero da parte di Federico. La grande espansione della produzione siciliana di zucchero si verificò soltanto nel secolo XV: C. Trasselli, *Storia dello zucchero siciliano* (Caltanissetta-Roma 1982); è difficile dimostrare una continuità significativa dall'inizio del Medioevo. Sul più ampio contesto, cfr. A. M. Watson, *Agricultural innovation in the early Islamic world* (Cambridge 1983), pp. 83, 184-5.

l'indaco e l'alcanna è in questo senso significativo. Ma le sue politiche nei riguardi dei mercanti esteri hanno fatto sorgere perplessità. Gli italiani del nord non erano affatto scomparsi dopo che Genova fu privata dell'esenzione dalle tasse e del controllo di Siracusa nel 1220; è stato in verità supposto da James Powell che il commercio dei genovesi soffrisse relativamente poco per l'iniziale affermazione da parte di Federico dell'autorità regia.[57] Un esame dei registri notarili genovesi indusse Powell a concludere che fu solo nel 1230 che il commercio genovese in Sicilia crollò, mentre Genova gravitava sempre più nelle vicinanze della Lega lombarda.

In effetti, è essenziale mettere in evidenza l'importanza delle considerazioni politiche nell'insuccesso di quella che era stata, sotto i Normanni, una relazione commerciale molto stretta. Così il rifiuto genovese di presenziare all'incoronazione di Federico a Roma fu un primo indizio del fatto che Genova non si sarebbe impegnata nella difesa degli interessi di Federico nell'Italia settentrionale e centrale. Quello che Powell dimentica di dire è che i genovesi che continuavano a commerciare in Sicilia nel decennio tra il 1220 ed il 1230 erano guidati dai rappresentanti di quelle famiglie che si erano legate all'imperatore, famiglie come i della Volta che venivano sempre più emarginate nelle questioni politiche della città.[58] Federico favoriva sempre alcuni genovesi scegliendo i suoi ammiragli dalle famiglie dominanti della città come gli Spinola e i de' Mari, ed evitando di tenerli a freno perfino nell'ambito delle flotte genovesi, con conseguenze drammatiche quando l'ammiraglio Ansaldo de' Mari catturò molti alti prelati della Chiesa Romana nel 1241.[59] I de' Mari e i della Volta avevano stretto un'alleanza particolarmente forte tra loro, ed anche con l'imperatore.

Inoltre, Federico non abrogò i privilegi commerciali genovesi nell'Impero nel corso degli anni '20, anche se si deve ammettere che si è tutt'altro che certi di quali vantaggi reali questi privilegi fossero portatori: con ogni probabilità essi erano in gran parte teorici. Vale anche la pena di ripetere che nel 1230 Federico scrisse ai propri ufficiali portuali per ordinare loro di imporre ai genovesi le stesse tasse sul commercio che erano state imposte sotto Re Guglielmo; ad essi non furono negati i loro antichi diritti, perfino dopo le espropriazioni del 1220.[60]

L'atteggiamento di Federico nei riguardi di Genova si basava sulla

---

[57] J. M. Powell, *Genoese policy and the Kingdom of Sicily, 1220-1240*, in « Medieval Studies », 38 (1966), pp. 346-354.
[58] Imperiale di Sant'Angelo, *Genova*, cit., p. 47.
[59] Abulafia, *Federico II*, cit., pp. 288-9.
[60] *Acta imperii*, 1. n. 758.

supposizione che, sostenendo la fazione pro-imperiale nella città e nei vicini centri liguri, egli potesse esercitare sul governo genovese una pressione sufficiente a portarlo sotto la sua influenza ed a mantenerlo al di fuori del campo d'azione di Milano e del papato. Tale concetto era errato: il fatto che gli alleati di Federico a Savona fossero in grado di evadere dal controllo genovese aveva l'unico effetto di rafforzare l'opposizione genovese a Federico; ed anche la sua interferenza negli affari della Sardegna ebbe un effetto decisivo sulle questioni politiche genovesi, spingendo la città perfino verso un'alleanza con la sua vecchia avversaria Venezia e con il papato nel 1238-39.[61] Il punto importante è che il suo atteggiamento nei confronti dei genovesi, e degli altri italiani, era guidato da considerazioni politiche che si estendevano ben oltre i confini del *Regno*. I suoi problemi in Lombardia, con il papato ed anche nel regno di Gerusalemme, avevano tutti un ruolo nel determinare l'atteggiamento di Federico; ed i suoi passati motivi di lagnanza contro i genovesi a Siracusa come altrove erano solo una parte delle sue difficoltà con loro. Perciò sarebbe errato ipotizzare che Federico fosse impegnato in un programma di riforma economica avveduto quando privò i genovesi dei loro eccessivi privilegi. Allo stesso modo, egli era perfettamente consapevole del fatto che i redditi regi fossero nella condizione di essere danneggiati se gli abitanti del nord Italia potevano portare via impunemente grano ed altri prodotti senza pagare tasse.

È comunque interessante constatare che il trattato stipulato da Federico con i veneziani (nel 1232) era in parte ispirato dal desiderio che essi esportassero « quelle cose che hanno la propria origine nel Regno »; lui, Federico, non era particolarmente interessato a mostrare indulgenza nei riguardi del loro trasporto-merci attraverso la Puglia.[62] Purtroppo, l'accordo commerciale con i veneziani non si dimostrò durevole; nel giro di pochi anni, il Doge di Venezia era diventato un saldo alleato del papato e del comune di Genova, la stessa città che aveva combattuto aspramente contro Venezia per difendere gli interessi dei pirati genovesi e del sedicente Re di Creta, Enrico conte di Malta.[63] Una caratteristica di questo accordo con Venezia era il suo tentativo di proteggere gli interessi commerciali dei mercanti indigeni perfino mentre incoraggiava le attività di quelli stranieri. Quelli che erano in rapporti di compravendita con i mercanti veneziani sarebbero stati esentati dall'obbligo di pagare tasse

[61] Imperiale, *Genova*, cit., pp. 33-48.
[62] Abulafia, *Federico II*. cit., p. 183.
[63] Sui rapporti di Federico con Venezia, cfr. Chone, *Handelsbeziehungen*, cit.

X

alla corona. Sarei indotto a ritenere che questa clausola fu inclusa su suggerimento dei veneziani, come meccanismo per assicurarsi che la tassazione invisibile non avrebbe avuto luogo, cosa che sarebbe potuta accadere se i mercanti del posto fossero stati tassati ed avessero scaricato la tassa sui veneziani compagni in affari, incorporandola nel prezzo dei loro beni; la clausola permise inoltre ai veneziani di offrire a minor prezzo dei concorrenti nelle vendite ai *regnicoli.* Venezia, comunque, sembrava ancora in grado di incamerare bottini più ricchi, quali il possedimento di intere città pugliesi, tramite l'alleanza con il papato e con Genova contro Federico negli anni '40. Federico poteva rispondere soltanto con embarghi sull'esportazione di grano verso Venezia, ma perfino questi ultimi erano ignorati con il tacito assenso imperiale.[64] Verso l'inizio del secolo XIII Venezia tendeva ad usare la costa orientale dell'Adriatico come rotta principale verso il Levante: in tal modo l'ostilità di Federico era senza dubbio fastidiosa ma mai paralizzante.

Pisa, al contrario, tendeva da lungo tempo a sostenere gli Hohenstaufen. In parte il sostegno pisano poggiava su un atteggiamento negativo: che i genovesi ed in ultima analisi anche i veneziani fossero avversari dell'imperatore. Ma i pisani consideravano Federico non semplicemente un re siciliano. Egli confermò il loro diritto di commerciare liberamente nell'Impero; provò a proteggere i loro interessi in Terrasanta. I pisani ed altri toscani ottennero il diritto di esportare grandi quantità di grano, sebbene a condizioni piuttosto rigide. Nel gennaio del 1240 a quattro uomini d'affari pisani fu permesso di esportare frumento valutato a 520 once d'oro, del peso di 1.300 *salmae* (una salma era circa 263 libbre). Ma essi avevano tempo soltanto fino all'inizio di marzo per caricare le loro navi, e dovevano farlo a Palermo o a Trapani.[65] Nel 1239 i toscani provenienti da Poggibonsi e perfino i mercanti genovesi furono autorizzati a godere di diritti analoghi, sotto un controllo egualmente stretto.[66] In ciò Federico sfruttò la sua forte posizione di proprietario di estesi domini terrieri in Sicilia, nei quali veniva prodotto gran parte del frumento destinato all'esportazione. Impiantò istituzioni per un sistema di controlli che sopravvisse sotto gli Angioini e gli Aragonesi.[67] Erich Maschke ha affermato correttamente: « l'esportazione di viveri stava al centro degli interessi commerciali del governo ».

[64] *Registrum Friderici,* 418.
[65] *Registrum Friderici,* 313.
[66] *Registrum Friderici,* 278.
[67] David Abulafia, *Sul commercio del grano siciliano nel tardo Duecento,* in « La società mediterranea all'epoca del Vespro. Atti del XI Congresso di Storia della Corona d'Aragona », Palermo-Erice-Trapani 1982 (Palermo 1983), 2: 5-22, ristampato in Abulafia, *Italy, Sicily and the Mediterranean,* cit., capitolo 7.

Federico chiariva in maniera fin troppo effervescente le proprie priorità. Il Registro del 1239-40 afferma ripetutamente che l'imperatore ha bisogno di elevare significativamente il proprio reddito: « specialmente poiché il denaro ci è adesso necessario per gli attuali contrasti in Lombardia ».[68] Sotto Federico II il problema consisteva nella scarsezza di denaro contante disponibile subito piuttosto che in una totale carenza di fondi. Ad un paggio reale non potevano essere forniti i fondi per pagare i due scudieri ed i tre cavalli di cui aveva bisogno, « dal momento che nelle nostre Casse non c'è attualmente abbastanza denaro per pagare le sue spese », malgrado la somma in questione consistesse soltanto in quattro once d'oro. Una volta che si trovava nell'Italia meridionale, ordinò perfino che a parecchi banchieri ai quali era stato restituito il capitale ma nessun interesse fosse pagato quel che era ancora loro dovuto: una scrupolosità che nondimeno suggerisce anche che il denaro era difficile da ottenere alla sua corte e nelle tesorerie provinciali.[69] In effetti i prestiti che Federico riceveva dai banchieri dell'Italia settentrionale dovevano tutti, per quel che si può vedere, essere ripagati nel *Regno* dalle tesorerie provinciali, sia in denaro che, di quando in quando, in natura. Il metodo adottato prevedeva aumento di prestiti in Lombadia e Toscana contro futuri rimborsi nell'Italia meridionale. Nel novembre del 1239, mentre Federico era ancora a Lodi, prestiti che ammontavano in totale a circa 2.270 once d'oro furono concessi da venti associazioni di banchieri romani.[70] Certamente è impressionante il numero dei banchieri di Roma che non erano convinti che Gregorio IX potesse sconfiggere Federico II. Questi banchieri erano essi stessi di famiglie nobiliari, perfino *papabili*: i Pierleoni, i Sinibaldi, i Cenci; ed i cittadini di Roma avevano già dimostrato al papa che egli non poteva fare affidamento sul loro sostegno contro Federico II. Neanche la presenza di banchieri della Cremona imperiale è una sorpresa. Più insolita è la presenza del mercante viennese Heinrich Baum, che fornì a Federico un migliaio di marchi d'argento in valuta di Cremona e Colonia. Ad Arezzo nel gennaio del 1240 Federico riconobbe un debito di 1.400 once d'oro, somma per restituire la quale egli era in difficoltà, specialmente poiché aveva ricevuto metà del prestito solo un mese prima a Parma. Propose così un metodo ingegnoso di restituzione. A Baum veniva concesso di esportare 4.462½ *salmae* di frumento – abbastanza per riempire due grandi navi – dalla Puglia verso qualsiasi luogo tranne che nell'ostile Venezia. Il frumento do-

---

[68] Abulafia, *Federico II*, cit., p. 273.
[69] Abulafia, *Federico II*, cit., pp. 273-4.
[70] *Registrum Friderici*, 265-7.

veva essere fornito dal governo, da nuove scorte, e non doveva essere imposto alcun tributo per l'esportazione.

Il prezzo speculativo del frumento doveva essere di un terzo di oncia per *salma*, in modo tale che l'esportatore viennese avrebbe ricevuto frumento per un valore di 1.487½ once (avrebbe anche risparmiato almeno 300 once in tasse), ed il suo debito di 1.400 once sarebbe stato ripagato con un interesse di 87 once e 1/2, cioè del 6,25%. In effetti, dieci tari per *salma* era un prezzo piuttosto alto da pagare per il frumento, così Federico non stava neanche concludendo malamente l'affare.[71] Anche meno bene se la cavarono alcuni mercanti di Poggibonsi ai quali era garantito il diritto di esportare 1.000 salme di frumento da Palermo o Trapani, per 13 tari ogni *salma*. Federico accordò il privilegio nel novembre 1239 a Cremona, ma l'esportazione avrebbe avuto luogo nel febbraio 1240.[72] In altre parole, egli dirottava il loro denaro nell'Italia settentrionale, per usarlo per le sue guerre; e li stava ripagando in natura, in Sicilia, dalle scorte regie di grano.

Federico vedeva negli approvvigionamenti di grano di Sicilia e Puglia una fonte essenziale per i fondi di guerra. Nel dicembre 1239, mentre si trovava a Pisa, mandò istruzioni in Sicilia per una migliore gestione delle riserve siciliane di grano: il grano regio avrebbe dovuto essere mandato nel Nord-Africa ed in Spagna, perché lì era valutato di più; il lido di Eraclea avrebbe dovuto essere equipaggiato per consentire un facile imbarco di navi. E in febbraio Pier delle Vigne era in grado di scrivere a nome di Federico a Nicola Spinola, l'ammiraglio genovese della flotta siciliana, encomiandolo per un progetto di vendita di 50.000 *salmae* di grano per 40.000 once d'oro in Tunisia, afflitta a quel tempo da una grave carestia, ma, in quanto punto d'arrivo dei carichi d'oro provenienti dall'Africa occidentale, relativamente ricca d'oro; un prezzo, cioè, di non meno di 37,5 tari per *salma*, quasi quattro volte quello che Baum doveva pagare.[73] Questo era un colpo enorme per la corona siciliana, e fu necessario chiudere i porti per fare in modo che nessun mercante potesse esportare grano prima che le navi di Federico salpassero; Nicola Spinola sapeva che esisteva ancora il pericolo che mercanti privati volessero colpire la corona siciliana in Tunisia. I suoi agenti lo avevano informato che i genovesi andavano acquistando in Sicilia partite di cereali che venivano poi smistate al sultano di Tunisi. Federico, sempre infastidito dalle sotterranee ma-

---

[71] *Registrum Friderici*, 321.
[72] *Registrum Friderici*, 278.
[73] *Registrum Friderici*, 355-6.

novre dei genovesi, non vedeva ragione di consentir loro di realizzare un profitto che, a sapersi destreggiare, poteva finire nelle sue tasche. Né il suo leale ammiraglio genovese pensò minimente di favorire i propri compatrioti. Può darsi che l'iniziativa di Spinola esulasse dalla normale prassi dei traffici mercantili siciliani e che l'imperatore raramente imponesse embarghi talmente rigorosi; quel che è chiaro è che il grano era visto come una risorsa finanziaria, e che la guerra inaspriva il bisogno di Federico di usare il grano per coniare valuta. Federico II era talmente abile (come Rumpelstiltzkin) da trasformare la paglia in oro.[74] La continua emissione di *augustales* era resa possibile dal costante arrivo di oro africano, nelle nuove condizioni di carestia.[75] Il re era, quindi, un mercante: può essere fatto un utile paragone con il contemporaneo re di Aragona-Catalogna, Giacomo il Conquistatore, che pure si impegnava nel commercio; come Federico, la sua principale attività commerciale era probabilmente il noleggio di navi regie a mercanti stranieri in tempo di pace, una pratica che continuò nell'Italia meridionale sotto i re angioini.[76]

Il Registro del 1239-40 contiene chiare istruzioni agli ufficiali di Federico riguardo alle tasse sul grano: il valore di un quinto del carico in Puglia o Sicilia, dove il grano era abbondante, ma di un settimo nelle meno dotate regioni di Calabria o Abruzzo.[77] Queste istruzioni furono date in risposta alle domande dei portolani che erano insicuri sulle esatte regole da applicare. I mercanti indigeni avrebbero dovuto pagare tanto quanto i forestieri? Avrebbero potuto esportare a Venezia, anche se agli altri (e a maggior ragione ai veneziani) era proibito farlo? Ai portolani di Garigliano fu dato ordine che una tassa di un settimo avrebbe dovuto essere imposta anche sui cavalli e sui muli: come il grano, il bestiame, la carne ed il sale erano strettamente sorvegliati.[78] Dietro questi chiarimenti di politica governativa si cela la causa urgente della massimizzazione delle entrate dal *Regno*. Accurati ordini vennero dati per la trasmissione dei redditi ad una sede centrale, spesso la tesoreria di Messina, a volte invece la corte itinerante. Le voci che correvano, secondo le quali gli ufficiali provinciali negli Abruzzi, per esempio, non restituivano correttamente i

---

[74] Punto per il quale sono in debito con Bianca Susanna Abulafia.
[75] Cfr. le intuizioni di R. S. Lopez, *Back to Gold, 1252*, in « Economic History Review », ser. 2, 9 (1956-7).
[76] J. H. Pryor, *Foreign policy and economic policy: the Angevins of Sicily and the economic decline of southern Italy, 1266-1343*, in *Principalities, Powers and Estates. Studies in medieval and early modern government and society* (Adelaide 1980), pp. 43-55.
[77] Cfr., ad es., *Registrum Friderici*, 405-6.
[78] Abulafia, *Federico II*, cit., pp. 275-6. Sull'atteggiamento di Federico riguardo al bestiame, compresi cavalli e muli, cfr. Abulafia, *Federico II*, cit., p. 277.

redditi del commercio, erano fonte di preoccupazione; mentre nella Catalogna contemporanea erano i problemi della responsabilità degli agenti governativi che stimolavano l'esatto mantenimento della documentazione.[79] E qualche volta, in verità, gli ordini sembrano quasi superflui: nel maggio 1240 Federico ricordò ai suoi rappresentanti in Sicilia che una tassa di un quinto avrebbe dovuto essere imposta sulle cibarie che passavano attraverso Augusta e Milazzo, ma il dovere degli ufficiali regi di fornirgli questi redditi era reso evidente da ordini precedenti.[80] Qualsiasi segno che il sistema stesse crollando era attentamente notato a corte, ed ammonimenti o sollecitazioni venivano rapidamente inoltrati.

Nell'ottobre 1239 Federico pubblicò la sua *Ordinanza concernente i nuovi porti nel Regno dai quali le cibarie devono essere esportate*; essa fu debitamente copiata nel Registro.[81] Undici porti furono aggiunti alla lista esistente di porti ufficiali dai quali il grano poteva essere esportato via mare, e nei quali i portolani dovevano sorvegliare il movimento di beni. L'idea era di ridurre le restrizioni al movimento di merci che potevano produrre considerevole reddito per la corona. C'è da dire che pochi tra i nuovi porti avrebbero avuto un futuro brillante. Trapani (in effetti già menzionata come porto regio nel 1231) doveva emergere, quantunque ben oltre il 1300, come uno dei maggiori porti di grano della Sicilia, ubicato in modo ideale per l'accesso ad Africa, Sardegna, Spagna ed alle coste di Francia e dell'Italia del Nord. Pescara era ben ubicata per il commercio nell'Adriatico. Ma altri, come San Cataldo di Puglia, erano soltanto centri secondari superati di gran lunga dai centri tradizionali. Ai portolani fu lasciata anche una certa libertà d'azione: il trasporto di beni a Venezia non era assolutamente proibito ai sudditi di Federico, purché ciò non diventasse di dominio pubblico – anche se è difficile dire in che modo tale informazione dovesse essere tenuta all'oscuro dei veneziani. Soltanto i nativi del *Regno*, comunque, dovevano intraprendere questo commercio.[82] Sembra che il fascino del lucro avesse la precedenza sul cattivo stato d'animo di Federico nei riguardi dei suoi amici di un tempo nell'Italia settentrionale.

In questa sede è stato possibile considerare soltanto alcune delle

---

[79] T. Bisson, *The fiscal accounts of Catalonia (1151-1213)*, 2 volumi (Berkeley-Los Angeles 1985), e *Medieval France and her Pyrenean Neighbours. Studies in early Institutional History* (Londra 1989); non v'è dubbio, tuttavia, che il caso catalano mostri un'attenzione molto più rigorosa alla questione della responsabilità dei funzionari regi.

[80] Abulafia, *Federico II*, cit., p. 276.

[81] *Registrum Friderici*, 416-18.

[82] *Registrum Friderici*, 418.

espressioni pratiche dell'interesse di Federico nell'economia. La legislazione sull'usura contenuta nelle *Costituzioni di Melfi* fornisce un esempio dell'interesse di Federico nell'economia ad un livello differente, e forse largamente idealistico; studiato peraltro a lungo nella monografia di Powell. Il tono più pragmatico delle lettere conservate a Marsiglia e di quelle del Registro un tempo conservato a Napoli, fa orientare verso tre conclusioni. La prima è che il coinvolgimento di Federico II in attività economiche era guidato da interessi di natura fiscale: il bisogno di produrre denaro per la difesa dei suoi regni e dell'impero, ed il desiderio di tornare alla posizione di solvibilità finanziaria che era presumibilmente esistita sotto Guglielmo il Buono. In secondo luogo, parecchie caratteristiche delle politiche di Federico spesso considerate novità, come gli embarghi e l'interesse mostrato nei confronti di merci specifiche, hanno antecedenti normanni. Ed infine, manca un grande piano complessivo; i controlli sono effettuati in maniera approssimativa – a volte soltanto in alcune regioni, a volte con scarso successo. Un punto di vista siffatto era accettato da James Powell quando insisteva sul fatto che l'intenzione primaria della legislazione economica di Federico era quella di assicurare che gli antichi diritti della corona fossero riacquistati. I mezzi per questo recupero non erano di fatto coerenti ed uniformi. Se è possibile ridurre tutto questo ed un principio singolo, quel principio sembra consistere in un'insistenza sugli inveterati ed incontestabili diritti della monarchia siciliana, che nessuno può pensare di calpestare; se eccezioni dovranno essere fatte all'esercizio del controllo centrale, sarà (almeno in teoria) a causa del fatto che il sovrano abbia disposto in tal modo; la questione non è l'utilità economica dei diritti regi, e perfino il loro valore fiscale può passare in secondo piano di fronte alla volontà del sovrano di esercitare appieno la propria autorità. Dai sudditi di Federico ci si aspettava che rendessero lealmente a Cesare ciò che era di Cesare; e pochi aspetti dell'attività economica sfuggivano allo sguardo attento del sovrano.

(Traduzione di Giuseppe Giarratana)

XI

THE KINGDOM OF SICILY AND THE ORIGINS
OF THE POLITICAL CRUSADES

There has been an expansion of interest in those types of crusade that were not directed, at least as immediate objective, at the Holy Land, but against Muslims in Spain, pagans in Prussia or heretics in southern France. The concept of the crusade has increasingly been portrayed as one that depended primarily on papal justifications for the fighting of holy wars, and only secondarily on the popular appeal of the recovery of Jerusalem [1]. Particular interest attaches to crusades whose target was not the infidel at all but the enemies of the papacy within Christian Europe. Thus in the analysis offered by Norman Housley of the "Italian crusades" during the late thirteenth and early fourteenth centuries, we find that at one level we are looking at an alliance of the Angevin kings of Naples with popes and Guelfs anxious to secure primacy in Italy; but on another level we observe the application of crusade indulgences which transformed the conflicts into a series of holy wars as important as those being fought in the eastern Mediterranean [2]. The papacy frequently stated that it was conferring the same privileges as were bestowed on those going to help the Holy Land; although the terms of service might be stricter in the case of non-Holy Land crusades, the moratorium on debts, the remissions of sins and the inviolability of property during absence on crusade were all gener-

---

[1] See for instance the works of J. RILEY-SMITH, *What were the crusades?*, London, 1977; *The Crusades: a short history*, London, 1987; and the *Atlas of the Crusades*, London, 1990, edited by the same scholar.

[2] N. HOUSLEY, *The Italian Crusades. The papal-Angevin alliance and the crusades against Christian lay powers, 1254-1343*, Oxford, 1982.

ally present: to a canonist participants in such wars could not but be crusaders.

The new orthodoxy goes further by rejecting criticism of these crusades as a "perversion" of or "deviation" from a purer ideal. The term traditionally used to describe such wars is "political crusades"; Hippolyte Pissard stated in 1912: "I call by the name political crusades those crusades in which the primary aim of the church is not the suppression of heresy", and he pointed to a distinction in a gloss on the Decretals between the heretical enemies of the faith and those who fight against the Church without being heretics [3]. But the term "political" crusade also suggests a misuse of the crusading privilege for political ends; the crusade launched by Pope Boniface VIII against his rivals in Roman politics, the Colonna, is often cited as proof of such behaviour [4]. Despite Housley's rejection of the negative view of these crusades, and despite his preference for the cumbersome term "crusades against Christian lay powers", the term political crusade retains its usefulness as a description of holy wars fought, often within Italy, for political ends [5].

Analysis of this institution has often concentrated on the period after the death of Frederick II [6]. There are good grounds for this: the links between the house of Anjou and the crusades fought inside Italy (or indeed against Aragon in 1285) are so close that the late thirteenth and early fourteenth century can be labelled the high point of the movement. The result of such an emphasis has been the assumption that it was fully formed when Innocent IV and his successors called the armies of Christ into action against the Hohenstaufen in southern Italy. The argument here will be that the papacy experimented with ways of licensing war against its political foes, and that the use of the full force of crusading instruments

---

[3] H. PISSARD, *La guerre sainte en pays chrétien. Essai sur l'origine et le développement des théories canoniques*, Paris, 1912, repr. New York, 1980, pp. 121-2, citing *Decretals* 5.7.13v.

[4] PISSARD, *op. cit.*, p. 136.

[5] For a spirited attempt to re-establish more traditional views, see C. J. TYERMAN, *The Holy Land and the crusades of the thirteenth and fourteenth centuries*, in *Crusade and settlement. Papers read at the First Conference of the Society for the Study of the Crusades and the Latin East and presented to R. C. Smail*, ed. P. EDBURY, Cardiff, 1985, pp. 104-12.

[6] Apart from HOUSLEY, *op. cit.*, see J. STRAYER, *The political crusades of the thirteenth century*, in *History of the Crusades*, 6 vols, Madison, 1969, vol. 2, pp. 487-518, repr. in J. STRAYER, *Medieval statecraft and the perspectives of history*, Princeton, 1971.

against the Hohenstaufen and the Ghibellines was not the result of an even linear development [7].

Moreover, the papacy had reason to doubt the enthusiasm of western Christians for such wars. The cost of these wars had to be borne by financial impositions at a time when European monarchs (notably Philip IV of France) were increasingly wary of papal pretensions to tax their subjects without reference to their own needs. At times, then, the papacy had to compromise and to comply with attempts by princes or cities to divert funds collected for one objective towards one that suited the wishes of the pope's allies. Here lay the seeds of decay for the political crusades. Finally, the papacy was concerned that attempts to fight on too many fronts – in the eastern Mediterranean and southern Spain against the Muslims, in Lithuania and Estonia against the pagans, and within Europe against the pope's foes – could deny it the chance of victory anywhere. Resources, human and financial, were in danger of being spread too thinly, just as the ability of the papacy to exercise real control was undermined.

It is striking that the Sicilian kingdom appears again and again as target or source of the political crusades. One explanation for this lies in the simple fact that the papacy claimed lordship over the Regno. Kings of Sicily who effectively denied papal claims to primacy in southern Italy could easily be classed as rebels against the Church. The continued existence of Muslims in Sicily until the early thirteenth century, and at Lucera in Apulia from the 1220s to 1300, was cited as a means to convince potential crusaders that a war in the south would be a struggle against the infidel and his allies [8]. In the third place, the strategic position of the Regno as the last western kingdom on the route to the Holy Land, and as a major source of the grain, ships and other supplies that an army would need, appeared to link expeditions in the Regno to the ultimate objective of recovering Jerusalem.

---

[7] For accounts of the evolution of the institution up to 1250, see A. GOTTLOB, *Kreuzablaß und Almosenablaß. Eine Studie über die Frühzeit des Ablaßwesens*, Stuttgart, 1906; W. KOESTER, *Der Kreuzablaß im Kampfe der Kurie mit Friedrich II.*, Inaugural-Dissertation, Munster, 1913; PISSARD, *op. cit.*, pp. 122-35; E. KENNAN, *Innocent III, Gregory IX, and political crusades: a study in the disintegration of papal power*, in *Reform and authority in the medieval and Reformation Church*, ed. G. F. LYTLE, Washington, D.C., 1981, pp. 15-35.

[8] HOUSLEY, *op. cit.*, pp. 16, 19, 40; and see below.

The linkage between the road to Jerusalem and the papacy's military plans within Italy actually precedes the First Crusade. Gregory VII laid elaborate plans for a campaign that would flush Robert Guiscard out of southern Italy and that would subsequently head east to Byzantium, to give military support against the Turks, who had recently scored their major victory at Manzikert [9]. It is generally agreed that Urban II's calling of a holy war in 1095 owed much to Gregory's earlier formulation of plans to aid the Byzantine Empire, but during the First Crusade southern Italy played a positive role as a furnisher of men, notably Bohemond of Taranto, for the crusader armies. Paschal II's later encouragement to Bohemond in his plans to invade the Byzantine Empire shows that the papacy did conceive of Apulia as a base from which holy wars could be launched against schismatics [10].

The link between south Italian affairs and the Holy Land was expressed differently under Innocent II, at the Council of Pisa in 1135. Innocent proclaimed the struggle against Anacletus II and his ally Roger II to be a holy war; he promised the same remission of sins to those who came by land or sea to liberate the Church as his predecessor Urban II had conferred on those who joined the expedition to Jerusalem; this was the culmination of a long propaganda campaign against Roger [11]. Hehl remarks: "it is the first time that the papacy mentioned the Jerusalem indulgence as a reward for the struggle against its enemies within the Christian world" [12]. Some capital could be made out of the fact that Roger II had large numbers of Muslim subjects, including Muslim soldiers and administrators. However, it is hard to find evidence for the application of this privilege. The Pisans may have benefited, as the reference to those who joined the attack by sea suggests. They had already benefited from similar promises during their campaign against the Balearic

---

[9] H. E. J. COWDREY, *Pope Gregory VII's "crusading" plans of 1074*, in *Outremer. Studies in the history of the crusading kingdom of Jerusalem presented to Joshua Prawer*, ed. B. Z. KEDAR, H. E. MAYER, R. C. SMAIL, Jerusalem, 1982, pp. 27-40.

[10] J. G. ROWE, *Paschal II, Bohemund of Antioch and the Byzantine Empire*, in "Bulletin of the John Rylands Library", vol. 49, 1966-7, pp. 165-202.

[11] N. HOUSLEY, *Crusades against Christians: their origins and early development, c. 1000-1216*, in *Crusade and settlement*, cit., pp. 22-3; D. GIRGENSOHN, *Das Pisaner Konzil von 1135 in der Überlieferung des Pisaner Konzils von 1409*, in *Festschrift fur Hermann Heimpel*, Göttingen, 1972, vol. 2, pp. 1099-1100.

[12] E. D. HEHL, *Kirche und Krieg im 12. Jahrhundert. Studien zu kanonischen Recht und politischer Wirklichkeit*, Stuttgart, 1980, p. 42.

islands in 1113-15, which Paschal II may well have recognised as a crusade [13]. It is likely that the declaration at the Council of Pisa was another shot in the propaganda war against the king of Sicily and his ally the "Jewish" pope; and this shot does not seem to have struck its target.

These attempts to use crusades within Europe were not followed through by later popes. The late twelfth century is noticeable for the lack of attempts to declare a crusade within Europe even when the papacy was exceptionally embattled. Alexander III made no move to turn his struggle against the excommunicated Frederick Barbarossa into a crusade [14].

Most historians look to events several decades later to identify the "first political crusade". For Elizabeth Kennan, Innocent III's campaign against Markward von Anweiler, in 1199-1200, "opened a new era in the relations between spiritual and secular powers in Europe" [15]. Innocent III was deeply concerned at the usurpation of power by Markward, just as Innocent II had been concerned at the usurpation by Roger II. The central theme was the defence of the legitimate interests of St Peter in southern Italy. It is not necessary to postulate any direct influence of Innocent II on Innocent III.

The crusade against Markward was never widely publicised; it is only in two letters, one to Capua of Spring, 1199, and one to Sicily late the same year, that the pope raises the possibility of a war for the defence of the Sicilian kingdom. In the first letter he says that, "if it should be necessary", he will grant the same remission of sins to those who oppose Markward as he had already granted to "all who girded themselves against the treachery of the Saracens for the defence of the eastern province" [16]. Indeed, Markward actually hinders the provision of aid to the Holy Land, since he is tied by bonds of friendship to the Muslims of Sicily. He is a second Saladin, who will give Sicily back to Islam, and then there will be not an ounce

---

[13] *Liber Maiolichinus de gestis Pisanorum illustribus*, ed. C. CALISSE, in "Fonti per la Storia d'Italia", Rome, 1904, p. 9, lines 74-5. There is some difficulty knowing exactly what this passage signifies: Pontifex tribuendo crucem, romanaque signa militi ducibusque...

[14] HOUSLEY, *Crusades against Christians*, p. 24.

[15] E. KENNAN, *Innocent III and the first political crusade: a comment on the limitations of papal power*, in "Traditio", vol. 27, 1971, pp. 231-49; cf. H. ROSCHER, *Papst Innocenz III. und die Kreuzzüge*, Göttingen, 1969, pp. 87-92, 253-9.

[16] INNOCENT III, *Register*, ed. O. HAGENEDER et al., Graz/Rome, 1964-, vol. 1, no. 555, 809.

of hope of recovering Jerusalem. Finally, in his letter of November 1199 to Sicily, Innocent fulfilled his threat and offered the Sicilian people the indulgences normally available to those who travelled east in defence of the Holy Land; he cast Markward as "a worse infidel than the infidel" [17].

It is hard to know whether the crusade materialised. Walter of Brienne led a papal army into southern Italy. He had earlier taken vows to go to the Holy Land, and it is likely that he assumed he could commute them by offering service to the papacy against Markward. His army included the young Francis of Assisi, who apparently thought he was fighting in a crusade [18]. Innocent made ambitious use of the crusading instrument, notably in his attempt to topple the southern French lords who were seen as protectors of heresy. Around 1205, the conflict over control of Viterbo was also justified by papal insistence on the liberty of the Church and the defence of St Peter, even though crusade privileges were not issued [19]. Innocent had no doubts that the papacy could launch such wars if it judged it necessary to do so; the decree *Excommunicamus* of the Fourth Lateran Council confirmed that feudal lords who were placed under the ban of the Church had a year and a day in which to make amends, before their vassals were released from the bonds of fealty. Canon law provided express grounds for the just war against the enemy of the Church, above all against heretics [20].

The crusade against Markward, if it ever even existed, had no progeny. Although Kennan insists that it marks the start of a new era, it was not to be for another forty years that an explicit attempt was made to launch a full crusade against the enemies of the papacy. It is possible that the defence of England against Prince Louis VIII of France in 1216 was treated as a crusade, but the issue is clouded by the fact that there were knights present who had earlier vowed to go to the Holy Land [21]. But the war fought by Gregory IX against Frederick II in 1228-9 was not licensed as a crusade; in-

---

[17] INNOCENT III, *Register*, vol. 2, no. 212, p. 414.

[18] J. N. STEPHENS, *The conversion of St Francis*, in *City and Countryside in late medieval and Renaissance Italy. Essays presented to Philip Jones*, ed. T. DEAN and C. WICKHAM, London, 1990, pp. 31-43.

[19] Contrary to what is suggested by PISSARD, *op. cit.*, p. 135.

[20] F. H. RUSSELL, *The Just War in the Middle Ages*, Cambridge, 1975, p. 196.

[21] S. LLOYD, *"Political crusades" in England, c. 1215-17 and c. 1263-5*, in *Crusade and Settlement*, cit., pp. 113-20.

deed, its interest lies precisely in the way the papacy tried to formulate a novel type of holy war based on the institutions of the crusade, but in certain crucial respects quite distinct from the crusade. The most noticeable similarity between the war of 1228-9 and a crusade lies in the financial mechanism behind the war: the papacy attempted to levy a clerical tithe in northern Europe, in aid of the war. In the province of Canterbury, Stephen of Anagni was nominated as collector in England, Scotland and Ireland [22]. The pope urged Stephen to be thorough in gathering funds, even if "it is known to form part of the Holy Land subsidy". Other collectors were active in Sweden and northern France; in Arles and Provence, funds collected for the Albigensian Crusade, now to all intents at an end, were diverted to this use. It is striking that the pope was ready to transfer money committed to the crusade to his war against Frederick II, a point which suggests his desperate need for funds [23].

Additional means had to be found to raise money. Stephen was given the authority to grant absolution for crimes, apparently in return for contributions to the war fund. When ecclesiastical property was being assessed for taxation, Stephen must watch to ensure that no fraud is committed, and will be allowed to excommunicate those who try to cheat the papacy of funds. In fact, Master Stephen encountered stiff resistance from the English clergy. In late 1228 Gregory IX wrote to the bishop, dean and chapter of Sarum stressing the danger that would result from delay in provision of the tithe. But even in June 1229 the money had yet to materialise.

The historian Roger of Wendover offers a possibly tendentious account of Master Stephen's activities. At a meeting with Henry III and his barons, bishops and abbots, in April 1229, Stephen read out the papal letters requiring the payment of a tithe from all laymen and clerics in his British lands. Henry said nothing, and Roger suspected a secret deal with the pope which would allow the king to appoint his own man to the archbishopric of Canterbury [24]. In any case, the barons were angry at the pope's demands. The clergy pointed to the danger that England would be placed under interdict, and after much wrangling Stephen had his way.

[22] W. E. LUNT, The valuation of Norwich, Oxford, 1926, pp. 19-26.
[23] STRAYER, op. cit., p. 349.
[24] ROGER OF WENDOVER, Flores historiarum, ed. H. O. COXE, 4 vols, London, 1841-4, vol. 4, pp. 201-2.

It is easy to see why resistance was so bitter. Lunt calls Gregory "the first and only pope to ask for an aid from English laymen for his own purposes", and stresses that there was no offer of an indulgence to those who gave [25]. Absolution was made available to penitent sinners, but there was no general reward; indeed, there was some sympathy for Frederick II, who had good relations with the English court and whose own crusade had recently won back the city of Jerusalem.

Roger of Wendover is of special interest because he stresses the linkage between the affairs of the Holy Land and the war he is fighting in southern Italy; even if not a crusade, the campaign against Frederick is intimately ticd to Frederick's own false crusade, as well as being financed after the manner of a crusade. Other connections were made. Rainald of Spoleto had invaded the papal state with the help of Saracen troops from Lucera, which was itself seen as a clear advertisement of Frederick's sympathy for Islam; the papal letters talk of "our faithful, impiously slaughtered by the Saracens" [26].

It is in the later stages of Gregory's war with Frederick, in late September and early October 1229, that signs can be found of a shift of emphasis towards the idea of the political crusade. In October 1229 the pope implored aid from the Lombards, by way of the archbishop of Milan; soldiers must be sent, "for the remission of their sins" [27]. In September 1229 the archbishop of Lyons was asked to bring troops to Italy "for the remission of your sins, and the sins of those who come with you to aid the Church, so long as you hurry to come to us in person without delay with a good supply of soldiers" [28]. The same letter accuses Frederick of subverting the *negotium Terrae Sanctae*; and a similar message went to the bishop of Paris [29]. Even so, it is far from clear that the pope was conferring a crusade indulgence on those who participated in the war. A vague reference to remission of sins does not transform the

---

[25] W. E. LUNT, *Financial relations of the Papacy with England to 1329*, Cambridge, Mass., 2 vols, 1939-62, vol. 1, p. 190.

[26] *Epistolae Saeculi XIII e Regestis Pontificum Romanorum selectae*, ed. C. RODENBERG, vols 1-2, in "Monumenta Germaniae Historica", Berlin, 1883-7, vol. 1, no. 376, p. 293.

[27] RODENBERG, *op. cit.*, vol. 1, no. 405, p. 324.

[28] RODENBERG, *op. cit.*, vol. 1, no. 403, p. 322-3.

[29] RODENBERG, *op. cit.*, vol. 1, no. 404, p. 323-4.

pope's favours into a full crusading privilege. Although the letters mention the Holy Land, they do not state that identical benefits will be conferred on those who join the campaign as are conferred on those who take crusade vows.

The most obvious sign that a soldier was also a crusader was the wearing of a cross. But it was the keys of St Peter that were displayed on the banners and coats of the papal army. This was not a novelty, but the comparison between key-bearers and cross-bearers struck contemporaries; Riccardo di San Germano wrote of the *clave signati* or *clavigeri hostes* and pointed out that Frederick fought these foes using his own *crucesignati* who had just returned with him from the east [30]. The use of the papal keys emphasises the underlying theme of this war: not a crusade, but a war in St Peter's interests that was at least as justifiable as a crusade and that could be funded by the same means. At first the pope assumed that he would achieve his objectives by simply persuading Christendom to provide subventions; this aspect of the campaign met with a degree of success. Even so, it is hard to agree with Joseph Strayer's eulogy: "the pope had discovered the way to finance his military operations, to pay for the secular support which he had to have in order to achieve his political objectives. For the first time, the papacy could afford a first-class war" [31]. But Gregory needed men as well, and his eventual pleas to the Lombards and to the French bishops show a significant shift towards the language of crusading. Even so, remission of sins did not make the soldiers into crusaders.

It was during his second war with Frederick II, in 1239, that Gregory completed the transformation of his War of the Keys into a crusade. Again there were appeals to the English clergy, involving a tax of as much as one fifth in certain cases. Again there was strenuous opposition [32]. Matthew Paris portrays a cringing, weak Henry III who was readier to support the papacy (and betray his kinsman by marriage, the emperor) than the clergy was; their view was that Gregory had promised never to reiterate his demand for a tenth to pay for the earlier war against Frederick. They were worried that a custom was about to be established. They knew that Frederick had

---

[30] Ryccardus de Sancto Germano, *Chronica*, ed. C. A. Garufi, Riss², vol. 7, part 2, Bologna, 1938, p. 160; cf. ibid., p. 153; Koester, *op. cit.*, p. 17.

[31] Strayer, *op. cit.*, p. 349.

[32] Lunt, *op. cit.*, pp. 197-205.

never been formally condemned for heresy [33]. Some funds were collected by Pietro Rosso (Petrus Rubeus) the papal emissary, despite vigorous counter-appeals from Frederick.

Some of this treasure, Lunt has surmised, may have been aboard the Genoese ships captured, along with sundry prelates, by Frederick II in 1241 [34]. It is important to note that this fleet had some crusading characteristics: the leading ship was adorned with a white crucifix, and all the vessels had white sails bearing red crosses. When the enemy came in sight, many of the Genoese took crusading vows [35].

Gregory's final act of transformation of his war into a crusade occurred in early 1240, when Rome itself was under threat. The comparison with Jerusalem could be stressed; a second holy city was under threat. Gregory processed with the relics of Saints Peter and Paul, and he urged the Romans to take up arms in defence of the *libertas* of the Church. This time it was crosses that were distributed to be worn as battle badges [36]. Milan, still cowering after Cortenuova, also received offers of crusade privileges [37].

A Europe-wide attempt to secure allies was then initiated. In February, 1241, Gregory addressed a letter to Giovanni de Civitella, who had been sent to Hungary to preach the cross against Frederick; the pope encouraged Hungarians to commute their vows to go to the Holy Land into vows to fight Frederick. This caused some difficulty in a kingdom that had to contend with an infidel threat of its own, that of the Mongol hordes [38]. Gregory's actions are, of course, the logical sequence of his attempts in 1228-9 to divert money collected for Holy Land crusades towards the War of the Keys against Frederick II.

A brief mention of the later development of the political crusade

---

[33] MATTHEW PARIS, *Chronica Majora*, ed. H. R. LUARD, in "Rolls Series", 7 vols, London, 1872-83, vol. 4, p. 10.

[34] LUNT, *op. cit.*, p. 204.

[35] For this series of events see the discussion by KOESTER, *op. cit.*, pp. 31-2; cf. MATTHEW PARIS, *op. cit.*, vol. 4, p. 121; *Annali Genovesi di Caffaro e de' suoi continuatori*, ed. L. BELGRANO and C. IMPERIALE DI SANT'ANGELO, in "Fonti per la Storia d'Italia", Rome, 1890-1929, vol. 3, 113-5; RODENBERG, *op. cit.*, vol. 1, no. 813, pp. 714-6; RYCCARDUS DE SANCTO GERMANO, *op. cit.*, pp. 208-9.

[36] STRAYER, *op. cit.*, pp. 352-3.

[37] KOESTER, *op. cit.*, pp. 20-1.

[38] A. THEINER, *Vetera monumenta historiam Hungaricam sacram illustrantia*, vol. 1, Rome, 1859, no. 327, p. 178; KOESTER, *op. cit.*, 28-9.

will make Gregory's key role plain [39]. After the election of Innocent
IV in 1243, the scale of the conflict enlarges greatly. With the depo-
sition of Frederick at the Council of Lyons, the crusade against the
Hohenstaufen is preached vigorously in Germany and northern
Italy, with promises of the same remission of sins as had been conferred on those going to fight in the Holy Land. Material as well as
spiritual rewards were on offer: lands in southern Italy, franchises
for the Campanian towns, exemptions in Germany from the tight
rules concerning the right to marry within prohibited degrees.
Frisians who had planned to join the crusade of Louis IX to Egypt
were urged to commute their vows and to stay in Germany, resist-
ing the Hohenstaufen: "for this they receive the same indulgence as
if they were going to Jerusalem". The papal registers suggest that
rather few did so: five Frenchmen here, fifteen Germans there [40].
On the other hand, Denmark and Poland were added to the list of
areas where the cross was being preached against Frederick. Italian
prelates north of the Alps were taxed exceptionally severely. The
problem was that traditional sources of supply, such as England,
were drying up [41]. In the summer of 1246 Henry III banned the
transmission of further funds to the pope, though there were, according to Matthew Paris, secret agreements to supply small numbers of knights or money for the maintenance of knights [42].

The problem was that it was easy for even pious contemporaries
such as Henry III and Louis IX to see the war with the Hohenstaufen as a conflict for political control in Italy; the pope's attempt
to unseat the greatest European monarch was bound to send shiv-
ers down the spines of other kings too. Later events proved that the
political crusade won most support within northern Italy from
those who stood to gain from papal policies: the crusade against
Ezzelino da Romano in 1254 won widespread support in the Vene-
to, but crusades against the Colonna under Boniface VIII and
against Venice under Clement V were too obviously bound up with

---

[39] KOESTER, op. cit., pp. 34-56.

[40] D. ABULAFIA, Federico II. Un imperatore medievale, Turin, 1990, pp. 320-1, based
on Vatican Register 21. See RODENBERG, op. cit., vol. 2, nos. 168, 178, 462, pp. 126-7,
135, 330-1, for examples.

[41] See MATTHEW PARIS, op. cit., pp. 519-21, 527-36, for an account of Henry's difficulties with the papacy; also LUNT, op. cit., pp. 214-9.

[42] MATTHEW PARIS, op. cit., pp. 536-7.

papal territorial ambitions, in the one case in the Roman Campagna and in the other case in Ferrara [43].

In the late thirteenth and early fourteenth centuries the emphasis on the defence of the Regno re-emerges as a major theme of the political crusades. Charles of Anjou's conquest of the Regno was itself, of course, a crusade, the final act in the series of crusades against the Hohenstaufen that had begun under Gregory IX. In the preaching of Charles' crusade, much emphasis was laid again on the existence of a nest of infidels at Lucera, even though it took the Angevins until 1300 to disband the Saracen colony. In 1258 the English nobles assented to Henry III's plans to launch an army against Manfred of Sicily; all vows to go to the Holy Land could be commuted to vows to support this campaign, and "this can be done with honesty because of the town of Lucera in Apulia, which is inhabited by infidels" [44]. Emphasis was also laid on Sicily as the strategic key to the Holy Land. This theme was subsequently strengthened when, in 1277, Charles purchased the title to the kingdom of Jerusalem, even though his claim to its crown was contested. During the War of the Sicilian Vespers, and again during Robert of Anjou's attempts to recover the island of Sicily, these themes linking the political crusade to the recovery of the Holy Land were constantly cited [45].

It is thus unwise to assume .that a continuous line of development can be traced from the crusade-like campaigns of early twelfth-century popes through Innocent III to Gregory IX, Innocent IV and later pontiffs. Under Gregory IX and Innocent IV we see a broadening of the concept of holy war, at first not explicitly linked to the crusade, but later, from 1240, expressed as a Europe-wide struggle against the enemy in Christendom's midst. Subsequently there was a narrowing of aims, but the connection with the fate of the papal state, the Regno and, ultimately, that of Jerusalem, was re-established as a central theme in many campaigns – even, in-

---

[43] N. HOUSLEY, *The Avignon Papacy and the Crusades 1305-1378*, Oxford, 1986, pp. 5, 75-6; IDEM, *Pope Clement V and the crusades of 1309-10*, in "Journal of Medieval History", vol. 8, 1982, pp. 29-43; and, for Ezzelino, IDEM, *Italian crusades*, pp. 167-9. But for a different view of the setting of the Ferrara crusade, see D. ABULAFIA, *Venice and the Kingdom of Naples in the last years of Robert the Wise, 1332-1343*, in "Papers of the British School at Rome", vol. 48, 1980, 187-8.

[44] MATTHEW PARIS, *op. cit.*, vol. 5, pp. 680-1.

[45] HOUSLEY, *Italian crusades*; IDEM, *Avignon papacy*, passim, makes this plain.

deed, in the disastrous French crusade against Aragon of 1285. Though this was fought primarily in Catalonia its target was still the heir to the Hohenstaufen, the Aragonese conqueror of Sicily [46].

Papal conflict with the rulers of Sicily moulded the political crusade. Later, papal co-operation with the kings of Naples gave the institution a continued life, in Sicily, Lombardy and elsewhere.

---

[46] J. STRAYER, *The crusade against Aragon*, in "Speculum", vol. 38, 1953, pp. 102-13, repr. in J. STRAYER, *Medieval statecraft and the perspectives of history*, Princeton, 1971.

XII

Ethnic Variety and Its Implications: Frederick II's Relations with Jews and Muslims

Frederick II lived at a time when attitudes to Jews, Muslims, and pagans were undergoing important transformations in Western Europe. He was himself a victim of criticism that labeled him a friend of Islam, during and after his crusade; he actively defended the Jews of Germany against accusations of the slaughter of Christian children. Yet it was the same Frederick who imposed discriminatory legislation on the Sicilian Jews and who helped launch the Teutonic Knights on their war of conquest and conversion in the pagan lands of Eastern Europe. It is thus important to recall that Frederick was king of no less than three states that lay on the edge of the Latin Christian world: Sicily, Germany, and Jerusalem. Each elicited a specific response to the problem of the infidel living next door to, or in the midst of, Christians. Frederick combined the traditional tasks of a medieval emperor, such as the promotion of crusading and missionizing, with the outlook of a Sicilian king brought up on the physical frontier between Islam and Christianity, ruler over Jews, Greeks, and Muslims. It is therefore hard, and perhaps wrong, to try to isolate a common line of thought developed by Frederick to deal with Jews, Muslims, and pagans in all his kingdoms. However, alongside a dislike for persecution for its own sake, we do find a pragmatism and traditionalism that sets Frederick apart from some leading contemporaries such as Saint Louis.[1] It will be argued here that Frederick's approach to Judaism and Islam was in fact quite conservative, part of an established western tradition of toleration (rather than tolerance), which had its roots in the theology of Saint Augustine and in the verdicts of the canon lawyers. And, on a more practical level, his approach was also guided by past practice in each of his kingdoms.[2]

I

In order to understand where Frederick stood, it is essential to outline the principal attitudes to the status of the Jews and Muslims in late twelfth- and thirteenth-century Europe.[3] Clearly, there was a wide spectrum of opinion, and popular hatred for the Jews during the early crusades went far beyond what the Church was prepared to permit; but an "establishment" view of the Jews held by the papal curia and influential church leaders (such as Saint Bernard) can be roughly defined, which in addition provided a basis for attitudes to Muslims. The cornerstone of twelfth-century treatment of the Jews was the view that their very existence was a testimony to the truth of Christianity (testimonium veritatis). Relics of the religion of Jesus' time, they would be converted at the end of time; they were obstinate, and wrong, but they were also part of the divine scheme. The roots of this doctrine lay in Saint

Augustine, and its application had, for instance, helped save many Rhineland Jews threatened with forced conversion or massacre at the start of the Second Crusade.[4] The right to practice Judaism did not give immunity from peaceful attempts at the conversion of Jews, and there was a growing tendency to criticize the Jews as unreasonable because they would not acknowledge Christian "truth." The Christian study of the Talmud and other Jewish sources began by the middle of the twelfth century, under the aegis of Peter the Venerable, abbot of Cluny; from this time, there slowly emerged a new insistence that modern Judaism was based on corrupt texts and on texts offensive to Christians, and that it had ceased to be the religion of Jesus' time.[5] Popular attitudes also took a turn for the worse, with the emergence, first of all in England in the 1140s, of tales that Jews were putting Christian boys to death at Passover.[6]

Papal legislation, reiterated at the Fourth Lateran Council in 1215, confirmed the right of Jews to live in peace but reiterated too the Church's veto on the erection of new synagogues. Neither Jews nor Muslims could own Christian slaves: the linkage of the two groups in the decrees of 1215 is interesting for two reasons. In the first place, this was part of a process whereby disabilities applied to Jews were also applied by extension to Muslims. In the second place, this legislation serves as a reminder that only Christians could assume authority in society; Jews who held power over Christians, whether as royal officials (as so often in Spain) or as slave owners, intrinsically contradicted the view that Jews were in the Augustinian state of servitude.[7] The roots of these ideas and laws lay in late Roman law codes, which (without the help of Saint Augustine) had again adopted a minimalist approach to the preservation of Judaism. Jews must be distinguished from the surrounding population by costume and even by a special badge.[8] This concern to mark out Jews indicated a fear that they would "contaminate" Christian society with their beliefs, even to the extent of trying to convert Christians. In 1222 an English cleric was burned at the stake for having accepted Judaism after falling in love with a Jewess.[9] In any case, marriage between Jews and Christians was proscribed

as strongly by the Christian as by the Jewish authorities.[10] The hunt for heretics in southern France was rapidly extended to include both Jewish converts to Christianity who kept up their ancestral practices and Jews who interfered with Christianity by supposedly encouraging Cathar and other heretics.[11]

In the thirteenth century the attack by the Roman Church on Jewish belief was intensified. The Paris Disputation of 1240 and the subsequent Talmud burnings were symptomatic of a new mood not merely at the French royal court.[12] Popes Gregory IX and Innocent IV also condemned the Talmud from 1239 onward; the Jews of the thirteenth century were increasingly seen as Judaic heretics who had broken away from their ancient beliefs, which had pointed the way to Christianity. Because the rabbis had failed to impose true orthodoxy on their fellow Jews, it was legitimate for the Christian authorities to do so.[13] In other words, the Christian authorities, well read in their Josephus, could see a large gap between Jewish practice of the years around 1200 and that of Temple times; the Jewish authorities, steeped in the Talmud, were more inclined to stress the continuities with the remote past. The Karaite accusation that Judaism had been distorted by rabbinic reinterpretation of the divine law stung the rabbis of the Rabbanite mainstream and may have come to the attention of Christian critics of Judaism; it is, at least, certain that the violent theological and philosophical debates of the Spanish and southern French rabbis over the opinions of Maimonides were known to Christian opponents of Jewish practices.[14]

Current historical debate addresses the problem of the role of the friars in changing attitudes to the Jews and stresses the importance of the debates between Jews and Christians that took place close to the Christian frontier in Spain, at Barcelona, Majorca, and elsewhere.[15] James I of Aragon and Catalonia (1213-1276), king over Christians, Jews, and Muslims, had to confront the practical and theoretical problem of rule over a very large non-Christian population, particularly after the invasion of Valencia in the 1230s. He guaranteed the safety of his Jewish subjects in newly conquered Valencia; he made regular use of Jewish officials; he established peaceable relations with the Moorish élite; but he also fostered conversionist campaigns and permitted the papacy to send friars into the mosques and synagogues of his realms in order to preach to a reluctant forced gathering of infidels.[16] James thus represents a transitional phase in attitudes to the Jews, strongly influenced by the traditions that molded the attitude of his contemporary Frederick II, but enthusiastic too about the vigorous conversion campaigns led by the friars. Both James and Frederick tend to be lauded as tolerant figures who befriended Jews and Muslims; it is important to realize that their stance was not the same.

The Muslims were able to benefit from the tradition of controlled toleration for the Jews. Christian understanding of Muslim belief was tenuous, despite, or maybe because of, Peter the Venerable's commission of a translation of the Koran; and the notion that Islam was some sort of extreme Christian heresy was articulated.[17] Sinibaldo de' Fieschi, the future Pope Innocent IV (1243–1254), gave much thought to the question of whether it was licit for Christians to attack and seize Muslim lands. A particularly important argument was that the infidel could not be deprived of his property and of his rule over fellow infidels simply because he was not Christian. A Christian ruler could legitimately judge infidels where they failed to observe the natural law to which all men were subject. The pope (Innocent argued) also had authority to approve the removal of infidel lords who persecuted Christians, which meant, of course, licensing a crusade against them. What was important was that infidels could not be attacked simply because they were infidels; even their government had a certain legitimacy, if it operated in accordance with natural law.[18]

II

It remains to define Frederick II's place in relation to these developing views. He defined and perpetuated the status of the Jews as *servi nostre camere*, whether in Sicily or Germany, and applied it also to the Sicilian Muslims. But, whereas the king of Aragon had acquired a massive number of Muslim subjects by conquest, from 1229 onward the king of Sicily presided over the virtual extinction of Sicilian Islam. As under James of Aragon, Jewish scholars were active in translation work, but there is no evidence that disputations were held at Frederick's court; nor, in general, was the intellectual life of the Sicilian and South Italian Jews as lively as that of the Catalan and Aragonese ones—they were certainly less well equipped than the rabbis of Girona and Barcelona to debate with Christians. Nor did Sicilian Jews play the role in administration that their Sephardi brethren played in Aragon and Castile, not even to the extent of replacing Muslims in the administrative offices the Muslims had vacated.[19]

Frederick in fact continued the process of Christianization of Sicily that had been begun by his great-grandfather Roger I and continued by his grandfather Roger II, one of whose aims, late in life, was (according to a reasonably reliable chronicler) the conversion of Jews and Muslims: "Circa finem autem uite sue secularibus negotiis aliquantulum postpositis et ommissis, Iudeos et Sarracenos ad fidem Christi conuertere modis omnibus laborabat, et conuersis dona plurima et necessaria conferebat."[20] Roger II thus appears to have offered financial rewards, which was a practical, though strikingly unsubtle, approach to the problem of how to persuade people of the truth of his religion. Later evidence from France and England indicates that conversion could cause financial embarrassment if patrons failed to provide a livelihood for converts; a moneylender, for instance, would find himself subject to ecclesiastical censure if he continued to ply his trade once converted to Christianity.[21] A Muslim source, from 1184–1185, the travel diary of ibn Jubayr, indicates that in Norman Sicily conversions took place for a wide variety of motives:

Should a man show anger to his son or his wife, or a woman to her daughter, the one who is the object of displeasure may perversely throw himself into a church, and there be baptised and turn Christian. Then there will be for the father no way of approaching his son, or the mother her daughter.[22]

According to the same writer, were ibn Hammud, leader of the Muslims in western Sicily, to convert to Christianity, most Muslims would certainly follow him.[23]

Three factors transformed Sicily from

being an island with a Muslim majority into one in which, by 1240, Islam had to all intents ceased to exist.[24] One was the emigration of leading Muslims, who resettled in North Africa and Spain; the Muslim religious authorities disapproved of Muslims living under Christian rule, for they were well aware of the restrictions this would place on free practice of Islam; and, more important, they identified the practice of Islam with the exercise of real political authority. The conquest of Sicily and the Holy Land, and the Spanish *reconquista,* resulted for the first time in large numbers of Muslims falling under Christian authority; and both religions found it hard to adjust to the new reality. A second reason for the decline of Sicilian Islam was extermination. There certainly were pogroms, and Frederick II's tough repression of the last Muslims in Sicily was not a novelty.[25] A third reason was conversion, not so much by Latin missionaries as by a slow process of osmosis that brought Muslim peasants into the local Greek churches; this is demonstrated by the gradual transformation in personal names from those of Islam to those of Greek Orthodoxy.[26] An élite of administrators, often non-Sicilian Muslims like Philip of Mahdiyyah, accepted Christianity; and some, like Philip, were probably not sincere converts.[27] At Messina the civil servant Abd al-Massih told ibn Jubayr: "You can boldly display your faith in Islam. . . . But we must conceal our faith, and, fearful of our lives, must adhere to the worship of God and the discharge of our religious duties in secret."[28] It is true that ibn Hammud, an unconverted Muslim, held a government office; this reflected his exceptional standing in the Muslim community, and yet he still suffered expropriation and persecution.[29] For the other Muslims in government, Palermo was well worth a mass. By Frederick II's reign, Muslims played no part in the royal administration, though Uberto Fallamonaco, *secretus* of western Sicily, appears to have been of Muslim descent. The writing skills of Arabic speakers were still required at the start of the thirteenth century; by the late Middle Ages they had to be supplied as special services by Arabic-speaking Jews or by inhabitants of the Sicilian-Hafsid condominium of Pantelleria.[30]

In other words, by the time Frederick came of age, Sicily no longer stood beyond the Latin Christian frontier; that frontier now lay at Pantelleria and Tunis. A massive immigration of "Lombardi," settlers from northwestern Italy, Campania, and elsewhere, had helped fill some of the gaps left by the disappearance of Muslim cultivators. The decline of the Muslim population did, however, lead to a collapse in specialized agriculture based on Arab technology: the sugar industry, for instance, went into a crisis.[31] The island became even more of a center for grain production, though just when the North Africans were desperate for additional food supplies. The loss of Sicily's Muslims did not therefore lead to a break in contact with North Africa; in a sense it even enhanced that contact, at a commercial level, in the form of massive grain shipments.[32]

Since the 1190s the Muslims were in revolt; the harsh economic régime to which many were subject, and the sudden imposition of the overlordship of the archbishops of Monreale around 1180, created a violent reaction. Old autonomies were stripped away by William II; but on his death the royal government also became greatly enfeebled, and German warlords, Genoese pirates, and others seized what they could in Sicily.[33] The Muslims, too, looked for a radical solution: the recreation of a Muslim state in the mountains of western Sicily. A Sicilian *intifada* broke out, consisting of rebels hopeful of support from Africa and determined to shake off what they saw as foreign rule. The rebels even minted their own coins in defiance of the royal minting laws; they were not mere guerrillas but had actual charge of mountainous territory in western Sicily.[34]

Frederick II's reassertion of royal power in the 1220s involved the merciless destruction of the Muslim rebellion. In 1222 Frederick launched an attack on Iato, where ibn Abbad (or Benaveth), the leader of the rebels, was based. An eight-week siege was sufficient to bring about the surrender of the Saracens. In a famous episode, ibn Abbad was taken to Frederick's pavilion, a prisoner; he prostrated himself before Frederick and begged pardon, but Frederick in his fury struck ibn Abbad with his spur and tore his body open. Soon after, ibn Abbad was publicly hanged at Palermo.[35]

At first sight, Frederick's solution to the problem of the Muslim rebellion has no obvious parallels elsewhere in Western Europe. He created a Saracen colony at Lucera in Apulia, at the other edge of the Sicilian kingdom; he expelled the Christian population of Lucera, even including the bishop, and turned Lucera into a garrison town. There is no evidence that it ever became an important center of Islamic culture, though it is certainly true that Frederick often resided at his castle there and enjoyed the company of his belly dancers and Muslim musicians (who were not, or not all, Lucerans; some were certainly black slaves).[36] The castle at Lucera was a composite structure consisting of a royal palace built on top of a massive glacis; clearly, Frederick felt the need to defend the palace from potentially restive Lucerans.[37] The discovery of Chinese celadon ware in the British excavations at Lucera castle is some indication of the contacts Frederick, or an immediate successor, enjoyed with the East, though even then the pottery probably reached the Sicilian court via Egypt; it is not evidence of the quality of life in the town of Lucera.[38] Although many of the Lucera Saracens were certainly soldiers, some remained active as pastoralists and others were lured back to the soil by promises of plow teams. In the imperial register of 1239–1240, Frederick is found offering one thousand cattle to the Lucera Muslims, with the aim, he says, of binding the Saracens to the soil "as was the case in the time of King William."[39] Frederick sought to create an economically viable community in an area that, like Sicily, was not already very densely settled; but he also sought to isolate the Lucera Muslims from the Islamic world. Thus he permitted them freedom from commercial tolls in the whole of southern Italy (from the *plateaticum, jus dohane, passagium*), but not in Sicily; and he instructed his officials to ensure that Saracen shepherds did not cross to Sicily.[40] The island was to be empty of Muslims; in fact, this was far from easy to ensure, since Muslim rebels held out in the hills, few in number but still a source of trouble as late as the 1240s.

Some outlying territories, too, notably Malta, retained a high proportion of Muslims even though an attempt was made to deport rebel Christians, from Celano in the Abruzzi, into their midst.[41] Forced deportation thus was a tool not merely in the management of Muslims but also in that of Christians. This again was a phenomenon of the frontier: as in Spain, mass population movements, for security, or to increase agricultural productivity, had long been a fact of life. Frederick's deportations from Sicily bear comparison with the expulsion of the Muslims from newly conquered Cordoba, Seville, and other Andalusian towns by the Castilian king in the 1230s and 1240s (though new Muslim settlement was, interestingly, permitted in Cordoba later on). There, too, expulsion of one group was matched by settlement by another. Contemporaries, at the papal curia most notably, viewed Castilian policy with surprise.[42] It is notable that in the Castilian case the Moors were expelled out of Christian Andalusia, toward Muslim Granada or North Africa; in the Sicilian, they were condemned to "internal" exile. Only in 1287, with the Catalan conquest of Minorca, was virtually an entire Muslim population not merely expelled but enslaved.[43] Frederick's policy at Lucera is much less radical—original insofar as it was applied to non-Christians, but traditional insofar as it was a standard Mediterranean solution, known in southern Italy at least since Byzantine times, to the problem of how to deal with a disaffected population. Frederick's actions recall the Byzantine practice of deporting large populations from one side of the empire to another; in the tenth and early eleventh centuries, this policy had brought Armenians and even Bulgars to Apulia. Occasional voluntary mass movements of north Italians and Provençaux into Sicily and southern Italy in this period may also have stimulated ideas about less than voluntary transfers within the *regno*.[44]

It is a moot point whether Lucera was intended to remain a lone beacon of Islam in Italy. Lucera was a long way from the Muslim world, about as far away from Africa as anywhere in the *regno*. The Muslims of Lucera, unlike those of Sicily, could not expect to maintain close religious contact with Tunisia, let alone to receive military aid against Frederick, as had happened during difficult phases of the Sicilian revolt. Isolated in Apulia—"in media christianorum planitie"—the Luceran Muslims would surely experience the same assimilation into the surrounding Latin society that so many Sicilian Muslims had experienced in the twelfth century. Many already understood Italian. Moreover, there is some evidence of conversion campaigns. In 1233 Gregory IX solicited Frederick's help in ensuring that the Dominicans be allowed to preach Christianity to the Lucerans.[45] Frederick insisted that he, too, was keen to convert all the Saracens in Lucera and that many had already converted. James Powell suggests that the pope was worried that the Lucerans spoke the same language as their Christian neighbors and that they might therefore infect them with Islam.[46] This is perhaps one element, assuming that *intelligunt* really does mean "they speak" as well as "they understand"; but more important was the feeling that this self-contained group of Muslims was ripe for conversion, at a moment when Gregory IX, Ramon de Penyafort, and others were beginning to plan still more ambitious preaching campaigns against Jews and Muslims, based on the close study of Arabic and Hebrew in special language academies set up for training missionaries.[47] The prospect of an easy kill against Islam in Apulia must have seemed too good to miss, especially since just now Frederick and the papacy were on reasonably good terms.

A second letter of Frederick II indicates that his concern for the Christianization of Lucera was still alive in 1236. Now we find him insisting that one-third of the population had decided to turn Christian already, and rebutting accusations that he has been neglectful of the need to convert them. Interestingly, he claims credit not merely for deporting the Saracens from the Sicilian mountains to Apulia, which he obviously saw as a positive achievement for Christianity; he also claims credit for Christianizing western Sicily by strengthening Christian settlement there and by removing the Muslim menace from the island. Lucera has to be seen as a two-pronged policy, both arms of which are intended to benefit the Christians.[48] As Powell says, the letter of 1236, "which has been cited to show that Frederick had little interest in the conversion of the Luceran Muslims actually demonstrates the opposite."[49]

The problem of the loss of the agricultural skills of the Islamic world after the disappearance of Islam from Sicily also had to be faced. Frederick sought to attract North African settlers to Sicily, turning not to the Muslims but to the Jews. This again was not unheard of: in Seville, Majorca, and elsewhere contemporary Spanish kings actually encouraged them to settle, bringing in Jews from northern Spain, southern France, and North Africa.[50] It is not unlikely that Frederick was consciously imitating Spanish practice. The imperial register of 1239–1240 lays out Frederick's plans to bring Jewish settlers, possibly from the island of Jerba, who would know how to plant and tend date palms and who could introduce to Sicily indigo, henna, and "other various seeds which grow in North Africa and yet are not now seen to grow in Sicily."[51] This remark seems to confirm the evidence from the Monreale estates that agricultural skills brought to Sicily by the Arabs had declined seriously since about 1200.[52] Half of the Jews' produce was to be paid to the crown, and, like other Jews, the settlers were to be treated as "serfs of the chamber"; they were liable to the poll-tax, of Muslim origin, and to taxes on wine and what appears to be kosher slaughter. The *secretus* of Palermo, Uberto Fallamonaco, was worried that too many settlers might come; he placed severe limits, insisting, for instance, that the palm grove was to be leased to them for only five or ten years. No doubt he hoped that local imitators who had learned the appropriate technology could then take over.[53] The North African Jews were specially conceded the right to have their own synagogue, no doubt because their customs differed from those of Sicily, but it was preferably to be an old disused one, a symbol (perhaps) of the desuetude of the "Old Law."[54] Even the repair of old synagogues had met with disapproval in the Roman law codes, but the wish to ensure that they do not build one afresh certainly fits into the spirit of traditional Roman and papal legislation concerning the Jews. Toleration did not mean encouragement.

III

Frederick's legislation in Sicily contains important clues to his outlook toward Jews and Saracens. Interestingly, he sometimes couples the two, insisting twice in the Constitutions of Melfi of 1231 that both are too severely persecuted at the moment: in other words, some disabilities can be imposed, but this must not extend so far that they are denied access to proper exercise of justice. "We do not," he says, "desire them to be persecuted simply because they are Jews or Saracens."[55] He even exempts the Jews from a general prohibition on the charging of interest, since Christian laws against usury do not apply to Jews;[56] in fact, his decree mirrors that of the Fourth Lateran Council.[57] On the other hand, earlier legislation of 1221 demanded that Jews wear a distinguishing costume, again in line with the decrees of the Fourth Lateran Council. Similar restrictions were placed on prostitutes, for both groups consisted of outsiders who could not really belong to a Christian society and yet were entitled to protection by Christian rulers.[58] Frederick's approach to the Jews of Germany provides important parallels. Accusations from Fulda that Jews had crucified Christian children to pour scorn on the Passion led Frederick to investigate the charge with a thoroughness that is generally assumed to reveal his skepticism about the whole notion. He saw clearly that such a charge, already known from other areas of Europe, would affect the status of all Jews in Christendom and would unleash great violence against the Jews far beyond Fulda. He summoned a tribunal which failed to agree on the matter, and Frederick himself then took direct charge.[59] He wrote to Christian rulers elsewhere in Europe asking that Jewish converts to Christianity be sent to Germany; their knowledge of Jewish law and practice would surely settle the matter once and for all, while their new commitment to Christianity would mean that they would not automatically defend Judaism. The converts demonstrated that Jewish law did not permit human sacrifice, and Frederick then accepted that the charges were a fabrication: "We can surely assume that for those to whom even the blood of permitted animals is forbidden, the desire for human blood cannot exist, as a result of the horror of the matter, the prohibition of nature, and the common bond of the human species in which they also join Christians."[60] The reference to the common bond of the human species was not a mere throwaway line, at a time when Christians were denigrating Jews and other non-Christians as less than human, or incompletely human, because of their obstinate refusal to heed the reasonable arguments of those who sought to convert them. It is interesting, too, to find that one of the sources upon which Frederick's judgment depended was the Talmud. It was described in neutral terms as a book of Jewish "decrees," and it is thus clear that at this stage growing suspicion of the Talmud, in France and at the papal curia, had not significantly influenced Frederick II.

In July 1236 Frederick issued a privilege in favor of the Jews, describing the accusations against the Jews and their refutation, forbidding others from repeating the libel, and stating that the Jews were under the special supervision of the emperor, as *servi camere nostre*.[61] They were thus in general exempt from interference by other great lords, while the emperor could hope to enjoy revenues from their economic activities. The state of "chamber serfdom," as it is often, perhaps wrongly, translated, was a privileged condition of dependence as well as a sign of the subservience of Jews to Christian authority.[62] Such dependence was certainly in Frederick's mind, too, for in a privilege to Vienna of 1237 he insisted that Jews should not hold office in the city government since imperial authority has imposed perpetual servitude upon the Jews as punishment for their crime: "cum imperialis auctoritas a priscis temporibus ad perpetrati Iudaici sceleris ultionem eisdem Iudeis indixerit perpetuam servitutem."[63] However, the terms *servus* and *Knecht* did not have entirely negative connotations in the Hohenstaufen period.[64] The state of *Kammerknechtschaft* was in certain respects analogous to the state of immediacy in which imperial cities and, later on, the Swiss stood; it was a guarantee of relative safety in the much-fragmented political world of medieval Germany. Frederick II's privilege was soon paralleled by grants from German princes, notably that awarded by Frederick II von Babenberg in Austria in 1244; the duke's desire to guarantee the physical safety of the Jews in his principality is emphasized again and again.[65] The parallels can be extended further if we look at the copious documentation from Spain in the same period, again guaranteeing the physical and economic well-being of the Jews.[66]

On the other hand, Frederick did not mention the Jews in his more widely ranging Landpeace of Mainz in 1235. The separation of the Jews from other beneficiaries of the emperor's grace in Germany has excited comment, not least since a major concern of the document was the prevention of private warfare within Germany; the consequent assumption is that the lack of reference to the Jews made them more vulnerable.[67] However, it is likely (as Dietmar Willoweit has suggested) that the Mainzer Landfriede was intended to be binding on all who inhabited Germany, Jew or Christian, male or female, lord or peasant. The Landpeace had little explicit to say to merchants, peasants, and women, so that Jews were not the only apparent omission.[68]

The papacy joined in the condemnation of the ritual murder charge.[69] Once again, we find that Frederick's position is in many respects close to that of the papal curia; the great distance is that between papal thinking and the emerging popular image of the Jew as the vengeful and bloody enemy of all Christians. On the other hand, as has been seen, the papacy was becoming deeply hostile to the Talmud. Innocent IV's brief repetition of Frederick's refutation shows that even a decade after the Fulda libel there were constant accusations against Jews of child murder.

IV

Frederick's contact with Jews and Muslims did, of course, exist on other levels. He was capable of expressing himself in Arabic, and his respect for Islam puzzled the Muslims he met in Jerusalem during his remarkable crusade.[70] As a young man he had been exceptionally enthusiastic about going on crusade, and an interest in the fate of the Holy City remained with him throughout his life.[71] But as king of Sicily his involvement in the politics of the Muslim world naturally took on a more complex character; commercial ties to Egypt and Tunisia, and political ambitions in

Jerba and Tunis inherited from the Normans, meant that he had a deeper understanding of the Arab world than other crusaders—an understanding that paid off triumphantly when he negotiated the surrender of most of Jerusalem, Nazareth, and Bethlehem to the kingdom of Jerusalem.[72] His ability to play Middle Eastern politics does not, of course, qualify him for the role attributed to him by Gregory IX and, above all, Innocent IV as a secret ally of Islam.[73]

It is worth adding that the reconquest of Jerusalem by Frederick II's deft diplomacy resulted not in Jewish settlement but in the expulsion of the city's Jews. It is possible that Frederick himself was not involved in the decision, which was little more than a reenactment of twelfth-century practice. After a few years the emperor's representative permitted a single Jewish dyer to live within the walls of Jerusalem, so as to provide aid to Jewish pilgrims who came by day to pray at the Western Wall.[74] The many Muslims of al-Quds were also obliged to leave the Old City, but the Temple Mount remained in Muslim hands. Such a solution to the problem of the ownership of Jerusalem naturally satisfied no one.

V

The other main area of contact he had with Jews and Muslims lay in the intellectual sphere. It is doubtful whether any Muslim scholars spent more than the briefest time at his court, and then only on embassies from Egypt and elsewhere.[75] In this respect Roger II's court provides a far better example of Christian patronage of Arab learning (including that of native Arabs).[76] In fact, much the same qualification applies to Jewish scholars too; his meetings with Judah ha-Cohen and other Spanish Jews were rare, and the native Sicilian Jews played no identifiable role in the translation work which did go ahead. The translators appear to have been organized by Michael Scot, Frederick's astrologer, and were drawn from a common background: they were mostly members of the ibn Tibbon family, Provençal Jews of Spanish origin, or their close associates.[77] Jacob Anatoli, brother-in-law of Moses ibn Tibbon, translated Ptolemy's *Almagest* and works by Averroes; but to imagine him frequenting the imperial court on easy terms is to stretch the evidence too far.[78] The Jewish scholars who worked for Frederick were thus products of Spanish and southern French Hebrew learning; they were not torchbearers of south Italian Jewish scholarship.

It is likely, too, that the famous questions about the nature of the universe sent to Muslim scholars by Frederick II were as much part of a diplomatic initiative in the 1240s toward the Almohad rulers of Morocco as they were an act of philosophical inquiry.[79] The replies from the philosopher ibn Sab'in of Ceuta were somewhat scornful of the knowledge Frederick had displayed; nonetheless it is certainly striking that a medieval emperor should have entered into correspondence with Muslim scholars as far afield as Ceuta and the Yemen, without any apparent intention of converting them to Christianity.

It is also clear that Frederick's *De arte venandi cum avibus* was influenced by Arab zoological learning and hunting treatises. Michael Scot's successor, Master Theodore, translated Moamyn's *De scientia venandi per aves*, and Frederick spent the six-month siege of Faenza in 1240–1241 checking Theodore's draft. The illuminations of the beautiful Vatican manuscript of part of the hunting book of Frederick II perhaps show the influence of Arabic models. But the ultimate source of Frederick's method lay with Aristotle, whose *De animalibus* he knew well. His taste for the natural sciences is part of a tradition going back to Roger II, but it must be stressed that the physical universe in which he believed was most emphatically a Christian one. The questions he posed to Michael Scot reveal a wish to obtain a literal description of where God sits and what his angels and saints continually do before him. It is a complete, integrated universe in which Heaven and Hell are geographically defined spaces.[80]

VI

Nearly everything we know about Frederick's religious outlook suggests that he saw himself as a Christian. His view of the crusades was far from unconventional; he associated with Cistercians and Franciscans; he insisted in his law code on his appointment by God to rule over mankind. He, or more likely his advisers, flirted with radical movements critical of the wealth of the Church; but, though Frederick's attitude to the papacy was much complicated by his violent quarrels with Gregory IX and Innocent IV, he did not believe that the papacy and the empire were necessarily opposed. It is thus hardly surprising that his treatment of Jews and Muslims was guided by traditional papal practice and recommendations; even the creation of Saracen Lucera was less original than is generally assumed. His approach to unbelievers was conservative rather than (as sometimes assumed) lax or sympathetic; it was fully in line with his overall policy of restoring the rights of his predecessors as kings of Sicily and as Christian Roman emperors.

XII

NOTES

1. William C. Jordan, *The French Monarchy and the Jews* (Philadelphia, 1989), 147–150, emphasizes Louis IX's deeply felt hostility to Judaism.

2. For a fuller assessment of Frederick's aims, see David Abulafia, *Frederick II: A Medieval Emperor*, 2d ed. (New York, 1992).

3. My understanding of this subject owes much to Anna Sapir Abulafia and to the studies she is undertaking for her forthcoming book on *The Jews and the Twelfth-Century Renaissance*.

4. Saint Bernard in Patrologia Latina 182, Ep. 567, col. 567c; compare Rabbi Ephraim of Bonn, "Sefer Zekhirah," trans. Shlomo Eidelberg, *The Jews and the Crusaders: The Hebrew Chronicles of the First and Second Crusades* (Madison, Wis., 1977), 122: "whosoever touches a Jew to take his life, is like one who harms Jesus himself"; however, the view of Gillian R. Evans, *The Mind of St. Bernard of Clairvaux* (Oxford, 1983), 32, is rather exaggerated.

5. Robert Chazan, *Daggers of Faith: Thirteenth-Century Christian Missionizing and Jewish Response* (Berkeley and Los Angeles, 1989), 23–24; Evans 1983, 226–227.

6. Augustus Jessopp and Montague R. James, *The Life and Miracles of St. William of Norwich* (Cambridge, 1896).

7. The same question, in a modern guise, is sometimes said to affect the refusal of the Vatican to recognize Israel as a sovereign state.

8. Edward A. Synan, *The Popes and the Jews in the Middle Ages* (New York, 1965), appendix 7, title 68, 233, 235.

9. Frederic W. Maitland, "The Deacon and the Jewess," in Frederic W. Maitland, *Roman Canon Law in the Church of England* (London, 1898), 158–179; the church council that dealt with this matter also reaffirmed the decisions of the Fourth Lateran Council on the role of the Jews in a Christian society.

10. There is a conundrum here: Jewish law also encouraged social separation, especially at meal times, and the wearing of beards by men. But it appears that around 1200 Jews wore similar clothes to Christians and that their identity was not immediately obvious. In works of art of the thirteenth century, Jews were occasionally distinguished by their features (notably, by giving them large noses), but this was far from universal and may not even represent reality: Bernard Blumenkranz, *Le juif médiéval au miroir de l'art chrétien* (Paris, 1966), 24–25, 28, 32. The use of grotesque noses by artists may simply be an attempt to make Jews look ugly. For a bizarre discussion of noses, see the eccentric book of Arthur Koestler, *The Thirteenth Tribe* (London, 1976), 168–170.

11. Jeremy Cohen, *The Friars and the Jews: The Evolution of Medieval Anti-Judaism* (Ithaca, N.Y., 1982), 42.

12. Chazan 1989, 33–34. Hyam Maccoby, *Judaism on Trial: Jewish-Christian Disputations in the Middle Ages* (Rutherford, N.J., 1982), 19–38, contains a translation of the 1240 debate; the editor's introduction is, however, flawed.

13. James Muldoon, *Popes, Lawyers and Infidels: The Church and the Non-Christian World, 1250–1550* (Philadelphia, 1979), 10–11, though the discussion can be taken rather further.

14. Cohen 1982, 52–60; Bernard Septimus, *Hispano-Jewish Culture in Transition: The Career and Controversies of Ramah* (Cambridge, Mass., 1982); Bernard Septimus, "Piety and Power in Thirteenth-Century Catalonia," in *Studies in Medieval Jewish History and Literature*, ed. Isadore Twersky (Cambridge, Mass., 1979), 197–230.

15. See Cohen 1982 and Chazan 1989, the latter of which makes better sense. Maccoby 1982, 97–150, translates the Hebrew and Latin reports of the 1263 debate. The *Decretum* of Gratian also encouraged disputations between Christians and other unbelievers in the hope that by reason they would be drawn to Christianity: Muldoon 1979, 4, referring to *Corpus Iuris Canonici*, ed. Emil Friedberg, 2 vols. (Leipzig, 1879–1881), vol. 1, *Decretum*, C.23 q.4 c.17.

16. Cohen 1982, 80–84, 109–110.

17. Richard W. Southern, *Western Views of Islam in the Middle Ages* (Cambridge, Mass., 1962), 32–37.

18. Muldoon 1979, 6–14.

19. David Romano, *Judíos al servicio de Pedro el Grande de Aragón (1276–1285)* (Barcelona, 1983) shows that the Aragonese court became more hostile to the Jewish officials during the thirteenth century; James I was more benign than his son Peter the Great, who was under great pressure from the nobles during the War of the Sicilian Vespers.

20. Romuald of Salerno, *Chronicon*, ed. Carlo A. Garufi, Rerum Italicarum Scriptores, ser. 2, 7:1:236.

21. Jews who became Christians could find themselves in financial difficulty because they were cut off from their previous business associates; those involved in moneylending might be in special difficulty. See Jordan 1989, 149–150.

22. *The Travels of ibn Jubayr*, trans. Ronald J. C. Broadhurst (London, 1952), 359.

23. Ibn Jubayr, 360.

24. For a fuller discussion, see David Abulafia, "The End of Muslim Sicily," in *Muslims under Latin Rule, 1100–1300*, ed. James M. Powell (Princeton, 1990).

25. Hugo Falcandus, *La Historia o Liber de Regno Sicilie e la Epistola ad Petrum Panormitane Ecclesie Thesaurarium*, ed. Giovanni B. Siragusa, Fonti per la storia d'Italia (Rome, 1897), 73, reveals the bloodthirsty approach of the king's kinsman Roger Sclavus to the Muslims in the mid-twelfth century.

26. A detailed account of this process by Jeremy Johns is in press; the outlines of his approach can be seen in his article "The Monreale Survey: Indigenes and Invaders in Medieval West Sicily," in *Papers in Italian Archaeology 4: The Cambridge Conference*, part 4,

Classical and Medieval Archaeology, ed. Caroline Malone and Simon Stoddart, British Archaeological Reports, International series 246 (Oxford, 1985), 215–221.

27. Ibn Jubayr reports that some Latin women at the royal palace in Messina actually converted secretly to Islam: ibn Jubayr, 341. However, ibn Jubayr himself admits that there were many strange stories circulating about the court of William II.

28. Ibn Jubayr, 342.

29. Ibn Jubayr, 358–360; also Hugo Falcandus, 119. For information about his business activities, see David Abulafia, *The Two Italies: Economic Relations between the Norman Kingdom of Sicily and the Northern Communes* (Cambridge, 1977), 247–249.

30. Henri Bresc, "Pantelleria entre l'Islam et la Chrétienté," *Cahiers de Tunisie* 19 (1971), 105–127; Henri Bresc, *Un monde méditerranéen: Économie et société en Sicile, 1300–1450*, 2 vols. (Rome and Palermo, 1986), 2:582–584; also compare 2:622–623. Malta also remained as an island of Arabic in the Sicilian kingdom. This may reflect the longer survival of Islam there than in other parts of the kingdom and a greater continuity in population (even after conversion to Christianity) than in many areas of Sicily proper. Maltese Arabic was the language of the peasantry, but the late medieval nobility, partly of non-Maltese origin, spoke a form of Italian.

31. Henri Bercher, Annie Courteaux, and Jean Mouton, "Une abbaye latine dans la société musulmane: Monreale au XIIᵉ siècle," *Annales: Économies, sociétés, civilisations* 34 (1979), 525–547.

32. Tunis became a Sicilian protectorate, probably not for the first time, and acquired a vast, though generally transient, Christian population: Robert Brunschvig, *La Berbérie orientale sous les Hafsides des origines à la fin du XVe siècle*, 2 vols. (Paris, 1940–1947), 2:431–472. The literature on Frederick II's grain exports to Africa includes James M. Powell, "Medieval Monarchy and Trade: The Economic Policy of Frederick II in the Kingdom of Sicily," *Studi medievali*, ser. 3, 3 (1962), 420–524, and Erich Maschke, "Die Wirtschaftspolitik Kaiser Friedrichs II. im Königreich Sizilien," *Vierteljahrschrift für Sozial- und Wirtschaftsgeschichte* 53 (1966), 289–328, reprinted in *Stupor Mundi: Zur Geschichte Friedrichs II. von Hohenstaufen*, ed. Gunther Wolf, 2d ed. (Darmstadt, 1982), 349–394; Abulafia 1988, 331–332.

33. David Abulafia, "Henry Count of Malta and His Mediterranean Activities, 1203–1230," in *Medieval Malta: Studies on Malta before the Knights*, ed. Anthony Luttrell (London, 1975), 104–125, reprinted in David Abulafia, *Italy, Sicily and the Mediterranean, 1100–1400* (London, 1987), no. 3.

34. Franco D'Angelo, "La monetazione di Muḥammad ibn ᶜAbbād emiro ribelle a Federico II di Sicilia," *Studi Magrebini* 7 (1975), 149–153; see also Jeremy Johns, "Monte Guastanella: Un insediamento musulmano nell'Agrigentino," *Sicilia archeologica* 16:33–51. See now Ferdinando Maurici, *L'Emirato sulle montagne: Note per una storia della resistenza*

musulmana in Sicilia nell'età di Federico II di Svevia (Palermo, 1987).

35. Abulafia 1988, 144–145.

36. Abulafia 1988, 146–148.

37. See the contribution by Gary M. Radke, "The Palaces of Frederick II," in this volume.

38. David B. Whitehouse, "Ceramici e vetri medioevali provenienti dal Castello di Lucera," *Bollettino d'arte* 51 (1966), 171–178.

39. *Constitutiones regum regni utriusque Siciliae, mandante Friderico II Imperatore per Petrum de Vinea Capuanum Praetorio Praefectum, et Cancéllárium . . . et Fragmentum quod superest Regesti eiusdem Imperatoris Ann. 1239 & 1240*, ed. C. Carcani (Naples, 1786), 307; Abulafia 1988, 334–335.

40. *Acta Imperii inedita saeculi XIII et XIV*, ed. Eduard Winkelmann, 2 vols. (Innsbruck, 1880–1885; repr. Aalen, 1964), 1:763; and Carcani 1786, 295.

41. For the Maltese population, see the document in *Acta Imperii*, 1:938; Anthony Luttrell, "Approaches to Medieval Malta," in *Medieval Malta*, 1–70, esp. 36–40; David Abulafia, "The State and Economic Life in the Kingdom of Sicily under Frederick II," in *Frederick II: Theory and Practice of Government*, paper distributed at the Centro E. Majorana, Erice, Sicily, 18–24 September 1989 (Italian edition in press, Palermo); Abulafia 1990. Celano is mentioned in *Ryccardi de sancto Germano notarii Chronica*, ed. Carlo A. Garufi, *Rerum Italicarum Scriptores*, ser. 2, 7:2:112–113, in only one version of the text.

42. Felipe Fernández-Armesto, *Before Columbus: Exploration and Colonization from the Mediterranean to the Atlantic, 1229–1492* (Philadelphia, 1987), 51–60; Muldoon 1979, 111–119. Both cite Oldradus de Ponte, *Consilia* (Venice, 1571), 126–127: the despoliation of the Moors was "openly contrary to the precepts of charity."

43. Fernández-Armesto 1987, 36; Elena Lourie, "La colonización cristiana de Menorca durante el reinado de Alfonso III 'El Liberal,' Rey de Aragón," *Analecta sacra Tarraconensia* 53–54 (1980–1981), 135–186; Ramón Roselló Vaquer, *Aportació a la història medieval de Menorca: El siglo XIII* (Ciutadella, 1980); Micaela Mata, *Conquests and Reconquests of Menorca* (Barcelona, 1984), 9–62. In a paper at the 13th Congress of the History of the Crown of Aragon, Palma de Mallorca, September 1987, Henri Bresc argued that the events of 1287 were a novelty, marking a new attitude to the Muslims among Christian Mediterranean rulers.

44. Vera von Falkenhausen, *Untersuchungen über die byzantinische Herrschaft in Süditalien vom 9. bis ins 11. Jahrhundert* (Wiesbaden, 1967), 23–24, which tends, however, to suggest that settlement rights in Byzantine Apulia were as often a favor as a punishment.

45. Jean L. A. Huillard-Bréholles, ed., *Historia Diplomatica Friderici Secundi . . .*, 6 vols. (Paris, 1852–1861), 4:452.

46. James M. Powell, "The Papacy and the Muslim Frontier," in *Muslims under Latin Rule* (hereafter Powell 1990).

47. Cohen 1982, 107.

48. Huillard-Bréholles, 4:831.

49. Powell 1990.

50. Fernández-Armesto 1987, 23, 66-67.

51. Carcani 1786, 290-291.

52. Bercher and others 1979.

53. Abulafia 1988, 336.

54. Carcani 1786, 290-291.

55. Constitutions of Melfi (1231), title 18 (21), in Carcani 1786.

56. Constitutions of Melfi (1231), title 6 (9), in Carcani 1786.

57. Synan 1965, appendix 7, pp. 232, 234, title 67, *De usuris Judaeorum*, speaking of "si de cetero quocumque praetextu Judaei a Christianis graves et immoderatas usuras extorserint."

58. *Ryccardi de sancto Germano notarii Chronica*, 96-97; Abulafia 1988, 143-144.

59. Monumenta Germaniae Historica, *Leges*, sectio IV, 2:274-275; here Frederick explains the course of events.

60. Translation from Robert Chazan, *Church, State and Jew in the Middle Ages* (New York, 1980), 125-126, by kind permission of Professor Chazan.

61. Monumenta Germaniae Historica, *Leges*, sectio IV, 2:274-275.

62. There is now some agreement that the important work of Guido Kisch, *The Jews in Medieval Germany*, 2d ed. (New York, 1970), 142-153, exaggerated the novelty of "chamber serfdom" and misunderstood some aspects of its meaning. See Dietmar Willoweit, "Vom Königsschutz zur Kammerknechtschaft. Anmerkungen zum Rechtsstatus der Juden im Hochmittelalter," in *Geschichte und Kultur des Judentums: Eine Vorlesungsreihe an der Julius-Maximilians-Universität Würzburg*, ed. Karlheinz Müller and Klaus Wittstadt (Würzburg, 1988), 71-89, esp. 80-86.

63. Cited by Willoweit 1988, 82, and Kisch 1970, 149, from Friedrich Keutgen, *Urkunden zur städtischen Verfassungsgeschichte* (Berlin, 1901) 211, §165.

64. Willoweit 1988, 84: "Der Begriff *servus*, Knecht, hat in der Stauferzeit noch keinen eindeutig negativen Gehalt."

65. Text (in English) in Chazan 1980, 84-88.

66. Chazan 1980, 69-75, for examples of 1115, 1149, 1170, 1239.

67. Abulafia 1988, 245.

68. Willoweit 1988, 81, 86.

69. Élie Berger, *Les registres d'Innocent IV*, 4 vols. (Paris, 1884-1921), 1:§2815, §2838, §3077, all of 1247; 2:ccxvii-ccxx.

70. For the reactions of the Muslims in the Middle East, see for instance the collection of texts translated by Francesco Gabrieli, *Arab Historians of the Crusades* (Berkeley and Los Angeles, 1969), 267-275.

71. Abulafia 1988, 120-122.

72. Abulafia 1988, 183.

73. The main account of Frederick's Eastern policy is the Polish study (with a German summary) of Jerzy Hauzinski, *Polityka orientalna Fryderyka II Hohenstaufa*, Uniwersytetu Adama Mickiewicza w Poznaniu Serie historica (Poznan, 1978).

74. Joshua Prawer, *The History of the Jews in the Latin Kingdom of Jerusalem* (Oxford, 1988), 90-91; Mustafa A. Hiyari, "Crusader Jerusalem, 1099-1187," *Jerusalem in History*, ed. K. J. Asali (Brooklyn, N.Y., 1989), 170.

75. Charles H. Haskins, *Studies in the History of Mediaeval Science* (Cambridge, Mass., 1927), 252-253, a point that Haskins clearly finds embarrassing to his general argument.

76. For the overall picture, see Abulafia 1988, 251-270; see also 48-52 on the Norman comparison.

77. Colette Sirat, *A History of Jewish Philosophy in the Middle Ages* (Cambridge, 1985), 212-232. On Scot, see Lynn Thorndike, *Michael Scot* (London, 1965).

78. Haskins 1927, 251-252, again exaggerates the closeness of contact with Frederick II.

79. Haskins 1927, 264; Abulafia 1988, 258, 263.

80. Abulafia 1988, 258-259, 262.

XIII

Monarchs and minorities in the Christian western Mediterranean around 1300: Lucera and its analogues

Writing from Anagni in August 1301, King Charles II of Naples expressed the fervent wish that "the Holy Mother Church be venerated and the Christian faith be cultivated in praise of God where once the profane rite of the Synagogue of the damnable Prince Muhammad" had been conducted, in Città Santa Maria, formerly known as Lucera.[1] The words were apparently not his, but those of his principal minister, the protonotary Bartolomeo da Capua, who was one of the most skilled Latinists of his day, and perhaps too much should not be made of the rhetorical reference to the mosque of Lucera as a synagogue. In fact, the equation of the biblical Sarah with the Christian Church and of Abraham's handmaid Hagar with the rejected Synagogue was current at this time, and coincided with an awareness among Christian authors that Islam traced its origin to Hagar and her son Ishmael.[2] When the terms *Synagoga* and *Muscheta* were used interchangeably, this was not necessarily the result of ignorance or of overblown rhetoric. It is one period in the coming together of attitudes to Jews and Saracens that this essay seeks to analyze, concentrating mainly on what might be termed "official" attitudes at certain royal courts, and concentrating on Jews and Muslims who found themselves under Christian rule.

The chronological limits of this essay are set by a series of events and non-events during a twenty-year period: the destruction of the Muslim enclave of Minorca, in 1287; the expulsion of the Jews from Anjou and Maine, in 1289; the mass conversions of Jews in southern Italy, from about 1290; the destruction of the Muslim colony at Lucera in southern Italy in 1300; the decision by the kings of Majorca and Naples not to expel the Jews from the Balearics, Roussillon, and Provence in 1306. The geographical limits of the essay are set within the western Mediterranean (with one obvious exception), a region

---

[1] *Codice Diplomatico dei Saraceni di Lucera*, ed. P. Egidi (Naples, 1917) (hereafter: *CDSL*) no. 611; the same words are used in *CDSL* no. 654 of 10 January 1302; here Nicola de Friczia, Bartolomeo da Capua's deputy, lifts large passages from his master's text in no. 611. See also Egidi 1915; this originally appeared in the *Archivio storico per le province napoletane* between 1911 and 1914: 36 (1911): 597–694; 37 (1912): 71–89, 664–96; 38 (1913): 115–44, 681–707; 39 (1914), 132–71, 697–766. References here are to this edition.

[2] Zacour 1990.

XIII

where Angevins of Naples and Aragonese of Aragon–Catalonia, Majorca, and Sicily competed but also at times collaborated, so that marriage alliances brought Spanish princesses to southern Italy and vice versa. The inclusion of one northern French territory, Anjou–Maine, in this conspectus is justified by the retention of the counties in the hands of the royal house of Naples until 1302, and by the close interest that the Angevins of Naples retained in their original patrimony. In any case, it is also clear that policy towards the Jews in Capetian France had great influence on their treatment in the lands of both Aragon and of Anjou.

I

The Muslim colony at Lucera was founded in the 1220s, at the same time as the kings of Aragon and Castile were beginning a victorious drive southwards. The deportation of the Muslim rebels who had held out in the mountains of Sicily against Frederick II began six years before James the Conqueror added Majorca to the lands of the house of Barcelona, and the last phase of deportations was probably completed in the 1240s, around the time that the Castilians seized Seville. What was original about Lucera was that it did not simply involve the expulsion of the Muslims out of the conquered lands, as happened in parts of Andalucia; the entire Muslim population of Sicily of 15,000–30,000 was supposedly uprooted and taken far into the northeast of the Sicilian kingdom, to a point whence access to the Islamic world would be exceptionally difficult. The Lucera Muslims were deliberately isolated. They had, while in Sicily, received succor from North Africa. Henceforth they would be all but forgotten by the Muslim world.[3] Thus this case falls half way between the mass expulsions often carried out by the Castilians and the policy of retention of the *mudéjar* population characteristic of Aragon.[4]

Even so, the apparent oddity of the Lucera colony must not be exaggerated. The south of Italy was dotted with small communities of Greeks, Bulgars, and others, whose origins in some cases lay in earlier deportations by the Byzantine rulers of Langobardia. The deportation of Lucera thus fits into an ancient local tradition of population transfers, irrespective of what it reveals about Frederick's attitude to Muslims. In the second place, a small Christian community continued to exist there, if only in the suburbs; and there were Dominican attempts to convert the Muslims which met with official imperial approval, and which may even have produced some results. It is possible

---

[3] This is still in a sense the case: there is no heading *Lucera* in the *Encyclopaedia of Islam*, second edition.

[4] For the variations in policy, see the surveys by J. O'Callaghan (for Castile and Portugal) and by R. I. Burns (for Aragon) in Powell 1990.

that Frederick saw the isolation of the Saracens at Lucera as a means of assimilating them into the Christian world; all alone *in media christianorum planitie* the Luceran Muslims would surely experience the same assimilation into the surrounding Latin society that so many Sicilian Muslims had experienced in the twelfth century. Many already understood Italian. In 1233 Gregory IX solicited Frederick's help in ensuring that the Dominicans be allowed to preach Christianity to the Lucerans.[5] Frederick insisted that he too was keen to convert all the Saracens in Lucera, and that many had already converted. It has been suggested that the pope was worried that the Lucerans spoke the same language as their Christian neighbors, and that they might therefore infect them with their misbeliefs.[6] This was a stock accusation against heretics and Jews; but more important was the feeling that this self-contained group of Muslims was an obvious first candidate for conversion, at a time when Gregory IX, Ramon de Penyafort, and others were beginning to plan still more ambitious preaching campaigns against Jews and Muslims, based on the close study of Arabic and Hebrew in special language academies set up for training missionaries.[7] The prospect of a quick strike against Islam in Apulia must have seemed too good to miss, especially since just now Frederick and the papacy were on reasonably good terms.

A second letter of Frederick II indicates that his concern for the Christianization of Lucera was still alive in 1236. Now we find him insisting that one third of the population has decided to turn Christian already, and rebutting accusations that he has been neglectful of the need to convert them. It has to be said that, even if as much as one third had really expressed an interest in Christianity, there is no evidence that the number of converts was anywhere nearly as high. Interestingly, though, Frederick claims credit not merely for deporting the Saracens from the Sicilian mountains to Apulia, which he obviously saw as a positive achievement for Christianity; he claims credit for Christianizing western Sicily by strengthening Christian settlement there, and by removing the Muslim menace from the island. Lucera has to be seen as a two-pronged policy, both arms of which are intended to benefit the Christians.[8] As Powell says, the letter of 1236, "which has been cited to show that Frederick had little interest in the conversion of the Luceran Muslims actually demonstrates the opposite."[9] But the great majority certainly

---

[5] J. L. Huillard-Bréholles, *Historia diplomatica Friderici Secundi*, 6 vols. in 12 parts (Paris, 1854–61; reprinted 1872–83), IV.452.

[6] James M. Powell, "The Papacy and the Muslim frontier," in Powell 1990: 195, where Powell assumes that *intelligunt* means "they speak," rather than the more probable "they understand."

[7] Cohen 1982: 107. In general, the interpretation of Chazan 1989 is preferable; on this point, see *ibid.* 29–30.

[8] Huillard-Bréholles, *Historia diplomatica*, IV.831.

[9] Powell 1990: 196.

XIII

remained Muslims until 1300, though how strong their commitment was is unknown.

The Lucera Muslims were given the task of cultivating a potentially fertile area whose wheat and barley became one of the prized assets of the Angevin kings of Naples. It is generally assumed that the Saracens all lived in Lucera City; however, some of the lands they cultivated were several miles from Lucera, and the presence of resident Saracens, officially or otherwise, in the surrounding countryside should not be discounted.[10] There were significant numbers of cattle and sheep, even a few pigs, on their land; skilled craftsmen in the town were given commissions by the Sicilian king, and some at least of the male Lucerans became soldiers, serving as far afield as northern Italy, Albania, and Tunis during the thirteenth century. The city was not a major cultural center, though the royal palace in Lucera was a favorite residence of Frederick II and his successors. In fact, many of the Saracen dancers and trumpeters in the emperor's service were probably Muslim slaves brought from overseas, not local Lucerans, though they may in time have added to the Luceran population.

Frederick's legislation of 1231 provides a valuable clue to the status of these Muslims. Frederick's laws speak of Jews and Saracens in the same breath, and insist that both groups must not be deprived of royal protection because their religion is hateful to Christians. Later documents reveal that the Saracens in the *Regno* are *servi camere nostre*. The phrase is adapted from the similar label attached to the Jews. Applied to Muslims, the label is apparently devoid of the complex theological background that was held to justify its use when applied to Jews. There simply did not exist a long history of Saracen subjection to Christian rulers, and the transfer of the term from Jews to Muslims was at least as much a practical political and fiscal convenience as it was a statement about the nature of Christian relations with Islam. Frederick had appropriated the community and had planted it on royal demesne lands; the Lucera Muslims were royal property, working on royal property. Their status thus differed markedly from that of those *mudejares* in Spain who had entered into a treaty, however unequal, with Christian conquerors. Like the Jews, they did not lack an internal political organization, under Muslim officials; this evolved into a Saracen *universitas* in all major respects similar to other south Italian *universitates*: a municipal government that was charged with the collection of local taxes and day-to-day affairs. A further feature of Luceran autonomy was the way the Sicilian administration countenanced the exclusion of the local Christians from all or most of their churches within Lucera; church lands were taken into the royal demesne to be handed on to the Muslims, but the churches that lost lands did receive other estates in compensation.

---

[10] The most recent study of Lucera concentrates on these aspects: Martin 1989: 797–810.

Lucera was rapidly cited by the papacy as evidence of Frederick's multi-faceted faithlessness. The emperor surrounded himself with Saracens and brought them on his campaigns in northern Italy. The existence of a Muslim community in southern Italy provided a central justification for the launching of a crusade against Manfred in 1258; the English nobles agreed that all vows to go to the Holy Land should be commuted in order to help Henry III conquer southern Italy on behalf of his son Edmund; "this can be done with honesty because of the town of Lucera in Apulia, which is inhabited by infidels."[11] When Charles of Anjou became papal champion, the existence of Lucera remained a prominent justification for his crusade against the Hohenstaufen. His failure to destroy the colony, despite its vigorous resistance to the Angevin usurpation, suggests a practical awareness of its value to the crown. The poll tax as well as taxes on local produce could not be ignored by a king who came to the throne already deeply in debt. Besides, the Muslim troops included effective archers and specialists in siege warfare, tent-making, and any number of other valuable skills. If he had to use further force against them, he would be faced with a costly struggle against a highly competent foe that had already held Frederick II at bay in Sicily for several decades. Charles did attempt to attract Provençal settlers to the Capitanata, near Lucera, and may have seen the resettlement of the region by an all-Christian population as a long-term objective.[12] Otherwise, Charles's anti-Muslim policy within his kingdom was probably limited to the expulsion, perhaps towards Lucera itself, of the last Muslims on Malta. In other respects, he took care to guarantee the rights of the Lucera *universitas*.

The integration of the Lucera Saracens into the administrative structure of the kingdom was also indicated by the apparently paradoxical policy of making *servi camere nostre* into knights. Salem Garuyno and Salem son of Ninabet were decorated *militari cingulo* by Charles II in 1291.[13] The knight Abraham was explicitly said to be liable *pro feudali servitio*.[14] Adelasisius or Abd-al-Aziz of Lucera, a member of what was clearly the wealthiest and most powerful family in Lucera, received a fief at Tortivoli near Lucera in 1296, and in fact his family was able to retain many of its possessions after the fall of Saracen Lucera since he and his relatives converted to Christianity.[15]

Although there are hints in the documents of unrest in Lucera during 1299 and early 1300, and although there was some tension between the Muslims and

---

[11] Huillard-Bréholles, *Historia diplomatica* V.680–1; Housley 1982: 65; Maier 1995.
[12] It is possible that the Franco-Provençal-speaking settlements in the hinterland behind Lucera represent the surviving residue of the colonization arranged by the early Angevin monarchs, but there are other explanations for their origin too. See most recently Kattenbusch 1982: 14–22; Castielli 1978: 7–21.
[13] *CDSL* no. 58.
[14] *Ibid.* no. 142.   [15] *Ibid.* nos. 206, 242, 323, etc.

XIII

their Christian neighbors, the destruction of the colony by order of Charles II was sudden and unexpected. On 4 August Bartolomeo da Capua wrote to the Lucerans advising them of the need to appoint new city officials. This was a routine exercise, not by any means unique to Lucera; there was no hint that strong action was in the king's mind. It is true that in June Bartolomeo da Capua had written a strongly worded letter to the king's subjects condemning the fact that the inhabitants of Lucera were Muslims and insisting that those who became Christian would be exempt from all taxes for the rest of their lives.[16] This letter may reflect a belief that the Lucerans should be given a further chance to find the true faith before their expropriation; what is important is that at no point does the letter suggest that the Saracens face expropriation and sale as slaves.

The blow fell suddenly on 24 August 1300. Charles's men occupied the town rapidly; the Muslims were all arrested; deportations began at once; the town was renamed Città Santa Maria, a name which failed to stick. By 4 September 444 Saracens had already been taken in captivity to Naples. Charles declared in the same breath that the Saracens were to be taken away and that Christians were to be settled there: *iugiter in animo gessimus depopulare et exhabitare terram ipsam Sarracenis eisdem, deinde christicolis habitandum* (we arranged that the land be depopulated and evacuated by those same Saracens, and then to be inhabited by Christians).[17] The policy was carried out swiftly, efficiently and relentlessly, under the eye of Giovanni Pipino, a trusted royal minister, who later gained virtual lordship over much of the area. At least 10,000 Lucerans seem to have been deported, but the number may be much higher; Frederick II appears to have brought about twice that number to Lucera in the first place.

For Egidi there was a single explanation of the sudden abandonment of royal tolerance towards the Saracens: "il movente primo ed essenziale della distruzione della università dei Saraceni fu l'avida brama di confiscare i loro beni e di far denaro delle loro persone" (the first and essential motive for the destruction of the community of the Saracens was the avid desire to confiscate their goods and to make money from their persons).[18] A more recent writer has assumed that the fall of Lucera was "almost certainly a last desperate measure to gain a financial respite."[19] It is certainly striking that very nearly the first letters in the Angevin archives to deal with the Lucera Saracens after their expulsion in late August address the problem of where the cattle of the Lucerans have gone to.[20] Egidi's judgment has the force of finality since he

---

[16] *Ibid.* no. 294.
[17] *Ibid.* no. 318. The document was drawn up by Nicola de Friczia of Ravello, Bartolomeo da Capua's deputy.
[18] Egidi 1914: 697.
[19] Housley 1982: 243.   [20] *CDSL* nos. 320–1.

XIII

based his conclusions on over 800 documents, nearly all from the State
Archives in Naples which were destroyed in the Second World War. The
Angevin registers consisted of administrative records to a high degree
concerned with the state of royal finances and the rights of the crown over
south Italian vassals. It is thus hardly surprising that the vast majority of
the material examined by Egidi dealt with the disposal of the property of the
Lucera Saracens after their dispersal in 1300, with the profits from the sale as
slaves of Lucera Saracens, with the transfer of wheat and other supplies from
Lucera to the royal army then fighting in eastern Sicily, with arrangements
to resettle the land and to restore agricultural production, with the rights of
ecclesiastical landlords in the Lucera region.[21]

Egidi argued that the destruction of Lucera resulted from a desperate
financial emergency in 1300; the Angevins were making a vigorous, but
horrendously expensive, attempt to recover the island of Sicily from Frederick
of Aragon, at a moment when Frederick had been left politically isolated
by deft papal diplomacy. It was a good moment to move against Sicily, yet
Charles II had not received the substantial aid he had once naively expected
from James II of Aragon, supposed ally of the Angevins after 1297. Charles
thus sought a short-term objective: the realization of massive funds by the
seizure of the persons and property of at least 10,000 Lucera Saracens. As has
been seen, even the wheat and barley of Lucera was the subject of detailed
orders, prompted by grain shortages during the summer of 1300 that left the
Angevin armies poorly supplied. And, in defence of Egidi, it is noticeable that
Charles II sought not to convert the Saracens and to keep them in place as
Christians, but to take all that they had, including their bodies.

It is clear, nonetheless, that Muslim Lucera had been a valuable source of
profit to the crown. Charles II recognized this in 1296 when he said of the
Lucera Saracens: *hoc presertim tempore vexari nolimus et gravari, tum quia
oportuni et utiles ad ipsius terre custodiam reputantur.*[22] Such remarks are
reminiscent of the positive statements made by the Aragonese kings about the
Muslims of Valencia, as late as the reign of Ferdinand the Catholic. Were
the area to be resettled by Christians, the poll tax could not be levied on them.
There are plenty of signs that the Lucera Saracens, like the Jews throughout
Europe, suffered a significantly higher rate of taxation when asked to
contribute to royal *collecta*. The sheer fact that Lucera lay in a fertile area of
Apulia and that the Muslims had cultivated the restricted area of their settle-
ment so intensively meant that these lands, and the population that worked

[21] There are ready comparisons to be made, for instance with the expropriation of the French Jews
in and after 1306, notably the destruction of the princely house of Narbonne which (like Abd-
al-Aziz's family) held lands and possessed a sort of noble status.
[22] *CDSL* no. 196.

XIII

them, were a major asset of the crown. To depopulate the area might produce short-term profit, but it was also certain to damage long-term revenues. New settlers would in addition need to be promised tax exemption and help with their travel expenses from other parts of Italy or Provence. Even the transformation of the mosques into churches was to cost the crown a handsome sum. Finally, the increasingly close links between the Florentine banks and the Angevin court resulted in a flow of credit into Charles II's treasury and proved an effective way to meet war costs and court expenses.[23] Indeed, the Florentines were much attracted by the wheat of Lucera, which was of high quality and which met some of the food needs of their expanding home city in Tuscany.[24]

It is worth asking what evidence exists for a less crudely materialistic explanation of what occurred. It has been seen that there was a last-minute attempt to encourage Saracens to convert to Christianity from their *profanato seu dapnate secte ac scismatis immo perfidie seu credulitatis errore.*[25] In fact there is evidence also for other recent attempts to win Saracens to Christianity. In 1294 (a year after Dominican preachers had been active among the south Italian Jews) Charles II gave the Dominicans approval in their attempts to search out Christians who had denied their faith and had fallen under the spell of the Muslims.[26] Most likely these "heretics" were relapsed Muslims who had been converted during previous preaching campaigns and had now abandoned their new religion. The Dominicans had also attempted a year and a half earlier to investigate new Jewish settlers in Lucera (the only evidence that Jews inhabited the town at this period).[27] Among the friars prominent in this program was Guglielmo di Tocco, already prominent in the anti-Jewish preaching taking place in southern Italy.[28] These Jews were described as protectors of heretics, which probably means that they were actively trying to wean back to Judaism some of the many recent converts won over by the Order of Preachers. These converts apparently assumed that Lucera was a safe place where the friars would be unable to touch them, though the Inquisition had for some time insisted that its rights extended over Jews who led Christians, including New Christians, astray.

Dominican attempts to penetrate Lucera can be traced back to Frederick II's correspondence with Gregory IX, cited earlier. But, as Kedar has remarked, there is virtually no evidence of sustained preaching campaigns in Saracen

---

[23] Abulafia 1981: 377–88.
[24] *CDSL* nos. 389a, 404, 434, 470a, 489, 517, 529, 534a, 559, 578, 581, 613a, 619, 640, 642, 644, 659.
[25] *Ibid.* no. 294.
[26] *Ibid.* no. 99.
[27] *Ibid.* no. 85.
[28] See the discussion *infra* of the persecution of the Jews in southern Italy around 1290.

Lucera.[29] It is hardly surprising that Lucera should have attracted the attention of so passionate a promoter of conversionist campaigns as Ramón Llull, as Angevin documents of February and May 1294 reveal.[30] They thus coincide with the Dominican initiative against relapsed Muslims in Lucera. Even so, it is uncertain whether Llull actually went to Lucera, which is not mentioned in his short semi-autobiographical *vita*. That he was in Naples during 1294 is clear, and that he encouraged Charles II to join in his schemes to send preachers to the infidel is also certain. The first royal letter concerning Llull dates from 1 February 1294 and is in the name of Charles, king of Hungary, that is, Charles II's eldest son, Charles Martel, claimant to the Hungarian throne. Addressed to the *capitaneus* or governor of Lucera, the Christian knight Enrico Girardi, the letter orders Girardi to provide all necessary help to Llull.[31] The letter was written in Naples and was clearly the result of Llull's own attempts to impress his aims on the royal family.

In the second letter, it is Charles II himself who writes, this time to the castellan of Castel dell'Ovo; the date is 12 May 1294, three and a half months after the first letter. Here the king is ordering facilities to be provided so that Llull may preach to the *Sarracenis in predicto castro morantibus*, that is, to Muslims detained for some reason in Naples.[32] The most likely candidates for the role of Saracen inmates in Castel dell'Ovo are leading Luceran Muslims arrested after outbreaks of arson and other trouble in the Lucera region the previous year.[33] Llull's interest in Lucera is, however, in accord with his attempts to organize preaching in synagogues and mosques in the lands of the king of Aragon. Here he was generally less energetic than the Dominicans, and the main target of his own campaigns was, as is well known, the Muslims of the Islamic world rather than non-Christians already under Christian rule. In 1293 he had been trying to persuade Pope Celestine V to encourage missions to the Muslims, Mongols, and other nations beyond the Latin frontiers.

The evidence for conversionist campaigns in Lucera is thus very patchy. On the other hand, the evidence that Charles II and his advisers saw the destruction of the colony as a worthy religious objective is fuller than Egidi allowed. Egidi made little reference in his monograph to the simple fact that the Lucerans were Muslims. He did not attempt to draw parallels with the treatment of Muslims in other western Mediterranean kingdoms, nor with the treatment of Jews in southern Italy. His assessment of Charles's aims no doubt reflects the pragmatic outlook of the new *Italia laica* of the 1910s in which he lived.

It is not surprising that royal letters concerned with administrative

---

[29] Kedar 1984: 145.
[30] *CDSL* nos. 98, 100.   [31] *Ibid.* no. 98.
[32] *Ibid.* no. 100.   [33] *Ibid.* nos. 90, 91, 92, 97.

243   Lucera and its analogues

arrangements in Lucera, such as the rounding up of the cattle of the Saracens, have little to say about Islam. The strength of royal feeling about the Muslims is expressed in the more general statements of policy contained in the orders to disband the colony and to erect a new, entirely Christian city on its site. Thus in his letter of 24 August 1300 to Giovanni Pipino, ordering the arrest of the Lucera Saracens, Charles II stresses that it is hardly surprising if one who has such devout ancestors as he does should aim to increase the Catholic faith. The presence of Saracens in his kingdom has long appeared to him to derogate from the Christian faith; it is to the honour of the King of Kings that he commits this act, and it is to the Virgin Mary that he dedicates the new, Christian city. While the letter avoids detail on the way in which these orders will be carried through, a single precise provision is made: the conversion of "that place known in Arabic as the *musquitum*, in which the said Saracens pray and are accustomed to come together for prayer" into the principal church of the city.[34]

In a letter of 8 September 1300 these themes are taken further. The Saracens had *proh pudor!* profaned and polluted the land; the king explicitly justifies his actions by saying that he considers it for the *bonum commune, salutem provincie et comoda subiectorum* (common good, safety of the province and advantage of the subjects) that the seed of Belial should be uprooted and wiped out in Capitanata.[35] This biblical language becomes the refrain of another major letter.[36] The presence of the Saracens endangered the whole kingdom and threatened to become a major scandal.[37] Their removal was necessary "because of many horrendous and detestable things inimical to the Christian name" that the Saracens regularly committed out of irreverence for God.[38] Islam was a contagion that threatened to become a plague in Apulia.[39] Charles's efforts were commended by Pope Boniface VIII, who wrote to Franciscan petitioners in 1301 to say that the obscene works of the Saracens had now been put to an end.[40] In the pope's eyes, Giovanni Pipino had achieved a great victory over perfidy.[41] Charles II was probably glad to have impressed a pope on whose support he must count if Aragonese power in the Mediterranean was to be restrained.

Charles's wish for an easy triumph over Islam is not difficult to explain. He was a very devout man, from a very devout family, nephew of St. Louis of

[34] *Ibid.* no. 318.
[35] *Ibid.* no. 323.
[36] *Ibid.* no. 325; *ibid.* nos. 611 and 654 also repeat the same phrases from one another, but are less obviously derived from biblical models.
[37] *Ibid.* no. 324.
[38] *Ibid.* no. 342; interestingly, one of their major crimes was the recent burning of the forests by Saracen rebels.
[39] *Ibid.* no. 655.
[40] *Ibid.* no. 470; Reg. Boniface VIII no. 4012.
[41] *CDSL* no. 478a; Reg. Boniface VIII no. 4070.

France and father of the future St. Louis of Toulouse, who renounced his claim to the throne in order to become a Franciscan. He was also nominal king of Jerusalem; the Angevins from 1277 entitled themselves *rex Jerusalem et Sicilie*, even when they owned neither, and they bore the arms of Jerusalem alongside those of cadet princes of France on their shield. The fall of Acre in 1291 is known to have deeply moved the Neapolitan court. Charles II was deeply conscious that he had failed to defend his most prestigious kingdom while distracted by the War of the Sicilian Vespers. His elaborate plans for the recovery of the Holy Land reveal an ambitious policy of linking the conquest of Sicily to a new crusade to the east; his projects have a good deal in common with those of Ramón Llull.[42]

The prospect of an easy victory against Islam within southern Italy was too good to miss; Lucera lay at the king's mercy. Moreover, the disbanding of Lucera involved the fulfilment of promises made thirty-five years earlier by Charles II's father Charles of Anjou when he entered southern Italy as a crusader against Manfred and his Saracen troops. There is thus some reason to accept Charles's insistence in his instructions to Giovanni Pipino during August 1300 that he had long been hoping to suppress the colony.[43] To insist on the importance of religious motives is not to deny that Charles was enthused by the prospect of making short-term profits from the sale of the inhabitants, their livestock and their crops, to help pay his war costs.

In January 1304 the king was at Foggia, near Lucera, and Bartolomeo da Capua wrote on his behalf to Giovanni Pipino to praise the overthrow of the *Sarracenici ritus et cultus fermentum vetus* (the old ferment of the Saracen rite and religion); the city now pullulated with new, Christian settlers (a claim that is contradicted by other evidence).[44] Yet an apparent contradiction in Charles's actions is the continued existence of Islam in southern Italy after 1300. The Lucerans were sold as slaves; they were not forcibly converted; forcible conversion was rarely regarded as permissible. The motive behind the suppression of the Lucera colony does not therefore seem to be the induction into Christianity of thousands of Muslims; the Christianization of Apulia would be engendered by the arrival of thousands of new Christian settlers from war-ravaged Calabria (where they were under threat from Aragonese armies) and from further afield. In fact, those Saracens who converted to Christianity after August 1300 could not be sure of their release from captivity. Some of the leading Saracens secured the return of their property, even a quantity of Saracen slaves, through baptism: Abd-al-Aziz and his family had been baptized within two years of the fall of Lucera.[45] Lucerans who had become

---

[42] Schein 1991: 108–10, where, however, a more skeptical view of Charles II's motives appears.
[43] *CDSL* no. 318.
[44] *Ibid.* no. 748.   [45] *Ibid.* no. 680.

Christian before the fall of the city were to be singled out and sent under safe guard to Naples; whether it was feared they might escape, or whether they were thought to be in danger from the king's subjects, who ruthlessly massacred fugitive Muslims, is unclear.[46] Most likely they were going to be interrogated to see if they were free of the taint of "heresy," that is, backsliding into Islam. But those Muslims who had rushed to the baptismal font between the destruction of the colony and their capture were in an even more difficult position. Asked what should be done with such people, Nicola de Friczia answered that "since the taking of baptism does not confer freedom on the slave (servo)" they should be treated like everyone else.[47] It is important to stress that this reply accords with practice elsewhere in the Mediterranean, notably at Genoa in the late thirteenth century. There were several categories of Christian slave in Christian lands, such as pagans who converted on being brought to western Europe and enslaved rebels against the Church.[48] Where canon law and secular rulers were tougher was in cases of Christian slaves owned by Jews or Muslims under Christian rule.

In a sense, the king had not enslaved the Saracens when Lucera fell. They were all already slaves. It has been seen that the Lucerans were *servi camere nostre*. The term was apparently understood by Bartolomeo da Capua and his colleagues to mean not just that they were serfs on the royal demesne; they were the property of the crown, and they and their goods could be disposed of by the crown. The interpretation of their status was closely modeled on what Roman law texts had to say about the lack of rights of a slave.[49] It is no coincidence that Naples was at this period a major center of study of the civil law. It will be necessary to return to this fundamental point later in this essay. The animals of the Lucerans were *curie nostre* too. As assets of the crown, many Lucerans were sold in the international slave markets for the profit of the *curia: in multo ex ipsorum Sarracenorum spoliis accrevit erarium* (the treasury grew greatly from the spoils of these Saracens).[50] But many became agricultural laborers, sold to new owners in southern Italy. In a sense, the Lucerans had been privatized. Once the slaves had been sold, the monarchy no longer insisted on its rights over them.

Despite an order in September 1300 not to permit groups of more than ten Saracens to remain together on estates in Capitanata, the crown later reversed

---

46 *Ibid.* no. 460.
47 *Ibid.* no. 498; cf. the slightly earlier no. 459 where a baptized Saracen and his mother are freed.
48 Heers 1981.
49 See Buckland 1908. In fact, the sections of Neapolitan legal treatises edited so far have little to say about slavery; see E. M. Meyers, *Iuris interpretes saeculi XIII curantibus scolaribus leidensibus* (Naples, 1924), where the passages by Bartolomeo di Capua dealing with *servi* such as pp. 203–4, nos. 49–50, clearly refer to serfs.
50 *CDSL* no. 324.

its policy.[51] In an attempt to strengthen Egidi's argument that the fall of Lucera was motivated by financial motives alone, R. Bevere cited a document of June 1302 in which Charles II tolerated the establishment of a new Saracen settlement, consisting of 200 hearths, in Capitanata (quite near Lucera itself), and did not insist that these Muslims be converted to Christianity.[52] Thus, Bevere argued, Charles was not guided by religious motives when Lucera was disbanded. However, his belief that Charles II was explicitly tolerating the survival of Islam close to Lucera itself is given the lie by the wording of the king's instructions.[53] The Muslims were forbidden to have a mosque or to form a religious congregation; the call to prayer was forbidden too. Interesting is the reference to the fact that the Saracens might be either *liberi* or *servi*. Perhaps some Saracens had already managed to purchase their manumission, as Bevere hints.[54] The appearance of free Muslims poses problems: in Aragon it was assumed that even free Muslims were ultimately the property of the crown; this issue deserves further comparative study.[55] There remained Muslims in southern Italy under Charles II's son Robert the Wise (1309–43); in 1336 the king forbade their persecution so long as they did not themselves abuse the Christian faith; Robert even stated that he had heard that the Saracens played a useful role in the economy of Apulia.[56] There is little reason to doubt that most of these Saracens were free or unfree descendants of the Lucera community, though there were probably small groups of Muslim merchants present in several south Italian ports, comparable to the free Muslim merchants Elena Lourie has identified in thirteenth-century Majorca.[57]

II

It is now necessary to search for parallels to the treatment of the Lucera Saracens. There are two obvious directions in which to look: the treatment of other non-Christians (namely, the Jews) in southern Italy and the other lands of Charles II and his dynasty; and the treatment of Muslim enclaves elsewhere in the western Mediterranean. The major instance of the suppression of a Muslim territory contained within another western Mediterranean Christian kingdom is the conquest of Minorca in 1287 and the enslavement of its population. As Lourie has said, the Minorcans were denied the chance to become *mudéjares*.[58] There are some important analogies with Lucera: like Lucera, Minorca was a tolerated notch of Muslim-inhabited land within a Christian kingdom. It had submitted to James the Conqueror in 1231, in the wake of his conquest of

---

[51] *Ibid.* no. 327.   [52] Bevere 1935: 222–8.
[53] *Ibid.* 225.   [54] *Ibid.* 227.
[55] Burns 1973: 250.   [56] *CDSL* no. 818.
[57] Lourie 1970: 624–49.   [58] Lourie 1990a: 2–6.

Majorca, and was in Catalan eyes a fief held by its headman from the king of Aragón and/or Majorca.[59] Its inhabitants were originally permitted the free practice of Islam, and were even encouraged to come to Majorca, in the hope, it appears, that contact with Christians would be to their spiritual benefit. On the other hand, Minorca was not an artificial settlement like Lucera, but the rump of a disappeared Muslim state in the Balearics; it was not particularly fertile, but its pastoral products were valued in trade and as a major part of the annual tribute to the Aragonese kings.[60]

The dispersal of the Minorca Muslims once again is part of the side-history of the War of the Sicilian Vespers. The Aragonese had fought back against the French invasion of 1285 by attempting to dispossess James II of Majorca, brother of Peter of Aragon but apparent ally of Philip III and IV of France. Majorca and Ibiza were occupied in 1285 by the Infant Alfonso and there was fighting in the Majorcan-held lands in the Pyrenean foothills that separated Catalonia from Languedoc.[61] The Muslims of Minorca were suspected of plotting with the north African emirs against the Aragonese, notably during Peter's assault on Collo in north Africa which preceded his successful invasion of Sicily in 1282; besides, there was a danger that the French or Angevins might try to use the island, with its superbly endowed port at Maó (Mahón) as a base from which to attack Aragonese positions.[62] In 1287 Alfonso, now king of Aragon, invaded Minorca by way of Maó.[63]

The broad facts about the fate of the Minorcans are related in the chronicle of Ramón Muntaner, who was generally more interested in heroic deeds than in the niceties of Muslim–Christian relations. His insistence that Alfonso "se pensà que gran vergonya era de la casa d'Aragon que l'illa de Menorca tenguessen sarraïns, e així que era bo que els ne gitàs, e que la conqueris" (thought that it was a great shame for the house of Aragon that the island of Minorca contained Saracens, and thus that it was good that he should throw them out and conquer them) must be understood as part of his wider attempt to project a view of his masters as paragons of chivalry. He even papers over the deep gulf between Alfonso III and his uncle the king of Majorca by pretending

---

[59] Strictly, from James I of Aragon and Majorca till 1276; from James II of Majorca from 1276 to 1285; from Peter III of Aragon and his heir Alfonso III for the remaining couple of years.

[60] Jaume I, "Crònica o Llibre dels Feits," in Ferran Soldevila, ed., *Les Quatre Grans Croniques* (Barcelona, 1971), 59–61, caps. 117–23; Abulafia 1994: 65–8.

[61] For an outline of the make-up of the Majorcan kingdom, see Abulafia 1994: 34–55.

[62] Ramón Muntaner, "Crònica," in Ferran Soldevila, ed., *Les Quatre Grans Croniques* (Barcelona, 1971), 819, cap. 170.

[63] *Ibid.*, 820–2, cap. 172; Mata 1984: 9–62, especially 30–1 where stress is laid on the betrayal by the Muslim ruler of Minorca of Peter the Great's plan to attack Collo in 1282, and the conquest is explained as punishment for this betrayal; Rosselló Vaquer 1980, where details are given of links with Majorca before 1287. E. Lourie's studies in Lourie 1990a add much new documentation from the Arxiu de la Corona d'Aragó in Barcelona.

that a victory in Minorca would serve James II of Majorca's interests; the opposite was the case.[64] More revealing of Alfonso's outlook is what he did on his arrival in the island. Once he had reached the capital, Ciutadella, he "féu pendre totes les fembres e els infants de tota la illa, els hòmens qui romases eren vius, qui eren assats pocs, que en la batalla foren tots morts" (ordered to be taken all the women and children of the entire island and the men who remained alive, who were few in number, for all had died in the battle). Muntaner estimates the number of captives at 40,000, which may be a considerable exaggeration. The entire population was to be sold into slavery in Majorca, Sicily, and Catalonia.[65] Exceptions were made for those who could pay a ransom for themselves, who were nonetheless obliged to leave the island, which was to be repopulated "de bona gent de catalans" (good Catalan people). In fact, as Elena Lourie has discovered, some Muslims were retained on the island as agricultural laborers, but they were few and they were needed because of the great difficulty the kings of Aragon (and, after 1298, the restored kings of Majorca) had in attracting settlers to their wind-blown conquest.[66] These laborers were "ni esclaves ni libres" (neither slaves nor free), in Lourie's view.[67]

Recently, the mass enslavement of the Minorcan Muslims has been singled out by Henri Bresc as an important moment in the development of western attitudes to slavery. This was not just an expulsion, but an appropriation of human bodies and of their possessions, notably their lands, cattle, and sheep.[68] Even if earlier isolated examples of similar conduct can be found, the clearance of a whole territory in this manner cannot be paralleled, whether or not Muntaner greatly exaggerated his figure of 40,000 captives.[69] For Bresc, the assertion of royal rights over the Minorcans is an expression of the growing power of the state. The reappearance of slavery in the Christian Mediterranean world is thus seen as a symptom of the centralization of government during the late thirteenth and fourteenth centuries. Untidy exceptions such as enclaves of Muslims within Christian territories lay under threat from powerful unitary governments.

The occupation of Minorca was undoubtedly prompted by immediate political considerations. Alfonso III, like Charles II, had financial motives, and hoped to raise large sums from the sale of so many slaves.[70] The king seems to

---

[64] See the commentary by Soldevila (p. 975) on Muntaner, "Crònica," 819, cap. 170.
[65] Muntaner, "Crònica," 821, cap. 172.
[66] Lourie 1970: 622–3; idem 1983: 135–86; also repr. in idem 1990.
[67] Lourie 1983: 135.
[68] Bresc 1989–90: I.89–102.
[69] It is still unclear what happened to most Majorcan Muslims after 1229; the lack of a Muslim (as opposed to a Jewish) aljama in Majorca prompts the thought that a great many were unfree. See Abulafia 1994: 56–64.
[70] Lourie 1990b: 2–6.

XIII

have been of the opinion that he was free to dispose of the Minorcan Muslims since they were faithless on two counts: as Muslims, certainly, but also as people who had placed his father in jeopardy by alerting the north Africans to Peter's plans five years before. In a sense, then, they were war captives; captivity in war was an established justification for enslavement in Spain.

Whether the enslavement of the Minorcans influenced the enslavement of the Lucerans cannot be said. There is no sign of an argument that the Lucerans were war-captives, though this argument could have been pressed on historical grounds: they had, after all, been rounded up as rebels and dumped there by Frederick II. However, the basic idea of disposing of Muslims in this fashion may have been transmitted directly from the Aragonese lands to Naples. The royal house of Majorca built close ties to the Angevins of Naples, as the papacy tried to knit together the rival dynasties into a single clan that would be permanently at peace with its members. James II of Aragon married Blanche of Naples in 1295, while Robert of Anjou, the future king of Naples, married first Violante of Aragon in 1297, then Sancha of Majorca in 1304.[71] The personal and cultural links among the courts of Naples, Majorca, and Aragon were thus very close around 1300. The royal families shared an interest in the Spiritual Franciscans, while Queen Sancha of Naples displayed a hostility to the Jews that was moderated by the more benign outlook of King Robert, who continued the Angevin tradition of patronizing Jewish translators.

III

Patronage of Jewish translators did not automatically mean benevolence to the wider Jewish community. Court Jews were frequently exempted from legal requirements such as the wearing of a Jewish badge. If natives, they belonged generally to an elite group of families, who were recognizably the aristocracy of their people, and (like Abd-al-Aziz of Lucera) were recognized as such by monarchs who had a keen sense of nobility of birth.[72] The elite was also probably seen as a prime source of converts, whose baptism would act as an effective example to the wider population of Jews. In fact, many Jewish translators in southern Italy were not native-born, but originated in southern France or Spain.[73] Admittedly, some of Charles of Anjou's helpers were from Sicily (Faraj of Girgenti and Moses of Palermo), but Charles himself never took up residence on the island before he lost it, and Arabic-speaking Sicilian Jewry had a different cultural history from the communities of mainland

---

[71] Musto 1985: 182–5, where allusion is also made to the period when Robert was living as a hostage in Catalonia; his knowledge of Aragonese affairs must have been quite full.

[72] Suarez Fernández 1983: 113 describes how "d'authentiques aristocrates" developed at the Spanish courts, families such as de la Cavalleria, Benveniste, Abulafia, and ibn Shoshan.

[73] Abulafia 1988: 255.

southern Italy.[74] The status of the court Jews was thus quite different from that of the vast majority of south Italian Jews, who were a town-dwelling population of artisans, active in the textile and dyeing industry and similar pursuits. These Jews were mostly regarded as *servi camere regie*, as they had been in Frederick II's day, but several communities, such as that of dyers at Salerno, had been granted to the Church, whose *servi* they then became.[75]

The south Italian Jews were probably not the first Jewish subjects of Charles II to suffer from royal hostility. In December 1289 the Jews of Anjou and Maine were expelled.[76] Charles's action coincided with a wave of local expulsions in northern France, but had distinctive characteristics. Once again, the Sicilian Vespers affected the course of events. The settlement of the ransom demanded by his Aragonese captors was only possible with friendly help from Edward of England, who the previous year expelled the Jews from Gascony, and a few months later expelled the Jews from England. Charles II was thus in serious financial difficulty, and there is general agreement that the expulsion from Anjou was partly at least motivated by the need for money; the comparison with Lucera is obvious. What is striking is that much of this money was to be raised not from the Jews but from the Christians, who were to pay the count-king for the privilege of having their Jews removed.

Charles directed his decree of expulsion at the Jews, the Lombards, and the Cahorsins, but he singled out the Jews for especially lurid description: the document is quite plainly a denunciation of the Jews with an attack on the Italian and southern French usurers inserted as a bonus, perhaps at the prompting of the ecclesiastical and secular advisers who are said to have assented to the hearth and poll taxes (and who stood to suffer least from them). Alongside deep disapproval expressed for the usury practiced by all three groups, Charles condemns the Jews for the "subversion" of the Christians; they are "enemies of the life-giving Cross and of all Christianity," and they are the source of "crimes odious to God and abhorrent to the Christian faith." Charles recognizes that the Jews bring him financial benefit, but he says that he prefers "to provide for the peace of our subjects rather than to fill our coffers with the mammon of iniquity." While the goods of the Cahorsin and Lombard usurers are to be seized by local lords, whose help is solicited by the count, the goods of the Jews appear to fall to the count's officials, who will then presumably collect them for Charles. If this is the case, it reflects the special status of the Jews as the ruler's property. However, the principal source of profit to the

---

[74] Roth 5706: 93–5 for Faraj ibn Salim (Ferragut ben Solomon).
[75] Monti 1934: 174 made the error of assuming that *servus camere regie* was a title of honor applied (in this case) to Ribamelis, a Jew condemned by Bartolomeo dell'Aquila and another Dominican inquisitor.
[76] Chazan 1973: 184–6, with a partial translation of the decree of expulsion: Chazan 1979: 313–17, with a fuller translation; Jordan 1989: 181–2, 230.

XIII

count-king was to be a capitation tax of six *deniers* and a hearth tax of three *sous*, in return for which the debts to the Jews would apparently be cancelled.

As well as the corruption of usury, the Jews are held responsible for another form of pollution. "What is most horrible to consider, they evilly cohabit with many Christian maidens." The Jews have worked to impoverish the Christian population by "devious deceits" resulting in the loss of their goods and their reduction to the ranks of beggars. There is no doubt that, alongside the material gain that attracted Charles to the scheme, the decree exudes a contempt for the Jews that stands in the tradition firmly established at the court of Charles II's uncle Louis IX of France.[77] It is noticeable that Edward I also took the opportunity to claim a grant from his subjects when he expelled the Jews of England, and that he laid heavy stress on Jewish usury when explaining his action.[78] This curried favor with his subjects, and it is likely too that the expulsion from Anjou–Maine was greeted with some satisfaction by the count's subjects there.[79] Yet it would be a mistake to underestimate the sense that these rulers had that their expulsions were an act of piety.[80] Charles II was perhaps all the more inclined to acts of piety as a thank offering for his release from Aragonese captivity; the inception of his direct rule after his release must show that he aimed to reach a high moral standard in his methods of government. Usury was seen as a threat to the whole fabric of society, as well as being immoral because those who practiced it gained wealth without any input of labor.[81] The idea of usury as something destructive of the social and economic fabric is expressed with crystal clarity in Charles II's decree. While his levy of an expulsion tax on the Christians shows some originality, the attitudes underlying his action in 1289 closely reflect the hardline approach to the Jews that was gaining currency not merely in northern France and England at this time. To its impact in the crown of Aragon and in the southern lands of the house of Anjou it is now time to turn.

IV

On 9 November 1304 the Tuscan firebrand preacher Giordano da Rivalto described to his audience in the church of Santa Liperata in Florence how it had come to the attention of King Charles of Naples that the Jews were guilty of human sacrifice. They had supposedly put to death a boy in mockery of

---

[77] Jordan 1989: 181, stressing the importance of the image of the unnatural and beastly Jew at princely courts.

[78] *Ibid.* 182; Chazan 1979: 317–19.

[79] Chazan 1973: 186, speaks of the 'utilisation of anti-Jewish sentiment' by Charles II.

[80] Jordan 1989: 255–6, emphasizes the awareness of the French rulers that the Jews were a moral problem, as usurers and in other ways.

[81] Le Goff 1988 expounds the concept of the "Thief of Time."

Christ's Passion. The king had heard of this "perhaps fourteen or fifteen years ago, or a little more or a little less," that is, around 1290.[82] Thus the "re Carlo" to whom Giordano refers must be Charles II. Moreover, Giordano states that Charles heard of this accusation "per bontade d'un franco frate Bartolomeo, ch'era ministro"; Bartolomeo had reputedly found the Jews making "human sacrifices," and therefore claimed that there were ample grounds to kill or expel the Jews. It will be seen that there are good grounds for supposing this person to be Bartolomeo da Capua, who was first minister of Charles II in 1290, in 1304 when Giordano spoke, and under Charles's successor Robert.

The king accordingly arrested all Jews in "Puglia," that is, southern Italy, and gave them the option of converting to Christianity or of being exterminated. More than 8,000 Jews accepted baptism "dopo lungo consoglio"; those who had not been arrested fled the country, with the result that there were no longer any Jews in the kingdom. One of the converts had become a Dominican friar, like Giordano, and was a friend of his, but apparently lived in Naples.

Giordano's tale forms part of a wider attack on the Jews in this and other sermons. He insisted that the Jews constantly vilified and crucified Christ, blaspheming against Christ three times a day and cursing the Virgin as well. Giordano claimed to have studied their books and to have found evidence of their hostility to Christianity: not a new accusation by 1300. According to Giordano, they worship the wrong God, because they have lost the Bible which was once theirs; they circumcise Christian children, deface images of Jesus, desecrate the host and every year they are said to crucify a Christian child; he is glad to see them put to death for their crimes.[83] Jews are held to have no place in Christian society. Giordano's popular preaching is thus in certain respects reminiscent of themes present in Charles II's decree for the expulsion of the Jews from Anjou. Their corrupting influence on society is emphasized in both cases. But Giordano's medicine is far stronger, and his insistence on conversion or death is absent from the decree.

There is circumstantial evidence that Giordano's story of a mass conversion has a basis in fact.[84] The existence after the start of the fourteenth century

---

[82] Giordano da Rivalto, *Prediche* (Florence 1831), II.231; Delcorno 1975: 283–4, no. 62 [partial transcription].

[83] Giordano da Rivalto, *Prediche*, II.220–32; Cohen 1982: 238–41, identifying Bartolomeo dell'Aquila as the moving force in Naples (rather than Bartolomeo da Capua). It is to Cohen's credit that he has gone beyond the single passage that has attracted most attention among earlier writers, namely the description of the mass conversion in southern Italy, to look at the entire sermon.

[84] The basic study of this event is Umberto Cassuto 1912: 389–404; later studies by Cassuto add to and refine the original argument: U. Cassuto, 1931/2: 172–80; Moshe David Cassuto (his Hebrew name) 1950: M. D. Cassuto 1942: 139–52, which is an updated restatement of the original article of 1912. See also Ferrorelli 1915; Roth 5706: 100–1; Munkácsi 1940. There is valuable additional material in Starr 1946.

XIII

not merely of converts, *neofiti*, but of *universitates neofitorum*, and the transformation of synagogues into churches, notably in Trani, is well attested. Later
Hebrew sources knew that there had been an attempt at mass conversion but
were unsure when in the thirteenth century it had occurred. In the sixteenth
century a story was current that the son of Frederick II had been told by his
dying father to reward the Jews for their loyalty, and had been advised by
his counsellors that the best possible reward they could receive was the
salvation of their souls. The Jews tried to bargain with the king, and agreed to
be baptized only on condition that marriages would be arranged between themselves and the nobility of southern Italy. To their surprise, the king assented to
this and many were coerced into conversion. Others were massacred.[85] One of
the synagogues in Naples became the church of Santa Caterina (this part of the
tale seems to be true). The Hebrew chroniclers seem to date this event to 1250
or thereabouts, but in all likelihood this tale mirrors truer circumstances around
1290. The supposed intermarriage of the Jews and the nobility may reflect the
adoption at the font by *neofiti* of the family names of their noble patrons. This
was common practice in contemporary Spain.

On the other hand, the existence of converts to Christianity, not always
sincere, is attested from the time of Charles I of Anjou, when a more
enthusiastic convert named Manuforte urged the king to suppress Judaizing
neophytes.[86] In 1288 there was an attempt to disperse converts among the
population so that they would be more rapidly assimilated into the Christian
community.[87] Jews had become the victims of the inquisitors during
Charles II's reign. Partly as a result of Manuforte's reports to the king, and
partly as a result of similar measures taken by his brother the king of France
and by recent popes, Charles I ordered his own officials to go to the houses
of the Jews, in company with high-ranking ecclesiastical figures, and to
confiscate the Talmud and other books deemed harmful to Christianity.[88]

The spasmodic acts of hostility to the Jews in southern Italy were transformed into a concentrated campaign for mass conversion when Charles II
returned to Naples after his captivity in Aragonese hands. There is little
evidence for popular hostility to the Jews, whose communities in Apulia were
very ancient. All the signs are that this campaign was led from the front, by the
royal court and by the Dominicans, and that it dated to the period around 1290

---

[85] Solomon ibn Verga, *Shevet Yehudah*, ed. A. Shohat (Jerusalem, 1946), 66–7; Samuel Usque,
Consolaçam ás tribulaçoens de Israel (Coimbra, 1906–8), pp. Xa–XIb and no. 11; Samuel
Usque 1964: 178–80; Joseph ben Joshua ha-Cohen, *'Emeq ha-Bakha*, ed. M. Letteris
(Jerusalem, 1967), 64–5; Joseph Hacohen and the Anonymous Corrector, *The Vale of Tears*
(*Emek Habacha*), trans. Harry S. May (The Hague, 1971), 40–1; Cassuto 1912: 396–400.

[86] Starr 1946: 203.

[87] Starr 1946: 203; Caggese 1922–30: I.299.

[88] Starr 1946: 204; Caggese 1922–30: I.298–9.

to 1294, when close investigation of dubious converts was frequently ordered; it will be recalled that in December 1292 the inquisitors were trying to trace Jews who had fled to Muslim Lucera.[89] Described as *hereticorum receptatores, fauctores et defensores*, these Jews were evidently being accused of trying to wean back to their old faith some of the recent converts to Christianity; in this capacity they fell under the remit of the inquisitors.[90]

Among the figures who planned this campaign can be identified two Bartolomeos: the Dominican inquisitor Bartolomeo dell'Aquila and the protonotary Bartolomeo da Capua. Jeremy Cohen assumes that the former is the figure mentioned by Giordano da Rivalto, "un franco frate Bartolomeo, ch'era ministro" (a free brother, Bartolomeo, who was a minister). On the other hand, Delcorno, in his recent study of Giordano, provides several arguments to confirm the more common assumption that the "minister" intended by Giordano was Bartolomeo da Capua. Bartolomeo da Capua was a good friend of the Dominicans, even if he was never a member of the order; he was in fact married and a layman. He had been a pupil of Thomas of Aquinas and was later to give evidence in the process for the canonization of St. Thomas. Giordano perhaps never visited Naples, but he had close links with those who knew the Neapolitan court well.[91] In support of this argument it is possible to show that Bartolomeo da Capua was involved in royal policy towards the Jews; indeed, there were few aspects of royal policy in which he was not involved. An order of 1294 freeing the neophytes of Naples from the obligation to pay general subventions, *collecta*, and other taxes comes from his hand.[92] The motive was obviously to encourage conversion from Judaism. So too was Bartolomeo da Capua responsible for an act of February 1299 concerning a lapsed convert, Bonusmirus of Bari.[93] Thus Bartolomeo of Capua was active in the persecution of the Jewish communities, just as he was later to be active in the suppression of Lucera Saracenorum.[94]

Giordano's claim that Judaism had been suppressed in the *Regno* had lost whatever validity it had ever possessed by the time he delivered his fiery sermon in 1304. Inscriptions recovered from Jewish sites in Trani, a major Jewish center in medieval Apulia, indicate that Jews were still living and dying openly as Jews in 1293.[95] Although the *Universitas Judeorum* of Trani disappeared early in the fourteenth century, to be replaced by a *Universitas*

[89] *CDSL* no. 85.
[90] Cohen 1982: 48 rightly stresses the importance of accusations that Jews were aiding heretics, including Judaising ex-Jews.
[91] Delcorno 1975: 25, 234.
[92] Cassuto 1942: 152 doc. B.
[93] Monti 1934: 178–9.
[94] Bartolomeo dell'Aquila appears only in the margins of the events at Lucera: *CDSL* no. 142.
[95] Cassuto 1931/2: 172–8.

Neofitorum, Jewish settlements were still in existence elsewhere in the kingdom in the early years of the reign of Robert the Wise (1309–43). It is possible that as many as 8,000 Jews converted, as Giordano claimed, but Jews were still being taxed as such in Naples in 1294–5, and the king around this time permitted some fugitive Jews to return to the kingdom.[96] At most, there can only have been a period of a year or two in which it was impossible to live openly as a Jew in the *Regno*. Like his French counterparts, Charles II moderated his fury against the Jews; on the basis of French evidence, Jordan has argued persuasively that this "erraticism" in royal conduct damaged the social relations between Jews and Christians still further, since the king's subjects were unsure what was permitted of them, or the Jews.[97]

On the other hand, the conversionist campaigns continued throughout the 1290s, with a strong emphasis on the hunt for lapsed neophytes and on Jews who supposedly subverted the faith of new converts. Most likely the "mass conversion" was achieved more successfully in some areas of dense Jewish settlement, notably the major towns of Apulia (Giordano attributes the ritual murder to "Puglia" but the term was sometimes used for all the kingdom of Naples). Trani was certainly a center of the neophytes, and several synagogues, notably the *Scola Nova*, were seized from the Jews. The *Scola Nova*, built in 1247, still survives as the church of Santa Anna.[98] On the other hand, some old synagogues were not apparently expropriated, since at the end of his reign Robert of Naples guaranteed the right of Jews to keep the old ones but required the destruction of new ones.[99] He also expressed concern at mixing between neophytes and Jews, and it is clear that the neophytes long remained identifiable, and subject to suspicion, in the *Regno*: the parallels with fifteenth-century Castile are striking.[100]

It is now possible to suggest an explanation of the known events. Soon after his return to Naples from France, Charles II and the two Bartolomeos took advantage of renewed accusations of ritual murder to turn against the Jews of southern Italy. The emphasis of the campaign does not seem to have been on their involvement in usury, which was much less important an economic activity among the south Italian Jews than it was in Anjou and Maine; the legislation of Frederick II permitting Jewish moneylending in southern Italy under certain restraints should not lead to the conclusion that moneylending, rather than their industrial activities, was the main source of income to the Jews of the *Regno*. The driving force behind the campaign was a hatred for the

---

96 Starr 1946: 208, 210; Roth 5706: 259; Ferorelli 1915: 54.
97 Jordan 1989: 257–8.
98 Cassuto 1931/3: 178–80; Munkácsi 1940: 72–8. For a Neapolitan case, see Cassuto 1942: 161–2, doc. A.
99 Monti 1934: 179; Caggese 1922–30: I.309.
100 Vitale 1926: 233–46.

Jewish religion, accentuated by evidence that Jews were trying to draw back into their faith neophytes who had been converted in the wake of Manuforte's activities a few years earlier. The ritual murder accusation was apparently taken seriously, and past denunciations of it by Frederick II (though in Germany) and by the papacy were ignored. But ritual murder was seen as the most horrible and relatively rare manifestation of a daily cult of abuse of Christian beliefs. Judaism was believed to be impregnated with contempt for Christ; its character was thought to be that of a plot against Christ, a constant reaffirmation of the killing of Christ by the Jews. Thus the reasons given by Giordano da Rivalto for annihilating Judaism conform in striking measure with the passages in the decree of expulsion from Anjou–Maine where the count–king denounces the Jewish religion.

V

In view of his hostility to the Jews in Anjou and Naples, it is surprising that Charles II did not suppress the Jewish communities of Provence, a region that was in many ways his favorite possession. Indeed, Jews arrived in Provence during 1306, having just suffered the ignominy of expulsion from Capetian France. It has been suggested that it was the moderating influence of the royal heir Robert that prevented tougher action against the Provençal Jews than insistence that they should wear a badge, separate their markets from those of the Christians and not be approached for medical treatment by Christians; the ban on Jewish physicians treating Christians was, interestingly enough, also discussed by Bartolomeo da Capua in his commentary on the laws of Frederick II.[101] In fact, Charles spent 1306 and 1307 mainly occupied with Provençal affairs.[102] He seems simply to have lost his passion for the "Jewish problem." It was Robert who adopted a tough stance, and who ordered inventories to be made of Jewish property; Charles himself put an end to the scheme for their expulsion.[103] On becoming king, Robert merely confirmed his father's policy. Certainly, the Jews of Provence had close links to the former Occitan communities, and the count–king may have calculated that the Jews would generate wealth. More importantly, the towns of Provence had in several cases (notably Marseilles) granted special privileges to the Jews, with whom the Christian population generally lived in harmony.[104] On the other hand, the inquisitors were active in Provence against converted Jews, and on

---

[101] Jordan 1989: 230; Trifone 1921: cxcii, citing Bartolomeo da Capua on Constitutions of Melfi, book 3, cap. 46.
[102] Léonard 1967: 249.
[103] Kriegel 1978: 8.
[104] Shatzmiller 1990 shows that in 1317 Jews and Christians in the Marseilles business community had some esteem for one another.

XIII

one occasion the Provençal Jews persuaded Charles I of Anjou to restrain these investigators.[105] The Provençal communities thus survived by a hair's breadth, and were the beneficiaries of the "erraticism" in policy towards Jews observed by Jordan.

Similar plans for expulsion also nearly engulfed the Jewish communities of Roussillon and the Balearics, subjects of James II of Majorca, who was, as has been seen, deeply beholden to the French kings.[106] The Majorcan Jews continued to be subjected to royal fines, dispossession of their synagogues and other severe vexations, and were saved more by the greed of King Sancho, James's successor, than by adherence to any principles of *convivencia*.[107] As in Provence, the hope of financial benefit may have led the monarchy to tolerate the settlement in Roussillon of fugitive southern French Jews. The Majorcan Jews were expected to pay well for the right to live as a protected community. Equally, they were defended by the king himself against the sort of charges that had wrecked their security in southern Italy; in 1309 James II of Majorca instructed his officials to act against rumors of child murder, which were malicious nonsense.[108]

VI

There are some common threads in this evidence. The suppression of the Saracens of Lucera, like that of the Jewish communities in Anjou and southern Italy, has been attributed to the religious fervour of a king who sought divine support in his plans to recover Sicily, and ultimately the Holy Land. He was bitter in his denunciation of the supposedly corrupting influence of Jews and Muslims on the Christian inhabitants of his lands. In this policy he had the warm support, even the prompting, of the Dominicans, and also of his counsellors both in Anjou–Maine (as the expulsion decree makes plain) and in southern Italy. But he was not alone in adopting so aggressive an approach to his non-Christian subjects, as the case of Minorca indicates, and as the French and English precedents for his Jewish policy also suggest.

Just as the enslavement of the Minorcans, and by extension that of the Lucerans, has been associated by Henri Bresc with the growing power of the state, so too the expulsions of the Jews in the late thirteenth century and after have been seen by Maurice Kriegel as a stage in the definition of state authority. The ruler sought to win the approval of his subjects by persecuting an often unpopular minority; but rulers also sought a religious uniformity

---

[105] Kriegel 1977: 315–23.
[106] Kriegel 1978: 7–8.
[107] Abulafia 1992; Moore 1976; Pons 1957–60; the older work of Isaacs (1936) has a useful register of documents, though the text is very dated.
[108] Isaacs 1936: 241, doc. 87.

which would harmonize with their attempts at greater governmental centralization. There was little room for minorities; Valencia may appear the obvious
exception, but there it was the Christians who were numerically the minority in
their own kingdom. The Jews in southern Italy were a scattered community and
had few means of defence; the king, and some of the prelates to whom Jewish
communities had been granted in the past, were *de jure* their defenders. If the
king abandoned such a position, the Jews had little future in the *Regno* as Jews.
Less implacable than the Ashkenazi Jews, who had preferred death to
conversion, many Italian Jews went to the font, but not all those who did so
abandoned their loyalty to the God of their fathers.[109]

The Muslims were in certain important respects in a similar position. Their
status as royal *servi* was ruthlessly exploited by a government anxious to
possess their goods. Islam was suppressed, in the sense that those who survived
in southern Italy were denied the use of mosques; but forcible conversion
seems not to have occurred. The crown sought the conversion of the Muslim
leaders, and generally did not release from slavery those who converted after
their capture. Yet it has been seen that in the case of Lucera religious motives
of a different type cannot be discounted. Enslavement was a punishment for
generations of obstinate commitment to Islam, just as expulsion and the threat
of massacre was a punishment against Jews who for centuries had supposedly
maligned Christ.

It is being suggested here that the royal court harnessed Roman law to argue
that the state had the power and right to enslave its Muslim subjects. Indeed,
they were already slaves before they were sent into slavery. The importance
of the literal interpretation of the term *servus*, in *servus camere regie*, to
mean "slave" in the sense understood by Roman law, cannot be underestimated. In many ways, the use of Roman law to defend royal rights was what
made possible that assertion of state control that Kriegel and Bresc have
associated with the enslavement of Muslims and the expulsion of Jews. It is
thus necessary to stress that at Charles II's elbow there stood one of the
most eminent Roman lawyers in Italy, Bartolomeo da Capua. As royal protonotary, from June 1290, he had a direct role in the enactment of decrees
against Jews and Muslims. His influence and that of his circle deserve
examination.

Bartolomeo was a product of a distinguished legal family. His services to the

---

[109] The different outlook of the Mediterranean Jews to the problem of forced conversion is perhaps
expressed most clearly in the Letter on Persecution and Letter to Yemen of Moses Maimonides,
written in the late twelfth century to deal with rare instances of forcible conversion by Muslim
rulers; his pragmatic approach opened the door to insincere conversion which masked crypto-
Judaism.

XIII

crown earned him lands and wealth.[110] It has been said of him that for forty years he was the fulcrum of all Angevin legislative initiatives; he was "la mente direttiva della loro azione politica."[111] He was at the core of a group of Roman lawyers who insisted on the fullness of royal authority; *rex in regno suo est imperator*: the idea was articulated in Naples, as in France, to fend off papal and (in the case of Naples) imperial assertions of authority over the *Regno*.[112] He prepared glosses on the laws of Frederick II and his successors, which were incorporated in the glosses of his colleague Andrea da Isernia, another vigorous protagonist of the autonomy of the *Regno*.

A fuller study of Bartolomeo's legal writings, many of which remain unedited, is needed, all the more so when legal historians insist so emphatically on his importance. Yet what is significant in the glosses on the Sicilian law codes is not his originality. The glosses prepared by Andrea da Isernia under his influence repeat with approval the position on the rights of Jews established in canon law: Jews are *peioris conditionis quam Christiani et debent esse*. Jews may not have authority over Christians.[113] They state too that *privilegia data Catholicis denegantur Iudaeis, et omnibus qui non sunt membrum Catholicae ecclesiae seu fidei*.[114] A law of Charles II of Naples states *quod Iudaeis, qui sunt vassalli ecclesiae nulla officia committantur, nec aliae oppressiones, vel gravamina inferantur*.[115] Andrea was clear that both Jews and Saracens lived *sub protectione principis, ne vindicta sua auctoritate quis recipiat*.[116] As has been seen, Bartolomeo was of the view that Jewish physicians are not to treat Christians; indeed, Christians are not even to receive food and drink from Jews.[117] As Roman lawyers, then, the close advisers of Charles II could add something to the odium for non-Christians that Bartolomeo apparently shared, if (as Giordano da Rivalto suggested) it was he who turned the king against the Jews in about 1290. When it came to the expropriation of Saracen property, or the condemnation of the Jews for insulting Christians and supposedly murdering children, the Jews and the Muslims faced the full force of Roman law. The slave condition of the king's non-Christian subjects placed them under his protection, as the glosses said, but also at his mercy.

---

[110] The best recent description of his career is by Walter and Piccialuti in the *Dizionario biografico italiano*, s.v. His family connections and administrative functions are explained in Minieri Riccio 1872: 135–48, and tables at end.

[111] Trifone 1921: xx.

[112] Monti 1941: II.13–54; Ullmann 1949: 1–33.

[113] Andraeas de Isernia *et al.*, *Constitutiones regni utriusque Siciliae, Glossis ordinariis, Commentariisque excellentiss. I.U.D. Domini Andraeae de Isernia, ac D. Bartholomaei Capuani, atque nonullorum veterum*, ed. Gabriele Sarayna (Lyons, 1568), 32.

[114] *Ibid.*

[115] Capitula Regis Caroli II, in *ibid.*, 316; Trifone 1921: 99, no. 59 (101).

[116] Andraeas de Isernia *et al.*, *Constitutiones*, 47.

[117] Trifone 1921: cxcii, citing Bartolomeo da Capua on Frederick II's Constitutions of Melfi, book 3, cap. 46.

The years around 1300 saw, therefore, the coming together, at the court of Naples of the theme of the demonization of the Jew and the Saracen and the Roman law tradition that emphasized the subjection of *servi* and the rights of rulers over their property and persons. Roman law bolstered the authority of the state, but it also confirmed the lack of rights of non-Christian subjects, all the more so when they had for generations been called *servi camere regie*.[118]

REFERENCES

PRIMARY SOURCES

Andraeas de Isernia *et al. Constitutiones regni utriusque Siciliae, Glossis ordinariis, Commentariisque excellentiss. I.U.D. Domini Andraeae de Isernia, ac D. Bartholomaei Capuani, atque nonullorum veterum*. Ed. Gabriele Sarayna. Lyons, 1568.
Codice Diplomatico dei Saraceni di Lucera. Ed. P. Egidi. Naples: Pierro & Figlio, 1917.
Giordano da Rivalto. *Prediche*. 2 vols. Florence: Magheri, 1831.
Huillard-Bréholles, J. L. *Historia diplomatica Friderici Secundi*. 6 vols. in 12 parts. Paris: Henricus Pl., 1854–61. Reprinted 1872–83.
Jaume I. Crònica o Libre dels Feits. In Ferran Soldevila, ed., *Les Quatre Grans Cròniques*. Barcelona: Selecta, 1971.
Joseph ben Joshua ha-Cohen. *'Emeq ha-Bakha*. Ed. M. Letteris. Jerusalem, 1967.
Joseph Hacohen and the Anonymous Corrector. *The Vale of Tears (Emek Habacha)*. Trans. Harry S. May. The Hague, Nijhoff, 1971.
Meyers, E. M. *Iuris interpretes saeculi XIII curantibus scolaribus leidensibus*. Naples: F. Perralla, 1924.
Muntaner, Ramón. Crònica. In Ferran Soldevila, ed., *Les Quatre Grans Cròniques*. Barcelona: Selecta, 1971.
Matthew Paris. *Chronica Majorca*. 7 vols. Rolls Series, 1872–83.
Samuel Usque. *Consolaçam ás tribulaçoens de Israel*. Coimbra: Franca Amado, 1906–8.
Consolation for the Tribulations of Israel. Ed. and trans. Martin A. Cohen. Philadelphia: Jewish Publication Society of America, 1964.
Solomon ibn Verga. *Shevet Yehudah*. Ed. A. Shohat, Jerusalem: Mosad Bi'alik, 1946.

SECONDARY REFERENCES

Abulafia, David 1981 Southern Italy and the Florentine economy. *Economic History Review* ser. 2 33: 377–88. Repr. in David Abulafia, *Italy, Sicily and the Mediterranean, 1100–1400*. London: Variorum reprints, 1987: Essay VI.

[118] My understanding of these issues has been greatly enhanced by discussion with Anna Sapir Abulafia and with Norman Zacour, the latter of whom very kindly explored the resources of Trinity Hall Library, Cambridge, on my behalf, in pursuit of the almost non-existent civil law texts on Saracen slaves. Professor Zacour pointed out to me that Azo on Codex 1.11 states that when Justinian refers to pagans, Saracens are to be understood, *qui deos innumeros, deasque imo demones colunt et adorent*.

261   Lucera and its analogues

1988 *Frederick II. A Medieval Emperor.* London: Allen Lane.

1992 From Privilege to Persecution: Crown, Church and Synagogue in the City of Majorca, 1229–1343. In David Abulafia, Michael Franklin, and Miri Rubin, eds., *Church and City, 1000–1500. Studies in Honour of Christopher Brooke*, 111–26. Cambridge: Cambridge University Press.

1994 *A Mediterranean Emporium. The Catalan Kingdom of Majorca.* Cambridge: Cambridge University Press.

Bevere, R. 1935 Ancora sulla causa della distruzione della colonia saracena di Lucera. *Archivio storico per le provincie napoletane* 60 (n.s. 21): 222–8.

Bresc, Henri 1989–90 L'Esclavage dans le monde méditerranéen des XIVᵉ et XVᵉ siècles: problèmes politiques, réligieux et morales. In *XIIIᵒ Congrès d'història de la Corona d'"Aragó*, I: 89–102, 4 vols. Palma de Mallorca: Institut d'Estudis Balearics.

Buckland, W. W. 1908 *The Roman Law of Slavery.* Cambridge: Cambridge University Press.

Burns, Robert I. 1973 *Islam under the Crusaders. Colonial Survival in the Thirteenth-Century Kingdom of Valencia.* Princeton: Princeton University Press.

Caggese, Romolo 1922–30 *Robert d'Angiò e i sui tempi.* 2 vols. Florence: R. Bemporad & Figlio.

Cassuto, Moshe David 1942 Hurban ha-Heshivot be-Italyah ha-deromit ba-Me'ah ha-13. In Simhah Assaf and Gerschom Gerhard Scholem, eds., *Studies in Memory of Asher Gulak and Samuel Klein* (Hebrew), 139–52. Jerusalem: Hebrew University.

1950 Od ketubot ivrit me'ir Trani. *Alexander Marx Jubilee Volume*, Hebrew section: Jewish Theological Seminary of America.

Cassuto, Umberto 1912 Un ignoto capitolo di storia giudaica. *Judaica. Festschrift zu Hermann Cohens 70. Geburtstag*, 389–404. Berlin: Verlag von Bruno Cassirer.

1931/2 Iscrizioni ebraiche a Trani. *Rivista di studi orientali* 13: 172–80.

Castielli, R. 1978 Saggio storico culturale. In M. Melilli, ed., *Storia e cultura dei Francoprovenzali di Colle e Faeto*, 7–21. Manfredonia.

Chazan, Robert 1973 *Medieval Jewry in Northern France. A Political and Social History.* Baltimore: Johns Hopkins University Press.

1979 *Church, State and Jew in the Middle Ages.* New York: Behrman House.

1989 *Daggers of Faith. Thirteenth-Century Christian Missionizing and Jewish Response.* Berkeley/Los Angeles: University of California Press.

Cohen, Jeremy 1982 *The Friars and the Jews. The Evolution of Medieval Anti-Judaism.* Ithaca, N.Y.: Cornell University Press.

Delcorno, Carlo 1975 *Giordano da Pisa e l'antica predicazione volgare.* Florence: L. S. Olschki.

Egidi, Pietro 1911–14 La colonia saracena di Lucera e la sua distruzione. *Archivio storico per le provincie napoletane* 36 (1911): 597–694; 37 (1912): 71–89, 664–96; 38 (1913): 115–44, 681–707; 39 (1914), 132–71, 697–766.

1915 *La colonia saracena di Lucera e la sua distruzione.* Naples: Pierro & Figlio.

Ferorelli, N. 1915 *Gli ebrei dell'Italia meridionale dall'età romana al sec. XVIII.* Turin: Il Vessillo Israelitico; new edn., Naples, 1990.

Heers, Jacques 1981 *Esclaves et domestiques au moyen-âge dans le monde méditerranéen.* Paris: Fayard.

Housley, Norman 1982 *The Italian Crusades. The Papal–Angevin Alliance and the Crusades against Christian Lay Powers, 1254–1343.* Oxford: Oxford University Press.

Isaacs, A. Lionel 1936 *The Jews of Majorca.* London: Methuen.

Jordan, William Chester 1989 *The French Monarchy and the Jews. From Philip Augustus to the Last Capetians.* Philadelphia: University of Pennsylvania Press.

Kattenbusch, D. 1982 *Das Franko-Provenzalische in Süditalien. Studien zur synchronischen und diachronischen Dialektologie.* Tübinger Beiträge zur Linguistik 176. Tübingen: G. Narr.

Kedar, Benjamin Z. 1984 *Crusade and Mission. European Approaches toward the Muslims.* Princeton, N.J.: Princeton University Press.

Kriegel, Maurice 1977 Prémarranisme et inquisition dans la Provence des XIIIᵉ et XIVᵉ siècles. *Provence Historique,* fasc. 109: 313–23.

1978 Mobilisation politique et modernisation organique. Les expulsions de Juifs au bas Moyen Age. *Archives de sciences sociales des religions* 46: 5–20.

Le Goff, Jacques 1988 *Your Money or your Life. Economy and Religion in the Middle Ages.* New York.

Léonard, Emile 1967 *Gli Angioini di Napoli.* Milan: dall'Oglio.

Lourie, Elena 1970 Free Moslems in the Balearics under Christian Rule in the Thirteenth Century. *Speculum* 45: 624–49. Repr. in Lourie 1990: Essay VI.

1983 La colonización cristiana de Menorca durante el reinado de Alfonso III "el Liberal", rey de Aragón. *Analecta Sacra Tarraconensia* 53/4: 135–86.

1990a. *Crusade and Colonisation. Muslims, Christians and Jews in Medieval Aragon.* Aldershot: Variorum.

1990b Anatomy of Ambivalence: Muslims under the Crown of Aragon in the Late Thirteenth Century. In Lourie 1990a: Essay VII.

Maier, C. 1995 Crusade and Rhetoric against the Muslim Colony of Lucera: Eudes of Châteauroux's *Sermones de rebellione sarracenorum Lucerie in Apulia. Journal of Medieval History* 21.

Martin, Jean-Marie 1989 La Colonie sarrasine de Lucera et son environnement. Quelques réflexions. *Mediterraneo medievale. Scritti in onore di Francesco Giunta,* II: 797–810. Soveria Mannelli: Rubbettino.

Mata, Micaela 1984 *Conquests and Reconquests of Menorca.* Barcelona.

Minieri, Riccio C. 1872 *De' grandi uffiziali del Regno di Sicilia dal 1265 al 1285.* Naples.

Monti, Gennaro M. 1934. Da Carlo I a Roberto d'Angiò: ricerche e documenti. *Archivio storico per le province napoletane* 59.

1941 La dottrina anti-imperiale degli Angioini di Napoli. I loro vicariati imperiali e Bartolomeo da Capua. In *Studi di storia di diritto in onore di A. Solmi,* II: 13–54. 2 vols. Milan: Giuffre.

Moore, Kenneth 1976 *Those of the Street. The Catholic Jews of Mallorca.* Notre Dame, Indiana: University of Notre Dame Press.

Munkácsi, E. 1940 *Der Jude von Neapel.* Zurich: Verlag "De Liga."

Pons, Antonio 1957–60 *Los Judíos de Mallorca durante los siglos XIII y XIV.* 2 vols. Palma de Mallorca: Miguel Font.

Powell, James M. 1990. *Muslims under Latin rule, 1100–1300*. Ed. James M. Powell. Princeton, N.J.: Princeton University Press.

Musto, Ronald G. 1985 Queen Sancia of Naples (1286–1345) and the Spiritual Franciscans. In J. Kirshner and S. F. Wemple, eds., *Women of the Medieval World*, 179–214. Oxford: Blackwell.

Rosselló Vaquer, Ramón 1980 *Aportació a la història medieval de Menorca. El segle XIII*. Ciutadella de Menorca.

Roth, Cecil 5706 [= 1946] *The History of the Jews of Italy*. Philadelphia: The Jewish Publication Society of America.

Schein, Sylvia 1991 *Fideles Crucis. The Papacy, the West and the Recovery of the Holy Land 1274–1314*. Oxford: Oxford University Press.

Shatzmiller, Joseph 1990 *Shylock Reconsidered. Jews, Moneylending, and Medieval Society*. Berkeley and Los Angeles: University of California Press.

Starr, Joshua 1946 The Mass Conversion of Jews in Southern Italy (1290–93). *Speculum* 21: 203–11.

Suarez Fernández, Luis 1983 *Les Juifs espagnols au moyen âge*. Paris: Gallimard.

Trifone, R. 1921 *La legislazione angioina*. Naples: L. Lubrano.

Ullmann, Walter 1949 The Development of the Medieval Idea of Sovereignty. *English Historical Review* 64: 1–33.

Vitale, Vito 1926 Un particolare ignorato di storia pugliese: neofiti e mercanti. *Studi in onore di Michelangelo Schipa*, 233–46. Naples.

Zacour, Norman 1990 *Jews and Saracens in the Consilia of Oldradus de Ponte*. Toronto: Pontifical Institute of Mediaeval Studies.

XIV

Le attività economiche degli ebrei siciliani attorno al 1300

La documentazione notarile siciliana comincia a divenire consistente a partire dal tardo Duecento; i primi cartolari notarili, opera di Adamo de Citella, notaio di Palermo, datano dal 1286 al 1287 e dal 1298 al 1299. Poco dopo, Giovanni Maiorana, notaio di Erice (Monte San Giuliano) compilò il suo preziosissimo registro di atti, fra i quali molti trattano della comunità ebrea della cittadina. Grazie alla nuova magnifica edizione curata da Aldo Sparti[1], il registro di Giovanni Maiorana occupa un posto preminente fra le fonti siciliane del periodo subito dopo il Vespro. Già soggetto di un mio studio, pubblicato nelle riviste «Zion» (in ebraico) e nell'«Archivio storico per la Sicilia orientale» (in italiano), non tenterò di ripetere tutti gli argomenti che risalgono dallo studio di questa fonte ericina: il buon rapporto fra ebrei e cristiani, già notato dal primo redattore, Antonino De Stefano; la mancanza nella città di un quartiere specificamente ebreo; il sistema di tassazione degli ebrei attraverso

---

Legenda per le abbreviazioni usate nel testo.

Il numero del documento segue l'indicazione dell'edizione, p.es. B:464 = Burgarella, doc. n. 464.

B = P. BURGARELLA, *Le imbreviature del notaio Adamo de Citella a Palermo (1° registro, 1286-1287)*, Fonti e Studi del Corpus membranarum italicarum, serie 3, 1, Roma 1983. Vedi con la stessa numerazione dei documenti: P. BURGARELLA, *Il protocollo del notaio Adamo de Citella dell'anno 1286-7*, in «Archivio storico per la Sicilia orientale», 75 (1979), 435-553.

G = P. GULOTTA, *Le imbreviature del notaio Adamo de Citella a Palermo (2° registro, 1298-1299)*, Fonti e Studi del Corpus membranarum italicarum, serie 3, 3, Roma 1982.

Z = R. ZENO, *Documenti per la storia del diritto marittimo nei secoli XIII e XIV*, Torino 1936.

[1] *Il registro del notaio ericino Giovanni Maiorana*, a cura di A. SPARTI, Palermo 1982.

una propria università autonoma². Fra gli ebrei di Erice, forse 400 in numero, vediamo macellai, fisici, fabbri, viticoltori, ma quasi mai l'immagine classica dell'usuraio, perché, come in tanti altri luoghi del Mediterraneo, il rifornimento del credito non fu solo nella mano di questo gruppo.

Vale la pena di chiedere se le altre fonti notarili siciliane della stessa epoca rivelino lo stesso rango di occupazioni, lo stesso netto rapporto fra ebrei
e cristiani. La documentazione palermitana già riferita ci offre venti documenti caratterizzati dalla loro inconsistenza: vendite di schiavi, certo, ma anche di case; cooperazione fra ebrei e cristiani nell'opera della seta; il possesso
da parte dei cristiani di proprietà nel quartiere ebreo di Palermo; rimane, così, un'immagine non molto lontana da quella fornita dagli atti ericini, una conferma che attorno al 1300 gli ebrei siciliani rimanevano integrati nell'economia siciliana, anche se siamo a questo momento sull'orlo dell'imposizione di
una serie di leggi che cominciarono a costringere i rapporti sociali ed economici fra ebrei e cristiani [su questo vedi *Cod. dipl. Giudei* 1.1:34]. Rimango-
no, purtroppo, importanti lacune nelle fonti, per esempio la mancanza di informazione sulla comunità maghrebina stabilita a Palermo sotto Federico II
con lo scopo di sviluppare la produzione dell'indaco dell'ennè e di altre derrate specializzate conosciute dalla Sicilia islamica.

Il primo fenomeno rilevante nei documenti palermitani è il mancato ruolo
degli ebrei nel commercio oltre la Sicilia. Fino ad un certo punto, deve essere
un *argumentum ex silentio*; ma l'imponente gruppo di documenti lasciati da
Adamo de Citella sulle attività di commercianti toscani, genovesi, catalani in
Sicilia parla quasi mai di investimenti dagli ebrei. Eccezionale, ma di massimo interesse, è un documento del 16 gennaio 1287, nel quale vediamo un
ebreo e un cristiano, ambedue di Messina, che organizzano un viaggio da Palermo a Genova. Trattiamo di un documento in tutti i suoi termini paragonabile ad altri *mutui*: Markisius speciarius de Messana riceve da Syminto *iudeo*
quaranta libbre di moneta genovese da restituire entro otto giorni dalla data
dell'arrivo della nave di Matteo de Thermis chiamata *Sanctus Iohannes* 'aput
Ianuam seu in quocumque loco ipsa navis divertet presenti viagio non muta-
to' [Z:1, p. 1; B: 69, p. 56]. Di don Matteo di Termini sappiamo qualcosa;
fu evidentemente una figura di qualche importanza nella navigazione siciliana, perché appare nella documentazione con una seconda nave diretta a
Genova, la "Bona Parti", sulla quale un mercante di Poggibonsi in Toscana, ora

---

² *Yehudei Erice (Monte San Giuliano) shebeSitsiliah, 1298-1304*, in «Zion. A quarterly for
research in Jewish history», 51 (1986), pp. 295-317; *Una comunità ebraica della Sicilia occidentale: Erice 1298-1304*, in «Archivio storico per la Sicilia orientale», 80 (1984), pp. 7-39.

residente a Palermo, e un mercante di Messina hanno l'intenzione di caricare un gran numero di pelli di coniglio [B:113, p. 81; B:285, p. 173]. Un fatto che colpisce è che, quando possediamo una testimonianza dell'investimento di un ebreo nel commercio marittimo con l'Italia settentrionale, l'ebreo non è un palermitano ma un messinese, abitante di una città conosciuta per le sue attività commerciali in ogni canto del Mediterraneo[3].

È possibile che lo stesso Syminto riappaia nella documentazione. Un atto del 27 agosto 1287 consiste in un conto finale di una società costituita un po' meno di due anni prima per l'esercizio della seta; i soci furono Leone de Iannacio, cristiano, cittadino di Palermo, e un certo Symanto *iudeus*; è *iudeus* 'de' qualche luogo, ma a questo punto il manoscritto non si legge. Leone de Iannacio si trova menzionato in moltissimi documenti del cartolario, e fu uomo di affari con un interesse nel trasporto delle uve e nella manifattura delle botti (possibilmente per il vino) [per uve: B:10, pp. 23-24; 21, p. 30, 38; pp. 39-40, 63; p. 53, 67; p. 55, 126; pp. 87-88, 127; p. 88, 134, pp. 91-92, 162; p. 106, 171; p. 111, 199; p. 126, 212; p. 133, 221; p. 137, 230; p. 142; per botti: B:58, p. 51]. Nella funzione di testimone, Leone compare anche nel testo del documento di Syminto e Markisius da Messina, e nel testo del documento che parla del carico di pelli di coniglio da essere trasportate sulla nave di don Matteo di Termini [B:69, p. 56; B:113, p. 81], fatti che suggeriscono l'esistenza di un legame professionale con Syminto/Symanto. Testimonia a un contratto per l'esercizio dell'arte della seta fra un Palermitano cristiano e un Senese [B:66, p. 54]; s'impegna in una società per l'acquisto e la vendita di merce nella bottega di Runcio de Pulcari. Dalla documentazione traspare che questo associato dell'ebreo fu uomo ricco, attivo nel commercio e nell'organizzazione della raccolta delle uve, con interessi in altri settori come il commercio dell'orzo e degli schiavi [B:189-191, pp. 121-122; cfr. per altri affari, 215, p. 134; 228, p. 141; 236, p. 145-146; 249, p. 153; 301, p. 183; 308, p. 187; 309, p. 188; 322, p. 195; 334, p. 202].

La partecipazione degli ebrei nel commercio degli schiavi fa parte di un commercio più esteso, che coinvolgeva gli ebrei catalani e maiorchini, un commercio testimoniato nella Sicilia oltre Palermo, nel cartolario ericino di Giovanni Maiorana. Il 3 aprile 1287 a Palermo, Busayc, cioè Abu Ishaq, Nachui, descritto come ebreo e cittadino di Palermo, vendé una schiava negra saracena, di nome Miriem, per 5 onze 22 tarì e mezzo, prezzo medio per le schiave

---

[3] Per il commercio di Messina a quest'epoca, vedi D. ABULAFIA, *The merchants of Messina: Levant trade and domestic economy*, in «Papers of the British School at Rome», LIV (1986), pp. 196-212.

sul mercato siciliano a quest'epoca. Miriem fu comprata da un altro palermitano, il cristiano Costantino Speciali [B:229, p. 142]. Si trovano anche vendite di schiavi da cristiani a ebrei: Cesario de Natali, cittadino di Palermo, vendè una schiava saracena bianca, Gaylam, per il prezzo di cinque onze il 27 aprile 1287, a Bulchyar Binamera Gerbi, ebreo [B:271, p. 166]. La documentazione ericina dimostra la presenza fra i schiavi saraceni di Berberi provenienti da Monte Barca in Cirenaica, fonte importante degli schiavi attorno al 1300. Questo commercio di schiavi coinvolgeva i Catalani, già così una notevole presenza nel Maghreb, e, anche prima del Vespro, di una crescente importanza nella Sicilia. La vendita da Domenico Lugrillo, mercante barcellonese, di una schiava negra chiamata Asona, al prezzo di quattro onze 22 tarì e mezzo, a Bonafos ebreo testimonia l'internazionalità di questo commercio; anche Bonafos fu mercante di Barcellona. [B:267, p. 164]. Vediamo qui un segno del ruolo centrale dei porti come Palermo e anche Maiorca come basi per il commercio degli schiavi africani nel Mediterraneo. Vediamo anche nella documentazione l'espressione di un problema importante: il possesso di schiavi o servitori cristiani viene vietato dalla legislazione di Federico III di Sicilia, dal 1310 in poi; per gli ebrei, gli schiavi musulmani possedevano una utilità speciale per il lavoro domestico. Così Chackim b. Shimaria, ebreo di Messina, venne a Palermo nell'agosto del 1287 per comprare da Ferrer, mercante catalano, una schiava bianca chiamata Shemsi, al prezzo di quattro onze [B:400, p. 239].

Da un altro punto di vista, è notevole quanto pochi siano i riferimenti al commercio degli schiavi in mano degli ebrei nei cartolari di Adamo de Citella. Il primo cartolario rivela quattro vendite di schiavi nelle quali furono coinvolti ebrei; il secondo cartolario è privo di qualunque riferimento al commercio ebreo degli schiavi, che rimase, certo, appannaggio di altri mercanti, cristiani e musulmani.

Il registro del 1298-1299, più denso nella sua documentazione, mette in luce altri aspetti della vita economica degli ebrei palermitani meno conosciuti dal primo registro. La vendita di case in quartieri ebrei è rappresentata nel primo registro da solo due documenti: nell'uno, si tratta infatti di una casa a Termini, non a Palermo, venduta da Charufa vedova di Sibbet de Barashun de Castronovo e i suoi figli, Symcha e Salamone, a Samuele di Barashun di Termini, della stessa famiglia, per il prezzo di sei onze. La casa era vicina a quella di Amran Farrah di Termini; fra i testimoni troviamo un certo Chaluf Cattanus (ha-Kattan) de Thermis. Tutto ciò conferma l'esistenza di un gruppo terminerese di ebrei con stretti rapporti palermitani [B:354, pp. 213-214]. Nell'altro documento, una casa è trasferita in dote dalla sposa cristiana

Toscana, figlia del fu Orlando Toscano, al suo marito Bandino de Avico, pisano di Palermo; la casa in questione si trova nel Cassaro, nel mezzo in effetti del quartiere degli ebrei, 'iuxta domum Iacob iudei ex una parte et domum Chayoni iudei ex altera' [B:104, p. 76]. Mentre non è certo che questi toscani intendessero effettivamente abitare nella loro casa, il documento attesta la presenza in Palermo di quei grandi gruppi di toscani, orgogliosi delle loro origini (fino al punto di chiamare la figlia 'Toscana') che già dominavano il commercio della città attorno al 1300, e con i quali, in quest'epoca di 'dopo-Geniza', gli ebrei di Palermo non potevano concorrere.

Dal secondo registro risulta abbastanza chiaramente che, come a Erice, ebrei e cristiani abitavano nelle stesse strade. Nel Cassaro si trovò la casa di Haaron o Aharan l'ebreo e della moglie (o di Haaron o di un altro) Ioye, ma dall'altra parte si trovò l'eredità del fu Giovanni Inglisii, forse di origini inglesi [G:133, pp. 102-103, del 29 nov. 1298]. Il fondaco di un artigiano non-ebreo fu situato nel mezzo della 'contrata Iudayce' entro le proprietà della cattedrale di Monreale e del convento di S. Maria della Martorana, che stava molto vicino [G:248; p. 196; cfr. 356, pp. 276-277].

Nel Cassaro cristiani vendevano le loro case agli ebrei, come nel caso di Simone Nicolay di Lucca, altro toscano, ma cittadino di Palermo, che vendé una casa nella strada chiamata *Zucac Essabun* all'ebreo Mushi Maylim. La casa fu situata fra quelli di Sibet Levi, ebreo, e le due case di Giorgio Ricio. È verosimile che questi cristiani abitavano in altri quartieri della città, e che furono solo i proprietari delle case vendute. Ma non può essere esclusa la possibilità di una vera e propria convivenza fisica nel Cassaro. L'insediamento ebreo in questo quartiere al centro della città fu, pure, in pericolo di trasferimento ad un luogo fuori dal centro della città. Le lettere pubblicate negli *Acta Curie Felicis Curie Urbis Panormi* parlano nel 1311-1312 di un quartiere vuoto, del 'recessum Iudeorum de Cassaro'; in conseguenza, 'dictum quarterium cassarj videatur exhabitatum' [*Acta Curie*, 1, p. 94]. I tentativi di riunire tutti gli ebrei di Palermo in un sobborgo riservato, analogo all'istituzione catalana della *Call*, fanno parte di una politica anti-giudaica seguita alla corte di Federico III, sotto la forte influenza del movimento radicale dei francescani spirituali[4].

A Palermo, come ad Erice, vediamo un alto livello di interesse fra gli ebrei

---

[4] Per un esempio contemporaneo di *Call* (termine derivato dalla parola ebraica Qahal, non dalla parola spagnuola Calle), vedi D. ABULAFIA, *From Privilege to Persecution: Crown, Church and Synagogue in the City of Majorca, 1229/1276-1343*, in *Church and City 1000-1500. Studies presented to Christopher Brooke*, Cambridge 1992, pp. 111-126.

nel vino e nelle uve, risultato, forse, dell'obbligo rituale di fornire vino *kasher* alla comunità ebrea. Ma risulta della documentazione che gli ebrei s'interessavano non solo delle uve raccolte da e per ebrei; Buschac Shimilel di Palermo comprò due centenari di uve bianche da Giovanna vedova di Gentile Archerio [G:111, pp. 85-86, del 13 nov. 1298]. Leone *bankerius*, ebreo, si costituì fidejussore per una quantità di uve bianche vendute da un cittadino palermitano ad un altro [G:131, pp. 101-102, del 28 nov. 1298]. Più tardi Muchi figlio di Iacob Dachac di Palermo garantì due centenari di uve bianche e nere [G:390, pp. 301-302]. Il commercio del vino oltrepassò i bisogni della religione; si vede sviluppare un commercio al dettaglio di vini e di uve nelle comunità di ebrei della Sicilia. Altro commercio al dettaglio fu forse quello dei tessuti, seconda una possibile interpretazione di un contratto di vendita del 1286 [B:40, p. 40].

Mentre manca ogni riferimento alle attività usurarie fra gli ebrei di Palermo, non manca una documentazione sui mutui da cristiani a ebrei. (Possiamo escludere dall'analisi il documento già riferito sull'investimento di un ebreo nel commercio con Genova, che non differisce in nulla da altri investimenti fra cristiani). Nel febbraio 1298, Antonio Sacerdoti, cioè ha-Cohen, ebreo di Napoli, residente a Palermo, riceve da Guglielmo de Pistillono, forse un toscano, da Pistoia, otto tarì, soggetti al pagamento di un livello d'interesse descritto con la frase *'ad ebdomadas cinque pro rata'*. Per confermare il contratto, l'ebreo 'tacta lacinia vestimenti ad legem mosaycam iuravit', espressione che si trova in altro luogo nello stesso cartolario [G:229, pp. 179-180, cfr. G:316, pp. 247-248]. Credo che trattiamo qui della frangia o *tsitsit* del vestimento dell'ebreo, con la quale in mano egli procede al giuramento.

In effetti, l'altro documento che fa menzione delle *lacinia* è di un interesse particolare. Alla fine di marzo 1299, Maymum Diba e Bracha Firchel, macellai ebrei di Palermo, concordarono che tutte le pelli con la lana di tutti gli arieti di tre o quattro anni che sarebbero state scorticate nel macello della *Iudayca*, sarebbero vendute a Leone de Vivo, conciatore cristiano della città, al prezzo di un tarì e un grana ciascuna, e con un pagamento anticipato di sei onze, cioè il prezzo di un po' più di 163 pelli. Il contratto avrebbe avuto termine alla fine di giugno, e inizio alla 'Pasca Resurrectionis': strana espressione da ricercare in un documento che parla della macelleria *kasher* di Palermo; una spegazione possibile è la necessità di fare distinzione fra la data della Pasqua o *Pesah* degli ebrei e la Pasqua cristiana [G:316, pp. 247-248; cfr. per la macelleria *Acta Curie* 1, p. 324].

Meno ricche, certo, della documentazione ericina, le fonti palermitane possiedono importanti punti in comune col registro di Giovanni Maiorana. La

comunità che si osserva è un gruppo di artigiani, integrati nella società e nel-
l'economia di Palermo e di Termini a quest'epoca, concentrata, certo, nel Cassaro, ma abitatori di un quartiere già in parte nelle mani di non-ebrei. Pochi
sono gli esperti del gran commercio internazionale, e l'epoca della geniza in
questo senso è da lungo tempo finita. Dobbiamo ricordare, inoltre, che la comunità cristiana a Palermo — come si vede bene nei cartolari di Adamo de
Citella — fu dominata da immigrati toscani, genovesi, catalani, ed altri latini; gli ebrei siciliani, stabiliti da lunghi secoli sul suolo siciliano, costituivano
un elemento ancora più antico nella popolazione dell'isola. Fino ad un certo
punto, possiamo dire che la distinzione fondamentale fra ebrei e cristiani non
fu una distinzione di funzione economica, come per esempio nella Francia
settentrionale, ma in gran parte una distinzione di culto, e, certo, di lingua
(l'arabo).

XV

Die Verfolgung der Juden in Süditalien und Sizilien (1290–1541)[*]

Das Problem der Behandlung der Juden in Süditalien und Sizilien ist voller Paradoxien. Einerseits gab es die Gesetze Friedrichs II. gegen übermäßigen Wucher seitens der Juden des *Regno*; andererseits spricht nur wenig dafür, daß sich die Juden Süditaliens und Siziliens vor 1400 auf die Geldleihe spezialisiert haben: Thomas von Aquin hat diesbezüglich die Situation in Italien mit der in Brabant kontrastiert. Einerseits erlebte das angevinische Königreich Neapel eine der wohl heftigsten Judenverfolgungen im spätmittelalterlichen Mittelmeergebiet; andererseits erholten sich die jüdischen Gemeinden von dem Schock der Vertreibung und Zwangstaufe und erhielten in der Folge königliche Vergünstigungen. Einerseits schützte König Ferrante von Neapel seine jüdischen Untertanen im späten 15. Jahrhundert und hieß sogar Flüchtlinge aus Spanien willkommen; andererseits weitete Ferdinand der Katholische die spanische Vertreibung in den Jahren 1492/93 auch auf die Insel Sizilien aus, von wo viele Juden übers Meer in die Sicherheit von Ferrantes Neapel flohen. Einerseits plante Ferdinand die Vertreibung auch der süditalienischen Juden, nachdem er im Jahre 1503 das Königreich Neapel erlangt hatte; andererseits erlaubte er einer Anzahl relativ wohlhabender Juden zu bleiben und vertrieb zusammen mit den ärmeren Juden die *Converso*-Bevölkerung, die er aus Spanien selbst niemals zu vertreiben gesucht hatte. All dies soll uns daran erinnern, daß es keinen Zweck hätte, nach einer konsistenten Judenpolitik spätmittelalterlicher Herrscher zu suchen oder eine solche zu erwarten, da letztere die Juden manchmal als eine Gruppe religiöser Dissidenten und dann wieder als materielle Aktivposten betrachteten. Es war die Spannung zwischen diesen beiden Einstellungen, welche die Geschichte der Juden im spätmittelalterlichen Mittelmeerraum wesentlich mitgestaltet hat.

I.

Süditalien präsentiert sich während des gesamten Mittelalters als ein Land voller ethnischer und religiöser Vielfalt: Griechen, Armenier, Slawen, Muslime in Lucera, franco-provenzalische Siedler, später dann Albaner und eine neuerliche Welle von Griechen[1]. In dieser fluktuierenden Bevölkerung zählten die Juden durchaus zu den

---

[*] Ins Deutsche übertragen von Gerd MENTGEN.
[1] GIURA, Vincenzo: Storie de minoranze Ebrei, Greci, Albanesi nel regno di Napoli, Napoli 1984;

beständigeren Elementen – waren sie doch schon seit den Zeiten der Römer in Süditalien präsent. Sie bildeten also einen integralen Bestandteil eines Mosaiks von Völkerschaften und Religionen. Dieses Faktum trug zum Schutz der Juden bei. Sie waren hier, anders als im nördlichen Europa, keine Außenseiter, die an den Rand der Gesellschaft gedrängt und gezwungen wurden, unpopuläre Tätigkeiten wie die des Geldleihers auszuüben, noch handelte es sich bei ihnen um Immigranten wie im Falle so vieler jüdischer Gemeinden des späten Mittelalters in Norditalien. Trotzdem wäre es falsch, ihre Lebensumstände als Idylle zu beschreiben. Daß die Juden eine so große Rolle im Tuchfärbehandwerk spielten, mag von der für Byzanz typischen Praxis herrühren, körperlich unangenehme Arbeiten wie Gerberei und Färberei von den Juden erledigen zu lassen. Außerdem wurden diejenigen, die im Lande Herrschaft ausübten, durch den Profit, den die Monarchie aus den Juden ziehen konnte, ermutigt, die Juden ihrem direkten Schutz zu unterstellen. Die Vorgänge im 15. Jahrhundert zeigen, daß antijüdische Ressentiments einen gefährlichen Grad erreichen konnten, wenn Juden offenbar von einer allgemeinen Steuer befreit waren – sogar wenn sie im Gegensatz zu den Christen zu anderen Steuerleistungen verpflichtet wurden. Obschon die angevinischen Monarchen gelegentlich ein Beispiel für Judenverfolgungen gaben, deuten Zeugnisse aus dem 15. Jahrhundert darauf hin, daß antijüdische Ausschreitungen im allgemeinen durch im Volk verbreitete Feindschaft gegenüber den Protegés des Königs verursacht wurden. Es kann sehr wohl sein, daß solche Übergriffe viel damit zu tun hatten, daß die Juden dem König in gewissem Sinne gehörten. Wie in den Jahren 1494/95, die für das Königreich Neapel eine Zeit politischer Turbulenzen waren, konnten solche Angriffe indirekt auf die Monarchie selbst zielen.

Die Zeit der Hohenstaufen und Anjou war in der Geschichte der Judengemeinden Süditaliens und Siziliens von entscheidender Bedeutung. Sie war gekennzeichnet durch die Rezeption neuer, härterer Haltungen gegenüber Juden und Judentum aus dem nördlichen Europa[2]. Das Zeitalter relativer Toleranz (wenn nicht selbst dieser Begriff zu optimistisch sein sollte) endet im 13. Jahrhundert, und es beginnt eine neue Periode von Zwangskonversionen und -migrationen, in die Monarchie und Kirche sehr stark verwickelt waren. Obzwar das 14. und das 15. Jahrhundert teilweise eine Rückkehr zu günstigeren Bedingungen brachten, muß der gefährliche Charakter der Zeit von Friedrich II. bis zu Robert von Anjou († 1343) betont werden.

ROGNONI, Andrea, ARCIONI, Marco F.: Altre Italie. Tradizioni e costumi delle minoranze etniche italiane, Milano 1991.

[2] Für eine ausführlichere Diskussion s. ABULAFIA, David: Ethnic variety and its implications: Frederick II's relations with Jews and Muslims, in: Intellectual life at the court of Frederick II Hohenstaufen, hg. von William TRONZO, Washington D.C. 1994 (Studies in the History of Art; 44 / Symposium papers, Center for Advanced Study in the Visual Arts 24), S. 213–221; ABULAFIA, David: L'epoca svevo-angioina, in: L'Ebraismo dell'Italia meridionale peninsulare dalle origini al 1541, hg. v. Cosimo D. FONSECA, Michele LUZZATI, Giuliano TAMANI, Cesare COLAFEMMINA, Potenza 1996, S. 65–78; COHN, Willy: Juden und Staufer in Unteritalien und Sizilien. Eine Sammlung verstreut erschienener Schriften aus den Jahren 1919–1936, Aalen 1978.

In seinem Gesetzeswerk von 1231, dem ein grundsätzlicher Charakter beizumessen ist, warnt Friedrich davor, Juden und Muslime zu verfolgen, die dasselbe Recht haben müßten, gerichtliche Schritte einzuleiten, wie jeder andere und die momentan zu heftig verfolgt würden. Beide Gruppen, Juden und Muslime, wurden als *servi camere regie* angesehen – ein Begriff, mit dem sich zunehmend pejorative Konnotationen verbanden im Sinne einer Herabwürdigung des Juden zum bloßen Besitztum des Herrschers[3]. Solche Vorteile für die Krone wurden durch die Praxis, *giudecche* Bischöfen zu übertragen, begrenzt, wenn auch die Juden von den Bischöfen wie von der Krone Schutz ihrer Person und ihres Besitzes erwarten durften. Friedrichs Erlasse hinsichtlich des jüdischen Wuchers spiegeln die einschlägigen päpstlichen Bestimmungen wider und können nicht als zutreffende Beschreibung der zeitgenössischen wirtschaftlichen Aktivitäten der sizilischen Juden angesehen werden.

Während Friedrich in seinen deutschen Landen den Talmud in positiver Weise zur Widerlegung der Blutbeschuldigung von Fulda zitiert hatte, bedeutete die Ankunft der angevinischen Dynastie im Jahre 1266 das Anbrechen einer neuen antitalmudisch bestimmten Einstellung zum Judentum, die sich insbesondere in den Kreisen König Ludwigs IX. von Frankreich herausgebildet hatte[4]. Unter der Herrschaft Karls I. organisierte der Täufling Manuforte antijüdische Predigten und inquisitorische Aktivitäten gegen die weniger standhaften Konvertiten bzw. *neofiti*; im Jahre 1288 wurde ein Versuch unternommen, die Konvertiten unter der übrigen christlichen Bevölkerung zu verteilen, um ihre Bande zum Christentum zu stärken[5].

Sporadische Angriffe dieser Art verwandelten sich in eine regelrechte Kampagne gegen die Juden, als Karl II. 1289/90 aus seinem aragonesischen Gefängnis zurückkehrte. Er hatte den Weg über Anjou genommen und von dort die Juden unter der Beschuldigung des Wuchers und angeblicher sexueller Exzesse vertrieben. Soweit ersichtlich, scheint in der Bevölkerung jedoch kaum Judenfeindschaft verbreitet gewesen zu sein. Die Initiative ging von der Krone aus, und das Verlangen nach moralischer Reform brachte Kampagnen gegen die Juden und andere hervor – namentlich die Sarazenen von Lucera oder die Lombarden und Kawertschen mit Leihbanken im Anjou. Und doch: War es das Bild vom Juden als einem im übertragenen Sinne blutsaugenden Wucherer, das die Vertreibung aus dem Anjou dominierte, so war es das Bild des buchstäblich blutsaugenden jüdischen Mörders, das anscheinend die Verfolgungen beherrscht hat, die sich nun nach der Rückkehr des Königs nach Süditalien ereigneten.

---

[3] Zum Problem der „Kammerknechtschaft" vgl. ABULAFIA: Ethnic variety (A. 2), S. 219.
[4] STARR, Joshua: The mass conversion of Jews in southern Italy (1290–93), in: Speculum 21 (1946), S. 203; ABULAFIA, David: Monarchs and minorities in the late medieval western Mediterranean: Lucera and its analogues, in: WAUGH, Scott L., DIEHL, Peter D. (Hg.): Christendom and its discontents. Exclusion, persecution and rebellion, 1000–1500, Cambridge 1996, S. 234–263, mit einem Vergleich der Behandlung der Juden und der in Süditalien verbliebenen Muslime.
[5] STARR: Mass conversion (A. 4), S. 203; CAGGESE, Romolo: Roberto d'Angiò e i suoi tempi, Bd. 1, Firenze 1922, S. 299.

Von den auf circa 1290 zu datierenden Ereignissen wissen wir aus einer mehrere Jahre später von Giordano da Rivalto in Florenz gehaltenen Predigt: Giordano behauptete, daß einer der Minister des Königs, wahrscheinlich der herausragende Jurist Bartolomeo da Capua, herausgefunden habe, daß die Juden Menschen opferten, und erklärt habe, es sei daher legitim, die Juden zu töten oder zu vertreiben[6]. Vor die Wahl zwischen Konversion und Vernichtung gestellt, entschlossen sich – so wird uns berichtet – 8.000 Juden zur Annahme der Taufe, während die anderen flohen, so daß nun keine Juden mehr im *Regno di Puglia* gewesen seien. In der Tat ließ sich Giordano kaum eine Möglichkeit entgehen, die Juden zu verleumden. Er bestand darauf, in jüdischen Büchern gelesen zu haben und zu wissen, wie in den jüdischen Gebeten dreimal pro Tag Flüche gegen Jesus und Maria ausgestoßen würden. Genauso wie sie christliche Kinder beschnitten, wählten sie eines aus, um es zum Spott zu kreuzigen; er wäre glücklich, die Juden alle niedergemetzelt zu sehen[7]. Andere Zeugnisse legen durchaus nahe, daß es in jener Zeit zu zahlreichen Konversionen in Süditalien gekommen ist[8]. Gemeinden von Konvertiten – *neofiti* – entstanden, die mitunter wie regelrechte *universitates* mit Gerichtsfunktionen ausgestattet waren und parallel zu den *universitates* der Altchristen existierten, von denen die süditalienischen Städte regiert wurden; einige müssen die Erben der alten *giudecche* gewesen sein, die offenkundig auch dann als eigene rechtliche Körperschaften weiterexistieren durften, wenn ihre Mitglieder sich hatten taufen lassen. Das Zentrum der Konversionen bildete anscheinend die Stadt Trani. Mindestens eine der dort erhaltenen Kirchen war bis zum späten 13. Jahrhundert nachweislich eine Synagoge, und Dokumente aus dem Jahr 1294 belegen die Exemtion von 310 Familienoberhäuptern von den königlichen Steuern in Trani, während die Zahlen für das übrige Süditalien niedriger liegen[9]. Das waren Jahre – so sollte später Samuel Usque sagen –, in denen die italienischen Juden „Unglück erlitten, das schlimmer war als der gewaltsame Tod."

---

[6] Giordano da Rivalto: Prediche, Florence 1831, Bd. 2, S. 231; DELCORNO, Carlo: Giordano da Pisa e l'antica predicazione volgare, Florence 1975, Nr. 62, S. 283f. (Teiltranskription).

[7] Giordano da Rivalto (A. 6), Bd. 2, S. 220–232; COHEN, Jeremy: The Friars and the Jews. The Evolution of Medieval Anti-Judaism, Ithaca, New York 1982, S. 238–241, der Bartolomeo dell'Aquila eher als die zentrale Figur ansieht als Bartolomeo da Capua.

[8] CASSUTO, Umberto: Un ignoto capitolo di storia giudaica, in: Judaica. Festschrift zu Hermann Cohens 70. Geburtstage, Berlin 1912, S. 389–404; DERS.: Iscrizioni ebraiche a Trani, in: Rivista degli studi orientali 13 (1931/32), S. 172–180; CASSUTO, Moshe David (der hebräische Name des Autors!): Od ketubot ivrit me'ir Trani, in: Alexander Marx Jubilee Volume, New York 1950; DERS.: Hurban ha-Jeshivot be-Italyah ha-deromit ba-Me'ah ha-13, in: Studies in memory of Asher Gulak and Samuel Klein, Jerusalem 1942, S. 139–152. Siehe auch FERORELLI, Nicola: Gli ebrei nell'Italia meridionale dall'età romana al secolo XVIII, hg. von F. PATRONI GRIFFI, Neapel 1990, S. 66–72 (diese Edition ist allen anderen Drucken des Buches vorzuziehen); ROTH, Cecil: The History of the Jews of Italy, Philadelphia 1946, S. 100f.; MUNKÁCSI, Ernst: Der Jude von Neapel. Die historischen und kunstgeschichtlichen Denkmäler des süditalienischen Judentums, Zürich 1939; STARR: Mass conversion (A. 4), S. 203–211.

[9] ROTH: History (A. 8), S. 101; vgl. FERORELLI: Gli ebrei dell'Italia (A. 8), S. 72, zu anderen Zahlungen in dieser Zeit.

Tatsächlich liegen aus Trani selbst Beweise vor, daß nicht alle Juden, die die Taufe verweigerten, umgebracht wurden. Ein Grabstein von 1293 spricht dafür, daß damals weiterhin jüdische Begräbnisse stattfanden[10]; in Neapel zahlten Juden 1294/95 weiter ihre Steuern als Juden, und bezeichnenderweise wurden Verordnungen ausgegeben, die geflüchteten Juden die Rückkehr ins Königreich erlaubten[11]. So konnten sich die jüdischen Gemeinschaften schrittweise erholen: Robert der Weise ermutigte sogar jüdische Kaufleute aus Mallorca im Jahre 1329, in sein Königreich zu kommen und sich dort niederzulassen[12]. Es scheint daher, daß die Juden nur in dem kurzen Zeitraum von 1290–1292 ihre Lage so unerträglich fanden, daß sehr viele flohen oder konvertierten.

Die dieser Politik zugrunde liegende Motivation muß in dem Versuch der angevinischen Könige gesucht werden, ein Image ihrer selbst als christliche Monarchen zu artikulieren, die christliche Untertanen regieren; somit war auch für die muslimische Kolonie von Lucera kein Raum mehr, die im Jahre 1300 brutal aufgelöst wurde. Die Bewohner verkaufte man als Sklaven[13]. Die christliche Identität des Königreichs bot nach dem Chaos des zwanzigjährigen Kriegs im Gefolge der Sizilischen Vesper eine Plattform für eine Politik der Zentralisierung und Durchsetzung der königlichen Autorität. Wie Clifford Backman kürzlich gezeigt hat, kann im aragonesischen Sizilien ein ähnlicher Trend unter dem Reformer Friedrich III. festgestellt werden, der sich ebensosehr durch die kirchliche Gesetzgebung wie durch spanische Beispiele dazu anregen ließ, die Aussiedlung der Juden aus der Cassaro-Gegend von Palermo und ihre Konzentration in einer neuen *giudecca* zu verfügen; ferner wurde es den Juden verboten, mit Christen zu speisen und zu trinken oder christliche Sklaven bzw. Diener zu besitzen[14]. Diese Art physischer Separation muß als eine Form „interner Vertreibung" gesehen werden; weitere zeitgenössische Beispiele, die König Friedrichs Gesetze inspiriert haben mögen, wurden aus anderen Ländern der Krone von Aragon geliefert, besonders aus dem Königreich Mallorca, wo Alfons von Aragon die Bildung eines jüdischen *Call* im Jahre 1286 initiiert hatte, und zwar innerhalb eines rechtlichen Rahmens, der wesentlich restriktiver war als im Falle des *Calls* von Barcelona. Eine Judenpolitik dieser Art machte kurz vor den Vertreibungen der Juden halt, die im nördlichen Europa so ungezügelt praktiziert wurden. Der Krone ermöglichte sie, weiterhin ein

---

[10] Cassuto: Iscrizioni ebraiche (A. 8), S. 172–178.

[11] Starr: Mass conversion (A. 4), S. 208, 210; Roth: History (A. 8), S. 269; Ferorelli: Gli ebrei dell'Italia (A. 8), S. 67.

[12] Ferorelli: Gli ebrei dell'Italia (A. 8), S. 73, basierend auf dem verlorenen registro angioino 1329B, fol. 180v, aus Neapel; zur Handelsgeschichte der Balearen, der Rolle der Juden und den Beziehungen zwischen Mallorca und Neapel s. Abulafia, David: A mediterranean Emporium. The Catalan Kingdom of Majorca, Cambridge 1994.

[13] Abulafia, David: From Privilege to Persecution: Crown, Church and Synagogue in the City of Majorca, 1229–1343, in: Church and City, 1000–1500. Essays in honour of Christopher Brooke, hg. von David Abulafia, Miri Rubin, Michael J. Franklin, Cambridge 1992, S. 111–126.

[14] Backmann, Clifford R.: The decline and fall of medieval Sicily: politics, religion and economy in the reign of Frederick III, 1296–1337, Cambridge u.a. 1995, S. 148–153.

Einkommen von den Juden zu beziehen, was besser war als einfach ein für allemal ihre Güter zu konfiszieren, wie dies bei so vielen Vertreibungen geschah. Zu dem Wunsche, die Juden im Land zu behalten, mögen freilich Hoffnungen beigetragen haben, daß sie durch Konversion doch noch zu brauchbaren christlichen Bürgern würden; schließlich lebte man im Zeitalter von Ramón Llull, der in seiner langen Karriere sowohl Süditalien als auch Sizilien persönlich besuchte.

Ohne Zweifel nahm die Marginalisierung der sizilischen Juden im 14. Jahrhundert zu; in Erice scheint es spätestens Ende des 14. Jahrhunderts eine *giudecca* gegeben zu haben. Auch sind Anzeichen dafür vorhanden, daß die dortige Judengemeinde durch eine Kombination von Pest, harter Besteuerung und Wirtschaftskrieg zwischen Juden und Christen – z.B. 1374, als die Christen die Juden beschuldigten, während einer Hungersnot Getreide zu horten – verarmt war[15]. Der Faktor, der bei der Verschlechterung der Lage der Juden am schwersten wog, war der Einfluß von neuen Einstellungen, die man aus Spanien übernahm.

Die schrecklichen Pogrome, die als Resultat ungestümer judenfeindlicher Predigten in den spanischen Städten 1391 Kastilien und Aragon erschütterten, breiteten sich überall in den Ländern der Krone von Aragon aus, so daß 1392 auch Sizilien mit dem Bazillus völlig infiziert war. Zwar hatte es im 14. Jahrhundert schon in vielen sizilischen Städten sporadische Ausbrüche von Gewalt gegen Juden gegeben; 1392 erfaßte diese Gewalt jedoch ein viel größeres Gebiet mit wesentlich stärkerer Intensität. In Erice wurden die Juden, die während des Pogroms von 1392 zwangsgetauft worden waren, der Amtsgewalt des Bischofs von Mazara unterstellt, so daß Spuren ihres alten Glaubens ausgerottet werden konnten[16]. Aus Sicht der Monarchie war dies ein Pyrrhussieg. Die illoyalen Untertanen König Martins hatten sowohl in Sizilien als auch in Spanien das Eigentum der Krone, die *servi nostre camere,* schwer geschädigt: Die Judengemeinden in Katalonien und auf Mallorca haben sich von diesen Angriffen niemals wirklich erholen können. Auf Sizilien andererseits deuten stärkere Anzeichen auf eine Erholung hin, vielleicht weil die Insel von ihrer Randlage in einem Staatenverbund profitierte, der – zumindest bis zu den italienischen Siegen von Alfons dem Großmütigen im 15. Jahrhundert – von der westlichen Peripherie aus kontrolliert wurde[17].

II.

In den Jahren um 1400 begann ein wichtiger Transformationsprozeß im südlichen Italien, in dem neue jüdische Siedler eintrafen, deren Schutzbriefe ihnen das Recht garantierten, Pfandleihhäuser zu führen. Diese Juden ließen sich insbesondere im

---

[15] ABULAFIA, David: Una communità ebraica della Sicilia orientale: Erice 1298–1304, in: Archivio storico per la Sicilia orientale 80 (1984), S. 184f.
[16] Ebd., S. 185.
[17] Zu diesem Herrscher s. RYDER, Alan: Alfonso the Magnanimous. King of Aragon, Naples, and Sicily, 1396–1458, Oxford 1990.

äußersten Norden des *Regno* nieder, z.B. in L'Aquila[18]. Die königliche Begünstigung jüdischer Geldhändler wurde jedoch aufgewogen durch die Angriffe auf die jüdische Religion und die ökonomischen Aktivitäten der Juden, die sich, ausgehend von Mittelitalien, in dieser Zeit bis in den Süden ausbreiteten[19]. Ein frühes Beispiel für die Bedrängung von Juden kann in Trani ausgemacht werden, wo sich die jüdische Gemeinde offenbar von den Verfolgungen Ende des 13. Jahrhunderts halbwegs hatte erholen können, wo der Bischof jedoch in den Jahren um 1380 den Juden hohe Steuern auferlegte und ihre Synagogen konfiszierte, woraufhin viele Juden die Stadt verließen. Der Franziskaner Giovanni da Capestrano gewann am Hofe der willensschwachen Königin Johanna II. beträchtlichen Einfluß und veranlaßte sie, die angevinischen Privilegien für die Juden zu widerrufen einschließlich des Rechts der Geldleihe gegen Zins[20]. Aufgrund weitverbreiteten Protests, an dem sich sogar die päpstliche Kurie beteiligte, nahm Johanna II. ihre antijüdischen Dekrete tatsächlich zurück und erlaubte den Juden wieder einen Zinsfuß von 45 % p.a. bei ihren Geldgeschäften. Die Lage der Juden blieb jedoch weiterhin prekär, weil die Monarchie geschwächt und von 1435 bis 1442 zwischen René von Anjou und Alfons von Aragon heftig umkämpft war. Der hl. Bernardin von Siena hielt im Jahr 1438 in L'Aquila in Gegenwart Renés eine Reihe von Predigten[21]. Perioden schwacher Königsgewalt erhöhten die Wahrscheinlichkeit von Angriffen auf die Juden. Dies hatte sich schon im Jahre 1411 gezeigt, als in Tarent ein Tumult ausbrach und die Amtsträger der Königin sich als unfähig erwiesen, die *giudecca* vor der Plünderung zu bewahren[22].

Die Ankunft von Alfons von Aragon als Eroberer von Neapel im Jahre 1442 stellte für die Juden in Süditalien, anders als die Ankunft Karls von Anjou, keine große Bedrohung dar[23]. Alfons und sein Nachfolger Ferrante waren sich noch des finanziellen Nutzens durch den Judenschutz bewußt, wie er so lange im heimatlichen Spanien praktiziert worden war. Etwas änderte sich jedoch: der Grad der Einflußnahme der Krone auf die Kontrolle und Besteuerung der jüdischen Geldleihe. Hierin wird eine Kombination königlicher fiskalischer Bedürfnisse mit langfristigen Veränderungen innerhalb der jüdischen Gemeinschaft deutlich; die aragonesischen Herrscher hatten zu Hause in Spanien seit Jahrhunderten Abgaben und Bußen von den Juden für die Erlaubnis zur Zinsleihe erhoben. So erneuerte Alfons bereits im Juni 1452 das Recht der Juden, Zinsleihe zu betreiben, nachdem die süditalienischen Juden eine Abgabe von 1.000 Dukaten hatten zahlen müssen[24]. Die

---

[18] FERORELLI: Gli ebrei dell'Italia (A. 8), S. 74f.

[19] Ebd., S. 75.

[20] Ebd., S. 76. Siehe auch STARR, Joshua: Johanna II and the Jews, in: Jewish Quarterly Review n.s. 31 (1940), S. 67–78.

[21] Zitiert von FERORELLI: Gli ebrei dell'Italia (A. 8), S. 77.

[22] Vgl. zur ersten Information MILANO, Attilio: Storia degli Ebrei in Italia, Turin 1963, S. 187.

[23] Den besten Überblick über die Geschichte Süditaliens zu dieser Zeit bietet GALASSO, Giuseppe: Il Regno di Napoli, Bd. 1: Il Mezzogiorno angioino e aragonese, in: Storia d'Italia, hg. von G. GALASSO, Bd. 15, Torino 1992, S. 561–775.

[24] Über die aragonesische Zeit informiert außer FERORELLI: Gli ebrei dell'Italia (A. 8), S. 89–198,

Kunst lag darin, die Juden stark genug zu besteuern, um die Finanzen des Königs in gutem Zustand zu halten, ohne zugleich den Wohlstand der jüdischen Gemeinden zu zerstören[25]. Die Juden von Neapel, Aversa und Capua beschwerten sich so im Jahre 1464 über die von ihnen verlangte *vigesime*, die so bedrückend sei, daß vielen von ihnen nichts übrigbleibe als zu packen und das *Regno* zu verlassen. Der König entschied, dies sei gegen jedermanns Interesse: die Juden müßten *humanamente* behandelt werden[26]. Anläßlich der Hochzeit der Tochter des Königs sahen sich die Juden von Terra di Lavoro einer Steuerforderung in Höhe von 1.050 Dukaten gegenüber; ähnliches geschah, als die Türken Otranto angriffen und als französische Truppen 1494 in Italien einmarschierten[27]. Das Problem war, daß die Juden durch diese Belastungen zu verarmen drohten, so daß einige der Juden von Kalabrien sagten, sie sähen keinen anderen Ausweg mehr, als sich nach Sizilien einzuschiffen, obschon auch dort die raffgierige Regierung darauf bedacht war, ihren Reichtum auszubeuten.

König Ferrante versicherte den Juden 1468, sie könnten in ihren Wohnorten dieselben Rechte und Privilegien genießen wie die örtlichen Christen; später wurde ihnen außerdem versprochen, zu außerordentlichen Steuern, die den Christen auferlegt würden, nicht automatisch mit herangezogen zu werden[28]. Der fundamentale Grundsatz bestand darin, daß die Monarchie im Besitz der Judengemeinden war und diese Kontrolle in ihren Entscheidungen darüber, wann, wo und in welcher Höhe die Juden zu besteuern seien, zum Ausdruck kam[29]. Konträr dazu gingen die örtlichen Christengemeinden die Juden andauernd um Beiträge zu Sondersteuern an, wodurch sich die Regierung zu fortwährenden Anordnungen veranlaßt sah, daß die den Juden gewährten Exemtionen eingehalten werden müßten[30]. Solche Dispute bauten zwischen Juden und Christen Spannungen auf und können sehr wohl als ein wichtiger Grund für Animositäten der christlichen Bevölkerung gegenüber den Juden im Süditalien des späten 15. Jahrhunderts angesehen werden[31]. Daß getrennte Besteuerung und totale Exemtion von der Steuerpflicht in keiner Weise dasselbe waren, stellte ein großes Problem dar; in den Kommunen glaubte man anscheinend,

---

BONAZZOLI, Viviana: Gli ebrei del regno di Napoli all'epoca della loro espulsione, 1. Tl.: Il periodo aragonese, 1456–1499, in: Archivio storico italiano 137 (1979), S. 495–559; SILVESTRI, Alfonso: Gli Ebrei del Regno di Napoli durante la dominazione aragonese, in: Campania Sacra 18 (1987), S. 21–77, und PETRALIA, Giuseppe: L'epoca aragonese, in: L'Ebraismo dell'Italia meridionale (A. 2), S. 79–114.

[25] Die Ernennung Francesco Martorells zum *baiulo generale a vita* über die *giudecche* des Regno im Jahre 1456 fügt sich gut in Alfonsos politische Strategien ein; vgl. BONAZZOLI: Gli ebrei (A. 24), Tl. 1, S. 524f.; vgl. ebd., S. 541f.

[26] FERORELLI: Gli ebrei dell'Italia (A. 8), S. 167.

[27] Ebd., S. 168f.; vgl. BONAZZOLI: Gli ebrei (A. 24), Tl. 1, S. 543.

[28] FERORELLI: Gli ebrei dell'Italia (A. 8), S. 170f.; zu Ferrantes Zinspolitik s. BONAZZOLI: Gli ebrei (A. 24), Tl. 1, S. 539f.

[29] Vgl. COLAFEMMINA, Cesare: La tutela die giudei del regno di Napoli nei „Capitoli" del sovrani aragonesi, in: Studi di storia meridionale 7 (1987), S. 297–310.

[30] FERORELLI: Gli ebrei dell'Italia (A. 8), S. 171.

[31] Siehe dazu die exzellenten Ausführungen von PETRALIA: L'epoca aragonese (A. 24), S. 79–114.

die Juden würden sich den von Neapel auferlegten regulären Steuerlasten entziehen[32].

Die Juden Süditaliens konnten 1465 von der Wiedererstarkung der Königsgewalt profitieren, als sie bei der Krone um eine umfangreiche Serie von Privilegien nachsuchten, die solche der früheren Regenten bestätigen und die Bewegungsfreiheit für jüdische Händler garantieren, aber auch einige aktuelle Befürchtungen überwinden helfen sollten. So sollten die städtischen Regierungen Verantwortung tragen für jüdisches Eigentum, falls ein Judenviertel geplündert würde, es sei denn, sowohl die Juden als auch die Christen der Gegend wären beraubt worden[33]. Besonders auffällig ist eine Klausel, die inhaftierten Juden erlaubte, am Sabbath oder an religiösen Feiertagen gegen Kaution das Gefängnis zu verlassen[34]. Diese Bestimmung zeigt wohl am klarsten die Inspirationsquelle der königlichen Politik gegenüber den Juden Süditaliens: Es handelte sich weniger um lokale Traditionen als um die Gesetzgebung früherer Könige von Aragon. Jakob I. von Aragon hatte seinen jüdischen Untertanen z.B. 1239 in Valencia ähnliche Rechte eingeräumt, kurz nachdem die Stadt in aragonesisch-katalanische Hände gefallen war; dort wurden Juden zwischen Freitag nachmittag und Montag morgen aus dem Gefängnis entlassen[35]. Nichts könnte die spanischen Ursprünge von Ferrantes günstiger Einstellung gegenüber den Juden besser verdeutlichen; ihre Wurzeln lagen in der traditionellen königlichen Politik, auch wenn sein Cousin und Namensvetter, der König von Aragon, im Jahre 1492 mit dieser Tradition vollständig brechen sollte.

Die positive Einstellung der aragonesischen Könige, besonders Ferrantes I., gegenüber den Juden spiegelt sicherlich ein Bewußtsein ihrer großen Produktivität wider. Giuseppe Petralia hat diesen Standpunkt ohne Umschweife auf folgenden Nenner gebracht: „gli ebrei erano per il re moneta"[36]. Solche Schlußfolgerungen schließen die Möglichkeit nicht aus, daß Herrscher aus dieser Dynastie die neuen Verfolgungen in Spanien, Norditalien und Deutschland aufrichtig verabscheuten. Letzten Endes machte der Wille König Ferrantes, die Juden auch in einem Zeitalter unbarmherziger Verfolgung und europaweiter Vertreibungen weiterhin zu schützen, ihr Überleben möglich. Dies war freilich nicht notwendigerweise das, was sich alle

---

[32] Zu den kleineren Städten s. die grundlegenden Studien von COLAFEMMINA, Cesare, insbes. Ebrei e cristiani novelli in Puglia. Le comunità minori, Bari 1991.

[33] COLAFEMMINA, Cesare: I capitoli concessi nel 1465 da Ferrante I ai giudei del Regno, in: Studi storici meridionali 12 (1993), S. 302.

[34] Ebd., S. 298 (7.).

[35] BAER, Fritz: Die Juden im christlichen Spanien, I. Urkunden und Regesten, 1. Aragonien und Navarra, Berlin 1929 (ND Farnborough 1970), S. 91; ASSIS, Yom Tov: The Jews of Spain: From Settlement to Expulsion, Jerusalem 1988, S. 62 (5.).

[36] PETRALIA: L'epoca aragonese (A. 24), S. 79–114. Vgl. allgemeiner zur Wirtschaftspolitik Ferrantes ABULAFIA, David: The Crown and the economy under Ferrante I of Naples (1458–1494), in: City and countryside in late medieval and Renaissance Italy. Essays presented to Philip Jones, hg. von Trevor DEAN und Chris WICKHAM, London 1990, S. 125–146, wiederabgedr. in: ABULAFIA, David: Commerce and Conquest in the Mediterranean, 1100–1500, Aldershot 1993.

süditalienischen Christen wünschten. Denn um 1490 waren die dominikanischen und franziskanischen Prediger so beflissen wie eh und je, das Christenvolk zu ermahnen, die Juden zu isolieren oder gar anzugreifen: Frate Gaspare, ein Dominikaner, reiste 1491 durch die Städte der Abruzzen, um seine Botschaft *contra hebreos* zu verkünden; Ferrante sah sich veranlaßt, von den Städten, die als Folge eines Besuches von Gaspare Maßnahmen gegen die Juden verabschiedet hatten, die Rücknahme dieser Anordnungen zu verlangen[37].

Im Jahre 1492 erhob ein namentlich nicht genannter Prediger in Tarent seine Stimme gegen Juden und Neophyten. In Tropea in Kalabrien und in anderen Städten wurden Juden am Karfreitag mißhandelt, weshalb allen, die bei irgendeiner Gelegenheit Juden schlecht behandelten, Strafgelder angedroht wurden[38]. Manchmal gerieten die Ereignisse auch außer Kontrolle: Schon 1463 waren die Judenviertel von Bari und Lecce geplündert worden. Der Druck auf die Juden, sich taufen zu lassen, wuchs; allein, wie schon in der Vergangenheit bewahrte die Neuchristen auch die Annahme neuer, nichtjüdischer Namen nicht vor dem Verdacht, insgeheim Juden geblieben zu sein.

III.

Wie wir sehen, kam es im 15. Jahrhundert in den sizilischen Städten zu immer regelmäßigeren Attacken auf die Juden. Im frühen 15. Jahrhundert wurden diese Angriffe von Forderungen nach Konversion, Segregation oder Vertreibung begleitet; die Bewohner von Vizzini überredeten die Königin von Aragon, die Juden zu vertreiben; Moses de Bonavoglia, der *Dienchelele*, hatte sich 1430 gezwungen gesehen, dem König nach Spanien nachzueilen, um den Widerruf von Regelungen zu erreichen, die von den Juden verlangten, Bekehrungspredigten zu hören und nur in ihnen zugewiesenen Stadtbezirken zu wohnen. Dennoch hielten die Versuche, die jüdischen Freiheiten zu begrenzen, an, so daß z.B. 1447 jüdischer Grundbesitz verboten wurde. Gerade die erratische Natur derartiger Verfügungen war eine Saat von Kalamitäten für die Juden, da ihre Situation zwischen königlicher Gunst und Anfeindung des Volkes oszillierte. Häufig kam es zu Ausschreitungen an Ostern, namentlich in Polizzi, und fortwährend wurden die Juden unter Druck gesetzt, ihre Synagogen oder Häuser aus der Nähe von Kirchen zu entfernen, wie etwa in Taormina und Mdina auf Malta. In Trapani wurde die Judengemeinde hart bestraft, weil sie die Tochter einer jüdischen Mutter und eines christlichen Vaters als jüdisch anerkannte – stießen doch jüdisches und christliches Recht hier direkt zusammen[39]. Dies war allerdings nichts im Vergleich zu dem Massaker des Jahres 1474 in Modica, das sich in die zahlreichen Beschuldigungen gegen und Angriffe auf Juden in sizilischen Städten einreihte. Der Pogrom in Modica fand am Festtag Mariä

---

[37] FERORELLI: Gli ebrei dell'Italia (A. 8), S. 192; BONAZZOLI: Gli ebrei (A. 24), Tl. 1, S. 50.
[38] FERORELLI: Gli ebrei dell'Italia (A. 8), S. 193.
[39] ROTH: History (A. 8), S. 248–251.

Himmelfahrt statt und forderte mindestens 360 Menschenleben, von den Nach-
ahmungsunruhen, die sich in der Folge u.a. in Erice, Sciacca und Noto ereigneten,
ganz zu schweigen[40]. Die Feinde der Juden beharrten darauf, daß letztere anti-
christliche Blasphemien lehrten; christliche Prediger verbreiteten diese Vorstel-
lungen auf der ganzen Insel. Der Sturm, der die Judengemeinden Siziliens traf, hatte
tatsächlich zwei Ursprünge: zum einen die immer erbitterteren Verleumdungen der
Juden, die auch auf dem italienischen Festland kursierten – oft in Verbindung mit
Angriffen auf das Wuchergeschäft, aber darüber hinaus durchtränkt von Invektiven
gegen die Juden als Feinde des christlichen Glaubens und Mörder Christi oder gar
christlicher Kinder; zum anderen – typisch für die antijüdische Politik in Kastilien
und Aragon – die Furcht, daß die andauernde Gegenwart von Juden auf christlichem
Boden Proselyten irremache, die durch die nichtkonvertierten Juden verleitet
würden, zu ihrem Väterglauben zurückzukehren. Die Krone bot den Judenhetzern
keine Unterstützung. Die Anführer der Erhebung in Modica wurden sogar hinge-
richtet. Das Vergehen, dessen sie sich schuldig gemacht hatten – dies muß betont
werden –, war eher gegen die Autorität des Königs gerichtet, dessen Schatz die
Juden waren, als gegen die Juden selbst.

Es gibt zwei Erklärungen dafür, warum die Juden aus Sizilien vertrieben wurden,
eine schaut auf Sizilien, die andere auf Spanien. Die Unruhen durch die antijüdischen Tumulte; die Unbeliebtheit der Juden selbst, die von einer kleinen, aber
einflußreichen Gruppe fanatischer Gegner – Bettelmönche und Geschäftsrivalen –
immer mehr dämonisiert wurden; lokale Vertreibungen der Juden aus kleinen
Städten: all dies kann als Zeichen dafür angesehen werden, daß die Repräsentanten
des Königs auf Sizilien unter Druck waren, die Insel von allen Juden zu säubern.
Eine Anschuldigung, die Juden hätten im Dezember 1491 ein Kreuz geschändet,
während man es durch die Straßen einer kleinen Stadt im östlichen Sizilien getragen
habe, wurde später als Grund für die Vertreibung genannt[41].

Der Befehl kam jedoch aus Spanien. Er war kein Bestandteil des ursprünglichen
Vertreibungsedikts bezüglich der Juden von Aragon und Kastilien aus dem März
1492, auch wenn sich die Juden Siziliens kaum der Illusion hingegeben haben
dürften, von der Vertreibung der Sephardim unbeschadet zu bleiben[42]. Die Ver-
treibungsorder für die Juden von Sizilien wurde erst Mitte Juni veröffentlicht, und
die Krone nahm den Juden alles, was sie hatten, einschließlich ihrer Synagogen und
Kultgegenstände. Die Juden wurden praktisch um die Chance gebracht, in den drei

---

[40] Ebd., S. 251f.
[41] Ebd., S. 254.
[42] Zur Vertreibung s. insbes. ASHTOR, Eliyahu: La fin du Judaïsme sicilien, in: Revue des études juives
142 (1983), S. 323–347, eine Kritik an TRASSELLI, Carmelo: Sull'espulsione degli ebrei della
Sicilia, in: Annali della Facoltà di economia e commercio, Università di Palermo, Bd. 8, 1954, und
C. TRASSELLIs Vorlesung „Gli ebrei di Sicilia", abgedr. in: DERS.: Siciliani fra Quattrocento e
Cinquecento, Messina 1981, S. 135–157. Auf je verschiedene Weise revidieren sowohl Ashtor als
auch Trasselli die Schlußfolgerungen von Roth, Milano und anderen Autoritäten. Siehe auch
RENDA, Francesco: La fine dell'ebraismo siciliano, Palermo 1993 (Biblioteca siciliana di storia e
letteratura 31).

Monaten, die ihnen für ihre Ausreise blieben, wenigstens für ihren Lebensunterhalt zu arbeiten; nichtsdestoweniger strengte sich der Vizekönig an zu gewährleisten, daß Juden in ihren Ortschaften, bevor sie sie verließen, nicht mißhandelt wurden. Ein vereinzeltes Zugeständnis wurde gemacht des Inhalts, daß die Juden Sizilien vor dem 12. Januar 1493 nicht verlassen mußten. Möglicherweise wurden die Befehle zur Beschlagnahme jüdischer Güter weithin ignoriert, denn die notariellen Verträge, die von den Juden aufgesetzt wurden, um ihre Verhältnisse vor dem Verlassen der Insel zu regeln, beziehen sich selten auf diesen Akt der Enteignung[43]. Ein kluger Weg, für eine sichere Zahlung zu sorgen, war, um Begleichung der Rechnung nicht in Sizilien, sondern in Neapel zu bitten; gelegentlich suchten die Juden um Bezahlung in Form von Waren nach; sie rechneten damit, Zucker, Leder oder sogar Florentiner Tuche als Ertrag dieser Transaktionen exportieren zu können[44]. Es gab allerdings auch noch einen anderen Ausweg: Täuflinge sollten ihr Eigentum zurückerhalten. Wie in Spanien hatte für die Krone nicht die Vertreibung, sondern die Konversion Priorität. Massenemigration bedeutete schließlich auch den Verlust handwerklicher Fertigkeiten; es ist eine vieldiskutierte Frage, ob die Vertreibung aus Spanien dem Land schweren ökonomischen Schaden zugefügt hat; in Sizilien indes waren sich die Zeitgenossen über diese Gefahr im klaren. Die Magistrate von Palermo und Catania, aber auch die eigenen Repräsentanten auf Sizilien legten der Krone eindringlich dar, daß der Verlust jüdischen Sachverstands nicht gutgeheißen werden könne, während König Ferrante von Neapel nur darauf wartete, die Handwerksspezialisten zu übernehmen, die andere hinausgeworfen hatten[45]. Die Monarchie verschloß sich solchen Argumenten in der Regel nicht: Ferdinand von Aragon vertrieb zeit seines Lebens die Muslime von Valencia nicht, da sie eine so wertvolle Quelle von Handwerkskunst und Einkommen waren[46].

Es ist eine offene Frage, ob das Vertreibungsdekret in der Konversion einer bedeutenden Zahl von Handwerkern resultierte, denn entgegen der herkömmlichen Ansicht, daß vornehmlich die Elite geblieben und die Taufe akzeptiert habe, hat Ashtor argumentiert, daß es auch konvertierte Handwerker in nennenswerter Zahl gegeben habe und daß es die reichen Gemeindemitglieder gewesen seien, ganz besonders die Ärzte, die am ehesten das Land verließen; seiner Ansicht nach hätten sich 20 % der sizilischen Juden tatsächlich taufen lassen. Auch nach Meinung von Trasselli gab es eine größere Zahl von Konvertiten als Historiker wie z.B. Roth annahmen, aber Trasselli gewann den Eindruck, daß es die Armen waren, die gingen, während die Reichen blieben[47]. Sicherlich führte das Vertreibungsedikt zu einer Welle von Konversionen in letzter Minute; gelegentlich waren es Männer, die übertraten, während ihre Ehefrauen, deren religiöse Überzeugungen stärker waren,

---

[43] ASHTOR: La fin (A. 42), S. 326.
[44] Ebd., S. 330.
[45] Ebd., S. 324; TRASSELLI: Siciliani (A. 42), S. 152.
[46] MEYERSON, Mark D.: The Muslims of Valencia in the age of Fernando and Isabel: between coexistence and crusade, Berkeley, Los Angeles 1991.
[47] ASHTOR: La fin (A. 42), S. 332f.; TRASSELLI: Siciliani (A. 42), S. 151–157.

ins Exil gingen[48]. In der herausragenden Familie Sala aus Trapani war es so, daß die Witwe des Bankiers Sadone und mehrere junge Kinder die Straße ins Exil beschritten, während einer von Sadones Söhnen, Paolo, Christ wurde; viele trapanesische Exulanten kamen aus gutsituierten Familien und steuerten eigentlich alle den wohlwollenden Empfang in Neapel an[49]. Ashtors Ansicht, daß arme und reiche Juden konvertierten, wird gestützt durch die Angaben zum Sozialstatus der *neofiti*, die in den Notariatsakten Siziliens nach der Vertreibung erscheinen; alte jüdische Handwerkskünste, wie die Produktion von Zucker oder das Einpökeln von Thunfisch, wurden in den neuchristlichen Familien weiter tradiert. Die Anwesenheit einer großen Zahl von *neofiti* in Palermo war im Jahre 1516 zu einer Quelle sozialer Spannungen geworden; wie in Spanien ärgerten sich Altchristen über den leichten Zugang von Neuchristen zu Möglichkeiten, die den Juden verschlossen gewesen waren. Gern gesehen waren Konvertiten, wenn sie Aufgaben im lokalen Handel weiterführten, an denen sich die Juden lange beteiligt hatten. Anfangs verdächtigte die Inquisition, wie 1516 in Palermo, die Konvertiten, von denen sie – wohl zu Recht – glaubte, daß jüdische Praktiken unter ihnen lebendig blieben. Ob das Phänomen des Kryptojudentums – nach außen das Christentum bekennend, insgeheim aber dem Judentum treu bleibend – auf Sizilien in einem Ausmaß fortlebte, wie es in Ländern wie Portugal und Mallorca sichtbar war, erscheint zweifelhaft, trotz kürzlicher Behauptungen des Gegenteils[50]. Die sizilische Inquisition verlor Mitte des 16. Jahrhunderts das Interesse an den Juden und konzentrierte sich zunehmend auf Protestanten, Hexen, Sodomiter und vereinzelte Muslime[51].

Die mit der Vertreibung aus Sizilien verbundene Demütigung wurde noch vertieft durch die Strenge der Dekrete hinsichtlich dessen, was die Juden mitnehmen durften; alle Anzeichen sprechen indes dafür, daß die harten Bestimmungen in der Praxis abgemildert wurden. Nicht einmal den *tallit*, ihren Gebetsschal, sollten die exilierten Juden über das Meer mitnehmen dürfen. Einige Feudalherren nahmen den Juden ihre Besitztümer und inhaftierten sie, als sie entdeckten, daß sie nicht länger als finanzieller Aktivposten angesehen werden konnten[52]. Ein anderer Faktor, der die sizilischen Juden vielleicht in ihrem Entschluß bestärkte, waren die engen Verbindungen zu Nordafrika, die ihnen Hoffnung auf ein neues Zuhause im Süden machten, während

---

[48] ASHTOR: La fin (A. 42), S. 331.
[49] Ebd., S. 336f.; TRASSELLI: Siciliani (A. 42), S. 151.
[50] Verschiedentlich wurde behauptet, daß auf Sizilien auch in der Gegenwart noch Marranos leben, doch ist dies in keiner Weise zu vergleichen mit dem außergewöhnlichen Überleben von Marranos im portugiesischen Belmonte. Siehe RENDA, Francesco: I marrani di Sicilia, in: Storia d'Italia, Annali, Bd. 11: Gli Ebrei in Italia, hg. von Corrado VIVANTI, Tl. 1: Dall'alto medioevo all'età dei ghetti, Turin 1996, S. 679–705.
[51] MONTER, William: Frontiers of Heresy. The Spanish Inquisition from the Basque lands to Sicily, Cambridge u.a. 1990, S. 181. Andererseits war der Inquisitor G. Di Giovanni in seinem Werk „L'ebraismo della Sicilia ricercato ed esposto", Palermo 1748, noch in der Mitte des 18. Jahrhunderts darauf aus zu demonstrieren, was ihm als große Gefahr erschien: dem Judentum zu erlauben, seine alte Stärke auf der Insel wiederzugewinnen; nichtsdestotrotz bleiben seine Forschungen ein Ausgangspunkt für Studien zur Geschichte der Judengemeinden Siziliens.
[52] Zu den Ereignissen 1491/93 s. z.B. ROTH: History (Anm. 8), S. 255–261.

ein weiteres Moment das unerschrockene Willkommen blieb, das ihnen Ferrante von Neapel entbot. Reggio Calabria wurde der Brennpunkt der Einwanderung, und rasch bildete sich eine eigene sizilische *judeca* neben der existierenden jüdischen Gemeinschaft. Es überrascht nicht, daß die Juden in Reggio mit feindlichen Amtsträgern unterer Ränge konfrontiert wurden, wie dem, der im Mai 1492 einen Verweis erhielt, weil er sizilischen Juden Barthaare ausgerupft hatte; die *Summaria* in Neapel unterstrich, daß der König ob solcher Nachrichten äußerst aufgebracht sein würde[53].

IV.

Besonders auffällig ist der Kontrast zwischen Ferdinand II. von Aragon, „dem Katholischen", der, zusammen mit seiner Frau Isabella, die Vertreibung der Juden aus Spanien und Sizilien angeordnet hatte, und seinem Namensvetter und Cousin Ferrante I. von Neapel. Im Jahre 1476 gab Ferrante seiner eigenen Beurteilung der Juden Ausdruck: *nos tamen ipsos iudeos et quemlibet ipsorum amamus atque diligimus, et ipsis iudeis et cuilibet eorum favori et auxilio semper fuimus et erimus*[54]. Wie zutreffend dies war, trat zutrage, nachdem die Juden Spanien und Sizilien lieber in Scharen verlassen hatten, als die Taufe zu akzeptieren. Trotz der enormen praktischen Schwierigkeiten bei der Überquerung des Mittelmeers, wo skrupellose Schiffskapitäne ihre Passagiere als Sklaven verkauften oder sogar niedermetzelten, war es in Neapel, Reggio und anderen süditalienischen Städten, wo sie am aufrichtigsten willkommen geheißen wurden.

Ferrante nahm diese Ereignisse vorweg. Bereits am 20. April 1491 versicherte er neu angekommenen Juden, sie würden sich derselben Privilegien erfreuen wie die *antiqui* und ganz genauso behandelt, als wenn sie im *Regno* geboren worden wären. Der vielleicht aufschlußreichste Teil dieser Anordnungen ist das Beharren des Königs darauf, daß seine Amtleute nicht nur verzeichnen sollten, wieviele Juden mit ihren Schiffen woher angekommen waren, sondern *de che artificio o mercancia sia* jeder Haushaltsvorstand. Einmal auf süditalienischem Boden angelangt, hatten die Juden frei zu sein bei der Wahl ihres Wohnortes, so daß sie Lebensmittel kaufen, Handel treiben und Güter produzieren konnten ohne Behinderung. Im Bewußtsein der Gefahr für die öffentliche Ordnung, wenn Juden in großer Zahl in Städten eintrafen, in denen es früher schon Unruhen gegeben hatte, verbot der König feierlich jedwede Gewalthandlung gegen Juden; diese mußten *vivere soptu la protecione de la prefata Maiestà*. Sie waren letztlich Eigentum des Königs, und Ferrante sah sie als zusätzliche Quelle wirtschaftlichen Nutzens für ein Königreich, dessen Gewerbe und (nicht zuletzt) Finanzen er zu fördern versuchte[55]. Seine Motive, die Ankunft der Juden zu begrüßen, wurden viel diskutiert. Für Petralia „gli

---

[53] COLEFEMMINA, Cesare: The Jews of Reggio Calabria from the end of the fifteenth century to the beginning of the sixteenth century, in: Les juifs au regard de l'histoire. Mélanges en l'honneur de Bernhard Blumenkranz, hg. von Gilbert DAHAN, Paris 1985, S. 255–262.

[54] FERORELLI: Gli ebrei dell'Italia (A. 8), S. 194.

[55] Ebd., S. 93f.

ebrei sono qualcosa di affine alle *coses vedades*, armi, metalli, monete, pece, risorse di cui si limata l'uscita et di cui si facilita l'entrata", während der bedeutende Theologe Louis Jacobs Ferrante als einen der „righteous among the nations" ansieht, inspiriert von einem aufrichtigen Wunsch, die enormen Leiden der jüdischen Flüchtlinge zu begrenzen. Seine Versuche sicherzustellen, daß Juden ihre Toten nachts begruben, um das Wissen um einen Ausbruch der Pest zu verheimlichen, werden als Akte, die sich aus hohen humanitären Prinzipien speisten, erklärt[56]. Eigentümlich ist bei Ferrante, daß seine Äußerungen über die Juden – neben seinem unbezweifelbaren Interesse an dem finanziellen Ertrag, den er von den größer gewordenen Judengemeinden erwarten konnte – eine echte Sympathie offenbaren, die weit über die pragmatische Großzügigkeit seiner Vorfahren, der Könige von Kastilien und Aragon, hinausgeht.

Schätzungen bezüglich der Zahl sephardischer Flüchtlinge, die im *Regno* eintrafen, sind besonders schwierig, da auch nach ihrer Ankunft noch viele von der Pest dahingerafft wurden. Es ist möglich, daß die Sephardim, einschließlich der Sizilianer, zahlenmäßig den süditalienischen Juden gleichkamen, die allerhöchstens 5 % der dortigen Bevölkerung ausmachten. Überdies stießen die Juden, bei ihrem Versuch, sich in diesem oder jenem Ort niederzulassen, auf Schwierigkeiten. In Pozzuoli gab es 1489 schon eine kleine Judengemeinde, aber als die Zahlen wuchsen – eventuell auch unter dem Druck des Ortsklerus –, erging im Januar 1493 der Befehl zu ihrer Ausweisung aus der Stadt. Es erstaunt nicht, daß die Krone einen Gegenbefehl erließ; allein, die Haltung der *Università* von Pozzuoli war symptomatisch für weiter verbreitete Einstellungen innerhalb des *Regno*. Der Judenhaß konnte extrem sein: Ein spanischer Priester behauptete, ein mirakulöses Täfelchen gefunden zu haben, das die Ausrottung der süditalienischen Juden befehle; doch König Ferrante ließ sich nicht täuschen[57]. Die Feindseligkeit gegenüber den Juden verschärfte sich nicht nur als Resultat der Einwanderung spanischer und sizilischer Flüchtlinge in großem Maßstab[58]. Ein politischer Sturm braute sich zusammen, der jahrzehntelang über Süditalien bleiben sollte: Ferrante I. starb im Jahr 1494, während Karl VIII. von Frankreich sich anschickte, alte angevinische Ansprüche auf das *Regno* geltend zu machen. Während der kurzen Regentschaft Alfonsos II. gab es keine nennenswerte Änderung in der königlichen Politik gegenüber den Juden, doch blieben Ausschreitungen in jedem Winkel des *Regno* an der Tagesordnung: in Salerno, Lecce, Altomonte, San Serverino[59]. Königliche Befehle, die Rechte der Juden zu respektieren, wurden in Bari, Bitonto und Tricarico in eklatanter Weise ignoriert[60]. Wenige Tage bevor Karls Armee Neapel erreichte, im Februar 1495,

---

[56] JACOBS, Louis: The Book of Jewish Belief, New York 1984, S. 44; KIDWELL, Carol: Pontano, Poet and Prime Minister, London 1991, S. 238, 392.
[57] Ebd., S. 287.
[58] LOPEZ, Pasquale: Napoli e la Peste 1464–1530, politica, istituzioni, problemi sanitari, Napoli 1989 (Storia e diritto/Studi 23), S. 91–22, bes. 101–122.
[59] BONAZZOLI: Gli ebrei (A. 24), Tl. 1, S. 500.
[60] FERORELLI: Gli ebrei dell'Italia (A. 8), S. 199.

wurden die Juden von Neapel Opfer feindseliger christlicher Horden, denen es gelang, das Judenviertel zu plündern und dabei die Bibliothek des großen Gelehrten und königlichen Vertrauten Isaac Abravanel zu vernichten[61]. Nicht nur unter den Juden, sondern auch unter den Neuchristen machte sich Panik breit; und der König, Ferrandino (Ferrante II.), war unfähig, etwas zum Schutz der Juden zu tun. Auch andernorts brachen Pogrome aus, als sich die Nachricht vom Fall Neapels an die Truppen Karls VIII. am 22. Februar 1495 verbreitete[62]. In Lecce bellte die Menge: *moiarono, moiarono li iudei, hover se facciano cristiani* und überfiel die Synagoge[63]. In ganz Apulien wurde enormer Schaden angerichtet: Steuerakten der unmittelbar folgenden Jahre spielen immer wieder auf die Armut der Juden und ihre Unfähigkeit an, noch irgendwelche Steuern zu entrichten. Gelegentlich gibt es, wie etwa in Barletta, Anzeichen dafür, daß die jüdischen Pfandleihgeschäfte zu den Streitpunkten gehörten, die Haß entfachten; dort waren die Juden erschrocken genug, um ihre Schuldenverzeichnisse zu zerstören, aber sie unterließen es, die Pfänder zurückzugeben, woraus ein Aufruf an Karl VIII. resultierte, die Vertreibung der städtischen Judengemeinde zu erlauben. Die neue Regierung indes untersagte – zweifellos zum Erstaunen der Christen von Barletta –, daß irgendjemand vertrieben werde[64]. Karl VIII., „un re senza ebrei" (um Petralia zu zitieren), führte aber nicht einfach die Judenpolitik seiner aragonesischen Vorgänger fort: jüdisches Eigentum wurde an Christen rückübertragen, und die Juden wurden eindeutig als ein Symbol der alten aragonesischen Ordnung betrachtet[65].

Das für die Juden vielleicht Schlimmste an diesen Jahren war das dauernde Hin und Her in der Regierung, als die Aragonesen zurückkehrten, die Franzosen erneut einfielen und die Spanier endgültig die Macht übernahmen[66]. Fünfzig Jahre lang hatten die Juden außerordentlich von der kontinuierlichen Existenz einer autonomen aragonesischen Regierung profitiert, die ihre Privilegien nicht nur respektierte, sondern ausweitete; nach 1494 aber ließ sogar die Begeisterung der Aragonesen für die Unterstützung der Juden nach, die sie nun, da das Haus Aragon alles daransetzte, die Loyalität der süditalienischen Mehrheit zurückzugewinnen, als eine Hypo-

---

[61] BONAZZOLI: Gli ebrei (A. 24), Tl. 1, S. 501, zu Ferrandinos Versuchen, die Judenhasser von Neapel zu beschwichtigen. Zu den Ereignissen des Februar 1495 vgl. ebd., S. 502.

[62] Generell zu diesen Vorgängen s. LABANDE-MAILFERT, Yvonne: Charles VIII et son milieu. (1470–1498). La jeunesse au pouvoir, Paris 1975, S. 327–377; DIES.: Charles VIII, Paris 1986, S. 287–327, und – wie stets – Francesco GUICCIARDINIs Storia d'Italia, auf den auch rekurriert: ABULAFIA, David: Introduction. From Ferrante I to Charles VIII, in: The French descent into Renaissance Italy, 1494–95. Antecedents and Effects, ed. David ABULAFIA, Aldershot 1995, S. 14–25.

[63] BONAZZOLI: Gli ebrei (A. 24), Tl. 1, S. 499, macht darauf aufmerksam, daß es schon an Ostern 1494 beinahe zu einem Gewaltausbruch in Lecce gekommen war, als die Christen gegen die Abschaffung des Judenzeichens protestierten. .

[64] BONAZZOLI: Gli ebrei (A. 24), Tl. 1, S. 504f.

[65] FERORELLI: Gli ebrei dell'Italia (A. 8), S. 203–205.

[66] Zu den letzten vierzig Jahren jüdischer Existenz in Süditalien s. BONAZZOLI, Viviana: Gli ebrei del regno di Napoli all'epoca della loro espulsione. II parte: Il periodo spagnolo (1501–1541), in: Archivio storico italiano 139 (1981), S. 179–287.

thek betrachteten. Außerdem sahen die aragonesischen Könige die Juden nicht mehr in dem Maße wie früher als wirtschaftlichen Aktivposten an, weil ein Großteil ihres Reichtums enteignet oder zerstört worden war. In seinem Testament äußerte Alfonso II. Zweifel an der Weisheit der besonderen Großzügigkeit von seinen und seines Vaters Privilegien für die Juden[67]. Darüber hinaus führte Ferrandinos Rückkehr nach Neapel nach dem Abzug der Franzosen im Juli 1495 nicht zu einer unmittelbaren Verbesserung im Status der Juden; Gerüchte von einer bevorstehenden Vertreibung von Juden und Neuchristen kursierten; es kam zu neuen lokalen Ausweisungen und in einigen Städten, wie in Cosenza, zu zahlreichen Konversionen[68]. Der venezianische Gouverneur von Monopoli enteignete die Judenschaft ihres Geldvermögens und ihrer Güter[69]. Das Problem war dabei, daß die Christen daran gewöhnt waren, die Juden um Kredite anzugehen; plötzlich wurde offenbar, daß die Juden letzten Endes nützlich waren, und langsam begann sich das Klima wieder zu verbessern. Der Gouverneur von Bari wurde gebeten, die Juden von der Pflicht, ein besonderes Abzeichen zu tragen, zu befreien – eine Auflage, die unter den Aragonesen gelockert worden war[70]. Federigo, der letzte aragonesische König von Neapel, billigte sogar die Vertreibung der Juden aus seiner Hauptstadt im Jahre 1496 in der Hoffnung, seine christlichen Untertanen in einer Zeit immensen Aufruhrs zu besänftigen; innerhalb weniger Monate jedoch verkehrte sich seine Politik in ihr genaues Gegenteil, und die Juden von Kalabrien und Apulien empfingen großzügige Privilegien, während ihren Glaubensgenossen von Neapel erlaubt wurde, in Frieden weiterleben zu können. Federigo war sich dessen bewußt, daß er erst jetzt unangefochten die Macht in seinem Reiche ausüben konnte[71]. Somit kann das Schicksal der Juden als Barometer verwandt werden, um den Erfolg der Krone bei der Behauptung ihrer Autorität zu messen.

Die Eroberung Süditaliens durch Ferdinand den Katholischen, die im Jahre 1503 abgeschlossen war, brachte bald darauf neue Unwägbarkeiten. Die Existenz einer steigenden Zahl von Neuchristen, einige davon spanischer Herkunft, resultierte in einer akuten Angst vor intensiveren Aktivitäten der Inquisition im *Regno*. Und diejenigen, die offen Juden geblieben waren, wußten nur zu genau, daß Judenvertreibungen nicht nur in Kastilien und Aragon, sondern auch in dem der Krone von Aragon unterstehenden Teil Italiens und in nordafrikanischen Städten, die von den Spaniern erobert worden waren, stattgefunden hatten. Die katholischen Könige

---

[67] BONAZZOLI: Gli ebrei (A. 24), Tl. 1, S. 506. Ferrandino selbst hatte allerdings keinen Zugang zu diesem Dokument.

[68] FERORELLI: Gli ebrei dell'Italia (A. 8), S. 201, 206–211; BONAZZOLI: Gli ebrei (A. 24), Tl. 1, S. 506.

[69] FERORELLI: Gli ebrei dell'Italia (A. 8), S. 208. Vgl. COLAFEMMINA, Cesare: Documenti per servire alla storia degli Ebrei in Puglia nell'Archivio di Stato di Napoli, Bari 1990, Nr. 63, S. 80, zu früheren Belegen von Juden in Monopoli (1490). Über eine andere Küstengemeinde in Apulien vgl. DERS.: Ebrei e cristiani novelli (A. 32), S. 65–73 (Molfetta).

[70] BONAZZOLI: Gli ebrei (A. 24), Tl. 1, S. 509.

[71] FERRANTE, B.: Gli statuti di Federico d'Aragona per gli Ebrei del Regno, in: Archivio storico per le province napoletane 97 (1979) S. 131–184; FERORELLI: Gli ebrei dell'Italia (A. 8), S. 210; ABULAFIA: Crown and economy under Ferrante (A. 36), S. 137.

entschieden sich zunächst, die süditalienischen Juden zu vertreiben, doch wurde die Anordnung innerhalb weniger Monate suspendiert[72]. Andererseits bedeutete der Tod Isabellas im Jahre 1504, daß die Juden es nurmehr mit dem pragmatischeren Ferdinand zu tun hatten, der sich schon geweigert hatte, die Muslime von Valencia in den Prozeß der Spanien auferlegten religiösen Säuberung einzubeziehen[73]. Indem er die Muslime schützte, schützte er seinen eigenen Geldbeutel. Dieser Pragmatismus zeigte sich erneut, als den Juden im Jahre 1510 befohlen wurde, Süditalien zu verlassen[74]. Tatsächlich durften 200 Familien bleiben, von denen eine jährliche Kontribution von 3.000 Dukaten verlangt wurde, und es scheint, daß viele andere es schafften, sich an ihre Schoßröcke zu hängen[75]. Ferdinand beharrte somit nicht auf dem Prinzip, daß Süditalien *judenfrei* sein müsse. Allein, wie in Spanien war er sehr besorgt darüber, daß die Neuchristen es nicht vermochten, aufrichtige Konvertiten zu werden, daher wurden in den Jahren 1514/15 auch sie vertrieben (wozu es in Spanien niemals kam)[76]. Die Verarmung der Juden und Neuchristen hatte die meisten von ihnen entbehrlich gemacht; indessen war sich der König völlig bewußt, daß es immer noch einen Rest von ihnen gab, der in der Wirtschaft weiterhin eine wertvolle Rolle spielen konnte.

Tatsächlich tröpfelte sogar nach 1510 noch der Strom jüdischer Immigranten: In Lanciano wurde den Juden erlaubt, wenigstens die Jahrmärkte zu besuchen; einige Juden kamen 1515 aus Dubrovnik an, nachdem sie von dort vertrieben worden waren; wirkungsvoller mag das fortwährende Beharren von Städten darauf gewesen sein, daß sie wieder ihre Juden bräuchten – die Einwohner von Neapel versuchten, der Krone im Jahre 1520 klarzumachen, *il bisogno grandissimo che teneno de li hebrei*[77]. In Apulien offenbarte es sich, daß ohne jüdische Geldleiher christliche Wucherer die Lücke füllten; diese aber kamen ihren Kunden weit weniger entgegen. Ein königliches Edikt Karls V. vom 23. November 1520 bestätigte daher den Juden, die im *Regno* lebten, das Recht auf Handel und Wandel dort und auf die Eröffnung von Leihbanken, wofür eine Abgabe von 1.500 Dukaten pro Jahr fällig war[78]. Versuche, die Juden zu konvertieren, fanden statt, dennoch war das Bemühen um Konversion der restlichen Juden bis zur Ankunft des Vizekönigs Pedro von Toledo

---

[72] Siehe ABULAFIA, David: Le communità di Sicilia dagli arabi all'espulsione (1493), in: Storia d'Italia, Annali, Bd. 11: Gli Ebrei in Italia, ed. Corrado VIVANTI, Tl. 1: Dall'alto medioevo all'età dei ghetti, Turin 1996, S. 47–82; ABULAFIA, David: Gli ebrei di Sardegna, ebd., S. 85–94; zu den Vertreibungsplänen von 1503/04 s. BONAZZOLI: Gli ebrei (A. 66), Tl. 2, S. 182f.

[73] MEYERSON: Muslims of Valencia (A. 46).

[74] Über die Auswirkungen in Gravina (Apulien) unterrichtet COLAFEMMINA: Ebrei e cristiani novelli (A. 32), S. 24–28.

[75] FERORELLI: Gli ebrei dell'Italia (A. 8), S. 213f.

[76] FERORELLI: Gli ebrei dell'Italia (A. 8), S. 219. Einige *neofiti* hatten 1510/11 z.B. Gravina verlassen; COLAFEMMINA: Ebrei e cristiani novelli (A. 32), S. 25f., 33 (doc. Nr. 6).

[77] FERORELLI: Gli ebrei dell'Italia (A. 8), S. 220; BONAZZOLI: Gli ebrei (A. 66), Tl. 2, S. 204.

[78] FERORELLI: Gli ebrei dell'Italia (A. 8), S. 221; BONAZZOLI: Gli ebrei (A. 66), Tl. 2, S. 204. Die Stimmungsänderung könnte auch die Ankunft eines neuen Monarchen reflektieren, der, obschon er den Juden gegenüber keine Sympathie empfand, die letzteren nicht durchgängig aus seinen zahlreichen Landen vertrieb.

im Jahre 1533 kein Hauptanliegen[79]. Nach Ansicht von Don Pedro war der Grund, warum die Monarchie jemals das Überleben des Judentums im *Regno* gestattet hatte, die antizipierte Konversion der wenigen dort verbliebenen Juden. Folglich befahl Pedro von Toledo den Juden, sich taufen zu lassen oder zu gehen; und obschon das Edikt von 1533 bis zur endgültigen Vertreibung von 1541 keine Rolle spielte, brachten die nächsten Jahre den Juden andauernde Versuche, den Druck auf sie zu erhöhen, z.b. indem ihre jährlichen Abgaben auf 2.000 Dukaten erhöht und die Bestimmungen zum Betrieb von Leihbanken verschärft wurden. Auch die Regelungen der jüdischen Tracht wurden erweitert; Männer beispielsweise mußten ein rotes oder gelbes Barett tragen[80].

Insgesamt bestimmte also die Monarchie das Schicksal der Juden in Süditalien und Sizilien in hohem Maße. Aber auch andere Faktoren konnten ins Spiel kommen und den Standpunkt von Herrschern wie Karl II. von Anjou und – wenn auch nur kurz – Johanna II. beeinflussen: das Beharren der Kirche, vor allem der Franziskaner und Dominikaner, auf der Notwendigkeit, die „Unverschämtheit" der Juden zu beschränken und sie zum Christentum zu bekehren; die Verurteilung – abermals durch die Bettelmönche – des Wuchers, wobei die Kampagne auf die jüdischen *banchieri* abzielte; judenfeindliche Manifestationen des Volkes, die sich anscheinend dann am stärksten regten, wenn die Juden ihre ökonomischen Aktivitäten auf die Geldleihe verlagerten, die aber auch von Ressentiments wegen des Sonderstatus der Juden herrührten. Eine entschlossene Monarchie konnte – unter den Aragonesen – diejenigen in Schranken weisen, die die Position der Juden zu attackieren suchten. Eine resolute Monarchie konnte aber auch Ressentiments hervorrufen, und die Juden, die man als Agenten dieser Monarchie wahrnahm, wurden allzu leicht als erstbestes Angriffsziel auserwählt. Je mehr Ferrante seine offenkundige Sympathie für die Nöte seiner jüdischen Untertanen erkennen ließ und je mehr er ihren Wert für die Finanzen der Krone betonte, desto stärker gerieten die Juden in den Brennpunkt der Ressentiments. Im übrigen war der Standpunkt der aragonesischen Könige von Neapel, wie wir sahen, in gewissem Grade importiert, ein Relikt traditioneller spanischer Einstellungen gegenüber den Juden im 13. Jahrhundert; er vertrug sich schlecht mit dem Antagonismus innerhalb der christlichen Bevölkerung Süditaliens im späten Mittelalter. Insbesondere stand er in merklichem Kontrast zu der neuen Welle von Emotionen, die sich gegen die Juden richtete und Ferdinand den Katholischen dazu bewegte, die Juden aus Spanien zu vertreiben, und die mit

---

[79] FERORELLI: Gli ebrei dell'Italia (A. 8), S. 224; eine ausführliche Betrachtung der spanischen Politik findet sich in RUIZ MARTIN, Felipe: La expulsión de los Judíos del Reino de Nápoles, in: Hispania 9 (1949), S. 28–76 und 179–240; s. auch PALADINO, Giuseppe: Privilegi concessi agli Ebrei dal viceré D. Pietro di Toledo (1535–1536), in: Archivio storico per le province napoletane 38 (1913), S. 611–622.

[80] Zu den Privilegien vom 25. November 1535 und 24. November 1536: BONAZZOLI: Gli ebrei (A. 66), Tl. 2, S. 266–271; das Dokument von 1535 ist abgedruckt in PALADINO: Privilegi (A. 79), das von 1536 in BONAZZOLI, a.a.O., S. 267–270; s. auch FERORELLI: Gli ebrei dell'Italia (A. 8), S. 224–233. Vgl. USQUE, Samuel: Consolation for the tribulations of Israel, ed. and transl. by Martin A. COHEN, Philadelphia 1965, S. 209f.

XV

einer weiteren Order zur Vertreibung der Juden auch Sizilien einholte. In einem Zeitalter der Ambivalenz hinsichtlich der Nützlich- oder Wünschbarkeit, den Judengemeinden das Verbleiben im Lande zu gestatten, überrascht es nicht, daß *ein* aragonesisches Reich, das von Neapel, den Juden sein Willkommen entbot, während ein anderes, das in Spanien beheimatet war, nur die Wahl zwischen Vertreibung oder Konversion ließ.

XVI

THE ROLE OF THE JEWS IN THE CULTURAL LIFE OF THE ARAGONESE KINGDOM OF NAPLES

I

Until the late fifteenth century, southern Italy and Sicily contained by far the greatest part of the Jewish population of Italy [1]. There is thus no need to plead a case for offering a study of the cultural outlook of the Jews in the Aragonese kingdom of Naples. That said, the results of this investigation may seem unpromising. The evidence for interest in humanism and the classical tradition cannot be pressed very far, despite the importance of such themes in the cultural history of Italian Christians at this period. The impression remains, both in southern Italy and Sicily, of rather somnolent communities, which were no longer able to match the glories of the tenth century, when Oria in particular had been a major centre of Jewish learning, associated with the physician and Hebrew scholar Shabbetai Donnolo among others [2]. In the famous parody of Isaiah's words: 'from Bari comes forth the law, and the word of God from Otranto'. The major examples of innovations in Jewish scholarship in southern Italy during the period between 1475 and the French invasion of 1494 both came from outside Italy, and are quite different in character: the development of the printing press, with the result that Naples became the prime centre of Hebrew printing around 1490, and the brief career in Naples, and later on in Monopoli, of the Iberian scholar and statesman Don Isaac Abrabanel [3]. It is on the evidence concerning the arrival and expansion of Hebrew printing that I propose to concentrate, though some comments will also be

---

1. David Abulafia, "Il Mezzogiorno peninsulare dai bizantini all'espulsione (1541)", in *Storia d'Italia, Annali*, vol. 11, part. 1, *Gli Ebrei in Italia*, ed. C. Vivanti (Torino 1996), 5-44; also, id., "Le comunità di Sicilia dagli arabi all'espulsione (1493)", *ibid.*, 47-82.

2. A. Sharf, *The Universe of Shabbetai Donnolo* (Warminster 1976), 120-1.

3. Benzion Netanyahu, *Don Isaac Abravanel, statesman and philosopher* (2nd ed., Philadelphia 1968), remains the standard life of this figure, even though it is tainted by its author's strong political prejudices. Uncertainties about fifteenth-century Sephardi pronunciation (and a confusion common to Castilian Spanish and some forms of Sephardi Hebrew between 'b' and 'v') have resulted in several transliterations of his family name: Abrabanel, Abravanel, Abarbanel; the name probably meant 'little Abraham'.

necessary on Abrabanel's role in south Italian Jewish cultural life. In the case of printing, just as in that of Abrabanel, we are looking at the impact of arrivals from outside the *Regno*: editors, proof-readers, publishers, from as far afield as Germany and Aragon. This does not take us very deeply into the cultural interests of the south Italian Jews themselves, though here the evidence concerning the market for printed books, and of course the titles of those books that are known to have been printed, will be of help. However, the surviving evidence does allow us to say something about the contact, friendly and otherwise, that existed between Jews and Christians in the kingdom of Naples at this period.

A second major feature of this paper is that its subject matter has a long scholarly tradition behind it, accessible in the work of such scholars as Nicola Ferorelli, Joshua Bloch, Cecil Roth, Renzo Frattarolo, A.K. Offenberg and many others [4]; and yet, with the exception of recent research by Eva Frojmovic [5], much of the best research on the origins of Hebrew printing in Naples is far from recent, beginning with the remarkable studies of Johannes Bernardus de Rossi, published as the *Annales hebraeo-typographici* in Parma in 1795 [6]. His own view of the catholicity of tastes in fifteenth-century Naples was stated clearly: 'libri autem omnis generis suscepti, biblici, liturgici, talmudici, morales, juridici, historici, philosophici, grammatici, medici' [7]; it is the intention here to look a little more closely and to see whether this generous assessment is entirely deserved. Since de Rossi, most research has soberly concentrated on identifying the works actually printed in Naples, and by whom they were printed; much attention has been paid to the fascinating problem of the woodcut borders shared by Jewish and Christian printers in and beyond Naples; less attention, with the notable exception of articles by Bloch and Mehlman, has been paid to the actual importance of the works chosen for printing in the intellectual life of the southern communities [8]. Even then, of course, the severe difficulty remains that what survives is very probably only a small fraction of the total output of the Hebrew printing presses of Naples; Ferorelli considered that most of what was printed was lost in the disasters that afflicted the Jewish communities of southern

---

4. N. Ferorelli, *Gli Ebrei dell'Italia meridionale dall'età romana al secolo XVIII*, new ed. by F. Patroni Griffi, Napoli 1992, with helpful additional bibliography on Hebrew printing, 282-3; *Hebrew printing and bibliography. Studies by J. Bloch and others*, ed. C. Berlin, New York 1976; C. Roth, *Studies in books and booklore. Essays on Jewish bibliography and allied subjects*, Farnborough 1972, and the individual items reprinted there which will be mentioned later; R. Frattarolo, *Tipografi e librai, ebrei e non, nel Napoletano alla fine del secolo XV*, Firenze 1956; A.K. Offenberg, "Hebreeuwse Incunabelen in de Bibliotheca Rosenthaliana", *Studia Rosenthaliana. Tijdschrift voor Joodse Wetenschap en Geschiedenis in Nederland*, 14 (1980), 176-90.

5. E. Frojmovic, "From Naples to Constantinople: the Aesop workshop's woodcuts in the oldest illustrated printed Haggadah", *The Library*, ser. 6, 18 (1996), 87-109.

6. J.B. de Rossi, *Annales hebraeo-typographici*, Parma 1795.

7. Rossi, *Annales*, XIV.

8. J. Bloch, "Hebrew printing in Naples", *New York Public Library Bulletin*, 46 (1942), 489-514, repr. in *Hebrew printing and bibliography*, ed. C. Berlin, 113-38 [page references here are to the reprint and not to the original]; I. Mehlman, "The first fruits of Hebrew printing", *Thesaurus Typographiae Hebraicae saeculi XV*, ed. A Freiman, *Supplement*, Jerusalem, 1967-9 [printed without pagination].

Italy from 1494 to their final extinction in 1541 [9]. On the other hand, enough copies of major works, such as the Psalms with Kimhi's commentary or Rashi's Torah commentary, are still in existence in such deposits as Cambridge University Library and the Bodleian to suggest the dominating role of several big printing projects of the Naples presses [10].

II

Before closing in on these issues, it will be helpful to examine two aspects of the wider setting: the cultural activities patronised by the court of Naples in the late fifteenth century; and the evidence concerning royal policy towards the Jews in the Neapolitan state. Neapolitan culture under the Aragonese has been the subject of close attention in the last few years, with studies by Carol Kidwell of the neo-classical poetry produced in court circles, by Allan Atlas of music at the Aragonese court, and by Jerry Bentley and Alan Ryder of the ways the Aragonese kings used their patronage of humanist scholars to project an image of themselves as legitimate rulers cast in the Roman imperial mould [11]. Reference back to classical sources, notably to the image of Alfonso the Magnanimous as a new Julius Caesar or Augustus, was complemented by a close attention to the works of Seneca, himself, like Alfonso, a Spaniard. Indeed, the latest research suggests that the Aragonese kings took especial delight in comparing themselves to Hispano-Roman models, so that Trajan, along with several silver age classical writers, were placed under emphasis as the precursors of Alfonso of Trastámara [12]. Bentley has shown how the Aragonese kings sought to accommodate the ideas of the Italian humanists who gravitated to the royal court,

9. Ferorelli, *Gli Ebrei nell'Italia meridionale*, 280-2.

10. It is important also to bear in mind the rich literature on Latin and Italian language printing in Naples, such as: T. de Marinis, "Per la storia della tipografia napoletana del secolo XV", *La Bibliofilia*, 4 (1902-3), 101-3; T. de Marinis, *Catalogue de livres anciens, rares et précieux, incunables et livres à figures, précédent des documents inédits pour l'histoire de l'Imprimerie à Naples au XV siècle*, Firenze 1907; M. Fava and G. Bresciano, *La stampa a Napoli nel XV secolo*, 2 vols., Leipzig 1911-12; L. Correra, *Saggi della tipografia napoletana nel secolo XV*, Napoli 1911; R. Frattarolo, *I tipografi meridionali dalle origini al secolo XVIII*, Roma 1955; M.G. Castellano Lanzara, "Origine della stampa e biblioteche di Stato nelle Due Sicilie", *Studi in onore di Riccardo Filangieri*, 2 vols., Napoli 1959, I, 75-105; C. De Frede, *Biblioteche di giuristi e medici napoletani del Quattrocento*, Napoli 1973; M. Santoro, *La stampa a Napoli nel Quattrocento*, Napoli 1984. A good bibliography is to be found in Ferorelli, *Gli Ebrei nell'Italia meridionale*, 283.

11. C. Kidwell, *Pontano. Poet and Prime Minister* (London, 1991); José Carlos Rovira, *Humanistas y poetas en la corte napolitana de Alfonso el Magnánimo*, Alicante 1990; Allan Atlas, *Music at the Aragonese court of Naples*, Cambridge, 1985; Jerry Bentley, *Politics and Culture in Renaissance Naples*, Princeton, NJ 1987; A.F.C. Ryder, *Alfonso the Magnanimous King of Aragon, Naples, and Sicily 1396-1458*, Oxford 1990; on the artistic representation of these rulers see conveniently A. Cole, *Art of the Italian Renaissance Courts*, London 1995; M. Hollingsworth, *Patronage in Renaissance Italy*, London 1994; C. Woods-Marsden "Art and political identity in fifteenth-century Naples: Pisanello, Cristoforo di Geremia, and King Alfonso's imperial fantasies", in C.M. Rosenberg (ed.), *Art and politics in late medieval and Renaissance Italy, 1250-1500*, Notre Dame, IN 1990, 11-37.

12. I owe this observation to work in progress at the British School at Rome by Peter Stacey.

and who were to some extent influenced by the republican tradition of Florence, to the needs of monarchy.[13] Public building projects under the Aragonese kings, notably the triumphal arch in the Castelnuovo, gave further emphasis to imperial imagery, and stressed the victories of the royal house over its French rivals who, of course, remained serious challengers for the loyalty of the south Italian barons [14]. The Neapolitan court also looked northwards for inspiration; cultural links to Flanders were accentuated by diplomatic contacts with the Burgundian dukes and other rulers; particularly in music, Ferrante showed himself dependent on Flemish models [15]. However, one famous dancing master who took employment for a time with Ferrante was a converted Jew: Guglielmo Ebreo da Pesaro, also known as Giovanni Ambrosio [16].

There is no need here to examine the often tiresome disputes among the scholars at the royal court, where Valla, Facio and Panormita (Beccadelli) vied for influence under Alfonso the Magnanimous; in the later years of Ferrante the dominant scholar at court was Giovanni Gioviano Pontano, 'poet and prime minister' [17]. The writing of laudatory histories of the dynasty's achievements was an important activity of several of these scholars. There does, however, seem to have been a significant change of emphasis under Alfonso's heir in Naples, his illegitimate son Ferrante or Ferdinand, whose lengthy reign, from 1458 to 1494, saw a growing interest in more practical learning, particularly the study of law; in this light, it is not surprising that the king gave active encouragement to the University of Naples, to the extent that he (rather than Frederick II) perhaps deserves most credit for generating it into life [18]. He also extended his protection to the German printers who were arriving in his kingdom; one of the early works to appear off the presses in Naples, in 1475, was Sixtus Rießinger's edition of the so-called *Liber Augustalis* (1231), the major collection of laws issued by Frederick II for the kingdom of Sicily [19]. Other early books included the *Epistola magni Turci* of Mehmet II, printed in 1473 by Arnaldus of Brussels, and an edition of Beccadelli's *Epistolae familiares*, from the presses of Rießinger. The northern printer based in Naples M. Moravus printed works by Pontano in 1481, 1490 and 1491 [20]. The royal librarian Giovanni Brancati prepared several encomia of the monarchy and was himself responsible for gathering together an imposing collection of books, including several magnificent illu-

13. Bentley, *Politics and Culture*, 288-9.

14. G.L. Hersey, *The Aragonese arch at Naples, 1443-1475*, New Haven, CT 1973.

15. Atlas, *Music at the Aragonese court*, 58.

16. Guglielmo Ebreo of Pesaro, *De pratica seu arte tripudii. On the practice or art of dancing*, ed. A. Sparti, Oxford 1993.

17. Bentley, *Politics and Culture*, 84-137.

18. David Abulafia, "Introduction: from Ferrante I to Charles VIII", in David Abulafia (ed.), *The French descent into Renaissance Italy*, Aldershot 1995, 13; similarly, David Abulafia, *The Western Mediterranean Kingdoms 1200-1500. The struggle for dominion*, London 1997, 234.

19. *Constitutiones regni Siciliae 'Liber Augustalis' Neapel 1475*. Faksimiledruck mit einer Einleitung von Hermann Dilcher, Glashütten/Taunus 1973.

20. Copies are in the Bodleian Library, Oxford.

minated volumes, handwritten or printed on vellum [21]; a fraction of this collection is now preserved in the Biblioteca General of Valencia University and the Bibliothèque Nationale, but much of its contents can be traced to contemporary catalogues, which formed the basis for an impressive modern reconstruction of the royal library by de Marinis [22]. Books dedicated to the king or his son and heir Alfonso II included an Italian translation by Landino of Pliny the Elder's *Natural History*, printed in Venice in 1476 [23], Flavio Biondo's *Decades* (Naples, 1494) [24] and Andrea Contrario's *Reprehensio sive objurgatio in calumniatorem divini Platonis* of 1471 [25] as well as a Latin and an Italian version of part of Livy for Alfonso of Calabria [26]; other books that can definitely be linked to the court included Duns Scotus' *Quaestiones* on the *Sentences* of Peter Lombard [27], and copies of the works of Vergil and Horace [28]. Brancati in one of his encomia of King Ferrante laid much emphasis on the quality of the Greek authors, though it was a Neapolitan baron, Antonello Petrucci, who perhaps possessed the most thorough collection of Greek manuscripts [29].

How many Hebrew books were in the original collection? To judge from the contemporary catalogues the royal library contained none, neither among the manuscript collection nor among the printed books. De Marinis' catalogue, updated by Denise Bloch and others, offers only one Hebrew text, on the very tenuous basis of the Aragonese royal arms which appear on an early page: this is the celebrated Sarajevo Haggadah, which it is more likely to have remained in Jewish hands at this period, and no case can be made for placing it in the royal collection [30]. That it passed through Italy on its long journey from Spain to Bosnia is clear, but there is no safe link to Naples. Some Arabic

21. For Brancati see Bentley, *Politics and Culture*, 65-71, 169-71, 181-2, 214-15. Several of the volumes referred to here, from the libraries of Alfonso and Ferrante, are included in the catalogue of an exhibition in London and New York: J.J.G. Alexander (ed.), *The Painted Page. Italian Renaissance book illumination, 1450-1550*, London/New York 1994.

22. T. de Marinis, *La biblioteca napoletana dei re d'Aragona*, 4 vols., Milano 1947-52; *La biblioteca napoletana dei re d'Aragona: supplemento*, ed. D. Bloch et al., 2 vols., Verona 1969.

23. Bodleian Library, Oxford, Bod. Arch. G. b. 6.

24. Staatsbibliothek, Munich, Clm. 11324.

25. Bibliothèque Nationale, Paris, BN lat. 12947.

26. British Library, London, Harley 3694; Biblioteca Universitaria General, Valencia MS 386.

27. British Library, London, Add MS 15270-2; Bibliothèque Nationale, Paris, BN lat. 3063.

28. Biblioteca Universitaria General, Valencia, MSS 891, 837.

29. De Marinis, *Supplemento*, I, 247-53; his library included orations by Brancati, with whom he corresponded: Giovanni P. Carratelli, "Un'epistola di Giovanni Brancati sull'arte retorica e lo scriver latino", *Atti dell'Accademia Pontaniana*, n.s. 2 (1948/9), 109-23 [using Biblioteca Universitaria General, Valencia, MS 774]. Petrucci was the son of a peasant gardener: Bentley, *Politics and Culture*, 31-2, 214-15, 281-3; but other nobles of bluer blood also had good collections of books: *Supplemento*, I, for the libraries of Anghilberto del Balzo, Pietro di Guevara and other great princes toppled in 1485 after the second baronial revolt.

30. *Supplemento*, I, 54; *Sarajevo Haggadah*, facsimile, Belgrade/Sarajevo 1983) f. 3r; on the arms, see E. Werber, *The Sarajevo Haggadah*, Sarajevo 1988, 22, credibly ascribing the original ownership of the MS to the Barcelona Jewish élite.

texts in translation, such as the hunting book of Moamyn (a favourite of Frederick II as well) were in the library. Josephus' *De bello Judaico*, which was not, of course, used by Jews in the Middle Ages, appears among a group of printed books pawned by the king in 1481, to raise money for the struggle against the Turkish occupiers of Otranto [31]. But most of the books were classical or patristic texts, in some cases probably duplicates. The works of Abrabanel, with their flattering references to the king, do not feature in any library catalogue, even though those of Christian courtiers such as Beccadelli, Carafa and Pontano could be found.

Among the Neapolitan nobility, who suffered massive confiscations of their books and other property after the baronial rebellion of 1485, items of Jewish interest are also hard to find. Angilberto del Balzo, count of Ducente, owned a manuscript copy of a work which was to feature among the early printed texts of Naples: the letter attributed to Rabbi Samuel of Fez, sent to Rabbi Isaac of Sijilmasa *De adventu Messiae*; the count's copy was bound with the work *De fide in Christum adversus Judeos et Sarracenos* of the converted Jewish aristocrat Pedro de la Caballeria [32]. Pietro di Guevara, prince of Sirignano and Marchese del Vasto, possessed a copy of a work which, as will be seen, Jewish physicians in Naples also used: Avicenna's *Canon*; however, this was a manuscript copy of Gerard of Cremona's translation from the Arabic, whereas the evidence for Jewish use concerns a printed Hebrew edition [33]. Lest it be thought that de Marinis and his successors simply failed to look for Hebrew manuscripts and incunabula in the Neapolitan royal and noble libraries, it should be stressed that the catalogues that survive from this period are often quite detailed, and show close attention to the language in which books were written. The conclusion must therefore be that the warm feelings that the monarchy showed towards the Jews were in no way matched by a serious interest in Jewish learning, such as had occasionally been shown by earlier rulers of southern Italy, and such as could be found in some parts of northern Italy, notably in the circle of Pico della Mirandola, where close attention was being paid to the kabbalistic texts of Abraham ben Samuel Abulafia [34].

III

The second issue that needs to be examined at this point is the status of the Jewish communities in Aragonese Naples. The contrast with Spain, even in the difficult conditions that beset the Sephardim between the pogroms of 1391 and the expulsion of 1492,

---

31. *Supplemento*, I, 97, 101.

32. *Supplemento*, I, 185 [now Bibliothèque Nationale, Paris, BN lat. 3362]; cf. Ferorelli, *Gli Ebrei nell'Italia meridionale*, 181, illustrating the edition printed by Francesco di Dino, Napoli 1478-80 [Biblioteca Nazionale, Napoli S.Q. III. C.29]. See on the Fez letter O. Limor, "The epistle of Rabbi Samuel of Morocco: a best-seller in the world of polemics", *Contra Iudaeos. Ancient and medieval polemics between Christians and Jews*, ed. O. Limor and G.G. Stroumsa, Tübingen 1996, 177-94.

33. *Supplemento*, I, 193.

34. C. Wirszubski, *Pico della Mirandola's encounter with Jewish mysticism*, Cambridge, MA 1989.

is striking. The lack of a figure comparable to the *rab de la corte*, or of court Jews generally, was only altered with the arrival of Don Isaac Abrabanel from Spain in 1492. Despite the existence of wealthy *neofiti* in Apulia, strongly suspected of retaining a loyalty to the Judaism their ancestors had been forced to abandon around 1290, the Jewish communities of southern Italy do not appear to have produced the élite families which still exercised so much power and influence in *Sepharad*[35]. To a native community of artisans, often heavily engaged in the cloth industry, as dyers or weavers, was added from the early fifteenth century a new population of Jews who migrated southwards in search of *condotte* permitting them to establish loan banks in the south Italian towns, similar to those that were springing up in northern and central Italy[36]. The communities themselves were spread out across the kingdom, and Apulia, despite the depredations of the late thirteenth century, remained an important centre of settlement[37]. On the other hand, Calabria grew in importance with the arrival of large numbers of Sicilian Jews at the start of 1493, though Reggio, as will be seen, already had played a significant role in the history of Hebrew printing[38].

By the time of King Ferrante the involvement of the south Italian Jews generally in loan banking had become a marked feature of their economic life. Ferrante himself, true to the tradition of his Aragonese forebears, valued the Jews as an economic resource; even before the expulsion of the Jews from Spain and Sicily had been enacted, he was asking his officials to note the *artificio* of each immigrant Jew, hoping that their presence would further benefit an economy that, according to the latest research, was undergoing significant recovery in his reign[39]. Ferrante made a special effort to welcome the Jews expelled from Spain and Sicily, and it is possible that the new arrivals doubled the existing Jewish population of the *Regno*. This set off tensions, long latent, between Christians and Jews, accentuated by fears that the Jews were bringing disease with them from Spain. Ferrante's officials were constantly reminded that the king cherished his Jewish subjects, to whom he was prepared to grant considerable liberties, both in commerce and in citizenship rights: the phrase *amamus et diligimus* that he applied to the Jews was not, perhaps, simply a formality, but reflected his genuine concern that they should be treated *umanamente*[40]. Isaac Abrabanel responded to such gestures with the opinion that the Aragonese rulers were 'princes of mercy and righteousness'. From this outlook has developed a strong historiographical tradition, extending through Cecil Roth to Louis Jacobs' eloquent accla-

---

35. V. Vitale, "Un particolare ignorato di storia pugliese: neofiti e mercanti", *Studi in onore di Michelangelo Schipa*, Napoli 1926, 233-46.

36. Abulafia, "Il Mezzogiorno peninsulare", 26-9.

37. For the crisis of Apulian Jewry c.1300 see David Abulafia, "Monarchs and minorities in the late medieval western Mediterranean: Lucera and its analogues", Scott L. Waugh and Peter D. Diehl (eds.), *Christendom and its Discontents. Exclusion, persecution and rebellion, 1000-1500*, Cambridge 1996, 234-63.

38. C. Colafemmina, "The Jews of Reggio Calabria from the end of the fifteenth century to the beginning of the sixteenth century", in G. Dahan (ed.), *Les juifs au regard de l'histoire*, Paris 1985, 255-62.

39. Abulafia, "Il Mezzogiorno peninsulare", 37.

40. Abulafia, "Il Mezzogiorno peninsulare", 30, 36.

mation of Ferrante as one of the 'righteous among the Gentiles' [41]. He was anxious to suppress hostile rumours (in the age of Simon of Trent) against the Jews [42]; the contrast with many, though not all, north and central Italian courts, such as that of Ludovico il Moro, is instructive [43]. But the fact that Ferrante's realm was the last place east of the Turkish Balkans in which a policy of *convivencia* seemed to be practised does not mean that it was at this time the seat of a great Jewish scholarly tradition.

IV

It was into this setting that the eminent Sephardi courtier Isaac Abrabanel and his family came in the Summer of 1492, carrying a thousand gold ducats, his books and other valuables, on the basis of which he was able to restore his fortunes in Naples [44]. It is not surprising that Ferrante greeted his arrival with acclaim, and gave him a place at court, where he was to remain until January 1495, just as the French armies were poised to strike Naples, at which point he left in the company of Alfonso II for Sicily; widespread popular hostility to the Aragonese dynasty, which had been mounting over the years, was accompanied by growing menaces towards the Jews as protégés of the dynasty [45]. It would perhaps be artificial to separate out Abrabanel's writings in Naples, or those he produced during his seven and a half year stay in the Venetian held port of Monopoli in Apulia (beginning at the end of 1495), from his vast oeuvre. They were the product of his intellectual formation in Portugal and Spain, where he had, in the tradition of the Sephardi élite, been exposed to a wide range of learning, extending far beyond the traditional Hebrew syllabus; his knowledge of Seneca and Cicero, not to mention Jerome, and his ability to challenge the Aristotelian framework accepted by Maimonides, set him on a special level [46]. Netanyahu draws a flattering comparison between Pontano and Abrabanel, even though he can only speculate about how intimate their contact may have been; it has been seen that the royal library, at any rate, was bereft of Hebrew books. Certainly, Pontano was one of those courtiers who supported Ferrante's policy of protecting the Jews. But Netanyahu goes on to note that Pontano, like many leading Jewish scholars in Italy, was a 'confirmed Aristotelian', whereas Abrabanel's claim to fame rests in significant

41. Netanyahu, *Abravanel*, 186, 312; C. Roth, *The History of the Jews of Italy*, Philadelphia, 5706/1946, 275-9; Louis Jacobs, *The Book of Jewish Belief*, New York 1984, 44.

42. R. Po-Chia Hsia, *Trent 1475*, New Haven 1992, is disappointingly brief on the diffusion of the legend of Simon of Trent.

43. Daniel Bueno de Mesquita, "The Conscience of the Prince", *Proceedings of the British Academy*, 64 (1979), repr. in G. Holmes (ed.), *Art and Politics in Renaissance Italy*, Oxford 1993), 166-8.

44. Netanyahu, *Abravanel*, 60-4; his stay in Sicily, already *Judenfrei*, was only rendered possible by Alfonso's patronage.

45. Netanyahu, *Abravanel*, 68-71.

46. Netanyahu, *Abravanel*, 304, 309 for links, positive and negative, with Seneca's thought e.g. in *De Clementia*; cfr. the comment *supra* that Seneca's works had considerable influence on the outlook of the Aragonese rulers of Naples.

measure on his resistance to the Aristotelians. Netanyahu then asks about 'the extent to which Abravanel was influenced – if influenced at all – by any of the Neapolitan spiritual leaders'.[47] However, there is so little secure information about the outlook of the leaders of the Jewish community in this period that no conclusions can be reached.

Abrabanel's work in Naples does in some respects reflect his new circumstances. He completed his commentary on *Kings I and II* while in Naples, and took the opportunity to express fulsomely his regard for the king.[48] But his new king seems to have valued him for his political and financial skills more than his scholarly ones. Abrabanel also wrote on the nature of divine justice in the light of his and his contemporaries' experience of renewed exile and their sense of abandonment by God.[49] On the other hand, it is not always at all clear how his experiences in Naples affected the development of his thought, for example his attitude to monarchs and city republics, which is largely based on the constitution attributed to Moses in the Torah, and on the negative image of King Saul, as opposed to the positive image of King David; there is an added irony in this, since his was one of those Sephardi families that claimed descent from David.[50] 'The existence of a king is not at all essential for a people', he says, while the Venetian constitution wins his great praise: Venice is a 'princess among the nations'.[51] Just as well, perhaps, that the king probably did not try to understand what he was writing. His own interest in Seneca and Cicero might be expected to have fitted well with the outlook of several Christian scholars at court; Netanyahu, however, insists on placing his views about the imminent coming of the Messiah alongside the prophetic message of Savonarola.[52]

These views acquired added force after the French invasion of 1495, the destruction of much of his library by a hostile mob in Naples, his journey into Sicilian exile with King Alfonso II, and his period of residence in Monopoli; this town lay under Venetian control after the Venetians intervened in the war for Naples, and thus provided a reasonably safe haven, even though there too there had been anti-Jewish demonstrations at the time of French invasion.[53] The consensus appears to be that Abrabanel owed most to the classical tradition in a negative sense: his rejection of Aristotelianism and of the entire naturalistic

---

47. Netanyahu, *Abravanel*, 66.

48. Abrabanel's commentary on the earlier prophets was printed at Pesaro in 1511/12.

49. Netanyahu, *Abravanel*, 65, 316-17.

50. H.J. Zimmels, *Ashkenazim and Sephardim. Their relations, differences, and problems as reflected in the rabbinical responsa*, London 1958, 283: such claims were of course a way in which leading Sephardi families consolidated their authority.

51. Netanyahu, *Abravanel*, 169-70.

52. Without however offering any more than circumstantial evidence of influence by Savonarola upon Don Isaac: Netanyahu, *Abravanel*, 193, 242-7.

53. For Monopoli and its Jews, see Abulafia, "Mezzogiorno peninsulare", 40-1; C. Colafemmina, *Documenti per la storia degli Ebrei in Puglia nell'Archivio di Stato di Napoli*, Bari 1990, 80. For the Venetian presence, see C. Kidwell, "Venice, the French invasion and the Apulian ports", David Abulafia, *French Descent*, 295-308. But, contrary to what has been claimed, Monopoli was not actually a centre of Hebrew printing, even of Abrabanel's works: Ferorelli, *Gli Ebrei nell'Italia meridionale*, 279-83; Abulafia, "Il Mezzogiorno peninsulare", 33; cfr. Bloch, "Hebrew printing in Naples", 115-16.

interpretation associated with Maimonides' *Guide of the Perplexed*. A different case can be made, however, for his son Judah (Leone Ebreo), with his overpowering interest in the neo-Platonic tradition; since much of his work was composed after the fall of the Aragonese dynasty in Naples, it falls outside the period of this paper. A different case again can be made for a quite different scholar, Messer David ben Judah Leon, from Mantua, who studied in his father's *yeshivah* at Naples, but took a contrary position on Maimonides to Abrabanel; his own career took him beyond Italy to Vlorë in Albania, but it is clear that he imbibed deeply in philosophy and other aspects of more general culture. His family will be encountered again shortly, in the realms of the printing press. He is the best clue we have to the cultural outlook of the intellectual leaders of the Jewish community in Naples at this time, even though his own contribution to the intellectual life of that community was probably very limited.

At this stage, then, it can be concluded that Naples at the end of the fifteenth century was not in itself a major centre of Jewish scholarship, so much as a place to which, perforce, Jews from Spain, Sicily and also northern Italy were migrating, as the one haven of any size left in southern Europe, at a time of expulsions and mass conversions. Though Abrabanel brought with him substantial intellectual baggage, his response to the problems of the time was to emphasize the apocalyptic nature of the age, setting the expulsion from Spain alongside the French invasion of Italy and the constant menace of a massive Turkish war on Christendom. All this he saw as a sign that shortly the Messiah would come; he could even offer a date in the very near future. There are interesting similarities here with the situation two hundred years earlier, when the kabbalist Abraham Abulafia had gone to Sicily in the midst of the War of the Vespers also in the expectation that the promised time was nigh. [54]

V

The really substantial evidence for intellectual activity among the Jews of the *Regno* is to be found in an analysis of their printed books. In his *Thesaurus typographiae Hebraicae* of 1924-31, A. Freimann identified up to twenty-two printed Hebrew books from Naples in the period 1487 to 1492, though some of his identifications were speculative, and more can now be added. But the first Hebrew book to be printed in southern Italy, dating to 17 February 1475, was the work of Abraham ben Garton ben Isaac, printing at Reggio di Calabria; it was an edition of Rashi's very popular Torah commentary, and the strategic position of Reggio may have made it an ideal place from which to try to serve both the Sicilian and the south Italian book market. [55] This initiative had no known aftermath, and the initiative passed by the mid-1480's to the German family of Joseph ben Jacob Ashkenazi, known from his place of origin as Gunzenhausen. The

54. Abulafia, *Western Mediterranean Kingdoms*, 101-3; Moshe Idel, *The mystical experience in Abraham Abulafia*, Albany, NY 1988, 3.
55. *Thesaurus*, plate A 1, 1-3: Rashi, *Perush ha-Torah*, Reggio Calabria, 17 February 1475 [in rabbinic script].

first clear evidence for printing operations in Naples comes from a notarial act of 19 March 1487, a quittance drawn up in Latin by Marco Laudario on behalf of two Jews, Emmanuel de Cave and Elya Volgheri. [56] According to the notarial minute, they had set up an enterprise with *magistro Iacob hebreo et magistro Iosep hebreo theotonicis*; the aim of the investment was *ad Instampandum libros*, and it was Emmanuel who actually provided the money, while Elya, Joseph and Jacob were to provide 'their persons', that is, the necessary skills and labour. The time scale of the agreement is, somewhat strangely, not specified, but it is made plain that Elya agreed to renounce any share of the profits (*lucrum*), while Emmanuel rewarded Elya for his efforts with thirty *carleni* of silver. The agreement was witnessed by four non-Jews, the use by Jews of a Christian notary is not a great surprise, and was common, for example, in Catalonia and in Sicily as far back as 1300. [57] The Jewish printers Joseph and Jacob are almost without a doubt Jacob Landau, of whom more shortly, and Joseph Gunzenhausen. Indeed, the notarial act coincides fairly closely with the date of the earliest Gunzenhausen book recorded by Freimann, the edition of the Psalms with Kimhi's commentary dating to 28 March 1487. [58] However, older Gunzenhausen books do survive: the great project of continuing the Soncino edition of the Bible led to the production in 1486 of *Job, Chronicles I and II* and *Proverbs*. Copies of all these are in Cambridge University Library. [59] Bloch observed that the project of publishing these works from *Ketubim* was a logical accompaniment to the printing operations that had been going ahead in northern Italy, where the Bologna Torah had been followed in Soncino by an edition of the early and later prophets (*Nebi'im*), dating to 1485 and 1486. [60] The Naples edition of these sections of *Ketubim* was physically of the same size, and the letter faces too were very similar. How far this should be seen as a competitive attempt to corner the market in that part of the Bible which the Soncino press had still not produced it is hard to say. More probably it was part of what was seen as a great and holy collaborative exercise that one press alone would find it hard to complete without long delays. In fact, the Soncino press could not be maintained in the north of Italy, where conditions for the Jews were worsening, and the Soncino press was taken south; archival evidence shows that a press was being set up in Naples by the Soncinos in March 1489. [61] On 25 May 1490 Joshua Solomon Soncino issued his first Neapolitan product, an edition of the Sephardi prayer-book, to be

56. Text in Bloch, "Hebrew printing in Naples", 137-8; also 118, n. 17; first published by M. Fava and G. Bresciano, *La stampa a Napoli nel XV secolo*, 2 vols., Leipzig 1911), I, 191-2, doc. 18; see also Offenberg, 'Hebreeuwse Incunabelen', 179.

57. For example at Erice: David Abulafia, "Yehudei Erice (Monte San Giuliano) sheb' Sitsiliah, 1298-1304", *Zion: a quarterly for research in Jewish history*, 51 (1986), 295-317; [Italian edition: "Una comunità ebraica della Sicilia occidentale: Erice 1298-1304", *Archivio storico per la Sicilia orientale*, 80 (1984), 157-90].

58. *Thesaurus*, plate A 57, 1-2.

59. University Library, Cambridge. Inc. 3.B.11.14 [2103-2105].

60. Bloch, "Hebrew printing in Naples", 119 for the prayer-book; for later works, see Thesaurus, plates A 69, 73, 75, 98-100.

61. Frattarolo, *Tipografi e librai, ebrei e non*, 10-12; Offenberg, "Hebreeuwse Incunabelen", 179.

followed by editions of biblical texts and a *Mishnah* with Maimonides' commentary. [62]

Important as was the arrival of German printers, who were thus working in Naples alongside the other, non-Jewish, German printers such as Sixtus Rießinger who have already been mentioned, the Gunzenhausens themselves came with, or invited to Naples, an entourage of scholars. Samuel ben Samuel of Rome may have been involved in the production of some mysterious early Hebrew printed books attributed to Rome; Bloch speculated that the emphasis in Naples on the printing of Biblical texts (and, indeed, commentaries) rather than on liturgical works reflected the prior existence of printed prayer-books from other presses. [63] Hayyim ben Isaac ha-Levi Ashkenazi (who edited *Proverbs* with the commentary of Immanuel Romano) and Jacob Baruch ben Judah Landau were German members of the team, with Landau playing a major role as proof-reader. [64] But scholars came from elsewhere too, and Shemtob ibn Habib was a member of a distinguished Spanish family of rabbis. Indeed, one of the printers active in Naples in this period was himself a Spaniard, Isaac ben Judah ibn Katorzi (Quatorze) of Cala-tayud in Aragon, who was to publish Nahmanides' commentary on the Torah and Ki-mhi's 'Book of Roots' in 1490. [65]

Jacob ben Judah Landau was well aware of the responsibilities that lay with him, stating in the colophon to his edition of the Psalms, where he described himself as 'a German now sojourning in Naples':

> I, the undersigned, come to excuse myself. Having been appointed to superintend this work, to correct the book daily according to the custom of those who are engaged in this art, I say if errors are found in the punctuation of the text, they are due to two causes. One is that we who are engaged in this art have only recently taken it up as beginners, and that our fathers had no idea of this art. It has always been recognised that every beginning is difficult and we have had not as yet suffi-cient time to practise thoroughly as we ought in the matter of vowel points. The second reason is that in spite of our exertions we have not succeeded in finding the requisite codices. Hence if errors are found in it, they are few, more especially when compared with other books, which have hitherto been printed. [66]

Even a quick examination of the text reveals that there are abundant errors in the Hebrew text of the Psalms. [67] However, the letters *dalet* and *he* are sometimes confused in the printing, a simple enough confusion for someone working with tiny letters, which suggests that many of the errors resulted from lack of skill. Still, it is interesting to hear Judah Landau's complaint about the lack of availability of reliable texts; clearly the kin-

---

62. Bloch, "Hebrew printing in Naples", 121-2.

63. Bloch, "Hebrew printing in Naples", 118.

64. Bloch, "Hebrew printing in Naples", 120-2.

65. *Thesaurus*, plates A 65, 1-3 and 66, 1-2, correcting the printer's name to Katorzi (Quatorze), of Ca-latayud; see Offenberg, "Hebreeuwse Incunabelen", 182-3.

66. For the edition, see *Thesaurus*, plate A 57, 1-2. The text is from de Rossi, *Annales*, 48-9, in the tran-slation of Bloch, "Hebrew printing in Naples", 125.

67. University Library, Cambridge, Inc. 3.B.11.14 [2107]; this copy has censor's erasions.

gdom of Naples was not a repository of what could be regarded as sound copies of the Bible texts. The interests of the Hebrew printers were squarely fixed on the Bible, and yet they began to spread out to encompass key classics in medieval Jewish religious literature. Bahya ibn Paquda's *Hobot ha-Lebabot* ('Duties of the Heart') was produced in a quarto edition in 1489, while David Kimhi's *Sefer ha-Shorashim*, 'Book of Roots', came out in a folio edition during the following year; [68] this must have been rapidly exhausted, since a new edition followed only five or six months later. [69] Mehlman cites Bahya's ascetic message, implying that it was this that brought it great popularity in Italy at this time: I have seen that perfect union with God cannot exist when the heart of the believer is intoxicated with a love of the world. [70]

But the interest in grammatical works, visible in the attention paid to Kimhi, also had more modest expression in the work known as the *Makre Dardeke* ('Teacher of Children'), which consisted of glosses of biblical Hebrew words in Italian and Arabic, both, however, printed in Hebrew characters. [71] Versions of this text went back to the fourteenth century. It would be interesting to know what audience existed for the Arabic glosses; the Jews of Sicily had by this time generally abandoned their customary use of Arabic as a vernacular. [72] *Petah Debarai* ('The opening of my words') was another grammatical work, printed in 1492, that had more remote antecedents: the text originated in thirteenth-century Spain. [73] Such interest in Hebrew grammar no doubt reflects the needs of a *yeshivah* or similar institution in Naples itself in the 1480's. However, some works, such as Nahmanides' *Sha'ar ha-Gemul* ('Gate of Reward'), printed in 1490, were of particular interest to those who delved into kabbalah [74].

Bible commentaries were of course popular alongside the Bible texts themselves: it has been seen that Katorzi printed a copy of Nahmanides' commentary in 1490, and that the earliest south Italian Hebrew printed book was in fact an edition of Rashi's commentary on the Pentateuch. Among the early products of Joshua Solomon di Soncino in Naples, after the Soncino press moved southwards, was an edition of the *Mishnah* with the commentary of Maimonides, and elaborate accompanying diagrams

---

68. Both in Cambridge University Library: for Bahya, see Inc. 5 B.11.14 [2109], also *Thesaurus*, plate A 63, 1-3; for Kimhi, see Inc. 3 B.11.14 [2110], and also *Thesaurus*, A 66, 1-2.

69. The "Book of Roots" in its second, Soncino, edition of 1491 (*Thesaurus*, plates 69, 1a-b) shared a decorative border with the Nahmanides Torah commentary printed by Gunzenhausen in 1490 (*Thesaurus*, plates A 65, 1-3): Offenberg, "Hebreeuwse Incunabelen", 190.

70. Mehlman, "First fruits", *Thesaurus* supplement [printed without pagination].

71. *Thesaurus*, plates A 61, 1-2; Mehlman, "First fruits"; also Bloch, "Hebrew printing in Naples", 128-9; Offenberg, "Hebreeuwse Incunabelen", p. 182.

72. On which see the comments of Abraham ben Samuel Abulafia, *Ozar 'Eden ganuz*, edited in part by A. Neubauer, *Revue des études juives*, 9 (1884), 149; also cited by Roth, *History of the Jews of Italy*, p. 82, and in David Abulafia, "The end of Muslim Sicily", in J.M. Powell (ed.), *Muslims under Latin rule, 1100-1300*, Princeton, NJ 1990), 117-18, with further comments on the use of Arabic by Sicilian Jews.

73. Bloch, "Hebrew printing in Naples", 129.

74. *Thesaurus*, plates A 64, 1-2.

(1492). [75] Without examining the finer, and important, differences between Rashi, Nahmanides and other major commentators, it is clear that the Hebrew presses in Naples concentrated heavily on the production of the classic works of Jewish scholarship. Some exceptions to this general rule will be examined shortly. As a community placed between the different liturgical and rabbinic traditions of Sepharad and Ashkenaz, the Jews of southern Italy were open to influences from both directions, all the more so when Naples became a place of employment for German rabbis, and of refuge for Spanish ones.

A rare example of a Hebrew book printed while its author was still alive was the *Agur* of Jacob Landau, whose efforts in proof-reading have already been mentioned. Written around 1480, it was printed about a decade later, and was intended to offer a handy guide to the basic laws of Judaism, those that any lay person might be expected to observe; the framework was that of Ashkenazi Judaism. [76] Amram and Bloch thought it the last Hebrew book published in Naples, but other authorities indicate several later volumes. [77] The use in this volume of rabbinic approbations to recommend the book to readers was apparently unprecedented, borrowed from the practice of contemporary Christian publications. Eight rabbis, probably the learned core of the Naples community, added their *hechsher* to this book; the names themselves are interesting, containing that of the soon-to-be illustrious David ben Judah Messer Leon, as well as Messer Leon himself, and that of the Sephardi Moses ben Shemtob ibn Habib, whose role in proof-reading has already been cited. Other rabbis hailed from Jerusalem and from Marseilles. Messer Leon stated:

> Behold, I have seen that which our distinguished master and teacher Jacob Landau has wrought, who has compiled a valuable book called *Agur* wherein he has gathered and collected the laws of the daily service and of the festivals and all that is forbidden and allowed, and all matters thereunto appertaining. And it is a work that giveth goodly words concerning customs and important decisions. Therefore I have set my hand to these drippings of the honeycomb, these words of pleasantness. [78]

Indeed, the need for summations of Jewish practice was all the greater in an age when Jews were being forced to migrate or under constant pressure to convert, and there was a fear that Jews would lose touch with law and tradition.

More difficult to identify are works which come from the world of secular knowledge. Azriel ben Joseph Gunzenhausen issued a Hebrew edition of a key medical work,

---

75. *Thesaurus*, plates A 73, 1-8; complete and second partial copy in Cambridge: University Library, Inc. 2 B.11.16 [2111-12].

76. *Thesaurus*, plates A 67, 1-3. The decorative border used for the title-page was used again for the Soncino edition of the Psalms, Job and Proverbs of 12 December 1490 (*Thesaurus*, plates A 68, 1-4); see Offenberg, "Hebreeuwse Incunabelen", p. 189.

77. D.W. Amram, *Makers of Hebrew books in Italy*, Philadelphia 1909, p. 66; Bloch, "Hebrew printing in Naples", 22-3.

78. Cited in the translation of Amaram, *Makers of Hebrew books*, 66.

the *Canon* of Avicenna, published in five parts in 1491-2; [79] there was already a printed Latin version, published in Padua in 1472 by Bartholomaeus Valdezocchus and Martinus de Septem Arboribus. The Hebrew version is eloquent evidence for the role of the Jews in medicine within the kingdom of Naples; it is confirmed by Ferorelli's reconstruction of the career of Abramo de Balmes, who from 1466 onwards was exercising his skills, becoming by 1472 the physician for life of the royal family; the Balmes family also had the benefit of papal protection. [80] In 1472 Ferrante accorded Abramo de Balmes a pension of three hundred ducats per annum. He and his own family were exempted from various taxes, especially in their home base of Lecce; he himself died around 1489. Another Jewish doctor at court was Guglielmo di Portaleone. Their medical knowledge perhaps had some political importance, guaranteeing the favourable outlook of the crown towards the Jews; but, with the exception of this volume of Avicenna, it is rather difficult to see on what authorities their medical knowledge was based. Abramo's grandson and namesake, however, appears to have penetrated deeper into the secular culture of the time, taking a degree in medicine, with royal and papal approval, at the University of Naples in 1492. He left southern Italy around 1510, becoming known in the north of Italy, until his death in 1523, both for his medical skills and for his ability to expound Averroes (translating Hebrew versions of the Arabic originals). That he must have developed some of his interests as a young man in Naples seems very likely; but much of his output was stimulated by the patronage of Cardinal Domenico Grimani in Venice, and even so several major works, such as a study based on the work of the Arabic philosopher ibn Bajja (Avempace), were left in manuscript. It is impossible to locate his career as a philosopher and grammarian securely within the Aragonese kingdom of Naples, which had ceased to exist by the time he was active in scholarship. [81]

VI

No less difficult is the question how the books were distributed. A document of 10 May 1491, published in part by Ferorelli, shows Davit Bono the Jew, an inhabitant of Naples, and *mercator librorum de stampa*. He wishes to travel in person, and to send his agents, through the lands of the kingdom in order to sell his books. In view of King Ferrante's wish that 'per li libri de stampa non se paga diricto alcuno de dohana', the *Regia Camera della Sommaria* declares Davit exempt from any sort of tax, of which several are named, on his books, and insists that he can travel with and sell his books without impediment; any transgressor will be liable for a fine of 25 ounces (150 ducats) [82]. A similar pronouncement was made the same day for Graciadei Rout, another Jewish seller of printed books, who also came from Naples. Such orders were needed because, whate-

79. *Thesaurus*, plates A 71, 1-2.
80. Ferorelli, *Gli Ebrei nell'Italia meridionale*, 263-75.
81. C. Roth, *The Jews in the Renaissance*, Philadelphia 1959, 76-7; Amram, *Makers of Hebrew books*, 169-72; Ferorelli, *Gli Ebrei nell'Italia meridionale*, 263-75.
82. Ferorelli, *Gli Ebrei nell'Italia meridionale*, 134, 280.

ver the fine intentions of the royal government, the provincial administration paid them all too little attention. This was a particularly severe problem for the Jews; constantly the crown reminded its agents in the provinces that they must indeed respect the rights of the Jews and restore any damage done to them. Whether it was in particular Jewish booksellers who had problems making sure their tax exemptions were respected is uncertain; Ferorelli found an example of another merchant, a Venetian Christian named Alexandro de Ludovico, who in 1477 complained at the taxes charged him when bringing books from Venice through Trani to Naples. In 1491 some French Christian booksellers based in Naples asked for a certificate of immunity. [83] Such difficulties perhaps afflicted foreign merchants and Jews more than others.

In any case, the Jew Davit Bono had precisely the trouble he anticipated. He went to Molfetta with sixteen boxes of books which he intended to export from the kingdom. He presented the documents issued to him by the *dohanero* of Naples making it plain that he was exempt from sales tax on his books: all to no effect. He was charged 25 *carlini*, and the head of the customs house of Molfetta was ordered on 6 September 1491 to restore that sum to him. [84] It is interesting to see that he planned to take the books out of the *Regno*. From Molfetta he could have sent them north to Venice, across to Dubrovnik, or into Ottoman lands (Vlorë or Avlona, where Messer David ben Judah Leon was to be rabbi, was only a short run across the straits). [85] Not just books but woodcuts used in the printing industry were carried eastwards into Ottoman lands in this period, as Eva Frojmovic has shown in an elegant study of the few remaining leaves of a Haggadah printed according to the Sephardi rite in Constantinople, but containing woodcuts prepared in Naples for the workshop of Francesco del Tuppo. [86]

There is no reason to suppose Davit Bono traded solely in Hebrew books. Claims have been made that Jewish printers were also keen to print non-Hebrew books. That they would have possessed the requisite skills is not in doubt. In many respects Hebrew printing was more of a challenge, as Jacob Landau had indicated with his worries about the vowel points. Cecil Roth insisted that a Dante *Commedia* of 1477, preserved in the John Rylands Library in Manchester, was in fact the work of a Jewish printer; this is only the fourth printed edition of the work to have appeared, the others originating in Foligno, Mantua and Venice in 1472. [87] However, the Naples Dante is considered to have a more reliable text. Roth pointed to the existence of a slightly later Dante produced by the important Neapolitan printer Francesco del Tuppo around 1478. This edition contains a vitriolic letter to the city council of Naples which accuses the Jews of

---

83. Ferorelli, *Gli Ebrei nell'Italia meridionale*, 281-2.

84. Ferorelli, *Gli Ebrei nell'Italia meridionale*, 281.

85. For Molfetta and its Jewish connections, see footnote 32 *supra*.

86. University Library, Cambridge, MS TS AS 196.381 TS AS 197.323, TS Misc. 19.61, TS NS 168; Frojmovic, "From Naples to Constantinople", 87-109.

87. C. Roth, "A Jewish printer in Naples, 1477", *Bulletin of the John Rylands Library*, 39 (1956), 188-95; repr. in C. Roth, *Studies in Books and Booklore*, Farnborough 1972, 59-70, to which page references given here refer. In addition to the Rylands copy, there is another one in Oxford.

horrendous crimes, including specifically the murder of Simon of Trent in 1475, and then insists that a Jew had interfered in his plans to make an edition of Dante:
While I was wishing in these past days to print Dante, who is so bound up with our Faith (treating as he does the rewards of the blessed and the pains of the wicked), there arose against me an arrogant Jew, who is certainly one of those who called to Pilate 'His blood be on us and our children!' He from every side endeavoured to make me desist, finding plausible reason for this. [88]

He praises the city fathers for giving him their support, 'for which I am truly grateful'. Clearly he had serious problems with a Jewish printer, but it does not necessarily follow, as Roth assumed, that the Jewish printer had been engaged on a rival production of the *Commedia*; that is not by any means the only way of explaining del Tuppo's harsh words. There is no doubt that the Rylands Dante was printed in Naples in 1477. However, to attribute it to a Jew is hazardous: for one thing, it was completed on a Sabbath, 12 April 1477, and Roth's bizarre attempt to argue that this would have occurred after dark over a few festive drinks ignores the difficulty such an operation would have posed without the advantage of good lighting. [89] More credible is surely the idea that Francesco del Tuppo, like other printers, relied on a consortium of investors, one or more of whom may have been Jewish: as Roth was well aware, such joint enterprises existed in contemporary Spanish printshops. The story of del Tuppo's Dante is probably a variant on the story behind the notarial contract already cited, where Elya Volgheri withdrew, apparently amicably, from a contractual association. [90] Such an explanation fits well with his words: there has been an impediment placed in his way, such as might have arisen from the withdrawal of capital.

What is also striking is that del Tuppo made his peace with the Jews of Naples. The violent language he used when irate was compensated by some very positive images of the Jew in his famous *Aesopus Moralisatus* of 1485. [91] He also worked closely enough with Jewish printers in this period to provide them with decorative borders of his Aesop; these woodcuts appeared in the 1488 Naples Bible of Joshua Solomon Soncino [92]. The history of the repeated re-use of the decorated borders found in the Hebrew incunabula of Naples has been examined closely by a number of scholars: borders prepared for Christian works were adapted, sometimes clumsily, to the needs of books that opened in the other direction; they were carried abroad, often in pieces, and were kept in use for up to forty years. [93] However, the close study of the re-use of the decorated

---

88. Roth, "Jewish printer", 60.

89. Roth, "Jewish printer", 63.

90. Bloch, "Hebrew printing in Naples", 137-8.

91. Roth, "Jewish printer", 64, 66; Offenberg, "Hebreeuwse Incunabelen", 179.

92. Illustration of the Aesop and its borders in Roth, "Jewish printer", 65; illustrations of both the Aesop and of the 1488 Bible in Offenberg, "Hebreeuwse Incunabelen", 180-1.

93. C. Roth, "The border of the Naples Bible of 1491-2", *The Bodleian Library Record*, 4 (1953), 295-303; Frojmovic, "From Naples to Constantinople", 87-109; Offenberg, "Hebreeuwse Incunabelen", 180-1, 186-7.

borders has detracted somewhat from the study of the literary output of the printing presses in Renaissance Naples, and it does not need to be repeated here. What is worth noting is the use in these borders of figurative motifs of a pagan character, such as Cupids. These seem to have been found perfectly appropriate even for sacred texts.

VII

The cultural life of the Jews in the Aragonese kingdom of Naples was clearly based on traditional skills in Hebrew scholarship. Setting aside, of course, the exceptional case of Isaac Abrabanel, there is little sign of an interest in secular learning, except in the realms of medicine. The royal court did not apparently foster Jewish learning; Abrabanel was welcome there as a financier and statesman, rather than as a scholar; his books were not, unlike those of Brancati, Valla and Pontano, to be found on the king's library shelves; nor indeed were any Hebrew books considered worthy of an entry in the library catalogues. Moreover, the scholarly efflorescence of the Jews in Naples in this period was entirely the result of migration into Naples; the coming together of Sephardi, Ashkenazi and Italian rabbis was certainly fruitful, but it was an awareness of the rather free conditions in the Neapolitan *Regno* that brought them there, rather than any special reputation in scholarship, spiritual or secular, which the Jews of Naples possessed. The *Agur* of Jacob Landau is evidence for close attention to the strictures of Ashkenazi Judaism, just as the Sephardi prayer-book reveals the appeal of the Spanish version of the liturgy, an appeal which must have been greatly strengthened by the mass immigration of Spanish exiles in 1492. The printing presses were, apart from a brief false start, based exclusively in Naples; no one now accepts Ferorelli's view that some of Abrabanel's books were printed in Monopoli when the town was under Venetian rule. It is a limited picture, in which contact with the Christian humanist scholars of the Aragonese court appears to have been limited to Abrabanel alone. A few scholars who received part or all of their education in Naples showed an interest in wider secular scholarship later in life, when living beyond the kingdom's boundaries: the younger Abramo de Balmes and Messer David ben Judah Leon. Such figures made use of their studies of Hebrew grammar to build bridges across to secular philosophy and even the contemporary interest in rhetoric, and it has been argued that the Jews developed their own version of the return to the pure language of the classical past, using Biblical Hebrew in lieu of classical Latin. [94]

In any case, the freedoms the Jews enjoyed in southern Italy did not last. The French invasion put to an end the intensive period of Hebrew printing. Nothing more would come off the Hebrew presses, which seem to have been dispersed towards Venice and

94. A.M. Lesley, 'Jewish adaptation of humanist concepts in fifteenth- and sixteenth-century Italy', *Renaissance Rereadings. Intertext and Context*, ed. M.C. Horowitz, A.J. Cruz, W.A. Furman, Urbana/Chicago 1988), 51-66, especially 57-8. Allowing for references to authorities such as Cicero (cf. Abrabanel's knowledge of Seneca, supra), Messer Leon's arguments, as cited by Lesley, compare interestingly with the search for purer Hebrew in Umayyad Córdoba in the tenth century, where arabiyya rather than Latinitas had been the source of inspiration.

The role of the Jews in the cultural life of the Aragonese kingdom of Naples

Constantinople. The Jewish community lingered on, under increasing threat from a hostile Christian population, until a first expulsion in 1510 (which left behind some useful Jewish financiers) and a final one in 1541. The Sephardim and the Sicilians who had arrived in 1492-3 headed eastwards to a welcome in Turkish lands. Indeed, the destruction of Abrabanel's library by the Christian mob in 1495 symbolises the failure of a rich and broadly based scholarly tradition, using secular as well as sacred sources, to take root among the Jews of southern Italy during the Quattrocento.

The Aragonese Kingdom of Albania: An Angevin Project of 1311-1316

The theme of this study is the project launched by the Angevin king of Naples in 1311 to exchange the Kingdom of 'Trinacria', ruled by Frederick of Aragon, for a new set of Aragonese possessions consisting of a kingdom in Albania and lands in Achaia further south. The hope was to resolve by diplomacy the constant tension between Neapolitan aspirations to restore the rule of the house of Anjou in Sicily on the one hand and the wish of James II of Aragon to create a permanent peace in the western Mediterranean on the other hand. This is not simply, however, an episode in the history of Sicily and of the Balkans. Sardinia and Corsica were also eventually placed in the scales as it became evident that Frederick of Sicily was unconvinced by the offer of Albania; both islands had already been conferred on James of Aragon as part of the series of deals that brought the War of the Sicilian Vespers to an end between 1297 and 1302, but, remaining unconquered, they seemed to the court of Naples a suitable alternative to Sicily, Albania, and Achaia.

The project for the acquisition of Albania arose at an unpropitious moment for Aragonese involvement in the affairs of Greece and neighbouring lands. Paradoxically, the presence in Greece of the Catalan Company made the situation less, not more, stable as far as Aragonese interests were concerned. The Catalans had acquired the Duchy of Athens by battle without the direction of the king of Aragon (1311), though a year later the conquerors came to recognize the loose authority of Frederick of Sicily over them.[1] The Catalan duchy intruded itself into a political arena already characterized by bitter infighting

---

1. K.M. Setton, *The Catalan Domination of Athens, 1311-88* (Cambridge, MA, 1948); L.N. d'Olwer, *L'expansió de Catalunya en la Mediterrània oriental*, 2nd edn. (Barcelona, 1974); F. Giunta, *Aragoneses y catalanes en el Mediterráneo*, trans. J. Bignozzi (Barcelona, 1989).

2

between factions loyal to the house of Anjou, the king of France and indeed other masters in the Greek world. It was therefore a tall order to suggest that the king of Trinacria should abandon a relatively peaceful island kingdom, which had begun to recover from 20 years of bitter warfare with the Angevins, for lands in turmoil in Greece and for a shadowy Kingdom of Albania, which lacked any administrative structure and which was torn apart by a startling variety of local interests.

In Albania, this was a period of particularly acute uncertainty. The Albanian historian Pëllumb Xhufi sees in the period 1306-7 an intensification of the conflict in the zone around Durazzo (Dyrrachium) between the supporters of the Byzantine emperor Andronikos II Palaiologos and Angevin troops under the command of Philip of Taranto, who was the son of King Charles II of Naples, and lord of Achaia and of the Kingdom of Albania. One result was that Durazzo itself capitulated to the Angevins, but the root of the problem lay in the assumption among the Albanian nobles themselves that only the Angevins were capable of helping resist their enemies in the region, in particular the Greeks loyal to Emperor Andronikos.[2] In order to consolidate their position in the Balkans, the Angevins also sought closer ties with other Balkan neighbours, in particular with the rulers of Serbia. A quick look at the antecedents of this policy will help explain Angevin priorities in the region.

Towards the end of the reign of Charles II (1285-1309) the issue of Neapolitan control of the western Balkans had a particular significance, bringing with it the hope of establishing Angevin dominion over the eastern shores of the Adriatic and over the Ionian Sea, areas in which there was a very long tradition of involvement by the rulers of southern Italy. There were two fundamental aspirations at work here, which neatly coincided: the consolidation of Angevin naval power in the waters around the Neapolitan kingdom, creating a *cordon sanitaire* impervious to Aragonese or other intruders; and also the assumption of a prime role in the struggle against schismatic Greeks and Muslims in the aftermath of the fall of Acre in 1291, a period when the lack of a secure Latin base in the east (other than Cyprus) generated a variety of approaches to the problem of how to restore Latin authority in the eastern Mediterranean. Since the reign of Charles I of Anjou the kings

---

2. P. Xhufi, 'Albania and the Kingdom of Sicily in the time of Manfred Hohenstaufen and Charles I and Charles II of Anjou', *Journal of Medieval History*, forthcoming.

of Naples had taken a firm line opposing compromises with the Greeks, and supporting attempts to revive the short-lived Latin Empire of Constantinople; the creation of an Angevin dominion in Albania by Charles was part both of that policy and of a more restricted, Adriatic-based, policy of affirming Angevin hegemony in the central Mediterranean (a dimension of Angevin policy that tends to be forgotten under the overpowering glare of the attraction of Constantinople).

The recovery of Latin power within Greece after 1300 offered the opportunity to relaunch the eastern policy of the house of Anjou on the basis of existing power relationships in the Balkans; Charles II's plans did not, therefore, solely consist of dreams of a massive crusade in which the flower of European knighthood would participate. The practical manifestation of this policy was visible in attempts to subjugate the Despotate of Epiros, the territory just south of Albania proper, in a delicate position between the lands controlled by the Byzantine emperor, by the Serbs, and by the supporters of the house of Anjou in the western Morea.[3] It is evident that Philip of Taranto aspired to the realization of his presumptive rights in Albania, Epiros, and western Greece, rights acquired in a controversial enough setting following his marriage to Thamar (Catherine), daughter of Nikēphoros, despot of Epiros, in 1294.[4] Indeed, part of the anticipated arrangement was that Philip would in due course succeed his father-in-law as ruler of Epiros.

Donald Nicol has argued that the result of this alliance was nothing less than the virtually total subjection of Epiros to Charles II of Anjou, around 1300; the presence in the region of Angevin administrative

3. The fundamental study of Epiros is that of D.M. Nicol, *The Despotate of Epiros 1267-1479: A Contribution to the History of Greece in the Middle Ages* (Cambridge, 1984), pp. 60-61. For the earlier history of Epiros up to 1267 see D.M. Nicol, *The Despotate of Epiros* (Oxford, 1957), and the same author's valuable 'The Relations of Charles of Anjou with Nikephoros of Epiros', *Byzantinische Forschungen*, 4 (1972), 170-94. There is a powerful tradition among British historians of expounding the narrative history of late medieval Greece: W. Miller, *The Latins in the Levant: A History of Frankish Greece 1204-1566* (London, 1908); id., *Essays on the Latin Orient* (Cambridge, 1921); Sir Rennell Rodd, *The Princes of Achaia and the Chronicles of the Morea*, 2 vols. (London, 1907). Among recent studies see also A.E. Laiou, *Constantinople and the Latins: The Foreign Policy of Andronicus II* (Cambridge, MA, 1972), particularly for the Catalans in Greece and for the legacy of Charles of Valois.
4. Nicol, *Despotate of Epiros 1267-1479*, pp. 44-9; for a brief biography of this princess, see D.M. Nicol, *The Byzantine Lady: Ten Portraits, 1250-1500* (Cambridge, 1994), pp. 24-32.

officials confirmed that Neapolitan domination was a stark reality; meanwhile, the existence of Angevin power bases in Corfu and on Cephalonia (which was ruled by a line of Orsini counts formally dependent on Naples) meant that the house of Anjou had a stranglehold on the western coasts of Greece.[5] Yet succession rights in Epiros did not prove so easy to obtain. When Nikēphoros of Epiros died his widow Anna refused to place the despotate in the hands of the Angevins, with the result that the Neapolitans sent in an invasion force in 1304-6 under the command of Philip of Taranto, and acquired (at greater expense than the limited results justified) bases at Butrint, Lepanto (Naupaktos), and Vonitsa.[6] Still, these were gains that were valuable in the confirmation of Angevin naval hegemony, even if control did not extend any great distance inland. Further north, Philip's eyes alighted on the half-forgotten Albanian kingdom created by his grandfather Charles I, possession of which would put considerable pressure on any number of enemies: the rebel Epirotes to the south, the schismatic Greeks to the east.[7] Whereas Charles I clearly saw the possession of Albania as the opening of a back door leading towards Constantinople, Philip's aims seem at this point to have been more localized, with the assertion of Neapolitan control of the southern Adriatic and the Ionian Sea a particular objective. Yet this policy was subject to change; in 1309 Philip abandoned the unhappy Thamar who was accused, probably unjustly, of flagrant adultery, and found a new wife with an even more extensive, and even more contested, legacy in the East: Catherine of Valois brought with her the title to the Latin Empire of Constantinople, which had ceased actually to exist nearly half a century earlier. As a result, Philip's energies began to turn more towards the Aegean, and the difficult task he had been set of establishing a secure Angevin dominion in the western Balkans became much less attractive. As a result, a vacuum began to open up in the area of Albania and Achaia.

It was as a result of these changes in his fortune that Philip could contemplate the exchange of his own Albanian dominion for Sicily; this exchange after all brought him no obvious direct benefit in territory, since he was to give up his own lands and his brother Robert, the new king of Naples, was to be the beneficiary of the abandonment of Sicily

---

5. Nicol, *Despotate of Epiros 1267-1479*, p. 50.
6. Ibid., pp. 56-61.
7. Ibid., p. 68. The aid of the papacy was expressed in the wish to aid the Latin Church, in particular Latin priests said to have been oppressed by the Greeks.

by Frederick of Trinacria. It is thus essential to look more closely at the exact terms of the arrangement as recorded in the documents of the *Arxiu de la Corona d'Aragó*.[8] In the spring of 1311 King Robert of Naples wrote to James II of Aragon to present to him the text of an agreement dated 28 April 1311, between himself and Philip, prince of Achaia, *dominum regni Albanie et despotum Romanie*.[9] The king of Naples promised to try to *procurare seu obtinere* a modification to the treaty of Caltabellotta of 1302, according to which Frederick of Aragon had been permitted to hold the island of Sicily with the title 'king of Trinacria' for the duration of his life, without the possibility of passing Sicily to his heirs; Philip of Taranto indicated his own preparedness to sell to the king of Naples his rights in Albania:

> Regnum Albanie cum civitate et castro Durachii aliisque civitatibus terris et locis, castris, fortelliciis, hominibus, iuribus et pertinentiis eiusdem regni omnibus que nunc tenet seu que tempore dicte assignationis faciende tenebit, cum plenaria cessione et translatione omnium iurium et accionum eidem domino principi quocumque iure seu titulo pertinentium in ipso regno Albanie, tam in domaniis, quam in feudis et ceteris quibuscumque, tam eorum, que tenet et tempore dicte assignationis tenebit, quam eorum que per Grecos seu quoscumque alios scismaticos detinetur et detineretur.

From this it is abundantly clear that the acquisition of Albania did not offer the chance to gain control of a territory already securely under Angevin rule, for Angevin power was on the retreat in the region, and it is really rather doubtful whether the Angevins controlled anything beyond the environs of Durazzo.[10] Robert of Naples was unable to deny

8. *Acta et diplomata res Albaniae mediae aetatis illustrantia, collegerunt et digesserunt*, Ludovicus de Thalloczy, Constantinus Jireçek et Emilianus de Sufflay, Vol. I, annos 344-1343 continens (Vienna, 1913); H. Finke (ed.), *Acta Aragonensia. Quellen zur deutschen, italienischen, französischen, spanischen, zur Kirchen- und Kulturgeschichte aus der diplomatischen Korrespondenz Jaymes II. (1291-1327)*, Vol. II (Berlin – Leipzig, 1908).

9. Finke, *Acta Aragonensia*, No. 443, pp. 704-5 (summary); Thalloczy *et al.*, No. 597, pp. 177-9 (text).

10. For the origins of the Angevin dominion in Albania, see P. Xhufi, 'Shqiptarët përballë anzhuinëve (1267-1285)', *Studime Historike* (1987), 199-222, with a French summary; Nicol, 'Relations of Charles of Anjou'; also special mention must be made of the outstanding work of A. Ducellier, in particular *La façade maritime de l'Albanie au Moyen Age. Durazzo et Valona du XIe au XVe siècle* (Salonica, 1981).

6

that there existed on the ground a strong Greek opposition, led by the princes of Epiros, and that there were also Slav factions hostile to Angevin interests. A further complication was the crisis generated by the Catalan victory at Almyros in March 1311, when the duke of Athens, Walter of Brienne, lost his life fighting against the freebooting Catalan mercenaries whom he had once hoped (like so many others) to control; first of all he aspired to an opportunistic alliance with the Catalans, and then he found himself facing a ruthless and irresistible force which managed to take his entire duchy from under his feet. The foundation of a Catalan duchy of Athens further decisively altered the political map of Greece, resulting in the long term in a series of proxy wars between supporters of the Angevin and of the Catalan interest in southern Greece.

Interesting in the letter of King Robert is not just the concession to Frederick of the title 'King of Albania', but also of rights in the principality of Achaia. Philip was for his part to receive a handsome financial settlement: 70 thousand ounces of gold, a sum which would represent a large hole in the Angevin treasury but also a hole that could eventually be filled with the substantial revenues to be expected from a reoccupied island of Sicily. For the moment, the sum was to be drawn from the general taxes of the Kingdom of Naples, payable in four instalments, the first at the time of the assignment of the title to Albania and Achaia, and then a further quarter for each of three years. Yet there was a pessimistic awareness that such an arrangement might not turn out so well after all; Mediterranean politics were not so stable that the possibility of further war between the Aragonese and the Angevins could be excluded even within the next three years. Were such a conflict to break out between the kings of Sicily *ultra* and *citra* the Faro, Prince Philip was to be compensated for his co-operation in the project with a grant from the gabelles of the Kingdom of Naples. In any event, the king of Naples had only three years in which to convince Frederick of Trinacria to make the suggested exchange of territories, and if he failed, the prince of Taranto for his part would be absolved from all obligations arising from the treaty between him and the king of Naples, who was his *dominum* not merely in the principality but also in the Albanian kingdom, which up to now Philip had held from him as his subordinate. Behind this willingness to trade Albania and Achaia for a large pile of gold can be seen Philip's new and more ambitious plans in the East, consequent upon his marriage to Catherine of Valois and the re-activation of the Latin claim to Constantinople.

James II of Aragon had himself begun the process of exchanging Sicily for other territories towards the end of his own brief reign as ruler of Sicily between 1285 and 1296; on his accession to the throne of Aragon itself in 1291 he began to consider the return of Sicily to the house of Anjou, notwithstanding the growing evidence that the Sicilian baronage would rather retain him, or failing that his younger brother Frederick, as their ruler, both being seen as the heirs through their Sicilian mother to the house of Hohenstaufen. Boniface VIII agreed to the cession of the *regnum Sardinie et Corsice* after other possibilities had been considered, among them Cyprus which was occasionally targeted by the Aragonese as a possible acquisition, particularly since the local Lusignan dynasty was not held in high esteem by the papacy and by other Latin rulers. It is unlikely that James II saw his offer to return Sicily to the Angevins as anything more than a manoeuvre to obtain papal goodwill and a chance of peace in the western Mediterranean, since his relations with his brother Frederick were still cordial after Frederick had been elected king of Sicily by his supporters and after James had joined the Angevin war against Frederick; James's participation in this conflict was maintained in a generally low key, and his interest in Italian politics lay increasingly not in the submission of Sicily but in the accretion of influence in the central Italian cities. While the peace of Caltabellotta confirmed the title of Frederick to Sicily (if only as 'king of Trinacria'), the house of Anjou suffered a serious loss of income from what had been a major revenue-earning part of their old kingdom. Thus the peaceful cession of the island was bound to be an issue on the agenda even in 1311. A further important factor was the presence in Italy at this juncture of the Holy Roman Emperor Henry VII of Luxemburg, who began to develop warm ties with Frederick of Trinacria, and whose policies in the north of Italy clashed directly with the interests of the Guelf allies of the house of Anjou.[11] Thus the needs of the king of Naples were clear; the danger of being squeezed between an aggressive Aragonese king of Sicily and an aggressive Holy Roman Emperor were more than he could bear to face. What is perhaps more surprising is the relatively favourable attitude of the king of Aragon to the proposal to grant Frederick lands in the Balkans in lieu of Sicily. Already in 1309 James II had been hoping to

11. W.M. Bowsky, *Henry VII in Italy: The Conflict of Empire and City-State, 1310-1313* (Lincoln, NB, 1960), pp. 4-5, 14, 53, 124, 137, 157, 161-2, 169-70. The intensification of the relationship between the king of Trinacria and Emperor Henry in 1312 gave rise to great difficulties at the court of Naples; see the discussion of the theoretical as well as practical implications by K. Pennington, *The Prince and the Law: Sovereignty and Rights in the Western Legal Tradition* (Berkeley, Los Angeles, 1993), pp. 165-201.

arrange the cession to Frederick of the title to the lost Kingdom of Jerusalem (a title already contested, of course, between the kings of Naples and those of Cyprus).[12] What we see at work, therefore, is a tentative eastern policy designed to insert the Aragonese royal house into the confused political world of Greece, Cyprus, and the eastern Mediterranean.

In this light a letter written in Valencia by James of Aragon on 5 March 1312 makes sense; it was sent to Frederick of Trinacria ten months after the initial approach by Robert of Naples to James of Aragon.[13] This second letter makes it plain that the delay in negotiations had resulted from the death of Arnau de Vilanova, the famous mystic and medical practitioner who was active for some time at the court of Frederick of Trinacria. James's letter mentions the great if implausible advantages of the Albanian kingdom as related to him by Robert of Naples: the kingdom *es molt noble e rich*, and the cession of Albania would also involve the grant of Durazzo (just as well, considering that there was not really much more to grant). But James knew full well that the king of Trinacria had no intention of following this road: *e que vos, germa, non avets vulgut fer*. The king of Naples, according to James, was prepared to offer substantial subsidies for the conquest of Albania and Achaia, a point which must have seemed to confirm the genuine difficulty involved in gaining control of the kingdom: 'Encara nos ha fet saber en les dites letres lo dit G. que otra les coses damuntdites vos assignava de vostra vida lo rey Robert alguna part de les rendes de la isla de Sicilia en aiuda de conquerre lo regne Dalbania'. James's letter also makes it plain that the negotiations between the various parties were set on a different track when the problem of the future of the Kingdom of Trinacria was brought under discussion. Frederick was clear in his aspiration to found a new dynasty which would hold the island permanently, despite past agreements, and it was this, rather than the issue of Albania and Achaia, that came to dominate negotiations between Naples and Sicily. Frederick even seems to have advanced the position that the king of Naples was not genuinely hostile to the maintenance of an independent Aragonese

---

12. P.W. Edbury, *The Kingdom of Cyprus and the Crusades, 1191-1374* (Cambridge, 1991); N.J. Housley, *The Italian Crusades: The Papal-Angevin Alliance and the Crusades against Christian Lay Powers, 1254-1343* (Oxford, 1982), pp. 84-5; J.N. Hillgarth, *Ramon Lull and Lullism in Fourteenth-Century France* (Oxford – London, 1971), p. 66, n. 61.

13. Thalloczy *et al.*, No. 602, p. 180 (summary); Finke, *Acta Aragonensia*, No. 445, pp. 706-8 (text).

dynasty in Sicily; such delicate issues, and such vain hopes, soon created a fog around the Albanian project. Indeed, what mattered for Frederick was not the Albanian question, which obviously never seriously took his fancy, but the opportunity to create an open channel of communication with his Angevin rivals, through which he could make plain his extreme reluctance to allow his family's title to Sicily to lapse after his death, whatever might have been agreed in 1302.

Robert was not prepared to let go of Sicily so easily. By offering Frederick Albania and Achaia, Robert stood to regain the *part principal de nostre regne*, Sicily, as he stated in a letter written to James II on 3 February 1314.[14] At this point the crisis between Robert of Anjou and Henry of Luxemburg had been unexpectedly resolved, with the death of the emperor in 1313. Thus Robert renewed his hope for the recovery of Sicily, this time without having to defeat a great imperial-Ghibelline-Trinacrian alliance against him, as had seemed necessary in 1312-13. Looking the other way, Philip of Taranto's increasing wish to involve himself in the central Byzantine lands meant that Albania and Achaia were readily disposable to another ruler. If that ruler were to be Frederick of Trinacria, all well and good, since he would be so tied up in the internal politics of the western Balkans that he would surely never pose a threat to Angevin interests in either Italy or Byzantium. The aim, in other words, was to ensure that Frederick would become lost in the thickets of Balkan politics, out of which there was no known escape.

In reality, Frederick had not the slightest illusion about the difficulty in making royal authority real in Albania and in Achaia amid the conflicting interests of Greeks, Slavs, Albanians, and Franks; in any case, he was now working hard to extend his authority within Sicily after the 20 years of disorder generated by the War of the Vespers, which had resulted in severe dislocation of the economic, ecclesiastical, and political life of the island.[15] This is not to say that Frederick lacked an eastern policy; he gave his support to his cousin Ferrando of Majorca, who dreamed of re-establishing the principality of Achaia with the help of his wife Isabella, of Frankish ancestry, and of Frederick himself. Ferrando arrived in the region in 1308, hoping to bring the

---

14. Finke, *Acta Aragonensia*, No. 447, p. 712. The date of the letter is not absolutely certain.
15. On this see C. Backman, *The Decline and Fall of Medieval Sicily* (Cambridge, 1995), a study of the reign of Frederick III that places some emphasis on the reconstruction of royal authority in the island, and the serious problems involved in the reaffirmation of Aragonese power in Sicily.

Catalan Company under his control; and he came again in 1313, but his presence only increased the instability in a world characterized by sharp confrontations between the Catalan mercenaries, the Frankish lords, and the Greek irredentists.[16] King Frederick sent aid in 1315, hoping to confirm his own lordship in Achaia without the approval, support, or wish of the king of Naples. Thus just now the Aragonese of Sicily, the Angevins of Naples, and also allies of the king of France were all contesting the lordship of Achaia: when Ferrando lost his life at Manolada, in 1316, this Majorcan prince was fighting against the armies of Louis of Burgundy, supported by King Philip the Fair of France.[17] With the victory of the Burgundian faction the court of Naples was prompted to reconsider its policy, with the result that Robert reaffirmed his own direct control over the Achaian lands from 1317 onwards; Louis died soon after his victory, and his widow, Mahaut, was seized by the Neapolitans, who took her from Achaia to the Castel dell'Ovo in Naples, where she was kept securely under guard. Thus western Greece returned for a few years to the sphere of influence of the house of Anjou.[18]

At the same time, the king of Naples resumed his interest in a diplomatic solution to the problem of Sicily. Alain Ducellier has argued that the original project of 1311 was dead after 1314, since the three years stipulated in the original document for the settlement of financial and territorial claims were now past.[19] But in reality the king of Naples could not let go of the Albanian project, and rather than forgetting it he began to vary his approach, substituting other offers, such as the revenues from Tunis or Aragonese rights in Sardinia and Corsica, for the grant of Achaia and Albania. The Franciscan emissary Ponç Carbonell, sent to Palermo and Naples by James II of Aragon, was struck by the fact that both kings of Sicily, that of Naples and that of Trinacria, insisted on their peaceful intentions:

Noscat igitur vestra sublimis maiestas, ambos reges fore super facto pacis diversarum voluntatum, licet uterque dicat se velle

---

16. For a recent study of Ferrando, see B. Berg, 'The Moreote Expedition of Ferrando of Majorca in the Aragonese Chronicle of Morea', *Byzantion*, 55 (1985); see also the *Libro de los fechos et conquistas del principado de la Morea*, ed. A. Morel-Fatio (Geneva, 1885).
17. For a brief narrative of the events, see N. Cheetham, *Medieval Greece* (New Haven, 1981), pp. 143-6.
18. Ibid., pp. 146-7.
19. Ducellier, *La façade maritime*, pp. 331-2.

pacem et concordiam. Et maxime in hoc est controversia, quod dominus rex Fredericus nullo modo vult facere pacem, nisi insula libere sibi et suis filiis remaneret, et dominus rex Robertus nullo modo vult consentire, quod filii eius habeant, nec etiam ipsemet dominus rex Fredericus in vita sua, set, si forte haberet concedere, dicit, quod non concederet hoc etiam pro vita domini regis Frederici, nisi traderetur sibi aliqua castra Sicilie pro cautione et pactis firmius observandis.[20]

The solution was therefore to find another kingdom for Frederick and his sons, such as Sardinia and Corsica:[21]

Concedit etiam inter alia, quod, si videretur et placeret vobis ei concedere ius Sardinie et Corsice, que quidem adquirere ac adquisita retinere dificile videtur: tum propter communitatum potentiam, tum etiam propter condicionem terre non sanam, ipse libenter adquireret pro vobis vel uno filiorum vestrorum aliquod regnum in Romania, vel etiam illud, pro que me misistis, vel recompensaret in pecunia, secundum quod conveniens videretur, ita tamen, quod tradito regno Sardinie et Corsice domino regi Frederico vel eius filiis, quod propter propinquitatem, quam habet cum Catalonia, esset sibi forsitan magis gratum, insula Sicilie sibi libere redderetur.[22]

Sardinia, then, was a mixed blessing, an unhealthy land full of contending parties; but if James felt the loss was too great, Robert would gladly provide a piece of the former Byzantine Empire as compensation. But Robert's prime energies were naturally directed to Sicily; indeed, the king of Naples implored the aid of the king of Aragon (appropriately enough) in such a project: 'Et insuper, quod vos teneretis aliqua loca sive castra Sicilie pro huiusmodi adimplendis'.[23]

---

20. Finke, *Acta Aragonensia*, No. 448, p. 715.
21. For Aragonese and Angevin policies at this time in relation to the question of Sardinia, see F.C. Casula, *La Sardegna aragonese. 1. La Corona d'Aragona* (Sassari, 1990), pp. 106-10, where the author justly indicates that the years from 1314 to 1323 have been ignored by historians such as V. Salavert y Roca, *Cerdeña y la expansión mediterránea de la Corona de Aragón, 1297-1314*, 2 vols. (Madrid, 1956), and A. Arribas Palau, *La conquista de Cerdeña por Jaime II de Aragón* (Barcelona, 1952), who have concentrated on the prior or subsequent years.
22. Finke, *Acta Aragonensia*, No. 448, p. 716.
23. Ibid.

An interesting point in the discussions was the refusal of the king of Trinacria to accept the overall dominion of the king of Naples on the model of the relationship between the king of Majorca and his overlord the king of Aragon; this was hardly the most propitious model anyway:

> Dominus quoque rex non vult consentire, quod filii sui tenerent insulam pro domino rege Roberto vel suis, sicut regnum Maioricarum tenetur pro rege Aragonum, nec ullo alio modo senioritatis, set bene consentiret habere mutuam societatem adinvicem, quod excepta ecclesia et rege Aragonum ambo essent contra quocumque alium et mutuo se iuvarent.[24]

Naturally, for the king of Naples such a response was quite unacceptable. However, the king of Aragon did not abandon the project of acquiring Sicily by diplomatic means, presumably with little real hope of success.

Thus, between September 1316 and May 1317 Robert of Naples wrote to James of Aragon to propose formally the granting of Sardinia to Frederick of Sicily, together with the property of the Templars in southern Italy, which was valued at 50,000 ounces, with an additional 100,000 ounces of gold. Another possibility offered to Frederick was the island of Sardinia together with all the revenues received by the rulers of Sicily from the king of Tunis, but in that case he could not have the 100,000 ounces. In conquering Sardinia, he would be able to count on the aid of Robert, who would supply 30 galleys for five years, or otherwise would offer money to cover the cost of operating a similar fleet. This time Robert was asking for only half of Sicily, and was actually prepared to leave Frederick in charge of the other half of the island; for instance, one could have the Val Demone from Messina to Castrogiovanni (Enna), the other the rest. Robert apparently assumed that once he had a permanent foothold on the island it would be hard ever to displace him, all the more so while Frederick was absent campaigning in Sardinia. Another possible offer, still very much in Robert's mind, was the exchange of Sicily for Albania and Achaia, as before, but with the additional concession that half of Sicily would be left in Frederick's charge during his lifetime.[25] Thus the project of 1311

24. Ibid; on this relationship, see D. Abulafia, 'The Problem of the Kingdom of Majorca. 1. Political Identity', *Mediterranean Historical Review*, 5 (1990), 150-68; id., *A Mediterranean Emporium: The Catalan Kingdom of Majorca* (Cambridge, 1994), pp. 34-55.
25. Thalloczy *et al.*, No. 629, p. 186; Finke, *Acta Aragonensia*, No. 449, p. 718.

THE ARAGONESE KINGDOM OF ALBANIA 13

was far from forgotten, even if the principle was extended to other, perhaps more palatable, offers such as Sardinia. Not that Sardinia was so much more attractive than Albania, for it too was a land of competing factions, Pisan, Genoese, and home-grown, while past projects for its incorporation into either the realms of Aragon or those of Anjou had come to nothing beyond the grant of the title to Sardinia to James II in 1297.[26]

In reality the king of Trinacria well saw that the time was ripe for a return to more conventional ways of sorting out the rivalry of Anjou and Aragon within the Italian South. In 1316 the armies of the two kings clashed in Calabria, while Frederick laid plans for new naval projects in Greek waters.[27] The intention of Frederick was to force Robert's hand, to make it plain that the house of Aragon had no intention of abandoning its rights on the island to anyone else, and that he was perfectly capable of maintaining an active role in the politics of the east Mediterranean on his own, without having to rely on the patronage and authority of the king of Naples in Albania, Achaia, or any other corner of the now fragmented Byzantine Empire.

26. Abulafia, *Mediterranean Emporium*, pp. 235-48.
27. Finke, *Acta Aragonensia*, No. 450, pp. 718-26.

XVIII

GENOVA ANGIOINA, 1318-35: GLI INIZI DELLA SIGNORIA DI ROBERTO RE DI NAPOLI

I

La storia di Genova è stata scritta, giustamente, come storia di una Repubblica potente, libera, importantissima nella politica e nel commercio del Mediterraneo medievale. Qui propongo di esaminare un'altra Genova: la città che si rende soggetta a signori stranieri, che perde, abbastanza volontariamente, il suo status di territorio indipendente per associarsi ai regni più potenti della regione. Pensiamo alla dedizione volontaria ad Enrico VII Imperatore di Germania nel 1311; alla signoria di Roberto d'Angiò, re di Napoli e conte di Provenza, dal 1318; alla sottomissione a Carlo VI re di Francia alla fine del secolo (già oggetto di uno studio francese vecchio ma approfondito); e, naturalmente, ai vari episodi quando i Visconti di Milano signoreggiavano sopra Genova, al punto di sfruttare i vantaggi conseguiti dai Genovesi con la vittoria sopra Alfonso d'Aragona a Ponza nel 1435. La sottomissione di Genova è, infatti, un fenomeno ripetuto e importante della storia della città; un giorno, varrebbe la pena di fare uno studio comparato.

Posso aggiungere che il fenomeno non è ristretto a Genova; concorrenti come Firenze trovarono una forma di pace sotto Carlo di Calabria e il Duca d'Atene; di prima rilevanza è la ben documentata decisione del governo di Pisa di sottomettere la città a Giacomo II d'Aragona dopo la morte di Enrico VII, decisione che avrebbe, se realizzata, portato la città e le sue dipendenze sarde sotto la Corona d'Aragona. Non sorprende che la concorrenza aragonese-angioina sia marcata anche da tentativi angioini di allargare l'influenza napoletana nelle città marittime alla stessa epoca, tanto più perché gli Angioini presero il ruolo di capitani della Lega Guelfa in collaborazione con i loro alleati papali e fiorentini.

Comunque, esistevano altri motivi per lo sviluppo di una politica di intervento negli affari specificatamente di Genova. La vicinanza di Genova alla Provenza, e soprattutto a Nizza, Monaco e Ventimiglia, coinvolgeva i Genovesi, Guelfi e Ghibellini, nella politica della costa angioina. Già nell'epoca di Carlo I d'Angiò la politica genovese verso gli Angioini fu controllata non solo da fattori internazionali come il loro sostegno per il rinnovato greco, ma anche (come si vede chiaramente nell'opera classica di Georg Caro) dal comune interesse di Genova e del conte di Provenza nel controllo di Ventimiglia e dei suoi dintorni. Importantissimo, e molto studiato, è il legame fra i Grimaldi, signori guelfi di Monaco dopo il 1297, e la casa angioina: un rapporto che porterebbe al sostegno angioino alle attività piratesche dei Monegaschi contro le flotte non solo dei Ghibellini di Genova, ma contro le grosse galere veneziane.

Il confronto fra la situazione nel 1311, quando i Genovesi accettarono Enrico di Lussemburgo, e 1318, quando accettarono Roberto d'Angiò, rimane, pure, netto; nel 1311 *Januenses enim acceptaverunt in Dominum usque ad annos XX* l'imperatore, e *tanto minus, quanto prius decederet*: testimonianza degli acerbi contrasti fra gli *inanes malignas partes Gibellinorum et Geulforum*. Le parole sono quelle di Giorgio Stella, e la sua cronaca, nell'eccellente edizione di Petti Balbi, rimane la fonte più dettagliata sugli eventi della signoria angioina, scritta da un punto di vista abbastanza imparziale.

Per Stella, le discordie fra i Grimaldi, i Fieschi ed i Doria da una parte, e gli Spinola dall'altra, furono all'origine dell'intervento angioino. Vediamo in Stella un'enfasi non sul vantaggio di una signoria straniera, ma sulle *maligna et dura discordia inter Gibellinos et Guelfos Janue*, stimolate da interessi fuori della città. L'aiuto di *aliosque de Italia ipsarum partium coadjutores*, e in primo luogo dei Visconti di Milano, risultò nel prolungamento della guerra civile in Genova, in effetti finoi all'anno 1331.

Per mancanza di spazio, propongo di analizzare in primo luogo le ragioni della sottomissione dei Guelfi a Roberto, in secondo luogo le conseguenze di questa sottomissione, al tempo del confronto fra i Guelfi e gli Angioini da una parte, Matteo Visconti ed i suoi Ghibellini dall'altra. Per concludere, vorrei citare alcuni documenti fondamentali che mettono in luce i rapporti fra il governo guelfo-angioino e gli abitanti della riviera genovese. Rimane molto da fare su questo periodo; già nel suo *Breviario* di storia genovese Vito Vitale indicò la necessità di uno studio approfondito della signoria angioina a Genova, e gli storici del *Regno*, principalmente Romolo Caggese, sottolinearono l'importanza di questo episodio per la comprensione della politica napoletana del primo Trecento.

All'origine, il problema per i Guelfi genovesi fu il maggior potere dei loro nemici; la risposta alla crisi, nel 1318, fu appello a Roberto di Napoli, già, come insiste Stella, signore di gran parte del Piemonte, e in questo senso abituato alla politica dell'Italia nord-occidentale; ma anche un principe *maxime sensus et potentie multe*. Il ritorno di Asti alla signoria angioina nel 1314 indicò la rinascita del potere angioino in Piemonte a quest'epoca. Il re rispondeva all'appello dei Guelfi genovesi con l'invio di cavalieri da Napoli, che arrivarono il 20 luglio; furono di primaria utilità in un momento in cui una grande folla di Ghibellini assediava la città. La sparizione dei Ghibellini fu seguita dall'arrivo il 21 luglio di circa venticinque galere nelle quali si trovavano il re angioino, la regina, due principi della casa angioina *et strenuorum militum numero*, che entrarono nella città e presero alloggio nel convento domenicano.

Alcuni giorni dopo, il re ricevette la visita del podestà e di altri alti ufficiali, che *renuntiarunt in manibus dicti Regis* la loro autorità. I Guelfi di Genova a questo momento scelsero come *gubernatores et presides* della città non solo il re ma anche il Papa, Giovanni XXII, con il compito dell'amministrazione della giustizia, con *mero et mixto imperio*, e con ogni altra giurisdizione. La durata della concessione era di dieci anni, ma se il papa non fosse sopravvissuto, il re di Napoli avrebbe potuto assumere tutti i poteri; e se il re di Napoli fosse morto entro dieci anni, il suo figlio e erede, il Duca di Calabria (futuro signore di Firenze), avrebbe preso il suo posto. La verità, come osserva Stella, fu molto più semplice: *effectu tamen semper erat Dominus ipse Rex*. La preponderanza angioina fu espressa, agli occhi di Stella, dalla presenza di duecento cavalieri napoletani, già riferiti, ma anche da mille cento altri *milites equestres*, provvisti di sussidi fiorentini, bolognesi e senesi. L'analisi di Stella prosegue con l'osservazione che anche i Ghibellini trovarono un loro padrone, in Matteo Visconti, signore di Milano, aiutato non solo dai Pisani ma dai Veneziani, dai Lucchesi, da Cangrande della Scala di Verona e da altri Lombardi, *quidam palam et quidam occulte*.

In questo senso l'arrivo di Roberto di Napoli a Genova fu un altro episodio nella lunghissima storia delle risse fra Guelfi e Ghibellini, elevato, pure, ad un più alto livello dalla partecipazione diretta del re di Napoli; nella luce della storia recente di Genova, dominata da interessi pro-Ghibellini, l'adesione degli *Intrinseci* a Roberto segnò un gran passo avanti nella concentrazione del potere angioino nell'Italia nord-occidentale. Il possesso di Genova poteva essere una chiave per il controllo del Piemonte e per una estesa autorità angioina in Lombardia. Genova collegava i territori provenzali degli angioini con l'Italia settentrionale; ma la via fu bloccata dall'espansione del potere di Matteo Visconti, dopo il fallimento del tentativo di Enrico VII di realizzare il suo sogno della creazione di una pacifica conciliazione fra Guelfi e Ghibellini in Lombardia.

Un'altra spiegazione degli avvenimenti a Genova fu divulgata da Giovanni Villani, seguito da alcuni storici moderni come Argenti: che l'aiuto della flotta genovese porterebbe Roberto alla realizzazione del suo più grande sogno, la riconquista della Sicilia da Federico di Trinacria *quando avesse a queto la signoria di Genova*, dice Villani, *si credea racquistare l'isola di Cicilia, e venire al di sopra di tutti gli suoi nemici*. I costanti tentativi di Roberto durante il suo regno per la conquista dell'isola (già prima del 1318) rendono probabile, ma non certa, questa interpretazione; mentre il coinvolgimento nella guerra civile a Genova di Federico di Trinacria conferma che anche il problema genovese aveva un aspetto siciliano. Comunque, la politica angioina nelle acque vicine alla Provenza sempre possedeva una sua logica interna, tanto più quando il gran premio sarebbe stata la sconfitta dei Visconti e l'apertura di una via d'accesso per mare ai possessi angioini dell'Italia nord-occidentale.

II

La storia dell'assedio di Genova dagli *Estrinseci* Ghibellini si trova nella cronaca di Stella e fu ripetuta da Giustiniani ed altri; non vale la pena di riprendere i fatti. Quello che importa è la frequentissima presenza del re di Napoli a Genova (o almeno nelle vicinanze, in Provenza) e i suoi tentativi di formare un grande esercito con l'intento di forzare l'espulsione degli *Estrinseci* dai loro posti lungo la riviera ligure. Per esempio, nel mese di febbraio 1319 Roberto e i suoi alleati attaccarono per mare Sestri Ponente, dove speravano di penetrare più facilmente nelle linee ghibelline: *rus Sextus quidem locus erat, per quem Guelfi per mare aptius possent Gibellinos invadere; nam alia loca erant per Gibellinos fortius munita*. La battaglia di Sestri fu una vittoria guelfa, con il risultato che i più potenti Ghibellini del retroterra fuggirono; i Guelfi saccheggiarono Gavi, Sampierdarena, Sestri ed altri luoghi: eventi nei quali il cronista trovò prove della tragedia che stava distruggendo la sua città e quell'epoca. Da un altro lato, possiamo vedere che i tentativi dei Visconti di impadronirsi di Genova furono bloccati; in questo senso, la lotta fu fra Roberto e Matteo Visconti, e i Genovesi giocarono un ruolo secondario.

I rapporti con il papa furono forse più importanti di quanto non lo creda Stella; ciò perché fu nelle mani del papa il permesso di dirottare una flottiglia di navi angioine pronte a Marsiglia per il viaggio verso l'Egeo verso una nuova destinazione, Genova stessa.

La crociata contro i Turchi doveva prendere il secondo posto dopo la crociata contro i nemici della Chiesa in Italia; la guerra in difesa dei Guelfi genovesi faceva parte di una più grande crociata politica contro i Visconti.

Non sorprende, dunque, che Roberto di Napoli, già conosciuto per i suoi buoni rapporti con il papato, partisse dopo la battaglia per visitare il papa ad Avignone. A questo momento pareva che il re avesse risolto molti dei problemi della regione ligure. Aveva tra l'altro riconciliato le fazioni dei Doria e una parte degli Spinola. E lasciò un comandante napoletano, Riccardo di Gambatesa, nella città per assicurare la supremazia guelfa angioina. La verità fu alquanto diversa. Come l'indica il cronista, i Ghibellini rimanevano forti nel contado; anche se i Guelfi tenevano Recco, Rapallo, Chiavari, Moneglia ed altri paesi, *rura tamen supra ea loca sita tenebant Gibellini*. Infatti, i Guelfi tenevano una sezione della riviera ligure, ma all'ovest, anche sul mare, i Ghibellini furono predominanti, con alcune eccezioni abbastanza importanti: Ventimiglia, Monaco, Mentone, San Remo, Roquebrune rimanevano con i Guelfi; vedremo più tardi come il re confiscò i beni dei Ghibellini a Monaco nel 1319. Anche all'est, i Ghibellini tenevano una parte della *riparia*. La divisione dei territori conferma che l'adesione di Genova a Roberto in nessun modo poteva garantire l'adesione di tutti i territori della Repubblica. Questo fu vero perlomeno oltremare, ove la colonia genovese di Pera, dopo un breve conflitto, rimaneva ghibellina di colore, conscia che i vecchi legami con la casa dei Paleologhi possedevano gran valore in un tempo in cui gli Angioini persistevano con i loro tentativi di impadronirsi di Costantinopoli.

La seconda fase della lotta per il controllo di Genova cominciò nel 1319, e fu caratterizzata da battaglie fra le navi dei Guelfi, dei Ghibellini, e dei loro alleati: una guerra che minacciava di coinvolgere altri poteri mediterranei, come gli Aragonesi di Catalogna e di Sicilia. Giovanni Villani esprime con chiarezza i risultati politici dell'arrivo di Roberto a Genova: *per la venuta del re Ruberto in Genova, non affieboliò l'oste di fuori, ma maggiormente crebbe per l'aiuto de' signori di Lombardia di parte d'imperio, e rifecionno lega con lo'mperadore di Costantinopoli, e col re Federigo di Cicilia, e col marchese di Monferrato, e con Castruccio signore di Lucca, e ancora co' Pisani al segreto*. L'origine del contrasto si deve ricercare negli effetti dell'assedio di Genova stessa dagli *Estrinseci*. Già esisteva nel 1319 nella città una carestia di frumento; nell'ottobre dello stesso anno i Guelfi festeggiarono l'arrivo di dieci galere guelfe della Romania, che portavano grano, ma ogni arrivo doveva oltrepassare un blocco di navi ghibelline. Gli *Estrinseci* misero a fuoco tre grandi navi genovesi e tre catalane, già prese dai Guelfi. Nel maggio 1320 nove galere di Roberto d'Angiò *venients armate in Guelforum auxilium*, presero una grande nave dei Catalani piena di grano a Porto Pisano; in seguito gli *Estrinseci* la catturarono, e ne conseguì una serie di battaglie sul mare nelle quali le navi provenzali già riferite presero un ruolo distinto. Giorgio Stella offre tutto un catalogo di attacchi di Ghibellini su navi Guelfe e viceversa; è ovvio che la mancanza di grano nella città di Genova, ma anche fra i Ghibellini, fu il motivo principale.

I Ghibellini naturalmente volevano procurarsi il loro frumento dal loro alleato tradizionale, la Sicilia aragonese; lasciando a parte le attività dei pirati, vediamo una netta distinzione in questo momento fra Ghibellini commercianti in Sicilia e Guelfi commercianti in Napoli. Il problema fu che per raggiungere le due destinazioni le loro navi dovevano seguire una rotta abbastanza simile. Le occasioni di scontri furono frequentissime. Così nel 1320 Federico III di Sicilia armò delle galere per aiutare i Ghibellini, e una flotta genovese guelfa sotto Lanfranco Usodimare partì per un incontro a Ponza, senza successo; in settembre, i soldati siciliani arrivarono in Liguria, e combatterono con i Guelfi sul suolo ligure, ma, vedendo che gli *Estrinseci* non potevano far niente contro il potere degli *Intrinseci*, decisero di tornare in Sicilia. Il risultato più importante fu che il re Roberto da questo punto ebbe timore di un intervento siciliano, e che di conseguenza il teatro della guerra minacciava di allargarsi a tutto il Tirreno. Una seconda minaccia fu fornita da Castruccio Castracani, signore di Lucca, che occupava un punto strategico importantissimo fra Genova e la sua alleata Firenze. Un esercito fiorentino, che penetrò nelle terre lucchesi, impedì a Castruccio di intervenire in Liguria.

La guerra navale di questi anni fu, in primo luogo, una guerra *civile* navale su una scala forse senza precedenti; in secondo luogo, è chiaro che i Genovesi non potevano combattere da soli, ma dipendevano (se Guelfi) dall'aiuto dei Napoletani e Provenzali, o (se Ghibellini) dai Siciliani aragonesi. In un certo senso, le tradizionali risse fra Guelfi e Ghibellini, e le tradizionali rivalità fra le città della regione toscano-ligure, ed anche la tradizionale rivalità Angiò-Aragona, furono tutte in gioco, ma questa volta sul mare. Cronista di una città marittima, Giorgio Stella documenta gli effetti di questa guerra sul commercio, che non poteva quasi sopravvivere: parla sotto l'anno 1321 della grande gioia fra gli *Intrinseci* quando arrivano dieci grandi vascelli *cum vini aliorumque victualium magno onere a partibus Neapolis incedentes: vino quippe valde egebant Intrinseci.* Più tardi ricorda l'arrivo di navi provenzali e pugliesi cariche di grano, ma ricorda anche che gli *Estrinseci* bloccarono la via e che carne, formaggio, uova non poterono arrivare nella città. Fu necessario portare queste derrate al paese di Recco e poi caricare le provviste su un battello per accedere a Genova stessa. Non sorprende, dunque, che i cittadini di Genova si sollevassero qualche volta nel periodo di dominio angioino; il loro approvvigionamento dipendeva sempre più dalle razzie piratesche contro galere di Sicilia o dei Ghibellini; la storia della *Motta* genovese e delle attività dei Popolari deve essere riservata per un'altra relazione.

III

Il mio intento fino a questo punto è stato quello di tentare di spiegare in che cosa consisteva la signoria angioina a Genova. Dopo l'analisi dell'origine di questa signoria, è importante fermarsi un momento per una considerazione del rapporto fra il signore ed i suoi soggetti genovesi. Grazie ad un gruppo di documenti conservati negli archivi delle *Bouches du Rhône* a Marsiglia, e alla documentazione nell'archivio del palazzo dei Principi di Monaco, sappiamo qualcosa degli effetti dell'intervento angioino sulla riviera di Ponente.

Già nel 1319 gli Angioini avevano tentato di confiscare i beni dei Ghibellini in Liguria, senza dubbio nella speranza di creare un legame territoriale che si estendesse da Nizza angioina verso Genova. Il 16 aprile 1319 Roberto scrisse al castellano di Nizza dando istruzioni che i beni dei Ghibellini di Monaco, la Turbie e Roquebrune, e in particolare degli Spinola ghibellini, fossero trasferiti a collaboratori guelfi, e in primo luogo ai Grimaldi. Interessante è il fatto che il privilegio fu emesso nel nome di Roberto re di Gerusalemme e di Sicilia, conte di Provenza, Forcalquier e Piemonte, senza riferimento, nell'intitolazione del re, alla signoria su Genova; il documento fu stilato dalla mano di Matteo Filmarino di Napoli, giurisperito e luogotenente del promontorio del *Regno*.

Questo mandamento regio trova le sue origini in un processo verbale del marzo 1319, opera di un notaio provenzale, compiuto dopo l'esame dei testimoni nel palazzo regio di Nizza, *in domo seu porticu in qua Judex Nicie habitare consuevit.* L'inchiesta fu trascritta su un lunghissimo rotolo di pergamena oggi a Marsiglia. *Volentesque super valore annuo possessionum dicti domini Nicholosii Spinole et Guebellinorum predictorum habere informationem*, il documento fornisce un'immagine molto specifica dei beni dei Ghibellini nella zona di Monaco. Quello che è meno chiaro è il rapporto fra questi territori e Genova; gli Angioini non dimenticarono, certo, il richiamo di diritti provenzali su Monaco e i suoi dintorni, ma, giocando una politica molto delicata, basata sul sostegno dei Grimaldi per la loro signoria, non potevano incorporare definitivamente queste terre nella loro contea di Nizza. Già nel 1306 e nel 1310 i re Carlo II e Roberto offrirono la loro protezione ai Grimaldi e ad altri Guelfi che erano fuggiti nel territorio di Nizza, e gli atti del 1319 debbono essere letti come un tentativo di estendere il dominio provenzale verso la riviera ligure: che a lungo termine, i Grimaldi rifiutarono. In ogni caso, il possesso se non di Monaco almeno di Ventimiglia sarebbe stato molto apprezzato dagli Angioini; nel 1345 il Doge di Genova informò il papa che Roberto di Napoli aveva tolto la cittadina da Genova, prendendo vantaggio sulla signoria angioina su Genova: un commento che conferma l'importanza della politica locale provenzale nell'analisi della signoria angioina a Genova.

Un altro effetto della signoria angioina fu il riorientamento commerciale della città. Le cronache indicano la netta distinzione fra Guelfi commercianti a Napoli e Ghibellini commercianti in Sicilia, e gli atti notarili confermano l'esistenza di un rapporto commerciale fra gli *Intrinseci* e Napoli. Già prima dell'arrivo di Roberto a Genova troviamo indicazioni di un fiorente commercio napoletano-genovese: un atto notarile di Giacomo *de Sancta Savina* del 1315 parla di un cambio di £ 5.000 su Napoli (Cart. 127 f. 230v); nel 1326 (e non 1328 come nell'inventario) troviamo nello stesso cartolare una commenda per la piccola somma di £ 13 (Cart. 127 f. 310r). Troviamo un'indicazione della presenza di un agente fiorentino della società dei Bardi in un documento del 1323, che si riferisce, con nostro interesse, agli atti del notaio fiorentino Boccadibue di Biagio, figura molto vicina ai Bardi (Cart. 142 f. 122v-123r). L'impressione che si riceve dai cartolari di quest'epoca è, pure, che il commercio genovese fosse molto ristretto, e che la guerra civile concentrasse le attività mercantili nel campo dell'approvvigionamento. Gli effetti del mancato commercio dei Guelfi in Sicilia furono gravi anche per il re di Trinacria, che temeva di perdere le imposte sul grano esportato ogni anno dall'isola verso il Continente. Nel 1327, infatti, Federico III (nelle parole di Giustiniani, che segue Stella) *vedendo che, per mancare il traffico de' Guelfi in Sicilia, mancavano ancora i suoi redditi, concessi il tratto ossia il traffico a' Guelfi*; si sa che questa manovra politica e commerciale *vehementer displicuit* il re di Napoli.

IV

Chiaramente, l'imposizione di una signoria angioina non ottenne pace nella città; il re cercò non di riconciliare i Guelfi e i Ghibellini ma di assicurare una vittoria guelfa, nel classico modo di confiscare i beni dei Ghibellini e di combattere le flotte e le attività dei loro alleati milanesi e siciliani. La possibilità di una riconciliazione vera e propria, nella tradizione della politica ingenua di Enrico VII, non esisteva in questo momento. La signoria angioina a Genova fu il prodotto del confronto fra fazioni locali, certo, ma anche dell'intervento di Enrico di Lussemburgo e della rinascita di una politica ghibellina in Lombardia e in Toscana, sotto Matteo Visconti, Castruccio Castracani ed altri; fu il prodotto della visione abbastanza coerente del re, e del papa Giovanni XXII, della ripresa dell'egemonia guelfa e angioina nell'Italia settentrionale.

NOTA BIBLIOGRAFICA

Dipendiamo da una fonte di prima importanza: Giorgio STELLA, *Annales Genuenses*, a cura di G. PETTI BALBI, *Rerum italiacarum scriptores*, ser 2, vol. 17, parte 2a (Bologna, 1975); si può aggiungere Agostino GIUSTINIANI, *Castigatissimi Annali di Genova* (Genova, 1537; esiste un'edizione moderna, Genova, 1854). Poi la *Cronica* di Giovanni VILLANI (ho utilizzato l'edizione di Firenze, dal 1823).

Le fonti documentarie sono da cercare a Marsiglia e a Genova: Archives Départmentales du Bouches-du-Rhône, Marseille, B. 449, per il rotolo di marzo 1319. Ho sfogliato alcuni notai del periodo nell'Archivio di Stato di Genova: Cartolare Notarile 127 e Cartolare Notarile 142 hanno fornito dati utili.

Scrittori moderni che riferiscono agli evenimenti trattati qui sono: Philip ARGENTI, *The occupation of Chios by the Genoese, and their administration of the island, 1346-1566*, t.1 (Cambridge, 1958), pag. 37-57, 70-85, basato su GIUSTINIANI in primo luogo; e Romolo CAGGESE, *Roberto d'Angiò e i suoi tempi*, 2 tomi (Firenze, 1922-30), ii, 30-41; anche Vito VITALE, *Breviario della Storia di Genova* (Genova, 1955).

XIX

Consideraciones sobre la historia del reino de Mallorca: Mallorca entre Aragón y Francia

I

El fin de esta ponencia es reconsiderar algunos aspectos fundamentales de la relación entre el reino independiente de Mallorca y sus vecinos, desarrollando los argumentos presentados en mi libro *Un Emporio mediterráneo*. *El reino catalán de Mallorca*, que apareció por primera vez en inglés in 1994, y en español in 1996 (ABULAFIA, 1984, 1996). En ese libro ponía el énfasis en el plano internacional (tanto en política como en comercio) del reino de Mallorca, y pienso retener ese énfasis aquí. En uno de los primeros capítulos de ese libro analizaba bastante detenidamente los orígenes del reino en el testamento de Jaime I de Aragón, y destacaba el hecho evidente de que el legado de Jaime I fue afectado, en 1279, por la actitud de Pedro III de Aragón, que insistía en que su hermano Jaime II de Mallorca debería convertirse en su vasallo. El reino de Mallorca se encontraba en una especie de limbo donde, a pesar de ser reino en nombre, su autonomía era muy limitada.

En particular, voy a destacar aquí la importancia de las relaciones de familia entre las diferentes facciones a finales del siglo trece. El autónomo reino de Mallorca fue creado por Jaime el Conquistador en la esperanza de que su rey sería capaz de coexistir en armonía fraternal con su hermano mayor, el rey de Aragón (JAUME I, *Crònica*, cap. 563; ABULAFIA, 1996, pag. 54). Demostraré como, incluso en momentos de inminente conflicto, se recurría continuamente a los lazos familiares para evitar la guerra –ya que La Guerra de las Vísperas enredó a las distintas ramas de las muy enlazadas casas reales de Barcelona, Francia y Nápoles. En su crónica, Ramón Muntaner exageró la importancia de los lazos familiares en la creación de una armoniosa comunidad Aragonesa de reyes, gobernando sobre Aragón-Cataluña, Mallorca y Sicilia (MUNTANER, *Crònica*). Su interpretación de la Guerra de las Vísperas contenía fallos fundamentales al tratar de demostrar que Pedro el Grande y Jaime II de Mallorca eran amigos unidos por una alianza secreta, cuando en realidad estaban comprometidos en plena guerra abierta. Sin embargo, aunque la interpretación es equivocada, hay que subrayar su reconocimiento de la importancia fundamental que los lazos familiares tuvieron en las relaciones entre los muchos gobernantes que fueron absorbidos en la Guerra de las Vísperas. En cierto respecto, ésta fue una disputa de familia, aunque a gran escala, que se basó en cuestiones de herencia y honor.

De acuerdo con la perspectiva de mi libro, continúo aquí considerando el reino de Mallorca no simplemente como las islas Baleares con ciertas dependencias peninsulares, sino como un compósito entero: Mallorca, Menorca, Ibiza, Rosellón, Cerdaña,

Vallespir, Conflent, Capcir, Collioure, Montpellier, Aumelas, Carlat; sin embargo, deberíamos subrayar el hecho de que el estado de estos territorios variaba. Por ejemplo, permaneció controversial la cuestión de si Rosellón formaba estrictamente una parte integral del reino, o sólo un feudo en Cataluña que por circumstancia caía bajo el rey de Mallorca, delegado por la persona que también era su señor en las islas Baleares, es decir el rey de Aragón y conde de Barcelona. La insistencia en ver el reino como una totalidad, también evidente en el excelente trabajo de Antoni Riera i Melis, distingue mi forma de acercarme al tema de algunos de los estudios principales que se han concentrado, comprensiblemente, en la dimensión baleárica del reino, como por ejemplo la inestimable *Ejecutoria del reino de Mallorca* de Alvaro Santamaría (RIERA MELIS, 1986; SANTAMARÍA, 1990).

II

El problema político central al cual tuvieron que enfrentarse los reyes de Mallorca en sus relaciones exteriores fue, claramente, su posición de vasallos a los reyes de Aragón, desde 1279 en adelante. Propongo empezar con ciertos aspectos de esa relación. Se suele dar menos consideración a otra relación feudal que tuvo gran impacto en su conducta y sobrevivencia, la relación con los reyes de Francia, señores de la ciudad y baronía de Montpellier, y del pequeño *enclave* de Carlat en las periferias de Auvergne y Rouergue (aunque de vez en cuando, hasta los derechos franceses fueron desafiados por los aragoneses). El problema de las relaciones entre Francia y Mallorca sería un tema presente a lo large de esta ponencia, un tema que debería ser entedido en el contexto de la amarga rivalidad entre el rey de Aragón y Carlos d'Anjou en Sicilia, Provenza y el norte de África. (RUNCIMAN, 1958; ABULAFIA, 1997; DUNBABIN, 1998). Hace más de cien años el historiador frances Lecoy de la Marche descubrió los restos de los archivos reales de los reyes de Mallorca en los Archives Nationales en París, basando en ellos su estudio clásico *Les relations politiques de la France avec le royaume de Majorque,* (LECOY, 1892) un trabajo que tenía también en su agenda la presentación sistemática del argumento que las tierras mallorquinas, ahora parte de Francia (principalmente Rosellón y Montpellier), poseían un destino francés: a Pedro el Grande, con su ambición de recuperar el señorío catalán, no sólo allí sino también en Millau, Carcassonne y los otros territorios cedidos a Francia bajo el Tratado de Corbeil de 1258, se le adjudica el papel de malo; Lecoy habla, por ejemplo, de su 'énorme ambition, une nature jalouse, vindicative' (LECOY, i. 108, 162-3). Pedro tenía lazos familiares con la corte de Francia, y sus relaciones con el futuro Philippe le Bel fueron aparentemente cordiales; estos lazos asumieron una realidad política en 1285, cuando Felipe IV puso fin a la guerra francesa contra Aragón, durante la cual su padre cayó fatalmente enfermo. Para Lecoy, sin embargo, Felipe representaba una figura siniestra que evidentemente elegía a amigos siniestros.

Desde luego, Pedro fue consistente. Nada más haber aceptado los términos del testamento de Jaime I, separando así las tierras de Mallorca de las aragonesas, catalanas, y valencianas, llegó al acuerdo de 1258 con Luis IX de Francia. Es aparente en el documento del 13 de junio, 1262 (LECOY, i. doc. num.14), que Pedro esperaba que Rosellón, Cerdaña, Conflent y Vallespir, con varias otras tierras catalanas, como Llagostera en el Gironés y Besalú, fueran dote para su mujer Constanza de Hohenstaufen. Como la defensa de los intereses de Constanza en Sicilia y en el sur de Italia se convirtieron en obsesión para Pedro el Grande, es probable que vio la pérdida de estas tierras como otro ejemplo de la erosión de sus derechos básicos como heredero de las posesiones de las casas de Barcelona y Hohenstaufen. Perder Rosellón con Sicilia, las tierras del sur de Francia, y además Provenza, era demasiado. Además, la amenaza estratégica hacia Cataluña, resultante del incremento de la influencia francesa en Rosellón, podía ser potencialmente seria.

Sin embargo, fue sólo dos meses después de que Rosellón y Cerdaña hubieran sido asignados como dote a Constanza, cuando Jaime I de Aragón, el 21 de agosto de 1262, publicó un documento dividiendo su reino entre Pedro y Jaime, e insistiendo en que la paz debería preservarse entre los que él evidentemente veía como dos hijos rivales (LECOY, i. pag. 109-111; Archives Nationales, París, KK 1413 y P1354(1) num. 800; Bibliothèque Nationale, París, ms latin 9261, num. 6). Si Pedro hacía la guerra contra su hermano pequeño, entonces ciertas promesas, concernientes a la posible devolución de Rosellón y Cerdaña a los condes de Barcelona, serían automáticamente canceladas. De hecho, está claro en el documento de agosto 1262, que Jaime I no veía Rosellón y Cerdaña como partes integrales, o dependencias, del condado de Barcelona; las veía en cambio como separadas entidades, que serían adjudicadas a la persona del rey de Mallorca de manera similar a los lazos personales que unían el condado de Barcelona a la persona del rey de Aragón. (Para Lecoy, este y otros aspectos de la historia y geografía de esas regiones simplemente confirmaban su identidad francesa; pero en otros respectos está claro que éstas fueron vistas como tierras catalanas, separadas de Francia después del Tratado de Corbeil). Jaime era consciente de que hasta 1235 Rosellón había estado en manos de su asesor y ayudante (también su tío) Nuño Sanchez, y puede que haya imaginado una relación similar entre sus propios hijos.

Los arreglos hechos en este momento por Jaime primero se convirtieron entonces en motivo de vergüenza para el infante Pedro que, después de todo, había estado negociando una delicada alianza con Manfredi de Sicilia, una relación que era de por sí extremadamente controversial en vista de la lucha de Manfredi contra el Papa y las facciones Guelf en Italia. Las complicaciones aumentarían a gran paso una vez que Carlos d'Anjou, ya señor del previamente aragonés condado de Provenza, se hiciera rey de Sicilia por su victoria sobre Manfredi en la batalla de Benevento en 1266. Puede que Pedro haya visto el cambio de estado en las tierras que había esperado incluir en el dote como un insulto implícito a su propio honor. Pedro se vió obligado a negociar de nuevo sus relaciones con el conde de Foix, quien mantenía ciertas tierras suyas en los condados pirineos ahora asignados a Jaime de Mallorca (LECOY, i doc. num.15, 17 febrero 1263). Aunque el acuerdo con el conde tenía una clausula de devolución, la cual le daba a Pedro cierta esperanza de restablecer sus propios derechos, la pérdida de un vasallo tan poderoso como Roger-Bertrand de Foix no era facilmente acceptable. Las tierras y la influencia de Roger en el lado francés de los Pirineos le ofrecerian a Pedro la esperanza de restaurar los derechos de los condes de Barcelona sobre otros territorios más al sur, en los planos de Llenguadoc. Sin embargo, en el pasado, Roger se había inclinado más hacia Jaime de Mallorca, cuya esposa Esclarmonde era su hermana. Pedro trató de dar balance a esta situación, y pidió la mano de la hija de Roger de Foix para su propio hijo; la boda al final no tuvo lugar. No era un secreto para nadie la intención que Pedro tenía de recuperar derechos sobre tierras como Millau, que habían sido entregadas a la casa de Capet en el Tratado de Corbeil.

Más adelante, en 1276, Pedro tuvo que tragar su orgullo; él mismo publicó un edicto extraordinario en el que admitía que hacía tiempo que estaba asombrado por una serie de donaciones que su padre había hecho a sus seguidores, *multas donaciones, assignaciones et contractus quos dictus pater noster cotidie faciebat*, pero ahora quería aclarar que no tenía ninguna objeción a la concesión de Mallorca y los territorios continentales a su hermano Jaime. Este documento sería conservado por los reyes de Mallorca como prueba evidente de que el dirigente aragonés había aceptado la disposición hecha por Jaime primero en su testamento. Porque no escribió Pedro: *donacionem predictam, vobis factam a dicto pater nostro, laudamus et approbamus et confirmamus?* (LECOY, i doc. num.16; París, Archives Nationales KK 1413 f.58 y P 1354[1] doc. num. 801). La idea de que Pedro y Jaime debían aprender a coexistir disfrutando del mismo estado como reyes fue expresada con frecuencia; sin embargo es de destacar que la *Crònica* describiendo las últimas horas de Jaime I ponía énfasis, también, en el honor debido de un hermano más joven a otro mayor:

> ... después ordené a Pedro que amara y honrara a mi hijo, el infante Jaime, que era su hermano tanto por parte de padre como de madre, a quien ya había otorgado cierta herencia, de tal manera que no tengan ningún tipo de contienda. Y que puesto que a él le dábamos la herencia más grande y todo el honor, debía darse por bien pagado. Lo cual no sería dificil para él, ya que el infante Jaime, hijo nuestro, lo amaría y obedecería en todo lo que mande, ya que él es su hermano mayor (*Crònica*, cap. 563).

Tal actitud refleja las piedades de un moribundo, pero Jaime I sabía bien que la relación entre los dos hermanos era particularmente difícil.

En paralelo, podemos ver al infante Jaime adquiriendo más responsabilidades en las islas Baleares. En agosto de 1256, ya aparece confirmando los derechos otorgados por su padre a los habitantes de Mallorca; se le describe como heredero al reino de Mallorca y de Montpellier (*Montispessulani*) (LECOY, i. doc. num. 12); en 1257 Jaime transfirió a su hijo Jaime de Mallorca los derechos a Ibiza que antes había disfrutado Pedro de Portugal (LECOY, i. doc. num. 13), mientras que en noviembre 1270, le dio a Jaime de Mallorca el derecho de repudiar la moneda valenciana, reemplazandola con su propia moneda. Este privilegio solamente correspondía a Mallorca y a Ibiza, a pesar de que el documento describe a Jaime como heredero de Mallorca, Montpellier, Rosellón, Cerdaña, y Conflent (LECOY, i. doc. num. 17). Sin embargo tal moneda no apareció hasta el año 1300. En los años siguientes el rey de Aragón prestó mucha más atención a los asuntos de Mallorca, preparando su defensa, suministrándole con grano, construyendo un puerto, etcetera, todo en preparación para el día en que el independiente reino de Mallorca se hiciera una realidad (LECOY, i. doc. num. 18-23).

III

Pero como reino verdaderamente independiente iba a durar poco más de dos años. Al principio de su reino, Jaime de Mallorca se rodeó del típico esplendor regio, celebrando la coronación en Ciutat de Mallorca y las Corts en Perpiñán. Esto, sin duda con gran consternación del rey Pedro, atrajo a muchos barones no solamente de sus tierras, sino también de Languedoc, Cataluña, Gasconia y Aragón (de manera que estaban presentes los sujetos de no menos de cuatro reyes: Mallorca, Aragón, Francia e Inglaterra) (*Crònica* de Muntaner, cap. 30). Aunque su presencia y aceptación de regalos generosos no indicaba de ninguna manera su sujeción a Jaime, la aparición de un polo rival de atracción para los barones locales fue un asunto de verdadera preocupación para el rey de Aragón, sabiendo como sabía que había potencial para la discordia en los condados interiores de sus territorios. En Montpellier, el rey de Mallorca se cuidó de rendir homenaje al obispo de Maguelonne, aunque en las fuentes de información hay opiniones variadas acerca de la reacción de los ciudadanos de una ciudad que, como veremos más adelante, tenía su propia agenda política.

En contraste a todo esto, el acuerdo hecho en Perpiñan en enero de 1279 entre Pedro el Grande y Jaime, rey de Mallorca, representa todavía otra extraordinaria serie de comunicados que de alguna manera consigue presentar la sumisión de Jaime a Pedro como un acto de buena voluntad fraternal (LECOY, i. doc. num. 27). La importancia fundamental de este documento puede ser juzgada por la manera en que el rey Pedro IV resumió sus principales puntos en su crónica varias décadas después, reconociendo en la ruptura de sus condiciones suficientes bases para la invasión de Mallorca y Roussillon que él inició entre 1343 y 1344: la donación *fue immensa, y tol.lia major o gran partida del patrimoni de la Casa d'Aragó*; Pedro el Grande *no volia que de tal regalia fos la Casa d'Aragó despullada* (*Crònica* de Pedro IV, lib. 3, cap. 3). Aunque retuvo los derechos sobre alta y baja jurisdición (*ab tota juredicció alta e baixa*), el rey de Mallorca tendría todas sus tierras en feudo del rey de Aragón, y tendría entonces todas las obligaciones de un verdadero vasallo hacia su señor. El acuerdo no era, Pedro IV recalcó, simplemente uno entre hermanos, porque fue también firmado por los ciudadanos más notables de Perpiñan, Puigcerdà, y Ciutat de Mallorca. En su crónica, Pedro el Ceremonioso, después de su detallada descripción de los derechos de los aragoneses sobre el reino de

Mallorca, pasa inmediatamente a hablar de la ruptura del acuerdo por parte de Jaime II, al admitir este en sus territorios ejércitos franceses durante la Guerra de las Vísperas. De esta manera el mensaje quedaba claro, es decir, los aragoneses nunca habían roto su parte del acuerdo. Toda la responsabilidad por el conflicto entre los dos lados se le atribuyó al desleal Jaime II de Mallorca.

La realidad era que Pedro III estaba, desde el principio de su reino, seriamente preocupado ante el peligro de que un estado mallorquín, con importantes posesiones en los Pireneos y el sur de Francia, podría gravitar hacia el lado francés. Incluso insistió en quedarse con derechos sobre la baronía de Montpellier (Aumelas) y sobre Carlat; y más tarde los reyes de Aragón siguieron insistiendo que estos eran libres territorios, totalmente independientes de la jurisdición francesa. Jaime de Mallorca fue exento del juramento de homenaje, así como de tener que presentarse en las *Corts* del conde de Barcelona, pero sus herederos sí estarían obligados a hacerlo; de todos modos, el documento en sí era un sustituto más que adecuado por el acto de homenaje. Poco a poco el estado de Rosellón y los otros condados pirineos fue cambiando; de ser entidades separadas formando parte de una distinta entidad política, ahora se encontraban sujetas a las leyes y costumbres de Cataluña –no solamente las vigentes sino, y esto era crucial, las que se introdujeran en el futuro. Sólo la moneda de Barcelona circularía en los territorios peninsulares. En la isla de Mallorca, todavía se permitiría su propia moneda. Había algunos límites en la apelación judicial a la corte de Pedro, pero también había obligación de asistir al rey de Aragón en la defensa de sus tierras de los Pirineos. Por otra parte, el rey de Mallorca tenía la libertad de imponer sus propios impuestos dentro de las islas Baleares (y aquí el texto parece excluir los territorios peninsulares tales como el puerto de Collioure), mientras que estos impuestos no crearan conflicto con las promesas hechas por el rey Jaime I. El rey de Mallorca retendría su propio impuesto *bovatge*. Viviría de sus propios recursos.

Todo esto puso a Jaime segundo de Mallorca en una situación donde sus derechos como rey habían sido seriamente comprometidos, tanto que más tarde las autoridades mallorquinas insistirían en que tal concesión no tenía valor legal. Sin embargo había una ventaja importante. Había asegurado otra vez, con ciertas limitaciones, un acuerdo con Pedro por el que se respetaría la linea masculina de su sucesión en Mallorca. La obligación mutua de defenderse el uno al otro entre señor y vasallo fue citada por Jaime III en los últimos días del reino de Mallorca, presentando entonces a Pedro IV con un dilema serio de relaciones públicas. La incertidumbre en la mente de Jaime II acerca de la continua adherencia de su hermano a los mandatos del testamento del Conquistador, fue lo que le llevó a darse cuenta de que el acuerdo de 1279 era la única manera en que podría estar seguro de fundar un reino que fuera a durar. Tuvo que tragar su orgullo si quería continuar siendo rey. Pero, si hacía tantas concesiones, podría considerarse un verdadero rey?

Desde la perspectiva aragonesa, el rey de Mallorca había aceptado gobernar las tierras que le habían sido asignadas casi como un conservador de patrimonio del rey de

XIX

Aragón: en las palabras de Pedro IV, debería conservar el reino, los condados y las tierras en feudo para el rey de Aragón. Sin embargo los reyes de Aragón insistieron en que el testamento de Jaime I 'no era legalmente valido, porque la donación era inmensa y se llevaba la mayor parte del patrimonio de la casa de Aragón'; otra vez son éstas las palabras de Pedro el Ceremonioso. Así que el acuerdo de 1279 era esencial si la relación iba a desarrollarse y también tener una base legal segura. Aun así los aragoneses mantenían una vigilancia estricta para evitar abusos de los términos. Para Lecoy de la Marche esto fue el comienzo de los problemas que estaban a punto de explotar (LECOY, i. pag. 158). Lo que se había formado, ya no era un reino: 'son héritage n'était plus un royaume, mais un simple apanage' (LECOY, i. pag. 159). Aunque el concepto de reino sujeto no era exactamente novedad, la verdad es que las limitaciones impuestas al rey de Mallorca le dejaban con pocos atributos de rey. El rey de Sicilia, por ejemplo, a pesar de ser sujeto del Papa, no estaba tan restringido; y el único otro caso contemporaneo mostrando límites tales parece haber sido el intento de Duarte I de Inglaterra de imponer su autoridad sobre el rey de los escoceses.

A últimos de diciembre de 1280, se organizó en Tolosa una conferencia a la que asistieron los reyes de Francia, Aragón y Mallorca, y el heredero al trono angevino de Nápoles, y fue entonces cuando se vió claramente que los reyes de Mallorca iban quedando atrapados en una situación imposible entre los reyes franceses y aragoneses. Entre los asuntos tratados estaba el gobierno de Montpellier, el sino de los famosos infantes de la Cerda, y quizás la reclamación del trono de Sicilia por Pedro de Aragón. Muntaner, típicamente, pone énfasis en las relaciones amistosas entre el rey de Aragón y su pariente el rey de Francia: *e con fo en França fo reebut ab gran honor e goig e alegre que n'hac lo rei de França e la reina.* Es verdad que se habían prometido que nunca lucharían uno contra el otro, sino que se ayudarían mutuamente *contra tots hómens,* porque iban a actuar entre ellos como si fueran hermanos - Muntaner no alcanzó a percibir la ironía de esta situación. Hay muchas indicaciones de que la relación ya se había vuelto amarga; en parte la presencia del rey de Mallorca parece haber tenido la culpa, en parte la cuestión de los derechos a Sicilia de Constanza de Aragón. La fuente del conflicto fue Carlos de Salerno, el hijo de Carlos d'Anjou, rey de Sicilia, que había asistido a la conferencia en lugar de su padre. Pedro trató al príncipe napolitano con falta de respeto como hijo de un usurpador. Los reyes de Francia y Mallorca estaban tan preocupados con esta situación que fueron a ver a Pedro en su cámara y le recordaron lo cerrados que eran los lazos de sangre que unían a Carlos y a Pedro. De hecho, al mencionar la boda de Carlos d'Anjou con la condesa aragonesa de Provenza, sólo consiguieron empeorar la situación y escarbar una llaga que había sido creada por la pérdida de Provenza a la casa de Anjou. Jaime II trató de dar un buen ejemplo, regalando al joven príncipe con atenciones y llevándole a Montpellier donde se organizaron grandes festejos, aparentemente en su honor (*Crònica* de Muntaner, cap. 38).

¿Qué es lo que estaba tratando de conseguir Jaime II de Mallorca? Sin duda, estaba tratando de dar un buen ejemplo a un hermano que actuaba de una manera bruta hacia el rival de su hijo; también, sin duda, se daba cuenta de que una ruptura seria en las relaciones entre las casas de Anjou y Aragón traería conflicto en una escala masiva, no solamente a la isla de Sicilia (que estaba a punto de irrumpir en una revuelta más o menos espontánea) sino también a las tierras costeras del Mediterraneo occidental. Claramente, también estaba preocupado acerca de su pérdida de credibilidad con el rey de Francia si no se mostraba en simpatía con los intereses franceses. Y la razón por la que todo esto era importante no era simplemente un deseo de usar los franceses como contrapeso a Pedro de Aragón, sino la existencia de serias tensiones en las tierras que Jaime mismo tenía en feudo del rey de Francia. En los 1280 y los 1290, vemos el extraordinario espectáculo de una alianza entre Mallorca y Francia, a lo largo de la cual el rey francés iba aumentando su propia influencia en el sector mallorquín de Montpellier. Por tanto, no compensaría apoyar a los franceses durante la Guerra de las Vísperas Sicilianas.

IV

En verdad Muntaner parece haber cometido la simple falta de confundir o mezclar los eventos de 1280 con los de 1293, cuando Felipe IV de Francia adquirió los derechos del obispo de Maguelonne en Montpellier, concentrando los hechos de diez años en unos pocos d'años. Muntaner insiste en que el rey de Mallorca había sido engañado por los franceses y que los *prohomens* de Montpellier estaban enojados ante el reto a los derechos de su señor el rey de Mallorca. Muntaner continúa diciendo que a Jaime II le preocupaba que la resistencia de los ciudadanos de Montpellier podría minar sus relaciones con el rey francés; ell no volia haver desamistat ab lo rei de França, y sabía que el rey de Francia le trataría honorablemente si él actuaba corectamente hacia él. Aunque el análisis que hace Muntaner acerca de las relaciones entre los reyes rivales no es fidedigno, sí apunta al hecho de que el asunto de Montpellier continuaba vivo.

Indudablemente, en 1280, según fuentes documentales y la crónica local, los eventos en Montpellier eran motivo de preocupación. Anteriormente, en ese mismo año, un atentado tuvo lugar contra la vida del gobernador real, Pere de Claramunt, mientras estaba durmiendo en su cámara en el palacio real de Montpellier. Este asalto, cualquiera que fuera el motivo, sacó a la luz el problema de quien tendría jurisdicción sobre tales crímenes. Entonces se inició un debate sobre los derechos de los *Seneschals* franceses en las baronías que estaban situadas alrededor de Montpellier, con el argumento, de parte de los Mallorquines, que el señor de Montpellier siempre había ejecutado *merum et mixtum imperium* en los confines de su propio territorio. La frontera entre los territorios del rey de Mallorca y de los dominios reales franceses siempre fue fuente de disputa. Se empezó a cuestionar la permisibilidad de la apelación por parte de las cortes de Mallorca en Montpellier a las del *Seneschal* de Beaucaire. Los franceses estaban tratando de argumentar que las leyes diseñadas por los notarios en Montpellier deberían llevar el nombre del rey de Francia y no del rey de Mallorca. Estos asuntos que llevaban much tiempo sin tocarse irrumpieron en este momento porque la naturaleza de la jurisdición aragonesa sobre Montpellier no había sido discutida a fondo en el Tratado de Corbeil veinte y dos años antes, y no se podían discutir directamente mientras Jaime el Conquistador seguía vivo. Lo más lejos que se podía llevar el asalto contra los derechos aragoneses en Montpellier antes de 1276 sería tratar de crear en Aigues-Mortes un lugar alternativo para el comercio que venía del Mediterraneo y del norte de Francia, pero en realidad Aigues-Mortes se desarrolló bajo Felipe III y IV más como un puerto fuera de Montpellier, que como un centro comercial en su propio derecho (THOMAS, 1928/9).

Una real comisión de investigación nombrada por Felipe III de Francia estableció basicamente lo que los franceses ya sabían que era el caso, es decir los *Seneschals* de Beaucaire tenían ciertos derechos para revisar sentencias del juzgado en Montpellier; la costumbre era en realidad que los documentos se fecharan en el año real del rey francés sin ninguna referencia al rey de Mallorca. La existencia en Montpellier de un juez de apelación, actuando en el nombre del rey de Mallorca, era realmente un abuso (LECOY, i. pags. 172-4). Es admirable que los oficiales del rey Jaime de Mallorca insistieron en el rechazo de estas conclusiones e incluso en el derecho de los franceses a dirigir tal predispuesta *enquête*. La disputa continuó a lo largo de 1281, culminando con el intento del *Seneschal* francés Guillaume de Pontchevron en organizar un ejército que obligaría a Montpellier a doblegarse. Aunque el rey de Francia tenía dudas sobre la prudencia de usar la fuerza, los métodos de los *Seneschals* tuvieron su efecto: en julio 1282, heraldos públicos fueron enviados por los magistrados de la ciudad, y anunciaron en las calles de Montpellier que el nombre del rey francés iba a ser utilizado en los documentos públicos, y que el dinero del norte de Francia iba a ser legal en la ciudad. Como ni este hecho parecía ablandar el corazón de Pontchevron, el partido mallorquín envió emisarios a Nîmes para presentar el caso en contra, pero encontraron que Pontchevron estaba decidido bien a tomar la ciudad, o a forzar completa aceptación de todas las demandas francesas. En especial, el rey de Mallorca debería admitir a través de su embajador que Montpellier era parte del reino francés. Hasta se esperaba de él que entragara la ciudad a la corona francesa para recibirla de nuevo (es de notar cuán poca atención se consideraba necesario prestar al obispo de Maguelonne, que era el señor inmediato del rey de Mallorca en Montpellier). La concesión de Jaime de todos los derechos que pedían los franceses, aseguró que cuando Pontchevron entró en la ciudad fue en paz, como agente administrador del rey de Francia en lugar de como un general conquistador.

Al final Jaime II haría un acto de homenaje al rey francés, indicando claramente que Montpellier le pertenecía sujeto a la mayoría de las condiciones que habían sido causa del choque entre Pontchevron y los oficiales de la ciudad. Lecoy estaba confundido por la falta de pruebas de que Jaime había intervenido en la disputa, la cual él veía como muy seria, pero también una disputa que en esencia era 'une querelle toute locale entre leurs lieutenants ou leurs officiers'. Tenía razón que tal disputa no podía quitar que Jaime II mantuviera su fin principal de mantener relaciones amistosas con el rey francés (LECOY, i. pag. 182). Pero ésta fue una disputa que en su punto álgido tuvo a

Montpellier bajo amenaza militar, y que había sido el objetivo de una *enquête* de los oficiales del rey. La monarquía francesa podía ver claramente la debilidad de la situación de Jaime II, y estaba decidida a explotarla para reforzar su propia posición en el Midi. El rey francés no se mantuvo aislado, sino que él mismo anunció la *enquête* y sus resultados. Esto fue el principio de una serie de eventos que llevó a la adquisición, por parte de Felipe IV, de los derechos del obispo de Maguelonne en Montpellier, en 1293, con el resultado de que la autoridad francesa (incluyendo la real casa de la moneda) pudo introducirse en la ciudad, particularmente en Montpelliéret, distrito del obispo, que siempre había quedado fuera de la jurisdicíón mallorquina. En el area comercial podemos observar una larga historia de intentos por parte de los franceses de desviar comerciantes italianos de Montpellier hacia Nîmes, y una mejora gradual de los canales que iban desde el mar a Aigues-Mortes. La ciudad se inclinaba cada vez más hacia la órbita francesa. En 1339, ya no se veía claro si los comerciantes de Montpellier podían recibir reducción especial de impuestos en Mallorca, como ciudadanos de una ciudad donde el rey de Mallorca ejercitaba cada vez más una autoridad nominal.

De este modo el rey de Mallorca había sido forzado a una capitulación humillante al rey francés, sólo unos pocos años después de una sumisión humillante al rey de Aragón. En cualquier caso es evidente que la sobrevivencia de su reino dependía más de su habilidad de promocionar los intereses franceses que los intereses aragoneses. Es evidente la furia que Jaime de Mallorca sintió cuando, en 1304, su hijo Fernando se involucró en Carcassonne en un *coup* para deshacerse del dominio capeto y para reestablecer un autónomo Languedoc bajo su propia autoridad; esto sólo podía meter en compromiso la posición de Jaime como vasallo del rey francés. No considero necesario aquí examinar el precio tan alto que pagó Jaime II de Mallorca por su consentimiento a dar acceso a las tropas franceses que pretendían invadir Cataluña via Rosellón.

Los dramáticos hechos de estos años, culminando en la huida de Jaime del palacio real de Perpiñan a través de una sucia cloaca, mientras su hermano golpeaba la puerta atrancada de su cámara, fueron gráficamente descritos por Bernat Desclot en su crónica contemporanea (DESCLOT, *Crònica*, cap. 134-6). Es interesante ver que incluso después de la restauración de su reino en 1298, Jaime II se vió obligado de nuevo a reconocer al rey de Aragón como su señor en las Baleares además de en los condados catalanes. Las décadas siguientes mostraron lo imposible que era para un rey de Mallorca el romper con las restricciones que ésta dependencia le imponían. El estudio clásico de Riera sobre las disputas entre Aragón y Mallorca, alrededor de la imposición de impuestos comerciales a los comerciantes catalanes que llegaron a Mallorca y Collioure entre 1299 y 1311, revela que a largo plazo la corona de Mallorca no podría resistir la presión de los aragoneses. Exitos de poca importancia, como la creación de consulados mallorquines en el Maghrib, acentuaron la tension aún más, aunque produjeron dividendos considerables para los reyes de Mallorca.

V

La crónica de Pedro IV cuenta una historia interesante acerca de los últimos años del sucesor de Jaime II, Sancho (1311-24): Pedro dice que Sancho siempre ofrecía el debido homenaje al rey de Aragón (Jaime II), incluso asistiendo a las *Corts* catalanas cuando se le pedía que lo hiciera. Pero algunos señores franceses (bien nos gustaría saber cuales) pusieron en su mente la idea de que su predecesor Jaime II de Mallorca había recibido sus tierras en condición de libres y que el rey En Pere por su poder y fuerza las había subyugado convirtiéndolas así en un feudo, y que esto no era válido en la ley. El rey de Aragón entonces envió una carta colérica a Sancho en Perpiñan, proponiéndole que luchara contra su heredero Alfonso; afectó esto tanto a Sancho que ni pudo cenar, y se convenció de que por culpa de los malos consejos había perdido el reino. "*Eu hai haüt mal consell! Eu sui en mal punt nats! Eu hai perduda ma terra! Me han dado malos consejos!*" se quejó, "*He nacido en mala hora! He perdido mi tierra!*" (*Crònica* de Pedro IV, lib. 3, cap. 6). Hillgarth menciona que estas palabras muestran ciertos rastros del occitan, pero se pregunta como sería que el rey de Aragón hubiese oído tal parlamento privado (HILLGARTH, i, pag. 235). Sancho admitió a Jaime de Aragón que él había pensado en declararse libre de todas ligaduras a Aragón, pero que ahora lo había pensado de nuevo; asistió a las *Corts* en Gerona, ofreciendo veinte barcos para asistir en la conquista de Cerdeña, e ofreciéndose incluso a viajar allí en persona, aunque esto último no se consideró necesario. Desde entonces las relaciones entre los dos reyes quedaron restablecidas; de hecho, como reconocimiento al apoyo de Mallorca, los comerciantes de Mallorca y Rosellón recibieron privilegios generosos para comerciar con Cerdeña (*Crònica* de Pedro IV, lib. 3, cap. 6-7. Abulafia, 1996, pàg. 302-5).

En el horizonte se presentaban nuevos problemas; la inminente muerte de Sancho sin heredero, en 1324, presentaba el prospecto de una sucesión problemática. Jaime II de Aragón podría citar los términos del acuerdo hecho en 1279, renovado en 1298, por el que el reino de Mallorca y sus dependencias volverían al rey de Aragón si el rey de Mallorca moría sin heredero directo. Pero la sucesión de Mallorca pasó en 1324 al joven sobrino de Sancho, Jaime III. En ese momento el reino estaba peligrosamente cercano a un intento por parte de Aragón de hacerlo desaparecer del mapa. Los sucesos de 1343 podían haber ocurrido facilmente en 1324 o 1325. Así que no fue simplemente la actitud del adulto Jaime III lo que trajo desastre al reino; los asuntos constitucionales que el testamento de Jaime el Conquistador había sacado a la luz cincuenta años antes se negaron a desaparecer. Cuando el niño rey Jaime III sucedió al trono, escribieron una carta de su parte al rey de Aragón comunicando que él había recibido el trono de Mallorca; Jaime II de Aragón, deliberadamente, evitó hacer uso del título real en su respuesta. El punto de vista mallorquín estaba totalmente claro en que Sancho había tenido el derecho de designar a su sobrino como heredero. De este modo, al principio del reinado de Jaime III surgió la cuestión de hasta que punto los reyes de Mallorca eran dueños de su propio destino. La crónica de Pedro IV indica que dos semanas después de morir Sancho, las *Corts* hablaron de las implicaciones de su muerte en una reunión en Lérida. Decidido a convertir sus derechos en una realidad, Jaime de Aragón decidió enviar a su hijo Alfonso con un ejercito a Perpiñan para reconquistar las tierras que eran suyas por derecho. El efecto principal de esto fue levantar de nuevo una lucha faccional que continuó en activo hasta 1327. La presión papal y la continua distracción de los asuntos cerdeños finalmente llevaron a Jaime de Aragón a aceptar que acciones violentas no le ganarían amigos. En 1325 en las Cortes de Zaragoza, Jaime de Aragón reconoció la sucesión en Mallorca de Jaime III, y arregló una boda alianza; su nieta Constanza se casaría con el joven rey de Mallorca. En 1327, a la edad de doce años, trajeron a Jaime tercero a Barcelona para que prometiera observar las convenciones de los términos bajo los cuales el reino de Mallorca estaba sujeto al reino de Aragón. Pero los juegos políticos continuaron: durante la visita de Pedro IV de Aragón y Jaime II de Mallorca a la corte papal en Avignon, en 1339, el rey de Aragón se enfureció cuando un noble mallorquín golpeó su caballo, aparentemente porque andaba un poco por delante del del rey de Mallorca (*Crònica* de Pedro IV, lib. 3, cap. 37). Pedro confiesa que podría haber matado al rey de Mallorca en ese momento; pero se acordó del mucho afecto que el Papa le tenía a Jaime de Mallorca. La crónica de Pedro pone énfasis en la precedencia que tuvo el rey de Aragón en la corte papal: fue Pedro quien se sentó a la derecha del Papa y el rey de Mallorca a su izquierda. Pero ambos Pedro y Jaime estaban obsesionados por el protocolo y sus implicaciones, como se puede observar en las *Leges Palatinae* de Jaime, y en el apodo de Pedro, conocido como 'el Ceremonioso'. Por debajo de esta obsesión sin embargo, había profundas cuestiones políticas. Los lazos familiares entre Mallorca y Aragón, sellados una vez más por la boda de Jaime con la hermana del propio Pedro IV, nunca evitaron completamente el resentimiento creado por su relación política.

Montpellier continuó siendo un problema entre los reyes de Mallorca y Francia (*Crònica* de Pedro IV, lib. 3, cap.11). Antes de 1340 Jaime III parece haber disfrutado de buenas relaciones con la corte francesa; de hecho, en 1327 o 1328, la corte francesa reafirmó los derechos de tribunal alto de la corona de Mallorca dentro de Montpellier; pero después de 1340, la interferencia en los asuntos de Montpellier por Felipe VI llevó a Jaime a pedir ayuda al rey de Aragón. Jaime también empezó a tomar más interés en una alianza con Inglaterra. Pedro de Aragón rechazó estas iniciativas; tenía miedo, y con razón, de involucrarse en la rivalidad entre Inglaterra y Francia sobre el control de la cercana Gasconia. Lo aparentemente absurdo de la querella entre el rey francés y Jaime III en 1341 no debería engañarnos de todos modos. El asunto parecía ser acerca de si el rey de Mallorca podría organizar un torneo en Montpellier cuando el rey de Francia había prohibido este tipo de actividad para evitar la pérdida de vida; necesitaba sus nobles para guerras de verdad. La rebelión de Jaime ante esta regla casi trajo desastre a la ciudad, porque justo como en 1281 y 1282, Montpellier parecía estar a punto de ser invadido por Francia, mientras que Jaime se jactaba de que él podría organizar una alianza de los tres reyes contra los franceses (LECOY, ii. pags. 31-43). Pero los cónsules de la ciudad no estaban dispuestos a cooperar con el rey de Mallorca, el cual les había puesto en una situación my difícil: tenían que decidir si obedecerle a él, o a su señor en Montpellier, el rey de Francia. Además, como ha señalado Jan Rogozinski, en Montpellier las quejas se iban incrementando: allí el sistema de doble impuestos puesto en sitio por los dos reyes había generado, bajo el liderazgo de abogados competentes, protesta política (ROGOZINSKI, 1982).

Jaime empujó a Pedro de Aragón a buscarle justicia del rey de Francia, quien 'le estaba haciendo gran daño y cosas insoportables en la ciudad de Montpellier' (*Crònica* de Pedro IV, cap. 11). Pedro le aseguró que intervendría con el rey de Francia en su favor; incluso, como mandaban los acuerdos existentes, Pedro hubiera estado dispuesto a hacer guerra contra Francia si el rey de Mallorca hubiera tomado tal iniciative. Pero Hillgarth dice que esto no es creíble, porque en Mayo de 1341 Pedro había prometido a Felipe de Francia que no haría tal cosa (*Crònica* de Pedro IV, vol. i., pag. 238n). Jaime se hico más jactancioso, y Pedro se sentía cada vez más alarmado ante la posibilidad de que sus acuerdos con el rey mallorquín podrían arastrarle a una peligrosa e inútil guerra con los franceses. La crónica de Pedro muestra que el rey aragonés diseó una manera extraordinariamente ingeniosa de dar la vuelta a la situación en contra de Jaime III: llamándole a una reunión de las *Corts*, insistió en que Jaime explicara porque había roto su acuerdo con el rey de Aragón al acuñar su propia moneda en Rosellón. Una situación en que el vasallo pedía a su señor ayuda contra sus enemigos, fue transformada en la insultante situación del vasallo que no aparece cuando su señor le llama, y que se opone a los derechos soberanos de su señor. En este sentido la decisión de suprimir el reino de Mallorca por parte de Pedro, aunque ya venía preparándose por mucho tiempo, fue el resultado del comportamiento del propio Jaime. Al poner en peligro los intereses vitales de Aragón, estaba claro que había que evitar que Jaime siguiera una política exterior independiente, un momento acercándose a Francia y al siguiente a Inglaterra (sin mencionar sus ambiciones extrañas sobre las islas Canarias). Pero ni su autobiografía consigue esconder el subterfugio con el que Pedro llevó esto a cabo. Pedro indica con una sinceridad desarmante que se libró de sus obligaciones a su vasallo al insistir que fue el vasallo y no él mismo quien había sido contumaz. El relato que sigue, que describe su encuentro con Jaime de Mallorca, venido en barco a Barcelona en busca de un acuerdo, fue claramente un intento de justificación de su conducta hacia el rey mallorquín, y no hay suficientes razones para creer la historia que nos cuenta Pedro de que Jaime tenía un plan para raptarlo y tenerlo como prisionero en Mallorca.

VI

Este énfasis en las dificultades personales entre dos orgullosos y obstinados príncipes no pretende quitar fuerza a los otros aspectos cruciales del problema: ante la ley, los mallorquines podían mantener con credibilidad que su gobernante era un rey, y como otros reyes su autoridad era absoluta —*rex in regno suo est imperator*. La postura aragonesa también tenía ciertos puntos legales válidos, si los acuerdos de 1279, y de años pos-

XIX

teriores, entre los reyes de Aragón y Mallorca se consideraban válidos; y se podría, como se ha visto, llevar aún más lejos, con el argumento de que el rey de Aragón había excedido su autoridad cuando creó el reino de Mallorca. Lo que he tratado de demostrar aquí es el simple hecho de que las relaciones de familia entre reyes rivales no hicieron mucho para evitar las desavenencias entre ellos. Es más, los reyes de Mallorca consiguieron sacar poco partido de sus intentos de manipular la situación entre los franceses y los aragoneses. Los franceses tenían sus propios planes, y sus esfuerzos para adquirir Montpellier para Francia continuaron incluso cuando Mallorca era su aliada más cercana en la lucha contra la casa de Barcelona. Politicamente el reino de Mallorca era tan impotente que no podia ni organizar un enfrentamiento entre sus mayores rivales; y entre 1341 y 1343, mostró su total falta de habilidad al no poder hacer uso del conflicto entre Aragón y Francia, y esto resultó en su caída.

Bibliografía

Fuentes manuscritas. París, Archives Nationales
Chambre de Comptes, KK 1413 y P1354(1)
París, Bibliothèque Nationale ms latin 9261
Fuentes impresas primarias y secundarias

ABULAFIA, David (1994), *A Mediterranean Emporium. The Catalan Kingdom of Majorca*, Cambridge.
ABULAFIA, David (1996), *Un Emporio Mediterráneo. El reino catalán de Mallorca*, Barcelona.
ABULAFIA, David (1997), *The Western Mediterranean Kingdoms, 1200-1500. The struggle for dominion*, Londres.
DESCLOT, Bernat, *Crònica*, in: SOLDEVILA, F. (1971), *Les quatre grans cròniques*, Barcelona.
DUNBABIN, J. (1998), *Charles I of Anjou*, Londres.
HILLGARTH, J.N. y M., *Pere III of Catalonia, Chronicle*, 2 vols., Toronto.
JAIME I DE ARAGÓN, *Crònica*, in: SOLDEVILA, F. (1971), *Les quatre grans cròniques*, Barcelona.
LECOY DE LA MARCHE, A. (1892), *Les relations politiques de la France avec le royaume de Majorque*, 2 vols.
MUNTANER, Ramón, *Crònica*, in: SOLDEVILA, F. (1971), *Les quatre grans cròniques*, Barcelona.
PEDRO IV DE ARAGÓN (Pere III de Catalunya), *Crònica*, in: SOLDEVILA, F. (1971), *Les quatre grans cròniques*, Barcelona.
RIERA MELIS, A. (1986), *La Corona de Aragón y el reino de Mallorca en el primer cuarto del siglo XIV.* Vol. 1: *Las repercussiones arancelarias de la autonomía balear (1298-1311)*, Barcelona.
ROGOZINSKI, J. (1982), *Power, caste and law. Social conflict in fourteenth-century Montpellier*, Cambridge Massachusetts.
RUNCIMAN, S. (1958), *The Sicilian Vespers. A History of the Mediterranean World in the later thirteenth century*, Cambridge.
SANTAMARIA, A. (1990), *Ejecutoria del Reino de Mallorca*, Palma de Mallorca.
THOMAS, L.J. (1928/9), *Montpellier entre la France et l'Aragon pendant la première moitié du XIVe siècle*, "Monspeliensia. Mémoires et documents relatifs à Montpellier et à la région montpelliéraine publiés par la Société archéologique de Montpellier", vol. 1.

Resum

Consideracions sobre la història del regne de Mallorca: Mallorca entre Aragó i França

Aquesta comunicació vol reconsiderar alguns aspectes bàsics de la relació entre el regne independent de Mallorca i els seus veïns, desenrotllant els arguments del meu llibre "Un Emporio mediterráneo. El reino catalán de Mallorca", que havia sortit primerament en anglès l'any 1994, i llavors en espanyol l'any 1996. L'èmfasi d'aquest llibre era principalment en el panorama internacional (en àrees de política o comerç) del regne de Mallorca, i vull guardar el mateix èmfasi aquí, però tractant temes que no van ser tractats, almenys detingudament, en aquest llibre.

El llegat de Jaume I va quedar distorsionat per la insistència de Pere III d'Aragó que el seu germà, Jaume II de Mallorca, havia de ser vassall seu. Així el regne de Mallorca entrava en una situació tenebrosa —era un regne, però amb la seva autonomia visiblement limitada. Em proposo aquí reexaminar els motius de l'enemistat entre els dos hereus de Jaume el Conqueridor, mirant una sèrie de casos en els quals els reis de Mallorca es trobaven atrapats entre les seves obligacions als seus senyors, els reis d'Aragó, i la seva relació complexa amb els reis de França, qui eren els seus senyors en Montpellier i els seus aliats en qüestions de política mediterrània. Vull sobretot insistir en la importància dels vincles familiars en les relacions entre les diverses faccions al final del segle tretze. De fet, el regne independent de Mallorca fou creat per Jaume el Conqueridor amb l'esperança que el seu rei pogués viure en armonia fraternal amb el seu germà més gran, el rei d'Aragó. Veurem també que la relació de Jaume de Mallorca amb el rei de França fou compromesa per les ambicions del rei francès sobre Montpellier. Mostraré que encara quant un conflicte estava a punt d'esclatar, hi havia una apel·lació constant per el manteniment dels llaços de parentiu per evitar la guerra. I acabada la guerra, la qüestió de Montpellier continuava dificultant les relacions entre França i Mallorca, mentre que la successió al tron de Mallorca en 1324 plantejava problemes bàsiques que no s'havien resolt mai sobre la naturalesa de la dependència mallorquina d'Aragó. El que he intentat demostrar es el fet clar que la relació familiar entre els reis rivals no mitigava en res la seva enemistat. A més a més, els reis de Mallorca no sabien treure cap consol ni profit dels seus intents d'utilitzar els francesos en contra dels aragonesos. Els francesos tenien la seva pròpia agenda, i ni tan sols quan Mallorca era un fidel aliat en el conflicte amb la casa de Barcelona, havien deixat d'intentar prendre possessió de Montpellier. Del punt de vista política, el regne de Mallorca era tan dèbil que no podia fer enfrontar els seus gran rivals un contre l'altre; i als anys 1341-3, aquesta impotència per utilitzar Aragó contra França, va ser la causa del seu esfondrament.

Abstract

Considerations on the history of the kingdom of Majorca: Majorca between Aragon and France

The aim of this paper is to reconsider some fundamental aspects of the relationship between the independent kingdom of Majorca and its neighbours, taking further the arguments presented in my book *Un Emporio mediterráneo. El reino catalán de Mallorca*, which first appeared in English in 1994 and in Spanish in 1996. The emphasis of that book was heavily upon the international setting (whether in the realms of politics or trade) of the Majorcan kingdom, and I propose to retain that emphasis here, while examining themes that were not discussed, at any rate at any length, in the book. The legacy of James I was distorted by the insistence of Peter III of Aragon that his brother James II of Majorca should become his vassal, in 1279. The kingdom of Majorca entered a shadowy world where it was at the same time a kingdom in name, and yet distinctly limited in its autonomy. Here I propose to re-examine the grounds for the hostility between the two heirs of James the Conqueror looking at a series of cases where the kings of Majorca found themselves caught between their duty to their overlords the kings of Aragon, and their complex relationship with the kings of France, who were their overlords in Montpellier and their allies in Mediterranean politics. In particular, I shall stress the importance of family relationships in the links between different factions at the end of the thirteenth century. The autonomous kingdom of Majorca was itself created by James the Conqueror in the hope that its ruler would be able to co-exist in fraternal harmony with his elder brother the king of Aragon. I will also be seen too that the relationship between James of Majorca and the king of France was compromised by the French king's ambitions in Montpellier. I shall show how, even when conflict was about to erupt, there were constant appeals to family ties as a way of trying to prevent the outbreak of war. After the war was concluded, the issue of Montpellier continued to sour relations between France and Majorca, while the succession to the throne of Majorca in 1324 raised fundamental problems that had never been resolved concerning the nature of Majorcan dependence on Aragon. What I have sought to demonstrate here is the simple fact that the family relationship between the rival kings did nothing to alleviate the hostility between them. Moreover, the kings of Majorca gained little comfort or advantage fron their attempts to play off the French against the Aragonese. The French had their own agenda, and their attempts to acquire Montpellier for France were pursued even when Majorca was their close ally in the struggle against the house of Barcelona. Politically, the kingdom of Majorca was so feeble it could not even play off its greater rivals against one another to any great effect; and in 1341-3 its inability to use Aragon against France, or France against Aragon, resulted in its downfall.

ADDENDA ET CORRIGENDA

II

page 5 Mallorca fell under Almoravid rule as a consequence of the Pisan-Catalan attack, and was therefore one of the last surviving taifa states in Spain, as it had been the last part of al-Andalus to be conquered by Muslims, and as it would be the last Almoravid territory to be seized by the Almohads; on these issues see G. Doxey, *Before the Conquest: the Muslim Balearic islands and Christian Europe*, Leiden, 2001.

page 19 The view of Muslim Granada as a virtual colony of the Genoese must be modified in the light of the impressive work of Roser Salicrú i Lluch, notably her *Relacions de la Corona d'Aragó amb el regne de Granada al segle XV (1412–1458)*, Barcelona, 1997. Salicrú shows that the Catalan presence was also very significant; see also her contribution in Catalan to the *XVI Congresso della Corona d'Aragona*, on 'The Catalan-Aragonese commercial presence in the Sultanate of Granada during the reign of Alfonso the Magnanimous', to appear in English in the *Journal of Medieval History*, 2001; also her article jointly with B. Garí, 'Las ciudades del triangulo: Granada, Málaga, Almería, y el comercio mediterráneo de la Edad Media', in *En las costas del Mediterráneo occidental. Las ciudades de la Península Ibérica y del reino de Mallorca y el comercio mediterráneo en la Edad Media*, ed. David Abulafia and Blanca Garí, Barcelona, 1997, pp. 171–211.

page 65 The literature on portolan charts also includes the innovative study of Y.K. Fallo, *L'Afrique à la naissance de la cartographie moderne. Les cartes majorquines (14ème–15ème siècles)*, Paris, 1985.

III

A well researched and very readable account of the twelfth-century Balearics will be found in the work by G. Doxey mentioned *supra*.

IV

pages 61–6 D. Selbourne replied to critics who denied the authenticity of *The City of Light* in his 'Afterword to the paperback edition', London, 1998, pp. 441–51; he addresses one or two of very briefly (pp. 443–4) my own criticisms concerning which Italians would have been in Acre when Jacob supposedly visited the city. However, he relies here on general statements by J.F. Leonhard in the Italian edition of his book on Ancona (*Ancona nel medio evo*, Ancona, 1992), and does not address the known effects of the War of St Sabas; nor does he address the point that Aaron of Aragon is a complete absurdity.

VII
The study of the trade of Galicia has opened up new perspectives on the links between the Mediterranean and the Atlantic in this period: see Elisa Ferreira Priegue, *Galicia en el comercio maritimo medieval*, Santiago de Compostela, 1988, and the revealing documentation edited by the same author in her *Fuentes para la exportación gallega de la segunda mitad del siglo XV. El Peatge de Mar de Valencia*, Santiago, 1984.

X
A further very helpful work in this field is: James M. Powell, 'Economy and society in the kingdom of Sicily under Frederick II: recent perspectives', in *Intellectual Life at the court of Frederick II Hohenstaufen*, ed. W. Tronzo, Washington, DC, 1994 [the same volume in which essay XII appeared], pp. 263–71.

XIII
Valuable new light on the treatment of conquered Muslims in Spain has been shed by R.I. Burns, P. Chevedden and M. de Epalza in their *Negotiating Cultures. Bilingual surrender treaties in Muslim-Crusader Spain*, Leiden, 1999. For further discussion of the expulsion of the Jews from Anjou, this time from an English perspective, see R. Mundill, *England's Jewish solution. Experiment and expulsion, 1262–1290*, Cambridge, 1998.

XIX
On Perpignan, see now P. Daileader's innovative *True Citizens. Violence, memory, and identity in the medieval community of Perpignan, 1162–1397*, Leiden, 2000. On the political and economic links between Mallorca and North Africa in this period, see now the massive study by M.D. López Pérez, *La Corona de Aragón y el Magreb en el siglo XIV (1331–1410)*, Barcelona, 1995.

INDEX

Note: Certain constantly recurring terms, *Italy, Jews, Levant, Mediterranean, Muslims, Saracens*, have been omitted from the index. Place names in Dalmatia are given in their Croatian form, with the Italian version in brackets. Place names in Catalonia and the Balearic islands are given in their Catalan form with the Castilian version in brackets, with the exception of Ibiza (*Cat.* Eivissa) and places in French Catalonia.

For Product Safety Concerns and Information please contact our EU
representative GPSR@taylorandfrancis.com Taylor & Francis Verlag GmbH,
Kaufingerstraße 24, 80331 München, Germany

Printed and bound by CPI Group (UK) Ltd, Croydon, CR0 4YY
08/05/2025
01864370-0012